(Continued on back endsheets)

American Novelists Since World War II
Fourth Series

Dictionary of Literary Biography® • Volume One Hundred Fifty-Two

American Novelists Since World War II
Fourth Series

Edited by
James R. Giles
Northern Illinois University
and
Wanda H. Giles
Northern Illinois University

A Bruccoli Clark Layman Book
Gale Research Inc.
Detroit, Washington, D.C., London

Printed in the United States of America

Published simultaneously in the United Kingdom
by Gale Research International Limited
(An affiliated company of Gale Research Inc.)

The paper used in this publication meets the minimum requirements
of American National Standard for Information Sciences–Permanence
Paper for Printed Library Materials, ANSI Z39.48-1984. (∞)™

Library of Congress Cataloging-in-Publication Data
American novelists since World War II: fourth series / edited by James R. Giles and Wanda H. Giles.
    p. cm. – (Dictionary of literary biography; v. 152)
"A Bruccoli Clark Layman book."
Includes bibliographical references and index.
ISBN 0-8103-5713-5 (alk. paper)
    1. American fiction –– 20th century –– Bio-bibliography. 2. Novelists, American –– 20th century –– Biography –– Dictionaries. 3. American fiction –– 20th century –– Dictionaries.
I. Giles, James Richard, 1937- . II. Giles, Wanda H. III. Series.
PS379.A554   1995
813'.5409'03 –– dc20   95–141
[B]   CIP

10 9 8 7 6 5 4 3 2 1

Contents

v

Plan of the Series

The advisory board, the editors, and the publisher of the *Dictionary of Literary Biography* are joined in endorsing Mark Twain's declaration. The literature of a nation provides an inexhaustible resource of permanent worth. We intend to make literature and its creators better understood and more accessible to students and the reading public, while satisfying the standards of teachers and scholars.

To meet these requirements, *literary biography* has been construed in terms of the author's achievement. The most important thing about a writer is his writing. Accordingly, the entries in *DLB* are career biographies, tracing the development of the author's canon and the evolution of his reputation.

The purpose of *DLB* is not only to provide reliable information in a convenient format but also to place the figures in the larger perspective of literary history and to offer appraisals of their accomplishments by qualified scholars.

The publication plan for *DLB* resulted from two years of preparation. The project was proposed to Bruccoli Clark by Frederick C. Ruffner, president of the Gale Research Company, in November 1975. After specimen entries were prepared and typeset, an advisory board was formed to refine the entry format and develop the series rationale. In meetings held during 1976, the publisher, series editors, and advisory board approved the scheme for a comprehensive biographical dictionary of persons who contributed to North American literature. Editorial work on the first volume began in January 1977, and it was published in 1978. In order to make *DLB* more than a reference tool and to compile volumes that individually have claim to status as literary history, it was decided to organize vol-

umes by topic, period, or genre. Each of these freestanding volumes provides a biographical-bibliographical guide and overview for a particular area of literature. We are convinced that this organization — as opposed to a single alphabet method — constitutes a valuable innovation in the presentation of reference material. The volume plan necessarily requires many decisions for the placement and treatment of authors who might properly be included in two or three volumes. In some instances a major figure will be included in separate volumes, but with different entries emphasizing the aspect of his career appropriate to each volume. Ernest Hemingway, for example, is represented in *American Writers in Paris, 1920–1939* by an entry focusing on his expatriate apprenticeship; he is also in *American Novelists, 1910–1945* with an entry surveying his entire career. Each volume includes a cumulative index of the subject authors and articles. Comprehensive indexes to the entire series are planned.

With volume ten in 1982 it was decided to enlarge the scope of *DLB*. By the end of 1986 twenty-one volumes treating British literature had been published, and volumes for Commonwealth and Modern European literature were in progress. The series has been further augmented by the *DLB Yearbooks* (since 1981) which update published entries and add new entries to keep the *DLB* current with contemporary activity. There have also been *DLB Documentary Series* volumes which provide biographical and critical source materials for figures whose work is judged to have particular interest for students. One of these companion volumes is entirely devoted to Tennessee Williams.

We define literature as the *intellectual commerce of a nation:* not merely as belles lettres but as that ample and complex process by which ideas are generated, shaped, and transmitted. *DLB* entries are not limited to "creative writers" but extend to other figures who in their time and in their way influenced the mind of a people. Thus the series encompasses historians, journalists, publishers, and screenwriters. By this means readers of *DLB* may be aided to perceive literature not as cult scripture in the keeping of intellectual high priests but firmly positioned at the center of a nation's life.

DLB includes the major writers appropriate to each volume and those standing in the ranks immediately behind them. Scholarly and critical counsel has been sought in deciding which minor figures to include and how full their entries should be. Wherever possible, useful references are made to figures who do not warrant separate entries.

Each *DLB* volume has a volume editor responsible for planning the volume, selecting the figures for inclusion, and assigning the entries. Volume editors are also responsible for preparing, where appropriate, appendices surveying the major periodicals and literary and intellectual movements for their volumes, as well as lists of further readings. Work on the series as a whole is coordinated at the Bruccoli Clark Layman editorial center in Columbia, South Carolina, where the editorial staff is responsible for accuracy of the published volumes.

One feature that distinguishes *DLB* is the illustration policy – its concern with the iconogra-phy of literature. Just as an author is influenced by his surroundings, so is the reader's understanding of the author enhanced by a knowledge of his environment. Therefore *DLB* volumes include not only drawings, paintings, and photographs of authors, often depicting them at various stages in their careers, but also illustrations of their families and places where they lived. Title pages are regularly reproduced in facsimile along with dust jackets for modern authors. The dust jackets are a special feature of *DLB* because they often document better than anything else the way in which an author's work was perceived in its own time. Specimens of the writers' manuscripts are included when feasible.

Samuel Johnson rightly decreed that "The chief glory of every people arises from its authors." The purpose of the *Dictionary of Literary Biography* is to compile literary history in the surest way available to us – by accurate and comprehensive treatment of the lives and work of those who contributed to it.

The *DLB* Advisory Board

Introduction

The United States just after World War II assumed virtually a new identity, and the writing from the late 1940s sometimes seems to have come out of just about as many viewpoints, theories, memories, and readings as there were people living at the time. Writers dealt with the monumentality of experience: the end of the last "good war," the rise of the United States in international politics and commerce, the opening of the universities to nontraditional classes and ethnic groups, the expansion of the literary canon, the new freedoms and strengths of women and ethnic groups, the horror and power of weaponry, decolonization and the explosion of new nations with special relationships to one of the two great powers, and the Cold War that was a state of hostilities without declaration which nonetheless controlled world events and alliances.

In the postwar period prosperity increased, and large families became fashionable, affordable, and socially favored, as home and civic life became a myth that would call to, but baffle and elude, writers for the rest of the century, never providing its own, earlier unquestioned, definition. Crime and violence grew in stunning proportion to prewar experience, the juvenile delinquents of the 1950s leading eventually to the drive-by shooters and carjack burglars of the 1990s, a far move from the shoot-outs and urban violence of Mark Twain's West or Theodore Dreiser's and Frank Norris's cities and their psychological and economic cruelties.

And maybe at the beginning of all of this Technicolor, as Tom Wolfe would call it in the 1960s, when it began to dazzle and burn too brightly, stood one image that opened the time – the nurse and the sailor in Times Square celebrating the end of World War II with a kiss vibrant with youth, hope, optimism, strength, confidence, love, and the black and white of anonymity. What this couple conveyed in the 1945 *Life* photograph was not new to human experience, but the expressions of it, the vitality and confidence, came out of victory in this war, with the expansion and importance it handed to the United States. Moreover, photographs themselves became an American icon in a nation of cameras and their images, with family albums continuing their domestic popularity, but with new technological potential: television, forensic imaging, computer enhancement. World wars do not create literature; simply, they destroy nearly everything in their paths. But at the end there is that couple, kissing, laughing, dancing with the hope of a new age, the fearlessness of conquerors in a world where only two decades earlier they or their families were probably, like most Americans, isolated, rural, onlooking.

The undeniable logic behind the tradition of designating 1945 as the beginning of a new era of the American novel is that it was also the year when the United States discovered itself one of only two world superpowers. For the generation who had fought the Great War (1914–1918), home had always been reality. The trip that began with the attack on Pearl Harbor has never ended. Home *is* now the undefinable myth and the political battleground. James Jones tried to identify and mourn it in *Some Came Running* (1958), and he made a finer attempt from Paris – his collection, *The Ice-Cream Headache and Other Stories* (1968). Others would write from Europe, including Anaïs Nin, who made a pilgrimage and a reflection of her life, and James Baldwin, who learned early that his home nation would not open itself to him.

Writers who stayed in the United States would try to find homes. For instance, James Agee's lifework depended on an understanding of homes within individual lives, as in *A Death in the Family* (1957), and across a region, as in *Let Us Now Praise Famous Men* (1941). A poignant search was that of Native Americans, whose quest for self and place is complicated by enforced moves to white-directed reservations. Louise Erdrich details the alienation of Native Americans and Native Americans of mixed blood in *The Beet Queen* (1986) and *Tracks* (1988). J. D. Salinger's most famous character, Holden Caulfield of *The Catcher in the Rye* (1951), defined a generation opposed to "phoniness." Family is important beyond place; thus Robert Penn Warren's father extends throughout much of Warren's writing, most memorably as Judge Irwin, whose honor is central to *All the King's Men* (1946). That novel includes an icon of twentieth-century literature, Willie Stark, who is so brilliant and controlling a politician and so devastating in his fall that he functions as a relentless paternal figure who knows that all people are controllable, for "there is always something" – always a secret, always a price.

Americans became richer and busier than ever before. For some it was small changes – the replacement of chicken by steaks, the consumerism that assaulted the soul (Jones, *Some Came Running*; Updike, *Couples,* 1968). And the country no longer luxuriated in ignorance of international affairs. It could not continue looking on; now it made and implemented decisions. Under President Harry S Truman, Americans undertook the rebuilding of Europe, formerly the center of the worlds of intellect and style. The plan was to use Yankee technology and American generosity. But even as the most clearly powerful and intact of countries, the United States could not escape being touched by the profound insecurity and moral uncertainty that were a part of the war's legacy. The full disclosure of the horrors of the Holocaust forced the West to question as never before the inherent decency of human beings. The American technology that destroyed Hiroshima, John Hersey's ravaged city (1946), forced the nation to confront a newly discovered human potential: the extinction of all life, made possible by brilliant minds and malleable matter. Americans could hardly ignore the fact that the powerful instruments for human annihilation were the clear result of technology, in which they had for so long posited an almost religious faith. Information, the technology of the mind that would dominate the last years of the century, would often entrap and diminish its own believers, as happens when it overpowers Sherman McCoy in Tom Wolfe's *The Bonfire of the Vanities* (1987). Kurt Vonnegut, like many other young men, came home from the war to view his home country in freer language and logic than had been read before.

But such a development would take a while, and in the late 1940s the United States was a heroic nation-hero, working around the world to repair it after the war. After rebuilding some of Europe with the Marshall Plan, the nation assumed a responsibility to stop the spread of communism and thus involved itself in the only-somewhat-undeclared conflict with the Soviet Union, rung in by Winston Churchill in his "iron curtain" speeches of the 1940s and perhaps ended in the collapse of the Soviet bloc in 1989. For the United States the first crisis of the Cold War began just five years after World War II, earlier believed to be a defining, limiting event in international warfare. In 1950, when Communist North Korea invaded South Korea, U.S. troops went to aid the besieged Asian nation as part of a United Nations police action to force out the invading North Koreans. The Korean conflict lasted until its ambiguous ending in 1953, but forty years later, when the unconquered North Korea adapted the nuclear weaponry of World War II, the ambiguity was once more a live issue. Korea would be the first, but not the last, tragically indecisive, brutalizing post–World War II experience for the United States in Asia. By the end of the police action, more than 150,000 American casualties (killed and wounded) fell in Korea.

What happened in Korea from 1950 to 1953 was never officially called a war; it was the Korean conflict, a palatable political noun spoon-fed to a weary generation of only somewhat young men. Whatever it was called, it forced Americans to realize that there were real limitations to the power of even the strongest of nations, an idea that contributed significantly to a pervasive sense of instability and uncertainty in the United States, back wherever home was. In 1952 Americans elected as their president Dwight D. Eisenhower, the former commander in chief of the Allied forces in Europe; some of his political strength was his common touch, the famous smile that met a national need for reassurance and stability. But he was a general, not a father to the country; and the 1950s were haunted by another new kind of nightmare, and the dominant images were far from kisses – congressional committee rooms and microfilm in pumpkins. The tough, smug Roy Cohn and the finally exasperated counsel Joseph Welch, with his gentle outrage: "Have you no decency, sir?" Decency had once been a given in U.S. manners and morals; its loss, or at least diminution, was one of the grave blows of the postwar years. Joseph McCarthy, a senator from Wisconsin, had largely inspired the witch-hunt for Communists in places of influence in the United States, but he was joined readily enough by a still-unsettled and war-prone American nation. Writers and other creative people soon found themselves favorite targets of McCarthyism, with the blacklists that isolated friend from friend and destroyed the careers of suspected Communists, certainly including writers, in the motion-picture, radio, and television industries, and in academia. Ironically, Irwin Shaw, whose *The Young Lions* (1948) was the most optimistic of the major post–World War II novels because of Shaw's declared "faith in the decency of the American people," would be among those blacklisted.

The national insecurity and loss of faith in moral certainty inevitably touched the young American writers who began publishing in the late 1940s and early 1950s. Not surprising, several of them – Norman Mailer (*The Naked and the Dead,* 1948),

Jones (*From Here to Eternity*, 1951), and Gore Vidal (*Williwaw*, 1951) – first published war novels; and a recurrent theme in this early World War II fiction is a warning against the imminent danger of an American fascism. Mailer and Jones, in their first published novels, create American generals who openly and unapologetically preach the necessity that strong leaders control the weak and directionless masses. And this thematic concern was not limited to the war novelists; Saul Bellow's *Dangling Man* (1944), William Styron's *Lie Down in Darkness* (1951), and Chester Himes's *If He Hollers Let Him Go* (1945) express anxiety about the existence of grave internal threats to the preservation of American democracy. Salinger's *The Catcher in the Rye,* not an overtly political novel, presented Holden Caulfield – youth in rebellion against a corrupt society and the "phonies" who profited from it – an emblematic figure for his entire decade. And even Shaw, with his abiding faith in the common American, wrote, in short stories and *The Troubled Air* (1951), specific protests against McCarthyism and the repression of the freedom of people whose lifework was words.

In contrast Herman Wouk violated the fictional logic of his otherwise powerful and honest novel *The Caine Mutiny* (1951) by imposing on it an arbitrary ending that seems to advocate adherence to authority, however incompetent or even corrupt. It is impossible to estimate the cost during the 1950s of self-censorship to American literature and to American culture in general. What is clear, though, is that the spirit of the times – a decade now remembered for full-blown emphases on idealized family life, consumption of goods, and unquestioning adherence to newly created traditional values – caused serious American writers simply to retreat from any sense of involvement in, or commitment to, the dominant culture of the nation. The clearest example of a literary repudiation of mainstream American society came from the talented group of writers known as the Beat Generation. Jack Kerouac, Allen Ginsberg, and Lawrence Ferlinghetti were among the best known of the Beats, writers who sought in Zen Buddhism, jazz, and drugs antidotes to what they perceived as the sterile conformity of American life. California – specifically San Francisco, and even more specifically San Francisco's City Lights bookstore – was the center of the Beat movement, from which, more or less directly, came such underground classics as John Rechy's *City of Night* (1963), Hubert Selby's *Last Exit to Brooklyn* (1964), and, most important, Kerouac's *On the Road* (1957) and William S. Burroughs's *Naked Lunch* (1959). In a time of wide social conformity, Burroughs reflected a personal and verbal freedom that matched the sexual nonconformity that was important to these writers' lives and work. It would also go beyond brilliance and into destruction, both of self and others, but for a time it made a dazzling new light in a country beginning to seek wisdom from beyond Main Street.

In California and other less experimental parts of the country, Zen was a fascination during this period. But it was not the only foreign philosophy of significant influence on American literature and American culture in the years following World War II. French existentialism, with its emphasis on the absence of any ethical system in the external universe and the resulting need for each individual to discover or create individual moral truths, had a strong appeal for postwar writers. A kind of fiction that can be called existential realism began to appear on the American literary scene during the 1950s. The work of most of the important writers to emerge in the United States since 1945 contains at least existential overtones. For one remarkable example, perhaps the main consistency in the constantly evolving literary career of Mailer has been his self-definition as an American existentialist.

Despite the considerable importance of the 1950s to American literature, 1961 and 1962 more clearly represented the end of one era of the American novel and the beginning of another. In these two years, at the beginning of what would prove to be one of the most turbulent decades in American history, Ernest Hemingway committed suicide and William Faulkner died. The work of these men constituted the triumph of modernism in American fiction; and they had dominated the national literary scene for more than three decades. Indeed, only the American Renaissance writers (Nathaniel Hawthorne, Herman Melville, Ralph Waldo Emerson, Henry David Thoreau, and Edgar Allan Poe) had been so central and vital to American literature for so long as the Lost Generation. They had moved American fiction beyond William Dean Howells's "reality of the commonplace," but now they were gone and were for a long time, if not forgotten, then obscured by technical experimentation and also by their own fame and familiarity, which despite such accolades as Nobel Prizes (in the cases of Faulkner and Hemingway) also included drunkenness, broken marriages, and self-indulgence. The experience of writer as celebrity was introduced and wore itself down with these writers and others who shortly followed them; Mailer and Jones particularly suffered from the overexposure of writer to hype.

Whatever the reasons – and they were complex and possibly still not understood – by the 1960s the Hemingway-Faulkner literary legacy had begun to have an inhibiting effect on the American novel. It was increasingly difficult to surpass the innovations in modernist technique found in such modernist masterpieces as Faulkner's *The Sound and the Fury* (1929) and *Absalom, Absalom!* (1936) and Hemingway's *The Sun Also Rises* (1926). A result of the brilliance of these works was that, to later American writers, modernism was the only valid mode for the twentieth-century novel, but a few had already rebelled against the limitations of modernist technique. Bellow, who had published two novels during the 1940s that conformed to the narrative and structural conventions of modernism, rediscovered in *The Adventures of Augie March* (1953) the formal freedom inherent in Twain's nineteenth-century legacy of the frontier picaresque novel. American novelists searched for narrative structures that would liberate them from the restraints of modernism throughout the 1960s.

The social and political turbulence of that decade contributed to the intensely felt need of many writers to escape virtually any kind of limitations on their art. Few, if any, periods in American history have begun so hopefully or ended so chaotically as the 1960s. In 1960 John F. Kennedy, the country's youngest president, was elected. Kennedy's youth, his search for a New Frontier, and his often-quoted inaugural appeal seemed to promise a revival of American idealism. The young, academically brilliant administration perceived no limits: the nation was promised a man on the moon within the decade. And existing technology was there for the using: television had in the 1950s become the primary source of entertainment and information for most Americans; and, despite critical lamentations over its genuine potential for superficiality, Kennedy grasped its potential for forming public opinion through the visual sharing of public experience. He had achieved the presidency in part because his appearance against Vice President Richard Nixon in a series of debates had won him the confidence of the American television audience, and he performed masterfully on television throughout his brief term in office.

This administration was confronted with the civil rights movement, symbolized in Dr. Martin Luther King Jr. but led by many – the most nearly realized twentieth-century example of Thomas Jefferson's expected internal revolution. Not wanting to offend the southern wing of the Democratic Party, the president first offered only verbal support to the cause of civil rights.

But – when pictures of Freedom Riders and other civil rights protesters in the South under attack by water hoses, clubs, police dogs, and tear gas began to dominate the national news on television screens throughout the nation – the civil rights movement quickly became the central beneficiary of the youthful idealism to which Kennedy had appealed. The president and Attorney General Robert Kennedy, his brother, saw the inevitability of a direct role in the struggle for American civil rights, which in some ways climaxed on 17 June 1963, when King delivered his "I Have a Dream" speech to a crowd of more than two hundred thousand in Washington, D.C., and such heroes of the movement as Bernice Reagon of Sweet Honey in the Rock demanded freedom.

Their torment expressed the smothering brutalities of real experience that had found passionate voice in such novels as Richard Wright's *Native Son* (1940), William Attaway's *Blood on the Forge* (1941), and Ann Petry's *The Street* (1946) and that would later find literary voice in Toni Morrison, who in 1993 received the first Nobel Prize for literature awarded to a black American. Words came to be the most effective weapons for the people struggling in the civil rights movement. With the witness of these men and women, Washington came to see the necessity of passing a federal civil rights bill aimed at ending the barriers – and the bloodshed – legitimized by racial segregation in this country. The civil rights struggle inspired a new activism among Americans – writers, artists, entertainers, students, housewives, clergy, teachers – and Pete Seeger's song "Wasn't That a Time?" expresses the peculiar combination of innocence, wonder, and corruption that the creative community experienced and translated. Novels of the 1960s by black authors, preceded in the recent past by the occasional work by Willard Motley (such as *Knock on Any Door,* 1947) or the many popular novels of Frank Yerby, came out of the earlier struggle of such writers as novelist and essayist Baldwin (*Go Tell It on the Mountain,* 1954; *Notes of a Native Son,* 1955) and Ralph Ellison, whose great work, *Invisible Man* (1952), emerged with a clarity and brilliance of voice rarely seen in his own country.

The nation was in a state of turmoil when on 22 November 1963 President Kennedy was assassinated. Frame 313 became the new American icon, and few events have been so devastating to the American sense of spirit as this murder and those that followed it in Dallas in the next three days. By the end of the weekend a young policeman would also die by gunfire, and so would the alleged assassin – another young, undefined man, someone who may once have heard Kennedy's call to do what he could for his country. In the young president's death there was no second chance, no relief, no easy comprehension. The nation gathered in living rooms, churches, schools, and even department-store furniture showrooms, watching the ceremony of grief. In an extended television event, the last for this television president, the country found some shared solace in watching the lying in state, the funeral, and the processions leading to his burial.

The murders that followed, however, introduced other kinds of shock. Officer J. D. Tippitt was an American Everyman: young, married, with children; he could have been anyone. And when, on live television, Kennedy's accused assassin, Lee Harvey Oswald, was shot to death by a Dallas nightclub owner, the killing was an early example of the power of television to stun its audience through the immediacy of image and the quickness with which chaos emerged from the high energy and political commitment of the dead president. Some people were already wondering whether such a passive medium as the novel could remain viable to an audience trained to respond so quickly. Oswald's death, moreover, intensified an already-present element of doubt and uncertainty first expressed by the artistic community. Further, it seemed impossible that so slight and insignificant a figure as Oswald could have a significant or decisive effect on American history, and suspicion of conspiracy in the president's death will possibly always haunt the American mind. In years that followed, several books with assassination-plot motifs appeared, among them Bryan Wooley's *November 22* (1981) and Vance Bourjaily's *The Man Who Knew Kennedy* (1967).

The nation seemed briefly to rediscover some stability and moral certainty when Kennedy's successor, Lyndon B. Johnson, a Texan who was expected to sympathize with the segregationist South, brilliantly secured the passage of the 1964 Civil Rights Act in a Congress he knew profoundly. Thus the old-style southern politician provided the legislative centerpiece so long sought. That a new stability had arrived seemed especially certain when Johnson was reelected in 1964 in a landslide victory over conservative Barry Goldwater, a Westerner who had voted against the civil rights bill. But it was a short triumph, a small domestic peace. Events overseas would quickly shatter the national recovery and war on poverty.

Years after Americans first read Hersey's *Hiroshima,* events had begun in Southeast Asia that would bring a new war, one that devastated the spirit in a way not earlier experienced by Americans. Few people knew or noticed that in the 1950s the United States, in an attempt to halt the spread of communism in Asia, had committed itself to defending a corrupt and authoritarian regime in a small Southeast Asian half-nation. As the political situation deteriorated, President Kennedy sent American military advisers to South Vietnam, and after the Johnson election in 1964 the United States became heavily involved in a miserable, confusing war in a country that few Americans had known previously. Throughout the next four years increasing numbers of American resources and troops were poured into a struggle doomed from the first – and with the historic example of the French fall in Vietnam shouting the futility to those who could listen.

The horror and hopelessness of the American effort was, again via television, brought home to the nation in 1968. Amid repeated assurances by the U.S. government and military that the war was going well, the North Vietnamese forces launched a devastatingly effective offensive against American and South Vietnamese forces during a term of negotiated cease-fire. As it did throughout the war, television brought shattering images of horror and destruction into the homes of Americans – the naked, crying Vietnamese girl whose clothing had been burned away by napalm, running toward the cameras of a nation who had supplied it; a South Vietnamese general (thus on the side of the United States) executing a bound prisoner with a pistol pressed to his head. For the first time in the century – in a national mood far from the loyalty, cooperation, and sacrifice of World War II – a reaction, and even revulsion, against the nation's involvement in a military action took to the streets, the newspapers and journals, even the classrooms of the mid 1960s.

More and more young Americans of draft age refused to accept induction into the armed services, and antiwar demonstrations became almost a ritual of daily life on college campuses across the nation. Hardly noticed in its beginnings, a counterculture of young men and women devoted to opposition to the war, experimentation with sex and drugs, and rebellion against everything associated with middle-class tradition ("the establishment") was highly visible throughout urban America. The residential section of San Francisco surrounding Haight and Ashbury Streets was soon identified as the center of the youth-dominated counterculture. It was the "Age of Aquarius" in San Francisco (and on the stages of *Hair* [1967] productions in New York and London), the time of a "dirty little war" in Southeast Asia. The dirtiness of the war, besides the massive casualties suffered, had to do with a new kind of racial conflict that ripped apart the fabric of national unity in the last half of the 1960s: African Americans, especially in the urban centers in the North and on the West Coast, were outraged by the disproportionate number of young black men being drafted to serve in Vietnam ground forces and in addition came to believe that resources of potential use in America's inner cities were being wasted in Southeast Asia. The Watts section of Los Angeles in 1965 and the black neighborhoods of Detroit in 1967 suffered massive outbreaks of rioting and looting, and television images of the late 1960s were often of body bags and coffins coming off planes at the edges of burning cities.

All the tensions that had been building throughout the 1960s seemed to explode in the years between 1968 and 1970. On 4 April 1968 Martin Luther King was assassinated in Memphis; and on 5 June of that same year Robert Kennedy, during a campaign for the presidency, was shot and killed – on television – in Los Angeles just after winning the California Democratic primary. In the summer, national television audiences saw the spectacle of antiwar demonstrators at the Democratic National Convention in Chicago under assault by armed officers in what the federally ordered Walker Report later called a "police riot." In 1970 National Guard troops fired on and killed student protesters at two universities, Kent State in Ohio and Jackson State in the Mississippi capital.

In 1969 an American did indeed land on the moon; still, Neil Armstrong's walk there, hard to celebrate as first anticipated in the early 1960s, represented one of the few seemingly unequivocal triumphs for American technology in the decade. Yet for the novelist, and especially for the writer of science fiction, even this revolutionary scientific breakthrough had ominous overtones. Now what had recently belonged to the world of fantasy had become one more aspect of reality; like so many other major historical events during the 1960s, Armstrong's adventure on the moon was visible on television as it occurred. From then on – indeed, from Alan Shepard's 1961 *Gemini* rocket ride – *astronaut* became a part of the vocabulary of ordinary Americans rather than a concept reserved for science fiction. Space science was always national news, but, until the walk on the moon, television images were limited primarily to takeoffs and landings.

Inevitably a decade marked by such relentless turmoil dramatically affected the American novel. It in fact called into even more serious question than in the previous decade the traditional mimetic role of the novel; American writers and critics began to wonder whether fiction could hope to capture such an elusive reality. Even at the beginning of the decade, Philip Roth expressed genuine doubt on this question:

> The American writer in the middle of the 20th century has his hands full in trying to understand, and then describe, and then make *credible* much of the American reality. It stupefies, it sickens, it infuriates, and finally it is even a kind of embarrassment to one's own meager imagination. The actuality is continually outdoing our talents, and the culture tosses up figures almost daily that are the envy of any novelist.

Throughout the rest of the 1960s echoes of Roth's pessimistic analysis, usually with some variations in emphasis, became commonplace in literary magazines. Mailer, among others, wondered whether the mass media's daily barrage of information and news effectively buried any objective and potentially verifiable reality that might exist. In the 1960s it became somewhat fashionable to issue pronouncements on the death of the novel. It was, after all, a time of so much death.

But a genre that had been so central to Western culture for so long would not pass quickly into oblivion. Already seeking alternatives to modernism and traditional realism, American novelists began to invent ways to revitalize the novel. The most venturesome found routes to use the chaos and contradictions of the time creatively. First in short stories and then in a novel, *Snow White* (1967), Donald Barthelme perfected his technique of narrative collage, a device that deliberately appeared to echo the fragmentation and randomness of American culture and society. In his first novel, *V.* (1963), Thomas Pynchon transformed the national obsession with plots and conspiracies into an elaborate historical tour de force; in *Gravity's Rainbow* (1973), he would explore an even darker and more complex landscape. Two World War II novels, one published at the beginning and the other at the end of the 1960s and based on different modes of narrative experimentation, depicted what almost seemed another war than the one described in the late 1940s and early 1950s by Jones, Mailer, and Shaw. With the title of his first novel, *Catch-22* (1961), Joseph Heller coined a phrase that has since become part of the English and American vocabulary for the description of bureaucratic and technological irrationality and insanity. Vonnegut, a prisoner of war in Dresden, Germany – a city of irreplaceable cultural importance and no great military significance when the U.S. and British air forces destroyed it in a World War II technique known as firebombing – combined in *Slaughterhouse-Five* (1969) literary realism with science fiction to capture and convey the technological horror that he had witnessed. This was beyond the power of television, a smashing together of internal and external realities and voices incomprehensible through chronological reportage and images.

John Barth, in a 1967 essay provocatively titled "The Literature of Exhaustion," concisely expressed the rationale for the continuous search in the 1960s for innovation in fictional technique. Careless readers saw the essay as simply another pronouncement on the death of the novel; and Barth sometimes seems to encourage this kind of misinterpretation. At one point, for instance, he says that he is "inclined to agree" with those who believe that "the novel, if not narrative literature generally, if not the printed word altogether, has by this hour of the world just about shot its bolt." But the essay turns out to be a plea for the revitalization of the novel. Barth asserts that contemporary writers of fiction who ignore the work of such literary innovators as the Argentine writer Jorge Luis Borges, the Irish playwright Samuel Beckett, and the Russian-born novelist Vladimir Nabokov are doomed to create outdated and irrelevant fiction. Self-consciousness in narration is the key to creating the kind of art that Barth believes has validity; people need, he says "novels which imitate the form of the Novel, by an author who imitates the role of Author."

The self-conscious, experimental fiction that Barth advocated and that he, Barthelme, Vonnegut, Pynchon, Heller, and others wrote was given different labels, the most common one probably being *metafiction*. Assuredly their work marked a movement of the American novel away from modernism and toward postmodernism; where Hemingway and Faulkner had perfected techniques ranging from narrative minimalism to complex variations on the stream of consciousness to prevent any overt intrusion of an authorial presence that would destroy the reader's suspension of disbelief, the 1960s practitioners of metafiction devised elaborate methods to expedite such intrusions. In his 1971 critical study *City of Words,* Tony Tanner provides an analysis of the fascination that such elaborate and often self-reflective alternative "realities" as labyrinths, mirrors, and texts held for these writers. In many ways Barth's novel *Giles Goat-Boy* (1966) epitomizes 1960s metafiction in using a mode of ironic mysticism and a mock-academic setting.

Other writers, responding to the sense that contemporary reality had become too complex and chaotic to be captured by traditional realistic fiction, would attempt to erase the commonly accepted boundaries between fact and fiction. Describing contemporary events, Truman Capote in *In Cold Blood* (1965) and Mailer in *The Armies of the Night* (1968; he would use the technique in *The Executioner's Song,* 1979) combined objective reporting with fictional subjectivity to produce a genre variously called nonfiction fiction, faction, or the New Journalism, the latter the province of Wolfe, whose one novel, *Bonfire of the Vanities* (1987), would come out of years of observation of the complex realities of New York City life. Other writers – for instance, Styron in *The Confessions of Nat Turner* (1967) – chose instead to fictionalize the historic past. Styron's book is not at all the same thing as the popular historical novel; nor is it a glorious revelation of the mythic past, as was Ross Lockridge's *Raintree County* (1948). It is instead a meditation on the connections between past and present American racial hatred and guilt. Finally, for all the speculation during the 1960s that traditional literary realism could no longer capture external reality, it was that decade which saw the publication of at least two novels, Selby's *Last Exit to Brooklyn* and Joyce Carol Oates's *them* (1969), that have revitalized the tradition of American literary naturalism.

One must use care to avoid overgeneralizing the influence of the 1960s on the American novel. It is easy to find self-destructive artifacts. For example, Jones, far from his literary home, the U.S. Army, wrote in Paris *Go to the Widow-Maker* (1967) and *The Merry Month of May* (1971) – two novels that lessened his reputation and commented pessimistically on the fallen times. Still, the decade was a climactic and defining one for the novel and for American literature in general, an it at least resulted in a recognition of the need to reexamine long-standing assumptions about the viability of literary realism and modernism closely.

For the United States the 1970s, while eventually a calmer decade than the preceding one, still had traumatic moments. The Vietnam War left a legacy of division and recrimination that has yet to end. The men and women who served in Vietnam did not receive the kind of homecoming that had traditionally been the reward for returning American veterans of overseas combat.

Every war has produced disabilities among veterans; additionally, the wars after World War II have produced large numbers of addicted men and women, as the opiates of survival in other countries became the opiates of culture shock on return to a consumerist, unthreatened civilian nation. Drug addiction among veterans is a new phenomenon in the middle class; before the 1960s the few references to it came in occasional pieces. By 1985 the Kentucky teenagers in Bobbie Ann Mason's *In Country* would know more about "dope" in Vietnam than did the mothers of the men and women who went to war there. Tim O'Brien and Larry Heinemann as well as the prolific and successful Stephen King have written on the addiction of their generation as a result of Vietnam.

The conquering heroes of World War II changed in only eight years to the largely neglected forces returning home from Korea. The Vietnam veterans came home to a place where to be ignored was good fortune. The other option was to be openly denounced for having fought in an immoral war. No clear and easily comprehensible justification of the U.S. involvement in Vietnam was ever articulated. When the war ended inconclusively after the deaths of more than fifty-six thousand American soldiers, overwhelmingly of the lower class and often people of color ("Three-Five-Zero-Zero" in *Hair* is virtually whispered; the song about the dirty little war reflected a war that had become a dirty little secret), the nation wanted above all to try to forget the entire experience. It has never been forgotten, though in time acceptance of the experience and its responsibilities has begun to seem possible, and the building of the Vietnam War Memorial was one of the rare healing acts in the public art of this country. Talking and writing about Vietnam have come slowly, and only recently have such writers as O'Brien, Heinemann, and Mason been free to explore the experience of the U.S. fighting contingent in Vietnam and in the United States after the war.

It was U.S. mass media that began a realistic evaluation of the war and its legacy. Between 1978 and 1990 American movies explored the horrific nature of military combat in Vietnam and/or the postwar suffering of those who survived it; among the best are *The Deer Hunter* (1978), *Coming Home* (1978), *Platoon* (1986), and *Born on the Fourth of July* (1989). By the late 1980s even television, especially in the series *China Beach,* was beginning to examine the suffering, and the political and moral ambiguity, of the war. The Vietnam writers are still a small group, most of them Vietnam veterans; they have so far produced a small, distinguished body of war fiction. They have used a variety of literary approaches that echo both the early realistic-naturalistic World War II novels of Mailer, Jones, and Shaw and the

later postmodernist works of Heller and Vonnegut. Heinemann's *Close Quarters* (1977) and *Paco's Story* (1987) are written in a predominantly realistic mode, while O'Brien's *Going After Cacciato* (1978) experiments with postmodernist narration. Mason's *In Country* was the first novel to observe the domestic war: the returns to individual and civil ignorance of the horror of modern warfare; the mysterious sicknesses that followed the fighting; and the curious, insensitive, invasive, compassionate, and chaotic response of the people who stayed at home. The near helplessness of women after war has seldom been so uncompromisingly stated as in Mason's descriptions of the pot of geraniums held on Mamaw's lap in the long journey from western Kentucky to the Vietnam War Memorial in Washington, D.C., where she at first experiences the agony of not being able to "see" her son and then, with the help of unknown friends, places her flowers under his name.

The sense of national instability, severely affected by the resignation of President Richard M. Nixon in 1974, was not erased in the 1970s. The Nixon presidency was followed by the administrations of Gerald Ford and Jimmy Carter, which remained free of scandal but were nevertheless perceived as unfocused and ineffectual; and in 1992 Updike's title *Memories of the Ford Administration* would give readers pause: there was little to remember. But in the early 1980s a politician at least as adroit as John F. Kennedy in the use of television to create dramatic and instantaneous images assumed the presidency: Ronald Reagan, a former motion-picture actor called "the great communicator" because of his intuitive mastery of mass media, became the first American president since Eisenhower to complete two terms in office. The Reagan presidency represented a return to political conservatism and a repudiation of much of the liberal Democratic agenda that had dominated national politics since Franklin D. Roosevelt's New Deal and was the direct result of a national movement away from political activism. Thus, while it represented something of a new national consensus, it alienated many traditional liberals and much of the old intellectual community.

During this period of national malaise and nondirection, serious American writers became more alienated from the national mainstream than at any time since the 1920s. This alienation was partly, but certainly not entirely, the result of national politics. To a significant degree it was related to an evolving ideology in academic circles that denied the traditional role of the novel as the literary genre of the middle class. In fact, the influence of the French thinkers Michel Foucault and Jacques Derrida led to new theories — first structuralism and then deconstruction — that questioned traditional assumptions about the nature and purpose of literature and of writing itself. Most structuralists argued that literary texts were interrelated and were not primarily the creation of individual writers but the product of the structure of society's dominant ideas and values. Deconstructionists held that, because of the uncertainty of language itself, all writing inevitably negates its own apparent meanings. Since these two theories assert that the traditional belief in an individual author of a novel is merely a convention and that the elusiveness of language constantly negates the possibility of any consistent theme or intent in any piece of writing, they challenged and repudiated the traditional view of the novel as a controlled individual work designed to speak to a mass audience.

This new emphasis on the fundamentally arbitrary nature of literature and thus of critical judgments about it led to an extensive reexamination of the accepted canon of American literature. Beginning in the 1970s feminist critics, merging some aspects of structuralist theory with the ideas of the French psychoanalyst Jacques Lacan, argued that the canon had traditionally been established by white males and thus reflected an arbitrary and limited approach to American writing. The feminist critical agenda resulted in more than one kind of benefit for American literary studies. It led to the rediscovery of previously undervalued American women writers of the past, among them Kate Chopin, Tillie Olsen, Zora Neale Hurston, Anzia Yezierska, Meridel Le Sueur, Margaret Walker, and Dorothy West, whose 1995 novel *The Wedding* will almost certainly be the last novel written by a Harlem Renaissance writer. The works by women of the second half of the twentieth century are perhaps foreshadowed by the agonies of Sylvia Plath, whose writings have been almost overshadowed by her sensational death and the posthumous treatment of her works by her husband and mother.

The silencing or the distortion of women and their writing continued to inspire new thinking about the proper subject matter for the novel by asserting that books written by men have tended to undervalue, if not to ignore or misperceive completely, the value of women, even in their customary nurturing roles. Finally, it brought a new awareness of the stereotypes that male writers have often imposed on female characters and an awareness of contemporary women writing to counter such stereotypes.

The same impulses that have affected feminist literary thinking have inspired, especially in academia, a view of literature and the novel in particular as being most important as a form of cultural study. This approach to literature has resulted in a new interest in writers from traditionally marginalized social groups. Beginning in the 1970s such African American women as Toni Morrison, Alice Walker, and Gayl Jones began to exercise an influence on the American novel comparable to that already enjoyed by Bellow, Roth, and other Jewish American writers. Maxine Hong Kingston, Amy Tan, and many other young Asian American novelists have made their initial contributions to the national literature, as have Chicano writers Sandra Cisneros, Raymond Barrio, Rudolfo Anaya, and Rolando Hinojosa-Smith, among the first Hispanics to celebrate their ethnicity since John Rechy (*City of Night,* 1963). Finally the fiction and poetry, perhaps engendered by the 1930s writings of D'Arcy McNickle, of N. Scott Momaday, whose *House Made of Dawn* (1968) was the first contemporary Indian novel, and of later writers such as Erdrich, Gerald Vizenor, and James Welch have inspired a Native American literary renaissance.

The contemporary American novel reflects so rich a cultural diversity that it is difficult to think that until the postwar period scholars innocently defined the novel as a hidebound masculine work. The considerable benefit of newer, broader, and more precise thinking has inevitably resulted in the questioning of old assumptions about the role of the American novelist as the voice of national consensus. Few today speak of the national mission of the American writer with the confident assurance of Emerson or Howells. Fewer successfully play the part of a national man of letters as Edmund Wilson did. For different reasons and in different ways, postmodernist novelists such as Pynchon and even writers speaking for socially marginalized groups must assume that they are addressing much more restricted and limited audiences than the traditional middle-class readership of fiction. There are, in addition, more prosaic reasons for the contemporary alienation of the serious American novelist from the middle class.

Television has been the communications medium of choice for America for nearly five decades; and for almost that long writers and others have regretted its shallowness and superficiality. Inevitably the ubiquitous presence of television in America has trained its audience to respond more readily to instantaneous visual images than to the printed page. Since 1939 paperback reprints evolved as a means of making the novel accessible to the middle class, but the paperback-publishing industry has itself been adversely affected by inflationary pressures.

Still, in spite of all these pressures, some quite serious and important postwar novelists have tried to speak to, and sometimes on behalf of, middle-class America. Updike's centrality to the postwar American novel is due in no small part to his evocation, in four volumes, of the financial and spiritual troubles of his fictional Toyota dealer, Rabbit Angstrom – *Rabbit, Run* (1960), *Rabbit Redux* (1971), *Rabbit Is Rich* (1980), and *Rabbit at Rest* (1990) – in whose life Updike depicts the morally ambiguous social rise of an ordinary American and thus evokes the fiction of Howells and Sinclair Lewis.

Other postwar American novelists of impressive talent have revitalized old fictional genres traditionally associated with popular culture. Mailer would continue his flirtation with journalism in 1995, issuing with Gerald Schiller, who paired with him in *The Executioner's Song* (1979), *Oswald's Tale*.

Larry McMurtry seemed for a time to be the only novelist writing in a contemporary Western form. But regional writers continued to be strong throughout the postwar years. Warren wrote as knowingly of his native western Kentucky as contemporary Kentucky writer Ann Mason; George Garrett's works revisit the Southeast with a sure, clear vision; and Donald Harrington and Madison Jones write of their South.

The late 1950s and 1960s pronouncements on the novel's demise to the contrary, American fiction since World War II has been, and continues to be, vital indeed. Among Jewish American writers who write firmly and compellingly on the need to tell and retell the stories of survival, both of humanity and art, are Bernard Malamud, Chaim Potok, and Cynthia Ozick. One of the century's finest writers, Malamud has been criticized for a view of Jews as passive victims, and Potok has possibly been devalued because one of his novels, *The Chosen* (1967), was a popular success, and later *My Name Is Asher Lev* (1972) and others were considered too dependent on Jewish esoterica. Ozick has written in a wide range, but her novels are marked, like Malamud's, by an intellectual and stylistic brilliance and wit; they also, like his, bespeak an undying commitment to the ironies – and the love – of life. Across cultures, Flannery O'Connor's novels, *Wise Blood* (1952) and *The Violent Bear It Away* (1960),

come from a comparable religious and regional commitment.

One 1968 anthology of post-1945 American fiction – *How We Live: Contemporary Life in Contemporary Fiction,* edited by Penny Chapin Hills and L. Rust Hills – illustrates the vitality of post–World War II American fiction writers of significance. Almost thirty years later a much longer list could be compiled. This volume introduces several writers who have not earlier appeared in the *Dictionary of Literary Biography* and carries forward discussions of novelists who have appeared but who continue to write and to be read, sometimes with fresh critical perception.

–Wanda H. Giles and James R. Giles

Acknowledgments

This book was produced by Bruccoli Clark Layman, Inc. Karen L. Rood is senior editor for *The Dictionary of Literary Biography* series. George Anderson and Darren Harris-Fain were the in-house editors.

Production coordinator is James W. Hipp. Photography editor is Bruce Andrew Bowlin. Photographic copy work was performed by Joseph M. Bruccoli. Layout and graphics supervisor is Penney L. Haughton. Copyediting supervisor is Laurel M. Gladden. Typesetting supervisor is Kathleen M. Flanagan. Systems manager is George F. Dodge. Julie E. Frick is editorial associate. The production staff includes Phyllis A. Avant, Charles D. Brower, Ann M. Cheschi, Patricia Coate, Denise W. Edwards, Joyce Fowler, Stephanie C. Hatchell, Erica Hennig, Kathy Lawler Merlette, Jeff Miller, Pamela D. Norton, Laura S. Pleicones, Emily R. Sharpe, William L. Thomas, Jr., and Jonathan B. Watterson.

Walter W. Ross and Robert S. McConnell did library research. They were assisted by the following librarians at the Thomas Cooper Library of the University of South Carolina: Linda Holderfield and the interlibrary-loan staff; reference-department head Virginia Weathers; reference librarians Marilee Birchfield, Stefanie Buck, Cathy Eckman, Rebecca Feind, Jill Holman, Karen Joseph, Jean Rhyne, Kwamine Washington, and Connie Widney; circulation-department head Caroline Taylor; and acquisitions-searching supervisor David Haggard.

American Novelists Since World War II
Fourth Series

Dictionary of Literary Biography

James Agee
(27 November 1909 – 16 May 1955)

Victor A. Kramer
Georgia State University

See also the Agee entries in *DLB 2: American Novelists Since World War II* and *DLB 26: American Screenwriters.*

BOOKS: *Permit Me Voyage* (New Haven: Yale University Press, 1934);

Let Us Now Praise Famous Men, photographs by Walker Evans (Boston: Houghton Mifflin, 1941; London: Owen, 1965);

The Morning Watch (Boston: Houghton Mifflin, 1951; London: Secker & Warburg, 1952);

A Death in the Family (New York: McDowell, Obolensky, 1957; London: Gollancz, 1958).

Editions and Collections: *Agee on Film: Reviews and Comments* (New York: McDowell, Obolensky, 1958; London: Owen, 1963);

Agee on Film, Volume II: Five Film Scripts (New York: McDowell, Obolensky, 1960; London: Owen, 1965) — includes *The Blue Hotel, The African Queen, The Bride Comes to Yellow Sky, Noa Noa,* and *The Night of the Hunter;*

The Collected Poems of James Agee, edited by Robert Fitzgerald (Boston: Houghton Mifflin, 1968; London: Calder & Boyars, 1972);

The Collected Short Prose of James Agee, edited by Fitzgerald (Boston: Houghton Mifflin, 1968; London: Calder & Boyars, 1972);

The Collected Journalism of James Agee, edited by Paul Ashdown (Knoxville: University of Tennessee Press, 1985).

MOTION PICTURES: *The Quiet One,* narration by Agee, Museum of Modern Art, 1949;

The African Queen, screenplay by Agee and John Huston, United Artists, 1951;

James Agee (photograph by Florence Homolka)

Genghis Khan, narration by Agee, Italian Film Exports, 1952;

The Bride Comes to Yellow Sky (half of *Face to Face*), screenplay by Agee, RKO, 1952;

White Mane, script by Agee, Rembrandt Films and Contemporary Films, 1953;

The Night of the Hunter, screenplay by Agee, United Artists, 1955;

Green Magic, script by Agee, Italian Film Exports, 1955.

TELEVISION: "The Blue Hotel," script by Agee, *Omnibus,* NBC, late 1940s;

Abraham Lincoln, scripts by Agee, *Omnibus,* NBC, 1953.

OTHER: *Notes for a Moving Picture: The House,* in *New Letters in America,* edited by Horace Gregory (New York: Norton, 1937), pp. 37–55;

"Dream Sequence," edited by Victor A. Kramer, *Texas Quarterly,* 10 (Spring 1968): 38–46.

James Agee's literary work – poetry, journalism, criticism, screenplays – was not that of just a fiction writer. According to Father James Harold Flye, Agee's mentor, teacher, and surrogate father, Agee frequently talked of extending his unfinished autobiographical project, *A Death in the Family* (1957), into a Proustian novel that could never have reached completion. Agee's autobiographical remembrances summoned flights of the imagination. Throughout his literary career he remained fascinated with developing methods of observing, documenting, and appreciating the ordinary by means of his writing. Agee's storytelling for films, as well as his fictional works, reveals that he constantly sought to extend the range of what fiction accomplishes.

The details of Agee's birth in 1909 in Knoxville, Tennessee; his childhood; and the early loss of his father in May 1916 in an automobile accident became the basis of *A Death in the Family*. His subsequent education – at Saint Andrew's School (1919–1923), near Sewanee, Tennessee, where he met Father Flye, who taught him history; his eventual transfer to Phillips Exeter Academy (1925–1928) in New England; and his attendance at Harvard College (1928–1932), where he wrote for the *Harvard Advocate* – has been well documented. During the years of his education it was already clear that Agee could write tight poetry, prose, and fiction; but he also chose to step beyond predictable literary boundaries. He was consistently as interested in writing about fact as he was in constructing fiction.

The atmosphere at Phillips Exeter Academy was intellectually stimulating for the sixteen-year-old Agee. He became editor of the *Phillips Exeter Monthly,* and his own contributions to the periodical were so ambitious that one of his prep-school teachers later described him as phenomenal. He churned out poetry, prose, drama, and reviews; and while some of the work is immature, his enormous productivity demonstrates a multiplicity of interests.

Characteristics basic to his later successful literary production are already present in the writing completed at Exeter. An awareness of the transitoriness of human life and of man's fragility, a theme that later buttresses the poetry of *Permit Me Voyage* (1934), is especially evident. In his earliest fiction Agee shaped a sense of the frailty of human existence. In stories he published in the *Phillips Exeter Monthly,* – "The Bell Tower of Amiens" (December 1927) and "The Scar" (January 1926) – Agee delineates a young narrator's surprise when confronted with the devastation of war.

Some of the *Phillips Exeter Monthly* stories are set in Tennessee and have a humorous tone. "Knoxton High" (April 1927), obviously based upon memories of a year spent in Knoxville in 1924–1925, satirizes small-town provincialism. Agee's first attempt at stream of consciousness, the story pokes fun at the pride taken in a new school building. Other Tennessee stories are somber. In "The Circle" (April 1926), for example, the young hero is trapped, not only by his father's death but also by his own laziness and choice of a dull life in a small town. In another early story, "Minerva Farmer" (November 1925), Agee uses his knowledge of the University of Tennessee, as well as his memories of the grammar school where he had been a student, to tell the story of a woman who finally graduates from the university at age thirty-nine. "A Sentimental Journey" (March 1928), also written at Phillips Exeter and to some degree autobiographical, is about a young widow whose marriage had been considered undesirable by her family. Agee uses the stream-of-consciousness technique to build toward her choice of uncertainty, as opposed to the security of returning to family. Another of these earliest stories, "Bound for the Promised Land" (January 1928), provides an account of a black funeral. The satiric treatment of the clergyman and descriptions of both mourners and the deceased are similar to passages in *A Death in the Family*.

At Harvard, Agee was also able to prove himself as a writer, and he produced a good deal of prose and poetry; again he served as editor of a literary magazine, the *Harvard Advocate*. Much of his undergraduate writing, especially the prose, is now recognized as a foreshadowing of later accomplishments. The summer of 1929, which he spent as a day laborer and harvest hand in Oklahoma, Kansas, and Nebraska, was – like earlier fictional materials derived from memories of Knoxville, or a 1924 bicycle tour of Europe – a remembrance used in successful writing.

Agee at Harvard in 1932

Agee's earliest fiction reflects his keen appreciation of the world of experience. Indeed, Robert Fitzgerald, who was one of Agee's roommates at Harvard, once asserted that the abstract Harvard poetry never seemed to possess the rhythm and power of the fiction. Agee's best stories possess an immediacy that suggests he relied upon autobiographical material. Thus, in fiction which treats abstract ideas, he is less successful. For instance, in one story published in the *Harvard Advocate* a young father, horrified at what he feels and haunted by a sense of mortal sin, kills his unwanted child by hurling the infant over a cliff. In this concocted situation, ironically entitled "A Walk Before Mass" (Christmas 1929), the weight of Christianity and the teachings of the church are a burden to the story.

Stories written at about the same time that are rather limited in scope are nonetheless carefully realized accomplishments. One of the best examples is "Death in the Desert," published in the October 1930 *Harvard Advocate,* a story that limits itself in large part to the stream-of-consciousness revelation of its narrator, a young man who appears to be much like the Agee of age twenty. This compellingly presented story relates the experience of a summer hitchhiker who has gotten a ride across a hundred-mile desert with a dull couple from Okla-

homa. While sitting in the back seat of their six-year-old Buick, he enjoys meditating about the couple – mentally stripping them of their clothes and allowing two grotesque skeletons to guide the Buick. Part of these mental wanderings are presented in a style reminiscent of James Joyce, while what is achieved is a perceptive picture of a rather obnoxious college sophomore who is sophisticated enough to distance himself from his surroundings. In much of this early autobiographical fiction, such as "Death in the Desert," we see the first successes of an ambitious writer who sought ways to mold fiction from the ordinary experiences of life. Agee's need was to find an adequate technique to suggest the semblance of the flow of events.

What is clear from the competent writing which Agee did before he was twenty-two is that, without the economic crisis of the 1930s, he might have been able to support himself by writing fiction and poetry. Agee's capabilities as a beginning writer are most evident in his undergraduate fiction when the distance between him and his subject matter remains minimal. At that time he could not yet have fully realized that his talent was best suited for a personal evocation of actuality. His less successful undergraduate writing reflects an artist who sought ways of making abstract religious and philosophical beliefs meaningful. Although he was still learning his craft, in letters written during his college years he often asserts an enthusiasm about a possible literary career. He wrote in a 19 November 1930 letter to Father Flye that "I'm from now on committed to writing with a horrible definiteness." Upon his graduation from Harvard in 1932, Agee became a journalist for *Fortune* magazine, a job he would hold for seven years.

Agee worked at a feverish pace throughout his career, and this negatively affected both his personal life and his health. In the first of his three marriages, Agee wed Olivia Saunders in 1934. He married Alma Mailman in 1939, with whom he had a son, Joel, in 1940, but a year later the marriage was terminated. Agee married Mia Fritsch on 28 April 1944, and together they had three children – Julia Teresa, Maria, and John Alexander. Mia Agee once poignantly remarked that her husband wrote continually. She felt he seldom found time for relaxation in the late 1940s, when he so furiously worked as a Luce Publications feature writer and as a freelance scenarist.

Much of what Agee accomplished in the 1930s is the product of his refinement of a fascination with the complexity of ordinary emotion, experience, and consciousness. He sensed that careful observation might be the basis of many writing projects. He asked – in an unsuccessful grant application, "Plans for Work: October 1937," published in *The Collected Short Prose of James Agee* (1968) – whether fictional methods could be used in conjunction with analysis of the "pathology of 'laziness.'" Such an experiment, he continued, might include "fear, ignorance, sex, misinterpretation and economics" as contributing factors. Or why not write, he inquired in these same plans, a "new type of 'horror' story" about the horror "that can come of objects and their relationships"? Such experiments would concentrate "on what the senses receive and the memory and context does [*sic*] with it." Agee's proposals seem the logical outgrowth of what had already been observed as early as in a May 1931 *Harvard Advocate* story called "They That Sow in Sorrow Shall Reap," a study in ambiguity about the difficulty of interpreting events. These are also steps in a progression toward *Let Us Now Praise Famous Men* (1941), written in the late 1930s.

Agee's writing of the middle and late 1930s – scenarios, poetry, and prose – demonstrates how he slowly moved from insight to accomplishment as a fiction writer and began to realize that his own life would become his best subject material. By the mid 1930s he was writing outlines for scenarios, most of them never produced. One early screenplay, "The

House," was written in 1937 and is based on specific memories of the Knoxville neighborhood that nurtured him. Such memories finally gave rise to the manuscript pages that modern readers know as the novel *A Death in the Family*. A story left in draft during this period, "Before God and This Company; or Bigger Than We Are" (circa 1938), is a detailed, prolonged remembrance of an evening's party in a New York City apartment. Seemingly more fact than fiction, the story is contrived of rather mundane events. A young couple hurriedly exits a gathering and performs lovemaking preliminaries as they rush to elevator, taxi, and home.

The familiar prose sketch "Knoxville: Summer of 1915" was already written in 1936. It is among Agee's best fiction. (Sometimes, because the sketch has been retitled and printed as the preface to *A Death in the Family*, it has been mistakenly assumed to be part of the novel.) "Knoxville: Summer of 1915" is a fictional evocation of remembered summer evenings from Agee's childhood. Throughout the sketch there is a movement back toward all summer evenings, then a concentration on an almost static single evening. What Agee caught was an atmosphere that permeated the experience of those evenings. Interestingly, in "Knoxville: Summer of 1915," published first in the August–September 1938 *Partisan Review*, the narrator is the mature writer looking back upon moments apprehended in clarity by a child. The sketch is heavily rhythmic and harmonious, and the narrator makes it clear that while some of that mood can be caught with particular words, the sense of what had been experienced was nonverbal – something sensed, without talking, by all the family as it gathered on midsummer evenings.

Agee did therefore write, at least a little, about memories of Tennessee during the 1930s, but over a decade passed before he devoted any significant amount of energy to such fictionalizing. His journalism for *Fortune*, then the "documentary" *Let Us Now Praise Famous Men*, and considerable film criticism occupied most of his time before the late 1940s. Two *Fortune* articles are significant examples of his analytical journalism and demonstrate how an interest in honoring "actuality" was being refined toward the precision of the nonfiction method used for *Let Us Now Praise Famous Men*. The first of these, "Havana Cruise: Six Days at Sea" (September 1937), about a pleasure cruise to Havana, utilizes a method that Agee knew might be expanded. In his "Plans for Work" Agee had listed as a possible project "an account and analysis of a cruise: 'high'-class people," which would have as its technique the procedure "devel-

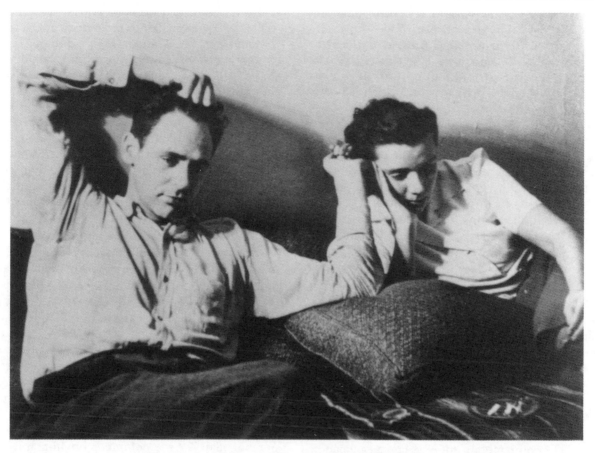

Agee with Mia Fritsch, his third wife (photograph by Helen Levitt)

oped part way in *Havana Cruise.*" In the article Agee reports the boredom and anxiety of cruise passengers, who try to act as though they are having a good time. How they simultaneously reveal fears and social background is fascinating, for it is as if Agee is writing fiction. The tone emerges from a recognition that the passengers cannot have a good time because they have lost any ability to accept life without accompanying complicated assumptions. In their desires to do the right thing at the right time, they forget other things. In being concerned about what costume to wear, they forget how to enjoy. The second *Fortune* article, which was rejected by the magazine as too subjective, was about the role of Brooklyn as appendage and bedroom to New York City and the deadening effect of urban life upon people.

Begun in 1936 as a project for *Fortune,* which the magazine later rejected, *Let Us Now Praise Famous Men* is Agee's deeply personal account of his six weeks' sojourn among three sharecropping families in Alabama. The genre of the book is not easily classified — it is perhaps in part a "nonfiction" novel; it is also a critical study about the impossibility of writing a book about a "typical" tenant farm family; and it is an experiment that is both a lyrical cry and a statement of fact that must be in some ways fictional.

In *Let Us Now Praise Famous Men* the opening "sketches" — reports about meeting black singers, observing persons on a deserted road, and seeing a trio consisting of a young couple and an older man who is startlingly odd in appearance — all are examples of Agee's reporting in such detail that facts are overtaken by imagination. Other whole sections of *Let Us Now Praise Famous Men* function the same way. Even when Agee restricted himself to "fact" within his part 2, called "Some Findings and Comments," fictionalization enters. The stark chapters about "Money," "Education," "Shelter," "Clothing," and "Work" retain their basis in fact; yet we know that Agee, as storyteller, makes us suffer a shock of recognition precisely because the individuals described are real persons who are like all persons. They refuse to be mere material for factual reporting. Archetypal patterns take over.

In 1939 Agee began his career as a film critic, first for *Time* and beginning in 1942 also for the *Nation.*

The columns he wrote until he resigned from both magazines in 1948 to devote himself to his own literary projects are regarded as America's first serious film criticism. During this period Agee also continued to write fiction. His most succinct literary treatment of the demise of individualism is a satiric 1946 short story, "Dedication Day (A Rough Sketch for a Moving Picture)." This bitter story satirizes the imagined dedication of a monument designed to commemorate the discovery of the atom's destructive power. As a parody of journalistic methods, the opening paragraphs of this report amass facts to document the fictional event. (There are no directions for the use of camera. If this work were more developed as a sketch for a film, some minimal suggestions for camera use would probably have been included.)

The story falls into two sections: first, the ceremony; and second, an incident which follows. The dedication is of a "heroic new Arch which was for all time to come to memorialize the greatest of human achievements." Representatives from all countries and faiths attend the bizarre ceremony that takes place between the Washington obelisk and the Lincoln Memorial. The second part of the story reveals how the memorial was planned and brings into focus the grotesque aspects of Agee's imagination. The entire monument – design, maintenance, and even dedication – is the result of hypocrisy and delusion. Only one person, a physicist who had been involved in the development of the bomb, emerges as admirable. "Dedication Day" is close to a parody of a news story. Unimportant details are self-consciously added, as in the description of the physicist's death: "Within a few minutes after the Dedication he was found next the great spool, dead by his own hand (by prussic acid)." This story stands as an indictment of a society in which any act of courage or heroism is interpreted as a deviation from the norm.

In "Dedication Day" Agee's method as fiction writer is to draw readers into the possibility of thinking that such a fantasy could actually have happened. Similarly, a 1948 draft of an unproduced screenplay for Charlie Chaplin depicts the days and weeks after the "Ultimate Bomb" had exploded, bringing the civilization which had produced it to an abrupt halt. Then, in Agee's draft for this script, which he called "Scientists and Tramps," out of the rubble emerge the tramp and the same scientists who had created the weapon. Little by little, the reader sees the individualism of the tramp squashed, as faith in science and scientists gradually regains strength.

The cultural shock of World War II (Agee wrote the *Time* magazine cover story about the Hiroshima atomic bomb) may have led to the kindling of Agee's interest in the American Civil War and stimulated his production of both verse and fiction about the earlier American conflict. His interest in John Huston's 1948 adaptation of Stephen Crane's *The Red Badge of Courage* (1895) for the screen may also have contributed to such a train of thought. An unpublished fragment of a short story about the Civil War provides insight into how soldiers on both sides, as well as a freed slave who is all alone, might have felt as they lived through the horror of a battle in that war.

In the fall of 1951 Agee wrote the stark fable "A Mother's Tale" (published in the July 1952 *Harper's Bazaar*), which functions as commentary about the age and all humankind but can also be interpreted as a symbolic statement about the author's own life. Such overtones are present, for it would have been impossible for Agee to compose "A Mother's Tale" and be unaware of parallels with the way his own energy had been consumed in distractions from serious artistic endeavors. The tale's title character is a mother cow who relates to her son how a steer once came back from the slaughterhouse and urged others to be aware of "the true ultimate purpose of man." As a comment on humanity in a harshly controlled society and man's herd instinct that emphasizes as well man's innocence and gullibility, the allegory is similar to Agee's earlier attacks on modern civilization expressed in works as diverse as *Let Us Now Praise Famous Men* and "Dedication Day."

Agee's partly autobiographical "1928 Story," another story also left in manuscript, was probably completed during the late 1940s. (It was published in the Spring 1968 *Texas Quarterly*.) It begins with an evocation of mood similar to that of some of his unpublished poetry of these years, and it reflects a cynicism similar to that of "Dedication Day." However, in technique and nostalgic tone it resembles the mature autobiographical fiction. The story catches the spontaneity, enthusiasm, and confusion of an adolescent; yet it also has value because it reveals significant facts about the mature Agee. It embodies Agee's ambivalent attitude about the role of the "artist" and is his first sustained attempt after *Let Us Now Praise Famous Men* to re-create a mood from his own life.

As the story opens in the 1940s, the writer Irvine listens to old records that remind him of his earlier years, when he had heard the same music in an altogether different atmosphere, one infused with adolescent confidence and the hopes of an aspiring artist. What the story suggests is that no moment can be clear; all moments become clouded by myriad emotions and reactions. The remembrance of the earlier confident state of mind is central to this story. To suggest the way the narrator feels during the present, as compared with some twenty years earlier, Agee elaborates a specific incident about observing a girl on the beach and about his reaction. The recollection implies that the confidence of adolescence stems largely from inexperience. A similar pattern exists in *The Morning Watch* (1951), a novella Agee wrote in 1950.

The Morning Watch is Agee's first fully sustained attempt to turn his back on the confusion of his own life and to re-create as carefully as possible a remembered moment through fiction. Much like Joyce's *Portrait of the Artist as a Young Man* (1916), Agee's novella catches the beauty of a hero confronted by different and conflicting drives, motives, and passions. Its twelve-year-old hero experiences a high point of religious emotion, but that moment is an ironic one. Indeed, *The Morning Watch* achieves success because of its focus upon a pinnacle of religious fervor that the reader senses will inevitably diminish. The book is about the special hours of the Maundy Thursday vigil and of the morning of Good Friday when students at a rural boarding school (based on Agee's remembrances of Saint Andrew's) are allowed to make visits before the exposed Blessed Sacrament in the Lady Chapel. Richard, the protagonist (his surname does not appear), has anticipated this vigil for months. He has hoped to pray extremely well during his chapel prayer visit. Yet his hopes are doomed; and the narrative is, in large part, a report of failure, even though he does experience genuine religious emotion.

This novella is emblematic of what all of Agee's best work accomplishes. He records facts (perhaps fictionally embellishes them as he goes), and then those individual facts come to stand for much more than just themselves. Agee came to believe that all lives (his, fictionalized as Richard's in *The Morning Watch* and as Rufus's in *A Death in the Family*) reflect archetypal patterns; further, each small detail – properly observed and fictionalized – also suggests archetypal patterns. Any event, properly beheld, can serve in a fictional context and radiate outward. Notes for *A Death in the Family* (written about 1948) include these significant words: "Being and doing archetypal things, and unaware of it." Such is Agee's best method of careful observation and fictional re-creation.

Much of the middle section of *The Morning Watch* – devoted to Richard's attempts to pray – is a record of his distracted mental state, a constant series of deviations from the path he so desperately hopes to follow. For instance, he is hardly in the chapel when its atmosphere of candles and flowers, which should allow him to think of God, drives his mind to remembrances of his father's funeral. When he tries to pray " 'Soul of Christ sanctify me . . . Blood of Christ inebriate me,' " thoughts immediately flash about the derivation of the word *inebriate,* and it is not long before he recalls "drinking soda pop in Knoxville [with] boys slightly more worldly than he [who] would twist the bottle deep into the mouth and cock it up vertically to drink . . . 'Ahhh, good ole whiskey!' "

Agee's working notes and the passages from his manuscript that he later cut support a reading of the novella that emphasizes the futility of the protagonist's attempt to sustain simple faith as it is intruded upon by all manner of things from sex to skepticism. In these notes Agee asked himself what he hoped to accomplish. His answers, as well as unused introductory and concluding passages, indicate that he felt the story should imply that innocence must yield to other ways of experiencing the world. Agee asked himself the following:

> What really am I after in this story, and is it worth doing? Religion at its deepest intensity of clarity of childhood faith and emotions; plus beginnings of a skeptical intellect and set of senses; how the senses themselves and sexuality, fed the skeptical or non-religious or esthetic intellect; efforts at self-discipline.

Realizing that he had overdeveloped too many elements, Agee in another note commented on "so many particularities. They drag, and they are all dull. I keep working for the maximum number, an inch-by-inch account, when what I am after is the minimum in word and image, and a short handing of action." For such reasons he may have developed the elaborate symbolism within the concluding pages. The locust shell that Richard finds and with which he is fascinated certainly connotes death and suffering; but Agee was doubtful about the effectiveness of such overt symbolism. Its function in the narrative suggests a change in the boy's awareness about suffering. Richard's awareness provides a basis for later development; but, as the book closes, he does not fully understand what the carapace signifies.

The concluding moments of the novella are fundamentally built on a boy's intently religious attitudes during hours that remain part of a religious feast. Agee's fear that his method of writing is perhaps too elaborate and "literary" also provides

*Dust jacket for Agee's novel, in which the character of a family is
revealed through the response of each member to the father's
unexpected death*

insight into his accomplishment – a sense of immediacy and evocation of emotion, but an emotion almost ready to disintegrate. In a related note, probably written in 1950, he suggested that "R's waking emotion and the hollowness of the dormitory beds must be as nearly immediate and simultaneous as possible." Any indirection, abstraction, or use of symbols, unless carefully integrated into the experience as a whole, would tend to detract from the immediacy of that moment. Agee experienced difficulty in deciding how to focus on Richard's emotion; many draft versions exist for alternate openings for this novella.

Agee had been seriously pursuing religious questions during the years immediately preceding his decision to write *The Morning Watch,* which he evidently wrote with a single spurt of energy during the spring of 1950. Agee had spent most of the win-

ter and spring on an essay about John Huston, published in *Life* magazine, and then in one week a draft for his "Maundy Thursday" story was finished. The book is, therefore, the product of a period preceded by religious awareness and a story written with relative speed. Ultimately, it should be considered part of the larger autobiographical project that led to *A Death in the Family.* The novel works the same way, with questions concerning religion, family, and sexuality placed below its surface.

In the opening moments of *A Death in the Family,* six-year-old Rufus Follet (with the help of the narrator) puzzles over a mysterious and beautiful world that is comforting and at the same time frightening. Thus, the opposition in the opening pages of *A Death in the Family* between the father, Jay, and the mother, Mary, is quietly addressed. But through the cumulative, incidental use of details, the reader senses, as did Agee, that if enough attention is paid to particulars, then a sense of a larger whole will also be felt.

Just as *Let Us Now Praise Famous Men* expresses the reality of what Agee had personally observed in middle Alabama, and just as *The Morning Watch* relied heavily upon autobiographical remembrance, Agee's final project, unfinished at his death, is systematically based on facts, for he consciously sought to reconstruct the atmosphere of his childhood. Thus, if *Let Us Now Praise Famous Men* is a memorial to tenant farmers, *A Death in the Family* became a memorial for the writer's family — and especially for the father. Agee's novel could not, however, be limited to accounts of father and son; the entire atmosphere sustained by the events and persons as remembered became material for this fictionalized remembrance. In one of the working notes for this project, Agee indicated that the days and months preceding the fictional death were as significant as those immediately surrounding the funeral.

As a tentative outline (1948?) Agee sketched this pattern:

> Begin with complete security and the simple pleasures and sensations. Develop: the deficiency in the child which puts them at odds: the increasing need of the child for the father's approval. Interrupt with the father's sudden death. Here either the whole family is involved, or it is told in terms of the child. At end: the child is in a sense and degree doomed, to religion and the middle class. The mother to religiosity. New strains develop.

Several such listings of possible episodes exist, and, as suggested earlier, the evidence suggests that Agee, early in the composition, had in mind a considerably longer work than the one readers now know as *A Death in the Family*. Had he lived to complete his project, or had he been able to continue in the natural direction in which his remembrances were leading, he might have amplified the atmosphere of family life preceding the death of the father; for most of the variant manuscript material is from Rufus's point of view.

Agee's story, while simple on the surface, confronts death as the negation of life but also as a necessary part of it. The book provides images of life that contrast with the change brought about by Jay Follet's sudden death. Commentators have described the novel as the fulfillment of a vision in which innocence and compassion meet. From its opening, when Rufus feels enclosed by his father's laughter, to the closing moments, when he is alone with his uncle, the focus remains on domestic love and family relationships. *A Death in the Family* is ultimately about all who have undergone similar experiences. What Agee experienced growing up in a comfortable neighborhood in a relatively small city with parents who combined urban and rural traits resembled the lives of millions.

The fictional method of *A Death in the Family* is an extension of Agee's continuing interest in documentation: everything remembered became potentially useful. A great respect for the commonplace, therefore, is at the base of what is accomplished; and Agee's remembrances take on significance simply because they grew out of the time and place he sought to describe. The word *poetic* occurs in descriptions of Agee's novel, and many perceptive insights about its form derive from the realization that *A Death in the Family* functions more like a conventional poem than a novel. Its open form provides a tension between the chaos of reality and the novelist's way of ordering his experience of the world.

A Death in the Family is primarily concerned with evoking and building upon earlier moments from Agee's own life. As he grew older he was increasingly aware that his identity had been formed under his mother's influence and in the absence of a father whom he associated with a rural background. In the novel the religion (and religiosity) of the fictional mother becomes a basic ingredient in her reaction to the death of her husband. The fictional parents had experienced tension in their marriage, "a gulf," the mother thinks, in an opening chapter, that had only recently begun to close; but the marriage had grown into a strong bond, beneficial to all of the family members.

The sketch "Knoxville: Summer of 1915," used as a prelude for *A Death in the Family,* was written at least a decade before Agee began his novel. It evokes the peaceful atmosphere Rufus and his family enjoy. Recollection of that peacefulness alone, however, is not the only mood that generated this novel. "Knoxville: Summer of 1915" recalls a time of unison with nature, as a city's noises are blended with natural ones. The actual mood which generated the novel is rather more evident from an excluded fragment, published posthumously in 1968 as "Dream Sequence." Relating a nightmare about a father brutally lost, the fragment suggests that through a work of art, harmony with the past can be achieved. The artist must first, however, exorcise the nightmare of contemporary life before such peacefulness can be created.

"Dream Sequence," which begins in nightmare, may well have been intended as the true introduction for this novel. It evokes the state of mind of an author driven to compose an autobiographical novel so that order can be made from memories that continue to affect him in the present. "Dream Sequence" has a completely different tone from the "Knoxville: Summer of 1915" sketch, for its narrator says he must return to the years of his childhood; in "Knoxville: Summer of 1915" he has already accomplished just that on a minor scale.

The closing quiet tone of "Dream Sequence," where, as part of the dream, father and son are united, is similar in its mood to the opening chapter of Agee's composite novel. Both passages evoke a peacefulness made possible when father and son are together. The opening chapter of the novel recounts a related evening when Rufus and Jay had gone to the movies and walked home. One basic idea in the novel is fundamental to this episode — the insistence that while one cannot be comfortable with the responsibilities of living, it is necessary to accept frustration. Agee's stress on different characters' acceptance when frustrated is the most important single theme in this novel.

Agee demonstrates how loneliness is part of a much larger pattern, which combines being alive with a sense of wonder, almost contemplative in quality, about life as something to be celebrated and honored — even if, inevitably, we must deal with the pain of being separate from others. All of the characters in this novel are remarkably alone. As Agee focuses on them, especially as they react to the death, loneliness is stressed. But, ironically, circumstances surrounding the death also allow individuals to be drawn together temporarily. Female characters are drawn together because of faith. The men, Uncle Andrew and the grandfather, react in anger, contempt, even pessimism; nevertheless, they, too, are momentarily drawn together. The accident of the death and circumstances of the moment also allow many individual acts of compassion. A pivotal scene, when the family gathers to await news about Jay, exemplifies how each individual can be drawn out of loneliness because of the needs of others. Mary's father, even though he is the skeptic of the family, does comfort his daughter. Agee gains a similar achievement by shifting the point of view within the main narrative, a move that allows him to avoid dependence on any single character. Thus, he can more easily celebrate the world as imagined. When, for instance, Hannah and Mary await news about Jay, Agee provides information through both their minds. After the family learns of Jay's death, Hannah, Mary, and Andrew each meditate about the meaning of death.

Agee lets his characters find a way to a realization of the truth by letting them talk, feel, and think within the immediacy of a particular situation, without narrational intrusion. Aunt Hannah perhaps best realizes how life must be lived. Her care not to push Rufus into making a decision about his new cap, like her restraint in not forcing ideas or opinions on Mary while they await news from Andrew, reflects Agee's own patience with the reporting and fictionalization of mystery. Hannah will let her niece come to whatever realization she must — but on her own. At the same time, Hannah comforts Mary as best she can, realizing that each person lives essentially alone. Agee amasses details to convey emotions, just as he had done in *Let Us Now Praise Famous Men*.

In *Let Us Now Praise Famous Men,* perhaps the keystone of his career, as well as in his autobiographical fiction, especially *The Morning Watch* and *A Death in the Family,* Agee's technique of fictionalizing the details of his own experience is his best way of revealing what others had not usually taken time to see. His respect for the unsung beauty of common lives, whether in rural Alabama or in his autobiographical musings, is finally prophetic of a new kind of nonfictional fiction, perhaps now best practiced by such diverse writers as Norman Mailer and Tom Wolfe. Walker Percy, working in a similar vein, acknowledged Agee's influence.

Agee's importance in modern literature rests on his ability to write poetic prose and fiction that go beyond traditional modes. Just as the poetry of his first book, *Permit Me Voyage,* utilized the Elizabethan flavor of its models yet went beyond to reveal Agee's immediate feelings, his nonfiction about sharecroppers went beyond any previous documentary produced in the 1930s because it insisted on the dignity of actuality. Agee's personal apprehension of actuality is therefore always at the base of his best writing. Thus, as novelist, he wrote in a manner reminiscent of Joyce in *The Morning Watch,* but the novella is about a crucial event from his memory; and the precision of *A Death in the Family* results from a fictionalization of the most ordinary kind of observations.

Agee's concern with innocence and individualism amid the complexities of modern society is reflected in the similarity of theme in all of his writing — poetry, journalism, fiction, screen adaptations. In each he taught readers to see beauty in the commonplace and to be aware of man's frailty and innocence. As one might expect, his influence is not just in literary areas. Robert Coles, who has produced numerous studies of deprived Americans, has documented his own reverence for Agee. Coles, active in the civil rights movement, asserts that Agee's work was crucial for many during the 1960s, when Americans first learned to see what had not been properly beheld before. Agee as storyteller, and as a novelist, was an observer whose careful attention to detail allowed him to reveal far more than just the surface.

Letters:

Letters of James Agee to Father Flye (New York: Braziller, 1962).

Bibliography:

Genevieve Fabre, "A Bibliography of the Works of James Agee," *Bulletin of Bibliography,* 24 (May-August 1965): 145–148, 163–166.

Biography:

Lawrence Bergreen, *James Agee: A Life* (New York: Dutton, 1984).

References:

Alfred T. Barson, *A Way of Seeing: A Critical Study of James Agee* (Amherst: University of Massachusetts Press, 1972);

Kenneth Curry, "The Knoxville of James Agee's *A Death in the Family,*" *Tennessee Studies in Literature,* 14 (1969): 1–14;

W. M. Frohock, "James Agee: The Question of Unkept Promise," *Southwest Review,* 42 (Summer 1957): 221 229;

Victor A. Kramer, *Agee and Actuality: Artistic Vision in His Work* (Troy, N.Y.: Whitston, 1991);

Kramer, *James Agee* (Boston: Twayne, 1975);

Kramer, "James Agee Papers at the University of Texas," *Library Chronicle of the University of Texas,* 8 (1966): 33–36;

Kramer, "Premonition of Disaster: An Unpublished Section for Agee's *A Death in the Family,*" *Costerus,* 1 (1974): 83–93;

Erling Larsen, *James Agee* (Minneapolis: University of Minnesota Press, 1971);

Michael A. Lofaro, ed., *James Agee: Reconsiderations* (Knoxville: University of Tennessee Press, 1992);

Dwight MacDonald, "Death of a Poet," *New Yorker,* 33 (16 November 1957): 224, 226, 229–230, 232–241;

MacDonald, "Some Memories and Letters," *Encounter,* 19 (December 1962): 73–84;

David Madden, ed., *Remembering James Agee* (Baton Rouge: Louisiana State University Press, 1974);

Genevieve Moreau, *The Restless Journey of James Agee* (New York: Morrow, 1977);

Peter H. Ohlin, *Agee* (New York: Obolensky, 1966);

Richard Oulahan, "A Cult Grew Around a Many-Sided Writer," *Life,* 55 (1 November 1963): 69–72;

Kenneth Seib, *James Agee: Promise and Fulfillment* (Pittsburgh: University of Pittsburgh Press, 1968).

Papers:

The Harry Ransom Humanities Research Center at the University of Texas at Austin has a large collection of Agee's literary manuscripts and correspondence.

William S. Burroughs

(5 February 1914 –   )

Leon Lewis
Appalachian State University

See also the Burroughs entries in *DLB 2: American Novelists Since World War II; DLB 8: Twentieth-Century American Science-Fiction Writers; DLB 16: The Beats: Literary Bohemians in Postwar America;* and *DLB Yearbook: 1981.*

BOOKS: *Junkie,* as William Lee, bound with *Narcotic Agent,* by Maurice Helbrant (New York: Ace, 1953; London: Digit, 1957); as William Burroughs (New York: Ace, 1964; London: Olympia/New English Library, 1966); unexpurgated edition as William S. Burroughs, *Junky* (New York: Penguin, 1977);

The Naked Lunch (Paris: Olympia, 1959); published as *Naked Lunch* (New York: Grove Press, 1962; London: Calder/Olympia, 1964);

The Exterminator, by Burroughs and Brion Gysin (San Francisco: Auerhahn, 1960);

Minutes to Go, by Burroughs, Sinclair Beiles, Gregory Corso, and Gysin (Paris: Two Cities, 1960; San Francisco: Beach Books, 1968);

The Soft Machine (Paris: Olympia, 1961; revised and enlarged edition, New York: Grove, 1966; second revision and enlargement, London: Calder & Boyars, 1968);

The Ticket That Exploded (Paris: Olympia, 1962; revised and enlarged edition, New York: Grove, 1967; London: Calder & Boyars, 1968);

Dead Fingers Talk (London: Calder/Olympia, 1963);

The Yage Letters, by Burroughs and Allen Ginsberg (San Francisco: City Lights, 1963; enlarged edition, San Francisco: City Lights, 1975);

Nova Express (New York: Grove, 1964; London: Cape, 1966);

Roosevelt after Inauguration, as "Willy Lee" alias WSB (New York: Fuck You Press, 1964; enlarged as *Roosevelt after Inauguration and Other Atrocities,* San Francisco: City Lights, 1979);

Health Bulletin: APO-33, a Metabolic Regulator (New York: Fuck You Press, 1965); published as *APO-33 Bulletin: A Metabolic Regulator* (San Francisco: Beach, 1966);

William S. Burroughs (photograph by Maarten Corbyn)

Time (New York: "C," 1965);

Valentine's Day Reading (New York: American Theatre for Poets, 1965);

So Who Owns Death TV?, by Burroughs, Claude Pélieu, and Carl Weissner (San Francisco: Beach, 1967);

Entretiens avec William Burroughs, by Burroughs and Daniel Odier (Paris: Belfond, 1969); translated, revised, and enlarged as *The Job: Inter-*

views with William S. Burroughs (New York: Grove, 1970; London: Cape, 1970; second revision and enlargement, New York: Grove, 1974);

The Last Words of Dutch Schultz (London: Cape Goliard, 1970; revised and enlarged edition, New York: Viking/Seaver, 1975);

Ali's Smile (Brighton, U.K.: Unicorn, 1971); published in an enlarged edition as *Ali's Smile/Naked Scientology* (Göttingen: Expanded Media Editions, 1973);

Electronic Revolution 1970–71 (Cambridge: Blackmoor Head, 1971; enlarged edition, Göttingen: Expanded Media Editions, 1972);

The Wild Boys: A Book of the Dead (New York: Grove, 1971; London: Calder & Boyars, 1972);

Exterminator! (New York: Seaver/Viking, 1973; London: Calder & Boyars, 1975);

Mayfair Academy Series More or Less (Brighton, U.K.: Urgency Rip-Off, 1973);

White Subway (London: Aloes, 1973);

Brion Gysin Let the Mice In, by Burroughs, Gysin, and Ian Sommerville, edited by Jan Herman (West Glover, Vt.: Something Else, 1973);

Port of Saints (London: Covent Garden, 1973; revised edition, Berkeley: Blue Wind, 1980);

The Book of Breeething (Ingatestone, Essex, U.K.: OU, 1974; Berkeley: Blue Wind, 1975);

Sidetripping, by Burroughs and Charles Gatewood (New York: Strawberry Hill, 1975);

Snack . . . , by Burroughs and Eric Mottram (London: Aloes, 1975);

Cobble Stone Gardens (Cherry Valley, N.Y.: Cherry Valley Editions, 1976);

The Retreat Diaries, with *The Dream of Tibet,* by Ginsberg (New York: City Moon, 1976);

The Third Mind, by Burroughs and Gysin (New York: Seaver/Viking, 1978; London: Calder, 1979);

Doctor Benway: A Passage from The Naked Lunch (Santa Barbara: Morrow, 1979);

Ah Pook Is Here and Other Texts (London: Calder, 1979; New York: Riverrun, 1982);

Blade Runner (A Movie) (Berkeley: Blue Wind, 1979);

The Soft Machine, Nova Express, The Wild Boys: Three Novels (New York: Grove/Outrider, 1980);

Cities of the Red Night (New York: Holt, Rinehart & Winston, 1981; London: Calder, 1981);

Early Routines (Santa Barbara: Cadmus, 1981);

The Streets of Chance (New York: Red Ozier, 1981);

A William Burroughs Reader, edited by John Calder (London: Pan/Picador, 1982);

The Place of Dead Roads (New York: Holt, Rinehart & Winston, 1983; London: Calder, 1984);

The Burroughs File (San Francisco: City Lights, 1984);

Queer (New York: Viking, 1985; London: Pan, 1985);

The Adding Machine: Collected Essays (London: Calder, 1985); published as *The Adding Machine: Selected Essays* (New York: Seaver, 1986);

The Cat Inside (New York: Grenfell, 1986);

The Western Lands (New York: Viking/Penguin, 1987; London: Pan, 1987);

Interzone (New York: Viking, 1989);

My Education: A Book of Dreams (New York: Viking, 1995; London: Pan, 1995).

PLAY PRODUCTION: *The Black Rider: The Casting of the Magic Bullets,* with songs by Tom Waits, Thalia Theater, Hamburg, 31 March 1990; New York, Brooklyn Academy of Music, December 1993.

OTHER: John Giorno, *You Got to Burn to Shine: New and Collected Writings,* introduction by Burroughs (New York: Serpent's Tail, 1994).

SELECTED PERIODICAL PUBLICATION – UNCOLLECTED: "My Purpose Is To Write for the Space Age," *New York Times Book Review* (19 February 1984): 9–10.

Fifty years after Allen Ginsberg, Jack Kerouac, and William S. Burroughs first met in Manhattan, New York University sponsored a conference celebrating the legacy of the Beat Generation. Burroughs, whose picture appeared prominently in several places on the elaborate brochure announcing the conference, was not listed as a participant. At the beginning of the main event, a series of performances at New York's Town Hall that included many of the prominent figures from the Beat Generation and those they influenced, Burroughs addressed the conference from his home in Lawrence, Kansas, through an amplified telephone hookup. Speaking in his trademark laconic style, he offered what *The New York Times* called "flinty, deadpan advice on writing and life." Once seen as a wild boy of beatitude, Burroughs at eighty appeared to be an elder statesman of an artistic impulse originally scorned by the literary establishment but now firmly a part of American literature.

The legend surrounding Burroughs's life has tended to deflect attention from his actual accomplishments while intertwining the life of the man with his work in ways that require knowledge of both to make either intelligible. His influence on musicians, filmmakers, computer hackers, and others with antiestablishment agendas has frequently overshadowed his importance as a writer. However, his employment of a Joycean stream-of-consciousness narrative; his prefiguring of postmodernism in his fusion of disparate modes; his development of a novel that does not depend on traditional methods of shaping plot, characters, and dialogue; and his creation of a distinctly singular voice that combines several strains of American speech while retaining its own characteristic qualities should ensure his place in twentieth-century literature. His abilities as a writer — in conjunction with his often-prophetic mapping of the direction of Western society in the last decades of the twentieth century and his scrutinizing examination of the life of an underclass of social outlaws and misfits — have kept Burroughs relevant while other practitioners of an extremist sensibility, as well as once-celebrated champions of more conventional literary forms, have receded from public consciousness.

William Seward Burroughs II was born in Saint Louis on 5 February 1914. His paternal grandfather, for whom he was named, perfected the first marketable adding machine that produced a printed record of results, and although his father, Mortimer Burroughs, sold his share of the company in 1929, sufficient funds were available to provide Burroughs with a comfortable home, adequate educational opportunities, and in his middle years a modest stipend. Burroughs recognized the safety net the regular arrival of the check provided and observed to biographer Ted Morgan that the value of his father's shares in the 1960s would have been "twenty million reasons not to write." His maternal grandfather, James Wideman Lee, was a circuit-riding minister who went to Saint Louis to head a prominent Methodist parish. Laura Lee, Burroughs's mother, was one of six surviving children that included Ivy Ledbetter Lee, a flamboyant promoter sometimes called "The Father of Public Relations" who counted among his clients John D. Rockefeller and Adolf Hitler. Burroughs recalls that among the circumstances leading to his vocation as a writer was a feeling that he had an obligation to redeem a language corrupted by manipulators such as his uncle.

During his childhood Burroughs felt estranged from the conventional expectations of his parents' position in Saint Louis society, irritated by .the requirements of mannered behavior, and insulted by the attitudes of those who felt his family was not quite rich enough. He described himself to Morgan as a "chronic malingerer" as a student at the private John Burroughs School, but he formed a friendship there with a popular young man named Kells Elvins that lasted until Elvins's death in 1962. Burroughs claims that he already knew then that he was homosexual, insisting that he was born with the predisposition, and while his friendship with Elvins was his first "love," it remained nonsexual, suggesting a pattern of desire for the unattainable that recurred with other significant figures in Burroughs's life.

In 1929 Burroughs's first published work appeared in the *John Burroughs Review* — an essay written in the investigatory mode of the skeptical examiner suspicious of the claims of those purporting to speak for official, acknowledged "wisdom." Burroughs had already begun to imagine a life as a writer, although his conception owed a good deal to the raffish depiction of the writer/adventurer of late-Victorian sensationalist fiction. The formation of his own sensibility proceeded on dual tracks: one directed toward the proper educational concerns of a young man, which placed him in the Los Alamos Ranch School in New Mexico, where his unathletic demeanor was supposed to be improved; and another, more personal course, which included reading Jack Black's *You Can't Win* (1926), a memoir of a professional thief and drug addict that Burroughs found congenial in its depiction of a subculture of outcasts with their own codes of honor and loyalty.

Burroughs continued to build the foundation of a solid classical education when he completed his last year of high school at an academy in Saint Louis that stressed the works of John Milton and William Shakespeare and entered Harvard University in the fall of 1932. There — although he studied with such esteemed professors as the Shakespearean scholar George Lyman Kittredge and the Samuel Taylor Coleridge expert John Livingston Lowes, whose course suggested some intriguing possibilities about the artistic use of mind-altering substances — Burroughs continued to feel like an outsider, cultivating various eccentric gestures (such as keeping a ferret and a .32-caliber revolver in his room) to establish an individual identity. He summarized his college experience in the prologue to *Junky* (first published as *Junkie,* 1953), "I hated the University and I hated the town it was in. Everything about the place was dead. The University was a fake English setup taken over by the graduates of fake English public schools. I was lonely. I knew no one, and strangers were regarded with distaste by the closed corporation of the desireables."

With a monthly stipend of two hundred dollars from his family, Burroughs was able to travel to

*Burroughs at age twenty-one, when he was a student at
Harvard University (Burroughs Archive)*

Europe, where he arranged a marriage to Ilse Krabbe in 1937 as a means of assisting her escape from the Nazis. He registered for some graduate courses in psychology at Columbia University upon his return to the United States in 1937, then in 1938 enrolled in a program in archaeology at Harvard, where he joined Elvins in an alternate-paragraph collaboration called "Twilight's Last Gleaming," a slapstick account of panic aboard a sinking ocean liner. Working with Elvins helped Burroughs overcome his self-consciousness about expressing his intimate feelings, and the piece introduced a "Dr. Benway," the prototype of the wild maverick who became the narrative consciousness of much of Burroughs's later writing. When *Esquire* rejected the mélange of surreal black humor and mordant satire as "Too screwy, and not effectively so for us," Burroughs was discouraged to the point that he did not attempt to write anything for the next six years. After a brief commitment for psychiatric care when he cut off the end of his left little finger to express

his anguish at the rejection of his affection by a man named Jack Anderson, Burroughs attempted to enlist in 1940 but was turned down by the navy as a "poor physical specimen," was turned down by the American Field Service because – he believed – he resided in the "wrong house" at Harvard, failed to complete flying school due to his poor eyesight, and after being drafted into the infantry in 1942 was given a psychiatric discharge arranged by his mother. When Lucien Carr, an old friend from Saint Louis, transferred to Columbia University in spring 1943, Burroughs went with him to New York.

The move essentially fixed the course of Burroughs's life. Through Carr he met Ginsberg, a freshman at Columbia, and Kerouac, no longer a student there but a part of a growing bohemian subculture that became the core of the Beat group that provided support and guidance for Burroughs as he began his life as a writer. In addition to their shared literary enthusiasms, Burroughs was fascinated by the unconventional, open-minded attitudes toward sex, drugs, politics, and art he encountered among these young people. The thirty-year-old Burroughs belonged to a generation they distrusted and despised, but they found his erudition and composure appealing.

Burroughs was comfortable enough with Kerouac to attempt another collaboration, a novel written in alternate chapters tentatively called "And the Hippos Were Boiled in Their Tanks," about Carr's killing of David Kammerer in self-defense. The book was turned down by every publisher who looked at it, and Burroughs, who unsuccessfully attempted to join the merchant marine as the war ended, experienced another rebuff from the respectable institutions of American society. His sense of himself as an underground man in combat with the straight world, combined with his ongoing interest in unusual conditions of psychic displacement, were factors in his involvement with a drug scene that left him hooked on heroin and driven to petty crime to support his addiction.

At the same time, although he was undeniably homosexual, Burroughs began an intimate affair with Joan Vollmer, a friend of Kerouac's first wife, Edie Parker. Morgan describes their union as a relationship "between two remarkable intellects." When Burroughs was arrested as an accessory to theft and given a four-month suspended sentence, the couple moved to east Texas to start a farm with money borrowed from his parents. Their son, William "Billy" Burroughs Jr. was born on 21 July 1947, and the family – including Vollmer's daughter, Julie – moved to Mexico City in 1949. Except for short visits, for the next twenty-four years he was in exile from the United States.

The arrival of Elvins in Mexico City led Burroughs back to his dormant but unrelinquished desire to be a writer, and with Elvins's encouragement he set down in a factual fashion "the only accurate account I ever read of the real horror of junk," as he wrote to Ginsberg when he began to send him fragments of the manuscript in 1951. Although the imaginative inventions in narrative structure, surreal poetic imagery, and uncharted psychic terrain characteristic of Burroughs's best work are not evident in *Junky,* the terse, laconic narration depicts a group of perversely fascinating fugitives from the straight world in search of some compensation for their alienation and discomfort. William Lee, Burroughs's pseudonym and protagonist, searches for a morphine high and attempts to understand and explain the sources of addiction. The circumstances of the addict's life – the score, the high, the with-

drawal, the evasion of the law, and the discovery of a new drug with enhanced visionary powers – function as an analogue for the life of the hipster, the rebel outsider who has rejected the square world and its constraints and is trying to find a more intense, more spiritual existence. Burroughs's avoidance of sentimentality and his frequent insertions of "scientific" data as a form of exposition give *Junky* a feeling of authenticity. Its open-ended, picaresque series of episodes is his initial attempt to expand the traditional principles of novelistic organization, and its presentation of the drug subculture is both a kind of historical journal and an incisive account of the lure and appeal of an alternative lifestyle.

After his previous failures Burroughs did not expect to see the novel published, but Ginsberg's friend Carl Solomon (the dedicatee of "Howl" [1956]) was working for A. A. Wyn, the publisher of Ace Books, and Wyn, Solomon's uncle, decided to combine the manuscript Solomon brought him with a reprint of a 1941 memoir, *Narcotics Agent,* by Maurice Helbrant. The news from Ginsberg in April 1952 that *Junky* had been accepted for publication cheered Burroughs to some degree, as did a visit from Kerouac, who arrived in May and stayed for two months.

The two books were bound in one paperback volume and sold for thirty-five cents. It was completely ignored by critics and reviewers, but Burroughs was paid an advance of one thousand dollars, which encouraged his dreams of a writing career. The book sold more than 100,000 copies in its first year, and Chandler Brossard recognized its originality and taught it in a class at New York University.

After realizing the possibilities of publication with *Junky,* Burroughs wrote his next book, *Queer* (1985), in response to a devastating event whose impact has continued to resonate through his life and work. Since his initial contact with the drug subculture in New York in the 1940s, he had been involved in a series of minor difficulties with the police, occasionally having to turn to friends, family, or lawyers for relief, but in spite of the stories about moments of violence included in his conversations with friends, he was a courteous, composed, and gentle man by nature. The effects of heavy drug and alcohol use for nearly a decade, however, led to an incident whose events are not entirely clear: on 6 September 1951 he accidentally shot and fatally wounded his common-law wife. In Morgan's biography, written with Burroughs's cooperation, the three men present – Burroughs, Eugene Allerton, and Eddie Woods, who had all been drinking – recount their version of Burroughs's attempt to demonstrate his marksmanship by firing at a glass balanced on his wife's head. In spite of some misgivings, no one resisted the idea, and the shot struck Vollmer.

In a retrospective evaluation of the event, Burroughs wrote in his introduction to *Queer,* "I am forced to the appalling conclusion that I would never have become a writer but for Joan's death, and to a realization of the extent to which this event has motivated and formulated my writing." He felt that the incident brought him directly into contact with a kind of hidden demon that had been shadowing him for years and that his only way to escape from its destructive influence was "to write my way out." Whether or not he realized this in 1951, he began writing *Queer* ostensibly to describe William Lee's withdrawal from drugs and their deceptive protection and to show how this left Lee vulnerable to an indefinite yearning expressed sexually. The character had become, as Burroughs wrote in the introduction, "disintegrated, desperately in need of contact, completely unsure of himself and his purpose in life." The object of Lee's (and Burroughs's) attention is Eugene Allerton (not his actual name), but the loss of Burroughs's wife is also clearly another source of longing and is camouflaged by transference, a strategy consistent with Burroughs's continuing interest in men throughout his relationship with Vollmer. Burroughs asserts that the book "is motivated and formed by an event which is never mentioned, in fact is carefully avoided: the accidental shooting death of my wife, Joan, in September 1951."

Burroughs was placed in custody by Mexican authorities after the shooting. He spent thirteen days in jail and was released after posting a bond of $2,312. The bail was a form of probation, and he had to register at the jail every week. His son was sent to live with Burroughs's family in Saint Louis, and Vollmer's daughter, Julie, was placed with Vollmer's parents. In December, with the prospect of additional funds required to keep him out of jail and little reason to remain, Burroughs left Mexico. After a brief stay in Palm Beach with his family, he headed for South America in search of the legendary hallucinogenic substance *yage,* which he hoped to use for psychic exploration and stress relief.

During the time he was in Colombia Burroughs maintained a correspondence with Ginsberg that the two men edited as "In Search of Yage," which was eventually published as part of an epistolary novel, *The Yage Letters* (1963). Again a form of collaboration enabled Burroughs to overcome his hesitancy about expressing his feelings in his writ-

ing. The letters continue the exploits of William Lee, with yage instead of morphine the goal of Lee's adventures. In a stylistic expansion that anticipates *Naked Lunch* (1959), Lee describes some of the visions produced by ingesting yage and includes some of the "routines" that Burroughs eventually made a central part of his work. His sojourn in South America was marked by sickness and discouragement, and he returned briefly to the United States to work with Ginsberg on the letters, then departed for Rome with writer Alan Ansen, who was briefly W. H. Auden's secretary. Rome did not interest Burroughs, and he decided to try Tangier, which he had read about in Paul Bowles's novels *The Sheltering Sky* (1949) and *Let It Come Down* (1952).

At first Burroughs found Tangier congenial, responding to the indifference of local authorities to private behavior concerning drugs and sex, the serious exploration of magic and psychic states in some quarters, and the low status or influence of women in society. The international mix of wanderers, dropouts, hustlers, and bizarre socialites temporarily amused him, and he met both Bowles and Brion Gysin, a Swiss-Canadian painter who became one of Burroughs's most important collaborative partners. Burroughs realized that it was unlikely he would ever be willing to work at any kind of conventional job, and his association with writers such as Kerouac and Ginsberg who had committed themselves to their work in spite of the difficulties they faced suggested that he might also devote himself totally to his craft.

As Burroughs wrote to Ginsberg, he hoped to get what he really meant down on paper but had "despair of ever doing so." A major part of the problem was his constant struggle with drugs and alcohol, which Ginsberg recalled as "his heroic battle with depression and junk." In letters written to Kerouac (18 August 1954) and to Ginsberg (17 May 1955) Burroughs captured both his enthusiasms and his frustration for the work he was doing: "I am having Serious difficulties with my novel. I tell you the novel form is Completely inadequate to express what I have to say. I don't know if I can find a form. I am very gloomy as to the prospects of publication." The manuscript on which Burroughs was working was the basis for *Naked Lunch,* and the letters to Ginsberg were another part eventually incorporated into the final version.

A feeling of exultation accompanied the project, once Burroughs realized that he had finally found his voice. Don Cotton, who lived next door, recalls wild laughter along with the typing, and Bowles tells of seeing the floor of Burroughs's room

Burroughs and Brion Gysin, one of his collaborators, in Paris, 1959

covered with hundreds of yellow pages torn from the typewriter, or written in longhand when Burroughs had to sell the typewriter to buy drugs, and flung onto the floor in a creative frenzy. Burroughs thought of the book as the release of a lifetime accumulation of experience and used as a working title "Word Hoard," although he also thought of the project as the book of the Interzone, imagining a shifting setting approximating Tangier with inhabitants caught between a disastrous past and an elusive dream of a more promising future.

Burroughs worried about how to organize his material, a problem not even partially resolved until just before the book was sent to Maurice Girodias's Olympia Press in Paris. Burroughs expressed his concern to Ginsberg – "The 'novel' is a dead form, rigid and arbitrary. I can't use it" – while trying to explain, both to Ginsberg and to himself, various methods for coherence. Recognizing that everything he was writing might be in some way relevant to his project, he wrote to Ginsberg in 1955, "I am selecting, editing and transcribing letters and notes from the past year." At the same time Burroughs envisioned possible principles of organization, such as the concept that "chapters form a mosaic, with the dream impact of juxtaposition," an idea somewhat

similar to Ginsberg's use of unusual associations in "Howl." Burroughs also worked on writing a piece on Tangier to sell – "When I don't have inspiration for the novel, I busy myself with hack work."

In 1956 Burroughs attempted to cure his narcotics addiction with John Dent, a physician in London. After completing treatment, while deciding how to proceed with his work, he invited Ginsberg and other friends to Tangier to enjoy the city and to assist in compiling his mass of material into a book that could be published. "The endless novel which will drive everyone mad" – as Burroughs described it, echoing James Joyce's reference to *Ulysses* (1922) as "this great monster novel" – began to take its ultimate shape when Kerouac arrived in February 1957 and offered to type a fair copy of the preliminary assemblage of texts and letters. Kerouac's title, "Naked Lunch," which Burroughs had considered using on various pieces, now became the working title. When Ginsberg arrived he brought all of the material Burroughs had sent him over the previous four years and retyped it, "separating personal-letter matter from imaginative improvisation and fantasy and routine matter." Burroughs had told Ginsberg, "Read it in any order. It makes no difference," but everyone sensed that some pattern was necessary, and each person – including Ansen, who also retyped sections – proposed a different chapter sequence. The resolution of the matter was delayed until 1959, when what Ginsberg calls "the final editing arrangement" was completed.

Ginsberg convinced Burroughs to submit a draft to Lawrence Ferlinghetti's City Lights Books, the publisher of *Howl,* but Ferlinghetti felt the manuscript was "too scattered." Ginsberg then sent eighty pages of the book to Irving Rosenthal, the editor of the *Chicago Review.* When University of Chicago authorities nervously suppressed the entire issue, in the spring of 1959 Rosenthal founded *Big Table,* which contained ten episodes of "Naked Lunch." Girodias, who had previously felt the work uncommercial, now requested that the manuscript be sent immediately, and by Burroughs's account in *Letters to Allen Ginsberg, 1953–1957,* "We worked away, sending pieces to the printer as soon as they were typed up.... The way it came off the typewriter was the way it worked." One month after Girodias decided to publish the book, *The Naked Lunch* (as it was called) was issued in an edition of ten thousand copies in July 1959. The "grand style" (in Ginsberg's words) of the book marked the emergence of the singular, striking, unprecedented narrative consciousness that has become Burroughs's signature, the first demonstration of what James Grauerholz, Burroughs's secretary since 1973, calls in *Interzone* (1989) "a man breaking through into unexplored literary territory."

This territory also includes Burroughs's mental landscape. As Jennie Skerl, one of Burroughs's most astute critics, has noted, the subject of *Naked Lunch* "is a state of mind," adding, "The action is the flow of consciousness." Skerl qualifies her comments by adding that since Burroughs is working "in a narrative form, he needs characters, action, and setting to convey his ideas." In *Naked Lunch* the four regions – South America, the United States, Interzone/Tangier, and Freeland (a "place of the living dead" modeled on what he thought Scandinavian socialism had produced) – correspond to four sections, and the four parties of the Interzone – Liquefactionists, Conferents/Senders, Divisionists, and Factualists – cover the spectrum of political possibility. While these ideas are not without interest, the essence of the book is the mind of the man who wrote it. The characters are manifestations of mental self-examination; if drawn from an external source, they are so shaped by the writer's sensibility as to be assumed into his psychic construct. The setting is so much an imaginative fusion of observation and the artist's responses to his environment that it too is essentially a part of the psychic geography of the writer. The satiric thrust of the novel and much of Burroughs's other work is directed against the massive powers of control exercised by the multiple tyrannies of the modern age. While this is a crucial modernist issue and one of Burroughs's central themes, it here depends on the narrative consciousness that was a product of Burroughs's experiences.

In *Naked Lunch* the linear tracks of Burroughs's life are intermingled in an extraordinary amalgam of diverse, apparently mutually exclusive cultural spheres. The old model of the learned, classically educated, ever-intrepid, never-flustered, self-effacing Victorian gentleman – which both appealed to and repelled Burroughs, who despised its reliance on status and privilege – was subverted by his fascination with the underworld of gangsters, junkies, sexual outlaws, and artistic rebels. At the heart of his struggle to find a suitable means of expression for all of these elements was the necessity for finding a voice that would not betray or exclude any of these features. An indication of his dedication was the composition of an almost entirely discarded section of the Interzone manuscript called "WORD" (later published from a temporarily misplaced collection as *Interzone* in 1989), in which Burroughs adopted, as Grauerholz puts it, "a manic, surreal, willfully disgusting and violently purgative regurgitation of seemingly random images." Grauerholz regards this as Burroughs's first breakthrough into his "own characteristic voice," but the angry tone of "WORD" is an echo of Henry Miller's own breakthrough in *Tropic of Cancer* (1934). Burroughs shared Miller's rage and his impatience with traditional conceptions of literary form, but he did not find the wrath that launched Miller a consistently comfortable mode.

Instead, in an introduction that did not appear in the original edition but that has been a part of U.S. editions since Grove Press published *Naked Lunch* in 1962, Burroughs presented himself as a man just awakened from "The Sickness" (drug addiction). While Miller challenged his readers to follow him through a world in decay, Burroughs invited his to enter the mental cosmos of an extraordinary mind that envisioned phenomena unimagined by most people and never before shaped into art. Some commentators have speculated that the introduction was written as a preemptive strike against censors – "Certain passages in the book that have been called pornographic were written as a tract against Capital Punishment in the manner of Jonathan Swift's *Modest Proposal*" – but he has never put anything in his books that did not satisfy his artistic purposes. The introduction includes his credentials for a journey into dangerous territory, testifies to the authenticity of his account, and suggests that one ignore him at one's peril since the germ of addiction is a genetic cornerstone of human genealogy. His list of the substances he has used is so esoterically extensive, a testament to and a parody of scientific expertise, and his blunt confession that "I have smoked junk, eaten it, sniffed it, injected it in vein-skin-muscle, inserted it in rectal suppositories" is such a mixture of braggadocio and apologia that unless a reader is disgusted by any mention of the subject, as many were, it is hard not to be captured by the knowledge, confidence, and compulsive enthusiasm of the author. At the conclusion of the introduction, Burroughs's interpolation of the phrase "Wouldn't you?" compels the reader's recognition that the forbidden and tantalizing world ahead must be seen, a strategy reinforced by a clever verbal re-creation of a drugged mood that encourages continued reading, as if language were the addictive agent. As Skerl points out, the term *addiction* is a metaphor for the human condition, and the cosmos of *Naked Lunch* is "an entire metaphorical world, or a mythology" where various aspects of behavior have been expanded or exaggerated to a stunning, often surreal, often absurd status that carries familiar tendencies toward a conclusion that reveals their real intent or back toward origins that uncover and explain their genesis. The "social structure mirrors the individual process of addiction/possession on a larger scale," Skerl explains, so the environment and its inhabitants resonate in a symbiotic rhythm of increasing outlandishness.

After the initial exposition, the remainder of the text is composed of what Burroughs originally called "skits" and then "routines," the terms suggesting a performance initially designed to entertain or hold someone's attention but for Burroughs a central outlet for the dynamic flux of associations and images surging through his mind. Grauerholz calls them "an absurdist form of soliloquy," and they may have begun as a means for the normally reserved, even shy, Burroughs to demonstrate his wit and ideas. "Twilight's Last Gleaming," his 1938 collaboration with Elvins, resembled a series of brief sketches built on exchanges of dialogue. As Burroughs's writing progressed the routines became much more deft and complex, and by the time *Naked Lunch* was being written, Burroughs was telling Ginsberg that the force of inspiration "shakes me like a great black wind through the bones." In explaining to Ginsberg how the routine worked, Burroughs said they are "uncontrollable, unpredict-

able, charged with potential danger for Lee. . . . [T]he routine is closest to bullfighting. The routine artist is always trying to outdo himself, to go a little further, to commit some incredible but appropriate excess." The routine opens a channel to the subconscious and requires that no data be restricted or censored – a fundamental part of Burroughs's creed as an artist.

The divisions or sections of *Naked Lunch* depend on the manipulation of language for their primary effect, with two controversial preoccupations threaded as leitmotivs through the book. Burroughs investigates the methods that people in positions of power or dependency use to influence others through the exertion of psychological, social, political, and sexual pressures, but most of the criticism directed at *Naked Lunch* by literary critics and legal authorities has focused on Burroughs's graphic presentation of coarse physical detail and his apparent lack of a clear moral base in his portrayal of deviant social activities. Burroughs's intentions, however, are neither to endorse nor directly to condemn the participants depicted in his routines, utilizing instead the shocking force of the portrayals as a means of undermining easy or habitual responses so that conventional judgment might be replaced by a new or deeper understanding of fundamental causes. The morality of his work is derived from his exploration of what he calls "The Algebra of Need" – a phrase pointing toward the cynical exploitation of human desperation that might be understood in terms of the root meaning of *algebra*. The concept of the Arabic *jebr* suggests the reunion of broken parts; thus Burroughs concentrates on social equations of power and control and also on the necessity for a reintegration of fragmented personalities so that destructive relationships of entrapment can be shattered.

The linguistic invention of the routines is directed toward this end. Burroughs mixes passages written in a burlesque of official complacency, often using upper-class British parlance, with the argot of the hipster; places cracker-barrel American slang amid elaborate quasi-Germanic medical and technical exposition; improvises hysterical diatribes parallel to surreal images flowing from a drug-induced haze; and interjects offhand commentary in a variety of voices, including the antic-parodic-professional prankster who twists familiar lines ("Why so pale and wan, fair bugger?") in a strategy that undermines familiar cultural assumptions.

The character of Dr. Benway, who some critics have regarded as a villain, is also a freewheeling projection of Burroughs's wildest nature – a cool,

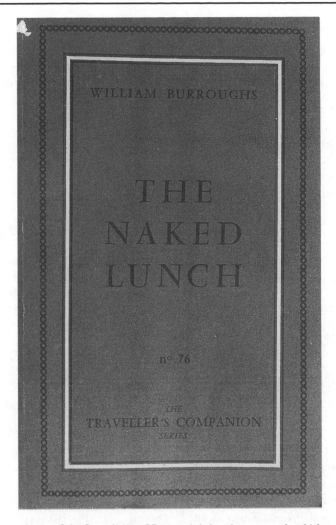

*Cover of the first edition of Burroughs's best-known novel, which
was published by the Olympia Press in Paris after many
rejections from American publishers*

self-composed, wryly amused manipulator. This du-
ality has confounded some readers and is also at the
crux of Burroughs's methods. The outrageous actions of many of the characters are partially justified
if not sanctioned by the massive idiocy and paranoia that pervade the setting, and Burroughs's tendency to present underdogs sympathetically, or at
least with a knowing understanding, corresponds to
an implicit philosophical assumption that for some
people – primarily the people for whom Burroughs
is writing – psychic survival in a world gone awry
might depend on altering one's mental state
through almost any means available.

    The last sections of the book, including the At-
rophied Preface – an unusual name for a "conclusion," indicating the cyclical nature of the structural
arrangement – draw back from the maelstrom, providing a reflective pause in which a point of balance

is momentarily achieved prior to another descent.
Speaking now as William Seward, a comfortably familiar presence, Burroughs muses about his methods, naming most of the characters and confiding
that they "are subject to say the same thing in the
same word . . . to be the same person." The flow of
consciousness, a series of images interspersed with
bits of conversation, continues, occasionally interrupted by the section's subtitle, "WOULDN'T
YOU?" – a mantra of complicity indicting the remainder of the world that would prefer not to notice
the activity Burroughs is writing about or admit its
genesis in fundamental human desire.

    Everyone involved with *Naked Lunch* antici-
pated difficulties with censors and realized that ad-
verse critical reaction was also likely. When Grove
Press issued the first American edition in 1962 the
book was prosecuted as obscene by Massachusetts,

and an illustrious group of artists – including Norman Mailer, John Ciardi, Ginsberg, and others – was called as expert witnesses to testify to its artistic objectives and values. In his book on the subject Michael Barry Goodman calls *Naked Lunch* "the last work of literature to be censored by the academy, the U.S. Post Office, the U.S. Customs Service, and the state and local government." In 1966 the Massachusetts Supreme Court declared the work not obscene based on national criteria.

Naked Lunch was widely reviewed upon its publication in the United States and Great Britain, with the entire spectrum of critical opinion represented. Herbert Gold, who had read aloud from the manuscript in Paris at an international avant-garde gathering in 1959, wrote a thoughtful, explanatory review for *The New York Times,* and appreciative, intelligent responses also appeared in *Newsweek* and the *New York Herald Tribune*. The review that had the most impact in beginning to establish the book's reputation was by Mary McCarthy for *The New York Review of Books*. McCarthy participated in a panel with Burroughs and Henry Miller at the Writers' Conference that John Calder, Burroughs's British publisher, organized for the 1962 Edinburgh Festival, at which Mailer called him "the only American writer who may be possessed by genius." McCarthy's essay on his style and comic technique compelled a more serious consideration of *Naked Lunch* than the chorus of disgust of many reviews, which attacked the author on grounds of moral depravity. The most strenuous discussion of the book's merits took place in Great Britain. John Wain thought Burroughs was a promoter of drug use, while John Willett in an unsigned review in the *Times Literary Supplement* titled "Ugh . . . " called for "the book world" to "clean up the mess." His attack drew a wide range of responses, from the most reactionary, as with Edith Sitwell, to the most enlightened, as with Eric Mottram, and in 1964 Burroughs contributed a typically clearheaded, sensible letter to the controversy. By 1965 *Naked Lunch* had become an important part of the literary landscape, with translations available in French, German, Italian, and Japanese.

Burroughs moved from Tangier to Paris in January 1958. In the fall of that year he became friends with Gysin, an acquaintance from Tangier whose casual cutting and rearranging of newspaper pages to form collages immediately struck him as a radical new technique for constructing literary texts. Burroughs also immediately recognized the literary precedents of this dissection and recombination of written materials, referring to T. S. Eliot's

The Waste Land (1922) as "the first great cut-up collage" and mentioning Tristan Tzara and John Dos Passos as others who had experimented with the practice. Burroughs observed that "cut-ups establish new connections between images, and one's range of vision consequently expands," but many writers remained skeptical, even ones such as Samuel Beckett, whose own work was radically experimental. Beckett told Burroughs that combining his writing with newspapers was not writing but plumbing.

Burroughs began to apply the cup-up or fold-in (where separate pages are folded together) to the mass of material that remained from his "word hoard" and eventually assembled three books – the "trilogy" *The Soft Machine* (1961), *The Ticket That Exploded* (1962), and *Nova Express* (1964) – using selected passages from juxtaposed texts, including both his own writing and other sources. The three books overlap in various ways and were rewritten between editions so that the 1968 British edition of *The Soft Machine* is actually an extension of some ideas presented in *The Ticket That Exploded.* The first critic in France to publish a study of Burroughs, Philippe Mikriammos, calls the three books a false trilogy better understood as a single entity in three versions.

Whereas *Naked Lunch* is something of a picaresque journey through a carnivalesque world, *The Soft Machine* has been described by critics as a sort of travelogue through what Skerl calls "five dystopias": the "anthropological fantasy" of a preliterate society in "Puerto Joselito," the "historical fantasy" of a repressive ancient civilization in the "Mayan Caper," the "contemporary-capitalist-consumer" society of "Trak Trak Trak," and the futuristic fantasy of a doomed earth in "Gongs of Violence." In all of these regions agents of control – the prototypical modern villain for Burroughs – appear as characters capable of mutant multiplication like a virus gone berserk, and in one scene the cut-up is a method for combating these forces by destroying the network built by various authorities to confine movement in time and space.

On the other hand the power of Burroughs's distinctive narrative voice(s) in *Naked Lunch* has been dispersed or replaced so that authorial consciousness vanishes as conventional concepts of identity are superseded by what Robin Lydenberg calls "technical detachment and awareness." While this might satisfy the literary theorist concerned with radical notions of textual meaning, Burroughs effectively reduced the range of appeal of his work, a fact reflected in the shift in critical response away from the general media and toward literary journals. Joan Didion in *Book Week* attempted to praise *The Soft Machine* by citing its "inventive, free, funny, serious, poetic, indelibly American" qualities, but more-detailed discussions of the trilogy appeared in professional journals or in serious magazines such as the *Nation* and the *New Republic,* as *Time* no longer felt it necessary to condemn Burroughs's writing.

During the 1960s Burroughs traveled between Paris, Tangier, and London, living primarily in England during this time. Among his friends there were two young Englishmen: Ian Sommerville, a computer expert, and Anthony Balch, a filmmaker, whose knowledge of the possibilities of their fields enabled Burroughs to incorporate aspects of spliced tape and photomontage in *The Ticket That Exploded,* the second part of which he wanted to be "a new mythology for the space age." He had also become temporarily interested in Scientology, an enthusiasm somewhat akin to his fascination with Wilhelm Reich's theories in the late 1940s, and he drew some of its lore into the context of his book about "the Nova conspiracy to blow up the Earth." One of Burroughs's projections of consciousness, Inspector Lee, provides a degree of narrative focus, and his combat with the Nova Mob is presented in terms of image patterns using the vocabulary of science fiction. The inconclusive nature of the book is illustrated by the separate endings of the British and American editions. Burroughs originally let the text almost disintegrate as words were replaced by Gysin's calligraphy, but in the revised edition another section, called "The invisible generation," addresses the applicability of the cut-up to political purposes.

Nova Express is both a recapitulation and extension of *The Ticket That Exploded* and carries some of Burroughs's main concerns — theories of addiction, esoteric solutions, conspiracies of control, bizarre characters drawn from the author's extravagant permutations of his own identity — further from the zany entertainments of *Naked Lunch* toward a more didactic, explanatory mode. Much of the material had been used before. The book is divided into eight routines, with specific subdivisions in each one. The shift from a cut-up section to more explicit narration is moderately clear, although throughout the text there are indications that the literal circumstances of the narrative are not necessarily representations of any literal truth. The character known as the Subliminal Kid (drawn from Sommerville and called, with characteristic mockery and affection, "Technical Tilly" in *The Ticket That Exploded*) consistently undermines the current reality of a situation by twisting the angle of observation with elec-

tronic and verbal devices, underscoring the artificial aspect of the narrative. The unifying conflict continues the struggle between the Nova Mob and the Nova Police, with the Nova Mob suggesting a version of the military-industrial complex grown huge even by contemporary standards and the Nova Police presented with some reservations as the supporters of valid social values in opposition to the controllers, since Burroughs has always spoken of the police as an "ambivalent agency." The thrust of the narrative is toward a state of freedom through awareness, a condition of existence achieved either through an alteration of consciousness or an education into the hipster's reality. In this case drugs are not offered as agents of transformation. Artistic perception, as exemplified in the cut-ups from *The Waste Land,* Franz Kafka's *The Trial,* and Shakespeare's *The Tempest,* replaces the addict's intense but self-enclosed vision, and there is a suggestion that Burroughs equates his own artistic power with Prospero's uses of magic to overcome evil in *The Tempest.* In this sense Burroughs argues that social change is irrelevant without a fundamental shift in consciousness, and the goal of the trilogy is to break the chains that have made this change impossible.

By 1964, when the trilogy had been published in its original editions, Burroughs had begun to spend more time in the United States, visiting his son, Billy, in Palm Beach at his parents' home, living primarily in New York, and gradually beginning to realize the kind of underground recognition that eventually made him a major cult figure. He gave several readings in lower Manhattan that drew some of the more prominent avant-garde figures, stunning and delighting audiences with his skillful, laconic, measured, and incongruously formal presentation of collage and cut-up routines, including his film-script adaptation, *The Last Words of Dutch Schultz* (1970). He was commissioned by *Playboy* to write a recollection of his childhood in Saint Louis; after the essay was rejected he published it in *The Paris Review.* In 1967 Burroughs was one of the figures depicted on the Beatles' *Sgt. Pepper's Lonely Hearts Club Band* album cover, and in 1968 he was hired by *Esquire* to cover the Democratic National Convention in Chicago with Terry Southern and Jean Genet.

Burroughs moved to London in 1966, and his sporadic contacts with the exploding rock music and pop art social scenes became a significant factor in the development of his writing. As John Tytell has observed, Burroughs is a superb raconteur, and the dissolution of narrative patterns in the trilogy represented a sacrifice of strength, even if it ad-

Burroughs in Paris in 1960

vanced Burroughs's aesthetic theories. The return to a more familiar narrative arrangement in the manner of the pulp fiction he read as a young man enabled him to concentrate and project some of the energy he drew from the cultural and political activities of the 1960s into a more direct and structurally cohesive kind of book.

In March 1967 Burroughs began work on *The Wild Boys: A Book of the Dead* (1971), the first unit in what might be seen as the second half of his oeuvre, which was inspired by and in sympathy with the efforts of young artists in every field to move toward the kind of freedom and independence of thought he admired. Reaching back to his own childhood, he began to develop the character of Audrey Carsons, a reflective figure for his sense of himself as a young boy. Initially, Carsons is depicted as an outcast out of step with social expectations and "normal" ambitions and desires. "He looks like a sheep-killing dog," Burroughs has a "St. Louis aristocrat" say about him, in a typical mixture of anguish and

amusement at his memories of his discomfort. At the opposite end of a continuum of personal expression Burroughs imagines the Wild Boys of the title — a gang of uninhibited, anarchic, compulsively sensual creatures unbound and roving like a band of avenging road warriors, a form of fantasy common to childhood's sense of its own limitations here run amok in the adult world of repressive authority and spirit-crushing control. Carsons is set on a course that carries him through several books toward the condition of utopian freedom the Wild Boys represent, and his journey is a demonstration of the power of spiritual liberation contained in the exercise of the artistic imagination. The twin strains of Burroughs's sensibility are at the poles of the narrative consciousness of the book, so that the Wild Boys, who are introduced about one-third of the way into the novel, remain as a hovering presence even when they are not depicted in violent action against the forces of control.

Both *The Wild Boys* and *The Last Words of Dutch Schultz*, which Burroughs was also working on in the late 1960s, incorporate many of the schematic devices of the cinema, which Burroughs now believed was a crucial instrument in the formation of contemporary consciousness. He used as many film techniques as he could in *The Wild Boys* and continued in *Exterminator!* (1973) to make explicit the film metaphor in which an image of film running out is used as a warning about the collapsing state of Western civilization.

As Skerl explains, *The Wild Boys* is structured in accordance with the montage theory of film editing and organization, so that "every scene is defined as an ephemeral 'set;' every narrative is a 'script;' every point of view is a 'camera angle;' every character is an 'actor' who frequently changes identities," and the separate narrative episodes fold into each other like reels of film spliced together. The eighteen brief chapters or routines are primarily narrative in form, while the cut-ups he includes are the product of considerable attention and revision to reduce the random juxtapositions of Burroughs's previous experiments in alternate approaches to readability. As he remarked in *The Job* (1970) about *The Last Words of Dutch Schultz* manuscript, which is subtitled "A Fiction in the Form of a Film Script," the incorporation of cut-ups results in "a perfectly straight film treatment," a comment reflecting his concern that in the trilogy he had "done writing that I thought was interesting experimentally, but simply not readable." In rewriting the books in the trilogy Burroughs, according to Oliver Harris, the editor of his letters, "instigated the restoration of generic conventions" of narration to overcome the incipient isolation inherent in the extremes of some of the strategies. In *The Wild Boys* Burroughs claimed he "was quite deliberately returning to older styles of writing," but in bringing the techniques of film to the novel, Burroughs was continuing the Joycean experiments with language at the heart of his philosophy of composition.

Speaking with his familiar insouciance, Burroughs said in his essay "My Purpose Is To Write for the Space Age" (1984) that "*The Wild Boys* could be considered a kind of homosexual *Peter Pan*" and described it as the beginning of a "new cycle that continued with *Exterminator!, Port of Saints* and *Ah Pook Is Here*," a grouping that Burroughs felt was "increasingly preoccupied by the themes of space travel and biological mutation as a prerequisite for space travel." Perhaps of greater significance was the introduction of the Audrey Carsons character, who appears in all of the books of the cycle as well as the first volume of Burroughs's 1980s triad, *Cities of the Red Night* (1981), eventually evolving into Kim

Carsons in the second volume of the triad, *The Place of Dead Roads* (1983). Carsons is used for Burroughs's imaginative excursions prior to his devastating experiences with drugs and thus is able to speak without the fascinatingly hip hard edge that is so much a part of Burroughs's narrative voice in *Naked Lunch*.

Consequently, a dual narrative consciousness develops in which a brilliant outcast youth, the dreaming idealist whose disappointments lead to the mature artist described by McCarthy as a "soured Utopian," can still envision a struggle toward an advanced state of being in which happiness is the result of a continuous struggle for one's dreams and desires – or, as Burroughs has said in "My Purpose Is To Write for the Space Age," "Happiness is a byproduct of function, purpose and conflict." The conflict of *The Wild Boys* is located in a vague future in which the population of the world has been reduced by various disasters and the Wild Boys act as a counterforce to the American army, a generic representation of the negative forces of conventional popular culture. Burroughs included many scenes of homosexual activity, and of his exclusion of women even as a necessity for reproduction he said he was following an "experimental line" in which "boys who had never had contact with women would be quite a different animal," but he also observed that he would have no objections "if lesbians would like to do the same."

The separated segments of much of Burroughs's work have often functioned as kinds of chapters in the longer fictional forms that he has used as a means of expanding the methods of narrative coherence in his novels. Nonetheless, it is more precise to describe *Exterminator!* as a collection of short pieces in spite of its subtitle, "A Novel," since it is composed of routines that could have appeared in other collections and essayistic examples of relatively straightforward reporting. "The Teacher," for instance, is a variant from the Dutch Schultz manuscript "The Coming of the Purple Better One," an excerpt from the *Esquire* coverage of the 1968 Democratic Convention.

In 1973 Burroughs also published *Port of Saints,* a sort of sequel to *The Wild Boys* that actually includes more Wild Boys material than the title work as well as many autobiographical references, although taken out of context and slightly disguised through shifts in names and key words. Audrey Carsons remains a recollective narrative sensibility, and some of Burroughs's expressions of self-satisfying fantasies of hero figures such as the lethal Tio Mate also appear again in film-sequence tableaux, with

*Dust jacket for the first American edition of Burroughs's 1959
novel. Because of its explicit depictions of drug use and sexual
acts, Massachusetts unsuccessfully attempted to ban the
book as obscene.*

Carsons eventually joining the Wild Boys in an escape from a confining "past" and the biological grip of mortality.

The Wild Boys was Burroughs's last book to receive widespread, generally positive reviews, notably by Josephine Hendin in *The Saturday Review* and Alfred Kazin in *The New York Times*. In the year of its publication British critic Eric Mottram completed a book-length, consistently incisive, and intellectually powerful study of Burroughs, *The Algebra of Need*. Tytell's landmark *Naked Angels: The Lives and Literature of the Beat Generation* (1976) combined biographical and analytical material on Burroughs. As a continuing counterpoint, negative commentary by reviewers for the popular press "professed disgust and boredom with Burroughs's characteristic imagery and fragmentary technique," according to Skerl, but these stand in sharp contrast to the extended, probing discussions of Burroughs's place in literary history appearing in the 1970s. Tony Tan-

ner and Cary Nelson, writing for an audience familiar with current concerns about literature, devoted chapters to Burroughs in their serious studies of fiction, establishing a pattern in which reviewers working for newspapers and weekly magazines complained about deviations from conventional forms while scholars familiar with Burroughs's intentions and accomplishments were able to write illuminating, discerning assessments of his efforts.

By 1974 Burroughs no longer wanted to live in London. The friendships he had made with various collaborators were suspended as they pursued their own projects, the relationships he had partially enjoyed with several young men had dissolved, and he grew increasingly annoyed with the city. When Ginsberg visited in 1973 he realized that Burroughs was in a state of stasis and retreat and approached City College in New York about Burroughs's participation in a three-month course to be offered by distinguished professors. Burroughs accepted an offer of seven thousand dollars for a February–May 1974 semester and moved to New York City. There, in February, Ginsberg introduced him to Grauerholz, a young man from Kansas, which led to a deep friendship and a satisfactory business arrangement as Grauerholz became an artistic collaborator, editor, business manager, and coordinator of Burroughs's performances. In April 1974 Burroughs had a successful reading at the Saint Marks Church in Greenwich Village and during the next ten years estimated that he gave about 150 readings at an average fee of five hundred dollars. At the same time that mainline critics such as John Updike or Anatole Broyard were expressing the establishment position that Burroughs was writing claptrap, a younger generation that was prepared to assume some of the prerogatives of artistic power had begun to respond to Burroughs's work significantly. The term *heavy metal* (from *Naked Lunch*) defined a whole genre of contemporary rock music, while other arcane items from *Naked Lunch* and elsewhere, such as the name *Steely Dan,* found their way into the culture. Burroughs appeared in Conrad Rooks's 1966 film *Chappaqua,* was interviewed by Robert Palmer of *Rolling Stone* in 1972, was featured in a brief story in *People* magazine in 1974, and in 1981, his last year in New York, was introduced by Lauren Hutton on NBC's *Saturday Night Live* as "America's greatest living writer."

As he began to respond to the growing demand for his cryptic reading style and his droll, sardonic sense of humor, Burroughs had a temporary experience of writer's block, but once again a fortunate meeting with a potential collaborator, Steve Lowe, who was a devotee of Burroughs's work, led to an arrangement in which Lowe would assist Burroughs on research into the life of pirates in the eighteenth century, material he planned to use in his next book, *Cities of the Red Night.* In 1975, as work got underway, Burroughs also received his first grant, four thousand dollars from the New York State Creative Arts Public Service, which provoked a predictable complaint from people who mistakenly assumed he was an heir to the adding-machine fortune, and lectured at Ginsberg's branch of the Naropa Institute in Colorado, where Ginsberg and poet Anne Waldman had founded the Jack Kerouac School of Disembodied Poetics. Maintaining his sharp eye for sham, Burroughs referred to the chief monk as a "whiskey lama" but was able to set up some readings there with his son, who was having serious problems. Among other things, heavy drug use necessitated a liver transplant

for Billy, and Burroughs spent a good deal of time with his son before Billy's death in March 1981. Despite the grief he felt about Billy's illness and the time he spent in Boulder, Colorado, where Billy was hospitalized, Burroughs was one of the prominent participants at the Nova Convention of antiestablishment celebrities and fellow travelers in December 1978 in New York and was able to continue work on *Cities of the Red Night,* which was ready for publication in 1981.

The book was dedicated to his old friend Gysin; to Lowe; to his publisher, Dick Seaver; to his agent, Peter Matson; and to Grauerholz, "who edited this book into present time." Seaver suggested revising the original manuscript, which contained forty-eight intercut sections switching every few pages between a narration about an idealized community founded by eighteenth-century pirates and events in the present time. According to biographer Barry Miles, Grauerholz "uncut the cut-ups" and proposed to Burroughs, "let's suppose we give the reader at least fifteen or twenty pages of each story. . . . I slowed the cutting pace and made it much more readable." The final version, which removed more than twenty-five hundred lines of the original manuscript, moves easily among three narrative threads: the exploits of the Wild Boys in the pirate utopia; the adventures of a hard-boiled private named Clem Snide, who is trying to unravel the mystery of a mutant virus run amok; and a quasi-historical account of a city ravaged by the "red plague" (echoing Edgar Allan Poe's "The Masque of the Red Death"), written as a precursor to recent cyberpunk science fiction. In "My Purpose Is To Write for the Space Age" Burroughs described his method in *Cities of the Red Night* as placing the characters "behind enemy lines in time [where] their mission is to correct retroactively certain fatal errors at crucial turning points." The virus that has infected the "city" of human civilization is a symbol of desperate, manic sexual frenzy leading to a despoliation of the body and a death of the soul, and each linear component of the narration points toward an antidote against its virulence. The pirate retreat represents a small community among other small communities allowing "maximum variation . . . as opposed to the uniformity imposed by industrialization and overpopulation," as Burroughs wrote in "My Purpose Is To Write for the Space Age." The vision of the "city" is similar to other descriptions of the "unreal city" in his work and stands as a forecast and warning, "one voice in a swelling chorus" of the apocalypse, as Burroughs put it.

Burroughs with Allen Ginsberg, Gregory Corso, and Anne Waldman at the Naropa Institute in Boulder, Colorado
(Ginsberg Collection, Stanford University)

The Clem Snide story uses the private investigator as a skewed figure for the artist who can examine contemporary reality, see its flaws, and in his reactions suggest means of protecting one's sensibility (or one's soul) by resisting absorption into the debased world of control administered by the manipulation of various addictions, including the lure of drugs, sex, and submission to authority. Much of the book is written in a conventional third-person omniscient narration, which lends an air of semiofficial wisdom to the account of the action. There is a considerable amount of dialogue, which gives the narrative paths a sense of immediacy and dramatic tension as well as providing a means of characterization through conversation. Snide in particular is revealed through his knowing, cryptic commentary on events as he pursues various leads and probes the decadence in his path. The Audrey Carsons figure – joining the Wild Boys as the author's agent on utopian excursions into imaginary worlds – is a foil for Snide, but, in a characteristic blending of modes, as the narration

progresses Snide and Carsons seem to fuse, and in the final chapters it becomes apparent that the entire text is the product of Carsons's imagination. The question of the artist's shaping of various realities remains unresolved, as none of the three narrative tracks reaches a denouement or conclusion, but it is implied that the story of the Wild Boys in the pirate gang enabled Carsons/Burroughs to revitalize spirits battered by the discouragement of finding oneself an outcast.

Cities of the Red Night was actively promoted by Seaver and sold twenty thousand copies in hardcover. It was one of Burroughs's last books to be widely reviewed in the popular press and was poorly received there. In *The Saturday Review* Anthony Burgess, while respectful of Burroughs's seriousness and ability, felt that the book was "rather monotonous" and suggested, "What Burroughs needs is a theology." J. G. Ballard, on the other hand, called Burroughs "the first mythographer of the twentieth century," and Steven Shaviro argued in *The Review of Contemporary Fiction* that, as Skerl puts it, Burroughs is "a thinker and theorist rather than a survivor of outrageous experiences."

Burroughs's career now extended beyond any single review, and his place in a larger context of artistic experience was demonstrated by Howard Brookner's 1984 film biography *Burroughs: The Movie,* which had been in preparation since 1978, and by Burroughs's induction into the American Academy and Institute of Arts and Letters in 1983. Ginsberg had been campaigning for Burroughs's election for several years, and Burroughs was pleased by the honor but not beyond remarking to a friend, "Twenty years ago, they were saying I belonged in jail. Now they're saying I belong in their club. I didn't listen to them then, and I don't listen to them now."

After living in New York since 1974, Burroughs had also decided, following Grauerholz's suggestion, to move back to the Midwest, and he visited Lawrence, Kansas, for six weeks in the summer of 1981. Burroughs felt comfortable in a moderately rural environment where he could practice his old hobby of target shooting without much restraint, and he found that he was able to write effectively there as well. Although he still traveled extensively, partially to supplement his royalties, which were not very significant, and partially to participate in events honoring his work and that of his colleagues, he found the idea of purchasing a home for the first time in his life appealing. In December 1981 he settled in "a small house on a tree-lined street in Lawrence, Kansas, with my beloved cat Ruski," he wrote to an inquisitive graduate student who imagined him "in a male whorehouse in Tangier." With the help of Grauerholz and other young friends he also established William Burroughs Communications in downtown Lawrence, with a word processor for converting Burroughs's typewritten drafts to disk.

Burroughs had begun the second book in the triad, *The Place of Dead Roads,* in New York and found that without the constant interruptions of the city he was able to progress quickly. Working with some of the material removed from *Cities of the Red Night,* he continued the evolution of the Audrey Carsons character by placing him at the center of the narrative and by calling him Kim Carsons, although eventually he discloses that Carsons is a pen name for William Seward Burroughs and that the overlapping autobiographical projections are all aspects of authorial consciousness. Burroughs had been talking about writing a Western for more than twenty years, and the form of *The Place of Dead*

Roads uses many familiar conventions both from cowboy adventure novels and from Western films and then undercuts convention with bizarre twists, such as the phrase "the blind Gun who zeroes in with bat squeaks." The narrative proceeds from the late 1800s, when the young Kim Carsons decides to become a "shootist" – an echo of Burroughs's youthful desires to take control over an unfriendly environment – and joins a gang of "Johnsons," people in 1930s underground argot who are trustworthy and admirable in terms of an outlaw's code of honor. Burroughs depicts the members of the gang as a continuation of the Wild Boys, here called the Wild Fruits in typical Burroughs self-reflective humor, and they, like Carsons, are expert marksmen who have carried their lethal skills into the realm of telekinetic perception and extrasensory awareness, transposing the setting at times into a space-time warp that includes the future and various outposts of the old British colonial empire.

In accordance with his strategy to carry his experience as a mature artist back to the days when his nascent artistic consciousness was in a formative stage, Burroughs uses his full capabilities as a writer to re-create the prelapsarian sensibility of his youth. The extensive descriptive passages and frequent use of spirited dialogue are patterned after the kind of Victorian saga in which intrepid gentlemen retain their composure in the face of any adversary or uncivilized horror, and Burroughs keeps shifting the narrative between an effective reproduction of the prototype and a parodic homage that is like a commentary on the events as they occur. The almost-constant interjections of bits such as the satirical thrust at the CIA in the stanza drawn from Lord Byron's "The Destruction of Sennacherib" help to avoid a didactic tone as the "Johnsons" are arrayed against all of the viral contagions threatening to turn the earth into a useless, barren wasteland (the "place" of the title).

When *The Place of Dead Roads* was published in a sixth draft that Grauerholz had reassembled from a working manuscript, *The New York Times* took a position that reflected both sides of the debate about Burroughs's worth as a writer, assigning Broyard, an old adversary, to a daily review, which castigated the book for its "indistinguishable acts of sodomy, its gloating over sadistic killings," and giving Perry Meisel space in the Sunday *New York Times* book section on 19 February 1984, where he described Burroughs as "a principal avatar of the liberationist esthetic he helped to create." The relatively shallow nature of these reviews was effectively established by the 1985 publication of Skerl's oft-quoted, comprehensive overview of Burroughs's life and work, which demonstrated how it was possible to examine the most serious issues of Burroughs's writing for both interested readers and scholars.

The death of Gysin in 1986 contributed to a period of depression during which Burroughs stopped work on *The Western Lands,* the third book of a triad now called "the Red Night trilogy" by Grauerholz. Using eight hundred pages of overflow from *The Place of Dead Roads,* Burroughs had begun *The Western Lands* in 1983, but Gysin's death, following the death of Burroughs's brother, Mort, and the loss of other friends, temporarily unsettled him. As he says on the third page of *The Western Lands,* "William Seward Hall sets out to write his way out of death." The title is taken from an Egyptian term for a paradise, which might imply a condition beyond physical death, but as Lydenberg pointed out in a perceptive review for the *Nation* (19 March 1988), "For Burroughs, the promised land is not a piece of commercial real estate but the self-sustaining and disembodied domain of reflective wisdom, in which the narrative consciousness is art." The novel was conceived as more relaxed, meditative, less agitated, and less frenetic than any of Burroughs's previous works. Although Joe the Dead seems to be the central character, the fusion of this figure with Kim Carsons (supposedly shot by Joe the Dead in the previous book) and with William Seward Hall and Hassan I Sabbah conveys a feeling of a multiple-voiced narrative in which variants of the author emerge in different spheres of time, space, and mood. Egyptology, wickedly funny demolitions of various opponents, and unusually evocative moments of spiritual longing and fulfillment flow through the narration as Burroughs recalls many of the elements of previous books while suggesting his own place in the great tradition of James Joyce, F. Scott Fitzgerald, Eliot, and other modern masters.

Some critics speculated that this would be Burroughs's last book. The somewhat elegiac tone does imply a kind of conclusion, but Burroughs has continued to write, publishing limited editions such as *Ghost of Chance* (1991) and telling a *Newsweek* interviewer in 1993 that he was editing and adding to a new six-hundred-page manuscript, a project that led to *My Education: A Book of Dreams* (1995).

By the late 1980s his reputation had grown to the point that he was something of a revered seer for a diverse grouping of scholars, artists, and others. Burroughs joined the late rocker Kurt Cobain on a compact-disc single, "The Priest They Called Him"; appeared in Gus Van Sant's movies *Drugstore Cowboy* (1989) and *Even Cowgirls Get The Blues* (1994); released an album with jazz artist Ornette Coleman in 1995; collaborated with Robert Wilson on the libretto for the opera *The Black Rider* (1990); joined performance artist Laurie Anderson for several shows and a 1986 film; lectured (unidentified) in a Nike shoe television ad in 1994; and continued to work on his painting, selling pictures for more than three thousand dollars each by 1990.

At the same time his position as an important part of twentieth-century American literature was emphasized by Lydenberg's *Word Cultures* (1987), which adeptly used contemporary literary theory in an examination of *Naked Lunch* and the *Nova Express* trilogy, while Lydenberg and Skerl's *William S. Burroughs at the Front* (1991) covered the critical reception of Burroughs's work from 1959 to 1989 in a convincing demonstration of the diversity of response to his work and the intense debate generated by its provocative nature. This dispute continues into the 1990s, as authors such as Gilbert Sorrentino describe Burroughs as a "unique, important and unquestionably subversive writer," (in his 1988 review of Morgan's biography in *The New York Times Book Review*) while the avant-garde Canadian magazine *Double Bill* in 1994 attacked Burroughs for his expressions of misogyny, an issue that has troubled many of Burroughs's admirers throughout his career. The publication of his letters in 1993, including an excellent introduction by Harris, reveals in greater detail the range and dimension of Burroughs's mind, suggesting that the wide spectrum of opinion about his life and art is not likely to be narrowed in the near future, if ever.

Nonetheless, the importance of Burroughs's writing is undeniable. The publication of *My Education: A Book of Dreams* — a part of his continuing examination of the flow of consciousness through an extraordinary artistic sensibility — was the occasion for an enthusiastic assessment of his entire career by James Wolcott in *The New Yorker,* a magazine that had previously ignored his existence, and drew an appreciative, respectful review from *The New York Times Book Review,* where Robert Cohen summarized a prevailing sentiment by calling Burroughs "arguably the most influential American prose writer of the last 40 years" among young authors. Beyond the provocative discussions about his influences and ideas, Cohen observes that at the end of Burroughs's career, "there is simply what there was in the beginning: a man alone at his desk, spinning dreams into words and words into dreams." It is this image of a writer at work that is likely to endure when talk about his escapades fades into oblivion.

Letters:

Letters to Allen Ginsberg, 1953–1957, edited by Ron Padgett and Anne Waldman, introduction by Ginsberg, preface by Burroughs (New York: Full Court Press, 1981);

The Letters of William S. Burroughs, 1945–1959, edited by Oliver Harris (New York: Viking, 1993).

Interviews:

Gregory Corso and Allen Ginsberg, "Interview with William Burroughs," *Journal for the Protection of All Beings,* no. 1 (1961): 79–83;

Conrad Knickerbocker, "William Burroughs," in *Writers at Work: The Paris Review Interviews, Third Series,* edited by George Plimpton (New York: Viking, 1967), pp. 143–174;

Robert Palmer, "Rolling Stone Interview: William S. Burroughs," *Rolling Stone,* 108 (11 May 1972): 48–53;

Gerard Malanga, "An Interview with William S. Burroughs," *The Beat Book,* 4 (1974): 90–112;

John Tytell, "An Interview with William Burroughs," in *The Beat Diary,* no. 5, edited by Arthur and Kit Knight (California, Pa.: unspeakable visions of the individual, 1977), pp. 35–49;

Victor Bockris, *With William Burroughs: A Report from the Bunker* (New York: Seaver, 1981);

Jennie Skerl, "An Interview with William S. Burroughs (4 April 1980, New York City)," *Modern Language Studies,* 12 (Summer 1982): 3–17.

Bibliographies:

Miles Associates, *A Descriptive Catalogue of the William S. Burroughs Archive* (London: Covent Garden, 1973);

Jennie Skerl, "A William S. Burroughs Bibliography," *The Serif,* 11 (Summer 1974): 12–20;

Michael B. Goodman, *William S. Burroughs: An Annotated Bibliography of His Works and Criticism* (New York: Garland, 1975);

Joe Maynard and Barry Miles, *William S. Burroughs: A Bibliography, 1953–1973* (Charlottesville: University Press of Virginia, 1978);

Goodman and Lemuel B. Coley, *William S. Burroughs: A Reference Guide* (New York & London: Garland, 1990).

Biographies:

Bruce Cook, "The Holy Monster," in his *The Beat Generation* (New York: Scribners, 1971), pp. 165–184;

Burroughs in 1983 (photograph by Kate Simon)

William Burroughs Jr., *Kentucky Ham* (New York: Dutton, 1973);

Ann Charters, *Kerouac: A Biography* (New York: Warner, 1974);

John Tytell, *Naked Angels: The Lives and Literature of the Beat Generation* (New York: McGraw-Hill, 1976), pp. 36–51, 111–140;

Ted Morgan, *Literary Outlaw: The Life and Times of William S. Burroughs* (New York: Holt, 1988);

Barry Miles, *William Burroughs: El Hombre Invisible* (New York: Hyperion, 1993).

References:

Alan Ansen, *William Burroughs: An Essay* (Sudbury, Mass.: Water Row, 1986);

Michael Bliss, "The Orchestration of Chaos: Verbal Technique in William Burroughs' *Naked Lunch,*" *enclitic,* 1 (Spring 1977): 59–69;

Clive Bush, "An Anarchy of New Speech: Notes on the American Tradition of William Burroughs," *Journal of Beckett Studies,* 6 (Autumn 1980): 120–128;

Gérard Cordesse, "The Science-fiction of William Burroughs," *Caliban,* 12 (1975): 33–43;

Laszlo Géfin, "Collage Theory, Reception, and the Cutups of William Burroughs," *Perspectives on Contemporary Literature,* 13 (1987): 91–100;

Michael B. Goodman, *Contemporary Literary Censorship: The Case History of Burroughs' "Naked Lunch"* (Metuchen, N.J. & London: Scarecrow, 1981);

James Grauerholz, *On Burroughs' Art* (Sante Fe, N.M.: Gallery Casa Sin Nombre, 1988);

Ihab Hassan, "The Literature of Silence: From Henry Miller to Beckett and Burroughs," *Encounter,* 28 (January 1967): 74–82;

Hassan, "The Subtracting Machine: The Work of William Burroughs," *Critique,* 6 (Spring 1963): 4–23;

Anthony Channell Hilfer, "Mariner and Wedding Guest in William Burroughs' *Naked Lunch,*" *Criticism,* 22 (Summer 1980): 252–265;

Richard Kostelanetz, "From Nightmare to Serendipity: A Retrospective Look at William S. Burroughs," *Twentieth Century Literature,* 11 (October 1965): 123–130;

David Lodge, "Objections to William Burroughs," in his *The Novelist at the Crossroads and Other Essays in Fiction and Criticism* (Ithaca, N.Y.: Cornell University Press, 1971), pp. 161–171;

Robin Lydenberg, *Word Cultures: Radical Theory and Practice in William S. Burroughs' Fiction* (Urbana: University of Illinois Press, 1987);

Lydenberg and Jennie Skerl, *William S. Burroughs at the Front: Critical Reception, 1959–1989* (Carbondale: Southern Illinois University Press, 1991);

Mary McCarthy, *The Writing on the Wall and Other Essays* (New York: Harcourt, 1970), pp. 42–53;

Frank D. McConnell, "William Burroughs and the Literature of Addiction," *Massachusetts Review,* 8 (Autumn 1967): 665–680;

Eric Mottram, *William Burroughs: The Algebra of Need,* revised edition (London: Boyars, 1977);

Cary Nelson, "The End of the Body: Radical Space in Burroughs," in his *The Incarnate Word: Literature and Verbal Space* (Urbana: University of Illinois Press, 1973), pp. 208–229;

Neal Oxenhandler, "Listening to Burroughs' Voice," in *Surfiction: Fiction Now . . . and Tomorrow,* edited by Raymond Federman (Chicago: Swallow, 1975), pp. 181–201;

Donald Palumbo, "William Burroughs' Quartet of Science Fiction Novels as Dystopian Social Satire," *Extrapolation,* 20 (Winter 1979): 321–329;

Alvin J. Seltzer, "Confusion Hath Fuck His Masterpiece," in his *Chaos in the Novel, the Novel in Chaos* (New York: Schocken, 1974), pp. 330–374;

Steven Shaviro, "Burroughs' Theater of Illusion: *Cities of the Red Night,*" *Review of Contemporary Fiction,* 4 (Spring 1984): 64–74;

Jennie Skerl, *William S. Burroughs* (Boston: Twayne, 1985);

Tony Tanner, "Rub Out the Word," in his *City of Words: American Fiction 1950–1970* (New York: Harper & Row, 1971), pp. 109–140;

Nicholas Zurbrugg, "Burroughs, Barthes and the Limits of Intertextuality," *Review of Contemporary Fiction,* 4 (Spring 1984): 86–107.

Papers:
Primary collections of Burroughs's papers are located at the Ohio State University, Arizona State University, the University of Kansas, Columbia University, and the University of Texas at Austin. Other locations include Northwestern University, Princeton University, and Syracuse University.

Sandra Cisneros

(20 December 1954 –)

Cynthia Tompkins
Arizona State University West

See also the Cisneros entry in *DLB 122: Chicano Writers, Second Series.*

BOOKS: *Bad Boys* (San Jose, Cal.: Mango, 1980);
The House on Mango Street (Houston: Arte Público, 1983);
My Wicked Wicked Ways (Bloomington, Ind.: Third Woman, 1987);
Woman Hollering Creek and Other Stories (New York: Random House, 1991);
Loose Woman: Poems (New York: Knopf, 1994);
Hairs: Pelitos (New York: Knopf, 1994).

PLAY PRODUCTION: *The House on Mango Street,* Chicago, Edgewater Theater, 16 October 1992.

SELECTED PERIODICAL PUBLICATIONS –
UNCOLLECTED: "Los Tejanos: Testimony to the Silenced," *Texas Humanist* (November–December 1984): 11–12;
"Cactus Flowers: In Search of Tejana Feminist Poetry," *Third Women,* 3, nos. 1–2 (1986): 73–80;
"Ghosts and Voices: Writing from Obsession," *Americas Review,* 15 (Spring 1987): 69–73;
"Notes to a Young(er) Writer," *Americas Review,* 15 (Spring 1987): 74–76;
"Do You Know Me? I Wrote *The House on Mango Street,*" *Americas Review,* 15 (Spring 1987): 77–79.

Sandra Cisneros (photograph by Rubén Guzmán)

Sandra Cisneros, poet and short-story writer, is best known for *The House on Mango Street* (1983), a Chicana novel of initiation, which won the Before Columbus American Book Award in 1985. In this lyrical novella Cisneros challenges the conventions of the bildungsroman by weaving the protagonist's quest for selfhood into the fabric of the community. Such a dual focus is usual in Cisneros's poetry and prose, in which a multiplicity of voices illustrate the ways the individual engages in the discourses and social practices of Chicano culture. Additionally, by focusing on the socialization processes of the female in Chicano culture, Cisneros explores racism in the dominant culture as well as patriarchal oppression in the Latino community.

Born to working-class parents (her father an upholsterer, her mother a factory worker), Cisneros grew up as the only girl among six brothers on Chicago's South Side. Out of necessity, she learned to make herself heard, recalling in an 11 January 1993 interview, "You had to be fast and you had to be funny – you had to be a *storyteller.*" Since her Mexican father missed his homeland and would frequently sojourn there for periods of time, the family

35

was often disrupted and moved from one ghetto neighborhood to another many times during her childhood. In 1969 her parents managed to buy a cramped two-story bungalow in a Puerto Rican neighborhood on the city's North Side, an ugly red house similar to the one Cisneros portrays in *The House on Mango Street.*

Responding to questions concerning the autobiographical nature of *The House on Mango Street,* Cisneros in the spring 1991 *Americas Review* observed, "All fiction is non-fiction. Every piece of fiction is based on something that really happened. . . . They're all stories I lived, or witnessed, or heard." Nevertheless, the central idea of her novel had a specific literary inspiration. In a seminar at the Iowa Writers Program, Cisneros participated in a discussion of Gaston Bachelard's *La Poétique de l'éspace* (1958; translated as *The Poetics of Space,* 1964) and realized that her unique experience of the intersection of race, ethnicity, class, and gender separated her from the other students.

The House on Mango Street tells the story of a child named Esperanza (Hope) and her gradual realization of her own separate being. The tale of maturation is supported by Cisneros's use of the house as a symbol of familial consciousness, and the novel also depicts the lives, struggles, and concerns of Esperanza's immediate family, neighbors, and friends. As Erlinda González-Berry and Tey Diana Rebolledo point out, "we see the world through this child's eyes and we also see the child as she comes to an understanding of herself, her world, and her culture."

In a manner somewhat comparable to that of Sherwood Anderson's *Winesburg, Ohio* (1919) and Jean Toomer's *Cane* (1923), Cisneros's work mixes genres, for while each section achieves, in Ellen McCracken's words, "the intensity of the short story," the forty-four interrelated stories allow for a development of character and plot typical of the novel. Julián Olivares quotes Cisneros on her intent: "I wanted to write stories that were a cross between poetry and fiction. . . . Except I wanted to write a collection which could be read at any random point without having any knowledge of what came before or after. Or that could be read in a series to tell one big story. I wanted stories like poems, compact and lyrical and ending with a reverberation."

The image of the house, as McCracken points out, is symbolic in three distinctive ways, first as it suggests a positive objectification of the self for Esperanza. Before her family moved into the house on Mango Street, Esperanza's teachers had made deni-

grating remarks about their living conditions. " 'You live *there?* ' . . . I had to look where she pointed – the third floor, the paint peeling, wooden bars Papa had nailed on the windows so we wouldn't fall out. . . . The way she said it made me feel like nothing. . . ." Sister Superior reveals her prejudices by suggesting that as a Mexican, Esperanza must live in "a row of ugly 3-flats, the ones even the raggedy men are ashamed to go into. . . ." Thus, though far from perfect, the family's new home, according to McCracken, "represents a positive objectification of the self, the chance to redress humiliation and establish a dignified sense of her own personhood."

Cisneros also successfully dramatizes both the individual and the communal significance of owning a house. Such a basic human desire and need is especially crucial for economically oppressed minorities. The house Esperanza dreams of beyond her family home will still have a communal function. She vows that "one day I'll own my own house, but I won't forget who I am or where I came from. Passing bums will ask, Can I come in? I'll offer them the attic, ask them to stay. . . ." In a third distinctive motif Cisneros establishes a link between the image of the house and creativity, not only in the bedtime stories Esperanza's mother tells, but also in the daughter's wish for "a house quiet as snow, a space for myself to go, clean as paper before the poem."

Despite the generally positive symbolism of the house, Cisneros does explore issues of patriarchal and sexual violence. During the course of the novel, a woman is locked in by her husband, a young girl is brutally beaten by her father, and Esperanza is raped. But even as she "mourns her loss of innocence" Esperanza understands, as critic María Herrera-Sobek points out, that by romanticizing sexual relations, grown-up women are complicit in the male oppression of their sex.

Several positive role models, McCracken observes, help guide Esperanza's development. Minerva, barely two years older than Esperanza, writes poetry when not dealing with her two children and an abusive husband. In fact, Esperanza realizes that Minerva's writing allows her to transcend her predicament. Also, Esperanza's bedridden aunt encourages her, "You must keep writing. It will keep you free." And "las comadres" (godmothers or women close to the family circle) tell Esperanza that her art must be linked to the community: "When you leave you must remember always to come back . . . for the others. A circle, you understand? You will always be Esperanza. You will always be Mango Street. . . . You can't forget who

*Dust jacket for Cisneros's 1983 novel, about a Chicana girl
growing up in Chicago*

you are." Writing, then, empowers Esperanza and strengthens her commitment to the community of Chicanas.

The House on Mango Street, in Ramón Saldívar's view, "represents from the simplicity of childhood vision the enormously complex process of the construction of [a woman's ethnic identity]. Posing the question of sexual difference within the urban working-class Chicano community, Cisneros's novel emphasizes the crucial roles of racial and material as well as ideological conditions of oppression." The need to address such pervasive conditions became clear to Chicana writers of the 1980s. After *The House on Mango Street* many Chicanas developed, according to Yvonne Yarbo-Bejarano, "a clear-sighted recognition of the unavoidably mutual overdetermination of the categories of race and class with that of gender in any attempted positioning of the Chicana subject."

Cisneros's willingness to experiment in different genres leads to stylistic and thematic crossovers. However, Cisneros regards writing poetry and prose as distinctly different: "writing poetry . . . you're looking at yourself *desnuda.* . . . [Y]ou've got to go beyond censorship . . . to get at that core of

truth. . . . When you think: 'Oh my goodness, I didn't know I felt that!' that's when you stop. . . . That's a poem. It's quite a different process from writing fiction, because you know what you are going to say when you write fiction. To me, the definition of a story is something that someone wants to listen to."

My Wicked Wicked Ways (1987), Cisneros's most widely known collection, contains the poems published originally in a chapbook titled *Bad Boys.* Discussing the title of her work in the *Americas Review,* Cisneros observed, "These are poems in which I write about myself, not a man writing about me. It is . . . my life story as told by me, not according to a male point of view. And that's where I see perhaps the 'Wicked Wicked' of the title." Citing her novel, Cisneros acknowledges, "A lot of the themes from *Mango Street* are repeated: I leave my father's house, I don't get married, I travel to other countries, I can sleep with men if I want to, I can abandon them or choose not to sleep with them, and yes, I can fall in love and even be hurt by men — all of these things but as told by me. I am not the muse."

Both Cisneros's fiction and her poetry emphasize some dominant themes. In discussing the quest for cultural identity, Cisneros asserts that "it's very strange to be straddling these two cultures and to try to define some middle ground so that you don't commit suicide or you don't become so depressed or you don't self explode. There has to be some way for you to say: 'Alright, the life I'm leading is alright. I'm not betraying my culture. I'm not becoming Anglicized.'"

In a 1993 interview Cisneros attributes her devotion to feminism, another recurrent theme, to her Mexican American mother: "My mom did things that were very non-traditional – for one, she didn't force me to learn how to cook. She didn't interrupt me to do chores when I was reading or studying. And she always told me, 'make sure you can take care of yourself.' And that was very different from other women, who felt they had to prepare their daughters to be a wife." Yet she remains aware of the price exacted by a revisionist approach to traditional mores, recalling in the *Americas Review,* "I felt, as a teenager, that I could not inherit my culture intact without revising some parts of it. That did not mean I wanted to reject the entire culture, although my brothers and my father thought I did. . . . I know that part of the trauma that I went through from my teen years through the twenties up until very recently, and that other Latinas are going through too, is coming to terms with what Norma [Alarcón] calls 'reinventing ourselves,' revising ourselves. We accept our culture, but not without adapting ourselves as women."

For a Hispanic the question of cultural identity often involves language. Growing up, Cisneros spoke Spanish with her father and English with her mother. Her practice of interspersing Spanish terms and phrases in her writing, especially notable in *Woman Hollering Creek and Other Stories* (1991), which was written since her move to San Antonio, stems naturally from her bicultural background. Cisneros asserted in the 4 August 1991 *Chicago Tribune* that "if you're bilingual, you're doubly rich. You have two ways of looking at the world."

Again dramatizing the interconnection between the individual and the community through her focus on gender in interpersonal relationships, Cisneros in the twenty-two stories of *Woman Hollering Creek* explores the San Antonio setting, contrasting the socialization processes of *Mexicanas de éste y el otro lado* (Mexican women on both sides of the border) with those of their Anglo counterparts. The book's three major sections suggest a developmental progression from childhood to adulthood, and the thematic motifs of time, love, and religion also function as organizing principles.

The experience of cyclical and parallel patterns of time especially seems to be the collection's major unifying concept, as repeated actions and rites of passage allow Cisneros to make thematic interconnections. Time, for instance, appears as a metaphysical dilemma in "Eleven." The experience of immanence leads the child narrator to explore the notion of chronology: "when you wake up on your eleventh birthday you expect to feel eleven, but you don't. You open your eyes and everything's just like yesterday, only it's today." Cisneros's narrator also views the passage of time in a context of behavioral expectations: "some days you might say something stupid, and that's the part of you that's still ten. Or maybe some days you might need to sit on your mama's lap because you're scared, and that's the part of you that's five. And maybe one day when you're all grown up maybe you will need to cry like if you're three." Finally, the child understands that the resolution of the paradox lies in conceiving time as a process of accretion: "when you're eleven, you're also ten, and nine, and eight, and seven, and six, and five, and four, and three, and two, and one."

In "One Holy Night" the paradox of time is reflected in the characterization of Boy Baby, who "seemed boy and baby and man all at once." Similarly, his refutation of time – "the past and the future are the same thing" – is set against his proclaimed attempt to reenact ancient Mayan ways. The young female protagonist is told that she will become "Ixchel, his Queen" after undergoing a rite of passage, which turns out to be a rape. The experience is described as a clear-cut separation from the past: "something inside bit me, and I gave out a cry as if the other, the one I wouldn't be anymore, leapt out." The irony is underscored when the narrator, now a pregnant teenager who feels suspended in the present, says, "I don't think they understand how it is to be a girl. I don't think they know how it is to have to wait your whole life. I count the months for the baby to be born." A contrasting view of time is evident in "Eyes of Zapata," in which time becomes destiny. Zapata's long-standing lover, Inés Alfaro, states, "I . . . see our lives, clear and still, far away and near. And I see our future and our past, Miliano, one single thread already lived and nothing to be done about it."

Parallel temporal paradigms are articulated in "*Bien* Pretty." According to the narrator, an educated Latina from San Francisco confused about her ethnic identity, "we have to let go of our present way of life and search for our past, remember our destinies." Conversely, her Mexican lover argues,

Dust jacket for Cisneros's 1991 collection of short stories set along the border between Texas and Mexico

"You Americans have a strange way of thinking about time. . . . You think old ages end, but that's not so. It's ridiculous to think one age has overcome another. American time is running alongside the calendar of the sun, even if your world doesn't know it."

Distraught at discovering that her lover must return to Mexico to tend to a wife, a mistress, and seven children, the narrator seeks solace in *telenovelas* (soap operas). However, she substitutes the "passionate *and* powerful, tender and volatile, brave" women she has known in real life for the passive models on the screen. As a result, self-confidence returns, and aesthetic pleasure leads her to focus on the present, her *being* in the world: "the sky is throbbing. Blue, violet, peach, not holding still for one second. The sun setting . . . because it's today, today; with no thought of the future or past."

In keeping with the stereotype of the passionate Latina, many of the stories in *Woman Hollering Creek* revolve around love, Cisneros's second major organizing motif. To the author's credit, however, her approach is, for the most part, unorthodox. In "One Holy Night" love is defined as "a bad joke,"

as "a big black piano being pushed off the top of a three story building [while] you're waiting on the bottom to catch it," as "a top . . . spinning so fast . . . all that's left is the hum," and as a crazy man who "walked around all day with his harmonica in his mouth. . . . wheezing, in and out, in and out." The male lead of "*Bien* Pretty" defines love by means of a paradox, "I believe love is always eternal. Even if eternity is only five minutes." On the other hand, under the spell of *telenovelas,* the protagonist of "Woman Hollering Creek" lives for a masochistic version of passion, firmly believing that to "suffer for love is good. The pain all sweet somehow." It takes female bonding to help her break away from her predicament as a battered woman.

The link between time and love is established through a pattern of cyclical repetition. "Never Marry a Mexican" focuses on unrequited love. Seeking revenge for having been seduced by her teacher and smarting from a protracted but essentially unfulfilling love affair, the female protagonist repeats the pattern by having an affair with her lover's son, who at that point happens to be her student. Seduction initiated by males, however, is more common in Cisneros's fiction. In "*Bien* Pretty" Flavio acknowledges the existence of a wife, a mistress, and seven children in Mexico. In "Eyes of Zapata" Inés Alfaro is aware of the numerous "pastimes" who, in addition to his wife, compete with her for the General's attention.

Moreover, patterns of cyclical repetition connect time to male violence. Inés Alfaro's mother was murdered after being gang-raped; Boy Baby appears to have murdered eleven women; and the battered wife of "Woman Hollering Creek" recalls grisly stories that point to a pattern of socially condoned practices – "this woman found on the side of the interstate. This one pushed from a moving car. This one's cadaver, this one unconscious, this one beaten blue." In a much less brutal and depressing way, female power also takes on a cyclical pattern. Inés Alfaro acknowledges, "My Tía Chucha, she was the one who taught me to use my sight, just as her mother had taught her. The women in my family, we've always had the power to see with more than with our eyes."

Religion, the collection's third major unifying theme, might more accurately be defined as a faith in the intercession of certain spiritual figures in human dynamics. Though this cultural marker is treated in "Mericans" and "Anguiano Religious Articles," it is most developed in "Little Miracles, Kept Promises," where Cisneros offers an array of ex-votos (petitions addressed to religious figures and accompanied by promises to do penance in return for the granting of requests). These offers of penance in their very nature contain the nuggets of stories. Local color emerges from the popularity of certain saints as well as through references to healers and African deities. The twenty-two pseudo ex-votos in the story come from a wide range of people, including three heads of households, four young women, three grandparents, and a gay man.

The narrator, a Chicana artist who has been reading the ex-votos, rejects the traditional representation of the Virgin of Guadalupe and the passive endurance of pain endorsed by her mother and grandmother. "I wanted you bare-breasted, snakes in your hands. . . . All that self-sacrifice, all that silent suffering. Hell no. Not here. Not me." Her struggle against traditional mores, class values, and sexism results in a redefinition of and a challenge to the Catholic icon: "When I could see you in all your facets, all at once the Buddha, the Tao, the true Messiah, Yahweh, Allah, the Heart of the Sky, the Heart of the Earth, the Lord of the Near and Far, the Spirit, the Light, the Universe, I could love you." Thus Cisneros proves faithful to her purpose,

as she defined it in a 20 May 1991 interview: "in my stories and life I am trying to show that U.S. Latinas have to reinvent, to remythologize, ourselves. A myth believed by almost everyone, even Latina women, is that they are passive, submissive, long-suffering, either a spit-fire or a Madonna. Yet those of us who are their daughters, mothers, sisters know that some of the fiercest women on this planet are Latina women."

Woman Hollering Creek won the P.E.N. Center West Award for best fiction in 1992. Also the winner of two National Endowment for the Arts Fellowships, Cisneros remarked on 20 December 1992 that "there are many Latino writers as talented as I am, but because we are published through small presses our books don't count. We are still the illegal aliens of the literary world." Cisneros has been a writer in residence at the University of Michigan in Ann Arbor and at the University of California at Irvine since she graduated with her master's degree from the writing program at the University of Iowa. Describing herself as "[n]obody's wife" and "nobody's mother" in 1993, the author currently "lives in a rambling Victorian painted in Mexican colors right on the San Antonio River amid pecan and mesquite trees."

Among other projects, Cisneros plans to write a second novel, "Caramelo," set in Mexico and the United States. In her December 1992 interview she said that her novel will focus on "Mexican love and the models we have of love." In a 4 August 1991 interview Cisneros asserted that she is also "particularly interested in exploring father-daughter relationships and aspects of growing up in 'the middle,' between Mexican and Mexican-American culture." She wants to examine the notions that one culture holds about the other, "what one said when the other wasn't around." But her dream, she admitted in December 1992, is to write a Chicana feminist *telenovela* because "It's a way to reach a lot of people." Today Cisneros is perhaps the most visible Chicana in mainstream literary circles. The vividness of her vignettes and the lyrical quality of her prose attest to her craft, about which Melita Marie Garza notes, "Cisneros is as exacting in her writing as she is brazen in her criticism. She rewrites even her shortest stories about twenty-five times."

By re-creating a Chicana child's perspective, Cisneros has already made a significant contribution to the development of the Chicano literary tradition. Moreover, by focusing on the socialization processes of the Chicana, she has criticized and challenged major stereotypes. Perhaps most important, Cisneros grounds her revisionist feminist perspective in everyday experience by highlighting the stamina of the women she has known in real life. Finally, the broad range of voices that appears in her texts – from historical figures such as Emiliano Zapata to fictional gay lovers – attests to her continued success in developing a flexible, yet personal, style.

As shown by the six reprintings of *The House on Mango Street* (1983, 1984, 1985, 1986, 1988, and 1992), Cisneros's reading public is steadily increasing. Her endorsement of bilingualism in *Woman Hollering Creek* as well as her focus on interfacing cultures and her willingness to adopt the popular soap-opera style suggest that, though Cisneros has already carved herself a niche in American literature, the best may be yet to come.

Interviews:

Pilar E. Rodríguez Aranda, "On the Solitary Fate of Being Mexican, Female, Wicked and Thirty-three: An Interview with Writer Sandra Cisneros," *Americas Review,* 18 (Spring 1991): 64–80;

Mary Ann Grossmann, "Caught Between Two Worlds: Mexican-American Writer Sandra Cisneros Walks a Thin Line between Two Clashing Cultures," *St. Paul Pioneer Press-Dispatch,* 20 May 1991, p. D7;

Adria Bernardi, "Latino Voice: Vignettes of Varied Neighborhood Life Come Straight From the Heart," *Chicago Tribune,* 4 August 1991, VI: 12;

Carol McCabe, "A Dazzling Group of Bicultural Writers," *Journal-Bulletin* (Providence, Rhode Island), 21 June 1992, p. A10;

Melita Marie Garza, "Writer Says She Succeeded Despite Chicago," *Chicago Tribune,* 20 December 1992, p. 2C;

Annie Nakao, "Voice of the Latina," *San Francisco Examiner,* 11 January 1993, p. C1.

References:

Erlinda González-Berry and Tey Diana Rebolledo, "Growing up Chicano: Tomás Rivera and Sandra Cisneros," *Revista Chicano Riqueña,* 13, nos. 3-4 (1985): 109–119;

María Herrera-Sobek, "The Politics of Rape: Sexual Transgression in Chicana Fiction," in *Chicana Creativity and Criticism: Charting New Frontiers in American Literature,* edited by Herrera-Sobek and Helena María Viramontes (Houston: Arte Público, 1988), pp. 171–181;

Ellen McCracken, "Latina Narrative and Politics of Signification," *Critica: Journal of Critical Essays,* 2 (Fall 1990): 202–207;

McCracken, "Sandra Cisneros' *The House on Mango Street:* Community-Oriented Introspection and the Demystification of Patriarchal Violence," in *Breaking Boundaries,* edited by Asunción Horno Delgado (Amherst: University of Massachusetts Press, 1989), pp. 62–71;

Julián Olivares, "Sandra Cisneros' *The House on Mango Street* and the Poetics of Space," in *Chicana Creativity and Criticism: Charting New Frontiers in American Literature,* pp. 160–170;

Ramón Saldívar, "The Dialectics of Subjectivity: Gender and Difference in Isabella Ríos, Sandra Cisneros, and Cherríe Moraga," in his *Chicano Narrative: The Dialectics of Difference* (Madison: University of Wisconsin Press, 1990), pp. 171–199;

Yvonne Yarbro-Bejarano, "Chicana Literature from a Chicana Feminist Perspective," in *Chicana Creativity and Criticism: Charting New Frontiers in American Literature,* pp. 139–146.

Louise Erdrich
(6 July 1954 –   )

Ruth Rosenberg
Brooklyn College

BOOKS: *Imagination* (Westerville, Ohio: Merrill, 1981);

Jacklight (New York: Holt, 1984; London: Abacus, 1992);

Love Medicine (New York: Holt, 1984; London: Deutsch, 1985; revised and enlarged, New York: Holt, 1993);

The Beet Queen (New York: Holt, 1986; London: Hamilton, 1987);

Tracks (New York: Holt, 1988; London: Hamilton, 1988);

Baptism of Desire (New York: Harper & Row, 1989);

Route Two (Northridge, Cal.: Lord John Press, 1990);

The Crown of Columbus, by Erdrich and Michael Dorris (New York: HarperCollins, 1991; London: Flamingo, 1992);

The Bingo Palace (New York: HarperCollins, 1994; London: Flamingo, 1994);

The Bluejay's Dance (New York: HarperCollins, 1995).

OTHER: "American Horse," in *Earth Power Coming: An Anthology of Native American Fiction,* edited by Simon Ortiz (Tsaile, Ariz.: Navajo Community College Press, 1984), pp. 59–72;

"A Sense of Place," in *A Place of Sense: Essays in Search of the Midwest,* edited by Michael Martin (Iowa City: University of Iowa Press, 1988), pp. 34–44;

Desmond Hogan, *A Link with the River,* preface by Erdrich (New York: Farrar, Straus & Giroux, 1989);

Michael Dorris, *The Broken Cord: A Family's Ongoing Struggle with Fetal Alcohol Syndrome,* foreword by Erdrich (New York: HarperCollins, 1989; London: Futura, 1992);

"The Bingo Van," in *Talking Leaves: Contemporary Native American Short Stories,* edited by Craig Lesley (New York: Dell, 1991);

Louise Erdrich (photograph by Michael Dorris)

"The Leap," in *How We Live Now: Contemporary Multicultural Literature,* edited by John Repp (Boston: Bedford, 1992);

The Best American Short Stories 1993, edited by Erdrich (Boston: Houghton Mifflin, 1993);

John Tanner, *The Falcon: A Narrative of the Captivity of John Tanner during Thirty Years' Residence among the Indians of the Interiors of North America,* introduction by Erdrich (New York: Viking Penguin, 1994).

SELECTED PERIODICAL PUBLICATIONS –
UNCOLLECTED: "On Excellence," by Erdrich and others, *Ms.,* 13 (January 1985): 84;

"Where I Ought to Be: A Writer's Sense of Place," *New York Times Book Review,* 28 July 1985, pp. 1–2;

"Bangs and Whimpers: Novelists at Armageddon," *New York Times Book Review,* 13 March 1988, p. 1;

"A Woman's Work: Too Many Demands and Not Enough Selves," *Harper's,* 286 (May 1993): 35–46;

"What My Mother Taught Me," *Ladies' Home Journal,* 110 (May 1993): 83–84;

"Skunk Dreams," *Georgia Review,* 47 (Spring 1993): 85–94.

The families Louise Erdrich first introduced in a short story, "The World's Greatest Fishermen" (1982) – the Kashpaws, the Lamartines, the Pillagers, and the Morrisseys – have also appeared in four of her novels. The focus of each changes as previously silent characters speak, revealing their secrets. Three generations interact in the Turtle Mountain Reservation of North Dakota and the nearby town of Argus. Erdrich claims she has no control over whose voice will emerge or what part of the past will be disclosed. Thus the story keeps growing, its truths changing as each new narrator adds an additional perspective. Readers discover a community of unpredictable people by overhearing their gossip, puzzling out their relationships through subtle clues. Despite their tragedies, they are exuberantly funny. Erdrich also possesses the gift of depicting spirits as vibrant presences, not transcendent beings. These forces emanate from stones, pulse from drums, rustle in the leaves of trees, can be summoned by medicines, or flow through fingertips. The forces under a lake, the power within a pipe, and the ancestors' dancing in the northern lights control the destinies of these people.

Louise Karen Erdrich was born on 6 July 1954 in Little Falls, Minnesota, the eldest of seven children. Her mother, Rita Joanne Gourneau Erdrich, had been born on the Turtle Mountain Chippewa Reservation, of which Patrick Gourneau, Erdrich's grandfather, had been tribal chairman. Her father, Ralph Louis Erdrich, of German descent, taught at the Bureau of Indian Affairs boarding school, where her mother also taught. The family lived in faculty housing at the edge of the small town of Wahpeton, North Dakota, three hundred miles away from the Turtle Mountain Reservation. Some aspects of her paternal grandmother, Mary Erdrich Korll, appear in *The Beet Queen* (1986) as well as in the poetry sequences called "The Butcher's Wife" in *Jacklight* (1984) and *Baptism of Desire* (1989). Her great uncle, Ben Gourneau, inspired some of the details for the characterization of Eli Kashpaw. Her mother had told her many of the stories in *Tracks* (1988), the first written but third published of her novels.

In a 1991 *Writer's Digest* interview, collected in *Conversations with Louise Erdich and Michael Dorris* (1993), Erdrich credits a childhood without movies or television for her narrative impulse:

> The people in our families made everything into a story. They love to tell a good story. People just sit and the stories start coming, one after another. You just sort of grab the tail of the last person's story: it reminds you of something and you keep going on. I suppose that when you grow up constantly hearing the stories rise, break and fall, it gets into you somehow.

Erdrich's tetralogy is comprised of chapters narrated by different speakers. The events, spanning a century, assume the form of a traditional Chippewa story cycle. As Erdrich explained to Malcolm Jones of the *St. Petersburg Times* in 1985:

> This reflects a traditional Chippewa motif in storytelling, which is a cycle of stories having to do with a central mythological figure, a culture hero. One tells a story about an incident that leads to another incident that leads to another in the life of this particular figure. Night after night, or day after day, it's a storytelling cyle.

Erdrich told Joseph Bruchac in *Survival This Way: Interviews with American Indian Poets* (1987) that she idolized her grandfather: "He is funny, he's charming, he's interesting." She respected his being able to live with dignity in two cultures – maintaining the old religion, speaking "the old language," doing pipe services for ordinations, knowledgeable about the ways of the animals. But he also attended mass, "gave Tricia Nixon an Anishinabe name, for publicity," and danced in powwows. In a 1986 interview with Nora Frenkiel of the *Baltimore Sun* she recalled how "he searched his fields for old stones used in tomahawks, and remade the entire beadwork." But above all, she says, "My grandfather was a great storyteller." Although none of her fiction is autobiographical, she has given her character Nector Kashpaw some of her grandfather's attributes. Nector's devoted wife, Marie, bears some resemblance to her grandmother, Mary Gourneau, who married at age fourteen.

Erdrich's father made the Depression era so vivid for her that she was able to fictionalize his accounts in *The Beet Queen.* She got the idea for the novel from his anecdote about his first airplane ride, which inspired a plot based on Adelaide's flight. He also gave her the idea for one of her poetry sequences, as she told Jan George in 1985: "My father is a terrific storyteller and made his relatives and the characters in the towns where he grew up

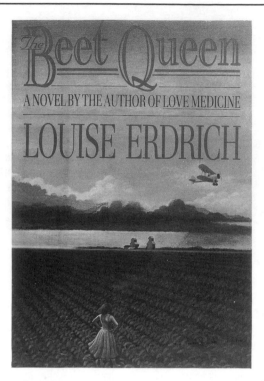

Dust jacket for the second novel in which Erdrich examines the lives of the Turtle Mountain Chippewa

almost mythic. I owe 'Step-and-a-Half-Waleski' in *Jacklight* completely to him. There really was a woman like her in his childhood." Erdrich's father also introduced her to William Shakespeare, playing and replaying records of *Macbeth* and *King Lear*. He encouraged her and her sisters to write by occasionally paying them a nickel for their stories. Her sisters Heidi and Lise are also published authors. When Erdrich was judging the entries for a volume of best American short stories, she regretted that the rules prevented her from accepting Lise's submission.

Except for a few years in a parochial school, Saint John's, in Wahpeton, Erdrich attended public school. One small detail that surfaced later in her fiction was her election to the B# piano club while she was taking music lessons with her teacher Sister Anita. Wallace Pfef in *The Beet Queen* is described as being a supporter of the B# piano club. Another incident, which she uses in *The Bingo Palace* (1994), had actually happened to her when she was fourteen. One May night she took her sleeping bag out to the football field and awoke at dawn with a skunk curled up on top of her. In a 1993 essay in the *Georgia Review* she wrote how she envied skunks their fearlessness. She wrote in the January 1985 *Ms.* that performing on the piano in public "terrified me to the point of nausea or paralysis."

In 1972 she entered Dartmouth College on scholarships as part of its first coeducational class.

That same year her future husband, Michael Dorris, had been appointed head of the Native American studies department. Their first collaboration was published in an Indian magazine, a children's story that he wrote and she illustrated. Dorris said in *The Broken Cord* (1989) that "her bold, quirky drawings" were "better than my text."

Her first publications were in Dartmouth literary magazines. One of her teachers, A. B. Paulsen, considered her a poet of unusually high talent. She finally felt credentialed when *Ms.* accepted one of her poems; an American Academy of Poets Prize in 1975 was further validation. After graduation she worked as poet in the schools for the State Arts Council of North Dakota, teaching "children, convicts, rehabilitation patients, high-school hoods and recovering alcoholics." The following summer James Wright, a Dartmouth history professor, invited her to serve as consultant on a documentary he was filming on Northern Plains Indians for Nebraska Public Television.

A variety of minimum-wage jobs followed, many of which found their way into her fiction later. Many of her characters are waitresses, as she had been, either "on the night shift in an all-night family diner" or "on the breakfast shift as a short-order cook." She prides herself on still being able to crack four eggs one-handed. She also weighed trucks on the interstate and worked as flagger on a construction site — both jobs she gave to characters.

She weeded beets, picked cucumbers, delivered newspapers, sold popcorn, and worked as an ad manager and as a bookstore distributor of small-press publications. The scenes in *Love Medicine* (1984) set in the elder-care center gain verisimilitude from her having worked in one.

In 1979 a fellowship at Johns Hopkins University enabled Erdrich to move to Maryland and concentrate on her writing. In a small apartment she worked on the poems she submitted as her thesis. After receiving her master's degree in 1980 she became editor of the Boston Indian Council newspaper, *The Circle*. In Massachusetts she wrote a textbook, *Imagination* (1981), for Merrill while waitressing at a pastry shop.

An invitation to read at Dartmouth led to her meeting Dorris again. As he wrote later in *The Broken Cord,* her reading left him "dazed, stunned." Her poems were "vivid stories, tight and condensed as black holes in space." They had time only to exchange addresses because he was leaving for New Zealand and she for the MacDowell Colony in New Hampshire. Their correspondence became an exchange of manuscripts, each writing long editorial comments on the other's drafts. After working at Yaddo, Erdrich was invited to serve as writer in residence at Dartmouth. Her arrival on campus in January 1981 coincided with Dorris's return. On 10 October 1981 they were married in a civil ceremony in the backyard of the house Dorris had shared with his three adopted children. Erdrich's mother had sewn the wedding gown and mailed it to Cornish, New Hampshire, from North Dakota.

To pay for repairs on their farmhouse the couple collaborated, under the pseudonym Milou North, on stories published in the British magazine *Woman*. Erdrich told the *Washington Post* in October 1988 that their first fictions were "not terribly deep, but they were uplifting. Always about a young woman under stress who resolved her crisis affirmatively."

Their next collaboration won the Nelson Algren Award, a five-thousand-dollar prize from *Chicago* magazine. Dorris's aunt Virginia Burkhardt had sent them the announcement of the contest early in January; the deadline was 15 January. In a single day Erdrich drafted the story of a family reunion "with events, but no conversation or details." As she finished each page at the kitchen table, she took it into the living room for Dorris's suggestions. After they mailed off "The World's Greatest Fishermen" they spent so much time discussing the revisions they would make when it returned that they had enough material for a novel. It became the opening chapter of *Love Medicine*. Two other chapters, "The Red Convertible" and "Scales," had already been published. When Anne Tyler selected "Scales" for *The Best American Short Stories 1983* she wrote of Dot Nanapush, "You think you won't care much about a gigantic, belligerent, pregnant woman who weighs trucks for a living? Just wait. By the time you see her violently knitting her orange and hot-pink baby clothes you'll care passionately."

For a year and a half the couple imagined scenarios for their characters, who, in the course of many conversations, became as familiar as relatives. The "Saint Marie" chapter gave them some problems. Dorris felt that it was not working in the nun's voice and suggested it be told by the novitiate. Erdrich went out for a long walk. "The next day," Dorris told Shelby Grantham of *Dartmouth Alumni Magazine* in 1985, "there was a new draft on my desk. We had no other words about it – it just appeared there. And it was absolutely right." Henry Abrams, who selected it for the 1985 O. Henry Awards, agreed.

When they sent *Love Medicine* to publishers it received polite responses but no offers. Dorris finally managed to place the manuscript with Holt by printing up stationery with the letterhead Michael Dorris Agency and promoting it himself. The novel became an immediate best-seller. The American Academy of Arts and Letters gave the thirty-year-old novelist the Sue Kaufman Prize for Best First Fiction, and distinguished writers acclaimed her achievement. Philip Roth praised her "originality, authority, tenderness, and pitiless wild wit." Toni Morrison wrote that "the beauty of *Love Medicine* saves us from being devastated by its power." Ursula K. Le Guin called Erdrich "a true artist and probably a major one," while the *Chicago Tribune* called her "the first novelist of her generation to have achieved front-rank writerly stardom."

The author who had seldom seen television was wooed by producers who saw possibilities in *Love Medicine* as a television serial; movie rights were also optioned. A measure of its worldwide appeal was its translation into eighteen languages. Native Americans wrote her thousands of letters, some of them asking how she could have known things that had actually happened to them. She appreciated their endorsement, especially those who told her she was the first writer who knew how Indians really talked. She acknowledged this at the New York Historical Society when the National Book Critics Circle honored her as the year's best novelist. It was the Chippewa who deserved the recognition, she said: "I accept this award in the spirit of

Erdrich and Michael Dorris, her husband and collaborator (photograph by James Woodcock)

the people who speak through the book." In 1984 she also won the Virginia Scully Award for Best Book Dealing with Western Indians and in 1985 the American Book Award from the Before Columbus Foundation.

A wide readership responded to promotions by the Book-of-the-Month Club and the Quality Paperback Book Club. An academic audience, the Great Lakes Colleges Association, conferred upon her its prize for Best First Work of Fiction. In 1985 she received a Guggenheim Fellowship.

In August 1985 Dorris went on sabbatical to research *The Broken Cord* while Erdrich worked on *The Beet Queen,* based on her father's people. The family moved to Northfield, Minnesota, to a six-bedroom Victorian house a block away from Carleton College.

Erdrich submits her work to continual revision. The first longhand drafts are passed back and forth between the couple for interlinear comments. Then Dorris triple-spaces the manuscript on his word processor, using a different font for each successive version. The final manuscript is spread out on a long table and read aloud page by page. They do not send it out until they have achieved consen-

sus on every word. Therefore they were surprised to find themselves still prompted to further revision after *The Beet Queen* seemed ready to send to the publisher. In a 1986 interview in the *North Dakota Quarterly* Erdrich said, "Right after Christmas, we started rewriting it from page 206 on. In a month, we rewrote pages 206 to 393, and made a whole new ending. The last 15 pages are completely new."

Some reviewers objected to the carefully reworked ending. Michiko Kakutani in the 20 August 1986 *New York Times* lamented its artifice in reassembling all the characters at a parade. Dorothy Wickenden in the 6 October *New Republic* wrote that "the coming together of all the characters and themes at the beet festival — complete with Dot's dramatic reliving of her grandmother's flight — is a contrivance." Josh Rubin in the 15 January 1987 *New York Review of Books* deplored the outlandish coincidences "in the novel's final set piece, which blatantly arranges the intersection of the redemptive return of wastrel Karl, the black-comic demise of Cousin Sita, and the rigged election of sullen Dot Adare as the 1972 Beet Queen of Argus, North Dakota."

The carefully contextualized conclusion arose from a spiderweb image in a mother's dream in the center of the novel. She notices "in the fine moonlight floss of her baby's hair, a tiny white spider making its nest. It was a delicate thing, close to transparent . . . throwing out invisible strings." The novel was spun out of that central metaphor. Erdrich's daughter Pallas, whose "passion is spiders" and who was delighted that one "spun a delicate web in an eave above her bed," inspired that passage.

The passages between the chapters lyrically describing the characters' dreams are the "invisible strings" making the episodes coherent. When the Bantam paperback edition failed to include these, Erdrich's lawyer, Charles Rembar, offered to share the expense of recalling the fifty thousand copies already in print. When they declined Erdrich changed to another publisher. HarperCollins paid an unprecedented six hundred thousand dollars for the paperback rights. From its third week after publication *The Beet Queen* was on *The New York Times* best-seller list. It was featured by the Book-of-the-Month Club as an alternate selection, was named by *Publishers Weekly* as one of the "Best Books," and was nominated for the National Book Critics Circle Award. It was published in England and translated into Danish, Norwegian, Finnish, Swedish, German, and French.

Erdrich's technical virtuosity impressed many critics. In the 15 January 1987 *New York Review of Books* Rubin wrote that her storytelling was so compelling that her authorial stratagems "don't undermine the story's forward momentum and emotional conviction." Robert Bly in the 31 August *New York Times Book Review* expressed "amazement and gratitude at this splendid, feisty talent, capable of bizarre comedy, ordinary Midwestern facts and vigorous tragedy." Russell Banks in the 1 November 1986 *Nation* applauded the "exquisite ironies" wrought from "a Bruegel-like realism" and the elegant orchestration of the multiple voices that "blend, as in a chorus, without ever losing their remarkable individuality. Erdrich has been able to give each of her characters their own tone, diction, pitch and rhythm, without letting go of her own."

For her third novel Erdrich returned to her student manuscript, *Tracks,* portions of which had already been published as short stories. "Fleur" had been doubly honored. In 1986 it was cited by Sharon Ravenel as a distinguished short story of the year, and in 1987 it was chosen by William Abrahams as the first-place winner of the *Prize Stories: The O. Henry Awards.* In *The Broken Cord* Dorris described its impact on him a decade before at Dartmouth: "Louise read a section of what she described as a

novel-in-progress: the tale of a Chippewa woman who bested a group of men in a card game in a butcher shop and their fury over the loss. It was alternately hilarious and terribly sad, a building swirl of impressions that clung to the imagination with incredible power." Erdrich said that rereading it led her to the realization "that it was now part of what the novel could be, and it eventually became the second chapter in the book." Dorris saw in the emerging trilogy three of the four natural elements. As the first novel had been governed by images of water, the second had reiterated references to air. The third would be dominated by images of earth, as the fourth would be by fire. The plot of *Tracks* is a conflict over the land. The Anishinabe are threatened by surveyors preparing for allotment as well as by loggers. Since it moved back into tribal history to events between 1912 and 1924 Dorris considered it a prequel to the other two novels. Alternately narrated by Nanapush and Pauline (who becomes Sister Leopolda in *The Beet Queen*), its silent auditor is the child Lulu (the matriarch of *Love Medicine*). The already-published short story "Snares," which had been selected for *The Best American Short Stories 1988,* became the fifth chapter.

Erdrich was reluctant to let this book, scheduled for publication in September 1988, go. She considers it her favorite because it gave her such difficulty, and she wishes she had had more time with it. In spite of her feeling that it was still incomplete, *Tracks* was widely praised, was adopted in college courses, and immediately ascended the best-seller lists. *Studies in American Indian Literatures* devoted two issues to it. Among the many topics discussed, that of dealing with ritual materials, of trying to transform an oral tradition into a written one, suggests why she felt *Tracks* posed such problems.

Erdrich uses the double-voiced narration again in her next book, *Baptism of Desire.* The Trickster voice is apparent in the "Potchikoo" cycle, while the convent voice can be heard in the Catholic poems. The two antithetical belief systems energize her poetry.

In 1990 Erdrich and Dorris collaborated on a travel book later printed in a limited edition. *Route Two* resulted from their family visits to relatives across the continent. They plotted their next project, the novel *The Crown of Columbus* (1991), on their drive through Saskatchewan described in *Route Two.* They had been intrigued by Columbus's multiple identities in the public mind for a decade, researching the complex personality of the man credited with "discovering" Native Americans. Erdrich undertook the task of reading every book that Colum-

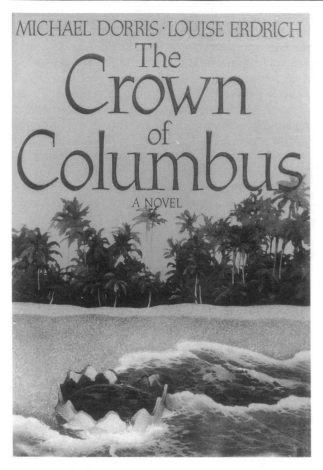

Dust jacket for Erdrich and Dorris's novel about the relationship between two twentieth-century characters doing research on Christopher Columbus

position within the text, since everything in the poem is paralleled in the novel and it therefore assumes structural importance.

Erdrich enjoyed the opportunity to write about literate characters in an academic setting, which allowed her to exercise her gift for parody. Her penchant for playing with forms made *The New York Times Book Review* writer uncomfortable. The book, he wrote, mixes too many genres: "domestic comedy, paperback thriller, novel of character, love story." Carla Freccero disagreed in the 17 October 1991 *Women's Review of Books:* "What has appeared to some critics as a helter-skelter fragmentary novel catering to popular tastes is in fact a highly structured, complex, symbolic rewriting of American history, framed by four parallel discoveries and four returns." With a first printing of 150,000 copies; excerpts in *Redbook, Mother Jones,* and *Caliban;* movie rights sold to Cinecom; and a two-hundred-thousand-dollar advertising campaign and author tours, the book became a resounding commercial success, and it was chosen as a Book-of-the-Month Club alternate.

In 1993 Erdrich was invited to serve as the guest editor of *The Best American Short Stories 1993.* Pam Lambert in the 15 November 1993 *People Weekly* noted that Erdrich fortified herself for the task of selecting from the 120 entries with "a case of licorice. 'I like the red better, but you feel more professional eating black.' " Reviewers praised the collection assembled by Erdrich, calling it "remarkably rich." Her criteria had been "intellectual pleasure" as well as "texture, place, aroma, succulence, and stiff particularity," she wrote in her introduction.

In November 1993 Holt issued an augmented version of *Love Medicine.* Erdrich's editor there, Marian Wood, justified the expanded edition because the series of which it forms a part is "organic," and its growth had to be accommodated. The four inserted chapters set up *The Bingo Palace.* Serving as transitions to this fourth novel are the chapters "The Island," "Resurrection," "The Tomohawk Factory," and "Lyman's Luck." Erdrich's explanation, in the 14 October *New York Times,* of the augmented edition is interesting for what it reveals about her methods of composition:

> When I started working on my new book, *The Bingo Palace,* I started sifting through these notebooks I have of handwritten manuscripts and notes of everything I'd done before. It's basically like a big compost pile. The notebooks not only suggested the shape for the new book, but they suggested that there were parts of *Love Medicine* that I had forgotten. . . . I felt that these voices needed to be included.

bus had mentioned in his diaries. Like the protagonist, Vivian Twostar, she worked in Dartmouth's Baker Library. At the time Erdrich was pregnant with their third daughter, Aza, as Vivian was with her baby, Violet.

The second narrator, Roger Williams, is writing an epic poem about Columbus. Erdrich described him in a 1991 *Mother Jones* article on the couple as "terribly self-important," and Dorris added that he is "a very fastidious, self-protective, established English professor." His joining the quest for the missing pages of Columbus's diary jolts him out of his academic isolation into the disorder of the everyday. As another of their pseudonymous publications Erdrich and Dorris submitted the poem about Columbus under the name Roger Williams to the periodical *Caliban,* admitting they were jealous of their invented author since he got printed with his first submission. The French publishers of the book wanted Williams's poem displaced to an appendix. However, Erdrich and Dorris defended its

Those voices – Lulu, Marie, and Lyman – give readers the background knowledge needed to understand Lipsha's accession to the Pillager powers in *The Bingo Palace*. Lulu tells how Lipsha's father, Gerry, was conceived by the medicine man, Moses Nanapush, who was Fleur's cousin – the only male Pillager who survived the epidemic depicted in *Tracks*. Marie tells of the ancestral pipe to be inherited by Lipsha, which, when its stem is joined to its bowl, connects heaven and earth. Lyman speaks of the profound mourning for his brother, Henry Lamartine, Jr., which will be resolved by his performance of the grass dance. The business acumen he inherited from Nector Kashpaw, which leads him to found not only a tomahawk factory but also a bingo palace, leads finally to tribal recognition of his paternity. The epic ends with a reconciliation of sons with fathers after the rivalry between Lipsha and Lyman is healed during a joint vision quest. Not only are the old ceremonies restored but even the old language, as Gerry tells his son where to find him in Anishinabec. Gerry is the fictionalized counterpart of the Chippewa hero Leonard Peltier, wrongly imprisoned for eighteen years. His martyrdom inspires the union of all tribal people in protest.

Erdrich had been working on a story cycle called "Tales of Burning Love," scheduled for publication in 1995, when *The Bingo Palace* came to her during a blizzard. She interrupted her work on the story cycle to draft the novel in six weeks. Then an invitation came to write an introduction for a captivity narrative that had long been a family favorite. She reminisced about the history of a boy who in 1789 was adopted by the Ojibwa:

> [T]he darkly bound narrative of the captivity of John Tanner stood upright on a shelf in my grandparents' Turtle Mountain Reservation home. It belonged to my grandfather Patrick Gourneau, and I first read it on the sun-soaked back steps of his house, just beyond the shade of the spreading woods where Tanner once joined an ill-fated early nineteenth-century Cree party. The story of Shaw-shaw-wa-be-na-se, or The Falcon, was a family touchstone especially cherished by my sister, Lise.

Erdrich is also considering a book about the kindly Father Damien. In preparation she is studying the lives of the saints and the history of the Jesuit missionaries as well as researching Catholic devotions. As she told Bruchac, "You never change once you're raised a Catholic. You've got that symbolism, that guilt."

Erdrich is also planning a book about Mustache Maude, a female cattle rustler, "a North Dakota maverick" about whom she had published a short story in *Frontiers*. "The story was, as early work often is, an experiment in voice and form," Erdrich explained to an interviewer.

Erdrich has compiled a book of nature essays, selected from the many she has published in magazines, called *The Bluejay's Dance* (1995). The conceit of dancing away the threat of death is an apt metaphor for survival humor. She writes of a baby bluejay that had escaped a swooping hawk by fluffing its feathers and dancing a "manic, successful jig – cocky, exuberant, entirely a bluff, a joke." All of Erdrich's life-affirming exuberance is in that image.

Interviews:

Jan George, "Interview with Louise Erdrich," *North Dakota Quarterly,* 53 (Spring 1985): 240–246;

Kay Bonetti, "Interview," *Missouri Review,* 11 (1988): 79–99;

Allan Chavkin and Nancy Feyl Chavkin, eds., *Conversations with Louise Erdrich and Michael Dorris* (Jackson: University Press of Mississippi, 1993).

Bibliographies:

Lillian Brewington, Norman Bullard, and R. W. Reising, "Writing in Love: An Annotated Bibliography of Critical Responses to the Poetry and Novels of Louise Erdrich and Michael Dorris," *American Indian Culture and Research Journal,* 10, no. 4 (1986): 81–86;

Mickey Pearlman, "A Bibliography of Writings by Louise Erdrich," *American Women Writing Fiction: Memory, Identity, Family, Space,* edited by Pearlman (Lexington: University Press of Kentucky, 1989), pp. 108–112.

References:

Nora Barry and Mary Prescott, "The Triumph of the Brave: *Love Medicine*'s Holistic Vision," *Critique,* 30 (Winter 1989): 123–138;

Peter J. Beidler and Helen Hoy, "*The Crown of Columbus:* Two Views," *Studies in American Indian Literatures,* 3 (Winter 1991): 47–55;

Joni Adamson Clarke, "Why Bears are Good to Think and Theory Doesn't Have to Be Murder: Transformation and Oral Tradition in Louise Erdrich's *Tracks,*" *Studies in American Indian Literatures,* 4 (Spring 1992): 28–48;

Daniel Cornell, "Woman Looking: Revisioning Pauline's Subject Position in Louise Erdrich's

Tracks," *Studies in American Indian Literatures*, 4 (Spring 1992): 49–64;

James Flavin, "The Novel as Performance: Communication in Louise Erdrich's *Tracks*," *Studies in American Indian Literatures*, 3 (Winter 1991): 1–12;

Louise Flavin, "Louise Erdrich's *Love Medicine:* Loving Over Time and Distance," *Critique,* 31 (Fall 1989): 55–64;

William Gleason, " 'Her Laugh An Ace': The Function of Humor in Louise Erdrich's *Love Medicine*," *American Indian Culture and Research Journal*, 11, no. 3 (1987): 51–73;

Helen Jaskowski, "From Time Immemorial: Native American Traditions in Contemporary Short Fiction," in *Since Flannery O'Connor: Essays on the Contemporary Short Story,* edited by Loren Logsdon and Charles W. Mayer (Macomb: Western Illinois University Press, 1987), pp. 54–71;

Pam Lambert, Review of *The Best American Short Stories 1993, People Weekly,* 40 (15 November 1993): 31;

Marvin Magalaner, "Of Cars, Time, and the River," in *American Women Writing Fiction: Memory, Identity, Family, Space,* edited by Mickey Pearlman (Lexington: University Press of Kentucky, 1989), pp. 95–108;

Julie Maristuen-Rodakowski, "The Turtle Mountain Reservation in North Dakota: Its History as Depicted in Louise Erdrich's *Love Medicine* and *Beet Queen*," *American Indian Culture and Research Journal*, 12, no. 3 (1988): 12–18;

Thomas Matchie, "Exploring the Meaning of Discovery in *The Crown of Columbus*," *North Dakota Quarterly,* 59 (Fall 1991): 243–250;

James McKenzie, "Lipsha's Good Road Home: The Revival of Chippewa Culture in *Love Medicine*," *American Indian Culture and Research Journal*, 10, no. 3 (1986): 53–63;

Louis Owens, "Erdrich and Dorris's Mixedbloods and Multiple Narratives," in his *Other Destinies: Understanding the American Indian Novel* (Norman: University of Oklahoma Press, 1992), pp. 192–224;

Catherine Rainwater, "Reading Between Two Worlds: Narrativity in the Fiction of Louise Erdrich," *American Literature,* 62 (September 1990): 405–422;

Ann Rayson, "Shifting Identity in the Work of Louise Erdrich and Michael Dorris," *Studies in American Indian Literatures,* 3 (Winter 1991): 27–36;

James Ruppert, "Mediation and Multiple Narrative in *Love Medicine*," *North Dakota Quarterly,* 59 (Fall 1991): 229–242;

Kathleen Sands, "Louise Erdrich: *Love Medicine*," *Studies in American Indian Literatures*, 9 (Winter 1985): 1–29;

Greg Sarris, "Reading Louise Erdrich: *Love Medicine* as Home Medicine," in his *Keeping Slug Woman Alive: A Holistic Approach to American Indian Texts* (Berkeley: University of California Press, 1993), pp. 115–146;

Lissa Schneider, "*Love Medicine*: A Metaphor for Forgiveness," *Studies in American Indian Literatures,* 4 (Spring 1992): 1–13;

Lydia A. Schultz, "Fragments and Ojibwe Stories: Narrative Strategies in Louise Erdrich's *Love Medicine*," *College Literature,* 18 (October 1991): 80–95;

Robert Silberman, "Opening the Text: *Love Medicine* and the Return of the Native American Woman," in *Narrative Chance: Postmodern Discourse on Native American Indian Literatures,* edited by Gerald Vizenor (Albuquerque: University of New Mexico Press, 1989), pp. 101–120;

Jean Smith, "Transpersonal Selfhood: The Boundaries of Identity in Louise Erdrich's *Love Medicine*," *Studies in American Indian Literatures,* 3 (Winter 1991): 13–26;

Margery Towery, "Continuity and Connection: Characters in Louise Erdrich's Fiction," *American Indian Culture and Research Journal*, 16, no. 4 (1992): 99–115;

Annette Van Dyke, "Questions of the Spirit: Bloodlines in Louise Erdrich's Chippewa Landscape," *Studies in American Indian Literatures,* 4 (Spring 1992): 15–27;

Victoria Walker, "A Note on Narrative Perspective in *Tracks*," *Studies in American Indian Literatures,* 3 (Winter 1991): 37–40.

Ernest J. Gaines

(15 January 1933 –)

Keith E. Byerman
Indiana State University

See also the Gaines entries in *DLB 2: American Novelists Since World War II, DLB 33: Afro-American Fiction Writers After 1955,* and *DLB Yearbook: 1980.*

BOOKS: *Catherine Carmier* (New York: Atheneum, 1964; London: Secker & Warburg, 1966);
Of Love and Dust (New York: Dial, 1967; London: Secker & Warburg, 1968);
Bloodline (New York: Dial, 1968);
A Long Day in November (New York: Dial, 1971);
The Autobiography of Miss Jane Pittman (New York: Dial, 1971; London: Joseph, 1973);
In My Father's House (New York: Knopf, 1978; London: Prior, 1978);
A Gathering of Old Men (New York: Knopf, 1983);
A Lesson Before Dying (New York: Knopf, 1993).

Ernest J. Gaines has since the publication of *The Autobiography of Miss Jane Pittman* in 1971 established himself as one of the most prominent of contemporary African American writers. The CBS television presentation of Gaines's most famous novel on 31 January 1974 helped bring to public awareness a history of black Americans that had been too long ignored. Two other works have also been made into televised dramas: "The Sky is Gray," a story from the *Bloodline* collection (1968) that was produced for public television in 1980, and *A Gathering of Old Men,* which appeared on CBS (10 May 1987). Gaines has received many awards, most recently a MacArthur Foundation award in recognition of his achievements (1993). Like one of his models, William Faulkner, Gaines has chosen to focus his fiction on a small portion of the South, discovering in his mythical Bayonne, Louisiana, a great richness of human experience. The fact that it is a world that had been largely ignored simply adds to his importance as an interpreter of American culture.

Gaines was born on the River Lake Plantation near Oscar, Louisiana; his parents, Manuel and

Ernest J. Gaines (photograph © Thomas Victor)

Adrienne Gaines, were sharecroppers. Gaines has described digging potatoes as a young child for fifty cents a day. His paraplegic aunt, Augusteen Jefferson, managed to feed, clothe, and discipline him and his brothers while their parents worked in the fields. The world of the plantation and nearby town, with its mixture of blacks, black and white Creoles, and Cajuns, has served as the setting for all of Gaines's fiction. His aunt has served as the model for the recurring figure of the strong older woman whose endurance, faith, and sacrifice have aided generations of struggling African Americans.

Gaines's parents separated when Ernest was eight, and he lost contact with his father, who served in World War II and then moved to New Orleans. After the war his mother moved to California to join her new husband, who was in the merchant marine. Ernest remained in Louisiana to help Aunt Augusteen with the younger children. In 1948, at the age of fifteen, he joined his mother and stepfather in Vallejo, California, because there was no black high school in Pointe Coupé Parish. While in high school he began extensive reading. The kind of people he had grown up knowing were missing from the stories of America and the South he read, and, while still relatively young, he began writing about their experiences. Some of his early models were nineteenth-century Russian novelists – Ivan Turgenev, Leo Tolstoy, Nikolay Gogol – who focused on the lives of rural people. His literary apprenticeship continued through his time at Vallejo Junior College and two years in the army. In 1956 his first stories were published in *Transfer,* a San Francisco little magazine, while he was studying at San Francisco State College. After he graduated in 1957, Gaines accepted a Wallace Stegner fellowship in the creative writing program at Stanford University (1958–1959).

His fiction focuses on the folk culture of rural Louisiana, including the small town he calls Bayonne. His characters are primarily those blacks who work on the plantations, but he also treats Cajuns and Creoles. Unlike other storytellers of the region, such as George Washington Cable, Kate Chopin, and Walker Percy, Gaines takes the perspective of ordinary black residents, often semiliterate and ignorant of the larger world. Nonetheless, the world he creates is richly multicultural, and he renders with care its complex race and class tensions and interactions. His decision to focus on the early and mid twentieth century means that he can examine racial oppression and also the methods blacks used to endure it during a time of transition. His world is one in which the modern problems of alienation and social change are played out in local terms.

Gaines depicts an organic society in which blacks and whites are both culturally and socially conservative. Strong figures, usually black males, emerge to challenge the existing order, especially on matters of race. They face resistance not only from whites, whose authority and sense of superiority are questioned, but also traditional blacks, who assume both the futility and danger of social disruption. Gaines refuses to simplify these struggles into categories of good and evil; instead, he explores the human meanings and implications of resistance and endurance. While those seeking change are depicted as heroic, they also are shown to endanger themselves and others. Those who endure rather than fight are often shown to preserve the stories of the heroes to inspire another generation. Thus, Gaines seeks to present a varied and complicated history of his small part of the South.

This complexity is evident in his first published novel, *Catherine Carmier* (1964), which is patterned after Turgenev's *Fathers and Sons* in its depiction of rural life and the tensions between generations. Its protagonist, Jackson Bradley, has returned to the plantation after years of education. This training has alienated him from the values of the rural black community and especially his Aunt Charlotte, a very religious woman who had hoped that he would return to teach in the local school. Jackson wishes to leave but finds himself imprisoned by his inability to tell Charlotte the truth and by the rekindling of his love for Catherine. The title character is the daughter of a black Creole farmer, Raoul, who believes himself racially and socially superior to blacks and who has forbidden his daughters to have anything to do with them, including Jackson. This isolates Catherine, who nonetheless feels a deep love for her father, a man she sees as courageously resisting the Cajun takeover of all the good farmland. Though she loves Jackson, she cannot leave Raoul. Thus, both Catherine and Jackson are immobilized by the pressures of this rural community.

These twin themes of isolation and paralysis give the novel an existential quality. Characters must face an unfriendly world without guidance and must make crucial choices about their lives. Raoul, an embittered, lonely man, works his land and restricts his daughters, not out of hope for a better future but because he defines his manhood in terms of his resistance to both Cajun greed and to what he sees as black acquiescence to that greed. He takes pride in both his family history and in his own ability to work hard and productively. His increasing age and lack of a son cause him despair over the future; though doomed to ultimate failure, he continues to struggle because it is the struggle that has given his life meaning.

Aunt Charlotte seems in many ways the opposite of Raoul. She has had two sources of hope in her life: her religion and Jackson. Her religion has given her the strength to endure the difficulties of her life because she believes that there is an underlying spiritual meaning to everything that has hap-

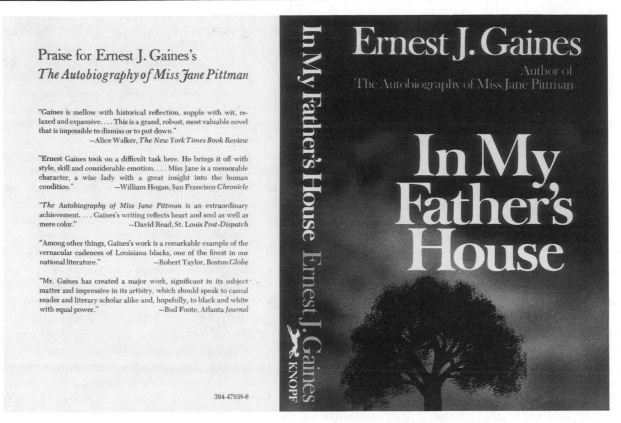

394-47938-6

Dust jacket for Gaines's 1978 novel, about a civil rights leader and his illegitimate son

pened. Unlike Raoul, she puts her faith in something outside herself. Her initial crisis comes when Jackson refuses to attend church services with her; she sees this as a possible judgment on her own faith and on the efficacy of her prayers. But because Jackson has returned, she has confidence that he will eventually completely reenter the community, including the church. The greater crisis occurs when he finally announces to her that he will not remain. We discover that Charlotte, like Raoul, has staked all of her hopes on a son. Her frustration is in some ways even greater because she has the son (psychologically if not biologically) and he fails to live up to her expectations. She feels so deeply betrayed that not even her religious faith can give her real relief from despair. She becomes physically ill, and even after she recovers she cannot fully accept the meaning of the experience.

Jackson, though he intends no harm to Aunt Charlotte, cannot help but hurt her because of his own lack of faith. His experience of the outside world has led him away from what he considers the parochial values of his aunt and her community. He cannot accept an unquestioning faith in a divine order when he has both learned the value of reason and has used reason to gain an understanding of

human behavior. And though not politically active, he rejects the idea that the existing racial order is either natural or unchangeable. His problem is that he has no new values with which to replace the old ones. His reason has left him with skepticism and not with hope. The source of his despair is thus the very opposite of that of Raoul and Charlotte. The future seems closed to them because there is no one to whom they can pass on their values; to Jackson, the future is far too open because he is young but has no direction. The story is in one sense Jackson's search for a home, a place he can have faith in and still be true to his reason.

He tries to create this place through his love for Catherine, but this effort is made extremely difficult by her attachment to her father. At first she rejects the idea that she even cares for Jackson, even though they had loved each other before he left. That separation was caused in part by Raoul's refusal to allow his daughter to have anything to do with young black men. While Jackson was gone for several years, the relationship between father and daughter deepened, to the extent that her mother, Della, claimed that Catherine was more of a wife than she herself was. While no incest is implied, Raoul's attitude toward his daughter is very much that of a jealous husband. He watches over her constantly and will not allow her to develop close ties to any other people in the community. When she falls in love with a young Creole man and bears his child, Raoul drives off the baby's father and isolates Catherine even more completely. Catherine accepts Raoul despite his fanatical behavior and even sees in him a kind of heroism for showing so much devotion to the land and to his family. She gladly becomes a substitute son for him, even though his actions virtually guarantee that the land will be lost to the Cajuns after his death.

Jackson disturbs this unnatural equilibrium by seeking and getting Catherine's love. But in place of Raoul's imprisoning devotion to land and family, the young man can offer escape to nowhere and nothing in particular. Catherine is torn between the desire for freedom and her love of father and the soil. Much of the book is devoted to an analysis of her fluctuating loyalties and to Jackson's uncertainties about the meaning and future of the relationship. Meanwhile the two of them continue to meet in secret, fearful of Raoul's anger. In a final confrontation, Jackson defeats Raoul in a fistfight and believes himself to have literally won Catherine. To his surprise, however, she insists that she must nurse her father back to health and that the conqueror must wait to gain his prize. Jackson's bitterness at this ironic turn is neutralized somewhat by Della's observation that he has in fact won; Catherine no longer sees her father as heroic, and her admiration has turned to pity. If the victor will be patient, he will have what he sought. Crucial to her understanding is the revelation that Raoul deliberately killed their son, Marky, the product of Della's extramarital liaison with a black man. In effect, what all the family now understands is that Jackson has exacted Marky's revenge and become the son that Raoul destroyed. Consistent with the naturalistic tone that dominates the work, the father acquires the son only by being beaten and supplanted, and the son can acquire a father and a family only by allowing himself to be imprisoned in the very life he wishes to escape. The end of the novel has Jackson waiting in the yard, "hoping that Catherine would come back outside. But she never did." The reader is left in a state of uncertainty, having to choose between Della's optimistic reading of events and Jackson's own despair. Neither possibility will bring him comfort. Either he has lost Catherine or, the deepest irony, he has succeeded in his quest, but at the price of his freedom.

Perhaps because of this ambiguity and pessimism, the book did not receive much attention when it was first published. Even with Gaines's increasing reputation, *Catherine Carmier* has been largely neglected. Those who have commented on it tend to see its pessimism as reflective of the influence of Hemingway, an influence which Gaines himself has conceded. It is considered the most despairing of his works and, perhaps for that reason, the least characteristic. While this latter point can be debated, given the tone of some later works, it is clear that *Catherine Carmier* is not entirely successful in presenting its major characters and their motivations. It is hard to understand, for example, what draws Catherine and Jackson together, given the experiences and values they have accumulated over the time of separation. Moreover, the revelation of the cause of Marky's death is unnecessarily melodramatic. On the other hand, Gaines does begin here to create a sense of the black community and its perceptions of the world around it. Shared ways of speaking, thinking, and relating to the dominant white society are shown through several minor characters. This element of Gaines's fiction continues to develop throughout his career; it is the very richness of this social fabric that calls into question the frustration and sterility of the major characters in this first novel.

Though *Catherine Carmier* was not a critical or financial success, Gaines steadfastly worked on his writing. Though he does not consider himself prolific, he wrote four novels (of which only *Catherine Carmier* was published) and a dozen short stories before *Of Love and Dust* brought him recognition in 1967. Some of the success of the new book can be explained by certain differences between it and his first novel. This new book deals much more directly with the black-white relationship, including miscegenation, and thus could be considered more accessible than the earlier work, which focused almost exclusively on black life. In addition, *Of Love and Dust* more clearly condemns the economic, social, and racial system of the South for the problems faced by its characters. While Gaines is not a protest novelist in the tradition of Richard Wright, his questioning of the southern political structure certainly would strike a chord at the socially tumultuous time it was published. Finally, hope, if not optimism, is apparent at the end of this work, which clearly was not the case with *Catherine Carmier*.

Of Love and Dust is narrated by Jim Kelly, a middle-aged black man who has gained a degree of respect on the plantation where he works. He is trusted by both the owner and the overseer to do his job well. Part of that job becomes the supervising of Marcus, a young man charged with stabbing

Dust jacket for Gaines's 1983 novel, a murder mystery in which each member of a group of old men claims to have committed the crime

another man and released into the custody of Marshall Hebert, the plantation owner. Jim is asked by Miss Julie Rand, another of Gaines's "aunt" figures and Marcus's godmother, to take care of Marcus while he is at the plantation. She believes him to be good despite his obvious bitterness, hostility, and insensitivity.

Sidney Bonbon, the white overseer on the farm, expects Jim to help break Marcus of his rebelliousness and arrogance by forcing him to labor in the fields under intolerable conditions. As a result, Marcus considers Jim a traitor to his race for cooperating with the white bosses and contemplates ways of getting even with the whites. While Jim tries to keep his promise to Miss Julie, he finds it difficult to deal with a man so unwilling to adapt to his conditions. All of the black community becomes alarmed when Marcus starts paying attention to Bonbon's black mistress, Pauline, with whom the overseer is very much in love. In fact, he cares more for her than he does for his white wife. One of the accomplishments of the novel is Gaines's presentation of the nuances of such a relationship. Everyone on the plantation, including Bonbon's wife, knows

of this love, yet no one can in any way acknowledge it, not even the two children that are its products. A very careful social etiquette is followed, by which everybody ignores what they all in fact know.

When Marcus is rejected by Pauline, he turns his attentions to Bonbon's wife, Louise, who desires revenge on her husband for his infidelity. The black community, represented in this instance by Aunt Margaret, is horrified by this development, not merely because of Marcus's motives, but more important because his action threatens the security of the whole community. If it is discovered that a black man is violating this most sacred of southern taboos, then every black man is a potential target of white violence. But even though he is repeatedly warned by Jim against such behavior, Marcus's desire for self-gratification overwhelms the need for community safety.

What in fact happens is that Marcus and Louise transcend their exploitative motives and begin to love each other, much like Pauline and Bonbon. They then plot an escape with the aid of Marshall Hebert, the owner, who has his own reasons for getting back at his overseer. Hebert then betrays the lovers by arranging Bonbon's presence at the moment of their leaving. Marcus is killed, Louise goes insane, and Bonbon and Pauline flee the plantation. Jim also must leave, because Hebert realizes that he knows too much to be fully trustworthy.

In the process of telling the story, Jim comes to understand two things. One is Bonbon's statement to him that they are all victims. Race is ultimately less important than one's position in the social and economic hierarchy. Hebert and the system he has created and maintained are vastly more powerful than any of the petty manipulations of Marcus and Bonbon. The second insight Jim gains comes from observing Marcus. While Marcus's motives were primarily selfish, he still displayed a courage and spirit that deserved respect if not emulation. Jim learns that he himself has been too willing to accept his victimization. Throughout the story he has been a blues performer, singing and talking of lost loves and opportunities. He has chosen to be self-pitying and self-protective, but Marcus has taught him that risk is necessary if one is going to live in dignity. Jim acknowledges this lesson when he refuses to accept Hebert's offer of a recommendation. Though it will make his life more difficult, he realizes that his integrity requires cutting all ties to such a man. Unlike Jackson of *Catherine Carmier,* Jim Kelly has hope at the end of the novel because he has found something to believe in – himself.

By moving to a first-person narrative in *Of Love and Dust,* Gaines renders life in rural Louisiana much more effectively. Jim Kelly both speaks in the idiom of the place and time and instinctively asserts the values of the black community. Thus, a much greater immediacy is apparent here than in *Catherine Carmier.* But beyond these benefits, the first-person narration also comes closer to the ideal of the folk storyteller and thus is more appropriate than omniscient narration to the folk materials Gaines uses in his fiction. He has said that the novel was inspired by a Lightning Hopkins blues song, "Mr. Tim Moore's Farm," and clearly Gaines's method of presenting the story comes closer than his first novel to resembling black folk stories of love and trouble. The book received decidedly mixed reviews. While Sara Blackburn asserted Gaines "is a writer of terrific energy; his characters have a dimension and authenticity that make us care about them" (*Nation,* 5 February 1968), James Lea found them to be stereotypical and unconvincing. He felt the book was "mustily reminiscent of innumerable novels of the down-on-the-old-plantation variety" (*Saturday Review,* 20 January 1968).

Some of Gaines's best use of folk material comes in the stories collected in *Bloodline.* Although this book came out in 1968, some of the stories were among the first of his work to be published. Three of the five, "A Long Day in November" (1958), "Just Like a Tree" (1962), and "The Sky is Gray" (1963), preceded *Catherine Carmier.* Nonetheless, some factors unify the collection. The sequence is determined in part by the age of the narrator or central figure: beginning with a six-year-old in the first story, these characters get progressively older until Aunt Fe, in the last story, is on the verge of death. Further, the action of each story is confined to a single day in the area around Bayonne, Louisiana. Thematically, the stories in *Bloodline* are about the relationships between younger and older generations; more specifically, they usually deal with a son's heritage from his father. Stylistically, they are presented in the folk idiom of rural southern blacks. Gaines displays in these stories a mastery of these speech patterns, giving them an authenticity that is seldom present in dialect writing.

The second story of the collection, "The Sky is Gray," reflects Gaines's career-long concern with the achievement of manhood within the context of community. The eight-year-old narrator of the story learns about social rules, in this case the rules about race relations and personal integrity. Gaines has said that this story is patterned after Eudora Welty's "A Worn Path," and the connection is clear in the journey motif and the need for certain rituals. The difference is in the level of experience of the central character: while Welty's Phoenix Jackson has taken her journey many times, this is the initial and thus most important journey for James.

He has already had several painful episodes in his young life when his mother sought to teach him crucial lessons in survival. Because his father is in the army, she is the only one who can provide for the family. Fearing that something might also happen to her, she wants James to be able to take care of the others. Out of this necessity, she one day forces him to kill two small redbirds he has caught in a trap. When he cries that they should be set free, she beats him until he stabs them. Since the birds make very little food, James fails to understand her actions until an aunt explains that the mother wants him to learn that survival is more important than sentiment.

When he develops a toothache, an opportunity develops for him to learn another lesson in survival, this time black survival in a white-dominated, racist society. What James must become aware of is the system of rules that dictates black-white relations. His grasp of the rules is evident when he gets on the bus and immediately moves to the back, past the "White-Colored" sign, before looking for a seat. What he will acquire in Bayonne is a sense of the complexity of the system and of the means of maintaining one's dignity under such conditions.

In the dentist's office he is presented with two different perspectives on social adaptation in a confrontation between an alienated, educated young man, much like Jackson of *Catherine Carmier,* and a black preacher who defends the principles of faith and humility. The young man rejects those principles in the name of reason and the harsh view of reality that reason has given him. In frustration over this attack on his way of life, the preacher strikes the young man. The preacher acts this way not only in order to protect what is for him a relatively successful compromise with the powers that be but also because the refusal to compromise could be a threat to the entire black community. This same fear was expressed in *Of Love and Dust.* The community would be doubly threatened if its children began to admire the spokesmen of such a view, as James does here: "When I grow up I want to be just like him. I want clothes like that and I want to keep a book with me, too."

When the dentist closes for lunch without attending to James, he and his mother must walk the streets in the bitterly cold weather. Not permitted to enter any of the white-owned restaurants, they have no way of keeping warm. James now receives another lesson in survival and racial etiquette. His mother takes him into a hardware store and positions him by a hot stove. She then asks to examine an ax handle. While she looks over several, she keeps glancing at James; when she sees that he is warm, they leave without buying anything. In this way, she provides him an example of how to get the necessities of life without giving whites the satisfaction of seeing her beg.

A third lesson that is social in nature comes in an encounter between mother and son and a white couple who sincerely desire to help them. The white woman wishes to give them food, but James's mother refuses to accept it as charity. They agree that the boy must work for the food by carrying around the garbage cans. Though he believes the cans to be empty, James is prevented by the women from opening them. After the meal James's mother wishes to buy a small amount of salt pork in the couple's tiny grocery and is offended when the owner attempts to give her a piece much larger than her quarter will buy. James's mother refuses to accept more meat than she can pay for.

This scene is important in showing the nuances of race relations. Even those people who wish

to transcend racial hostilities must do so in the context of the social rules. These two women cannot face each other candidly; they must play their socially assigned roles despite their personal desires. Moreover, in the charade of the garbage cans, they conspire to teach James that the maintaining of dignity in human contacts is a fragile process. That James may have started learning this and the other lessons is indicated in the mother's last words: " 'You not a bum,' she says. 'You a man.' "

While the first four stories in *Bloodline* feature male protagonists, the last story, "Just Like a Tree," treats a matriarchal figure. Although Aunt Fe has always lived on the land, her family fears for her safety and wants to move her to the city. The move seems necessary because Emmanuel, her grand-nephew, has been active in the civil rights movement; as a result, whites have started bombing black homes. The setting of the story is Fe's home the night before she is to leave. Family and friends have come for a final celebration of her life. The story is narrated by these visitors, following, as Gaines has noted, the structure of William Faulkner's *As I Lay Dying.* Significantly, the only characters we do not hear directly from are Emmanuel and Fe herself. The effect is to give us a broadly based sense of both the public and private meanings of one of Gaines's aunts. The voices of the old and the young, male and female, black and white offer a broad and deep sense of the quality of life for which the characters in the other stories have been searching. At the end of "Just Like a Tree," we see why that quest is so crucial. In an ironic play on the spiritual from which the title is derived, Aunt Fe "will not be moved": she dies after a night-long conversation with Aunt Lou, her lifelong friend. Her death, which seems willed, signifies that life for her is sustained by a time, place, and community that contain the richness of her experience. To leave all of that is to die spiritually, and for her physical life is nothing without the spirit.

Critics have seen *Bloodline* as a series of portraits of southern black rural life in which the characters search for manhood. While Gaines is praised for the effectiveness of his characterizations and settings, doubts are raised about his way of defining manhood as primarily aggressive, head-oriented behavior and about the apparent lack of resolution in the stories. Granville Hicks, for example, commented that "Gaines has trouble in winding up [some] stories. In spite of my reservations about the endings, they are strong stories" (*Saturday Review,* 19 August 1968). Gaines deliberately leaves his characters facing the future, trying to apply the lessons they have learned.

177

Lou Dimes

Remembering that I was still on the job, I took out
my pen and pad and jotted down a few notes:

"Fifteen old black men with shotguns--guns probably
old as they. Five or six women old as the men. Two of the
women wear faded head rags; couple other wear aprons of
gingham that has been washed so many times the cloth has
lost all its color, too. Two or three nappy headed barefoot
children sit with the men and women. A stubborn silence
prevails.

"Framed house--your typical plantation quarters's
house--gray from sun, rain, wind, dust, sits on leaning xxxxx
cement blocks half sunkend into the ground. House probably
fifty, maybe sixty, possibly seventy five-years old. Has
not seen an ounce of paint during half that time.(Note: must
ask Candy exactly age of house, also when last time painted.)
Tin roof. No loft between roof and porch, and in Summer porch
becomes an oven. Large cracks between the boards in the wall.
Originally chucked with mud; now paper and pieces of torn
cloth keep out cold in Winter, mosquitoes in Summer. Two of
the four steps leading from ground to porch missing. Weeds,
weeds, weeds. A small garden right of porch. Mustards,
turnips, cabbages, collards. Hog in backyard. Chickens

Page from the typescript for A Gathering of Old Men *(courtesy of Ernest J. Gaines)*

The time after the publication of *Bloodline* was devoted to the writing of what turned out to be Gaines's most effective and most popular work, *The Autobiography of Miss Jane Pittman* (1971). The novel started out as a communal biography, a fuller version of "Just Like a Tree." In writing, Gaines made the brilliant discovery of Jane's own voice, which radically changed the nature of the book. Through this point of view came both a fully rounded character and a folk history of the black experience in America from the Civil War to civil rights. One hundred and eight years old when she tells the story, Jane captures the experiences of those millions of illiterate blacks who never had a chance to tell their own stories. By focusing on the particular yet typical events of a small part of Louisiana, those lives are given a concreteness and specificity not possible in more general histories. Gaines accomplishes this by showing the impact of the larger events of those one hundred years – the war, Reconstruction, segregation, the civil rights movement – on individual blacks. But the work is not simply another historical novel, for the narrator enriches the story with elements of popular culture and folk experiences. Boxing and baseball on the radio, comic strips, sermons, voodoo, and superstitions all make their way into Jane's story. What we have, in effect, is the totality of life as lived by Jane; in the process, the author reveals what it is that gives his aunt figures, including Jane, Fe, and Charlotte, their stability and dignity.

The narrator structures her saga primarily through the experiences of a series of heroes, but she always presents them in the context of their nonheroic communities. Jane herself is shown to have heroic potential when, in the opening pages, she tells of beatings she suffered as a child because, though a slave, she insisted on being called by the name given her by a Yankee soldier who passed through the plantation. She also encourages a group of slaves to leave the plantation as soon as the war is over.

It is at this point that Gaines establishes a crucial tension of the text. The efforts of this group are challenged by those who are older because they question the value of radical change; they doubt that white hostility has lessened just because the war has ended. This more conservative group does *not* believe that whites necessarily know better or are better than blacks, but their experience tells them that confrontation produces trouble for both individuals and the community. They value security over the risks of freedom.

Their fears are realized when the departing group is attacked by a gang of Confederate veterans who kill all but Jane and the little boy Ned, who manage to hide. The incident also sets forth Gaines's use of the conventional idea of heroism. Big Laura, Ned's mother, dies fighting back against the white violence. Her story is one that Jane tells to Ned and others for years as one model of black courage. Thus, the hero advances the cause of freedom but at the cost of her/his life. Jane's role becomes that of the preserver of the legends which will inspire others.

Jane herself settles down after this experience into the relatively passive role of observer and bearer of stories. Ned, encouraged by Jane, follows in the steps of his mother. He goes away for education but then returns to teach and to encourage the community to claim its rights. He renames himself Ned Douglass as a way of claiming the mantle of the great orator and activist Frederick Douglass. The price of his dignity and leadership is his death; he is assassinated by a Cajun friend of Jane's, who is also a hired killer. Albert Cluveau, the killer, represents, as did Bonbon in *Of Love and Dust,* the white man caught in a system of racial oppression almost as much as the blacks. Cluveau cannot refuse to murder Ned; to do so would cost him his own life.

Another kind of heroism is symbolized by Joe Pittman, a man who sought economic rather than political freedom. Joe's antagonist is nature rather than racism. He defines his manhood by his ability to break wild horses; he does so even when the horse is one that Jane calls a "ghost." He dies in the effort to tame the untamable. Jane acknowledges his bravery by taking his name, even though they never were legally married.

Acquiring a fatalistic wisdom through these experiences, Jane both fears and admires courage. She herself is an important part of the community, but she retains a degree of individuality and independence that allows her to understand the heroes that enter her life. For example, she is made a church mother because of her devotion, but she loses that status when she prefers listening to baseball games over attending Sunday services. But what she listens to in part is the performance of Jackie Robinson of the Brooklyn Dodgers, whom she sees as another hero of the race.

The relationship between religion and heroism is made even more explicit in the story of the last of the book's legendary figures. From the time Jimmy Aaron is born, the old people label him The One, a modern Moses to lead them. They understand this in spiritual terms and carefully watch and train him to be the person they want. He then goes away for schooling and returns, prepared to lead.

But he wishes to lead them into the civil rights movement, not to the Promised Land. They cannot follow because of their deeply ingrained caution and their long experience with danger of confrontation. They fear losing everything with no guarantee of any improvement in their lives.

Jane, too, though she admires Jimmy and believes him to be right, doubts the effectiveness of his call to action, given southern racial conditions. When he is killed, her fears seem confirmed. But this time she decides that she must act. On the last page of the story, she faces the plantation owner, Robert Samson, who has said that anyone who marches will lose his home: "Me and Robert looked at each other a long time, then I went by him." Jane's action is, in essence, that of the black masses, who put aside very real fears and long-established habits of accommodation to white power in order to play their role in history, to become the heroes of their own story.

Though this work, like the earlier ones, leaves the character at the beginning rather than at the end of some experience, Gaines gives a much stronger sense of the character's probable success in whatever must be endured. This optimism is doubtless one reason why the book was both critically and financially successful. Consistently the work has been praised not only for its effective use of folk materials but also for its integration of political and artistic concerns. Jerry Bryant called Jane "a master of her people's language" who is "unsurpassed as a story-teller" (*Nation,* 5 April 1971). P. L. Gerber adds that Gaines's command of the Louisiana black and Cajun dialects is "masterful" (*Saturday Review,* 1 May 1971).

The popularity of the book was such that a television movie was made of it. Though Stacy Keach Jr. wrote the screenplay, Gaines was actively involved as a consultant. The production received high ratings and won praise from television critics. Because of key changes from the novel, however, the movie did stir some controversy in academic journals. The shift from a black to a white frame figure who interviews Jane, the revision of certain historical elements, and the revised ending, where Jane actually goes to Bayonne to drink from a segregated fountain, all have been cited as evidence that the producers of the film undercut the novel's message in order to make it more palatable to a largely white audience.

Gaines remained out of the controversy, preferring to return to his writing. He received a Guggenheim Fellowship (1973–1974) to continue his work. He began a novel, "The House and the Field," which he later put aside in order to write *In My Father's House,* which was published in 1978.

This novel returns to the father-and-son theme of the earlier works. As in *Catherine Carmier* a key character is a young man whose life is rootless and who seeks some meaning for his existence. But *In My Father's House* differs from the earlier works in its urban setting and the noncentrality of rural folk materials. The transition from rural to urban life has largely cut away such connections. Reflecting this change, the novel is set several years after the conclusion of *The Autobiography of Miss Jane Pittman.* Though the central character, Philip Martin, is a civil rights leader, the movement, like the black community, is in transition. Throughout, characters question the utility of protest and of white participation in the movement. The idealism that inspired Ned Douglass and Jimmy Aaron has dissipated.

The plot of the novel involves Martin's recognition of his illegitimate son and then his quest to find out the truth and consequences of his past life. In the beginning he is a highly respected, now rather conservative leader in the community whose reputation has been made in earlier nonviolent activism. His efforts for equality have necessarily shifted from social and political protests to less dramatic economic protests. In the process many people, including the black middle class represented here by schoolteachers, have become indifferent and cynical. In the midst of arousing enthusiasm for a new demonstration, Martin is confronted with the return of his son, who calls himself Robert X. The father is so shocked by this ghost from his past that he faints when he first sees the young man. Martin's inability to justify having abandoned Robert and his mother and Robert's hostility toward his father make communication between the two impossible. Nonetheless, Martin becomes obsessed with this aspect of his past, to the neglect of his civil rights activity. He returns to the plantation where he grew up, where he loved and lived with Johanna many years before. He then goes to Baton Rouge and encounters friends of his youth, including Chippo Simon, his alter ego, who has become as dissipated as Martin would have been if he had not found religion and civil rights. In a final dramatic scene, Martin learns that his son has committed suicide. He fights with Chippo over the question of responsibility for the past and achieves a tentative reconciliation with his wife.

In some ways *In My Father's House* is one of the most pessimistic of Gaines's books. All of the son figures are somehow misguided. Robert has been destroyed by his own hate and frustration; Billy, a

Dust jacket for Gaines's 1993 novel, in which a schoolteacher helps a condemned man recover a belief in his own humanity

young man Martin meets in Baton Rouge, has lost all contact with his father and has turned to suicidal revolutionary violence; and Jonathan, the young minister in Martin's church, refuses, in his arrogance and inexperience, to be guided by the wisdom of the past in his role as new leader. Given such characters, the future holds little promise. Moreover, the circumstances of Martin's tragedy suggest a rather strong destructive and deterministic aspect to human experience. Martin's final perception that nothing can be done about the past and that it does not necessarily bring life or enlightenment contradicts Jane Pittman's implicit assertion that history is full of meaning and that it gives vitality to the present.

This nihilistic undertone is perhaps responsible for some of the weaknesses of the book. Inadequate motivation is provided for Martin's immediate acceptance of Robert as his son and the resultant obsession with private responsibility to the neglect of social responsibility. He suddenly wants to be a father after abandoning Johanna and her children twenty years earlier. The son Martin sacrifices himself for is a flat, burned-out character whose psychological deadness is inadequately accounted for. The deterministic element gives the book a mechanical quality, with characters functioning more as opportunities for Martin to talk about fathers and sons than for effective dramatic action to take place. The resolution and hopefulness at the end seem imposed and not the natural product of the story's development. Critical response reflected discomfort with the novel's tone and theme. V. M. Burke noted that it has "a weak plot, stick figures, and flat redundant writing, except for runs of crackling dialogue" (*Library Journal*, 1 June 1978). Ellen Lippman, in the *Southern Literary Journal* (November 1978), generally praised it but felt that "Gaines' pace is a little slow, however, and, unfortunately, neither Martin's developing urgency nor Etienne's desperation rings true."

A Gathering of Old Men (1983) returns to the rural world of Gaines's earlier fiction, but its time is closer to the present. On the Marshall plantation the only ones left are the old blacks who have worked the land all their lives, the white Marshalls, and the Cajuns who are gradually displacing the blacks. In one sense the novel is a detective story. A Cajun work boss, Beau Boutan, has been killed in front of the cabin of Mathu, one of the blacks. Since the latter has a history of confrontations with the Boutan family, the case seems open-and-shut. But when Sheriff Mapes arrives on the scene, several black men are present with their recently fired shotguns. Moreover, Candy Marshall, in order to protect the old man who essentially raised her, claims that she is the guilty one. With an excess of suspects and the possibility of racial violence, Mapes is compelled to listen to all of their stories. Complicating the situation is the fact that the sheriff believes that none of the men except Mathu has enough courage to commit murder, and so he is baffled by this group compulsion to confess.

The emotional center of the novel is its collection of stories. Each man tells of the accumulated frustrations and injustices of his life – raped daughters, jailed sons, public insults, economic exploitation – that serve as sufficient motive for murder. Though Beau Boutan is seldom the immediate cause of their anger, he clearly represents the entire white world that has deprived them of their dignity and manhood. The confessions serve as ritual purgings of all the hostility and self-hatred built up over the years. If they did not literally kill Boutan, they symbolically did so many times, and thus their confessions are psychologically true. What makes their narratives especially poignant is their previous submissiveness and even impotence; in addition to Mapes, the Cajuns, Candy, and, most important, Mathu have always assumed that they are weak and insignificant. Through their stories they face their self-hatred and enter, at least metaphorically, their manhood. The actual murderer turns out not to be Mathu, as everyone, including all the "confessors," believed, but Charlie, who for fifty years has been the weakest of them all. He has always absorbed abuse and run away from trouble, even though he is the biggest and hardest working of the blacks. When he can absorb no more, he responds to Boutan's physical abuse by striking back in self-defense. He then tries to run, but Mathu threatens to beat him if he does. So he takes the old man's shotgun and kills the Cajun, who has come after him with his own gun. Then he runs again after begging Mathu to take the blame, which he does. But Charlie finds that something – his nascent manhood – prevents him from escaping. So he returns to accept responsibility and thus fully becomes a

man, a change which is acknowledged by everyone, including the sheriff, when they call him Mr. Biggs.

Meanwhile, change is also being experienced in the Cajun community. The Boutans are planning their usual revenge on the blacks, but they come up against certain modern realities. Gil, Beau's brother, plays football at Louisiana State alongside a black running back. They are known throughout the region as Salt and Pepper. Their success as a combination has made race largely irrelevant; working together, they have the possibility of becoming All-Americans. The possibility will be destroyed for Gil if he is linked to racial violence. In other words he has begun to measure his life by values different from those of his father and brother. His reluctance offends his father, Fix, who refuses to accept change, but at the same time the father will not act without the son. Both are frustrated, but the effect is to create a new order.

Neither father nor son can prevent the final explosion of racist violence, led by a family associate, Luke Will. He and others arrive at Marshall just as Mapes is taking Charlie away. The whites open fire, and the old black men, who have in a sense been frustrated because their confessions had so little effect, get their chance to do what they have only dreamed of. The ensuing battle blends the absurd with the heroic. Some of the blacks accidentally fire their guns through Mathu's roof, and all of them miss their targets. In the end only Charlie and Luke Will are killed. Charlie dies because he refuses to use the protection of darkness; instead he stands at his full height and openly challenges the whites to shoot him. He kills Luke Will while being shot himself.

One of the most effective devices of the book is the variety of narrators. Developing the technique he used in "Just Like a Tree," Gaines employs white, Cajun, and black voices. He thereby achieves a range of social values as well as different perspectives on the action. Significantly, as in the earlier story, the central characters do not narrate; the words and actions of Candy, Mathu, and Charlie are reported by others. The author creates in this way a communal rather than individual story. The narrative works best when focused on the black community; the Cajun scenes lack the same rich texture, and the killing off of Charlie and Luke Will seems more related to the author's moral imperatives than to narrative necessity.

The effectiveness of the narrative is evidenced by the fact that it too was made into a successful television movie, starring Lou Gossett Jr. and Richard Widmark. *A Gathering of Old Men* appeared without the controversy connected with *The Autobiography of Miss Jane Pittman*. The book received a California Commonwealth Award for Fiction, as well as generally positive reviews. The comment of Reynolds Price (*New York Times Book Review*, 30 October 1983) about Gaines is representative: "He has built, with large and single-minded skills, a dignified and calamitous and perhaps finally comic pageant to summarize the history of an enormous, long waste in our past – the mindless, mutual hatred of white and black, which, he implies, may slowly be healing."

Gaines's time after *A Gathering of Old Men* has been divided between Lafayette, Louisiana, where he teaches creative writing at Southwestern Louisiana State University, and San Francisco. During this period he also gained considerable recognition for his literary achievements. He received honorary doctorates from Brown University (1985), Bard College (1985), Whittier College (1986), and Louisiana State University (1987). Awards came from the San Francisco Arts Commission (1983), the Commonwealth Club of California (1984), and the American Academy and Institute of Arts and Letters (1987). In 1993 he was given a MacArthur Foundation "genius" grant and also was married to Dianne Saulney.

It was also in this year that he published *A Lesson Before Dying*, which continues the focus on manhood in its story of a young man, Jefferson, convicted of murder and condemned to die, and the teacher, Grant Wiggins, who is asked by the man's godmother to talk with him. As would be expected, Gaines concerns himself not so much with the fairness of the legal system as with the search for self-worth under conditions which work against it. The Hemingway value of "grace under pressure" has special resonance for Gaines's work, but to the personal struggle must be added the reality of racial oppression. Grant's task in the novel is not to save Jefferson but rather to convince him that he is not the "hog" he was described as being by his own lawyer in the trial.

Grant's problem is that he himself has little desire to be where he is and sees little value in trying to change Jefferson's perspective. He is another of the alienated young men of Gaines's fiction who has seen the larger world and has no faith in it or in his own ability to change it. But also like Jackson, Robert X, and others, he knows that he cannot return to the values and attitudes of the rural community he once belonged to. Grant only goes to Jefferson because he is urged to do so by his own aunt and by the woman he loves and with whom he wants to leave Louisiana with as soon as possible.

What happens in the interaction of these two men is that both are transformed by their experience. Grant attempts at first to offer some conventional wisdom and to understand Jefferson's position. The prisoner has become cynical in his self-hatred and hopelessness. He refuses to speak when others come to visit him, and he will not take solace in religion. Most of the novel is taken up with how each of them comes to see the other in human terms. Eventually, Jefferson is convinced to keep a journal that describes his feelings about his own life and about the people in it. The end result is that both men gain some sense of the value of their lives. With this recognition, Jefferson can die as a man rather than a hog, and Grant can be more sympathetic to the community he chose to leave.

The book was awarded in early 1994 the National Book Critics Circle Award as the best novel of 1993. The evaluation of Charles R. Larson (*Chicago Tribune*, 9 May 1993) demonstrates why it would be so recognized: "This majestic, moving novel is an instant classic, a book that will be read, discussed and taught beyond the rest of our lives."

The focus of Gaines on human dignity, especially African American humanity, has won him considerable recognition, critical praise, and financial success. In addition to the MacArthur award, he has received National Endowment for the Arts (1967), Rockefeller (1970), and Guggenheim (1971) grants. This recognition results not only from the quality of his storytelling but also because of his success at doing what many great writers have done: making a small world into a microcosm of universal human experience. Like William Faulkner, he has created a "postage stamp" of the South that represents the whole world.

Interviews:

"An Interview: Ernest Gaines," *New Orleans Review*, 1 (1969): 331–335;

Forrest Ingram and Barbara Steinberg, "On the Verge: An Interview with Ernest J. Gaines," *New Orleans Review*, 3 (1972): 339–344;

Ruth Laney, "A Conversation with Ernest Gaines," *Southern Review*, 10 (1974): 1–14;

Charles Rowell, " 'This Louisiana Thing that Drives Me': An Interview with Ernest J. Gaines," *Callaloo* (May 1978): 39–51;

Jeanie Blake, "Interview with Ernest Gaines," *Xavier Review*, 3, no. 1 (1983): iv–13;

Mary Ellen Doyle, "A *MELUS* Interview: Ernest J. Gaines – 'Other Things to Write About,' " *MELUS*, 11 (Summer 1984): 59–81;

Marcia Gaudet and Carl Wooton, *Porch Talk with Ernest Gaines: Conversations on the Writer's Craft* (Baton Rouge: Louisiana State University Press, 1990).

Bibliography:

Mary Ellen Doyle, "Ernest J. Gaines: An Annotated Bibliography, 1956–1988," *Black American Literature Forum,* 24 (Spring 1990): 125–150.

References:

William L. Andrews, " 'We Ain't Going Back There': The Idea of Progress in *The Autobiography of Miss Jane Pittman,*" *Black American Literature Forum,* 11 (1977): 146–149;

Valerie Melissa Babb, *Ernest Gaines* (Boston: Twayne, 1991);

Jerry H. Bryant, "Ernest J. Gaines: Change, Growth, History," *Southern Review,* 10 (1974): 851–864;

Bryant, "From Death to Life: The Fiction of Ernest J. Gaines," *Iowa Review,* 3 (1972): 106–120;

Keith Byerman, "Negotiations: The Quest for a Middle Way in the Fiction of James Alan McPherson and Ernest Gaines," in his *Fingering the Jagged Grain: Tradition and Form in Recent Black Fiction* (Athens: University of Georgia Press, 1985), pp. 41–103;

Callaloo, special issue on Gaines, 1, no. 3 (1978);

David Estes, ed., *Critical Reflections on the Fiction of Ernest J. Gaines* (Athens: University of Georgia Press, 1994);

J. Lee Greene, "The Pain and the Beauty: The South, the Black Writer, and Conventions of the Picaresque," in *The American South,* edited by Louis D. Rubin, Jr. (Baton Rouge: Louisiana State University Press, 1980), pp. 264–287;

Jack Hicks, "Afro-American Fiction and Ernest Gaines," in his *In the Singer's Temple: Prose Fictions of Barthelme, Gaines, Brautigan, Piercy, Kesey, and Kosinski* (Chapel Hill: University of North Carolina Press, 1981), pp. 83–137;

William Peden, *The American Short Story: Continuity and Change, 1940–1975* (Boston: Houghton Mifflin, 1975);

Barbara Puschmann-Nalenz, "Ernest J. Gaines: 'A Long Day in November,' " in *The Black American Short Story in the Twentieth Century: A Collection of Critical Essays,* edited by Peter Bruck (Amsterdam: B. R. Gruner, 1977), pp. 157–167;

Noel Schraufnagel, *From Apology to Protest: The Black American Novel* (De Land, Fla.: Everett/Edwards, 1973);

Frank W. Shelton, "Ambiguous Manhood in Ernest J. Gaines' *Bloodline,*" *CLA Journal,* 19 (1975): 200–209;

Kathleen Thames, "Lessons from Ernest Gaines," *La Louisiane,* 4 (Fall 1993): 18–24.

George Garrett

(11 June 1929 –   )

R. H. W. Dillard
Hollins College

See also the Garrett entries in *DLB 2: American Novelists Since World War II, First Series; DLB 5: American Poets Since World War II: Part One; DLB 130: American Short-Story Writers Since World War II;* and *DLB Yearbook: 1983.*

BOOKS: *King of the Mountain* (New York: Scribners, 1958; London: Eyre & Spottiswoode, 1959);

The Sleeping Gypsy and Other Poems (Austin: University of Texas Press, 1958);

The Finished Man (New York: Scribners, 1959; London: Eyre & Spottiswoode, 1960);

Abraham's Knife and Other Poems (Chapel Hill: University of North Carolina Press, 1961);

In the Briar Patch (Austin: University of Texas Press, 1961);

Which Ones Are the Enemy? (Boston: Little, Brown, 1961; London: W. H. Allen, 1962);

Sir Slob and the Princess: A Play for Children (New York: French, 1962);

Cold Ground Was My Bed Last Night (Columbia: University of Missouri Press, 1964);

Do, Lord, Remember Me (London: Chapman & Hall, 1965; revised edition, Garden City, N.Y.: Doubleday, 1965);

For a Bitter Season: New and Selected Poems (Columbia: University of Missouri Press, 1967);

A Wreath for Garibaldi and Other Stories (London: Hart-Davis, 1969);

Death of the Fox (Garden City, N.Y.: Doubleday, 1971; London: Barrie & Jenkins, 1972);

The Magic Striptease (Garden City, N.Y.: Doubleday, 1973);

Welcome to the Medicine Show: Flashcards / Postcards/Snapshots (Winston-Salem, N.C.: Palaemon, 1978);

To Recollect a Cloud of Ghosts: Christmas in England 1602–1603 (Winston-Salem, N.C.: Palaemon 1979);

Luck's Shining Child: A Miscellany of Poems & Verses (Winston-Salem, N.C.: Palaemon, 1981);

George Garrett

Enchanted Ground: A Play for Readers' Theater (York, Maine: Old Gaol Museum, 1981);

The Succession: A Novel of Elizabeth and James (Garden City, N.Y.: Doubleday, 1983);

The Collected Poems of George Garrett (Fayetteville: University of Arkansas Press, 1984);

James Jones (New York & San Diego: Harcourt Brace Jovanovich, 1984);

An Evening Performance: New and Selected Short Stories (Garden City, N.Y.: Doubleday, 1985);

Poison Pen; or, Live Now and Pay Later (Winston-Salem, N.C.: Wright, 1986);

Understanding Mary Lee Settle (Columbia: University of South Carolina Press, 1988);

Entered from the Sun (Garden City, N.Y.: Doubleday, 1990);

The Sorrows of Fat City: A Selection of Literary Essays and Reviews (Columbia: University of South Carolina Press, 1992);

Whistling in the Dark: True Stories and Other Fables (New York: Harcourt Brace Jovanovich, 1992);

My Silk Purse and Yours: The Publishing Scene and American Literary Art (Columbia: University of Missouri Press, 1992);

The Old Army Game: A Novel and Stories (Dallas: Southern Methodist University Press, 1994).

PLAY PRODUCTIONS: *Sir Slob and the Princess,* Houston, Alley Theater, 25 March 1961;

Garden Spot, U.S.A., Houston, Alley Theater, 25 April 1962.

MOTION PICTURES: *The Young Lovers,* screenplay by Garrett from the novel by Julian Halevy, M-G-M, 1965;

The Playground, screenplay by Garrett from *My Brother, Death,* by Cyrus Sulzberger, Jerand, 1965;

Frankenstein Meets the Space Monster, screenplay by Garrett, R. H. W. Dillard, and John Rodenbeck, Allied Artists, 1965.

OTHER: "The Reverend Ghost," in *Poets of Today IV,* edited by John Hall Wheelock (New York: Scribners, 1957), pp. 21–72;

New Writing From Virginia, edited by Garrett (Charlottesville, Va.: New Writing Associates, 1963);

The Girl in the Black Raincoat: Variations on a Theme, edited by Garrett (New York: Duell, Sloan & Pearce, 1966);

Man and the Movies, edited by Garrett and W. R. Robinson (Baton Rouge: Louisiana State University Press, 1967);

New Writing in South Carolina, edited by Garrett and William Peden (Columbia: University of South Carolina Press, 1971);

Film Scripts One, edited by Garrett, Jane Gelfman, and O. B. Hardison Jr. (New York: Appleton-Century-Crofts, 1971);

The Sounder Few: Essays From the Hollins Critic, edited by Garrett, R. H. W. Dillard, and John Rees

Moore (Athens: University of Georgia Press, 1971);

Film Scripts Two, edited by Garrett, Gelfman, and Hardison (New York: Appleton-Century-Crofts, 1971);

Film Scripts Three, edited by Garrett, Gelfman, and Hardison (New York: Appleton-Century-Crofts, 1972);

Craft So Hard to Learn: Conversations With Poets and Novelists About the Teaching of Writing, edited by Garrett and John Graham (New York: Morrow, 1972);

The Writer's Voice: Conversations With Contemporary Writers, edited by Garrett and Graham (New York: Morrow, 1973);

Botteghe Oscure Reader, edited by Garrett (Middletown, Conn.: Wesleyan University Press, 1974);

Intro 6: Life As We Know It, edited by Garrett (Garden City, N.Y.: Anchor/Doubleday, 1974);

Intro 7: All of Us and None of You, edited by Garrett (Garden City, N.Y.: Anchor/Doubleday, 1975);

Intro 8: The Liar's Craft, edited by Garrett (Garden City, N.Y.: Anchor/Doubleday, 1977);

Intro 9: Close to Home, edited by Garrett and Michael Mewshaw (Austin, Tex.: Hendel & Reinke, 1978);

Festival 88, edited by Garrett (Charlottesville: Virginia Festival of Film, 1988);

"Eric Clapton's Lover" and Other Stories from the Virginia Quarterly Review, edited by Garrett and Sheila McMillen (Charlottesville: University Press of Virginia, 1990);

Contemporary Southern Short Fiction: A Sampler, edited by Garrett and Paul Ruffin (Huntsville: Texas Review, 1991);

The Wedding Cake in the Middle of the Road: 23 Variations on a Theme, edited by Garrett and Susan Stamberg (New York: Norton, 1992);

Elvis in Oz: New Stories and Poems from the Hollins Creative Writing Program, edited by Garrett and Mary Flinn (Charlottesville: University Press of Virginia, 1992);

That's What I Like (about the South) and Other Southern Stories for the Nineties, edited by Garrett and Paul Ruffin (Columbia: University of South Carolina Press, 1993).

"When I was young and proud and poor and feisty," George Garrett wrote of himself in a 1985 essay on the group of southern writers known as the Fugitives, "and such things seemed to matter, I was vain about my independence, eager to be, if I

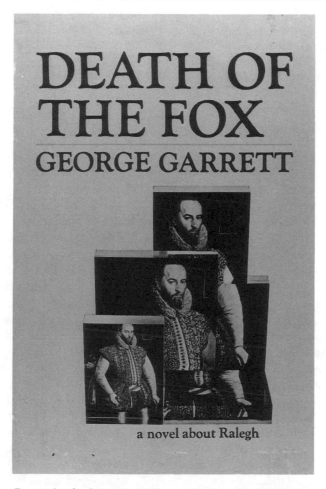

*Dust jacket for Garrett's 1971 novel, the first of his Elizabethan
trilogy, which provides the memories of Sir Walter Ralegh before
his execution*

could, like Mr. Faulkner, *the cat who walks alone.* . . .
And so, from time to time, I paid a price for the
privilege of my freedom." For over forty years, Garrett has maintained his independence – from literary camps and schools, from popular styles and positions, and even from repeating himself and his
own successes. He has published during that time a
collection of books, remarkable in number, in their
uniformly high quality and commitment to distinctive style, and in their wide-ranging explorations of
different genres and formal techniques. The list of
his books includes seven collections of poems, eight
collections of short fiction, two plays, four volumes
of literary biography and criticism, and the seven
novels for which he is most widely known.

He has also, since 1958, always been an editor
in one capacity or another. In addition to serving as
contributing editor for a number of journals, he
acted as poetry editor of the *Transatlantic Review*
(1958–1971), coeditor of the *Hollins Critic* (1967–
1971), assistant editor of the *Film Journal* (1970–
1973), and coeditor of *Poultry: A Magazine of Voice*
since 1980. He was the poetry editor of the Contemporary Poetry Series of the University of North
Carolina Press (1962–1968) and an editorial adviser
for the short-story series of the Louisiana State University Press (1966–1969). Garrett has also edited
or coedited twenty-two volumes since 1963. One
would be hard-pressed to find a more literarily active contemporary American writer.

The seven novels themselves reveal Garrett's
commitment to imaginative independence: a traditional, realistic novel of southern politics; a colloquial, first-person narrative of a soldier in Trieste,
Italy; a novel centered upon a southern revivalist,
using multiple points of view; three Elizabethan historical novels dealing with the life of Sir Walter
Ralegh, the succession of King James to the throne
of Elizabeth, and the murder of Christopher Marlowe, each of them constructed in radically different

ways; and a postmodernist satire of modern American political and public life. The sources of his literary and personal independence are many, but especially important to his development are his being the scion of a large and variously talented family, a southerner, a Protestant Christian, and a member of his particular generation of American writers.

The price he has paid for his freedom is ironically a product of that freedom — he has not been easy to categorize. His refusal to remain aesthetically in one place has resulted in a kind of literary camouflage; he has not offered an easy target for the sharpshooters of either critical or popular recognition. Garrett has not, therefore, received the celebrity status of many of the more easily placed writers of his generation — which is not to say that he has not achieved both kinds of success. Throughout his career, Garrett has been well received by reviewers and held in very high regard by other American writers. He was awarded the T. S. Eliot Award for Creative Writing by the Ingersoll Foundation in 1989 and the P.E.N. Bernard Malamud Award for Short Fiction the following year. His books have also sold well; *Death of the Fox* (1971) was a best-seller and a Book-of-the-Month Club main selection, and *The Succession* (1983), although not a best-seller, was featured by the Literary Guild. Perhaps even more tellingly, five of his seven novels are currently in print and readily available.

George Palmer Garrett Jr. was born in Orlando, Florida, on 11 June 1929 to George Palmer Garrett and Rosalie Toomer Garrett. He was one of four children, two boys and two girls, although his older brother died at birth. Garrett has written in *Whistling in the Dark* (1992) of the powerful influence both sides of his family had on him. The Toomers were an old aristocratic South Carolina family with roots deep in southern history; theirs was a heritage of inherited culture and privilege, of flamboyance and honor. The Garretts were a family who had come into their own in the meritocracy of the post–Civil War South, a family, as he put it, "hard to like but almost impossible not to admire." Garrett in the *Contemporary Authors Autobiography Series* has also noted that his father and his maternal grandfather were "the two most powerful influences and examples" on the development of his character: his father, a powerful, one-armed lawyer who successfully fought the influence of the railroads and the Ku Klux Klan and who taught his son "that our first and primary duty in whatever vocation we found ourselves was always service"; and Garrett's grandfather, Col. William Morrison Toomer, a man who

lived a life of grand gestures and "who made two fortunes and spent three."

In addition to these two exemplars of active and essential independence, there were a wide variety of artists, writers, and other daring individuals on both sides of Garrett's family to offer him encouragement and example for a life of writing. He has described many of his colorful uncles: "a cavalry officer who became one of America's first military pilots; a tap and ballroom dancer, who danced in several Broadway shows and on the great ocean liners while those bright floating palaces still crossed the Atlantic; a first-rate professional golfer; a very good musician or two. There was even a professional guide and mountain climber who disappeared forever into a sudden blizzard long before I was born." Garrett's great-uncle on his mother's side was Harry Stillwell Edwards, who wrote the prize-winning novel *Sons and Fathers* (1896) and the best-selling novella *Eneas Africanus* (1919). His aunt Helen Garrett wrote children's books, and his uncle Oliver H. P. Garrett was the author of numerous screenplays, among them *Street of Chance* (1930), *Manhattan Melodrama* (1934), the final shooting script of *Gone With the Wind* (1939), *Duel in the Sun* (1946), and *Dead Reckoning* (1947).

Garrett's growing up and living much of his life in the American South also had a great effect upon his literary independence. The Civil War, fought almost entirely within the borders of the region, not only freed the slaves and shattered the economic structure of the Old South, but it filled that part of the country with thousands of wounded soldiers and also inflicted the less tangible but still real scars that follow upon losing a war. It is no wonder that a region which depended upon a system of slavery, lost a major war, experienced occupation, and entered into a new era of racial tension and injustice should produce writers who are intensely aware of the past's continuing weight in the present and also who have little choice but to deal directly with questions of loss and change, of good and evil, of genuine individual moral responsibility.

Popular southern writers around the turn of the century like Thomas Nelson Page wrote romances of lost Eden and the "Lost Cause" in literary forms that were little changed from the early nineteenth-century models of Sir Walter Scott, but during the "Southern Renascence" of the early twentieth century serious southern writers tackled the hard issues head-on and became necessarily aesthetic rebels as well. Modernist formal experimentation found particularly fertile ground in a region which, while remaining politically conservative, had no choice but to reinvent itself from the ground up. One need think only of Ellen Glasgow, Thomas Wolfe, Erskine Caldwell, or especially William Faulkner to find artists who felt compelled to deconstruct and reconstruct the literary forms they inherited in order to make them fully expressive of the complex understanding that their growing up in the South had given them; it is no accident that so many of the formally innovative writers of fiction of that time came from this culture.

Garrett's novels *The Finished Man* (1959) and *Do, Lord, Remember Me* (1965) use southern locales and characters, but, more importantly, all of his novels, even the Elizabethan historical trilogy, are marked by this southern rebelliousness against the dictates of received opinion, whether they be political, aesthetic, or moral. His work certainly seems to indicate his complete agreement with Faulkner's commitment "to create out of the materials of the human spirit something which did not exist before."

An Episcopalian in upbringing and lifelong practice, Garrett is also a Christian writer whose Protestant belief has strongly influenced his literary independence of mind. His novels take place in fully realized times and places, but they gain much of their force and meaning by an underlying awareness that their particularity exists in the face and context of eternity. Acts of human vice and folly dwindle and diminish in that overwhelming presence to the point where forgiveness becomes not only possible but essential. Garrett's American Protestant understanding has not led him toward pietistic or allegorical fictions like those of C. S. Lewis or Charles Williams but rather toward a basically realistic fiction with an Augustinian understanding of the complex interrelationship of sin and grace, of failure and salvation. The characters who engage his abiding interest are neither sinners nor saints but rather sinners who are saints or saints who are sinners. For all their great differences, what draws John Riche of *Which Ones Are the Enemy?* (1961), Big Red Smalley of *Do, Lord, Remember Me,* and Sir Walter Ralegh of *Death of the Fox* (1971) together is that they are sinner-saints in whose individual stories the great issues of life and death are actively joined.

Garrett is also very much a member of his generation of American writers. Born in the year of the Wall Street Crash, growing up during the Great Depression and the Second World War, serving in the military during the early years of the Cold War, he came of age during a time of enormous instability and transformation. Garrett could very well have

been describing himself when, in *James Jones* (1984), he described the life of that slightly older American author as "the story, as seen through the life and character of an alert and sensitive individual of an America that is first fixed in its own past, as if drunk with the sweet wine of nostalgia, and then all of a sudden takes fire from all sides with change. It is hard for those who lived through it to remember back before World War II, to recall that world so different that it might have been dreamed or only visited, like a foreign country." No wonder, then, that Garrett's novels take place during times of social and moral uncertainty, that their characters always feel exiled from a world where things were once simply and solidly real, and that those characters see their lives and the lives of those around them less as clearly defined facts than as multilayered fictions. No wonder, too, that his novels grow increasingly complex in form as the twentieth century, blazing with change, moves toward its millennial conclusion.

As is so often the case with prolific writers, Garrett began writing as a child. He has commented on his beginnings in an introduction to two pieces of his juvenilia in Paul Mandelbaum's anthology *First Words* (1993): "I have been writing things all my life, beginning even before I could read or write for myself, when my patient father, in the evening after work and when we weren't all listening to the radio or something, took down my earliest stories in dictation." Garrett continued to write during his years at the Sewanee Military Academy, from which he graduated in 1946, and at the Hill School the following year. He entered Princeton University and began to make his mark as a poet before his graduation with a B.A. in English in 1952. He published no fewer than thirty-eight poems in the *Nassau Literary Magazine* in 1951 and 1952, and he was selected to represent Princeton in the Glasscock Intercollegiate Poetry Contest at Mount Holyoke College. He won the Glasscock Prize and met and struck up a friendship with the judge, Marianne Moore, to whom he was to dedicate his first collection of poems, "The Reverend Ghost," in 1957.

On 14 June 1952 in Philadelphia, Garrett married Susan Parrish Jackson, a musician. They are the parents of three children, William, George, and Alice, and the long-term stability of this marriage between equals has enriched Garrett's work. He is able in his fiction to examine insightfully the emotional ties as well as the tensions and struggles among men and women and within families.

A member of the Active Reserves of the United States Army (Field Artillery) from 1950

2X3X487

lightly armed horsemen. They disappear into the screening
[A]
[continue to]
of dust. From which cloud for a long time after they hear the
sound of the fifes and drums.

Now more dust swirls over Newmarket Road between the wind-
mill and Cambridge as the artillery, the field guns known as
the slings, and all the baggage train of high-loaded two-wheeled
carts straggles along, strung out far behind.

--Well, says one, after they are safely down and walking
home, I pity those poor rebellious farmers of Norfolk.

--God help the poor fools. They will never have seen or
imagined anything like that.

--Nor have I, he says. Thinking then it would be a glorious thing to be a soldier.

Not thinking that for long....

[CAME TO]
Only a few days into August when the news reached Cambridge from dirty, and bedraggled, white-eyed riders. How
Kett's rebels had completely defeated and routed Northampton's
forces. How many men, even including some of the gentlemen,
had died there. How the rebels now held Norwich. And soon enough
[Then]
behind the riders came a ragged straggle of the survivors,
most of their weapons and armor gone. Some hobbling in bloody
bandages. Those who could not walk were crammed in groaning
carts leaving trails of bloodstains, clot and gout, behind them.
All of them terribly thirsty, hungry enough to steal or to kill.
[The]
if they had to. Town and colleges mustered in arms, as much or
more against these desperate scarecrows as against any possibility

Page from the revised typescript for The Succession *(courtesy of George Garrett)*

through 1956, Sergeant Garrett spent two years during the Korean War on active duty in the Free Territory of Trieste and in Linz, Austria. In addition to insight into the military life which he would use to develop many of the important characters in the Elizabethan trilogy, his time in the army gave him the material for his novel *Which Ones Are the Enemy?* and many of his best short stories which were eventually to be collected together in *The Old Army Game* (1994).

Garrett returned from military service to Princeton to begin graduate study toward a doctorate in English, and there he received his M.A. in 1956. He went on to finish his classwork, pass his examinations, and begin work on a dissertation which was to be a full biography of Sir Walter Ralegh; his academic and writing careers led him in a different direction, but he was finally awarded his Ph.D. in 1985, when the first two novels of his Elizabethan trilogy were accepted as that dissertation.

His first published story, "Don't Take No for an Answer," appeared in *Coastlines* in 1956, and during his stay at Princeton he began to write and publish fiction regularly. His first book, however, was "The Reverend Ghost," which appeared along with two other collections by Theodore Holmes and Robert Wallace in *Poets of Today IV,* one of a prestigious series edited by John Hall Wheelock.

In 1957 Garrett left Princeton for a full-time teaching position in the English department at Wesleyan University in Middletown, Connecticut. In addition to his fiction and poetry, he began to write critical and scholarly articles, including studies of the poetry of William Faulkner, Joyce Cary, and Robert Penn Warren; Faulkner's literary criticism; and the fiction of Faulkner, James Gould Cozzens, and his great-uncle Harry Stillwell Edwards. He has continued writing literary and cultural analyses throughout his career — enough to be collected in two large volumes in 1992, *The Sorrows of Fat City* and *My Silk Purse and Yours* — but his essays became less traditionally academic year by year. The success of his poetry and fiction allowed him to make his creative work central to his academic career. He won the Sewanee Review Fellowship in Poetry in 1958 and the Rome Prize of the Academy of Arts and Letters (which included a year's stay in Rome) in 1959. A Ford Foundation Grant in drama in 1960 gave him the opportunity to spend a year at the Alley Theater in Houston, followed by a second year when he was also a visiting lecturer at Rice University. During those years he wrote two plays and worked closely with their production at the Alley: a children's play, *Sir Slob and the Princess* and a two-act comedy, *Garden Spot, U.S.A.*

Garrett's second collection of poems, *The Sleeping Gypsy,* and his first collection of short fiction, *King of the Mountain,* were both published in 1958. Each of his first three books was generally well received, setting the stage for the appearance of his first novel, *The Finished Man,* in 1959. In fact, James Stern said of *King of the Mountain* in the 2 March 1958 *New York Times Book Review,* "In some twenty stories he says more, and more forcefully, than is commonly said in as many full-length novels." The novel draws from those stories (one, "King of the Mountain," appears in it almost intact), from Garrett's own life and family history, and from the Florida senatorial primary in which George Smathers defeated the incumbent Claude Pepper to tell the story of its central character's disillusionment and coming of age in a time of political turmoil and changing standards and values. The book is strongly influenced by William Faulkner's complex structures and more specifically by Robert Penn Warren's *All the King's Men* (1946) in both content and form, but the style is Garrett's own. Edward Abbey, in a review in the *New Mexico Quarterly* (Autumn 1959), drew attention to Garrett's distinctive defining of character by image: "When Mike Royle's heart 'sagged in its net of veins like a rock in a sling,' no precise thesaurus word is necessary. And Jojo Royle, his wastrel brother, is seen as a 'cookie man waiting his turn in the oven,' a blurred picture which captures the essence of the unfinished man."

Mike Royle, the novel's central character, is a young man who becomes involved in the Democratic primary campaign of Sen. Allen Parker, a populist New Dealer who has double-crossed his political protégé and opponent, John Batten, and entered the race when he realized that Batten was being supported by his long-time enemies on the Right. Mike's difficulties are compounded when his father, Judge Royle, also enters the race and is used by Batten as a stalking-horse, the "moral" candidate who will draw votes away from Parker and force him to relinquish the high ground of the campaign. In the course of the novel, the young man must attempt to come to terms with his father's complicated character and death, his older brother's becoming a disillusioned and cynical drifter, and what Frank H. Lyell in the 11 October 1959 *New York Times Book Review* called his "loveless family. . . . an embittered lot, each one stuck in the 'furious, invincible rigidity' of his chosen form of isolation." But all of Mike's personal trials also take place in the public arena of modern politics.

Garrett's view of the political world is appropriate to his sense that postwar America is a country

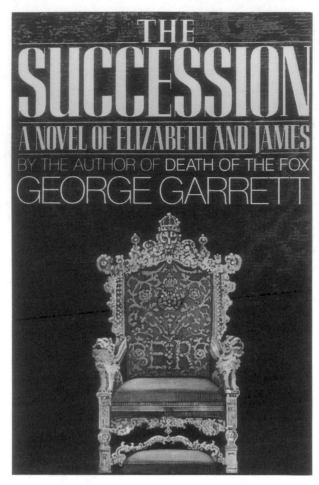

*Dust jacket for Garrett's second Elizabethan novel, based on the
succession of King James IV of Scotland to the English throne
on the death of Queen Elizabeth I*

foreign to the one in which he was born and which shaped his values. As he put it in a 1970 interview with John Graham and W. R. Robinson, "Something has happened, we've become less dimensional. We are less direct; we have rapport with an image." He has reiterated this belief time and again throughout his work, especially in the Juvenalian novel, *Poison Pen* (1986). Senator Parker is a product of prewar politics, distinctively individual, with features too exaggerated to be telegenic and too regional to be national. His younger opponent is a media creation, good-looking with all of his individual characteristics smoothed out: "John Batten's type wasn't regional; rather, since uniformity defined it, he was a man to be found most anywhere in the country today like the popular, attractively packaged foods available in supermarkets from Taos, New Mexico to the windblown coast of Maine."

Mike's decision at the end of the novel to defend a young black man who has attempted to assassinate Senator Parker after he allowed himself to be photographed with a leader of the Ku Klux Klan marks Mike's first serious step toward independence, away from the illusions of the past but not toward those of the "less dimensional" world of modern politics, which is "entirely a world of appearances, of two tight little dimensions." He acts to become the finished man of the title by moving, as the titles of the novel's three parts suggest, from witness to victim to actor.

Two of Garrett's first three books were published by Scribners, and he naturally expected to develop a long-term relationship with that publisher as had such prewar predecessors as F. Scott Fitzgerald and Ernest Hemingway. But he found out that the postwar world had changed the dynamics of publishing as well as politics. The new norm was for writers to move from publisher to publisher (as editors tended to become nomadic as well), and long-term writer-publisher relationships became increasingly rare. When he turned in the manuscript of his second novel to Scribners, the novel's colloquial, first-person narrative style is reputed to have so upset his editor that he accused Garrett of turning in a friend's manuscript under his own name. Scribners did not publish the novel, and when Garrett's next three books appeared in a three-week period in 1961, each was under the imprint of a different publisher.

Garrett's third book of poems, *Abraham's Knife and Other Poems,* was published by the University of North Carolina Press (where Garrett was to edit a poetry series from 1962 through 1968), and his second collection of stories, *In the Briar Patch,* by the University of Texas Press. His second novel, *Which Ones Are the Enemy?,* was published by Little, Brown and, as the editor at Scribners had noticed, marked a departure from his first novel in both form and subject. That the novel is strongly influenced by the slangy, disrespectful narrative voice of J. D. Salinger's *The Catcher in the Rye* (1951) was noted by more than one reviewer. David Slavitt in an unsigned review in the 1 May 1961 *Newsweek* noted that "Garrett's pert picaro, a DSC hero and habitué of stockades, has all of Holden Caulfield's bitter edge, and surely has more reason for it." Thomas E. Cooney in the 25 June 1961 *New York Times Book Review* placed the novel in a strongly American narrative tradition when he noted that the novel's narrator John Riche "sounds a little like Huck Finn and a lot like Holden Caulfield." But the recognition of this influence did not keep the novel from receiving uniformly positive reviews.

The reviewers focused on the fated love story of Riche and the Italian night club "hostess" Angela, but they also praised Garrett's knowledgeable rendering of the details of army life. C. E. Kilpatrick in the 15 May 1961 *Library Journal* found "a seal of authenticity in the portrayal of the army background that makes all ring true." Cooney also praised the novel's "startling picture of the peacetime military underworld of G.I. gangsters and black-market operators. This Army is different from Irwin Shaw's and Norman Mailer's, and it is even different from the one that James Jones knew before Pearl Harbor."

The events of *Which Ones Are the Enemy?* take place in the early 1950s in the Free Territory of Trieste, where the occupying American troops were in the command ironically named TRUST – Trieste United States Troops. Private John Riche is a professional artilleryman, decorated with a Distinguished Service Cross and a Purple Heart in Korea,

who knows how to soldier well, but who, in the moral wasteland of TRUST, lives by a credo of ethical and emotional detachment and self-interest. He meets Angela, a young Italian woman who lives by a code as rigid and amoral as his own, another survivor who has had more than her share of misfortune and does not plan to take any emotional risks. Piqued by Angela's scorn of his low rank and low pay, he sets out to buy a relationship with her at any cost to his independence and his credo. This decision causes him to become involved in the black market, dealing in drugs stolen from the army hospital. He and Angela might well have survived had they not begun really to care for each other. R. C. Healy in the *Lively Arts and Book Review* of the 21 May 1961 *New York Herald Tribune* praised Garrett's rendering of their transformative relationship as "a virtuoso performance, in which he proves in bravura style how something tender and fragile can blossom out of a romance between two such unlikely lovers."

Angela's death leaves Riche alone again, on his own in a tough world in which no one around him knows what really has happened or understands who Riche really is, and in which he will allow no one to see his feelings or know the truth. Garrett's use of the first-person narrative voice does, however, allow John Riche the consolation of a private confession on the page, and his readers are allowed to know what it is "to keep on standing up and asking for more (more *what?* well, trouble maybe) until I'm really out, horizontal, heels up, white-eyed."

In the fall of 1961, Garrett moved to Charlottesville, Virginia, where he remained as an associate professor of English until 1967. His productivity continued undiminished, for during this period he completed his next collections of short fiction and poetry, wrote his third novel, and wrote three screenplays as well. He flew to Los Angeles in the summer of 1963 to work closely with the producer and director Samuel Goldwyn Jr. during the production of *The Young Lovers* (1965), a college love story set during the early years of the American involvement in Vietnam. He also worked closely with filmmaker Richard Hilliard, a former Princeton classmate, on the independent production *The Playground;* this film, a metafictional black comedy about death, is Garrett's most original and distinctive contribution to the cinema. His only other screenplay, *Frankenstein Meets the Space Monster* (1965), the only one available on videotape, was written as a lark with two young colleagues at the University of Virginia.

The collection of stories, *Cold Ground Was My Bed Last Night* (1964), and *For a Bitter Season: New and Selected Poems* (1967) were both published by the University of Missouri Press. The title story of *Cold Ground Was My Bed Last Night* is a novella which, according to Garrett, was originally intended to be "a kind of curtain-raiser" for his third novel, *Do, Lord, Remember Me* (1965). When he finished the manuscript of that novel, for the first time in his career he found himself unable to find a publisher for a new book; the huge manuscript went from publisher to publisher, but Garrett could find no one to take a chance with it. Chapman and Hall finally published a radically shortened version of the novel in London, and Doubleday published a different, slightly bowdlerized, and even shorter version in the United States. The British version was eventually published in this country by the Louisiana State University Press in 1994, but the complete manuscript of this important novel unfortunately may never be reassembled and brought into print.

Do, Lord, Remember Me is the story of a tent revivalist and his gospel troupe who encounter in a small southern town both a chaotic explosion of human vice, lust, and greed and an equally devastating implosion of the Holy Spirit. Big Red Smalley is, like John Riche, a powerfully flawed man, a sinner-saint. According to Garrett in his interview with Graham and Robinson, he is a man with genuine mystical power who is faced with the dilemma that "whereas he has been given great gifts he can't really use them. His gifts are his undoing and, unfortunately for him, he knows it." He is surrounded by a group of equally flawed (if not so powerful) people, an earthy Chaucerian gathering of spiritual travelers: Miami, a somewhat reformed prostitute; Moses, a World War II veteran who may or may not be a Jew and who was traumatized by his mistakenly slaughtering a group of children during the war; and Elijah J. "Hookworm" Cartwright, a Tennessee mountain boy driven by a quest for money and sex. The events of the story are set into motion by the arrival of Judith, a sexually sick young woman whom Red had once healed some years before. The often wildly comical but ultimately terrible events that ensue lead to Red's death and the literal caging of his friends (except for Miami, who escapes), but they also lead to an understanding in the reader that, for all the vice and folly and outright evil that plague the world, it is made more bearable by love and by God's awful grace.

Garrett unfolds the narrative of the novel by using a multiple first-person point of view reminiscent of Faulkner's technique in *As I Lay Dying* (1930). In the 19 September 1965 *Book Week — The Sunday Herald Tribune,* Paul West described Garrett's method as "tellingly indirect. He sets the characters soliloquizing in turn, almost as if he's unpicking a part-song or a round; the voices don't overlap or clash, but their respectively imperfect, cranky versions of the story do, coinciding and colliding in the mind. . . . This is pretty much the method that Andrei Bely called 'symphonic,' and Mr. Garrett beautifully controls it." While West and others praised the novel highly, some reviewers paid little attention either to the novel's form or to its thematic complexity and misread or attacked it. Martin Levin in the 5 September 1965 *New York Times Book Review* dismissed it as merely a repetition of the story Sinclair Lewis had already told in *Elmer Gantry* (1927), a novel with which (except for their both being concerned with revivalists) Garrett's book has very little in common.

Undaunted by the mixed reception given to what many critics now view as a major work, Garrett started writing a kind of sequel or pendant to the novel, a novella that has been published in two versions: as "To Whom Shall I Turn Now in the Hour of My Need?" in *A Wreath for Garibaldi* (1969) and as "The Satyr Shall Cry" in *The Magic Striptease* (1973). He also began to work on a satirical novel to be called (after a tabloid newspaper headline) "Life with Kim Novak Is Hell," which grew to eighteen hundred manuscript pages. The entire novel remains unpublished, but many pieces of it did appear as short stories — including its beginning and end sections which compose the story "A Record as Long as Your Arm" in *An Evening Performance* (1985) — before its final radical transformation into the novel *Poison Pen* in 1986.

In a cavalier (but typically generous) gesture that his maternal grandfather might have admired, Garrett resigned his position at the University of Virginia in 1967 to protest the dismissal by the English department of a group of young assistant professors. He then moved to Roanoke, Virginia, where he directed the creative writing program at Hollins College from 1968 to 1971. There he also acted as coeditor of the journal *The Hollins Critic* and was the driving force and codirector of the Hollins Conference on Creative Writing and Cinema, a large gathering of writers, filmmakers, and students in the summer of 1970 which became known in the literary world as "Woodstock South." During this period he published a collection of stories in England, *A Wreath for Garibaldi,* and wrote and brought to publication the first of his Elizabethan novels, *Death of the Fox* (1971).

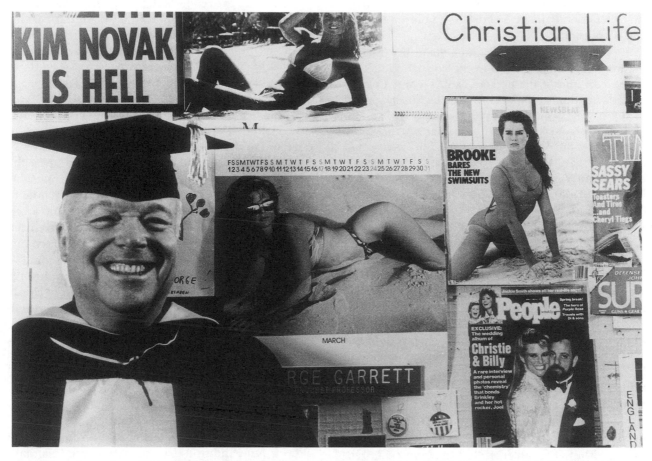

George Garrett in a publicity photograph for Poison Pen, *his satiric novel featuring letters to celebrities (photograph by Cathy Hankla)*

Garrett's serious interest in Sir Walter Ralegh began with his study of Ralegh's poetry at Princeton. He first planned to write a biographical dissertation on the poet, but as his research developed he began to see Ralegh as a central figure for an attempt to understand the entire Elizabethan Age. Ralegh was a poet and an important one, but he was also a historian, a soldier, a courtier, an explorer, a colonizer, and a father, among many other things, and his larger-than-life figure allowed Garrett the chance to attempt genuine imaginative contact with a past that is at once utterly foreign to us and is at the same time our own. The novel that resulted was such an innovative work, both in its stylistic and narrative techniques and in its historical insights, that it redefined the very notion of what a historical novel might be and accomplish. Reviewers were hard-pressed even to decide what to call it: A. Z. Silver in the 2 October 1971 *Saturday Review* called it "more epic poem than historical novel"; an unsigned review in the Spring 1972 *Virginia Quarterly Review* called it "a processional novel, touching all

the sacred places of Elizabethan England and imaginatively evoking the minds of its greatest people"; and J. R. Frakes said in the 24 October 1971 *Book World – Chicago Tribune* that it is "a lovesong to England, a threnody to mutability, a work of committed art, informed with a rare fusion of guts and spirit."

The *VQR* reviewer described the book's "narrative strategy [which] allows Garrett to evoke the man [Ralegh] in a stream of time by use of reveries of telescoped events, told in magnificent, long, rapid sentences, curiously broken up yet continuous – suggesting the baroque prose of the early seventeenth century without its obscurity or tedium." The narrative present of *Death of the Fox* spans only the last two days of Ralegh's life (28–29 October 1618) and lacks any semblance of a conventional plot. The novel does not restrict itself to the Tower of London and the events of those days; rather, it ranges far and wide throughout history and geography by means of a cloud of memories from a great variety of individuals, from named historical figures like Ralegh, King James I, and Sir Francis Bacon to three less-distinguished ghosts — a sailor, a soldier, and a courtier.

The book is, then, as much about the place of memory and imagination in the construction both of the past and of the present as it is about a particularly vital time and place. As Ralegh himself puts it in the novel, "All memory is vain and foolish and all history compounded of many memories, therefore all the more vain and foolish. Yet a man could do worse than remember such times." The struggle at the center of *Death of the Fox* is not between Ralegh and James, or Ralegh and Bacon, but between the author in his effort to raise and revivify the ghosts of an ancestral past and the intractable material of history. In his essay "Dreaming with Adam: Notes on Imaginary History" (1970), which is reprinted in *The Sorrows of Fat City,* Garrett explains that "I came to cling to the notion that the proper subject and theme of historical fiction is what it is — the human imagination in action, itself dramatized as it struggles with surfaces, builds structures with facts, deals out and plays a hand of ideas, and most of all, by conceiving of the imagination of others, wrestles with the angel (Wallace Stevens' 'necessary angel') of the imagination."

After the success of *Death of the Fox,* Garrett, upon the urging of Samuel Vaughan, his editor and the publisher at Doubleday, began planning an Elizabethan trilogy which, as it turned out, was not to be completed until nineteen years later. During the twelve years between the publication of *Death of the Fox* and the second of the Elizabethan novels, *The Succession* (1983), Garrett left Hollins College (in 1971), went to the University of South Carolina (1971–1974), and then, after a Guggenheim Fellowship (1974–1975), lived in York Harbor, Maine, where his wife became the administrator of York Hospital. In 1975 he began a decade of widely varied academic employment (including stays at Princeton, Columbia, Bennington, the College of Charleston, Virginia Military Institute, Hollins, and the University of Michigan) before his return in 1984 to Charlottesville and the University of Virginia, where he has remained as the Henry Hoyns Professor of Creative Writing. This peripatetic existence must surely have contributed to the slowing of the output of this prolific author. In the years between 1971 and 1983, he published only one volume of fiction, *The Magic Striptease* (1973), a collection of three novellas — one previously published, one revised from a previously published version, and a single new one. For the Olde Gaol Museum in York, Maine, he wrote *Enchanted Ground* (1981), a one-act play for reader's theater, which has strong connections in tone, content, and technique to his historical fiction. He did, however, return seriously to the writing of poetry, publishing two collections of new poems, *Welcome to the Medicine Show* (1978) and *Luck's Shining Child* (1981).

The Succession: A Novel of Elizabeth and James was initially conceived, as its subtitle indicates, as a novel about the succession of King James IV of Scotland to the throne of England upon the death of Queen Elizabeth, and it was to be based upon the bulky correspondence between the two monarchs, who never met face to face. In the prefatory note to the novel, Garrett says that "The gist of that story was to be, purely and simply, a narrative accounting of the two of them, Queen and King, exchanging letters over the years, each seeking to come to know and understand the other with a kind of urgent and thorough intimacy that even lovers seldom achieve." But just as Garrett's life of Ralegh had grown into a revivification of the Elizabethan age and a rumination upon the nature of memory, this novel became, as Maureen Quilligan put it in an unusually perceptive review in the 25 December 1983 *New York Times Book Review,* "a subtle, complex meditation on the poetry of time. . . . more purely antiphonal and more complex than *Death of the Fox.*" While the voices and visions of that earlier novel all flow around and find their sources in the final days of the character of Ralegh and are mediated by the controlling voice of the novel's unnamed narrator, those in *The Succession,* loosely bound by the central event of the succession but ranging back and forth in time in an apparently unordered succession from 1566 to 1626, form what Garrett called in a 1983 interview a "kind of simultaneity."

This radical form — no linear narrative progression, no single central character, no important events that are not reported in writing or examined, tested, and interpreted from at least one other perspective in time and/or space — not only differentiates the book from its predecessor in the trilogy but also presses the form of the historical novel much further into new ground. As Linda Wagner pointed out in the *Michigan Quarterly Review* (Summer 1984), "what seems to be an historical novel becomes, finally, a surfiction passing as an historical novel. Garrett has, deftly, unobtrusively, made his book into a commentary upon the genre, and he has done it chiefly by shifting points of view so as to keep 'fact' subjective rather than objective. . . . The effect is an intricate tapestry that draws the reader into the novel as a sleuth and fact-finder, rather than as a passive receptor of information."

Dust jacket for the last novel of Garrett's Elizabethan trilogy, in which two investigators probe the mystery of Christopher Marlowe's murder

The book is, appropriately enough for a book based upon Elizabeth and James's complex but purely epistolary relationship, a philosophically epistemological work, a book as much about the acts of reading and writing and of interpretation as it is about the Elizabethan succession. Even the actual letters of the two rulers are interpreted for us in the text by, as Quilligan put it, "Elizabeth's brilliant, devious and powerful secretary, Robert Cecil, a spymaster himself." A reader's engagement with this novel is an active exploration of knowing itself. And yet the texture of the novel, for all its philosophical complexity, is imaginatively rich and sensuous, full of the stuff of Elizabethan life and filled with engaging characters, ranging from the king and queen to Cecil to an outlawed Catholic priest on the run to a group of Scottish reivers to an actor and erstwhile spy to a drunken plowman silently wishing his queen a good night under the frozen stars of Christmastide. It is in no way a traditional historical novel (or a traditional novel, for that matter), but it still manages to be what D. H. Lawrence claimed the novel should be, "the one bright book of life."

For all its metafictional complexity, *The Succession* was both popularly and critically well received, but Garrett spent the years immediately following its publication on a variety of other projects rather than turning his hand directly to the projected final volume of the Elizabethan trilogy. He assembled sets of both published and previously unpublished poems and stories into two collections, *The Collected Poems of George Garrett* (1984) and *An Evening Performance: New and Selected Short Stories* (1985), and he completed two scholarly projects — the literary biography *James Jones* (1984) and the critical monograph *Understanding Mary Lee Settle* (1988). He also returned to the abandoned manuscript of "Life with Kim Novak Is Hell" and began the process of revising, cannibalizing, reconstructing, and transforming it into his sixth novel, *Poison Pen*.

In a review of *Poison Pen* in the *Hartford Courier* (15 June 1986), Kit Reed wrote, "This novel, if that's what it is . . . suggests that behind the elegant facade of the Elizabethan novelist there lurks Bad Georgie, a comic spirit waiting to be unleashed." At first glance *Poison Pen* does appear to be by a different author than the first two Elizabethan novels, even more extravagantly so than Garrett's *Which Ones Are the Enemy?* had appeared to the editor at Scribners. It is a wildly and brutally satiric novel, savagely anarchistic in its values, often vulgar in its language, and unrelenting in its analysis of the accelerating devolution of American society during the twenty years of its composition. A closer reading will show that its very complicated metafictional structure is not all that far from Garrett's earlier novels (although Madison Bell in the 29 July 1986 *Village Voice* found even its experimental form to be "a parody of experimental forms"), and its concern with the loss of dimension in American life has also been clearly present in Garrett's work since *The Finished Man*.

The novel has an absolutely double nature from start to finish. Even its central character, John Towne, is a dark double and comic alter-ego of the author; in the novel's opening section, "Psst . . . *a little preface*," Garrett claims that Towne *is* the author, while also admitting at the same time that he is just a character in "Life with Kim Novak Is Hell." As savage as the novel is, it is also quietly and seriously humane. As sleazy and vulgar as its characters and their language may be, they are also given a human depth that renders their hectic lives as tragic as they are comic. Its double nature led Thomas Fleming to comment in the 7 November 1987 *National Review*, "The only writer who combines the same loftiness of purpose with anything like this vulgarity of speech is Aristophanes. Rabelais doesn't even come close."

Poison Pen is an elaborately self-contradictory work, and that duplicity is essential to its structure and purpose. The novel purports to be a collection of the abandoned papers and letters of John Towne — a collection (written under a variety of pseudonyms) of abandoned novels and schemes for novels, advice columns (which he wrote as "Dr. Wisdom"), and a great number of poison pen letters to celebrities — all ostensibly edited by Lee Holmes, scrambling, as the "oldest Assistant Professor" at a small woman's college in southwest Virginia, for tenure. To make matters even more complicated, as Bell noted, "the whole scheme is deliberately undercut by George Garrett, who has interleaved the document with authorial intrusions, labeled as such."

In this age of celebrity when presidents, supermodels, and serial murderers exist at exactly the same level of reality (or unreality), Garrett launches a direct attack on the notion that ordinary citizens really know or even care very much at all about the people who dominate their lives, since none are very real to them. The very structure of the novel asserts the fictional quality of all public life, and therefore the difference between Garrett's sleazy con men and the political leaders and celebrities they parody or assault becomes increasingly difficult to ascertain — and increasingly unlikely even to matter. In the face of the inescapable and potent reality of our private lives, they are all fictions, including the author who prints his curriculum vitae conveniently in the novel and addresses a private letter to model Christie Brinkley, which the reader is told not to read.

In the books which followed *Poison Pen*, Garrett directly explored the complex interrelationship of fact and fiction in the human construction of external reality and even the internal reality of the self. For the concluding novel in Garrett's Elizabethan trilogy, *Entered from the Sun* (1990), he used the form of a murder mystery, that literary genre which most completely concerns itself with seeking solutions, with separating fact from fiction. After the completion of that novel, which is concerned with the mysterious life and death of Christopher Marlowe, Garrett then set out to solve the mystery of his own life in *Whistling in the Dark: True Stories and Other Fables* (1992).

Readers of the first two novels of the Elizabethan trilogy are aided in their quests for the truth about Ralegh and about the succession of King James to the throne of Queen Elizabeth by Garrett's narrative strategies. In *Death of the Fox* Ralegh is restored to life not only through the voices of its characters but also by means of the mediation of an authoritative narrative voice. In *The Succession* the reader is required to sift through the evidence and its various interpretations in different times without that central mediating narrative presence, but the data has been carefully put in place for the reader's assembling. The reader also knows, before both stories even begin, how they come out: Ralegh is executed in the Tower, and James succeeds to the throne. The reader of *Entered from the Sun,* however, does not know what will happen to its main characters (who are not known historical personages) and, further, does not know the answer to its central historical question: who killed Christopher Marlowe and why? As Tom Whalen noted in an essay on the novel in *To Come Up Grinning: A Tribute to George Garrett* (1989), "Garrett puts even more emphasis on the need for the creative participation of the reader in this novel than in the previous two."

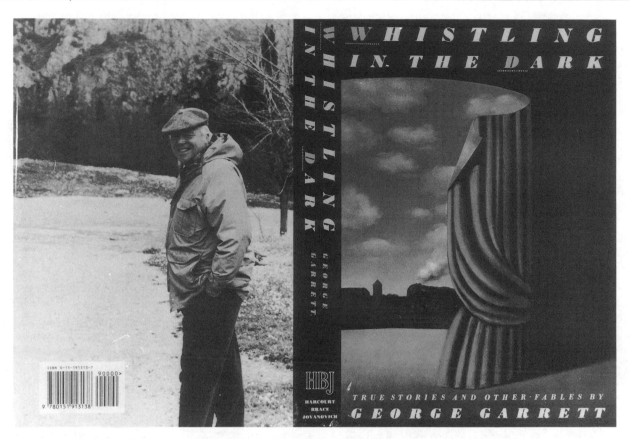

Dust jacket for Garrett's 1992 collection of short stories that explore how imagination transforms memory

Although it is, as Whalen suggests, as multi-layered and complex as either of its predecessors, *Entered from the Sun* uses formal elements which are in many ways quite familiar: it has fictional central characters and a clearly defined linear plot, and it uses many of the conventions of both classical puzzle mystery novels and hard-boiled detective stories. The reader must accompany two "detectives" who are trying in 1597 to discover the truth about Marlowe's violent death under mysterious circumstances in a Deptford lodging house on the evening of Wednesday 30 May 1593. But these men, Joseph Hunnyman, an actor, and Captain Barfoot, a battle-scarred old soldier, are throughout, figuratively and often literally, in the dark – not knowing that the other is on the case, not knowing why they have really been hired or even by whom, and certainly not knowing whether the facts they do manage to uncover will lead to the promised reward or a sudden death for themselves.

The danger and confusion into which they (and the reader) are cast are entirely appropriate to the dark side of Elizabethan life that Garrett chooses to explore in this novel; as he puts it in the "Author's Greeting" which opens the novel: "Not to forget, now or ever, the long-lost brightness and shine, the hope and glory of those times. But likewise to remember, keeping in mind, the other side of it. Stony discontent, cold despair, end-of-the-world indifference." They are also appropriate to the complicated life and death of Christopher Marlowe, poet and playwright, reputed heretic and homosexual, and active participant in shadowy politics and espionage to such a degree that it casts almost everything else that is known about him into question. It is interesting to note that Garrett's exploration of these dark doings reaches essentially the same conclusions that Charles Nicholl was to reach in his prize-winning historical study, *The Reckoning: The Murder of Christopher Marlowe* (1992), a solidly researched book that sheds light on the foundations of Garrett's historical imagination.

The characters of Garrett's exclusive making, Hunnyman, Barfoot, and the vigorous Widow Alysoun, are joined by others taken directly from history, including a striking appearance by Sir Walter Ralegh and even William Shakespeare, the man through whose imagination the era is best known.

The novel proper closes with an enigmatic speech by Touchstone in Shakespeare's *As You Like It* (circa 1599) which has long been considered a veiled reference to Marlowe's death, and the conclusion of the entire trilogy is Garrett's tribute (in "The Author's Farewell") to the power of imaginative language: "Christopher Marlowe's death may have been sudden and brutal and sordid and, finally, mysterious. But the greater and deeper and very joyful mystery is how, beyond all the known facts of his life and death, beyond the boundaries of the age he found himself living in, his living words, as best we can still recollect and resurrect them, thrive and flourish even here and now – *shining*!" It is this vital power of language in Garrett's own trilogy which Monroe K. Spears saluted in a review of *Entered from the Sun* in the Winter 1991 *Virginia Quarterly Review* when he said, "The trilogy as a whole re-creates an age . . . with wonderful vividness, completeness, and accuracy, and also, by implication, interprets it in relation to our own. It tampers with no facts, fictionalizes no history, but creates living characters who represent their own time and the universally human in any time."

The book which followed immediately upon the completion of the trilogy, *Whistling in the Dark: True Stories and Other Fables* (1992), contains a set of autobiographical stories which differ from a traditional memoir because of their open concern not with factuality but rather with the way those facts are remembered and interpreted. Just as he did not allow himself to return directly to the massive research that he had done for *Death of the Fox* during the composition of that novel, but rather concerned himself with the way the facts were transformed by his imagination into a fictive reality, so in this collection of stories he produced an imaginative revivification of his own life.

After the publication of *Whistling in the Dark,* Garrett began work on the first of a new trilogy of novels to be set in America. In "The King of Babylon Shall Not Come Against You," Garrett returns to the novella from *The Magic Striptease,* "The Satyr Shall Cry," and develops its account of the chaotic events (including a double murder) which took place in a small town in Florida into a full-scale novel by setting them on the day Martin Luther King Jr. was assassinated in 1968, possibly along the lines of Wright Morris's use of the day John F. Kennedy was killed in *One Day* (1965). According to Garrett, the novel, like the novella, will be "in various tongues and voices," but the novel's many voices will be orchestrated by a modern-day writer who has come to town to write a book that will at-

tempt to determine and make sense of exactly what did happen that day. The novels to follow will be set at the Columbian Exposition in Chicago in 1893 and at a football game in Florida in the fall of 1944. Garrett's use of these three significant dates would seem to indicate that he is planning a fictional examination of American social and cultural history quite as ambitious as his Elizabethan trilogy. It also seems clear that George Garrett, with unflagging energy, plans to continue to disregard literary fashion and to write novels that are distinctively his own.

Interviews:

John Graham and W. R. Robinson, "George Garrett Discusses Writing and His Work," *Mill Mountain Review,* 1 (Summer 1971): 79–102;

Graham, "Fiction and Film: An Interview with George Garrett," *Film Journal,* 1 (1971): 22–25;

John Carr, "Kite-Flying and Other Irrational Acts: George Garrett," in his *Kite-Flying and Other Irrational Acts: Conversations with Twelve Southern Writers* (Baton Rouge: Louisiana State University Press, 1972), pp. 174–198;

Charles Israel, "Interview: George Garrett," *South Carolina Review,* 6 (November 1973): 43–48;

Allen Wier, "Interview with George Garrett," *Penny Dreadful,* 4 (Fall–Winter 1975): 13–16;

Wier, "George Garrett," *Transatlantic Review,* 58–59 (1977): 58–61;

"An Interview with George Garrett" in *DLB Yearbook: 1983* (Detroit: Gale, 1984), pp. 157–161;

Paul Ruffin, "Interview with George Garrett," *South Carolina Review,* 16 (Spring 1984): 25–33;

Wyn Cooper and Kimberly Kafka, "George Garrett: An Interview," *Quarterly West,* 20 (Spring–Summer 1985): 54–63;

J. Argus Huber, "The Balanced Shelf: Understanding Beyond George Garrett," *Albany Review,* 2 (August 1988): 44–47;

Irv Broughton, "George Garrett," in his *The Writer's Mind: Interviews with American Authors,* volume 2 (Fayetteville: University of Arkansas Press, 1990), pp. 275–308;

Richard Easton, "An Interview with George Garrett," *New Orleans Review,* 17 (Winter 1990): 33–40;

David A. Maurer, *Charlottesville Daily Progress,* 23 July 1992, pp. C4–C5.

Bibliographies:

James B. Meriwether, "George Palmer Garrett," in *Seven Princeton Poets,* edited by Sherman

Hawkes (Princeton, N. J.: Princeton University Library, 1963), pp. 26–39;

R. W. H. Dillard, "George Garrett: A Checklist of His Writings," *Mill Mountain Review,* 1 (1971): 221–234;

Meriwether, "George Garrett," in *First Printings of American Authors* (Detroit: Gale, 1976), pp. 167–173;

Stuart Wright, "George Garrett: A Bibliographical Chronicle," *Bulletin of Bibliography,* 38 (1980): 6–19, 25;

Wright, *George Garrett: A Bibliography* (Huntsville: Texas Review, 1989).

References:

Richard A. Betts, " 'To Dream of Kings': George Garrett's *The Succession," Mississippi Quarterly,* 45 (Winter 1991–1992): 53–67;

Irv Broughton and R. H. W. Dillard, eds., *Mill Mountain Review,* special issue on Garrett, 1 (1971);

Fred Chappell, "Fictional Characterization as Infinite Regressive Series: George Garrett's Strangers in the Mirror," in *Southern Literature and Literary Theory,* edited by Jefferson Humphries (Athens: University of Georgia Press, 1990), pp. 66–74;

Dillard, *Understanding George Garrett* (Columbia: University of South Carolina Press, 1988);

William Peden, "The Short Fiction of George Garrett," *Ploughshares,* 4 (1978): 83–90;

Peden, " 'Swift Had Marbles in His Head': Some Rambling Comments about George Garrett's More Recent Work," *Southern Literary Journal,* 17 (Fall 1984): 101–106;

W. R. Robinson, "The Fiction of George Garrett," *Red Clay Reader,* 2 (1965): 15–16;

Robinson, "Imagining the Individual: George Garrett's *Death of the Fox," Hollins Critic,* 8 (August 1971): 1–12;

Paul Ruffin and Stuart Wright, eds., *To Come Up Grinning: A Tribute to George Garrett* (Huntsville: Texas Review, 1989);

David R. Slavitt, "George Garrett, Professional," *Michigan Quarterly Review,* 25 (Fall 1986): 771–778;

Slavitt, "History – Fate and Freedom: A Look at George Garrett's New Novel," *Southern Review,* 7 (January 1971): 276–294;

Monroe K. Spears, "George Garrett and the Historical Novel," in his *American Ambitions: Selected Essays on Literary and Cultural Things* (Baltimore: Johns Hopkins University Press, 1987), pp. 200–210;

Henry Taylor, "George Garrett: The Brutal Rush of Grace," in his *Compulsory Figures: Essays on Recent American Poets* (Baton Rouge: Louisiana State University Press, 1992), pp. 152–170;

Richard Tillinghast, "The Fox, Gloriana, Kit Marlowe, and Sundry," *South Carolina Review,* 25 (Fall 1992): 91–96;

Tom Whalen, "The Reader Becomes Text: Methods of Experimentation in George Garrett's *The Succession: A Novel of Elizabeth and James," Texas Review,* 4 (1983): 14–21.

Papers:

Garrett's papers and manuscripts are located at Duke University.

Donald Harington

(22 December 1935 –   )

Edwin T. Arnold
Appalachian State University

BOOKS: *The Cherry Pit* (New York: Random House, 1965; London: Gollancz, 1966);

Lightning Bug (New York: Delacorte, 1970; London: Gollancz, 1971); republished as *Sounds of a Summer Night* (London: Corgi, 1972);

Some Other Place. The Right Place. (Boston: Little, Brown, 1972; London: Cape, 1973);

The Architecture of the Arkansas Ozarks (Boston: Little, Brown, 1975);

Let Us Build Us a City: Eleven Lost Towns (San Diego: Harcourt Brace Jovanovich, 1986);

The Cockroaches of Stay More (San Diego: Harcourt Brace Jovanovich, 1989);

The Choiring of the Trees (San Diego: Harcourt Brace Jovanovich, 1991);

Ekaterina (San Diego: Harcourt, Brace, 1993).

OTHER: "Introduction," in *Interviewing Appalachia: The Appalachian Journal Interviews, 1978–1992,* edited by J. W. Williamson and Edwin T. Arnold (Knoxville: University of Tennessee Press, 1994), pp. xv–xix.

Donald Harington (photograph by Kim Harington)

Starting with his first novel, *The Cherry Pit* (1965), Donald Harington has concentrated his writings on his native Arkansas, especially the Ozark mountain region in the northwestern part of the state. In his second novel, *Lightning Bug* (1970), he introduced the semifictional hamlet of Stay More (sometimes called Stick Around: the name comes from the polite entreaty to guests to "stay more," even when the host is ready for solitude). Stay More is "*a community of some 113 souls in the Ozark mountains of Newton County, south of the county seat, Jasper, and the lovely village of Parthenon, west of the village of Spunkwater, north of Demijohn, Hunton, and Swain, east of Sidehill and Eden.*" The villagers are genially referred to as "Stay Morons." In Harington's books all roads lead to Stay More, although physically it is nearly impossible to reach the village, set beyond pavement and modern transportation and sometimes beyond history and time itself.

Harington is the topographer of an arcadian neverworld, a kind of hillbilly Macondo (Gabriel García Marquez is a major influence) inhabited by several prominent families of the Stay Morons who appear in most of his novels. "All of the worlds of my 'fiction' are invented, pastoralized, idealized, *fictionalized,* that is, made into art as opposed to 'life,' which is pretty dull stuff," Harington observed in a 1994 interview. The author himself, in various disguises or personae, also appears with regularity, for he is mediator between this comic, pastoral, romantic locus and the outside world of the reader. Harington has explained his "appearances" as being an aid to the reader: "If the reader can believe that the author himself was involved in the story, that diminishes the reader's own distance from the story.... To the extent that characters appearing in my books are based on me or offer allusions to me – they are presented as objectively as possible, as if I were writing from a psychic distance about a character not myself. The 'Harington personae' ... are usually depicted as comic characters, seen with a sense of humor that one would not ordinarily be able to apply to oneself."

In the tradition of such serious novelistic jokesters as Vladimir Nabokov and García Marquez, Harington requires that his readers join him in the telling of his stories: "In my effort to make the reader a participant in the creation of the imaginary world of 'reality,' I choose narrative techniques which require the reader not only to figure out the stories but also to investigate, usually with the benefit of a second or third reading, the multiple levels of 'existence,' meaning, allusion, 'reality.' ... And as long as I am in control of your perception while you're reading one of my books, I am going to use every trick I know to take you into realities where you've never been." As critic Tom D'Evelyn writes, "Donald Harington is the Fred Astaire of the contemporary novel.... Like Astaire dancing with a chair, Harington's grace and wit are such that he can turn the bare furniture of the form – the narrative voice, the sense of time passing, the imitation of unique individuality – into a dancing partner of exquisite grace."

Harington was born 22 December 1935 in Little Rock, Arkansas, the son of Conrad Fred and Jimmie Walker Harington. His mother's family came from a small village called Drakes Creek, located in the Ozark Mountains near Fayetteville. Although Harington lived and attended school in Little Rock, he was not fond of the city and spent his summers at his grandmother's home. In 1993 Harington recalled, "Some of the people in Drakes Creek treated me as a kind of outsider, but I was *Jimmie's boy*, and Jimmie, of course, my mother, she was a native. So being Jimmie's boy gave me a special cachet to be treated as a native even though they knew I was a city boy." Drakes Creek would figure strongly in Harington's creation of Stay More.

When he was twelve, Harington was stricken during a severe meningococcal meningitis epidemic and lost most of his hearing, a condition which plays a significant role in some of his books. While recuperating, first in the Little Rock hospital and later at Drakes Creek, he began reading "serious"

fiction: "My older brother Conrad, who at 18 was a college sophomore and fancied himself already an intellectual, the first in many generations of my family on either the paternal or the maternal side, determined to 'improve' my taste in reading and wean me from comic books. So he drew up a post-hospital reading list which included writers I'd never heard of: Dostoyevsky, Tolstoy, Faulkner, Conrad," Harington remembered in 1994. In addition he read Erskine Caldwell, Mickey Spillane, and other popular writers of the time, including cartoonist Walt Kelly, whose *Pogo* comic strip would also prove an important influence. "Throughout high school and college I did not do much serious reading of fiction, mostly things my brother had in his room at Drakes Creek.... Even when I took required college literature courses at the University of Arkansas, I was resistant to being *assigned* to reading fiction.... I seem to recall Drakes Creek as the place where I did most of my 'voluntary' (that is, pleasurable) reading of fiction."

Harington graduated from the University of Arkansas in 1956 and the following year married Nita Harrison, with whom he had three daughters, Jennifer, Calico, and Katy. He earned an M.F.A. in studio art from Arkansas in 1958 and an M.A. in art history from Boston University in 1959. He began a Ph.D. program in art history at Harvard University in 1959 but dropped out the next year: one of his professors had declared his work "too breezy and novelistic to be scholarship," he said in 1994. He was quickly hired to teach art history at Bennett College in Millbrook, New York, where he worked from 1960 to 1962. During that time, through a series of haphazard events, he decided to work seriously at becoming a writer.

Among the novels Harington had read for pleasure as a student at Arkansas was William Styron's *Lie Down in Darkness* (1951), "probably my first instance of reading contemporary fiction by a young novelist." In graduate school at Harvard in 1960, he bought a hardbound copy of Styron's *Set This House on Fire* (1960). He remembered, "Maybe ownership of the hardcover made it seem greater than it actually was, but I still believe that the reading of *Set This House on Fire* was probably the greatest single reading experience I ever had." When Harington later saw negative reviews of the book, he wrote Styron to praise it, and after Harington began teaching at Millbrook, he visited Styron at his home in nearby Roxbury, Connecticut, the result being the start of a long friendship and of Harington's career as a novelist.

Harington had begun "perhaps a dozen novels, never finished" in his youth. Now, inspired by Styron, he stopped teaching at Bennett, moved into a shack in Vermont, and wrote a book titled "Land's Ramble." Styron recommended the unread manuscript to his Random House editor Robert Loomis, who refused it but expressed interest in anything else Harington had to offer. Harington had by this time begun work on *The Cherry Pit*. Styron "made numerous valuable suggestions for it," Harington recalled in 1994. "He then offered me the summer-long use of his guest house, a famous building that had sheltered a number of writers, including Philip Roth and James Baldwin, to finish rewriting the novel. That summer in Roxbury was more idyllic than any of my summers in Drakes Creek." In 1964 Harington moved to Putney, Vermont, to begin teaching at Windham College, where he would remain until the college closed in 1978.

The Cherry Pit was published by Random House in 1965. Narrated in the first person, it is the story of Clifford Stone, a twenty-eight-year-old native of Little Rock, graduate of the University of Arkansas and Yale, and assistant curator for the Cabot Antiquities Foundation in Boston, "an organization devoted to the preservation of certain important relics, both tangible and intangible, of the Vanished American Past, or VAP as we abbreviate it around the office." Caught in an unhappy marriage, a dead-end job, and a minor scandal involving a coworker, Cliff returns to Little Rock, hoping to find his own personal VAP. Staying at his widowed father's home, Cliff slowly makes contact with people from his boyhood, when he was known as "Nub" Stone and famed as a small but skillful fighter. The most important of these are his former best friend, Doyle "Dall" Hawkins, a hill boy from the Ozarks who is now a police sergeant; Margaret Austin, a onetime girlfriend who has become an actress in local theater; and Napoleon "Naps" Howard, a black man approximately Cliff's age who acts as an unexpected ally during Cliff's two-week visit.

The Cherry Pit is an ambitious novel, comic in tone but serious in subject (as are most of Harington's works). It is among the most realistic of Harington's books, accurately reflecting a specific time and place (Little Rock in 1964). Dall Hawkins is a racist, outraged by the social changes forced on his region. Margaret Austin is fighting for her sanity and involved in a bizarre relationship with a local playwright of some renown, James Royal Slater. Naps Howard strives for a new social order with wit and courage; his business card reads

N. Leon Howard
Books, Religious and Otherwise
Agitating, Non-violent and Otherwise
Lunch Counters a Specialty

As Larry Vonalt has shown, Harington's use of doubling in *The Cherry Pit* is of major importance in the narrative. Not only are the adult characters compared with their younger selves – Cliff with "Nub" Stone, for example – but Harington also draws surprising parallels between other characters – Dall Hawkins and Naps Howard, Cliff Stone and James Royal Slater, or even Cliff Stone and Margaret Austin. Cliff's experiences in Little Rock are sometimes disturbing, even dangerous, but there is an overall sense of regeneration, forgiveness, and healing, although Cliff's fate remains uncertain at the end. As he leaves Little Rock and Margaret, she tells him, "You want to make history out of everything. If there were any word to describe the opposite of history, to mean for the future what history means for the past, then that would be my favorite word, my favorite subject. . . . Futurity? Would that do? Then you are lost in history, and I . . . I want to be lost in futurity." Clifford Stone does not reappear in any of Harington's later published novels (although he is the narrator of the unpublished "Farther Along," begun in 1976, wherein he surfaces as a cliff-dwelling hermit in *Stay More*), but as he tells Dall, "I'll be back. . . . I'll always keep coming home."

The Cherry Pit was generally well received by critics. Granville Hicks wrote in the *Saturday Review* (21 August 1965), "Harington has shown much ingenuity in devising adventures for Stone and his friends, and the incidents, if not always plausible, are entertaining. Harington writes well, sometimes brilliantly." But Hicks concluded that "like many first novelists, he writes as if he were never going to write another book and must say here and now all that he has to say," a concern which would prove unfounded. *The Cherry Pit* was nominated for the Pen-Faulkner award for best first novel but lost to Cormac McCarthy's *The Orchard Keeper,* also published by Random House in that year.

Harington's next project was a historical novel called "A Work of Fiction," centered on Albert Zebulon Pike, the Arkansas soldier, politician, and poet. In 1993 Harington recalled of the unpublished work that "some of its main characters came, like Dall Hawkins in *Cherry Pit,* from the Ozark mountains in Newton County. So I was already beginning to perceive Newton County as a possible setting for some future novel." Before he published his next novel, Harington formed a second important literary friendship with the aspiring novelist John Irving, who began teaching at Windham College in 1967 when Harington took a year's leave of absence in Europe. The two men discussed and shared their writings with each other, indulging in a certain amount of competition as well as mutual support. (The interrelated themes of imagination and reality, art and life are fundamental to both writers; likewise, both men incorporate elements of their own lives into their fiction and pay homage to similar influential authors.)

Reminiscing in 1993, Harington said he intended his novel *Lightning Bug* (1970), which he dedicated to Styron, as a "swan song to the Ozarks": "I thought once I'd gotten the Ozarks out of my system, or exorcised, by writing *Lightning Bug,* that would liberate me to write about the rest of the world. I discovered after writing *Lightning Bug* that I was hooked on the Ozarks." Whereas *The Cherry Pit,* for all of its inventiveness, is nonetheless a traditional novel, *Lightning Bug* gives first evidence of Harington's narrative play, of his postmodern approach to story. Rather than chapters, the book is divided into "Movements." The "Beginning" section is set dramatically: "*From a porch swing, evening, July, 1939, Stay More, Ark.*" The first sound is that of a screen door "*twanging*" open. The authorial voice is that of the novelist, who observes the scene as an adult from years in the future but who also experiences the scene as a small boy of "*five going on six*" whose name is Donald but is called "Dawny." The house belongs to Latha Bourne, the "*postmistress of this place — and the heroine, the demigoddess, of this world.*" The narrator says of the boy, "*Even when he is old, the thought of her will give him twitchings and itchings* [and the only way he will ever exorcise her, the only way she will ever give him any peace, is for him to write a book about her, who is, it should be obvious by this time, *the* Lightning Bug]." Latha Bourne, like the Ozarks themselves which she personifies and like the village of Stay More over which she presides, will appear at various ages and stages in all of Harington's later novels. In the same way, "Dawny" is the first self-acknowledged representative of the "Harington persona," the narrator who creates, recounts, and participates in his fiction.

The lengthy "Middling" movement of the book makes up the central narrative of Latha Bourne's story. It is divided into present-time sections, told in traditional third-person, past-tense style, which cover "Morning," "Noon," "Afternoon," "Evening," and "Night" of one full day in July 1939, when Every Dill, an insistent former suitor, returns as a revivalist preacher. Subsections, which separate these present-time events, relay the history of Latha and Every's relationship, but they are spoken in first-person, present tense, by a controlling, intruding authorial voice which often addresses Latha in the second person. From the interplay of these contrasting sections, the reader learns of Every's rape of Latha; his running away to war; the birth of their child, Sonora; Latha's breakdown and placement in an asylum; and Every's eventual rescue of Latha.

The last movement, "Ending," concentrates again on Dawny, who has run away and become lost in the wooded mountains nearby. At this point Harington shifts to future tense, a technique of special significance in his work. "I *hate* endings," he said in 1993. "Every one of my novels has shifted into the future tense . . . the future tense shift is specifically designed to help prevent the book from ending, because anything in the future tense does not end . . . my books are 'propped open' to a subsequent book and the reader can be assured that none of my books will end at that particular place, but that it will always be propped open to some future book." And so it is that Dawny, the child self of the adult narrator, is never found and remains in a timeless world. "So yes, it will have been just as well, it will have been nearly perfectly all right, that I shall never have been found," the author writes, moving into the imagined state of future perfect. "*The lightning bug flashes to find, and finds by flashes and is found by flashes. But is lost until found. The flashing is of loss, and yearning.*"

"Whenever people who haven't read any of my novels ask me which novel they should start with, I always say *Lightning Bug.* . . . It is full of flaws, of embarrassing things I wish I could rewrite if I had a chance. But it is the book that is closest to my heart," Harington admitted in 1993. Most reviewers found it inventive and winning. Martha Duffy, in *Time* magazine (17 August 1970), captured the mood of the book: "*Lightning Bug* is a modest but totally satisfying novel. . . . Like the late James Agee, [Harington] reveres the most ordinary aspects of the lives of unexceptional people, and with lyrical comedy and irony, he makes his joy infectious." Whether these people were "unexceptional" or not, Harington had, in this book, introduced to his readers a group of characters who would come to populate and dominate his fictional world.

Harington's next novel, *Some Other Place. The Right Place.* (1972), is his most complex narrative. As one reviewer observed, "There could not be a better illustration of the fact that novel-writing has no rules" (*Times Literary Supplement,* 31 August 1973). The influence of Nabokov looms large in the telling. "I didn't read *Lolita* until after I'd emerged from Faulkner's spell and had fallen under the spells of Styron and Agee, and I don't recall being enormously infatuated with *Lolita* at first reading," Harington noted in 1993. "Several years passed before I got around to *Pale Fire,* his masterpiece, and to the reading of his other books, and, eventually, to a close rereading of *Lolita,* which left me awed and forever imitative of it." Harington's homage to *Lolita* would come much later in *Ekaterina* (1993), but *Some Other Place. The Right Place.* shows his early fascination with Nabokov's narrative experimentation, even to the point of using a lengthy poem sequence to relate and comment on the story, as Nabokov did in *Pale Fire.*

Some Other Place. The Right Place. is a story of reincarnation, told in four movements, preceded by an "Overture" and concluded by a "Finale," thus underscoring the symphonic or even operatic blending of voices throughout. In the Overture a college student, Diana Stoving, reads a news article concerning an eighteen-year-old boy, Day Whittacker, who under hypnosis speaks in the voice of Daniel Lyam Montross, a poet born in Connecticut in 1880 and killed in Arkansas in 1953. Since Montross is Diana's grandfather, she sets out to discover the truth of this apparent spiritual possession. Together, she and Whittacker go in search of Daniel, first by finding the place, the ghost village of Dudleytown, where he was born and lived until the age of fifteen. They make camp (Day Whittacker is an Eagle Scout) in the forest, amid the remains of the town, and set about their exploration. In the First Movement, Diana, through the hypnotized boy, makes tapes of her dead grandfather as she hears his stories of growing up. At the same time, she and Day fall in love, although Diana can never be sure if it is Day or Daniel to whom she is attracted, or if there really is a Daniel beyond the one created by the imagination of the boy.

Following in the path of Daniel Montross's earlier journey, Diana and Day next travel to Five Corners, Vermont, in the Second "Unfinished" Movement. Other voices join the telling, but as Daniel's story develops, Diana and Day's relationship begins to unravel, and at the end of this section, Day apparently commits suicide. The Third Movement is a reproduction of *Selected Poems of Daniel Lyam Montross,* a sixty-page collection, complete with publisher's imprint and table of contents. These poems relate Montross's experiences in Lost Cove, North Carolina, before he then moves on to Stick Around, Arkansas, where he will die, killed by a state trooper when he kidnaps his three-year-old granddaughter, Diana herself, to raise her away from the corruption of civilization. The last sections of the book focus on the authorial persona, here called "G," a thirty-five-year-old deaf author and professor of art history who is given a sabbatical to pull his shattered life together. He is "like a town which is on the verge of becoming a ghost town" and decides to go home to Arkansas, the "right place" for him to be. There he reads of Diana Stoving's disappearance and decides to find her, tracking her finally to Stick Around, where he discovers her pregnant with Day's or possibly her own grandfather Daniel's child. For "G," the search is also a journey into his own past, his own identity, just as it was for Clifford Stone of *The Cherry Pit.*

One of the major themes of *Some Other Place. The Right Place.* is the solipsistic nature of fiction, and, by extension, of life. The novel constantly comments on itself as an imaginary work, through its shifting narrative voices, its uncertain "reality," its exaltation of the imagination. Although the reader may be tempted to see "G" as Harington himself, Harington claims greater identity with Montross or even Day Whittacker. The Fourth Movement is narrated by the dead Montross, a ghost who describes and directs "G"'s actions. At one point Montross even encounters "Dawny," the child from *Lightning Bug,* still lost in this fantasy wood. The boy, unnamed here, asks if Montross is a magician, and, as author, he of course is, as long as the reader is willing to believe in his "*gimmick.*" Literature, Harington seems to say, is magic. The author made a related point in a 1994 interview: "Something in the back of your mind always reminds you that [these characters] are not really alive, that only you exist, that all of those people are simply being pretended into existence by yourself (with the help of the author), but for the duration of your enjoyment of the book, you 'willingly suspend disbelief' and convince yourself you are moving among real people."

It is this question of imagined reality, of the individual as author of his or her life, that haunts this exceedingly complex work. Reviewers largely appreciated Harington's ambition and talent, although some questioned the overall accomplishment. One critic called it "an interestingly ambitious though a tediously difficult book. It may be that the structure of the whole novel calls attention to itself too often and too loudly" (*Best Seller,* 1 December 1973). However, the review concluded, "Read it by all means. Obviously, the author feels he's succeeded. The reader, though he may be somewhat reeling at the end, feels he has too." Clearly a tour de force on Harington's part, the novel remains an astonishing celebration of the mystery of fiction.

Harington's fourth novel, *The Architecture of the Arkansas Ozarks* (1975), is generally considered his best. ("If I could only be *remembered* for one book, it would have to be *The Architecture of the Arkansas Ozarks,*" Harington said in 1993.) In *Some Other Place. The Right Place.* Diana Stoving foretells that "G" will write a book with this unusual title, and the primary characters, the founders of Stay More, Jacob and Noah Ingledew, are first mentioned in *Lightning Bug.* (Latha Bourne, Diana, and Day Whittacker also appear briefly in *The Architecture of the Arkansas Ozarks.*) The book is a history of the village and of Arkansas itself, covering some 140 years from the 1830s to the 1970s and into Harington's habitual future tense. Although the Ingledews are fictional, they are based in fact, as are their exploits – Harington details his research in "Acknowledgments" at the end of the novel. But the novel is foremost an imaginary creation. "My characters . . . have wills of their own, even if I created them," Harington said in 1993. "If I did not endow them with free will, I would quickly become bored with what I *make* them do. It is no fun being a puppeteer, when one can play God with one's creations, and, like God, be solely responsible for their existence and completely aware of their foibles and frailties, but unable to stop them from doing anything they choose to do." Harington noted in 1994 that *The Architecture of the Arkansas Ozarks* "was greatly inspired by *One Hundred Years of Solitude* – all the way through, even beginning with the similarities of the opening paragraphs. . . . But at the time I wrote [*The Architecture of the Arkansas Ozarks*] I didn't know what 'Magic Realism' was. For that matter, I'm not sure I yet understand it. I just admired what Garcia Marquez had done and wanted to emulate it, but I took pains to make sure that everything which happened in [*The Architecture of the Arkansas Ozarks*] was possible, conceivable, believable. . . . So the 'magic' of Garcia Marquez might be missing."

Harington is once again a figure in the novel. As Michael Lund describes it, "Harington provides a logic for his narrator's ability to leap or look beyond his own story by casting him as a native of or regular visitor to Stay More, perhaps even the author himself." Indeed, the narrator has visited Stay

Dust jacket for Harington's 1993 novel, his homage to Vladimir Nabokov

More as a child, has written three novels about the region, and remembers characters from earlier Harington books. As the title indicates, the author uses an architectural motif to structure his novel. Each chapter is prefaced with a drawing by the author and a learned discussion of the construction and purpose of progressive dwellings and buildings in the Ozarks, starting with an Indian structure made of bent poles interwoven with reeds and other materials, moving to the first log cabin and including subsequent wagons, barns, mansions, mills, churches, and mobile homes. Each structure illustrates a stage in the rise and fall of Stay More and, primarily, of the Ingledew family. Harington's conflating of the actual history of Arkansas and his own high-spirited but convincing imagined history results in Jacob Ingledew's becoming governor of Arkansas after the Civil War. The first third of the novel is devoted to the founding brothers Jacob and Noah; the rest of the book follows the succeeding five generations down to the last of the Ingledews,

Vernon. Spanning these generations, and affecting each, is the peddler Eli Willard, a mysterious, magical figure (similar to Melquiades in *One Hundred Years of Solitude*). Also serving as a connecting device is the hymn "Farther Along," sung at the passing of each generation of Ingledews. The hymn underscores the humanely comic and vaguely religious tone of the book: "*Farther along we'll know all about it, / Farther along we'll understand why; / Cheer up, my brother, live in the sunshine, / We'll understand it, all by and by.*"

After the publication of *The Architecture of the Arkansas Ozarks* in 1975, it would be eleven years before Harington published another book and fourteen years before his next novel appeared. From 1976 to 1980 he worked on the unpublished novel "Farther Along" – which brought together Clifford Stone (*The Cherry Pit*), Latha Bourne (*Lightning Bug*), and Daniel Montross (*Some Other Place. The Right Place.*). Harington told *Contemporary Authors* in 1982 that in recent years he had encountered "every conceivable financial and personal problem inimical to writing." In 1978, the year Windham College closed and his friend John Irving (who had left the college in 1972) achieved resounding success with the publication of *The World According to Garp,* Harington began the difficult peripatetic existence of a visiting professor at, first, the University of Missouri-Rolla (1978–1980); then, the University of Pittsburgh (1980); and, finally, South Dakota State University, Brookings (1980–1981). Harington's novels continued to sell only modestly, despite their good reviews; he and his publisher were especially disappointed by the indifferent reception of *The Architecture of the Arkansas Ozarks.* Moreover, depressed by his separation from his wife in 1979 and the breakup of their marriage as well as the death of his father, Harington began to drink to excess. "I had prided myself for 20 years for being a very heavy but controlled drinker, but I lost that control," he said in 1994.

It was in this condition that Harington, like so many of his characters, returned to Arkansas for revival. He eventually moved to Fayetteville in 1982, where he has since 1986 taught art history at the University of Arkansas, his alma mater. He gave a fictionalized account of his life during this period in his next book, *Let Us Build Us a City: Eleven Lost Towns* (1986), and another version in his novel *Ekaterina* (1993). According to the fictional account while at South Dakota State, Brookings, he had received a letter from a reader, Kim Gunn, who admired his book *Some Other Place. The Right Place.* and proposed an investigation of dying or deserted

towns in Arkansas, similar to the journey undertaken by Day Whittacker and Diana Stoving. In *Let Us Build Us a City,* the Harington persona (here called "Harrigan") corresponds with "Kim"; it is not until near the end of her exploration of the towns mentioned in the subtitle that he joins her. In truth she and Harington had met in 1978 and during 1983–1984 made the entire trip together, recorded in photograph and word by Harington. Although by genre a photojournalistic work similar to Erskine Caldwell and Margaret Bourke-White's *You Have Seen Their Faces* (1937) or James Agee and Walker Evans's *Let Us Now Praise Famous Men* (1941), authors and works Harington admires, *Let Us Build Us a City* is by turns "truthful" journalism and high-flying fiction. For example, in Marble City, which has been turned into the "Dogpatch" theme park inspired by Al Capp's *Li'l Abner* comic strip, Kim meets former governor Orval Faubus among the deserted amusements. In the "Mound City" chapter, the reader learns about the explosion and burning of the steamboat *Sultana* in 1865 through a twenty-page story presented as fact but told through fictional devices. Each chapter includes the author's photographs which, in one sense, prove these "ghost towns" exist, yet the reader is never sure of the "truth" of the histories presented. In addition to being a travelogue, the book is also a love story, describing the growing relationship between "Harrigan" and "Kim." Thus, although *Let Us Build Us a City* is classified as nonfiction, it blurs the distinctions between fact and fiction as do all of Harington's novels. Harington and Kim Gunn soon married, and in 1987 *Let Us Build Us a City* won the Porter Fund Award for Literary Excellence, presented by the actress and native Arkansan Mary Steenburgen, who also optioned the film rights to *Lightning Bug* (presently unmade). In the same year his publisher Harcourt Brace Jovanovich began bringing out his earlier novels in paperback editions in their Harvest/HBJ series.

Although Harington had started his next novel, *The Cockroaches of Stay More,* in 1985, it was not published until 1989. Harington credited Kim and a friend, the writer Jack Butler, with helping him regain his confidence as a novelist through this book. *The Cockroaches of Stay More,* a comic, gently satiric fable dedicated to his three daughters and his new stepson, views Stay More and Stay Morons from the perspective of the insects who live there. Filled with fascinating facts about roaches, it manages to make them both appealing and affecting, no small achievement. At the same time, the story serves as a religious parable and an insightful commentary on the Cold War atmosphere of the mid 1980s. One group of insects considers itself descended from the line of old Jacob Ingledew and, despite their pitiful state, feels superior to the more common roaches. Another group, the "Manfearing Crustians," worships the few remaining Stay Morons as gods, their houses as temples. Led by the preacher Brother Chidiock Tichborne, they await the Rapture, which occurs when the drunken writer Larry Brace, who is in Stay More researching Daniel Montross, shoots the bugs with his pistol. Brace is in love with Sharon Ingledew, the granddaughter of Latha Bourne, who is remembered and adored by the roaches as the first woman from the "Ozark Golden Age of yore." Sharon lives in Latha's home, known as the "Parthenon." Also in the house is the cockroach Gregor Samsa Ingledew, known as Sam, who lives in the clock on the mantle and has been made deaf by the striking of the hours. Sam loves Tish Dingletoon, whose parents are disreputable lower-class with pretensions, but is too shy to make his feelings known to her.

With imaginative references to Franz Kafka's "The Metamorphosis," Thomas Hardy's *Tess of the d'Urbervilles,* and Don Marquis's "Archy and Mehitabel," among other works, the book is rich with animal, insect, and human characters, all of whom finally join together to give hope for all manifestations of life in a dangerous world. It ends with "The Mockroach's Song," a prayer for "love, dependency, survival": "Grow up, earn Love, like us conceive / a God to pray to and believe." *The Cockroaches of Stay More* earned Harington some of his best reviews. Donald McCaid declared him "a daring and confident writer" and the book "surprising and funny and frequently brilliant" (*Washington Post Book World,* 19 February 1989). Harry Middleton in *The New York Times Book Review* (23 April 1993), never a source of strong reviews for Harington, called it a "truly captivating and appealing book." It was reprinted as a Vintage Contemporary in 1990, the only one of his novels so chosen.

Harington's next work, however, proved a definite change of pace. "The novels written in Vermont were written out of a kind of desperate homesickness for Arkansas," he said in 1993. "It was almost as if I had to recreate . . . Arkansas and the Ozarks as an imaginary living place. Once I came back to Arkansas, it was almost as if I could make . . . the imaginary living place a real living place. That takes a little bit of the idealism off of your setting. . . . The Ozarks as they exist in my fiction since I have returned to Arkansas probably

aren't quite as mythologized. Maybe not quite as heroic, not quite as flagrantly Arcadian."

Such is certainly the case with *The Choiring of the Trees* (1991), which Harington calls his most realistic novel. Inspired by an actual event, as Harington explains in a prefatory note, the novel contains historical as well as fictional characters. Nail Chism, a native of Stay More in the early part of the twentieth century, a shepherd and a moonshiner, is falsely accused of rape by Dorinda Whitter, a young girl who has actually been assaulted by Sewell Jerram, husband to Nail Chism's sister. Jerram is also a county judge and with that political power has plans to market illegally his in-law's product, "Chism's Dew." Because Nail has confronted him over his infidelity and his treatment of Nail's sister, and because Nail refuses to cooperate in his schemes to market the moonshine, Sull Jerram is anxious to rid himself of his troublesome relative. Dorinda's accusation serves the purpose, and Nail is arrested and convicted.

The narration of the novel alternates between that provided by Latha Bourne, who is Dorinda's best friend but suspects that she is lying in accusing Nail of the crime, and by the Harington narrator, who concentrates on Nail's experiences in prison, his close escapes from execution, and his final freedom. In addition to Latha, Nail is supported by the efforts of Viridis Monday, a staff artist assigned to the execution for the *Arkansas Gazette.* Viridis comes from a prominent Arkansas family. Although she is self-sufficient, has studied art in Europe, and is now making her way as a career woman, she also has a sexual secret in her past which makes her sensitive to the complexities of Nail's case. Convinced of his innocence, she makes her way to Stay More to find evidence to overturn his conviction. There she meets Latha, Dorinda, and other Stay Morons from earlier novels (most importantly an unnamed old woman, Jacob Ingledew's lover in *The Architecture of the Arkansas Ozarks,* who followed him back to Stay More after his term as governor).

More so than in other novels, it is difficult to tell where fact and fiction diverge in this book. In this way the novel is similar to *Lightning Bug,* although *The Choiring of the Trees* is more obviously a work of historical imagination, and might, as Linda K. Hughes perceptively illustrates, be read as a darker, more mature companion to *Lightning Bug,* the earlier novel centered on Latha Bourne. The final success of *The Choiring of the Trees* probably depends on the reader's expectations. For some the relative "down-to-earth" quality of the novel, the sober realism, might be less rewarding than

Harington's more playful, exuberant tone. There is little comedy in this tale, and the story, largely deprived of a sense of wonder, of "magic," ironically makes it sometimes more difficult to suspend disbelief, despite the historical basis.

In 1993 Harington published his most recent novel, *Ekaterina,* his homage to Nabokov. "*Ekaterina* is not so much an inversion of *Lolita* as it is an apotheosis of it," Harington asserted. The story reflects both *Lolita* and *Pale Fire* and interconnects with several of Harington's own works as well. Ekaterina Vladimirovna Dadeshkeliani (Kat) is a refugee from Soviet Georgia, brought to the United States by the Fund for the Relief of Russian Writers and Scientists in Exile. She has been imprisoned in Moscow's Serbsky Institute and tortured by the evil Bolshakov, a sadist who follows her, intent on her assassination (recalling Nabokov's Jacob Gradus in *Pale Fire* or Claire Quilty in *Lolita*). A female version of Humbert Humbert, Kat has a desire for prepubescent boys. Arriving in America, she lives in a boarding house with several professors from the local university, one of whom is a visiting professor of creative writing from the "Bodark" mountains of Arkansas, an unsuccessful novelist who drinks heavily and is almost totally deaf. In the book he is identified by the initial "I.," which, the narrator says, stands perhaps for "Irresponsible, for Incognito, for Inept, for Indiscretion, for Inebriated"; the description, of course, roughly fits Harington himself (he is also called "Ingraham" and is another incarnation of "G" from *Some Other Place. The Right Place.*). Furthermore, the narrator for the first part of the book is, we later learn, the ghost of Daniel Lyam Montross of *Some Other Place. The Right Place.*

The first part of the book is set in (apparently) Pittsburgh, where Kat begins to write under the tutelage of the novelist Ingraham. Manipulated in part by the ghostly interventions of Montross, who takes the form of a cat, but also as a result of her seduction of the twelve-year-old son of the owners of the boarding house where she lives, Kat accompanies Ingraham to the Bodark mountains, followed by the evil Bolshakov. In Stick Around, Kat stays first with Diana and Day and their son, Daniel I. Stoving-Whittacker. There she works on her first novel, *Georgie Boy,* which becomes a best-seller. With her wealth she (emulating Nabokov) then takes over the top floor of the Halfmoon Hotel, an aging resort run by Latha Bourne's granddaughter Sharon. After years of reclusion, she is finally tracked down by Bolshakov, who kills Ingraham but is himself captured. Shortly thereafter Ekaterina, being inter-

viewed for the *Paris Review* (another nod to Nabokov), meets her own ambiguous end. Harington has suggested that the ghostly Montross brings Ekaterina to Stick Around so that she can be with him after death. "That's the most beautiful interpretation to put on the whole novel," he said in 1993. But he also uses the multiple "ghosts" in the book to comment on his concept of fiction: "Any invented fictional character is *per se* a ghost. There's a very thin line between your attempt to make a flesh and blood character and convince the reader that this apparition of words actually exists and to cross the line and say, no, this flesh and blood character of words did exist at one time but is now in the spirit world but still capable, like Montross, of using speech."

Ekaterina proved the occasion for a general reconsideration of Harington's work among many critics. The *Chicago Review* committed half of one 1993 issue to an interview with and four essays on Harington and also included excerpts from the new novel. D. M. Thomas, author of *The White Hotel* (1981), called the book "a superbly crafted, foxy, engaging, funny, joyous work" in the *Los Angeles Times Book Review* (18 July 1993). Peter Straub described Harington as "one of the most powerful, subtle and inventive novelists in America. Everywhere, his work is full of mystery and heartbreak kept afloat by high spirits, sensual pleasure and intellectual joy" (*Washington Post Book World,* 6 June 1993). He concluded that "Harington's seductive, artful novel is another reminder of the splendor this writer can offer us as long as we are willing to entertain the notion that the word 'reality' should always have quotation marks around it."

From January of 1993 to January of 1995 Harington battled with a cancer of the throat, which his doctors said was a much-delayed result of his earlier years of heavy drinking and smoking. He underwent months of chemotherapy followed by months of radiation, but these failed to remove the cancer, and in September of 1994 he had an apparently successful supraglottic laryngectomy, which spared his voice.

He had planned, since the completion of *Ekaterina,* that his next work would be a "medical" novel exploring the life of Doc Swain, Stay More's beloved physician who appears in several of his books. Harington had no inkling that during the writing of *Butterfly Weed* he would have so much firsthand exposure to the medical profession. He completed the manuscript of the new novel in the winter of 1995, simultaneously with his recuperation from the surgery and his return to full-time teaching.

Butterfly Weed is narrated from his deathbed by Vance Randolph, the eminent Arkansas folklorist whose own books have served as a valuable resource for Harington in all of his writing. A master collector of tall tales, Randolph seeks in *Butterfly Weed* to relate a grand tall tale which is possibly "true" and in the process to explore both his and Harington's lifelong preoccupations with the nature of fiction in relation to "truth." *Butterfly Weed* is also, according to Harington, whose publisher will bring the novel out in the spring of 1996 simultaneously in hardcover and trade paperback, "a grand retelling of some ancient Greek myths in an Ozark setting." The book takes its title from the Ozark plant which, according to Randolph's *Ozark Superstitions,* is a cure for tuberculosis, and it concerns Doc Swain's attempt to help a girl stricken with the disease. The title is also allusive to Nabokov and to Psyche.

With that novel behind him, Harington is now contemplating a return to the short story, which he occasionally wrote during the 1960s and 1970s but had abandoned in order to concentrate on the novel. He has in mind an eventual collection of Stay More tales, perhaps including one in which another Ingledew replaces Bill Clinton as governor of Arkansas. "Whatever the stories are about," Harington says, "they will all have to do with Stay More. If I live to be eighty-six and do a novel or a collection of stories every year, I would not exhaust Stay More as a subject."

Interviews:

Larry Vonalt, "An Interview with Donald Harington," *Chicago Review,* 38, no. 4 (1993): 60–77;

Edwin T. Arnold, "An Interview with Donald Harington," *Appalachian Journal,* 21 (Summer 1994): 432–445.

References:

Jack Butler, "The Ghosts of Stay More," *Chicago Review,* 38, no. 4 (1993): 120–126;

Tom D'Evelyn, "'Words are all the ghosts we need': The Fiction of Donald Harington," *Bostonia* (Fall 1993): 78–80;

Linda K. Hughes, "Knowing Women and the Fiction of Donald Harington," *Chicago Review,* 38, no. 4 (1993): 100–109;

Michael Lund, "Donald Harington's House of Fiction," *Chicago Review,* 38, no. 4 (1993): 110–119;

William J. Schafer, "All God's Chillun Got Wings (and Six Legs, Carapaces, Rube Accents)," *Appalachian Journal,* 17 (Spring 1990): 276–284;

Larry Vonalt, "Doubling and Duplicity in Donald Harington's *The Cherry Pit,*" *Critique,* 22, no. 1 (1980): 47–54;

Andy Winston, "On Donald Harington: An Introduction," *Chicago Review,* 38, no. 4 (1993): 58–59.

Papers:

Letters between Harington and William Styron can be found in the Styron collection in Perkins Library, Duke University.

Madison Jones

(21 March 1925 –)

Sandy Cohen
Albany State College

BOOKS: *The Innocent* (New York: Harcourt, 1957; London: Secker & Warburg, 1957);

Forest of the Night (New York: Harcourt, 1960; London: Eyre & Spottiswoode, 1961);

A Buried Land (New York: Viking, 1963; London: Bodley Head, 1963);

An Exile (New York: Viking, 1967; London: Deutsch, 1970); published as *I Walk the Line* (New York: Popular Library, 1970);

A Cry of Absence (New York: Crown, 1971; London: Deutsch, 1972);

Passage through Gehenna (Baton Rouge: Louisiana State University Press, 1978);

Season of the Strangler (Garden City, N.Y.: Doubleday, 1982);

Last Things (Baton Rouge: Louisiana State University Press, 1989).

From the publication of his first novel, the literary reputation of Madison Percy Jones Jr. has been solid, not just in America but in South America and Europe as well. Among his earliest American admirers were such respected literary figures as Flannery O'Connor, Allen Tate, James Dickey, Donald Davidson, and Andrew Lytle. M. E. Bradford compared Jones's third novel, *A Buried Land* (1963), favorably to Fyodor Dostoyevsky's *Crime and Punishment* (1866); Hayden Carruth praised *A Cry of Absence* (1971) highly, and Monroe K. Spears placed that novel in the company of the best writings by Sophocles, Jean Racine, Henrik Ibsen, Gustave Flaubert, Thomas Hardy, and William Faulkner. In recent years Jones's work has been the subject of many favorable reviews by such writers as Jesse Hill Ford and Madison Smartt Bell (who says he was named after Jones) and the subject of a growing number of scholarly articles, interviews, and reviews in such periodicals as *Sewanee Review, South Atlantic Review, Southern Review,* and *Georgia Review.*

Critics especially admire Jones's tight plotting and the robust power of his prose, which frequently rises to the level of poetry. Except for *A Cry of Absence,* which made *The New York Times* best-seller list, Jones has not yet attained the popularity among general readers that he deserves. But he has always been thought of as a novelist's novelist, a writer to whom other writers turn to learn their craft.

Jones's work is solidly in the American tradition of what Nathaniel Hawthorne on the title page of *The Scarlet Letter* (1850) called romance. In many of Jones's books the characters, plots, imagery, and settings are halfway between those found in purely allegorical works such as John Bunyan's *Pilgrim's Progress* (1678, 1684) and realistic novels such as those of Mark Twain or Henry James.

Jones often uses imagery to convey his themes. The conflicts between good and evil are often symbolized by his contrasting images of heat and cold, darkness and light, drought and rain, health and fever, naturalness and artificiality, and flesh and fleshlessness. In *A Buried Land,* for example, the rising floodwaters become an apt symbol for the rising tide of awareness that comes to the major character, and in *Passage through Gehenna* (1978) the burning fever of the protagonist marks his descent into sin.

Jones balances the realistic elements of the novel and the allegorical elements of the romance. His characters are given the psychological motivation and verisimilitude one expects to find in a realistic novel so that they seem to be real people while at the same time representing or becoming abstractions or ideas just as in pure allegory. For example, Lily in *Passage through Gehenna* represents Lilith, the classic seductress in legend, as well as the worldly experience that corrupts innocents who have not been prepared for it.

In Jones's best work there is a skillful balance of these opposing forces. The settings, characters, and plots are portrayed too realistically to be taken as pure allegory, yet not so realistically that they would not be subject to allegorical interpretation. Jones deliberately deemphasizes the literal level in

Madison Jones

order to explore more deeply his two favorite themes, the confrontation of good and evil and the clash between innocence and guilt. These recurring themes in his work come as much from his education and reading as from his upbringing.

Jones was born on 21 March 1925 in Nashville, Tennessee, and was raised on a farm by his parents, Madison Percy and Mary Temple Webber Jones. His family was well-to-do, affording Jones a private-school education founded in classical literature, a background that would later affect his novels, especially *A Buried Land* and *A Cry of Absence*. He is also a longtime admirer of Herman Melville, Joseph Conrad, and Dostoyevsky.

Just as his secular education was of great importance, so too was his early moral training, a strict Presbyterianism. "Our Presbyterian training had real teeth in it," he has said. "We grew up with moral consciences that today's vision could only see as overabundant." An important literary influence was the Bible: "If I were to have to say who the greatest influence on me was, I'd have to say, Moses. I'm not kidding about that — if he

wrote the Pentateuch, with all the wonderful stories about Abraham and Isaac and Jonathan and David."

One can certainly find in Jones's writings the Calvinistic combination of a strong emphasis on the rational processes of the mind and the desire for a direct connection to God. In the best of his writings these two forces of rationalism and mysticism are precisely balanced.

Jones studied writing under Donald Davidson at Vanderbilt University, where he received a B.A. degree in 1949. His undergraduate years were interrupted twice, once by a return to the family farm, where he worked eighteen months, and once to serve in the U.S. Army Military Police in Korea (1945–1946). After his military service Jones returned to Vanderbilt to resume study under Davidson. After graduation he went to study under an even more influential writer, editor, and critic, Andrew Lytle, at the University of Florida, where he received an M.A. degree in 1950. Jones married Shailah McEvilley of Cincinnati, Ohio, in 1951. They have five children.

*Dust jacket for Jones's novel about a young man who attempts to
stop the Tennessee Valley Authority from flooding his
childhood home*

Between 1951 and 1953 Jones completed all of
the requirements for a Ph.D. except the dissertation. He left the University of Florida without completing the dissertation or his degree in order to
write his first novel. A powerful and effective
teacher, Jones left the University of Florida for a
year at Miami University in Ohio. After a year off
to accept a *Sewanee Review* fellowship, he taught at
the University of Tennessee during the 1955–1956
school year. In 1956 he accepted an assistant professorship at Auburn University, where he remained
until his retirement in 1987, having attained the
rank of professor and alumni writer-in-residence.
He was awarded a Rockefeller Foundation fellowship in 1968 and a Guggenheim Fellowship that enabled him to spend some months in Ireland and in
Majorca in 1973–1974. He now lives on a small
farm outside Auburn, Alabama.

Jones's method is to write about one page a
day, to revise it while he is writing, then not to re-

vise much afterward. He does not work from outlines:

> I can't ever see the end. Usually, I have a situation and
> a main character maybe with just vague ideas about one
> or two other characters. I might see fifty pages of action,
> one action leading to a second action, and then a general
> idea that it ought to reach a certain point or a statement
> in the vague misty distance. But I never know how
> they're going to come out.

The two fundamental themes that have fascinated Jones throughout his career, the confrontation of innocence and guilt and the confrontation of
good and evil, commonly determine the stuff from
which he molds his characters. Many of his characters struggle to distinguish God from the devil.
Their spiritual selves battle their fleshly selves.
When their ideologies clash with reality, their psyches often suffer.

Jones's first novel, *The Innocent,* received a mixed reception. Some critics, such as the reviewer for *Commonweal,* did not like it, but so important a writer as O'Connor found it excellent. The novel establishes some of his major themes – the adulteration of innocence through experience and the corruption of the present by the past. The story concerns the return of Duncan Welsh to the southern land he inherited. After wandering about in the North for seven years he returns home to fight bitterly the vague, half-formed, pessimistic ideas of his sister, her liberal husband, and the other intellectuals who have replaced the rigid rural traditions of his ancestors.

In this battle Jones presents an evenhanded review of the ideas of the Agrarians, the group of southern writers – including John Crowe Ransom, Allen Tate, Robert Penn Warren, and Davidson – who championed a farming economy over industrial capitalism from the early 1920s to the early 1940s. Jones's presentation is so balanced, as is his assessment of racial tensions in *A Cry of Absence,* because his allegiance is never to ideas but to art.

In *The Innocent,* however, Jones's protagonist, Welsh, is a strict agrarian. He wants to restore his life and his community to a way it never really was, to a kind of idealistic pastoral. His own hubris drives his destruction. After the failure of his second marriage his vision is increasingly directed inward, toward the dark, obsessive side of his own soul. This is symbolized in the novel by his attempt to restore a nearly extinct breed of horse and by the sinister moonshiner, Aaron McCool, who embodies Welsh's dark self.

Welsh is seduced by McCool into savagery and by his own pride to justify that savagery. The penultimate result is the ultimate act of hubris, murder. The ultimate result is Duncan's and his alter ego's death. Though Duncan tries to stop McCool in the end, he discovers that he cannot reenter Eden, for, as Jones writes, "The 'Innocent' who tries to reenter the garden is destined to find that it is not God but Satan who walks there now." It is this lesson that many of Jones's characters learn, or fail to learn, in the novels and stories that follow.

Forest of the Night (1960) is a historical novel set in Tennessee in 1802. Its central theme is the corruption of innocence. Jonathan Cannon, the innocent, a devoted follower of Jean-Jacques Rousseau, hopes to find along the Natchez Trace (the pioneer road from Nashville, Tennessee, to Natchez, Mississippi, that follows an old Native American trail) living examples of the French philosopher's "natural man," uncorrupted by civilization. He gives up his

social position to stalk this shadow. As he does, he is in turn stalked by the infamous outlaws, the Harpe brothers – or by their comrades or by the memories of their exploits.

Cannon's journey into the wilderness is a voyage from innocence to experience. Like many of Jones's innocents, Cannon is too naive in the sense that he is so unprepared for reality that he is like a firefighter ignorant of the true nature of fire. Like many of Jones's subsequent protagonists, Cannon becomes the very thing he abhorred in theory, an outlaw so much like the Harpe brothers that even the woman who loves him thinks he is one of them. Eventually, Cannon, like John Locke and Edmund Burke, comes to the conclusion that society is a civilizing force.

One of Jones's two best novels is his third, *A Buried Land.* (The other is his fifth, *A Cry of Absence.*) Here the strength of the plot, symbolism, and character merge most portentously with the power of the word. The novel is set in the Tennessee Valley during the time when the Tennessee Valley Authority (TVA) was beginning to build the huge dams and change life along the Tennessee River. Percy Youngblood, a young attorney, returns to the land where his strict father raised him. As his name suggests, Percy returns to change the attitudes of the valley people, to raise their consciousness with the rising waters.

Gradually, he discovers that it is not his world that needs changing but himself. Like Jonathan Cannon, he thinks he can live outside civilization's governance, becoming the prototype of the new man in the new Eden. He tries to bury his own personal, racial, cultural, intellectual, historical, and emotional history. He discovers he can bury the past, but he cannot detach himself from it any more than the heart can detach itself from the body. The rising waters become a powerful symbol.

Also symbolic are Percy Youngblood's acts. He attempts to bury in the rising waters the young woman who dies aborting his baby. When he ultimately confesses to his crimes and his sins he begins to realize that conscience is not powerful enough to govern, for it is always tempered with hubris. With his confession he only begins to waken from the nightmare of history. He only begins to understand that human limitations overwhelm and enlightenment rarely removes one from one's own buryings.

Jones's fourth novel, *An Exile* (1967), was the basis of the Gregory Peck motion picture *I Walk the Line* (1970). It is a short, straightforward tale about a middle-aged country sheriff who abandons his career and his principles for the young daughter of a

*Dust jacket for Jones's 1989 novel, in which the protagonist
represents the decadent values of the New South*

bootlegger, who seduces him in an effort to protect her family's business. By the time the sheriff realizes the woman is more interested in protecting her father than in him, he is too ensnared to save himself.

With *A Cry of Absence* Jones achieved both critical acclaim and a modicum of financial success. It is a complex story about an aristocratic gentlewoman, Hester Glenn, and the Old South she represents. She deludes herself into thinking she is upholding old traditions that need to be upheld when she is in reality poisoning her sons' minds, failing to help her town grow progressively out of its past or to save her own marriage. In classical terms she cannot see above her own hubris.

A Cry of Absence is, in fact, a classical tragedy in its form. Jones, consciously or unconsciously, has structured his story in accordance with the principles set out by Aristotle in his *Poetics*. Hester's self-delusions lead her to teach her two sons what she considers to be old southern family values. These lessons, learned all too well by the younger son, lead him to the brutal killing of a young black activist. That her pride stints her virtues is symbolized by her older son's involvement with a family of self-righteous liberals who move to town from the North.

When the tragic reversal comes, some of the scales drop from Hester Glenn's eyes. She achieves the same kind of familial nobility of which Cassandra bitterly complains just before her death in Aeschylus's *Agamemnon*. Hester's younger son's crime leads her to achieve only partial awareness, a dangerous thing. It leads her to cause her son's suicide and to pay for it with her own suicide. At the end she still has too much hubris to put her fate into the hands of the gods. Like Clytemnestra, she must exact her own unlawful and sinful vengeance. Her tragedy is that she never knows herself and removes herself from the redeeming pain. She never achieves the ultimate insights of an Orestes.

Though the final scene has a haunting beauty achieved by the power of the prose, *Passage through Gehenna* is less successful than its predecessors. The characters are not as sharply drawn, and it is not a novel but a romance, an allegory about the corruption of innocence and the power of grace working through blood sacrifice. As in William Faulkner's *A Fable* (1954), the characterizations suffer because they are more abstractions of ideas or allegorizations than characters.

In a 1983 interview with David K. Jeffrey and Donald R. Noble, Jones said about *Passage through Gehenna,* "in the earlier books my goal had at least something to do with a cultural situation. I do, of course, try to create in that book the culture insofar as it relates to character. But *Passage* is pretty much what I set out to make it . . . a more cold-blooded attempt to deal with a bare confrontation of good and evil, of innocence and guilt."

Young Jud Rivers, who too early in his life renounced the sins of the flesh, is almost completely consumed by his own self-righteousness. Jud meets an unholy trinity consisting of a seductive older woman, Lily; a young hedonist, Meagher; and the town prostitute, Dorcas Poole, called Goldie. These three seduce him away from asceticism into sin, materialism, and crime. With them he falls into a wasteland. Not until he is saved through the grace of Hannah, a young woman who literally dies for his sins, is he redeemed out of Gehenna, which in this book is a combination of Christian hell (the place of damnation), Jewish Sheol (the place where he must suffer, learn, and pass through), and the classical underworld (a dreamlike world through which he moves unthinkingly, like a sleepwalker). The image of passing through Gehenna is highly appropriate for a book that chronicles a boy's coming of age, a romance in which plot and character development are subordinate to theme.

Though the publisher called it a novel in an attempt to boost sales, *Season of the Strangler* (1982) is really a group of interconnected short stories. It could be called a novel only in the sense that Sherwood Anderson's *Winesburg, Ohio* (1919) could be called a novel. The twelve powerfully written and beautifully constructed stories are interconnected. Together they tell a larger story.

Season of the Strangler is based loosely on an actual series of murders known as the Columbus (Georgia) strangler case. In Jones's adaptation of those terrible serial killings in 1969, five women are strangled in their beds in the little town of Okaloosa, Alabama. The crimes engulf the town in fear, straining family and racial tensions. These tensions cause the various people whose stories are told to examine their lives. All of them find that death and separation have strangled more lives in the city than the unknown killer. They have their memories, either overwhelming – strangling, to use the same metaphor – or inadequate to overcome the meaninglessness in their own dark souls. *Season of the Strangler,* in addition to being a gripping story, is a powerful examination of the racial, social, moral, religious, and philosophical tensions in modern America and deserves a wider audience.

Last Things (1989) is set in the New South, where whatever improvements the region carries are offset by drugs, the vehicle of destruction. The external danger is the disintegration of society; the internal danger is the failure of will; the eternal danger is the failure to separate the active from the passive self. This is a separation deemed nonexistent by the thinkers of the Western Enlightenment but deemed essential by Jones. Elsewhere Jones has written what could be taken for the theme of *Last Things:* "We are children of the Enlightenment, a movement promising among other things to replace with pure reason the darkness that has misguided traditional thinking." This has led to "moral relativism and finally cynicism. . . . The consequence of this condition, notably the disintegration of community, grows more apparent daily in our society." The novel concerns the disintegration of Wendell Corbin, who quickly becomes an adulterer, pusher, and murderer. The old woman he kills represents the old values and morals the modern world has cast away.

Jones has published a chapter of a forthcoming novel, "To the Winds," in the summer 1992 issue of *Sewanee Review,* where it won the Lytle Prize for short fiction. Two more chapters have appeared as short stories in *Oxford American Magazine*. He expects the novel to be published in 1995.

Readers have been surprised by the humorous nature of these chapters. Although those who know Jones personally have always valued his considerable wit and dry sense of humor, it is quite a change in direction for him to exhibit these traits in his published fiction. Although in the early 1970s he worked on a comic novel, he abandoned the project, in part because he was not entirely comfortable with the comic genre. Before and since, his vision has always been dark. After ninety lighthearted pages, "To the Winds" also returns to darkness.

The story is set in the 1950s, when a poor tenant farmer is trying to work ninety acres in Tennessee to keep his family of eight children fed. He is a good man, affectionate and kind, but has many strikes against him, not the least of which is that he is worthless as a worker and practical thinker. In fact, the only practical member of the family is the fourth son, who is always getting the family out of one comic scrape or another.

When Clarence, a long-lost uncle, shows up, Jones abandons the comic high ground. Soon the sheriff arrives to say that Clarence is wanted for murder. If the family harbors him they will be open to prosecution. If they turn him in they will violate their principles of family loyalty. After much debate the family decides to build Clarence a lean-to in the deep woods and to bring him food.

One of the brothers, Dud, sees in his uncle a way out of the family's financial troubles. He tells the sheriff where his uncle is hiding after exacting the sheriff's promise to give Dud the reward money. The sheriff hunts down Clarence with hounds and deputies. The uncle is wounded in the chase and dies a few days later in the prison hospital.

The sheriff, who represents the corrupting influence of human experience, will not give Dud the reward, which starts more family arguments. When Dud threatens to expose the sheriff's corruption, the sheriff in turn arrests him but then allows Dud to escape. But because he, like the other children, is so home loving, he sneaks back to the family farm.

Dud is shot, nearly captured by the sheriff, and found in the woods by hippies who nurse him and tell his youngest brother (who narrates the story, a new technique for a Jones novel) about Dud's mortal wound. The youngest brother rushes to see Dud and bring him home, but Dud dies before he can be moved.

Another brother, Coop, also intent on raising the family's sunken fortunes, tries to steal money from an old fortune-teller who makes her real money selling drugs. He ends up killing her in self-defense, but the sheriff begins to suspect Coop and comes to arrest him. When Coop, the only member of the family with practical sense, runs the sheriff through with a pitchfork and escapes, the disintegration of the family is accelerated.

This novel, like the eight that preceded it, reiterates Jones's dark observation that not only will innocence always be corrupted by experience but that the innocent deserve some blame for their ignorance of the reality of evil.

Interview:

David K. Jeffrey and Donald R. Noble, "Madison Jones: An Interview," *Southern Quarterly,* 21 (Spring 1983): 5–26.

References:

M. E. Bradford, "Madison Jones," in *The History of Southern Literature,* edited by Louis D. Rubin Jr. and others (Baton Rouge & London: Louisiana State University Press, 1985), pp. 523–526;

Sandy Cohen, "Images of Allegory: Madison Jones's *Passage through Gehenna,*" *South Atlantic Review,* 53 (January 1988): 67–81;

Monroe K. Spears, "A New Classic," *Sewanee Review,* 80 (January–March 1972): 168–172.

Erica Jong

(26 March 1942 –   )

Cynthia Tompkins
Arizona State University West

See also the Jong entries in *DLB 2: American Novelists Since World War II, DLB 5: American Poets Since World War II,* and *DLB 28: Twentieth-Century American-Jewish Fiction Writers.*

BOOKS: *Fruits & Vegetables* (New York, Chicago & San Francisco: Holt, Rinehart & Winston, 1971; London: Secker & Warburg, 1973);
Half-Lives (New York, Chicago & San Francisco: Holt, Rinehart & Winston, 1973; London: Secker & Warburg, 1974);
Fear of Flying (New York, Chicago & San Francisco: Holt, Rinehart & Winston, 1973; London: Secker & Warburg, 1974);
Here Comes & Other Poems (New York: New American Library, 1975);
Loveroot (New York: Holt, Rinehart & Winston, 1975; London: Secker & Warburg, 1977);
The Poetry of Erica Jong, 3 volumes (New York: Holt, Rinehart & Winston, 1976);
How to Save Your Own Life (New York: Holt, Rinehart & Winston, 1977; London: Secker & Warburg, 1977);
Selected Poems, 2 volumes (London: Panther, 1977, 1980);
At the Edge of the Body (New York: Holt, Rinehart & Winston, 1979);
Fanny: Being the True History of the Adventures of Fanny Hackabout-Jones (New York: New American Library, 1980; London: Granada, 1980);
Witches (New York: Abrams, 1981; London & New York: Granada, 1982);
Ordinary Miracles (New York: New American Library, 1983);
Megan's Book of Divorce: A Kid's Book for Adults (New York: New American Library, 1984);
Parachutes & Kisses (New York: New American Library, 1984; London: Granada, 1984);
Serenissima: A Novel of Venice (Boston: Houghton Mifflin, 1987; London: Bantam, 1987);
Any Woman's Blues (New York: Harper & Row, 1990);

Becoming Light: Poems, New and Selected (New York: HarperCollins, 1991);
The Devil at Large: Erica Jong on Henry Miller (New York: Random House, 1993);
Fear of Fifty: A Midlife Memoir (New York: HarperCollins, 1994).

PLAY PRODUCTION: *Fanny Hackabout-Jones,* by Jong and Susan Birkenhead, music by Lucy Simon, Long Wharf Theatre, New Haven, Conn., 4 June 1991.

OTHER: *Four Visions of America,* by Jong, Thomas Sanchez, Kay Boyle, and Henry Miller (Santa Barbara: Capra Press, 1977).

SELECTED PERIODICAL PUBLICATIONS – UNCOLLECTED: "Fear of Flirting," *Washington Post,* 6 December 1992, pp. C1–C4;
"Conspiracy of Silence," *New York Times,* 10 February 1993, p. 23;
"Liberté, Egalité, Sexualité!," *Playboy,* 40 (March 1993): 78ff;
"Sex Play," *Lear's* (November 1993): 59–60.

Erica Jong is primarily known for her six best-selling novels: *Fear of Flying* (1973), with twelve and a half million copies in print; *How to Save Your Own Life* (1977); *Fanny: Being the True History of the Adventures of Fanny Hackabout-Jones* (1980); *Parachutes & Kisses* (1984); *Serenissima: A Novel of Venice* (1987); and *Any Woman's Blues* (1990). In addition, Jong, who began her literary career as a poet, has published six collections: *Fruits & Vegetables* (1971); *Half-Lives* (1973), which received the Di Castagnola Award of the Poetry Society of America; *Loveroot* (1975); *At the Edge of the Body* (1979); *Ordinary Miracles* (1983); and *Becoming Light: Poems, New and Selected* (1991). She has also received the American Academy of Poets Award (1963), the Bess Hokin Prize from *Poetry* magazine (1971), the Borestone Mountain Award for Poetry (1971), the Premio In-

Erica Jong (photograph by Nigel Parry)

ternationale Sigmund Freud of Italy (1979), and the United Nations Society of Writers Award of Excellence (1994). Barnard College named her its Woman of Achievement in 1987, and from 1991 to 1993 she served as president of the Authors' Guild of the United States. Her works have been translated into twenty-seven languages, suggesting that they travel well and that her rapport with her audience is not culturally bound.

The second daughter of a painter mother, Eda Mirsky, and a musician-turned-businessman father, Seymour Mann, Jong was born on 26 March 1942 and grew up on the Upper West Side of Manhattan. As an undergraduate at Barnard College, she edited its literary magazine and produced poetry programs for the campus radio station. In 1965 she completed her M.A. in eighteenth-century literature at Columbia University. She eventually dropped out of the Ph.D. program to devote herself entirely to writing, but her fascination with the eighteenth-century novel would resurface in *Fanny*.

Fear of Flying, like many of Jong's other novels, includes obvious autobiographical elements. For in-

stance, Isadora Wing of *Fear of Flying* and Jong attended the High School of Music and Art, Barnard College, and the writing division of the School of the Arts at Columbia. Moreover, both had married – Isadora to Brian and Jong to Michael Werthman – before becoming involved with psychiatrists of Chinese descent. Finally, both Isadora and her creator taught English at the City College of New York before moving to Heidelberg, Germany, military posts where their drafted husbands were stationed. Jong has responded differently at different times to the charge of an extensive autobiographical dimension to her fiction, sometimes denying it, at other times admitting it.

Notorious at the time of its publication for its erotic content, *Fear of Flying* inspired many women to accept and even acknowledge their sexual fantasies, as Joan Reardon has analyzed. While John Updike's blurb on the novel's jacket promised "the most uninhibited, delicious, erotic novel a woman ever wrote," Jong perceived the book's now-famous "zipless fuck" as "a platonic ideal [in which] zippers fell away like rose petals, underwear blew off . . .

Jong in the early 1970s, at the time of her best-selling novel Fear of
Flying *(photograph by Peter Trump)*

like dandelion fluff. Tongues intertwined and turned liquid." *Fear of Flying* would foreshadow the boom of erotic literature produced by Latin American women writers in the 1980s.

Among the recurring themes in Jong's fiction is the plight of the female artist. In *Fear of Flying* Isadora's mother concisely states the dilemma of the female artist: "Women cannot possibly do both . . . you've got to choose. Either be an artist or have children." Isadora retorts, "With a name like Isadora Zelda it was clear what I was supposed to choose." Since she defines herself in terms of men, her lovers guide her along her quest for selfhood. Brian's "verbal pyrotechnics" and poetic worldview influence her desire to write; Bennett Wing's solitude and silence show her how to listen to her inner voice; and the idealized Adrian forces her, according to Reardon, "to salvage her life, hit rock bottom, and climb back up again."

Isadora attempts to discover herself by traveling through Europe, only to acknowledge in retrospect that the tour had been nothing more than "desperation and depression masquerading as freedom." She thus confronts her demons: "I was trapped by my own fears. Motivating everything was the terror of being alone." Her epiphany – "I wanted to lose myself in a man . . . to be transported

to heaven on borrowed wings" – reinforces her new resolution to put an end to "this nonsense of running from one man to the next [by standing] on [her] own two feet for once."

The process of rebirth in uncovering her previously buried identity involves analyzing journal entries on her marriage, examining her physical self in order to rekindle creativity as well as to reclaim identity – "every poem is an attempt to extend the boundaries of one's body. One's body becomes the landscape, the sky, and finally the cosmos" – and acknowledging the female tradition in literature. At one point, for instance, Isadora dreams that she is making love to the French author Colette in public. Analyzing the effect of Isadora's dream, Arlyn Diamond suggests that "the act of public affirmation of love for a woman, a writer, might be a way for Isadora to imagine a commitment to herself as poet, and a rejection of her former male-centered view of herself. . . ." Throughout the novel physiological cycles contribute to the discovery of selfhood. For instance, she says that "menstruation was always a little sad – but it was also a new beginning." Isadora does attain a higher level of awareness: "whatever happened, I knew I could survive it. I knew, above all, that I'd go on working. Surviving meant being born over and over. It wasn't easy, and it was al-

Cover for the first paperback edition of Fear of Flying, *Jong's
controversial novel about a woman's sexual self-discovery*

ways painful. But there wasn't any other choice except death."

Jong begins *How to Save Your Own Life* by chronicling the traumatic experience of Isadora's divorce, perhaps an echo of the novelist's separation from Allan Jong in 1975. There are other obvious autobiographical elements in the novel, including the author's retaliation for a bad review as well as her references to a never-produced movie adaptation of her best-selling book. Finally, the novel's reference to Jeannie Morton's suicide parallels Anne Sexton's, and the allusion to Kurt Hammer's struggle against censorship evokes Henry Miller's.

How to Save Your Own Life explores the ambiguity that results from the close interrelationship between experience and imagination through the persona of writer Isadora Wing, creator of writer Can-

dida Wong – the protagonist, in turn, of the best-selling *Candida Confesses*. As Isadora says:

> I had modeled Candida after myself, yet she was more and less than the real Isadora. . . . Yet my public insisted on an exact equivalency between her and me – because my heroine . . . had turned out to be amanuensis to the Zeitgeist. . . . Millions of copies later, I began to wonder whether I had created Candida or whether she had, in fact, created me.

In *How to Save Your Own Life* Jong continues, according to critic Robert J. Butler, to equate "life with motion and stasis with death"; analysis again plays a major role. The novel portrays the body as the site of memory ("I could tell the story of my life through the scars that mark my body"); and it emphasizes sexual experimentation, including a chal-

Jong in 1980 (photograph © Thomas Victor)

lenging lesbian relationship and an orgy. Isadora's divorce enables Jong simultaneously to chronicle her protagonist's emotional stages and her attempts to relate to other characters. The suicide of her friend, the "housewife/poet," shocks her into taking control of her life. The novel concludes with Isadora's being offered a fresh start with Josh, her young lover from the West Coast.

Jong's expertise on the eighteenth century comes alive with gusto in *Fanny: Being the True History of the Adventures of Fanny Hackabout-Jones.* Jong's Fanny Hill purportedly intends, in writing her autobiography, to answer John Cleland's slanderous version of her life in his *Memoirs of a Woman of Pleasure* (1748–1749), also known as *Fanny Hill.* Comparing these two texts, critic Mary Anne Ferguson remarks:

> Fanny neither abhors sex nor is reticent about it. From her earliest sexual experience – rape by her foster-father – she is able to distinguish between violence and true sexuality, between her love for her raper in his fatherly role and despair at his brutality. Thus Fanny starts with knowledge that separates her from the stereotype of sexual woman as masochistic and insatiable, an image emphasized in the famous 18th-century pornographic novel *Fanny Hill,* which Jong's *Fanny* parodies.

However, in keeping with the generic conventions of the picaresque tradition, according to critic James Mandrell, as Fanny looks "back over the course of her life [she] begins to convert herself into a literary character." Furthermore, the rewriting "for another woman of a canonical text of female pleasure written by a man for men" is reflected in Jong's cross-generational dedication in the afterword to her mother and daughter.

A feminist perspective is present in *Fanny* through a subplot concerning mother/daughter relationships. Since the generic conventions of the picaresque novel are conflated with those of the adventure novel, the plot is riddled with implausible coincidences, such as the reappearance of her mother, Alice, whom she had left for dead and who saves her by performing a cesarean section in defiance of the male establishment.

Jong portrays Fanny as a "very modern wench in eighteenth century dress," with her success depending on her courage. Ultimately, the novel's happy ending is contingent upon a major shift in the history of consciousness, since Jong suggests, according to Ferguson, that "women will succeed as women only in a world which values female wisdom."

After the break represented by *Fanny,* Jong returned to charting the development of Isadora that

Dust jacket for Jong's fourth novel about writer Isadora Wing, who was introduced in Fear of Flying

began with *Fear of Flying* and continued in *How to Save Your Own Life.* Jong has said:

> The reason I don't lie about my age is because I feel that if I am going to chronicle the stages of a woman's life honestly, the stages are different — different at 49 than at 39 or 29. It's always been my desire to be honest and to write the big book, the lifelong book about women that doesn't yet exist. I have to be honest about the place I'm at.

Parachutes & Kisses chronicles the plight of Isadora at thirty-nine, now a successful writer who happens to be a middle-aged baby boomer, a divorcée, and a single parent. "Possessed of a demoniacal sexuality — which has no need to justify itself with love," she looks back and concludes that a fundamental change has taken place in society: "For one thing, there is more oral sex. For another, more impotence. For a third, sex is ubiquitous and yet also

somehow devoid of its full charge of mystery. For a fourth, the world is definitely lurching to its end."

At times Isadora is self-congratulatory about the influence of her writing: the "book she wrote about [taking] off from Bennett Wing and running around with Adrian Goodlove gave women everywhere permission to do the same." Yet to a degree she also regrets her success: " 'That book of hers' haunts her. . . . On the one hand, *Candida Confesses* made her a 'household word.' . . . On the other, it bestowed upon her unsuspecting youth a strange sort of sexual smirch. Many people could see her only as the nymphomaniac of the literary world." Having completed the triangular path successful writers, actors, and media figures sometimes travel — Manhattan, Malibu, New England — Isadora settles down in Connecticut.

Echoes of confessional and self-help books appear in *Parachutes & Kisses,* as in this passage: "For the more she gave him, the more depressed he became, yet the more powerless she was to stop giving. It was as if she were desperate to make up the disparity between them – the disparity in ages, incomes, and power [because] she feels guilty about it, and he feels cheated." Her ultimate breakthrough is heralded by a reinterpretation of the Sleeping Beauty story, which is prompted by her daughter's question, "Mama – what if the Prince *doesn't* come?" Isadora replies, "Well then, darling, she just kisses herself and wakes *herself* up."

By focusing on the creative process, the novel becomes self-reflective. Isadora admits that writing is a lonely and increasingly difficult endeavor. During a trip to Russia intended for research on her painter grandfather's past in order to allow her to reclaim her roots, Isadora concludes that she need no longer search for his lost painting because she contains her identity in herself. Once again, and as in *How to Save Your Own Life, Parachutes & Kisses* concludes by offering Isadora a fresh start, this time by meeting Bean, a fellow sensation seeker, in Venice.

In *Parachutes & Kisses* intertextuality with the earlier Isadora novels can be detected in the protagonist's recollections about her pregnancy, a period during which she bloomed physically ("a radiant pink-cheeked blonde, with gray-blue eyes and enough life-force for three women") and intellectually ("she researched and wrote and wrote, and wrote and researched *Tintoretto's Daughter*"). These allusions were also echoed in the afterword to *Fanny*, where, in addition to thanking Jonathan Fast for having read the manuscript and for the suggestions she incorporated into the text, Jong points out that both "he and Lula Johnson took excellent care of . . . Molly [who in turn] helped by being the most amiable and unfretful of babies – born as she was between pages 303 and 304!" Moreover, both Fanny and Isadora undergo cesareans. Similarities may also be drawn between Isadora and her creator, since each divorces her third husband (Josh and Jonathan Fast), both of whom happen to be writers.

In 1987 Jong published *Serenissima: A Novel of Venice*, which focuses on the story of Jessica Pruitt, a beautiful actress who arrives in Venice and falls through a crack in time and finds herself in the sixteenth century, where she meets a young Will Shakespeare. Besides judging a film festival, Jessica has journeyed to Venice in order to come to terms with her mother's suicide, which took place in Venice years before, as well as with her own middle age and an absence of direction in her life. The novel's period setting allows her to become the inspiration for Shakespeare's sonnets to the Dark Lady as well as for Jessica, the daughter of Shylock in *The Merchant of Venice*. Jong, who identifies Virginia Woolf's

Orlando (1928) as the source of inspiration for *Serenissima*, argues that she attempted to convey the sense of living in the past, the present, and the future. Like Jong and many of her characters, Jessica is also a bright woman seeking wholeness in a society that limits women either to intelligence or physicality.

The familiar relationship between biography and fiction in Jong's work reappears in her next novel, *Any Woman's Blues*. As she revealed in an unpublished 1991 interview with Charlotte Templin:

> For me the turning point in my life, as in Leila's, . . . was when I began to enjoy my own solitude. I used to go to the country and sit alone and read, and walk, and write. . . . I had just come out of an abusive relationship, not so unlike the relationship in *Any Woman's Blues*, although that one is an exaggerated version of it – but I decided that if I never had another relationship with a man it wouldn't matter because I had found something in myself that was so profoundly fulfilling that I could live by myself forever.

The structure of *Any Woman's Blues* resembles a system of Chinese boxes, demanding active participation by the reader. In the novel's foreword the literary executrix of the late Isadora Wing, Caryl Fleishmann-Stanger, explains:

> *Any Woman's Blues, a conventional roman à clef about an artist called Leila Sand (who, at the outset of the book, is at once battling alcoholism and a sadomasochistic obsession with a much younger man), is punctuated passim with the interruptions of Isadora Wing arguing with Leila Sand (the author arguing with the protagonist – with herself, in short), which suggests the life that flowed alongside the novel.*

However, the foreword is repudiated in the afterword: "*Whatever Caryl Fleishmann-Stanger, Ph.D. may or may not have told you about 'me' or my 'last' novel, I am not dead, but back – I, Isadora White Stollerman Wing, alias Leila Sand, Louise Zandberg, Candida Wong, La Tintoretta, Antonia Ucello, und so weiter.*"

In addition to frame narratives that cancel each other out, characterization itself becomes a self-destructive category in *Any Woman's Blues*. For instance, the biographical sketch offered by Fleishmann-Stanger is undermined by Isadora: "*whether I am Leila, Isadora, Louise, Caryl, or even someone neither of us knows, is of the sheerest unimportance. All of these are merely masks . . . merely there to facilitate our understanding.*" Moreover, Fleishmann-Stanger's quoting of the interview Isadora granted in 1987 on the blurring of the lines between "reality" and fiction – "one tends to subsume in a book one is writing all the conflicts one is trying to resolve at a particular time" – can be read as a satire of literary critics who tackle the unwieldy genre of literary biography. Since in it the *"search for a way out of addictive love and toward real self-love"* is coupled with a penchant for *"the integration of body and mind,"* *Any Woman's Blues* proves to be a climactic point in the thematic struggle toward self-discovery that runs throughout Jong's novels.

The succès de scandale of *Fear of Flying* has tended to obscure the impact of Jong's poetry. However, critics such as Benjamin Franklin V, Ferguson, and Templin have devoted attention to it. Her most recent volume of poems, *Becoming Light: Poems, New and Selected,* appeared in 1991. Jong, among others, has noticed that issues tend to appear first in her poetry and then reappear in her fiction. Seeing the poet in a shamanic role as "the mediator between life and death," according to Templin, Jong has, says Ferguson, "from the beginning . . . shown an awareness of spiritual depths." Similarly, Ferguson continues, "her characteristic technical innovation, her concern for women's experience, and her wit are evident even in her teenage works." All of her work stresses the total female experience.

Jong's *The Devil at Large: Erica Jong on Henry Miller* (1993) is framed by the friendship that began with Miller's enthusiastic letter praising *Fear of Flying* in 1974. Though some critics have objected to the text's mixture of genres (Walter Kendrick attacking it as a confused mixture of biography, memoir, collection of letters, critical study, and soapbox rant), other reviewers point out her credibility in defending Miller in her admission that she could not help hating him, even after enjoying his company, for his "sexism, his narcissism, his jibes at Jews." However, she found his concern with spiritual discovery through physical pleasure sympathetic.

Jong's popularity is augmented by her academic reputation, which is on the rise, as documented by the steady increase in articles and dissertations on her work. A special session of the 1994 Modern Language Association conference, "Twenty Years of Feminism: Erica Jong's *Fear of Flying* as a Window on the History of a Political Movement," was well attended. Finally, Jong's place in the canon was addressed in Templin's *Feminism and the Politics of Literary Reputation: The Example of Erica Jong* (1995).

At present Jong is the mother of a teenage daughter. Married to Kenneth David Burrowes, an attorney, Jong, with her family, divides her time between Manhattan, Connecticut, Vermont, and Italy. Her most recent book is a best-selling memoir, *Fear of Fifty* (1994), and her essays on current issues make her a popular interpreter of and advocate for women.

Bibliography:

Charlotte Templin, *Feminism and the Politics of Literary Reputation: The Example of Erica Jong* (Lawrence: University Press of Kansas, 1995), pp. 205–220.

References:

Francis Baumli, "Erica Jong Revisited (or) No Wonder We Men Had Trouble Understanding Feminism," *University of Dayton Review,* 17 (Winter 1985–1986): 91–95;

John Bembrose, "Tropic of Eros: A Feminist Praises Henry Miller's Candor," *McLean's,* 106 (29 March 1993): 44;

Robert J. Butler, "Woman Writer as American Pícaro: Open Journeying in Erica Jong's *Fear of Flying,*" *Centennial Review,* 31 (Summer 1987): 308–329;

Arlyn Diamond, "Flying from Work," *Frontiers,* 2, no. 3 (1977): 18–23;

Mary Anne Ferguson, "The Female Novel of Development and the Myth of Psyche," *Denver Quarterly,* 17 (Winter 1983): 58–74;

Walter Kendrick, "Her Master's Voice," *New York Times Book Review* (14 February 1993): 10–11;

James Mandrell, "Questions of Genre and Gender: Contemporary American Versions of the Feminine Picaresque," *Novel,* 20 (Winter 1987): 149–170;

Gerald Nicosia, "A Grand Old Man of Lust and Letters," *Washington Post,* 6 June 1993, "Book World" section, pp. 4–5;

Joan Reardon, "*Fear of Flying:* Developing the Feminist Novel," *International Journal of Women's Studies,* 1 (May–June 1978): 306–320;

Charlotte Templin, *Feminism and the Politics of Literary Reputation: The Example of Erica Jong* (Lawrence: University Press of Kansas, 1995);

Templin, "Sources for the Aging Midget Cum Literary Critic in Erica Jong's *How to Save Your Own Life,*" *Notes on Contemporary Literature,* 21 (January 1991): 12.

Bernard Malamud

(26 April 1914 – 18 March 1986)

Joel Salzberg
University of Colorado at Denver

See also the Malamud entries in *DLB 2: American Novelists Since World War II, First Series; DLB 28: Twentieth-Century American-Jewish Fiction Writers; DLB Yearbook: 1980;* and *DLB Yearbook: 1986.*

BOOKS: *The Natural* (New York: Harcourt, Brace, 1952; London: Eyre & Spottiswoode, 1963);

The Assistant (New York: Farrar, Straus & Cudahy, 1957; London: Eyre & Spottiswoode, 1959);

The Magic Barrel (New York: Farrar, Straus & Cudahy, 1958; London: Eyre & Spottiswoode, 1960);

A New Life (New York: Farrar, Straus & Cudahy, 1961; London: Eyre & Spottiswoode, 1961);

Idiots First (New York: Farrar, Straus, 1963; London: Eyre & Spottiswoode, 1964);

The Fixer (New York: Farrar, Straus & Giroux, 1966; London: Eyre & Spottiswoode, 1967);

Pictures of Fidelman: An Exhibition (New York: Farrar, Straus & Giroux, 1969; London: Eyre & Spottiswoode, 1969);

The Tenants (New York: Farrar, Straus & Giroux, 1971; London: Eyre Methuen, 1972);

Rembrandt's Hat (New York: Farrar, Straus & Giroux, 1973; London: Eyre Methuen, 1973);

Dubin's Lives (New York: Farrar, Straus & Giroux, 1979; London: Chatto & Windus, 1979);

God's Grace (New York: Farrar, Straus & Giroux, 1982; London: Chatto & Windus, 1982);

The Stories of Bernard Malamud (New York: Farrar, Straus & Giroux, 1983; London: Chatto & Windus, 1984).

Editions and Collections: *A Malamud Reader,* edited, with an introduction, by Philip Rhav (New York: Farrar, Straus & Giroux, 1967; London: Chatto & Windus, 1982);

The People and Uncollected Stories, edited, with an introduction, by Robert Giroux (New York: Farrar, Straus & Giroux, 1989; London: Chatto & Windus, 1989).

Bernard Malamud, along with Saul Bellow and Philip Roth, holds a preeminence among Jewish American writers that has consistently been reaffirmed by recent critical assessments. Early in Malamud criticism, Alfred Kazin and Leslie Fiedler acknowledged the richness of Malamud's literary imagination in their responses to *The Assistant* (1957) – Kazin had praised Malamud in his review "Fantasist of the Ordinary" for his vivid characterization of his suffering schlemiels, and Fiedler's review "The Commonplace as Absurd" observed that the gray lives of Malamud's characters had their own kind of poetry. Over thirty years later, just after *The Stories of Bernard Malamud* (1983) appeared, Mark Shechner in "Malamud: The Still Sad Music" (reprinted in Joel Salzberg's *Critical Essays on Bernard Malamud,* 1987) compared Malamud's melancholic voice to the bleak pre-Holocaust photographs collected in Roman Vishnic's *Polish Jews* (1947):

> In his modest and laconic style of narrative, Malamud has found the exact prose equivalent of the dull light and gray tones of Vishniac's world, a world exhausted by siege and conscious of defeat.... *Collected Stories* is a book of mourning, an anthology, one might say of elegies. Even where there is no death, characters cloak themselves in talliths and recite Kaddishes for the living, as Salzman the matchmaker does for his client, Leo Finkle, in "The Magic Barrel" and Kessler the egg candler and Gruber the landlord do for themselves at the end of "The Mourners." Malamud has written stories of other kinds but has selected these for reissue, as if to honor that region of his imagination that is most accustomed to grief. The singularity of this grieving marks the book as a testament, a memorial, we may suppose, to the world that disappeared into the crematoria of Auschwitz, the memory hole of Russia, the suburbs of America. This book, then, is an act of Yiskor, an admonition to remember.

Like other Jewish American writers haunted by the experiences of their immigrant parents – a state of mind not exclusive to Jewish American writers

Bernard Malamud (photograph by John Bragg)

alone – Malamud's subject matter and themes were anchored in memories of the family past. The oldest son of Max (Mendel) and Bertha Malamud (née Fidelman), Bernard Malamud was born on 26 April 1914 at Williamsburg Hospital in Brooklyn to parents who had fled Czarist Russia separately and who subsequently met in the United States between 1905 and 1910. Eventually settling in the Gravesend section of Brooklyn, they became the owners of a barely surviving grocery-delicatessen. In their lives, Malamud found, the "solidity of specification" for many of his earliest characters, as well as his primal themes of gratuitous failure and suffering. These twin themes became for the author, moreover, a virtual obsession and found their way into many of Malamud's earliest short stories – as, for example, "The Armistice" (1940), "The Grocery Store" (1943), "The Place is Different Now" (*American Preface,* Spring 1943), "The Cost of Living" (*Harper's Bazaar,* March 1950), "The Bill" (*Commentary,* April 1951), and "Take Pity" (1956). As incremental repetitions of a past always present in Malamud's imagination, they achieve their artistic apotheosis in *The Assistant.*

Although the grief in Malamud's earliest stories is largely related to the futile and enervating quest of his own family for economic survival, three

critical events in the author's life intimate a subtext of suffering throughout his work for which there are no "objective correlatives" – or only the barest hints of them: the death of Bertha Malamud when Bernard was fifteen; his transformation into an unhappy stepson with a thin family life when his father remarried; and, according to his wife, Ann Malamud, the gradual assumption of moral and, later, financial responsibility for his handicapped brother Eugene.

If the grocery store and the neighborhood were living texts whose lessons he never forgot, there was also the more academic side to his education. After he completed grammar school at P. S. 181 in Brooklyn, Malamud went on to Erasmus High School and wrote short stories for the literary magazine *The Erasmian.* Similar to the journey made by other sons of immigrant Jews from the neighborhood ghetto to the city beyond, Malamud attended the City College of New York and received his B.A. degree in 1936, completing as well an M.A. degree in literature at Columbia University in 1942. His thesis, "Thomas Hardy's Reputation as a Poet in American Periodicals," while remote from the subject matter of his earliest work, served nonetheless as a momentary act of Emersonian self-improvement. In his autobiographical memoir *Long*

Work, Short Life, (1985) Malamud recalls his life as a graduate student in literature at Columbia: "I told myself what I was doing was worthwhile; for no one who spends his nights and days devoted to great works of literature will be wasting his time as a writer, if he is passionate to write." Economic constraints rather than the academic life was for Malamud the major obstacle to living the true life of the writer. Between 1939 and 1940 his desire to become totally self-supporting led to his becoming a teacher at Lafayette High School, but in the spring of 1940 he moved to Washington, D.C., where he obtained a position in the civil service. In that same year he received an appointment to teach evening courses as a "permanent substitute" at Erasmus High School to students who were for the most part recent immigrants.

While Malamud was attempting to balance night classes in New York and the writing of a first novel, "The Light Sleeper," which he eventually burned because he felt it was not good enough, he met Ann de Chiara, a woman of Italian descent, whom he married in 1945 after a three-year courtship. Her ethnic background added to Malamud's own knowledge of the Italian American experience, as well as helping him to become acquainted with the language and mores of Italian life for those of his stories situated in Italy. Marriage, however, brought with it new economic responsibilities during the time when he was still learning his craft. Feeling that college teaching would allow him more time for writing fiction, Malamud applied for a position teaching English at Oregon State College and was hired to teach freshman composition. In 1949 he left the New York high-school system and made Corvallis, Oregon, his home until 1961, the year he joined the Division of Languages and Literature at Bennington College in Vermont. His years at Oregon State College, however, were among the most productive in his career, nurturing such works as *The Natural* (1952), *The Assistant, The Magic Barrel* (1958), and *A New Life* (1961). Despite his new life in the pastoral innocence of the West, Malamud's imagination was still deeply obsessed with the settings and themes associated with the neighborhood of his youth. In his introduction to *The Stories of Bernard Malamud,* Malamud recalls the initially strained relationship with his father over his marriage to Ann de Chiara: "He [Malamud's father] had sat in mourning when I married my gentile wife, but I had thought it through and felt I knew what I was doing. After the birth of our son my father came gently to greet my wife and touch his grandchild. I thought of him as I began *The Assistant* and felt I

would be writing about Jews, in celebration and expiation, though perhaps that was having it both ways."

Despite the lack of a fully detailed biography and the unlikelihood that one will be available in the near future — Janna Malamud Smith, the daughter of Ann and Bernard Malamud, has been the chief family spokesman against one — the reader can discover a good deal about the author from his interviews and letters. Of particular interest are Malamud's letters to Harvey Swados and John Hawkes, written in the 1960s and 1970s, and a remarkably frank correspondence between Malamud and Rosemarie Beck, a New York–based artist, running intermittently from 1958 through 1985. These diverse sources reveal Malamud's disciplined commitment to the art of fiction, his sensitivity to public scrutiny, his oscillation between amiability and dourness, and the value he placed on some of his literary friendships.

While Malamud's literary influences — as, for example, Nathaniel Hawthorne, Henry James, Ernest Hemingway, James Joyce, Thomas Mann, Franz Kafka, Sholom Aleichem, and I. L. Peretz — invariably are reflected in his themes and literary strategies, the theme of self-transcendence bears his unique signature. Influenced as well by the ethical ideals of Judaism and Christianity, Malamud synthesizes them into his general theme of self-transcendence, which is imaginatively incorporated into character and plot almost throughout his entire canon. The following works are illustrative: Frank Alpine's desire in *The Assistant* to change his life; Abramowitz's attempts in "The Talking Horse" to discover whether he is a horse or a man inside a horse; and Calvin Cohn's efforts in *God's Grace* (1982) to evolve from a lower primate to a higher form of nature. For Malamud self-transcendence became the trait that defines humankind and is at the very center of his ethical vision. Expectedly, the various permutations of this theme have stimulated the major studies on Malamud in the 1960s and 1970s, represented by the work of Sidney Richman, Theodore Solatoroff, Robert Alter, Ben Siegel, Sanford Pinsker, and Sheldon Norman Grebstein, among others.

Although Malamud began publishing stories about poor Jews, Italians, and even nominal Irish characters in the 1940s, his first novel, *The Natural,* is on its surface an expression of an acculturated Bernard Malamud who, while growing up near Ebbets Field, became interested in the Brooklyn Dodgers and the lore of American baseball; at the same time it is also an expression of the learnedness of Bernard Malamud as City College student, who became interested in the Grail legend, and the ramifications of it, through his reading of Jessie L. Weston's *From Ritual to Romance*. Pirjo Ahokas in *Forging A New Self* suggests, moreover, that Arthurian legend, conflated with baseball, became the narrative ploy by which Malamud introduced himself to his readers at the beginning of his career both as an American and as a universal writer.

In Earl Wasserman's seminal essay "*The Natural:* Malamud's World Ceres" (1965), Wasserman asserted that Malamud's baseball novel was the necessary reference text for all of his subsequent fiction because of those recurring psychological and oneiric motifs that flow from it. In his detailed analysis of *The Natural,* Wasserman revealed how Malamud amalgamated in Roy Hobbs the moral struggle of the youthful Sir Percival, the Jungian concept of the infantile libido, and historical allusions to the baseball antics of Eddie Waitkus, Babe Ruth, and Shoeless Joe Jackson. Indeed, the story line itself invites the reader to respond to the narrative simultaneously at the literal and metaphoric levels as it playfully resonates between the two. On a train bound for Chicago, Hobbs, scheduled for a tryout with the Chicago Cubs, painfully confronts the questions of the seductive Harriet Bird and becomes involved in an unexpected test of his self-worth. In replying to those questions concerning his aspirations in life, Hobbs, thinking only of fame and money, feels "as if he had flunked a test." Once more playing the role of Sphinx in a Chicago hotel, Bird again interrogates him, but in this instance his answer results in his near destruction. She shoots him and then dances around his body in a ritual of triumph and despair. Fourteen years later, now a thirty-four-year-old rookie, Hobbs joins the New York Knights, and, with his talismanic bat Wonderboy, he rejuvenates his ailing team and its manager Pop Fisher. Hobbs's failure, however, to transcend his own desires for merely personal gratification eventually leads him to take a bribe and throw the decisive game of the pennant race in order to secure the affections of the materialistic Memo Paris. Juxtaposed to Memo Paris is Iris Lemon, who both lives and gives voice to the Malamudian theme of redemptive suffering. As these two women compete, as it were, for the soul of Hobbs, the plot takes on the structure of a morality play. Despite Hobbs's eventual change of heart, his inherent moral weakness and immaturity diminish his effectiveness as a baseball hero and culminate in the fracturing of Wonderboy, as Malamud's flawed hero literally and metaphorically strikes out.

As a thematic resource for other versions of Malamud's "failed" heroes, Hobbs embodies those preoccupations to which the author would continually return: parental death or abandonment, wasted youth, recurring failure, and fantasies of guilt. Hobbs's self-reflection — "Talk about his inner self was always like plowing up a graveyard" — indeed characterizes the state of mind of a line of Malamud characters that include S. Levin, Arthur Fidelman, Harry Lesser, and William Dubin.

Although Malamud's humanism has stimulated the largest body of criticism of his work, his earliest fiction reveals tendencies of a postmodern sensibility that have received, until recently, only passing attention. With their narrative experiments, self-reflexiveness, and disposition to intertextual parody, *Pictures of Fidelman: An Exhibition* (1969) and *The Tenants* (1971) are indicative of this other side to Malamud, whose writing began to reflect the ideological and literary controversies of the 1960s. Yet beneath the mythological treatment of baseball in *The Natural,* there is, according to Pirjo Ahokas, a subtext that addresses the very nature of literary construction. In short, while Malamud's narrative is a multimythic treatment of baseball, it is also a work of metafiction that introduces the reader to Malamud's philosophy of composition. Ahokas's comprehensive study represents a radical shift in critical direction from previous decades of humanist-modernist criticism, as she tests a variety of postmodern approaches to Malamud's work.

With *The Assistant* (1957) Malamud returned to the sources of inspiration for many of his earliest stories, the poverty and suffering of Jews and non-Jews imprisoned by their ghetto surroundings and wasted by the futility of their lives. Although this second novel recalls the immigrant and proletarian autobiographical fiction of the 1930s, such as Henry Roth's *Call It Sleep* (1934) or Michael Gold's *Jews Without Money* (1934), it is much more claustrophobic in its atmosphere and setting than its predecessors, to the point of rendering depressed economic circumstances as a timeless oneiric experience rather than the result of identifiable historical circumstances. Moreover, Malamud adds another turn of the screw to the suffering of his Jewish protagonist, Morris Bober, by situating him on the fringes of a Gentile community even as he lives among Jews from whom he is emotionally and morally detached. Malamud's early critics responded to the novel with almost universal praise, and over the years it has come to be received with not quite the adulation of Roth's *Call It Sleep* but nonetheless as a modern minor classic.

Dust jacket for Malamud's 1961 novel, which he called
"a romantic love story"

Although the title of the novel draws attention to Frank Alpine, the grocer's assistant, Malamud balances the plot between Alpine's submission to his emotional and biological urges and Morris Bober's unswerving adherence to the dictates of conscience dramatized in acts of selflessness and self-sacrifice. With an almost occult result, when Frank Alpine dons Morris Bober's apron, he becomes not only his assistant but also an apprentice to learning an ethical and psychological way of being that is as painful as it is exhilarating. Malamud, however, is writing a novel and not a moral tract; and in Alpine's characterization, he invents a character who is often contradictory and at odds with himself, reminiscent of Raskolnikov in Fyodor Dostoyevsky's *Crime and Punishment*. Indeed, this novel serves as the reference text for Malamud's version of "crime and punishment" in *The Assistant*. From such a perspective, Frank's periodic stealing from Morris's cash register, along with his rape of the grocer's daughter, engenders what is tantamount to a masochistic self-loathing, although at the same time these acts also serve as the catalysts for a new self. Laced with Malamudian irony, however, Frank's transformation into a moral and psychological version of Morris Bober involves a penitential assumption of the grocery and Helen's college education as Frank takes on Morris's selflessness, suffering, as well as the burdens of conscience intrinsic to his Jewish identity. Frank's circumcision at the conclusion, soon followed by his conversion to Judaism, remains an ambiguous form of moral transcendence. But such troublesome endings are repeated throughout Malamud's novels, suggestive of the unresolved philosophical tensions that have always characterized his most important work.

In its subject matter and themes, *The Magic Barrel* (1958), Malamud's first collection of stories, might be perceived in the chronology of his published work as a sequel to *The Assistant*; but twelve of its thirteen stories had appeared previously in such commercial and academic journals as *Partisan Review* and *Commentary,* among others. While some of them were preparatory for Malamud's writing of

The Assistant, in their evocation of ghetto neighborhoods harboring Jews and Italians, readers new to his fiction might have read these stories as spinoffs from this second novel rather than as the winding down of his experiments in Jewish and Gentile misery. The stories of this collection, even more than *The Assistant,* gained Malamud a widening readership propelled, no doubt, by his winning of the National Book Award in 1959 for *The Magic Barrel* — indeed, only the second instance in which a collection of stories had been the recipient of that award.

Any collection of stories invariably contains a few that stand out from the others in their inherent richness and imaginative impact. In this volume, apart from "The Magic Barrel" and "The Last Mohican," the most powerful stories are among the bleakest and are narrated by a laconic Jewish voice whose minimal rhetoric is at odds with the unrelieved suffering of the tale. In Malamud's narrative, time and place seem irrelevant as the reader enters an environment closer to folklore, legend, and fable than to the urban landscape in which these stories are ostensibly situated.

In the opening story of the collection, "The First Seven Years," Feld the shoemaker, immigrant father of a nineteen-year-old American-born daughter, desires a better life for her than his own has been, only to discover that she is attracted to his thirty-five-year-old assistant, a Holocaust survivor, rather than to a Jewish accounting student her own age whom he regards as a better prospect. For the father, the daughter's inexplicable attraction to the assistant is a dubious choice that will repeat the struggles and sorrows of his own past. Of greater moral and psychological complexity than this first story, "The Mourners" initially resembles Edgar Allan Poe's "The Imp of the Perverse," as a story of human personality mysteriously subverting its own interests. Such a Poesque theme is carried by the grotesque Jewish figure of Kessler, a former egg chandler. Gratuitously abandoning wife and children and lacking in remorse for thirty years, Kessler is belatedly shocked into a new awareness of his own impoverished humanity by the prospect of his eviction from his tenement apartment. Rending his own flesh in anguish and mourning, Kessler, as failed Jew and human being, suddenly emerges for Gruber the landlord as Gruber's moral double. Duplicating the behavior of his once-despised tenant, Gruber himself by his own enactment of mourning reveals in Malamudian terms that redemption is a reciprocal process. In an essay devoted largely to reader-response issues, Sharon Deykin Baris raises important questions as to how

one should respond to the weight of Malamudian suffering in this story: "In the double lights of postmodern theoretics and post-Holocaust paralysis, we read a work that thematizes inaction and yet demands reaction and pause to take note of its strange power." Although pertinent to "The Mourners," such questions need to be asked from a theoretical perspective about other Malamud stories that have been equally mesmerizing in their representation of grief. Engaging in a kind of personal mythmaking, Malamud in "Take Pity" extends his narratives of inexplicable human suffering on earth to a supernatural limbo. In the bitter domestic warfare between the recently widowed and long-suffering Eva and Rosen, the former coffee salesman, revealed through Rosen's painful account to Davidov, the census taker, Malamud creates one of his most powerful allegories of the unrelenting nature of all human suffering.

While at least half of the stories in *The Magic Barrel* dwell on Malamud's preoccupation with relentless suffering, Malamud often tempered it with his comic sense that embraced parody, farce, and black humor, illustrated, for example, in "The Magic Barrel," "Angel Levine," and "The Girl of My Dreams." Examining more fully the comic dimensions of "The Magic Barrel" than any other critic in recent years, Lawrence J. Dessner has fundamentally shifted the ground on which it has usually been read — that is, as an engaging but still poignant illustration of transformative suffering. Leo Finkle, a rabbinical student, attempts to secure a wife through the services of a marriage broker, Salzman, so that Finkle may more easily secure a pulpit. By nature and circumstance unloving and loveless, he suddenly and unpredictably is moved by a mislaid photo of Salzman's daughter, Stella — a prostitute — whose poignantly suffering image carries him to a previously unknown sense of spiritual ecstasy. Moving on to an essentially postmodern reading of the story, Dessner emphasizes Malamud's inclination to burlesque his literary sources as well as parody those very themes and conventions with which he has been so closely identified.

At the moment that Malamud's career was about to achieve a new impetus, the author paid homage to and also burlesqued the governing convention of one of his literary masters, Henry James, by inventing Arthur Fidelman, his own ethnic version of the American innocent abroad, first appearing in "The Last Mohican." Written in Rome in 1957, "The Last Mohican" is the first of a group of inter-related stories situated in Italy, and involving Arthur Fidelman, later to be called *Pictures of Fidel-*

man. "Behold the Key" and "The Lady of the Lake," also set in Italy, reveal Malamud rewriting himself, as well as James, by replacing New York Jewish suffering with Italian suffering. In the best intertextual study of Malamud's Italian stories in recent years (Salzberg, *Critical Essays on Bernard Malamud*), Guido Fink has shrewdly observed that Malamud's Italians are doubles, copies, or mirror images of Malamud's New York Jews.

In 1958, the same year that *The Magic Barrel* appeared, Malamud observed in an interview that his work in progress was following a different line from what he had previously written: "My next book will be an 'American' novel. It's different from anything I've done. . . . It'll be something new for my readers, and the first time for me: a romantic love story, with warmth and richness." The book turned out to be *A New Life* (1961), a radical break with the ethnic subject matter of *The Assistant* and *The Magic Barrel.* Malamud's love story, however, is anchored to the cultural and political contexts of the 1950s through allusions to the Cold War, the Korean War, Senator Joseph McCarthy, Whitaker Chambers, and Alger Hiss. Although he began to widen the boundaries of his fiction with a "romantic love story," the ironic ambiguity of this finished work superseded his stated intentions.

Malamud's love story became one element, albeit an important one, in a narrative that carried the resonances of the early Malamudian futility and despair. S. Levin's sadness in *The New Life,* reminiscent of T. S. Eliot's observations on Hamlet, is in excess of the narrative information Malamud supplies: a thieving father who dies in prison, a crazed mother who commits suicide, and a vague history of alcoholism. Such details, although Malamud's donnée, are best regarded as metaphorical equivalents of private griefs that originate with Malamud himself rather than actual chapters in Levin's personal history. Despite Levin's desire not only to possess a new life but also to be a new man, he nevertheless bears, both inwardly and outwardly, the stigmata of the old man. Such grief is often expressed in a kind of black humor. When Laverne, the barmaid, a figure of sexual interest for Levin, asks him why he wears a black beard, he replies: "Out of respect for the dead." Levin's self-directed levity is incongruous in the largely humorless schlemiel that Malamud has invented and seems more the superimposition of the author's own playful ventriloquy on Levin's generally self-effacing tone and language.

As an imaginative reworking of Malamud's own experiences at Oregon State College as eastern-er, humanist, and Jew, *A New Life* is essentially a comedy of manners. S. Levin comes to the American Northwest as another Malamudian innocent abroad. Reminiscent of Leslie Fiedler's own recollected culture shock after his migration to Montana in "Montana; or The End of Jean-Jacques Rousseau" (An End to Innocence, 1952) Levin, as did Malamud, experiences the flawless but disturbing beauty of the mountains and the weather in the arcadian state of Cascadia, Malamud's mythicized rendering of Oregon. Arriving at the town of Eastchester to take up his new life at Cascadia College, Levin alternately emerges as new Adam, schlemiel, eastern liberal, and, last but not least, lover of Pauline Gilley.

A New Life shares the satiric agenda characteristic of the academic novel. The narrative follows the career of the initially innocent and idealistic Levin through the intrigues and power politics of academic life in the Department of English at Cascadia College. Mistakenly believing that he has come to a liberal arts college, Levin discovers at the outset that Cascadia College was stripped of the liberal arts in 1880 and that the school is concerned mainly with science and technology. Instead of teaching the human spirit, Levin comes to realize that certain members of his department — in particular, Gerald Gilley, the director of freshman composition, and Professor Orville Fairchild, the author of *The Elements of Grammar* — are engaged in a collaborative effort to regiment, if not imprison, the soul. Emerging as a kind of maverick hero, Levin puts himself up as candidate for chairmanship of the department in order to prevent Gerald Gilley, who would stifle change in the curriculum, from gaining that position. Prior to arriving at this heroic stance, however, the initially meek and self-effacing Levin begins an affair with Gilley's wife, only to discover that in both roles — as departmental maverick and cuckolding lover of Pauline Gilley — he has become the ineffectual double of Leo Duffy, who was fired from the department before Levin arrived. While contributing to the plot, the academic politics of the novel are ultimately secondary to the emotional tone surrounding Levin who, like other Malamud characters, is stigmatized by perpetual grieving.

Halfway through *A New Life,* Pauline Gilley asks Levin what he wants from life, and his reply, "order, value, accomplishment, and love," largely sums up those aspirations that propel the protagonist through the complications of the plot; but those aspirations go largely unrealized or achieve only a momentary illusion of fulfillment. While the first three items of value in Levin's list are related to his quest for a new life, Levin's desperate need for love is the emotional priority that initially motivates his character. After his aborted sexual encounters with Laverne and Avis Fliss and an unfulfilling relationship with his student Nadalee Hamerstadd, Levin finds his version of Stella (of "The Magic Barrel") in Pauline Gilley. Levin and Pauline make love in the Edenic setting of a wood, and while their union seems to them to have a consecration all its own, in Malamud's world, if there is no manipulative trickster figure behind the scenes, reversing the expectations of his protagonists, Levin's own disillusionment is adequate to the task. Predictably, love becomes for Levin a burden and a dubious responsibility. Like Hawthorne's Edith and Edgar who leave Merrymount for the real world, Levin is obliged to accept the reality of life with Pauline: her menstrual eccentricities, past infidelity, adopted children, his own ambivalence, and the renunciation of a teaching career in college – the price imposed on him by Gerald Gilley. When Gilley asks Levin at the end of the novel why he is taking such a load, Levin's reply, "Because I can you son of a bitch," may carry more of Malamud's own existential morality than it expresses through characterization Levin as a man of principle. More mixed in its early reviews than *The Natural, The Assistant,* and *The Magic Barrel, A New Life* may ultimately be of interest to the reader as a bridge between the older and the newer Malamud.

From the beginning of his career, Malamud alternated writing novels with writing short stories because he liked the change of pace and form. "My rhythm," he observed in September 1966, "has usually been to do a novel, then a handful of short stories, then back to a novel." In the early 1960s his productivity in the short story as a break from novel writing eventually produced his second collection, *Idiots First* (1963), which comprises eleven stories and a scene of a play. In defending the human, or the idea of what it is to be humane, the keynote story of the collection, "Idiots First," is among the most powerful Malamud ever wrote. Mendel, who is suffering from a terminal illness, attempts to raise thirty-five dollars for a train ticket in order to send his retarded son Isaac to live with his eighty-one-year-old uncle in California. In the midst of his efforts to secure the money for Isaac's trip, the father, who has been granted a temporary reprieve from death by Ginzburg, the Angel of Death, is nonetheless continually pursued by this spectral figure. As Mendel arrives with his son at the station a minute before the train is to depart, Ginzburg, now in the guise of a ticket collector, is implacable in his refusal to allow Isaac to board the train. In his attempt to overcome death through what Malamud mythologizes as the superior force, the power of paternal love, Mendel momentarily overcomes the moral indifference and detachment of Ginzburg. Reflected in the father's eyes, however, is Ginzburg's "awful wrath," which also shames him into suspending his power. In its mix of realism and fantasy, Malamud creates a sequel to his earlier story, "Take Pity" (*The Magic Barrel*).

In "The Jewbird," Malamud creates a comic allegory of Jewish anti-Semitism. An assimilated American Jew contemptuously rejects the Yiddish-sounding European Jew symbolized as an unkempt blackbird or crow who stinks of fish. J. Gerald Kennedy's excellent treatment of the story (Salzberg, *Critical Essays on Bernard Malamud*) is significant not only for its intertextual study of Malamud and Poe but also for the light it sheds on the importance of parody in Malamud's development as a writer, a topic that is especially significant in connection with *Pictures of Fidelman.*

In addition to the three stories of *The Magic Barrel* set in Italy, Malamud's residence in Rome (1956–1957) nurtured four additional stories with an Italian setting collected in *Idiots First.* "Still Life" and "Naked Nude" continued the saga of Arthur Fidelman's attempt to find his new life through art. "A Maid's Shoes" added a variation to the cultural collision of the American abroad by putting a nervous, aging, and emotionally fastidious American professor into a relationship with an Italian maid whose personal problems and cultural mores only exacerbate his sensitivity toward personal involvement in the lives of others. In "Life is Better than Death," Malamud's main characters, a widow and widower, both Italian, by coincidence meet at a cemetery in remembrance of their respective dead. Malamud pays homage to his source, James's "The Altar of the Dead," while playfully burlesquing its solemn tone and elevated themes.

Idiots First is noteworthy for the political turn Malamud's writing was to take in the last story of the collection, "The German Refugee." In a September 1966 newspaper interview dealing with the genesis of *The Fixer,* (1966) Malamud explained his interest in writing "The German Refugee," the last story he wrote prior to the publication of that fourth novel: "It's about a man who has suffered under Hitler and then comes to this country and finds it hard to adjust. It's a story that is both historically and politically centered." Hired as an English tutor for Oskar Gassner, a German-Jewish émigré, so that he can deliver a lecture on the humanistic influence of Walt Whitman on German poetry, the narrator becomes an almost unwilling witness to the sources of Gassner's anguish – his struggle with English, the seeming triumph of fascism, and the murder of his now newly converted Jewish wife by the Nazis – that culminate in his suicide. "The German Refugee" is one of the most accomplished stories in Malamud's canon as it knits together text and subtext: the personal history of Oskar Gassner and the rise of fascism in Germany with the narrator's own transformation from youthful observer to an artist in the making.

The political, social, and cultural changes in the early 1960s may well have been the catalyst stimulating Malamud's own political consciousness, for this largely apolitical writer seemed to have felt the need to address issues in *The Fixer* that he usually reserved for his nonfictional writing. At the end of the novel, Malamud's hero, Yakov Bok, declares that "there's no such thing as an unpolitical man, especially a Jew." Malamud, who had himself shunned any activism as a student at City College and whose work prior to *A New Life* was often closer to the fanciful imagination of Marc Chagall than it was to Michael Gold's depiction of the Lower East Side, appears to have undergone something of a transformation almost similar to that of Yakov Bok. In the September 1966 interview, Malamud's comments on "The German Refugee" reveal his desire to write what amounts to a political novel: "I decided that I wanted to write about politics again – but with a broader base – freedom, injustice, something of that kind." He identifies the historical incident of Mendel Beiliss, an office manager in a Kiev brick factory, who was arrested for allegedly murdering a Christian boy for ritualistic purposes, as one of the sources for *The Fixer,* which specifically addresses institutionalized anti-Semitism. Malamud has also acknowledged that his inspiration for *The Fixer* came from both Jewish and non-Jewish sources – the Dreyfus case, the suffering of Sacco and Vanzetti, the Jewish persecution by the Nazis, and the experience of blacks in America. By coincidence, the very title of the novel was derived from a sign, "Jim The Fixer," that Malamud saw every day in Corvallis, Oregon, inadvertently including this Oregonian in his well-known metaphorical phrase, "All men are Jews except they don't know it."

Despite Malamud's use of a setting in *The Fixer* – prerevolutionary Russia – that is removed from his own time and experience, his hero remains fundamentally the mythical construct of the Jew evident in all his work. Like his predecessors, Yakov

Bok is initially the self-effacing Jew of the shtetl or the urban ghetto – orphaned at birth, afflicted by poverty, deprived of formal education, and bereft of hope. But unlike Isaac Bashevis Singer's saintly version of the schlemiel figure in "Gimpel the Fool," Yakov Bok – whose last name suggests that he is not only a goat but also a scapegoat, as the novel bears out – is filled with anger against both God and man. Married to a wife who is barren and who ultimately runs off with a musician, Bok, like his Malamudian counterparts, Arthur Fidelman and S. Levin, finally decides to break out of the prison of his ghetto and reinvent himself – at least outwardly.

As a Malamud hero, Bok follows certain patterns of characterization that almost amount to unchanging conventions. In works prior to *The Fixer,* his hero suffers from an excess of innocence and goodness, as with Morris Bober of *The Assistant,* or is a victim of the inscrutable powers that govern the universe, as with Mendel of "Idiots First." But whether an innocent victim or, in Bok's case, an angry apostate, all of Malamud's characters, even if they are Gentiles, are mysteriously caught up in the problematic experience of being a Jew. At his angriest and most despairing, Malamud regarded human suffering as gratuitous, but in *The Fixer* it is regarded not as the consequence of an indifferent God but rather as the result of history and politics.

From the moment *The Fixer* begins, the reader is immersed in the warp and weft of Czarist Russian history – references to the Jewish Pale, Cossack raids, the anti-Semitism of the Black Hundreds, ritual murder, and pogroms pervade the first few pages of the text. The setting possesses neither the abstractness of a Malamudian ghetto or Eden but rather the starkness of a place graphically visible in time – indeed, reminiscent of the black-and-white pictorial record of Vishniac's Eastern European Jews. Indeed, one of the reasons that Malamud gave for disliking Dalton Trumbo's film version of *The Fixer* was that Trumbo's use of color interfered with the concept of reality that Malamud wanted to convey: "The starkness of pre-revolutionary Russia," he observed in a June 1983 interview, "would have been more appropriately rendered in black and white." Yet Malamud's oneiric and mythic imagination is certainly as important an element in the success of the novel as is his rigorous commitment to the illusion of historical realism, especially in its placement of the hero within a culture of anti-Semitism.

At the beginning of Yakov Bok's journey, images of the irrational and the sinister surface as omens that foreshadow Bok's fate at the hands of Christians. As Bok makes his way to the holy city of

Dust jacket for Malamud's 1966 novel, which won both a
Pulitzer Prize and a National Book Award

Kiev dressed in a Russian cap and coat, he approaches a woman who stops before a crucifix at the side of the road, crosses herself, and then begins banging her head on the ground. Her self-flagellation is preparatory for his subsequent initiation into the cultural context of irrational Christian hatred directed against Jews generally and, later, Yakov Bok specifically. Malamudian realism is momentarily subsumed into myth as Bok, in order to get to Kiev, crosses at night the Dnieper River, the Russian equivalent of the mythological river Styx. Encountering a virulently antiSemitic ferryman, Bok listens impassively to the ferryman's final solution regarding the Jews, instinctively dropping his prayer things into the river and symbolically severing his connections to the God of the Jewish people. At this stage of the novel, Bok ironically collaborates with the ferryman's vision of Jewish annihilation in order to preserve the illusion that he will be protected if he remains anonymous and apolitical.

Soon after Bok takes up residence in the Lukianovsky district of Kiev as the foreman for Nikolai Maximovitch, the owner of a brickworks, he is arrested for living in an area forbidden to Jews; shortly thereafter, he is investigated for the murder of a Russian boy, Zhenia Golov, for ritual purposes. Thus begins another tale of Jewish suffering, and, moreover, a new chapter in Malamud's exploration of transformative suffering. In approximately the first half of the novel, Bok enacts the role of the passive Jew, recapitulating the historical and psychological ordeal of the Jew as perpetual victim. In the second half of the novel, he is gradually metamorphosed into the modern militant or "tough" Jew who has now become political.

While Bok waits for his indictment, he initially remains dependent on others for aid, supporting himself only with his Jewish legacy of self-directed mordant humor. Although B. A. Bibikov, the Investigating Magistrate, represents what is humane and civilized within the Russian legal system, in Malamud's conception of mankind all men are metaphorically Jews and, therefore, subject to fate and history. Thus, Bibikov himself falls victim to the political agenda of the state and is mysteriously hanged near Bok's cell as an object lesson. Feeling that his only source of hope has vanished, Bok can only cry out with the childlike despair: "Mama-Papa . . . save me! Shmuel, Raisl, – anybody – save me!"

From a combination of suffering, rage, and moral indignation, a new self begins to crystallize within Bok, but it is one, in fact, that has its original conception in the bleak confines of the shtetl. It is only in the literal prison, however, that Bok recovers the origins of that new self, through an act of memory, which prompts him to live out the recollected Spinozist philosophical precept on freedom. Musing over the beginning of his relationship with the fearful and timid Raisl, Bok attempts to vanquish her superstitious nature and thereby have her escape from her own sense of limitation: "If you want to be free," he asserts, "first be free in your mind." Having read Spinoza in the shtetl, Bok looks upon himself as a freethinker and has distanced himself from the religious constraints of orthodoxy; but even before his vision of freedom and politics matures, he is also capable of acting out a philosophy distilled from the essence of Judaism. Despite his attempt to dissociate himself from Jewish life and ritual, he nonetheless fulfills the covenantal relationship with a man whom, in Bok's view, God has abandoned: in coming to the aid of an old Hasidic Jew attacked by Russian boys before he is imprisoned; in accepting the paternity of Raisl's illegitimate child; and, finally, in enduring the suffering and humiliation of prison so that he can expose the inhumanity of the state against both Jew and non-Jew. Anachronistically, Malamud based his model for Bok less on the retiring Mendel Beiliss than on the emergence of Jews as radicals, revolutionaries, or Zionists.

In his September 1966 interview, Malamud considered *The Fixer* to be his strongest book to date, and a large number of earlier reviewers tended to agree. Many of the early critical affirmations of the novel allude to its density of texture, the authenticity of Bok's characterization, and Malamud's effectiveness in sustaining Bok's point of view. If the author's previous fiction did not possess the intellectual play of ideas of a Bellovian novel, such characters as Bibikov, Ostrosky, Bok's defense lawyer, and Bok himself introduce the kind of intellectual musings not found in Malamud's earlier work. It is not surprising, then, that in 1967 *The Fixer* won for

Malamud his second National Book Award as well as a Pulitzer Prize.

Pictures of Fidelman: An Exhibition (1969) reveals Malamud at his most experimental in narrative form and structure. While composing the first Fidelman story, "The Last Mohican," Malamud had been outlining ideas for a picaresque novel to be subsequently unified by the character of Arthur Fidelman, as he explained in a 1975 interview: "I wanted to see, if I wrote at intervals – as I did from 1975 to 1968 – whether the passing of time and mores would influence [Fidelman's] life." In another context, Malamud acknowledged that he was moved by Fidelman and had great affection for the stories. Indeed, in making Fidelman's struggle to find his artistic vocation comically grotesque, so far away from the facts of his own life, Malamud could render his own quest – under the Fidelman mask – unthreatening.

One of the epigraphs preceding the text of Malamud's novel is taken from Yeats's poem, "The Choice" – "The intellect of man is forced to choose / Perfection of the life, or of the work" – and offers the best point of entrance into the Fidelman character. Through Fidelman's response to Yeats's poem in the epigraph that follows, "Both," Malamud suggests an arrogance proportionate to the poetic justice of his failures in life and art, the seemingly affirmative conclusion notwithstanding. Fidelman's obsessive search for the girl of his dreams – for example, Annamaria in "Still Life," Esmerelda in "A Pimp's Revenge," or Margherita in "Glass Blower of Venice" – results invariably in brief and unfufilling encounters designed to illustrate some flaw in his nature. The last story, "Glass Blower of Venice," brings the sequence to its resolution by having Fidelman achieve sexual and artistic satisfaction in his relationship with Beppo, a glass blower, who sexually ravishes him as Fidelman has intercourse with Beppo's wife, Margherita. This new and unexpected relationship in which the glass blower makes Fidelman his apprentice in love and art is presumably redemptive, or so Malamud with innocence, real or feigned, would have the reader believe. In sending Fidelman back to America, where "he worked as a craftsman in glass and loved men and women," Malamud has taken a cue from his ironic master, Henry James, who provides the model of the exile's return as a form of chastening.

Just as Fidelman moves from relationship to relationship, he is equally mercurial in abandoning one artistic vocation for another. In "The Last Mohican," Fidelman, a self-confessed failure as a painter in America, becomes a failed art critic in

Italy. Taking up the vocation of painting in "Still Life," he experiments with both traditional and modern art. In "Naked Nude," he is forced to be a copyist, but narcissistically he falls in love with his own work. In "Pictures of the Artist," he works as an arrogant sculptor and then as a muralist translating into art a vision approaching the mystical.

In this black comedy we see Malamud at play, revealing in his less-guarded moments some of the darker corners of his own life. If all of the author's fiction tends to give the impression that he is trying to express the inexpressible or alternately to express and then repress it, then no work in his canon is as confessional and yet as secretive as *Pictures of Fidelman*. It is only when this work is read against Malamud's autobiographical reminiscences in interviews, along with his reflections on literature and art, that the reader can make sense of this puzzling and perverse collection of stories as a vehicle for self-parody. While the character of Fidelman may have been intentionally constructed as a vehicle for experiments with narrative, it also exists for Malamud as a mask for self-contemplation.

The best representative commentaries of *Pictures of Fidelman* begin with Robert Scholes's 1969 review, which judged the stories to be "Malamud's finest comic work" (Salzberg, *Critical Essays on Bernard Malamud*). Robert Ducharme offers the best discussion of the episodic structure of the sequence. Salzberg analyzes the tangled and sometimes obscure autobiographical issues — familial, humanistic, artistic, and literary — that govern Malamudian self-parody as the subtext of the work.

In representing the artist whose essential identity exists only through the practice of his vocation, *The Tenants* (1971) borrows its conception of character and some of its themes from *Pictures of Fidelman*. While Harry Lesser, writer, calls to mind many of Arthur Fidelman's problems — Lesser is haunted by his family past, inexplicably blocked in bringing his current novel to closure, and alternately preoccupied with the love of women and the demands of art — Lesser's character is born out of Malamud's attempt to represent the literary and political tensions between blacks and Jews of the 1960s. These tensions are personified in the confrontation between the Jewish Lesser and the African American Willie Spearmint, who later renames himself Bill Spear, apropos of his emerging self-image as a black revolutionary writer.

Lesser and Spearmint are the sole occupants of a decaying tenement, which turns into an ideological and human battleground. While Lesser asserts the importance of form in his dialogue with Spearmint, the black writer initially perceives Lesser's artistic principles as exclusively a white aesthetic and a barrier to completing his own fictionalized autobiography of the black experience. Spearmint declares that black experience is unique and cannot be universalized, a position diametrically opposed to Malamud's fundamentally humanistic belief that the universal lies in the particular, that the Jewish experience could be understood by and could apply to Gentile and Jew alike. Angry and frustrated by his own lack of literary skill, Spearmint allows himself to be influenced by Lesser's judgments on form, only to discover that Lesser's ideas have made him even more blocked as a writer than he was before. Out of revenge he destroys Lesser's irreplaceable manuscript. Thus, what was originally a confrontation of "black" versus "white" aesthetics ultimately turns into a racial confrontation in which Lesser puts an axe to Spearmint's head while the black writer castrates Lesser with a razor-sharp saber. The older Jewish writer and the younger black writer represent yet another dimension of the master/apprentice relationship, but rather than having redemptive value for each writer as in *The Assistant,* it carries Malamud to his most pessimistic conclusion prior to *God's Grace*. Intrinsic to the grimness of the novel is the irony that Irving Levenspiel, slum landlord of the decaying tenement, carries the word *mercy* throughout to the final apocalyptic conclusion. Whether a funeral, a sick wife, and a "knocked up daughter" are ruses by which the landlord tries to wring from Lesser mercy or indeed the landlord's own human realities, we never know; but caught up in the violence around him, the landlord seems as much a helpless victim as a con man. As Levenspiel witnesses Lesser and Spearmint's annihilation of each other, his cry for "mercy" trails off into an ideograph of fourteen rows of eight that literally moves the impassioned author's word (although seeming to emanate from the landlord) beyond what is signified as "*The End,*" beyond the fictional illusion itself.

Fueling the tensions between Spearmint and Lesser is their rivalry over Irene Bell (née Belinsky), initially Willie's girl and later to be Lesser's, but the drama of the triangular relationship is largely subordinated to the theme of art versus life. The psychological double of Lesser, Spearmint seeks fulfillment through his art while his life is put on hold. Thus Irene, lacking a future of love with Willy, breaks with him in order to find self-renewal in a loving relationship with Lesser. In his early encounters with Irene, Lesser perceives something of his original self as human being and Jew, nouns that are signifiers of life in Malamud's vocabulary. Lesser spontaneously greets Irene Bell with "Shalom," a word whose emotional undercurrents carry Lesser's renewed hunger for life. Soon after Lesser declares his love for her, Irene begins to recover her own sense of authenticity in their relationship, allowing her hair to return from blond to its original black and expressing her desire for a family rather than a career in acting. Lesser, however, like the thirty-five-year-old writer in his unfinished book, *The Promised End,* is not able to establish the priority of love over art. When Irene realizes that Lesser's book continues to take precedence over their relationship, she leaves a note for Lesser asserting her own value, "No book is as important as me," and moves to San Francisco.

In its thematic concern with the making of fiction and its intertextual play with writers and artists, *The Tenants* weds postmodern literary themes to Malamud's humanistic vision at its most enervated. The power of *The Tenants* resides as much in the author himself as in his invented characters. Despite its overt theme of racial conflict, *The Tenants* is largely self-reflective, revealing through the mask of Lesser the writer's (or Malamud's?) ongoing artistic preoccupations that at times are seemingly contradictory.

In his speculations on his inability to finish his third book, Lesser muses: "Each book I write nudges me that much closer to death." Toward the end of the novel, as Lesser remembers his family dead, he once again reflects on the meaning of writing, but in a different vein: "One thing about writing a book you keep death in place; idea is to keep on writing." In *Long Work, Short Life* Malamud reflects with some regret that as a young writer he had "felt the years go by without accomplishment." Indeed, through Lesser's belief that writing keeps death at bay, Malamud implies that authorial self-inscription is a form of immortality. In a 1975 interview he extends the idea, citing Robert Frost's definition of a poem as "a momentary stay against confusion." As though to embody these sentiments in the form of the novel, Malamud writes three different endings to the novel as an aesthetic and metaphysical defense against the very idea of closure.

"In the variety of their art, in the delicate and shocking juxtapositions of the personal and impersonal, the stories in this collection seem to me terrific," observed Leonard Michaels in a 20 September 1973 review of *Rembrandt's Hat* (1973) in the *New York Review of Books*. While not all reviewers of Malamud's third collection responded to it with the same enthusiasm, most were full of praise, and some considered it superior to his first two collections. Malamud's subjects, while not wholly unique to this collection, reveal in some instances an increased depth and range of treatment. Of the eight stories in *Rembrandt's Hat,* three explore the tortured relationships of fathers with sons; one concerns aging and desire, a new Malamud subject; two portray the relationship of Jewish artists with each other; one involves the near seduction of a young architect by the wife of his former professor; the last, a beast fable and existential comedy, addresses man's quest for knowledge and freedom.

Reminiscent of "Angel Levine" and "The Magic Barrel," the lead story of the collection, "The Silver Crown," reexamines the possibility of miracles once again emanating from the unlikeliest of sources. A retarded girl distributes a soiled card advertising cures for the sick and the dying, the advertisements of her wonder-working Rabbi-father. Gans, a biology teacher whose father is near death, comes to a point in his life when his rationalism fails him. Expiating his hatred for his father by purchasing a talismanic silver crown from the rabbi as a cure for the elder Gans's terminal illness, the son momentarily submits to a charitable impulse at odds with his own loveless nature. The impulse passes, however, and the biology teacher comes to believe that he has been conned by the rabbinical trickster, who admonishes the son to think of his father. True to his own nature, the son replies: "He hates me, the son-of-a-bitch, I hope he croaks." And indeed the wish, more efficacious than the original impulse to charity, is fulfilled one hour later in the death of the older Gans. While the story is one of many recurring instances of failed parent-child relationships in Malamud's fiction, the author here situates that failure within a historical and social context. At the beginning of the story, Malamud introduces oblique references to the sordidness of contemporary life — war, the atom bomb, pollution — linking the atrophy of the son's feelings to the wasteland condition of the historical moment.

"The Letter" introduces another unloving son, significantly called Newman, who grudgingly visits his father, a patient in a sanatorium. As the new man of the contemporary world, the son is incapable of responding compassionately to either his father or to Ralph and Teddy, father and son respectively, who are also patients in the same sanatorium. In contrast to Newman and his father they offer a touchstone for mutual sympathy. In his Sunday visits, Newman leaves the institution and passes Teddy, who hands him blank pages of a letter, which Newman routinely refuses to mail. Incapable of recognizing the needs of his own father, coded in a language that to all appearances seems irrational, he is even less capable of comprehending what the blank text of Teddy's letter signifies. The father and son, having fought in the First and Second World Wars, respectively, attempt to communicate to Newman truths of the human condition that the visitor, as yet himself untouched by human suffering, is unable to grasp. In its battery of verbal exchanges, Malamud's language resembles the absurdist banter to be found in a Beckett play.

War again is the backdrop for the third story, "My Son the Murderer." Dispensing with names, Malamud reduces the characters to their fundamental human roles, father and son, and reenacts their eternal drama of loss and alienation. While watching the Vietnam War on television and waiting to be drafted, the son has become increasingly remote from all human contact, including the love of his father. Desperately trying to find words that will bridge the emotional chasm of their relationship, the father, in the awkwardness of his Yiddish-accented English, becomes a figure of unsurpassed Malamudian pathos.

Broadly stated, "Rembrandt's Hat" and "Man in the Drawer" both deal with the responsibility of artists for the well-being of each other. In "Man in the Drawer," an assimilated Jewish American writer, Howard Harvitz, and a half-Jewish Russian writer, Feliks Levitansky, encounter each other in a manner reminiscent of Conrad's secret sharers. "A soft shalom I thought I heard," Harvitz narrates. Tentative and insecure in his relationships with his former wives, Harvitz is ill-prepared to take on the obligations presented to him by his Russian literary double: the smuggling of unpublished short stories out of the Soviet Union for publication in America. Like the untried captain in *The Secret Sharer,* Harvitz comes — in his case belatedly — to maturity by confronting the risks and challenges of human responsibility forced upon him by his double. In "Rembrandt's Hat" Rubin, a mediocre sculptor, and Arkin, an insensitive art historian, explore in an urban American setting what artists owe to one another in the way of sympathy and understanding. Failing to perceive the sculptor's low self-esteem, Arkin unintentionally insults Rubin by suggesting that the sculptor's headdress, a current mode of fashion, resembles Rembrandt's various painterly hats. Unknown to Arkin, Ruben is silently offended at an association with artistic eminence at odds with his own anguished sense of artistic mediocrity. Later, however, Arkin realizes that Rubin's hat more appropriately resembles the cap or beret of an assistant cook in Sam's diner, a recognition also made on Rubin's part, thinks Arkin, that further adds to the sculptor's sense of humiliation. Like his predecessor Arthur Fidelman, Arkin comes to recognize that he is limited in his sensitivity to others and correspondingly in his artistic acumen.

Sounding more like John Updike than Bernard Malamud, "Notes from a Lady at a Dinner Party," in representing the near seduction of a young architect by the wife of his former teacher, is probably the thinnest story of the collection. "Talking Horse," on the other hand, is among its most original and most powerful. An allegory of man's quest for dignity and freedom in a capricious universe that alternately rewards and punishes, the story employs "Q" and "A," signs for question and answer, to ground a Socratic dialogue into the body of the narrative. While the questioner, Abramowitz, unsure of whether he is a man in a horse or a horse that talks like a man, poses that question and similar ones pertaining to his existence, a blankness remains next to the "A" when the letter first appears in the text. Goldberg, Abramowitz's master, is a deaf mute, who has recently played ringmaster in a sideshow full of freaks and has now advanced Abramowitz to center ring. When Abramowitz participates in the act organized by Goldberg called "Ask Me Another," Goldberg's answers are either incomprehensible sounds or Morse-coded to Abramowitz through hard knuckle taps on the horse's head. Through an Abbott and Costello–like vaudeville routine, Abramowitz personifies man as the innocent naif or victim, abused by an alternately benevolent and violent owner-ringmaster. In Malamud's absurdist comedy, Abramowitz finally frees himself from the horse's body in a violent struggle with Goldberg, who mysteriously disappears. As a centaur, half man and half horse, Abramowitz's image serves Malamud as a metaphor of the problematic human condition.

In the Bernard Malamud memorial issue of *Studies in Jewish American Literature* (Fall 1988), Daniel Fuchs and Leslie Field reassess Malamud's accomplishment in *Dubin's Lives* (1979), and their respective readings of the novel recall some of the most sharply polarized of the earliest reviews. Fuchs asserts that *Dubin's Lives* is not "the *summa* Malamud wanted it to be," because it has lost its connection to the eloquence of his earlier Jewishness. Initially dissatisfied with it for other reasons, Field "began to see in the novel a denser complexity of thought and architectonic expressive style that had eluded . . . [his] earlier crude readings of the novel." Presenting a postmodern reading of *Dubin's Lives,* James Mellard's Lacanian approach emphasizes "just how sophisticated Malamud's art has always been" (Salzberg, *Critical Essays on Bernard Malamud*).

When it does not sound like Sir Thomas Browne's *Urn Burial* updated to the tone of an urban Jewish voice, Malamud's somber meditations on mortality and death belong to a tragicomic plot involving a May–December relationship. Fanny Bick, a young and attractive woman, is employed as a house cleaner for William and Kitty Dubin. Attracted to Dubin's wisdom, Fanny herself becomes sexually interesting to the fifty-six-year-old biographer when, appropriately, he finds himself blocked in distilling his most recent subject, D. H. Lawrence, into a short biography. As a man who initially sought out love as an existential need for meaning and commitment rather than passion, Dubin now finds himself without true knowledge of the emotion and consequently unequal to the task of representing the essential Lawrence. Increasingly preoccupied with his own mortality and depressed by the dearth of passion in his life – its absence being the very signifier of that mortality – Dubin finds in Fanny a counterbalance and compensation for his own and Kitty's death-tainted family histories. In a chance but fated encounter with Fanny in his study, Dubin relates to her something of his troubled past, the significance of his vocation as biographer, and his own philosophy of seizing the day. Their meeting ends with his gift to Fanny of his first book, *Short Lives,* Dubin's metonymic presentation of his own life, and eventually she responds in kind, offering her body in his study, which Dubin, out of respect for his wife Kitty, initially declines.

Attempting to recover his lost opportunity, Dubin arranges with Fanny a trip to Italy, informing Kitty that he is doing research on Lawrence – in its way a true statement. His erotic longings, however, are subsumed into a Chaucerian fabliau, as Fanny's stomach problem suddenly transforms the erotic moment into an excremental experience. But just prior to the fulfilling of Dubin's postponed consummation with Fanny, she capriciously makes of Dubin a cuckold by running off with an Italian gondolier, and Dubin returns to his home at Center Campobello. When Fanny's sexual adventures come to an end, she also returns to Center Campobello, and the relationship between the biographer and the much younger woman is rekindled. For a while Dubin experiences a sense of renewed life, but his affair with Fanny paradoxically propels him to a greater involvement in his biography on Lawrence, and as a consequence he begins to spend less time with Fanny, whose eventual departure throws Dubin into another bout of depression. Fanny's return once more to Center Campobello and to a renewal of their relationship produces in Dubin moments of sexual and creative energy, but increasingly Kitty becomes a victim of Dubin's secretiveness, guilt, and resulting impotence.

When she eventually takes up residence near the Dubins' home, Fanny's dwelling becomes Malamud's problematic embodiment of the life of passion, juxtaposed at the conclusion to the official Dubin residence, the life of moral responsibility – at least in Malamud's playful imagination. Coming to closure only in fantasy, with Dubin "holding his half-stiffened phallus in his hand, for his wife with love," Malamud's comic tableau represents the impasse to which author and character have come. Yet whatever dissatisfaction readers may have with Malamud's attempt to project on Lawrence's love ethic a Jewish ethic, the novel significantly broadens Malamud's fictional boundaries to include contemporary husbands and wives, parents and children, and aging men and sexually liberated women. Despite his reversion to an eroticized Chagallian ending, Malamud's authority among contemporary writers in rendering the state of psychological and spiritual loss remains unchallenged. While the elegiac tone of the novel may be pure Malamud, the closest approximation to it is in the fiction of Virginia Woolf, revealing an unexpected conjunction of sensibilities.

In June 1983 Malamud responded to a question concerning *God's Grace* (1982), his last published novel before his death in 1986, with the following caveat to his readers: "One of the misreadings of the novel, by the way, is that it ends in tragedy. Some reviewers have failed to recognize that a gorilla recites *Kaddish* for Calvin Cohn, and that is indeed a cause for optimism; the prayer itself is a vehicle of God's grace." These remarks indeed reflect Malamud's sense that the reviewers were not getting his novel "right," a feeling that is understandable given the wide spectrum of critical response it has inspired. Saul Maloff was, for example, impressed by Malamud's execution of this didactic fable which, despite its cuteness, culminates in a tragic vision (*Commonweal,* 5 November 1982). Alvin H. Rosenfeld was troubled by its unrelieved pessimism (*Midstream,* November 1982). On a much more negative note, Joseph Epstein judged the novel as artistically thin and an indication of Malamud's decline (*Commentary,* October 1982). Is the novel no more than a recycling of tired Malamudian conventions and themes updated as a

Dust jacket for the 1983 book in which Malamud collected short stories he selected from three earlier collections

black comedy, or is Malamud at his most daring and innovative in treating his apocalyptic subject, the termination of mankind through nuclear holocaust and flood?

Calvin Cohn, former rabbinical student turned paleontologist, rises from the ocean floor in a miniature submarine to discover that he is the lone survivor of a thermonuclear war and that God, in his anger over man's inability to use his free will constructively, has destroyed his own creation in a second great flood. As a result of a miscalculation, however, God has missed Calvin Cohn and several primate creatures who have also managed to escape his wrath. Although God manifests himself to Cohn and tells him to prepare for death — despite Cohn's appeal both to God's covenant with man and his own rabbinical arguments — Cohn is mysteriously spared imminent annihilation. Emerging as a new Adam and a new Moses, Cohn attempts to bring the primate creatures, through teaching and example, to a stage of evolution beyond their own animal natures, an effort that achieves mixed success.

Three of the primate creatures who become the inhabitants of Cohn's island are especially significant in developing the plot and themes of this fable: George, a male gorilla, who nurses Cohn back to health after his bout with radiation poisoning; Buz, a chimpanzee, capable of human speech, who becomes Cohn's adoptive son; and Mary Madelyn, a female chimpanzee who, under the influence of Cohn's humanistic and rabbinical teaching, transcends her own nature and becomes monogamously attached to this last man on earth, miraculously giving birth to their child, Rebekah. As Cohn develops his relationship with Mary Madelyn, while urging the chimpanzee males to sublimate, sexual jealousy of Cohn within the primate community begins to undermine the tenuous harmony of this new Eden. Foreshadowed by Buz's inclination to be at odds with his adoptive father, the chimpanzees ultimately revert to type and recapitulate the brutality of human history — murder and cannibalism — in the killing of Rebekah and Mary Madelyn. It has been suggested that Cohn himself fails civilization because of his egotism and inability to love, but this reading grasps only one strand, and hardly the most salient, in Malamud's morally complex version of creation. If, in fact, Cohn is as culpable as the primates for the failure of this new civilization, he is equally admirable as a spokesman for mankind in the face of an angry God.

Among the various biblical parallels that Malamud reworks into his apocalyptic fable is the story of Abraham and Isaac, which brings the novel to its strained and uncertain conclusion. In a reversal of the original story in tone and substance, Buz takes the part of Abraham and Cohn plays the role of Isaac as a sacrificial victim. Cohn, however, does not escape death, and the meaning of the ritual remains obscure; yet in the very nature of Cohn's death, Malamud seems to forsake both humanism and despair in order to embrace a theodicy, as Sidney Richman so persuasively suggests (Salzberg, *Critical Essays on Bernard Malamud*). Before Buz can apply the knife to Cohn's throat, blood spurts forth as though a divine hand had intruded, and followed by that event is a Kaddish intoned by George the gorilla, wearing a mud-stained white yarmulke. From such signs, Cohn acquires a spiritual tranquility, sensing an order beyond man's ability to fathom. Do the artistic pleasures of Malamud's text adequately support the burden of his thematic intentions as they have largely done in his past work? The answer is finally in the eye of the beholder.

The Stories of Bernard Malamud (1983), which appeared in Malamud's sixty-ninth year, reflects the author's selection and arrangement of stories chosen from his first three collections. Two of them, "God's Wrath" (*Atlantic,* February 1972) and "The Model" (*Atlantic,* August 1983), had not been previously collected. New to most readers, they were identifiably Malamudian in subject matter, style, and themes. "God's Wrath," echoing moments in "The Magic Barrel," sketches the mysteriously failed relationship between a retired sexton and a vulgar and uncommunicative daughter who inexplicably becomes a prostitute. In "The Model" Malamud portrays Ephraim Elihu, a self-effacing widower of seventy, who misses the pleasure of the youthful female body. Hiring a model to sit for a nude study, Elihu ineffectually attempts to paint her in order to gratify his voyeuristic needs. The model takes revenge on the would-be painter by insisting that he disrobe for her so that she can represent his aging image on canvas, subsequently blackening it in a gesture of contempt. Both stories are somewhat more direct in addressing sexual themes than Malamud's earliest fiction, and the unrelieved hopelessness connected with their protagonists is largely reminiscent of Malamud at his grimmest but not his most accomplished. Of additional interest to the reader in this volume is Malamud's autobiographical introduction, originally published as "The Making of a Writer: Pleasures of the Fast Payoff" in the *New York Times Book Review,* in which he provides a brief but intimate overview of his career in writing. Predictably, the majority of the reviews of this volume largely reaffirmed the high regard in which Malamud was held as a practitioner of the modern short story.

The ideal reader for Malamud's posthumous volume *The People and Uncollected Stories* (1989) is one who has known Malamud's previous work at its best, when inspiration and execution were fully realized. While the fiction in this book is not of the caliber of his first three collections, the selections are nonetheless interesting to students of Malamud for what they reveal about his imagination and Jewish sensibility in a life of unflinching commitment to the art of fiction, even through mortal illness. Because of its autobiographical subject matter, its very modern experiments with biographical fiction, and its all-too-familiar Malamudian themes and conventions, the book affords the reader an intimate glimpse of a writer doggedly practicing his craft in all seasons.

The People represents a first draft of a work still in progress which had not yet come close to artistic fulfillment. Although some of the stories in this collection had been previously published in magazines, Malamud chose not to include them in his earlier collections. According to Robert Giroux, ten of the sixteen stories in this volume were published between 1943 and 1985: "The Literary Life of Laban Goldman" (1943), "Benefit Performance" (1943), "The Place is Different Now" (1943), "An Apology" (1957), "An Exorcism" (1968), "A Wig" (1980), "Zora's Nose" (1985), "A Lost Grave" (1985), "In Kew Gardens" (1984–1985), and "Alma Redeemed" (1984). Six stories were found among Malamud's papers proper, none of which had been previously published: "Armistice," "Spring Rain," "The Grocery Store," "Riding Pants," "A Confession of Murder," and "The Elevator."

Philip Roth in "Pictures of Malamud" (*New York Times Book Review,* 20 April 1986) recalls the last time he saw Malamud prior to his death. It was also the occasion when Malamud read to him the opening chapters of the first draft of what was to be called *The People.* Roth's reaction was evasive, as indeed many of the reactions in the early reviews were to the unfinished novel. Malamud's protagonist Jozip carries his heavily accented Yiddish-sounding voice into unfamiliar territory, the Pacific Northwest. A former peddler who is now an unemployed carpenter, this new schlemiel abroad is chosen by an inscrutable fate to become morally responsible for an Indian tribe threatened with annihilation by the representatives of the white man's government. While Malamud's intention was to re-create the tragicomedy of his best work, the result is disturbingly closer to Jackie Mason's Yiddish-accented stand-up comedy. Whether Malamud could have, like his own protagonists, transcended his own limitations and transformed his first draft into a work of greater richness and force is problematic.

Many short stories in the collection are notable either for their fresh treatment of previously worked themes and conventions or for altogether new experiments with narrative. "The Exorcism," for example, adds a new twist to Malamud's stories of artists and writers in its relationship of an established but mediocre writer, Eli Fogel, and a young apprentice writer, Gary Simpson, who attempts to learn from and then destroy his literary father. Burlesquing Fogel's sexual ineptness with women in one of his own published stories, Simpson turns Fogel, his literary mentor, into a subject for ridicule. In what turns into an Oedipal struggle of mutual exorcism centered in literary and sexual jealousy, Fogel takes his revenge by burning Simpson's bus.

The two most interesting stories in the collection technically – "In Kew Gardens," which treats Virginia Woolf, and "Alma Redeemed," which has Alma Mahler as its subject – were ventures into what Malamud called "fictive biography." In these stories Malamud attempts to distill the lives of two fascinating women into a few pages. Malamud's intention for this new genre is cited in notes quoted by Robert Giroux in his introduction: "Method: start with a scene in one life, explicate that as fiction, then go into the biographical element and develop further. You come out, or should, with an *invention forward as a story,* limited but carrying the meaning of the life as a short story."

Malamud's serious interest in Virginia Woolf can be dated from his preparation for the spring 1979 course he taught about her at Bennington College, as he revealed in a 1986 interview. "I read a lot for the course," he observed, "and I became very much interested in Woolf, as a human being, a writer, and a genius." Malamud indicated that he felt a strong empathy both with the art and life of Woolf – indeed, with her own humanistic concerns.

"Alma Redeemed" might well be considered Malamud's intertextual sequel to his earlier thematic interest in the mystery of redemption. If Malamud in "The Magic Barrel" employs Stella as the unlikely vehicle for Leo Finkle's redemption, in "Alma Redeemed" he attempts to find within the boundaries of historical realism characters who are the fictional equivalents of Leo Finkle and Stella

Salzman. Such an unlikely pair as Gustav and Alma Mahler served his purposes. In the composer he found an Austrian renegade Jew who, like other Malamudian characters, rejects his past in order to invent a new life. In this instance Mahler discovered his redemption from his old life in the Gentile Alma, who devoted herself to cultivating other Jewish geniuses after Gustav's death. After recounting the history of Alma's relationships, and alluding to her death at eighty-five, Malamud concludes with the pronouncement, "Alma redeemed," which is playfully offered for the reader's meditation in the context of her relationship with Gustav Mahler and other Jewish artistic personalities.

Malamud's interest in biographical fiction, signaled by the vocation of William Dubin, biographer, and developed in "In Kew Gardens" and "Alma Redeemed," was an important new direction for his writing at a time when he may have felt that he was repeating himself; but its full potential was unfortunately unrealized before his death. *The People* aside, Malamud, with an assist from Joyce's Leopold Bloom, will be remembered for textualizing the Jewish experience, when that experience existed among Jewish and Gentile readers alike only as a vague or indeed repressed cultural memory. Indirectly he became a mentor to such Jewish American writers as Philip Roth, Cynthia Ozick and Norma Rosen who have in their own ways acknowledged their literary debt to Malamud's work. As one of his notable technical accomplishments, the Yiddish-sounding voice – modulated to fit the speech of Holocaust survivors, urban artists and writers, rabbis, or even God himself – must surely be compared to Mark Twain's contribution to the American idiom in *The Adventures of Huckleberry Finn* (1884). But Malamud also brought to the surface in the dissonant harmonies of Yiddish and immigrant English the subliminal memories of modern Jewish history. Ever mindful of the dangers of repeating himself, which he sometimes did, Malamud, at his best, created characters possessed of distinctive voices and sensibilities: S. Levin, Harry Lesser, Yakov Bok, William Dubin, and Calvin Cohn are illustrative. Two National Book Awards and a Pulitzer Prize are just a few examples of the literary honors bestowed on the author and his fiction over the years. Although Malamud criticism is presently not a growth industry as it was in the 1960s and 1970s, it will probably soon become more active, particularly as some of his neglected short fiction is reexamined in the light of postmodern theory. The tributes given at Malamud's death by Philip Roth and Saul Bellow testify to his significance in the making of postwar

American literature. And as new ethnic writers enlarge the canon of American literature, they and their critics may look to Bernard Malamud as a literary father who helped to make of that canon a truly magic barrel.

Interviews:

Conversations with Bernard Malamud, edited by Lawrence Lasher (Jackson: University of Mississippi Press, 1991).

Bibliographies:

Nathalie Kosofsky, *Bernard Malamud: An Annotated Checklist* (Kent, Ohio: Kent State University Press, 1969);

Robert D. Habich, "Bernard Malamud: A Bibliographical Survey, *Studies in American Jewish Literature,* 4 (Spring 1978): 78–84;

Joseph A. Grau, "Bernard Malamud: A Bibliographical Addendum," *Bulletin of Bibliography,* 37 (October–December 1980): 157–166, 184;

Grau, "A Further Bibliographical Addendum," *Bulletin of Bibliography,* 38 (April–June 1981): 101–104;

Joel Salzberg, *Bernard Malamud: A Reference Guide* (Boston: G. K. Hall, 1985);

Habich, "Bernard Malamud," in *Contemporary Authors Bibliographic Series: American Novelists,* edited by James J. Martine (Detroit: Bruccoli Clark/Gale, 1986), pp. 261–291;

Richard P. O'Keefe, "Bibliographical Essay: Bernard Malamud," *Studies in American Jewish Literature,* 7 (Fall 1988): 240–250;

Rita N. Kosofsky, *Bernard Malamud: A Descriptive Bibliography* (New York: Greenwood Press, 1991).

Biography:

Bernard Malamud, *Long Work, Short Life,* Bennington Chapbooks in Literature (Bennington: Bennington College, 1985).

References:

Edward A. Abramson, *Bernard Malamud Revisited* (New York: Twayne, 1993);

Pirjo Ahokas, *Forging a New Self: The Adamic Protagonist and the Emergence of a Jewish-American Author as Revealed through the Novels of Bernard Malamud* (Turku: Turun Yliopisto, 1991);

Iska Alter, *The Good Man's Dilemma: Social Criticism in the Fiction of Bernard Malamud* (New York: AMS, 1981);

Robert Alter, "Malamud as Jewish Writer," *Commentary,* 42 (September 1966): 71–76;

Alter, "Updike, Malamud, and the Fire This Time," *Commentary,* 54 (October 1972): 68–74;

Richard Astro and Jackson J. Benson, eds., *The Fiction of Bernard Malamud* (Corvallis: Oregon State University Press, 1977);

Sharon Deykin Baris, "Intertextuality and Reader Responsibility: Living On in Malamud's 'The Mourners,' " *Studies in American Jewish Literature,* 11 (Spring 1992): 45–61;

Jonathan Baumbach, "All Men Are Jews: *The Assistant* by Bernard Malamud," in his *The Landscape of Nightmare* (New York: New York University Press, 1965), pp. 101–122;

Baumbach, "The Economy of Life: The Novels of Bernard Malamud," *Kenyon Review,* 25 (Summer 1963): 438–457;

Samuel Irving Bellman, "Women, Children, and Idiots First: The Transformation Psychology of Bernard Malamud," *Critique,* 7 (Winter 1964–1965): 123–138;

Dorothy Seidman Bilik, "Malamud's Secular Saints and Comic Jobs," in her *Immigrant Survivors: Post-Holocaust Consciousness in Recent Jewish American Fiction* (Middleton, Conn.: Wesleyan University Press, 1981), pp. 53–80;

David Burrows, "The American Past in Malamud's *A New Life,*" in his *Private Dealings,* edited by Burrows and others (Stockholm: Almqvist & Wiksell, 1969), pp. 86–94;

Rafael Cancel-Ortiz, "The Passion of William Dubin: D. H. Lawrence's Themes in Bernard Malamud's *Dubin's Lives,*" *D. H. Lawrence Review,* 16 (Spring 1983): 83–99;

Sandy Cohen, *Bernard Malamud and the Trial by Love* (Amsterdam: Rodopi, 1974);

Lawrence Jay Dessner, "The Playfulness of Bernard Malamud's 'The Magic Barrel,' " *Essays in Literature,* 15 (Spring 1988): 87–101;

Robert Ducharme, *Art and Idea in the Novels of Bernard Malamud: Toward The Fixer* (The Hague: Mouton, 1974);

Edwin M. Eigner, "Malamud's Use of the Quest Romance," *Genre,* 1 (January 1968): 55–75;

Leslie [A.] Field and Joyce [W.] Field, eds., *Bernard Malamud and the Critics* (New York: New York University Press, 1970);

Field and Field, eds., *A Collection of Critical Essays* (Englewood Cliffs, N.J.: Prentice-Hall, 1975);

Harold Fisch, "Biblical Archetypes in *The Fixer,*" *Studies in American Jewish Literature,* 7 (Fall 1988): 162–176;

William Freedman, "From Bernard Malamud, with Discipline and with Love," in *The Fifties,* edited by Warren French (De Land, Fla.: Everett/Edwards, 1970), pp. 133–143;

Daniel Fuchs, "Malamud's *Dubin's Lives:* A Jewish Writer and the Sexual Ethic," *Studies in American Jewish Literature,* 7 (Fall 1988): 205–212;

Marcia Gealy, "Malamud's Short Stories: A Reshaping of Hasidic Tradition," *Judaism,* 28 (Winter 1979): 51–61;

Gealy, "A Reinterpretation of Malamud's *The Natural,*" *Studies in American Jewish Literature,* 4 (Spring 1978): 24–32;

Rita K. Gollin, "Malamud's Dubin and the Morality of Desire," *Papers in Language and Literature,* 18 (Spring 1982): 190–207;

Giles B. Gunn, "Bernard Malamud and the High Cost of Living," in *Adversity and Grace,* edited by Nathan A. Scott Jr. (Chicago: Chicago University Press, 1968), pp. 59–85;

Peter L. Hays, "The Complex Pattern of Redemption in *The Assistant,*" *Centennial Review,* 13 (Spring 1969): 200–214;

Jeffrey Helterman, *Understanding Bernard Malamud* (Columbia: University of South Carolina Press, 1985);

Sheldon J. Hershinow, *Bernard Malamud* (New York: Ungar, 1980);

Hershinow, "Bernard Malamud and the Jewish Humanism," *Religious Humanism,* 13 (Spring 1979): 56–63;

Gerald Hoag, "Malamud's Trial: *The Fixer* and the Critics," *Western Humanities Review,* 24 (Winter 1970): 1–12;

Marcus Klein, "Bernard Malamud: The Sadness of Goodness," in his *After Alienation* (Cleveland: World Publishing, 1965), pp. 247–293;

Josephine Z. Knopp, "Jewish America: Bernard Malamud," in her *The Trial of Judaism in Contemporary Jewish Writing* (Urbana: University of Illinois Press, 1975), pp. 103–125;

Wesley A. Kort, "*The Fixer* and the Death of God," in his *Shriven Selves* (Philadelphia: Fortress, 1972), pp. 90–115;

Shiv P. Kumar, "Marionettes in Talyim: Yiddish Folkfigures in Two Malamud Stories," *Indian Journal of American Studies,* 8 (July 1977): 18–24;

Norman Leer, "The Double Theme in Malamud's *Assistant:* Dostoyevsky with Irony," *Mosaic,* 4, no. 3 (1971): 89–102;

Brita Lindberg-Seyersted, "A Reading of Bernard Malamud's *The Tenants,*" *Journal of American Studies,* 9 (April 1975): 85–102;

Irving Malin, "*The Fixer:* An Overview," *Studies in American Jewish Literature,* 4 (Spring 1978): 40–50;

Herbert Mann, "The Malamudian World: Method and Meaning," *Studies in American Jewish Literature,* 4 (Spring 1978): 2–12;

James M. Mellard, "Malamud's *The Assistant:* The City Novel as Pastoral," *Studies in Short Fiction,* 5 (Fall 1967): 1–11;

Cynthia Ozick, "Literary Blacks and Jews," *Midstream,* 18 (June–July 1972): 10–24;

Sanford Pinsker, "The Schlemiel as Moral Bungler: Bernard Malamud's Ironic Heroes," in his *The Schlemiel as Metaphor* (Carbondale: Southern Illinois University Press, 1971), pp. 87–124;

Barbara Koenig Quart, "Women in Bernard Malamud's Fiction," *Studies in American Jewish Literature,* 3 (1983): 138–150;

Marc L. Ratner, "Style and Humanity in Malamud's Fiction," *Massachusetts Review,* 5 (Summer 1964): 663–683;

Sidney Richman, *Bernard Malamud* (New York: Twayne, 1966);

Earl H. Rovit, "Bernard Malamud and the Jewish Literary Tradition," *Critique,* 3, no. 2 (1960): 3–10;

Joel Salzberg, "Of 'Autobiographical Essence' and Self-Parody: Malamud on 'Exhibition' in *Pictures of Fidelman,*" *Genre,* 24 (Fall 1991): 271–295;

Salzberg, *Critical Essays on Bernard Malamud* (Boston: G. K. Hall, 1987);

Max F. Schulz, "Bernard Malamud's Mythic Proletarians," in his *Radical Sophistication* (Athens: Ohio University Press, 1969), pp. 56–68;

Helen J. Schwartz, "Malamud's Turning Point: The End of Redemption in *Pictures of Fidelman,*" *Studies in American Jewish Literature,* 2 (Winter 1976): 26–37;

Walter Shear, "Culture and Conflict in 'The Assistant,'" *Midwest Quarterly,* 7 (July 1966): 367–380;

Ita Sheres, "The Alienated Sufferer: Malamud's Novels from the Perspective of Old Testament and Jewish Mystical Thought," *Studies in American Jewish Literature,* 4 (Spring 1978): 68–76;

Marjorie Smelstor, "The Schlemiel as Father: Study of Yakov Bok and Eugene Henderson," *Studies in American Jewish Literature,* 4 (Spring 1978): 50–57;

Robert Solotaroff, *Bernard Malamud: A Study of the Short Fiction* (Boston: Twayne, 1989);

Fred L. Standley, "Bernard Malamud: The Novel of Redemption," *Southern Humanities Review,* 5 (Fall 1971): 309–318;

Tony Tanner, "A New Life," in his *City of Words* (New York: Harper & Row, 1971), pp. 322–343;

Frederick W. Turner III, "Myth Inside and Out: Malamud's *The Natural,*" *Novel,* 1 (Winter 1968): 133–139;

Earl R. Wasserman, "*The Natural:* Malamud's World Ceres," *Centennial Review,* 9, no. 4 (1965): 438–460;

Ruth R. Wisse, "Requiem in Several Voices," in her *The Schlemiel as Modern Hero* (Chicago: University of Chicago Press, 1971), pp. 108–124;

Paul Witherington, "Malamud's Allusive Design in *A New Life,*" *Western American Literature,* 10 (Summer 1975): 115–123;

Maurice Wohlgelernter, "Blood Libel — Fact and Fiction," *Tradition,* 8 (Fall 1966): 62–72;

Joan Zlotnick, "Malamud's *The Assistant*: Of Morris, Frank, and St. Francis," *Studies in American Jewish Literature,* 1 (Winter 1975): 20–23.

Papers:

Bernard Malamud's letters to John Hawkes are housed at the Houghton Library, Harvard University. His letters to Harvey Swados are in the Amherst Library Archives and Manuscripts, University of Massachusetts. A lengthy correspondence between Malamud and Rosemarie Beck is located in the Berg Collection of the New York Public Library. The Library of Congress holds Malamud's manuscripts.

Anaïs Nin

(21 February 1903 – 14 January 1977)

Philip K. Jason
United States Naval Academy

See also the Nin entries in *DLB 2: American Novelists Since World War II* and *DLB 4: American Writers in Paris, 1920–1939.*

BOOKS: *D. H. Lawrence: An Unprofessional Study* (Paris: Titus/Black Manikin, 1932; London: Spearman, 1961; Denver: Swallow Press, 1964);

The House of Incest (Paris: Siana/Obelisk, 1936; revised as *House of Incest* (New York: Gemor, 1947); published in *Winter of Artifice/House of Incest* (London: Owen, 1974);

The Winter of Artifice (Paris: Villa Seurat/Obelisk, 1939); revised as *Winter of Artifice* (New York: Gemor, 1942; enlarged edition, Denver: Swallow Press, 1961);

Under a Glass Bell (New York: Gemor, 1944; enlarged edition, London: Editions Poetry, 1947; New York: Dutton, 1948; revised edition, New York: privately printed, 1958);

This Hunger (New York: Gemor, 1945);

Ladders to Fire (New York: Dutton, 1946; revised edition, Denver: Swallow Press, 1963; London: Owen, 1963);

Realism and Reality (Yonkers, N.Y.: Alicat, 1946);

Children of the Albatross (New York: Dutton, 1947; London: Owen, 1959);

On Writing (Hanover, N.H.: Oliver, 1947);

The Four-Chambered Heart (New York: Duell, Sloan & Pierce, 1950; London: Owen, 1959);

A Spy in the House of Love (New York: British Book Centre, 1954; London: Spearman, 1955);

Solar Barque (N.p., 1958); enlarged as *Seduction of the Minotaur* (Denver: Swallow Press, 1961; London: Owen, 1961);

Cities of the Interior (N.p., 1959; revised edition, Denver: Swallow Press, 1961; enlarged edition, Chicago: Swallow Press, 1974; London: Owen, 1978);

Collages (Denver: Swallow Press, 1964; London: Owen, 1964);

The Diary of Anaïs Nin, 1931–1934, edited by Gunther Stuhlmann (New York: Swallow Press/Harcourt, Brace & World, 1966); published as *The Journals of Anaïs Nin, 1931–1934* (London: Owen, 1966);

The Diary of Anaïs Nin, 1934–1939, edited by Stuhlmann (New York: Swallow Press/Harcourt, Brace & World, 1967); published as *The Journals of Anaïs Nin, 1934–1939* (London: Owen, 1967);

The Novel of the Future (New York: Macmillan, 1968; London: Collier-Macmillan, 1968);

Unpublished Selections from the Diary, edited by Duane Schneider (Athens, Ohio: Schneider, 1968);

The Diary of Anaïs Nin, 1939–1944, edited by Stuhlmann (New York: Harcourt, Brace & World, 1969); published as *The Journals of Anaïs Nin, 1939–1944* (London: Owen, 1970);

Nuances (N.p.: Sans Souci, 1970);

The Diary of Anaïs Nin, 1944–1947, edited by Stuhlmann (New York: Harcourt Brace Jovanovich, 1971); published as *The Journals of Anaïs Nin, 1944–1947* (London: Owen, 1972);

Paris Revisited (Santa Barbara, Cal.: Capra Press, 1972);

Anaïs Nin Reader, edited by Philip K. Jason (Chicago: Swallow Press, 1973);

The Diary of Anaïs Nin, 1947–1955, edited by Stuhlmann (New York: Harcourt Brace Jovanovich, 1974); published as *The Journals of Anaïs Nin, 1947–1955* (London: Owen, 1974);

A Woman Speaks: The Lectures, Seminars and Interviews of Anaïs Nin, edited by Evelyn J. Hinz (Chicago: Swallow Press, 1975; London: Allen, 1978);

Aphrodisiac: Erotic Drawings by John Boyce for Selected Passages from the Works of Anaïs Nin (New York: Crown, 1976);

The Diary of Anaïs Nin, 1955–1966, edited by Stuhlmann (New York: Harcourt Brace Jovanovich, 1976); published as *The Journals of Anaïs Nin, 1955–1966* (London: Owen, 1977);

Anaïs Nin   (photograph by Marg Moore)

In Favor of the Sensitive Man and Other Essays (New York & London: Harcourt Brace Jovanovich, 1976);

Delta of Venus: Erotica (New York & London: Harcourt Brace Jovanovich, 1977); abridged as *The Illustrated Delta of Venus,* with photographs by Bob Carlos Clarke (London: W. H. Allen, 1980);

Waste of Timelessness and Other Early Stories (Weston, Conn.: Magic Circle, 1977);

Linotte: The Early Diary of Anaïs Nin, 1914–1920, translated by Jean L. Sherman (New York & London: Harcourt Brace Jovanovich, 1978);

Little Birds: Erotica (New York & London: Harcourt Brace Jovanovich, 1979);

Portrait in Three Dimensions (N.p.: Concentric Circle, 1979);

The Diary of Anaïs Nin, 1966–1974, edited by Stuhlmann (New York & London: Harcourt Brace Jovanovich, 1980); published as *The Journals of Anaïs Nin, 1966–1974* (London: Owen, 1980);

The Early Diary of Anaïs Nin: Volume Two, 1920–1923 (New York & London: Harcourt Brace Jovanovich, 1982);

The Early Diary of Anaïs Nin: Volume Three, 1923–1927 (San Diego: Harcourt Brace Jovanovich,

1983; published as *Journal of a Wife: The Early Diary of Anaïs Nin, 1923–1927* (London & Washington, D.C.: Owen, 1984);

The Early Diary of Anaïs Nin: Volume Four, 1927–1931 (San Diego: Harcourt Brace Jovanovich, 1985);

The White Blackbird and Other Writings, bound with *The Tales of an Old Geisha and Other Stories* by Kanoko Okamoto (Santa Barbara: Capra Press, 1985);

Henry and June: From the Unexpurgated Diary of Anaïs Nin (San Diego: Harcourt Brace Jovanovich, 1986; London: Allen, 1987);

Incest: From "A Journal of Love," The Unexpurgated Diary of Anaïs Nin, 1932–1934 (San Diego: Harcourt Brace Jovanovich, 1992; London: Owen, 1993).

OTHER: Henry Miller, *Tropic of Cancer,* introduction by Nin (Paris: Obelisk, 1934).

The stories and novels of Anaïs Nin are highly distinctive creations of a groundbreaking writer who helped to define a feminine tradition in literature. Daring and determined, she broke through the barriers of convention to address such themes as incest, homosexual desire, and erotic experimentation from a perspective of compassion and human development rather than of sensationalism. Informed by her readings of the major psychoanalytic thinkers, and with personal self-creation and transformation as her overarching theme, she struggled against the boundaries of formal conventions, especially those of realism and genre, seeking shapes and methods of expression that are essentially lyrical and nonlinear. Because her art is concerned with essences rather than surfaces, she sought to discover and employ techniques that would minimize dependence on abstraction and editorial narration. While she did not always succeed at this task, her best work sets a high standard, demanding and justifying new critical emphases for an expanded domain of literary art.

Nin, born near Paris to Joaquin Nin and Rosa Culmell de Nin on 21 February 1903, developed an international perspective at an early age. Her parents, both Cuban-born, traveled with their young children through various cultural capitals on the path of her father's career as a concert pianist. In the summer of 1914 her mother relocated from Barcelona to New York City, taking Anaïs and her brothers, the older Thorvald and the younger Joaquin, along. Just before leaving Barcelona, Nin began a diary (written in French until 1920) that she would continue for the rest of her life and that would become a notable part of twentieth-century literature. The move to New York separated the father from the rest of the family, a shaping event in young Anaïs's emotional life.

Her diary reveals a lively, precocious, and dreamy adolescent living in a close-knit, female-dominated Catholic family; in its pages her relationship with her absent father is continued in her imagination. In the diary the young Nin conducted a rigorous moral self-scrutiny, and she was moved by the color and feeling of Catholic ceremony. Adolescent infatuations, including one with her cousin Eduardo Sanchez, gave way to a deep and respectful romance with Hugh (Hugo) Guiler, whom she met at age eighteen and married two years later, in 1923, in Havana. In the year before her marriage she often worked as a model for artists and photographers.

Encouraged by her husband, Nin gave increasing attention to her aspiration to be a writer. On her twenty-first birthday she recorded that she had returned to work on a novel that would be critiqued by novelist John Erskine, who had been her husband's teacher at Columbia University and with whom, several years later, Nin came close to having an affair. By Christmas 1924, on Hugh's initiative,

his employer, National City Bank, transferred him to its Paris branch. As she turned twenty-two, Anaïs Nin Guiler resettled in the city of her birth and enjoyed a brief, pleasant reunion with her father. For the better part of the next fifteen years Paris served as the nurturing environment for her liberation from social convention and for her growth as an independent artist.

Although Nin began, completed, and abandoned a series of novelistic projects during the 1920s and 1930s, her art first developed and reached the public as prose poems, short stories, and novellas, with some pieces combining genres. Her first significant publication, however, was a response to D. H. Lawrence's fiction that critic Evelyn J. Hinz considered the seminal guidepost in her exploration of Nin's art. *D. H. Lawrence: An Unprofessional Study* (1932) is the place in which Nin first struggled to come to terms with what would become her own brand of modernism. As Hinz points out, the book is a creative, subjective criticism that more often "describes what she will do than what Lawrence has done." As such, it remains a proper starting point for understanding Nin's aesthetic orientation.

Given this ambitious preparation for her own fiction, it is surprising that five years passed before Nin made any notable achievement as a fiction writer. In part this delay stemmed from her indecisiveness about the proper avenue for the development and manifestation of her role as a woman artist. Also, as her personal life became increasingly frenzied and divided — wife to bank functionary and Spanish-dancing partner Hugh Guiler; mistress and helpmate to the destitute parasite-genius Henry Miller; bedmate to her own father; patient, assistant, and seductress of the brilliant psychotherapist and theorist Otto Rank — her diary became more and more the place in which some measure of integration took place. Moreover, she recognized in her stillborn attempts at fiction that she could not convincingly enter into the mind of another and that writing in the third person was unnatural for her. Transforming the diary, the created self, into fiction was clearly her best chance for success. But why transform it? Why not just publish it?

Questions such as these plagued Nin during the mid 1930s, with persistent pullings in one direction or another by her husband, by Miller, and by Rank complicating matters. Finally, her core concerns regarding creativity itself — sexual identity, narcissism, and incestuous longing, worked and reworked with suggestions from both Miller and Rank — sorted themselves into her two major titles

Nin, circa 1920

of the period: *The House of Incest* (1936) and *The Winter of Artifice* (1939).

House of Incest (as the book was retitled when revised in 1947) is marked by the influence of the French Symbolists and Surrealists. Best approached as a poetic sequence, it effectively mines archetypal patterns as it offers an equation between self-love and incest and searches for an escape from the confinements of both while brilliantly evoking their powerful narcotic attractions. Described by Benjamin Franklin V and Duane Schneider as Nin's "first, best, and most challenging volume of fiction," it is most notable for its intensity and originality.

The sections of *Winter of Artifice* (retitled with the 1942 revised edition) are somewhat more conventional fictions. The earliest part, "Lilith" (in later editions called "Djuna" and finally "Winter of Artifice"), is the thinly veiled refashioning of Nin's reunion with her father as recorded in *The Diary of Anaïs Nin, 1931–1934* (1966) and then more fully and shockingly revealed in *Incest: From "A Journal of Love," The Unexpurgated Diary of Anaïs Nin, 1932–1934* (1993). Bettina L. Knapp's detailed discussion shows how Nin attempted to fuse dream, reverie, and stream of consciousness in ways that defy the conventions of plot and characterization. In "The Voice," a more fragmented narrative, the central character is at a more mature stage of her development. This story, which carries echoes of Nin's relationship with Rank, depends even more than "Winter of Artifice" on dream motifs and techniques. The third story found in the original edition of *Winter of Artifice* is "Djuna" and deals, with minimal disguise, with the Nin–Henry Miller–June Miller triangle uncovered many years later in the diary excerpts collected as *Henry and June: From the Unexpurgated Diary of Anaïs Nin* (1986). (Though dropped from later editions, it is available, as "Hans and Johanna," in the 1989 issue of *Anaïs: An International Journal*.)

The Gemor (1942) and Dutton (1948) editions of *Winter of Artifice* are two-part versions, while the

Swallow edition (1961) adds a third section, "Stella," originally a section of Nin's *This Hunger* (1945) and of the first edition of *Ladders to Fire* (1946). For Nancy Scholar, "Stella," which is based on Nin's diary portrait of actress Luise Rainer, is the most successful of these three thematically repetitive works because it is the most emotionally intense and poetically concentrated.

Nin's three Paris publications received little notice, and when she moved to New York to escape the impending war she encountered the same indifference from commercial publishers that she had met when trying to market her work from Paris. Committed to sharing her art and building a readership, she founded her own imprint, Gemor Press, and began bringing out a small list of titles dominated by her own writings. Gemor was named for Gonzalo More, a Peruvian exile who was for a time her lover in Paris. He followed her to New York and became her principal assistant and titular manager of the press. Her first Gemor title, a shortened version of *Winter of Artifice* (1942), provoked the most significant early discussion of Nin's fiction – William Carlos Williams's " 'Men . . . Have No Tenderness': Anaïs Nin's 'Winter of Artifice' " (1942), in which he praises her search for a female approach to writing that is neither male-defined nor reactionary. Though he considers her achievement limited, successful only in isolated passages, he is appreciative of her intentions, direction, and promise.

Nin's Gemor Press first edition of *Under a Glass Bell* (1944), her collection of short stories, received a tremendous boost from Edmund Wilson in his 1 April 1944 review in *The New Yorker* but mixed notices on the whole. The 1948 Dutton edition, which also included the two-part "Winter of Artifice," received much more attention, but few of the reviews were enthusiastic. Nonetheless, many Nin critics consider several of the stories in this collection to be among her finest work. Oliver Evans, in the first book-length critical examination of her fiction, finds greater stylistic sophistication here than in the *Winter of Artifice* novelettes. Franklin and Schneider, who rank *Under a Glass Bell* second only to *House of Incest*, argue that her art lends itself best to shorter forms. They make a distinction between the original edition of eight stories, which they greatly admire, and the later thirteen-story version (1948 as part of the Dutton volume; 1958 separately), which they find diluted by significantly weaker material. Scholar generally echoes their sentiments, while other critics – Sharon Spencer and Knapp in particular – place a higher value on the

ambitious *Cities of the Interior* (1959) sequence. The stories most often singled out for praise are "Houseboat," "Under a Glass Bell," "Ragtime," "Birth," and "Hejda."

Nin had several false starts in developing what would be her first published novel. In 1945 she brought out *This Hunger* in a limited edition under her Gemor Press imprint. This title includes three sections: "Hejda," "Lillian and Djuna," and "Stella." Incoherent as a novel, *This Hunger* nonetheless projects itself as something more than the miscellanies of thematically or stylistically related materials that she had already published. Unwilling to base an extended piece on a central, elaborated plot, she continued to experiment with ways of bringing greater unity to compositions made of narrative fragments that could also have separate lives. Reviews remained mixed, but there were enough positive responses to her various Gemor Press titles to win her a contract with E. P. Dutton, her first commercial publisher.

Ladders to Fire (1946), Nin's first novel, is comprised of a first part that eliminates "Hejda" but reproduces the other two sections of *This Hunger* and of a second part called "Bread and the Wafer." For the final edition (1963) she discarded "Stella," which appears in the 1961 edition of *Winter of Artifice*. The section "This Hunger" here includes only the section formerly called "Lillian and Djuna," while "Bread and the Wafer" remains intact.

Essentially, *Ladders to Fire* gains its unity by establishing Lillian as its central character, focusing on different phases of her dilemmas. A pianist about whose career the reader learns nothing, Lillian is unfulfilled in her roles as wife and mother. A diminished sense of self results from these frustrations and leads her to experiments in less conventional relationships. As seen by her newfound friend and confidant Djuna, red-haired Lillian is a woman of strong, natural sensuality that had become paralyzed. Djuna, passive and enigmatic, serves as a kind of wise-woman alter ego. The two friends exchange intimacies and become engaged in a mutual courtship in which identities are tested and measured through rituals of gift giving and dressing alike. In a lesbian interlude Lillian's sense of self-worth is strengthened, and an adventuress is let loose. Lillian practices her more liberated femininity with Jay, a lover whose behavior is a combination of frustrating irresponsibility and a living in and for the present that proves tonic. A brilliant painter, Jay is also an ironist who tends to extract the humor of situations rather than the pathos. As sexual partners, Jay and Lillian are well matched.

*Nin with her husband, Hugh Guiler (wearing glasses), and her cousin Eduardo
Sánchez in the early 1930s*

"Bread and the Wafer" mysteriously transports the key characters from New York to Paris. The story of Lillian and Jay continues, with Jay's childlike nature receiving more attention, along with Lillian's confused attitude toward her nurturing role. This section is energized by the introduction of a fourth major character, Sabina, a discovery and obsession of Jay's who seems like a passionate manifestation of the hidden Lillian. A relationship between these two women develops that mirrors the Lillian-Djuna relationship of "This Hunger." Here, however, Lillian has the cooler, more contemplative role, as if she has absorbed or replaced Djuna and in turn been absorbed into the even more fiery (though blonde) Sabina. The Djuna character still exists, but she has been reduced in function and power. A party filled with minor characters provides a wry glimpse of Montparnasse decadence —

stunted beings whose psychic blocks keep them imprisoned, poisonous, and unfulfilled. Djuna, imprisoned in timidity and introspection, remains as a despairing witness who cannot even enter this sorry game. Here and in most of Nin's fictions outer events are sparse, and imagery does not function in accordance with realist technique. Instead, images seem to well up from internal sensibility and become projected into scenes and settings.

By 1947, when Dutton published *Children of the Albatross,* Nin had a clearer sense of her intentions. In a brief headnote she writes, "Some of the characters in the book have already appeared in *Ladders to Fire;* and some characters, such as Uncle Philip, make their first appearance here and will reappear in later volumes. The books can therefore be read separately or can be considered as parts of a tapestry." The tapestry simile suggests the spatial, plastic mode of her design. Whatever one reads next need not be taken as having happened next. As Spencer asserts in her introduction to the 1974 edition of *Cities of the Interior,* "A reader can begin with any of the five novels and move to the other four in any order." Nonetheless, the order in which they are offered in *Cities of the Interior* – including *Ladders to Fire, Children of the Albatross, The Four-Chambered Heart* (1950), *A Spy in the House of Love* (1954), and *Solar Barque* (1958; revised as *Seduction of the Minotaur* [1961]) – provides the most accessible path.

Children of the Albatross is made up of two parts that vaguely mirror their counterparts in the final version of *Ladders to Fire.* "The Sealed Room" depicts claustrophobic, introverted intimacies much like those in "This Hunger," while "The Café" offers a quasi-satiric social dimension that echoes the party scene in "Bread and the Wafer." While the ostensible setting remains Paris and its environs, the cast of characters is apparently American, and, besides a few haphazard place-names, the setting, aside from Djuna's home, barely figures in the first section. Indeed, the fact that the reader is traversing "cities of the interior" receives additional emphasis in this novel.

Djuna, with her mysterious interiority, is the focal character of the first section. She is given a background (including time spent in an orphanage), a vocation as a dancer, a tendency to live in dreams, strong memories of sexual threat, and an adolescent emotional nature that is at odds with her penetrating intellect. In "The Sealed Room," denoting more a psychic than a physical space, she is surrounded by young men who possess homosexual leanings or sexual uncertainty and who find her attractive and unthreatening. A major theme of this section is the threat and stultifying nature of male adulthood. Twenty-seven-year-old Djuna admires the malleability of the adolescent and fears the fixity of adulthood. For Nin fixity is spiritual death. The minor characters Donald, Michael, Lawrence, and Paul all have their roles to play in developing this theme. Though Nin is often accused of not sufficiently individualizing her characters, with this group at least she does so admirably. Most significant is Paul, whom Djuna shelters from the abusive and inhibiting strictures of obtuse parents. Here and throughout Nin's work Djuna serves as an exemplar of the struggle between wisdom and dogma. She strives to maintain a kind of innocence that does not deny experience.

"The Café" reconfigures Nin's trio of Djuna, Sabina, and Lillian and defines them against each other as partners for Jay. The café itself, Sabina's haunt, is depicted as the abode of the rootless. Perhaps nowhere else in all of Nin's fiction is the symbolic evocation of a Parisian setting put to better use. The major and minor characters are placed in brief vignettes that deepen their portraits and highlight their complicated interrelationships. After each vignette the characters make their way to the café, where Nin creates a group scene in which various degrees of contact and withdrawal, surrender and isolation, are portrayed.

The two parts of *Children of the Albatross* are connected by Nin's concern with the uncompleted search for emotional maturity and selfhood. While each section, as Franklin and Schneider have noted, has a firm structure, the bonding of the two lacks inevitability. Moreover, nothing exhibits the unifying centrality that Lillian provides for *Ladders to Fire.* One could argue that *Children of the Albatross* is Djuna's novel, but the attention given to Lillian and Sabina creates a diffuse, scattered effect, unless the reader begins to consider them less as distinct characters in the traditional sense and more as overlapping phases of a developing type of character whose possibilities are separately incarnated and abstracted under the three names. The two sections operate more effectively as movements in the whole *Cities of the Interior* enterprise than as halves of a self-contained novel.

As she explains in her preface to the 1974 edition of *Cities of the Interior,* Nin had hoped that Dutton would publish her third novel, *The Four-Chambered Heart,* soon after *Children of the Albatross* so that readers and reviewers could appreciate the continuity and interrelatedness of these efforts. However, when Dutton planned a four-year interval between books, she looked elsewhere for a publisher. Nonetheless, three years elapsed before Duell, Sloan & Pierce published *The Four-Chambered Heart.* In the interim Dutton published the first commercial edition of Nin's earlier fiction. This 1948 *Under a Glass Bell and Other Stories* includes thirteen short stories plus "Winter of Artifice," billed as a novelette with two parts separately titled "Djuna" and "The Voice."

At age forty-five Nin had reached a momentary peak in her career, a prestigious fiction writer with three titles in print from a respected trade publisher. By this time Nin had wearied of New York and began a process of reorientation, finally settling in California. A 1947 trip through the American Southwest and Mexico put a psychic and aesthetic distance between what she came to see as New York's frenzied tawdriness and these warmer, sun-

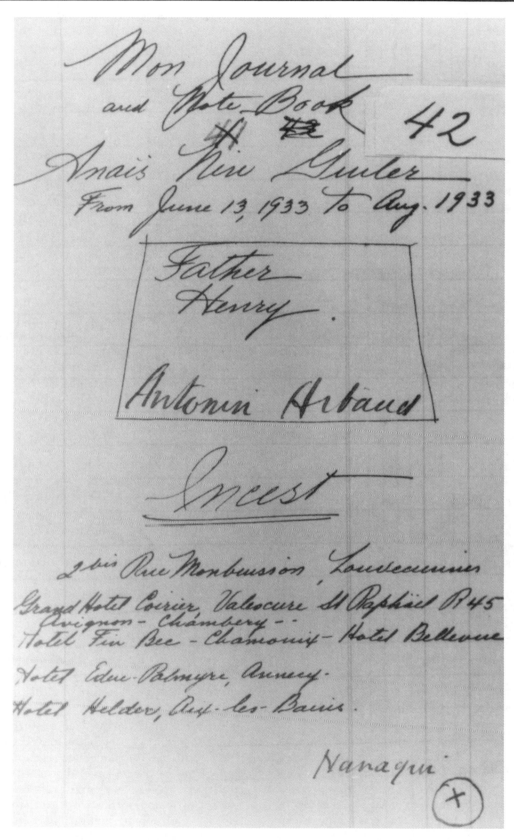

The cover page of book 42 of Nin's diary, which begins her account of her relationship with her father. (From Incest: From "A Journal of Love,"
The Unexpurgated Diary of Anaïs Nin, 1932–1934 *(1992); courtesy of the Anaïs Nin Trust).*

nier, friendlier, and less confining environments. These new settings figure importantly in her last two novels, but she had not yet finished writing about Paris and New York.

The Four-Chambered Heart can be considered as an exploration of the limits of union between human beings. Zora, the manipulative hypochondriac, represents the destructive side of the rebellious, earthy, and fatalistic Rango. Rango, who has taken up the role of gypsy musician, is depicted as endlessly torn by his conflicting creative and destructive urges. Djuna naturally identifies with and tries to nourish Rango's creative side. For her, Rango's bearlike manner and his easy physicality are a desired antidote to her cerebral mechanisms of judgment and delay. Through him and through absorbing the barge-home's communion with the river's flow she moves toward a greater sense of wholeness and spontaneity. Rango, through his growing commitment to political causes, finds a means to self-realization that is at odds with Djuna's concern with individual, inner revolutions. Zora remains a lost soul.

This novel shows a marked increase in Nin's concern for surface texture and dramatized event. It is thus more conventional and seems more polished than her first novels. Furthermore, the material is more tightly integrated. Djuna is not rivaled as the central character, and the two secondary characters, Rango and Zora, are drawn with care. The reader's interest stays with this triangular relationship from beginning to end, and the dominant setting of the barge-houseboat works well in both its literal and symbolic dimensions.

As her first three novels reappeared, Nin received a handful of accolades that were almost swamped by voices of disapproval. Her writing was called tedious, abstract, and obscure. Her characters were considered unattractive and self-absorbed. She was faulted for intrusive, editorializing narration. Her admirers — including Violet R. Lang, Hayden Carruth, and Charles Rolo — appreciated the fineness of her poetic style and her vivid rendering of sophisticated psychological insights. However, her career as a commercial novelist was not sustained by sales or critical acclaim. For her next novel she returned to what amounted to self-publication. In a 1965 essay James Korges called *The Four-Chambered Heart* the best of her work, "a fine achievement by a minor, flawed novelist." Although his commentary is largely negative, he finds here Nin's best "balance of intensity and control, of insight and art."

A Spy in the House of Love was published by the British Book Centre but with expenses underwritten by Nin. Aside from the diary volumes and her posthumous collections of erotica, the novel, perhaps her most experimental, became her greatest commercial success, with mass paperback editions by Avon (1958), Bantam (1968), Penguin (1973), and Pocket Books (1994). Its stylistic features are well-summarized by Knapp: "an attempt at further depersonalization of the main character; greater emphasis on cyclical time, thus delimiting the protagonist's vision and actions; repetitions of entire scenes, each time played out in a slightly different manner, thus heightening the ambiguity and multifaceted nature of life in general."

For *A Spy in the House of Love* Nin shifted the scene to New York and selected Sabina as her major character. An actress professionally and personally, Sabina is panicked by a fear of exposure of the intricate web of lies she has devised to cover her infidelities. Her fear and insecurity are projected into the device of the Lie Detector, a character who Sabina believes is scrutinizing her actions. Unfulfilled in her marriage to the tender and protective Alan, she is drawn into a series of relationships with a variety of men, each of whom satisfies, at least for a while, one aspect of her fluid, unstable personality. Constantly remorseful yet always ready for the next adventure, she serves to heighten an important theme of *Cities of the Interior* concerning the tension in each individual between psychic unity and multiplicity, integrity and dispersion. Nin asks if the psychological realities of modern life are susceptible to traditional moral judgments.

Perhaps more than Nin's other novels, *A Spy in the House of Love* depends on suggestive images that reinforce both theme and structure. One cluster of images — parasol, umbrella, and parachute — emphasizes the cyclical pattern of Sabina's behavior and thus of the novel's path. These images, with shapes at once rounded and segmented, also underscore the theme of unity versus multiplicity while suggesting by their functions the wish for protection and support, however fragile the instrument. Noteworthy also is the structure of allusions creating a musical motif.

Although it received enthusiastic attention from a few critics — notably Maxwell Geismar and Jean Fanchette — the immediate reactions to *A Spy in the House of Love* were generally hostile or indifferent, leaving Nin once again to rely on her own resources for bringing her work to the public. *Solar Barque,* the title that temporarily served as the final installment of *Cities of the Interior,* was self-published by Nin and later absorbed into the one-volume *Cities of the Interior.* Though a culmination of sorts, this publication also marked a decade of private publication following her limited commercial success of the mid-to-late 1940s. However, her publishing fortunes took a turn for the better two years later in 1961 when Alan Swallow, then a small but noteworthy publisher based in Denver, added *Cities of the Interior* and other Nin titles to his list. Also that year Swallow published her *Seduction of the Minotaur,* which included an augmented *Solar Barque* and completed *Cities of the Interior,* though no complete single-volume edition existed until 1974.

Seduction of the Minotaur returns to Lillian, who has accepted an engagement as jazz pianist in a Mexican resort town. Nowhere does Nin handle setting more evocatively than here, making the luxuriant natural scene as well as its social and cultural dimension an important force in the novel. The setting is a restorative force, an environment whose vivid colorations and natural rhythms help Lillian reach a high measure of self-understanding and inner peace. Though she meets a series of men, no passionate relationships develop. Each man provides a means for her to explore some aspect of her past and of her own psyche. As Spencer notes in *Collage of Dreams: The Writings of Anaïs Nin* (1981), a more mature Lillian "is now able both to experience and to control her emotions." Accepting and implementing the advice of Dr. Hernandez, she unravels the repetition impulse in her life as she prepares to give her marriage to Larry a second chance.

The last third of the novel, cast as a series of memories and observations during Lillian's plane trip home, brings both the novel and the sequence of novels to completion. To this end the narrator allows her to collect thoughts and judgments about the other main characters of *Cities of the Interior,* including Djuna, Sabina, and Jay. Nin signals Lillian's importance by having her open and close the cycle. The closing most clearly positions her between the remote, shy, introspective, and analytical Djuna and the hedonistic, spontaneous, sexually explosive Sabina. Knapp considers these other women to be aspects of Lillian, "satellite personalities" who live "as her mirror reflections." Lillian's movement toward balance is defined, here and throughout *Cities of the Interior,* as a narrowing oscillation between the extremes they represent, though each of the other women is portrayed as undergoing similar internal oscillations.

Once the majority of Nin's canon was in print, serious critical discussion began to grow. Between them Frank Baldanza's "Anaïs Nin" (1962) and Oliver Evans's "Anaïs Nin and the Discovery of Inner Space" (1962) established the poles of debate in Nin criticism. Baldanza accuses Nin of offering only a series of "pointless, rambling explorations of erotic entanglements and neurotic fears," while Evans champions her rhythmic language and her illuminating and luminous use of psychoanalytic insight. With Swallow's 1964 publication of Nin's self-proclaimed final novel, *Collages,* the opportunity for extended critical discussion that considered her fiction as a whole was at hand. Thus, Evans's *Anaïs Nin* (1968) became the first book-length study attempting to treat her work comprehensively. Evans deals with her fiction only; later criticism gradually shifted its focus, as did Nin, to her multivolume diary.

Collages was a departure for Nin in many ways. In it she abandoned the characters that had obsessed her for decades and took a lighter tone. While most of the stories involve Renate, an Austrian-born painter living in California, a few do not. Nonetheless, she is the binding force for a series of vignettes that touch upon Nin's theme of creativity and transformation while allowing wry glances at the culture of the western United States. There is even a note of self-mockery that provides a pleasant contrast from the somber mood of so much of her work. Most critics agree that while *Collages* has highly effective interludes and a buoyant spirit, its unity is weak. Many of the episodes are detachable and interchangeable, though by the analogy announced in the title and developed elsewhere one can consider this the most programmatically spatial of her fictional assemblages.

On the issue of how Nin's literary structures parallel the art of the collage and the mobile, Spencer's observations are most useful. While she considers Renate to be "the most fully developed example of Nin's concept of femininity and art," Nin's harshest critic, Scholar, finds Renate insufficiently developed. Evans believes that the many positive reviews of *Collages* attest to Nin's delayed recognition as an important writer rather than to the actual merits of this book. *Collages* is her most admittedly autobiographical fiction. The prototypes for Renate and other characters are not disguised; historical characters are mixed with fictional ones; and the diary sources are allowed to rise to the reader's consciousness, thus preparing the way for the publication of the actual diary volumes that began two years later.

Once the publication of Nin's diary was initiated, critical attention turned increasingly to this life project and away from her accomplishment as an inventive writer of fiction. Aside from the popular attention elicited by her erotica, nothing has sustained interest in Nin as much as the personal jour-

Nin setting the type for the revised 1942 edition of Winter of
Artifice, *which she published herself*

ney recorded in the diary. The seven-volume *Diary of Anaïs Nin,* the four-volume *Early Diary of Anaïs Nin,* and the several volumes of "unexpurgated" reeditings – including *Henry and June, Incest,* and the projected "Fire" – have dwarfed, somewhat unfairly, her achievement as an innovator in fiction.

Though properly seen as an appendage to the diary, Nin's fiction is nonetheless a significant achicvement, remarkable for its lyric intensity, its probing of previously taboo themes, its psychoanalytic orientation, its questioning of assumptions about gender, and its nonlinear structure. Indeed, some of the more provocative recent studies challenge the distinction between diary and fiction, viewing the Nin canon holistically from the perspectives of psychoanalytic and gender criticism. Taken together, the fiction and diary provide readers with an unparalleled example of the creative process and of the inadequacy of traditional genre studies to comprehend a truly unique artist.

Letters:

A Literate Passion: Letters of Anaïs Nin and Henry Miller, 1932–1953, edited by Gunther Stuhlmann (San Diego: Harcourt Brace Jovanovich, 1987; London: Allison & Busby, 1987).

Interviews:

Duane Schneider, *An Interview with Anaïs Nin* (Athens, Ohio: Schncider, 1970; London: Village, 1973);

Wendy M. DuBow, ed., *Conversations with Anaïs Nin* (Jackson: University Press of Mississippi, 1994).

Bibliographies:

Benjamin Franklin V, *Anaïs Nin: A Bibliography* (Kent, Ohio: Kent State University Press, 1973);

Rose Marie Cutting, *Anaïs Nin: A Reference Guide* (Boston: G. K. Hall, 1978).

Biographies:

Noël Riley Fitch, *Anaïs: The Erotic Life of Anaïs Nin* (Boston: Little, Brown, 1993);

Deirdre Bair, *Anaïs Nin: A Biography* (New York: Putnam, 1995).

References:

Frank Baldanza, "Anaïs Nin," *Minnesota Review,* 2 (Winter 1962): 263–271;

Patricia A. Deduck, *Realism, Reality, and the Fictional Theory of Alain Robbe-Grillet and Anaïs Nin*

(Washington, D.C.: University Press of America, 1982);

Oliver Evans, *Anaïs Nin* (Carbondale: Southern Illinois University Press, 1968);

Evans, "Anaïs Nin and the Discovery of Inner Space," *Prairie Schooner,* 36 (Fall 1962): 217–231;

Benjamin Franklin V and Duane Schneider, *Anaïs Nin: An Introduction* (Athens: Ohio University Press, 1979);

Evelyn J. Hinz, *The Mirror and the Garden: Realism and Reality in the Writings of Anaïs Nin,* revised edition (New York: Harcourt Brace Jovanovich, 1973);

Hinz, ed., *The World of Anaïs Nin: Critical and Cultural Perspectives* (Winnipeg: University of Manitoba Press, 1978);

Philip K. Jason, *Anaïs Nin and Her Critics* (Columbia, S.C.: Camden House, 1993);

Jason, "The Gemor Press," *Anaïs: An International Journal,* 2 (1984): 24–39;

Bettina L. Knapp, *Anaïs Nin* (New York: Ungar, 1978);

James Korges, "Curiosities: Nin and Miller, Hemingway and Seager," *Critique: Studies in Modern Fiction,* 7 (Spring–Summer 1965): 66–81;

Nancy Scholar, *Anaïs Nin* (Boston: Twayne, 1984);

Sharon Spencer, *Collage of Dreams: The Writings of Anaïs Nin,* revised edition (New York: Harcourt Brace Jovanovich, 1981);

Spencer, ed., *Anaïs, Art and Artists: A Collection of Essays* (Greenwood, Fla.: Penkevil, 1986);

William Carlos Williams, " 'Men . . . Have No Tenderness': Anaïs Nin's 'Winter of Artifice,' " in *New Directions No. 7,* edited by James Laughlin (New York: New Directions, 1942), pp. 429–436;

Robert Zaller, ed., *A Casebook on Anaïs Nin* (New York: NAL/Meridian, 1974).

Papers:
Major Nin materials are located in two collections. Northwestern University has drafts of Nin's book on D. H. Lawrence and almost all of her fiction (including unpublished works), while the University of California at Los Angeles has the manuscript diaries, correspondence, and extensive audiovisual materials.

Tim O'Brien

(1 October 1946 –)

Thomas Myers
Saint Norbert College

See also the O'Brien entries in *DLB Yearbook: 1980* and *Documentary Series 9: American Writers of the Vietnam War: W. D. Ehrhart, Larry Heinemann, Tim O'Brien, Walter McDonald, John M. Del Vecchio.*

BOOKS: *If I Die in a Combat Zone, Box Me Up and Ship Me Home* (New York: Delacorte/Seymour Lawrence, 1973; London: Calder & Boyars, 1973; revised edition, New York: Delacorte/Seymour Lawrence, 1979);
Northern Lights (New York: Delacorte/Seymour Lawrence, 1975; London: Calder & Boyars, 1976);
Going After Cacciato (New York: Delacorte/Seymour Lawrence, 1978; London: Cape, 1979);
The Nuclear Age (New York: Knopf, 1985; London: Collins, 1986);
The Things They Carried (Boston: Houghton Mifflin/Seymour Lawrence, 1990; London: Collins, 1990);
In the Lake of the Woods (Boston: Houghton Mifflin/Seymour Lawrence, 1994).

SELECTED PERIODICAL PUBLICATIONS – UNCOLLECTED: "Claudia Mae's Wedding Day," *Redbook,* 141 (October 1973): 102–103;
"Where Have You Gone, Charming Billy?," *Redbook,* 145 (May 1975): 81, 127–132;
"Landing Zone Bravo," *Denver Quarterly,* 4 (August 1975): 72–77;
"Speaking of Courage," *Massachusetts Review,* 17 (Summer 1976): 243–253;
"The Way It Mostly Was," *Shenandoah,* 27 (Winter 1976): 35–45;
"Keeping Watch by Night," *Redbook,* 148 (December 1976): 65–67;
"The Fisherman," *Esquire,* 88 (October 1977): 92, 130, 134;
"Calling Home," *Redbook,* 150 (December 1977): 75–76;
"The Nuclear Age," *Atlantic,* 243 (June 1979): 58–67;
"Civil Defense," *Esquire,* 94 (August 1980): 82–88;

"Underground Tests," *Esquire,* 104 (November 1985): 252–254, 256, 258–259;
"Enemies and Friends," *Harper's,* 280 (March 1990): 30–31;
"Field Trip," *McCall's,* 117 (August 1990): 78–79;
"The People We Marry," *Atlantic,* 269 (January 1992): 90–98;
"Loon Point," *Esquire,* 119 (January 1993): 90–94.

Tim O'Brien, a contemporary American novelist and short-story writer of immense imaginative power and range, freely admits that the Vietnam War was the dark, jarring experience that made him a writer. In a 1993 interview (unpublished) he described the war as the "Lone Ranger watershed event of my life," and the time before his induction into the United States Army as "a horrid, confused, traumatic period – the trauma of trying to decide whether or not to go to Canada." O'Brien went to Vietnam and served there in the Fifth Battalion, Forty-Sixth Infantry – the U.S. Army's Americal Division – from January 1969 to March 1970, patrolling the deadly Batangan Peninsula and the tragic villages of My Lai after the massacre there in March 1968. Unlike many of his peers, O'Brien returned to America sound of mind and body if not of spirit. He wrote of his war experience in a spare, poetically allusive, and classically toned personal memoir, *If I Die in a Combat Zone* (1973). His subsequent stories and novels, including the National Book Award–winning *Going After Cacciato* (1978), have all featured the Vietnam War as either a real or a ghostly presence. O'Brien examines the wrenching transformation of sense and sensibility in fictions that are evocative, challenging meetings of imagination and memory, of the created and the re-created, of the impossible and the possible.

Critics have often placed O'Brien within the somewhat limited category of "war writer." Milton J. Bates, assessing O'Brien's ongoing obsession with the myth of courage, places him "in the tradition of our great war novelists – Crane, Hemingway,

Tim O'Brien reading his work in 1988 (collection of Tim O'Brien)

Jones, Mailer, and Vonnegut." In Philip D. Beidler's *Re-Writing America,* Philip Caputo, himself a Pulitzer Prize–winning Vietnam writer whose memoir *A Rumor of War* reveals strong affinities with O'Brien's, finds his peer standing "solidly within the tradition of midwestern soldier-poets. Indeed, it is Ernest Hemingway that a reader hears most often in much of O'Brien's work — the spare, rhythmic repetition of key words and phrases; the hard, disciplined control of idea and emotion in sentences and paragraphs that are models of the stoic understatement; the darkly ironic gestures; and the classical imperatives of courage and cowardice, transgression and expiation, of Hemingway's best stories and novels.

Such comparisons, if containing more than an ounce of truth, are finally too easy and too constraining for a writer of O'Brien's thematic preoccupations and stylistic innovations. What a reader finds in his work, from the classical, meditative early memoir to the dazzling, metafictional *In the Lake of the Woods* (1994), is the remarkable education

and evolution of a writer whose fundamental themes, "discipline, honesty, integrity, understanding, acceptance, endurance," as Beidler notes, grant his work larger, even universal, significance. O'Brien certainly belongs to the small platoon of great American war writers that has walked through native mythic terrain, a literary outfit begun by James Fenimore Cooper, but in ambition and achievement he also demands induction into the larger unit of artists who are simply called important American writers. Like Mark Twain's Huckleberry Finn, O'Brien is a natural storyteller who can spin a tale with the best of them. Like Herman Melville's Ishmael, he is also a figure who would cast off from safe harbors and dive deeply into the primal American soul and psyche. If his diving is toward hot landing zones rather than the Leviathan, his frequent revisitations to the Vietnam War do not limit his thematic and symbolic reach. About the heart of his fiction the author in 1984 asserted, "My concerns have to do with the abstractions: What's courage and how do you get it? What's justice and how do you achieve it? How does one do right in an evil situation?" O'Brien has resisted the designation "war writer"; while admitting it was his Vietnam experience that demanded he become a writer, he calls the term "meaningless." The author of some of the most striking narratives of warfare, both real and imagined, in the entire corpus of American literature, O'Brien argues finally that "War stories aren't about war — they are about the human heart at war."

Beyond his war, any war, he recurrently explores a few specific subjects and themes: the continual interplay of fact and imagination in fiction and in life; the compulsive, absurd, noble quest for human truth; the difficulty in defining and obtaining the elusive quality of courage; and the ongoing human need for the fragile, made-up, explanatory device we call story. Indeed, O'Brien's prime theme finally is not that war maims and destroys — an obvious truism — but that storytelling explains, connects, and ultimately saves the teller and the listener. As O'Brien asserts in *The Things They Carried* (1990), "The thing about a story is that you dream it as you tell it, hoping that others might dream along with you, and in this way memory and imagination and language combine to make spirits in the head."

O'Brien's ability to dream his stories and novels and to make his readers dream them too has made him a major voice in American fiction since the early 1970s and has garnered him substantial recognition. In addition to the National Book Award, O'Brien has won *Esquire,* O. Henry, and Pushcart prizes for his short fiction; has been the recipient of awards from the National Endowment for the Arts, the Guggenheim Foundation, and the Massachusetts Arts and Humanities Foundation; and has seen his works translated into several foreign languages. Much more than a chronicler in fiction of a single, problematic war, O'Brien is now valued by critics and readers as a true American historian of the most valuable kind: the artist of the hidden recesses of the human heart and soul.

O'Brien does not deny the natural placement of his work within the larger corpus of war writing; indeed, considering his own writing in that context, he revealed in 1992 that "when I read the best things by Crane or Tolstoy, I feel a sense of confirmation." He faces, however, the ongoing paradox of the important literary artist, asserting that "a good writer must write beyond his moment, but he does have to be rooted to a lived-in world — like Conrad, Shakespeare, and Homer." If there does exist an American Joseph Conrad or a Homer of the Vietnam War, an artist who has melded that particular trauma with universal themes, that figure would seem to be Tim O'Brien, a writer who again and again has voyaged out into dangerous historical and imaginative waters only to return home with tales worth telling, unique American encounters with new cultural deceptions, with fresh hearts of darkness.

O'Brien's evolution as a storyteller seems the familiar stuff of the midwestern poet-novelist. Born on 1 October 1946 in Austin, Minnesota, he grew, as he relates in *If I Die in a Combat Zone,* "out of one war and into another. . . . My bawling came with the first throaty note of a new army in spawning." He matured in another Minnesota town, Worthington, where his father, William Timothy O'Brien, sold life insurance and his mother, Ava, raised him, his brother, Greg, and his sister, Kathy. His family life included a house full of books; as a boy O'Brien was a voracious reader who also tried his best to play Little League baseball and to grow into the sturdy young man his environment demanded. He attended Worthington Senior High School and Macalester College in Saint Paul, where he graduated summa cum laude in 1968, having earned a degree in political science. Despite having lived in the Boston area since 1970, when he entered the Ph.D. program in government at Harvard, O'Brien continues to see himself as a midwesterner. His decision to remain in the East after his early writing success, however, does reveal something about his ambivalent connection to the America of his boyhood. His early works, especially *If I Die in a Combat Zone* and his first novel, *Northern Lights* (1975), contain many passages that evoke the stolid provincialism that has recommended to many a young writer a permanent artistic and emotional exodus. Of his boyhood O'Brien said in 1992, "Writers are connected. I'm connected to my past, but we're connected to bad things, too. There were things about the Midwest that I liked. But my dominant recollection . . . is one of a kind of seething rage. Even as a kid I felt that way. Small town gossip and the values of those places."

In August 1968 after graduation from Macalester, O'Brien was drafted into the army, an event that produced a major emotional crisis for him. Finding the conflict morally reprehensible and emotionally unacceptable, he considered Canada or jail but finally did not choose flight or incarceration over Vietnam. He admits the prospect of losing friends and family and the censure of his culture overcame his personal objections, and he found himself dragged inexorably toward war. As he re-

O'Brien in August 1969, standing in a foxhole near the South China Sea, the site of Paul Berlin's guard tower in Going After Cacciato *(collection of Tim O'Brien)*

cords in his memoir, "in the end, it was less reason and more gravity that was the final influence."

His decision to accept induction into the armed forces might be seen as an American literary *felix culpa* (fortunate fault), for the war was the event that made him a writer. His service in Vietnam as an infantryman with the Americal Division presented him with jarring, traumatic material, but it also made writing a need rather than a choice. Seeing the many physical and emotional atrocities; watching friends destroyed or maimed in meaningless search-and-destroy missions and village searches; battling the fear, boredom, and deadliness of America's longest war, one to which he had pronounced moral objections – all of this and more supplied O'Brien with the two great themes that have powered all of his novels and short fiction: the ongoing quest to acquire or simply to define courage and the desperate need to attain redemption after sin. Careful to avoid cliché, O'Brien rejects the pat line "It was horrible but it makes a man out of you," finding in such sentiment "a certain B-movie quality."

Before Vietnam, O'Brien's commitment to the life of the writer was desultory at best. He wrote his

first story at the age of nine, a piece called "Timmy of the Little League." He credits "Miss Wiek, my junior high school English teacher," as a great writing influence but describes his overall commitment to his craft in high school and college as "a flickering rather than a burning desire." As a college student he wrote a novel set in Czechoslovakia, a "love story set within the political changes there" that remained, he is thankful, unpublished. In another familiar pattern of American fiction writers, O'Brien also served a literary novitiate as a journalist. Before Vietnam he worked as a sports reporter for the *Worthington Daily Globe;* between May 1973 and August 1974, while he was in the Ph.D. program at Harvard, he served two summers as a reporter for the *Washington Post,* learning the "discipline of the newspaper story, the importance of correct grammar and active verbs." Again, comparisons to the biographies of Crane and Hemingway are inevitable – the correspondent as storyteller who hones his spare, athletic prose with the tools of the working newspaperman. Although his lean, understated prose clearly puts him within the long tradition of the American journalist-fabulist, O'Brien has consistently forged his own imaginative and stylistic pathways through the rich terrain of the story and the novel.

O'Brien admits his debt as a writer to the modern pantheon of American writers that includes F. Scott Fitzgerald, William Faulkner, and Hemingway, but he also credits the influence of "a lot of nameless books." Critics have made much of O'Brien's intricate interplay of imagination, memory, and experience in his novels, his cutting back and forth through time, and as influences he points not only to Faulkner but also to James Joyce and Homer as masters of "nonlinear time, the experience of one's life as jumps and starts." He feels a strong kinship to such contemporary American writers as Robert Stone, Tom McGuane, and Philip Caputo because of the types of stories they tell and the chances they take: "A lot of fiction doesn't aspire high enough," says O'Brien of the contemporary scene. He admires fiction written without compromise, what he calls "all or nothing tales," and in the work of Stone and the others he finds strong analogues to his own artistic values and concerns. The writer O'Brien has mentioned most often, however, is neither American nor contemporary. As a writer who features themes of innocence and experience, transgression and expiation, O'Brien asserted, "I also have a lot in common with Conrad in many ways, especially when I think of *Lord Jim*. Good stories somehow have to do with the awakening into a new world, something new and true, where someone is jolted out of a kind of complacency and forced to confront a new set of circumstances or a new self " (*Missouri Review,* 1991). O'Brien is particularly attracted to fictions that feature heroes who sin or fail and then must make amends, figures who must live with memories that hurt and shame but that finally compel the bearer to evolve, to find forgiveness. He says, simply, "We write about the mistakes we make in our lives — we have to write about them."

After his return from Vietnam, O'Brien was at Harvard from 1970 to 1976 taking classes, passing his orals, making ends meet as a teaching assistant and a reporter, thinking about his dissertation, but mostly becoming a distinctive new voice in American letters. During his time at Harvard he published two books, the first of which was his memoir. O'Brien's achievement in *If I Die in a Combat Zone* was twofold. First, he established his literary voice by creating a striking personal meditation whose somber, classical tones and poetic effects immediately prompted critics such as Beidler to place his work "in the central tradition of American spiritual autobiography . . . the tradition of Edwards and Woolman, of Franklin and Thoreau and Henry Adams." In a more local historical way, however, *If I Die in a Combat Zone* was one of the key texts of the 1970s that placed Vietnam back within American historical memory just as cultural exhaustion and collective amnesia had become national conditions. Like Philip Caputo's *A Rumor of War* and Michael Herr's *Dispatches,* personal historical-artistic statements that would follow O'Brien's lead, in the memoir O'Brien offers a version of himself who is both a participant telling one man's story and a symbolic emissary of his culture who exchanges traditional and pop culture myth for the hard-earned knowledge of personal transgression and historical experience. O'Brien succeeds in joining the newly historical with the long-standing mythic, the particular with the general, the local with the universal in the memoir. Noting the book's striking, classical voice, Annie Gottlieb invoked the phraseology of Aristotle in her 1 July 1973 review in *The New York Times,* assessing O'Brien's first work as "a beautiful, painful book, arousing pity and fear for the daily realities of a modern disaster."

Early in the book O'Brien defines the memoir as both product and process with some key inquiries: "Do dreams offer lessons? Do nightmares have themes? . . . Can the foot soldier teach anything important about war, merely from having been there? I think not. He can tell war stories." O'Brien describes his own memoir not as autobiography but as a work of literary imagination. A poetic-philosophical sensibility controls the account of a young infantryman's passage through a year at war, always seeking the proper cultural touchstones for its experience and education: in the course of O'Brien's painful education at the firebases, in the jungle, and at the villages of My Lai is the desperate attempt to find reliable cultural explanations of the most jarring lessons of new history. There is also the necessary quest for models of proper behavior, a list that grows shorter as O'Brien finds various aspects of popular and classical myth inapplicable to his condition. The most concentrated part of the search is for an adequate definition of courage, the theme that is central to all of O'Brien's work. Despite the comparisons made by his critics, O'Brien asserted early in his career that his conclusions could not be a mere restatement of Hemingway. Considering the phrase most often attached to his predecessor, O'Brien reveals in the memoir that "grace under pressure isn't sufficient. It's too easy to affect grace, and it's too hard to see through it. . . . Grace under pressure means you can confront things gracefully or squeeze out of them gracefully. But to make those two things equal with the easy word 'grace' is wrong. Grace under pressure is not courage."

The great cultural irony of *If I Die in a Combat Zone* is that to find a proper standard of courage within a fragmented, postmodern war, one whose prime features are chaos and unreadability, O'Brien must swim back against the current of history to a time well before Hemingway and the modernist sensibility. To be hard-boiled and taciturn in the face of the kind of cultural tragedy Vietnam was for O'Brien was not enough. He returned in the memoir to older, dust-covered definitions of courage and virtue. Vietnam seemed to shatter many classical imperatives, and many World War I literary artists – Ezra Pound, Wilfrid Owen, Siegfried Sassoon and others – would nod in agreement with O'Brien when he asserts, "Horace's old do-or-die aphorism – *'Dulce et decorum est pro patria mori'* – was just an epitaph for the insane." But O'Brien, to be able to write about his war not only in his classical memoir but also in the more daring fictions to come, seeks and finds a standard with the help of another ancient thinker. He finds his man not in Shane, the mythic hero of the American West, not in Hemingway's Frederic Henry, but in a Greek philosopher.

Responding to the Socratic dialogue called *Laches,* O'Brien concludes, "Proper courage is wise courage. It's acting wisely, acting wisely when fear would have a man act otherwise. It is the endurance of the soul in spite of fear – wisely." Although he finds in Plato a meaningful four-part definition of virtue – courage, temperance, justice, wisdom – and an acceptable definition of courage as "wise endurance," he also discovers Vietnam to be nearly void of those necessary qualities. Instead of Socrates, he finds morally myopic chaplains; foolhardy, vicious, or cowardly commanding officers; increasingly brutal and brutalized peers. After one of many losses of personal and collective discipline in the field, he can only write that "it was good to walk from Pinkville and to see fire behind Alpha Company, just as pure hate is good" and can only nod in tragic agreement when his best friend in another area of Vietnam tells him in a letter that "what I see is evil."

If I Die in a Combat Zone is a remarkable first work, a moving attempt by one very literary "grunt" to reconcile ancient virtue with contemporary evil, but it was only the first chapter in O'Brien's ongoing quest to explore the ramifications of "wise endurance" in a contemporary land-

scape seemingly sandblasted of such noble imperatives. That critics see the memoir as a "real" story distinct from his subsequent fiction is to O'Brien a false distinction. Some of the characters in the memoir are real but others are invented; he describes the book as "eighty-five percent a work of the imagination." What he did discover in writing the memoir was the difference between facts and the truth, and it is the latter quality that O'Brien would pursue down innovative fictional pathways. Of that elusive prize in *If I Die in a Combat Zone* he said in 1984, "Truth doesn't reside in the surface of events. Truth resides in those deeper moments of punctuation, when things explode. So you compress the boredom down, hinting at it but always going for drama – because the essence of the experience was dramatic. You tell lies to get to the truth."

The next dramatic "lie" that O'Brien would tell would come in 1975 with his first novel, a long, darkly poetic, sometimes parodic story of two brothers and their ongoing quest for proper courage and personal virtue. The setting of *Northern Lights* is Sawmill Landing, a hard, cold Minnesota town where Pehr Lindstrom Peri, minister of Damascus Lutheran Church, tries to raise his two sons, Paul and Harvey Perry, to endure stoically whatever life may throw at them. Harvey, the athletic, physically courageous brother, goes to Vietnam and returns, like Hemingway's Jake Barnes, with a wound from the war. Paul, the softer, more passive sensibility, works ineffectually as a county farm agent and nestles in the sheltering arms of his wife, a maternal sexual presence with the symbolic name of Grace. Harvey returns from Vietnam as damaged goods both physically and psychically, and the brothers collide, antagonize, and test each other: in response to the father's apocalyptic obsessions (foreshadowing O'Brien's 1985 novel, *The Nuclear Age,* he is intent on building a bomb shelter); in a not-quite-defined rivalry for the affections of a beautiful, wild young woman named Addie; in opposition or adherence to untested cultural definitions or standards of courage, self-sufficiency, and manhood.

The novel contains some elements that O'Brien does not entirely harmonize. Part of the book is a long parody of Hemingway that some early critics took too seriously. Roger Sale in the 13 November 1975 *New York Review of Books* concluded that "*Northern Lights* is too literary much of the time, but fine when it is not" and, taking the parody to be serious imitation, asked, "Is it possible to read *The Sun Also Rises* too often? . . . O'Brien has read it too often, let it sink into him too deeply." Other reviewers also found the book too long, too self-conscious,

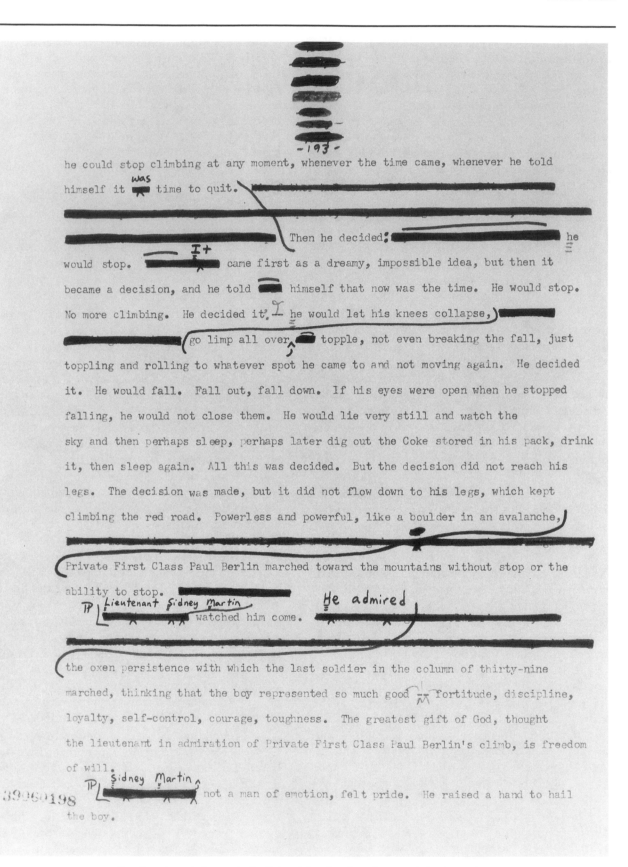

-193-

he could stop climbing at any moment, whenever the time came, whenever he told
himself it ~~was~~ time to quit.

Then he decided: he
would stop. came first as a dreamy, impossible idea, but then it
became a decision, and he told himself that now was the time. He would stop.
No more climbing. He decided it, he would let his knees collapse,
go limp all over, topple, not even breaking the fall, just
toppling and rolling to whatever spot he came to and not moving again. He decided
it. He would fall. Fall out, fall down. If his eyes were open when he stopped
falling, he would not close them. He would lie very still and watch the
sky and then perhaps sleep, perhaps later dig out the Coke stored in his pack, drink
it, then sleep again. All this was decided. But the decision did not reach his
legs. The decision was made, but it did not flow down to his legs, which kept
climbing the red road. Powerless and powerful, like a boulder in an avalanche,

Private First Class Paul Berlin marched toward the mountains without stop or the
ability to stop.
Lieutenant Sidney Martin watched him come. He admired

the oxen persistence with which the last soldier in the column of thirty-nine
marched, thinking that the boy represented so much good fortitude, discipline,
loyalty, self-control, courage, toughness. The greatest gift of God, thought
the lieutenant in admiration of Private First Class Paul Berlin's climb, is freedom
of will. Sidney Martin not a man of emotion, felt pride. He raised a hand to hail
the boy.

Page from the revised typescript for Going After Cacciato *(courtesy of Tim O'Brien)* and too artificially literary. Of the long parodic sequence O'Brien said, "I tried to make fun of Hemingway. I respect Hemingway's work, and some of it I love. But sometimes I find myself being irritated by a kind of macho simplicity and by the way women are treated almost as little pawns to be moved around from place to place. That's not always true of his women, but often it is true, I think" (*Missouri Review*, 1991).

The climax of *Northern Lights* is an arduous ski trip the two brothers undertake together that a killer blizzard turns into a physical and emotional stuggle for survival. Paul saves himself and his brother and begins to reconcile his feminine side that his father tried to expunge with traditional male definitions of heroism. In its deft exploration of gender in relation to identity, strength, endurance, and courage, the novel is an interesting one. Critics of O'Brien's work have sometimes complained that he fails to create three-dimensional female characters, but *Northern Lights* is an early attempt to isolate and explore both the male and the female in every human being, fictional or real. Of men and women, O'Brien said, "We're different, yes, but we're not *that* different. We all experience anger. We experience lust. We experience terror. We experience curiosity and fascination for that which repels us. All of us" (*Missouri Review*, 1991).

Although the original reviews of the novel were lukewarm at best, recent opinion has reversed this judgment somewhat. In perhaps the best specific reading of the novel, Bates concludes that "in its juxtaposition of masculine and feminine, woods and pond, apocalypse and salvation, endurance and love, it nevertheless has that 'mythic quality' O'Brien considers essential to a good story." Seeing the book over greater distance and within the context of O'Brien's evolving literary career, Beidler in 1991 assessed the novel sixteen years after its publication, finding in it "the stirrings of a stylistic experimentation of uncommon power and originality."

In retrospect, O'Brien calls *Northern Lights* "my training novel, my *Torrents of Spring*" and claims he would like to revise it, to cut it by eighty or ninety pages. At the time of its publication, critical reaction certainly gave no indication that within four years O'Brien would be the recipient of the National Book Award. Leaving Harvard with his degree unfinished, he was now committed full-time to his craft. "Instead of writing my dissertation," he says, "I was writing what I needed to write." Had he not become a writer, O'Brien feels he might have become a foreign service officer or an employee of the State Department, perhaps a government functionary of the type Melville or Conrad would have employed for dramatic, ironic effect. Without his Ph.D. and with his literary apprenticeship behind, O'Brien set to work on the novel that would show the true flowering of the "uncommon power and originality" Beidler and many other commentators would soon describe at length and with great enthusiasm.

O'Brien left Harvard but remained in the Boston area. With his academic ties cut, he devoted his full energies to a novel that would take many readers and critics off guard. Part reality, part memory, part fantasy or dream, *Going After Cacciato* (1978) established O'Brien as an important American writer whose subject happened to be the Vietnam War. To this day O'Brien insists it is not a war novel at all, but he also understands why the novel confused readers entering its stylistic terrain with specific if limited expectations. Playing the reader's role, O'Brien in 1984 commented, "if I were to pick up my own book and read it, my feeling would be that I wasn't really reading a war novel; I would perhaps feel that a trick had been played on me.... It's quirky. It goes somewhere else; it goes *away* from the war. It starts there and goes to Paris. A *peace* novel, in a sense."

What O'Brien offered his readers in 1978 was a novel that seemed a strange blend of the real and the fantastic, the remembered and the imagined, an elaborate literary game that was deadly serious about its subjects, a text in which time and space were arranged at odd angles, in nonlinear arrangements. The book is ostensibly the travel tale of a young foot soldier named Cacciato (Italian for "the hunter"), "dumb as a bullet," who decides one day to walk eighty-six hundred miles to Paris, but the real central character, the controlling narrative voice, is Spec Four Paul Berlin, who with his overaged, disaffected lieutenant and the rest of Third Squad, must track down the young deserter and bring him back to the war. The book begins with a somber, spare evocation of the tragic realities of the Vietnam War; O'Brien offers the reader a litany of the dead that quickly finds its opposite number in the celebration of the power of imagination to deal with the terrible facts of Vietnam. One of the lessons O'Brien offers in *If I Die in a Combat Zone* is that "soldiers are dreamers," the same epigraph from Sassoon that precedes the first chapter of *Going After Cacciato*. It is a well-chosen assertion, for what the reader discerns slowly is that this war novel is really an instruction manual on how to survive traumatic history through the power of imagination, through the need to tell a war story that is much more than a war story. Said O'Brien in 1984, "The very themes of the book are imagination and memory. In that sense it's about how one goes about writing fiction, the fictional process."

The novel is actually an elaborate frame tale, one in which the geometry often seems akin to the eye-fooling perspective of an M. C. Escher drawing. Author O'Brien creates the story of "author" Paul Berlin, a soldier afflicted with a major case of "fear biles," who while on guard duty one night by the South China Sea tells a story, an apparently fantastic tale about his and Third Squad's journey to Paris in pursuit of Cacciato. In his observation post, the present time of the novel, Berlin writes a novel of a certain kind, one that is an elaborate interpenetration of memory and imagination, hope and loss. The tripartite structure of the novel is at first puzzling, but a reader soon learns that memory and imagination, the real and the possible, affect the quality and nature of each other as Paul writes in the guard tower. The tragic realities and the unacceptable history of the Vietnam War affect the parameters and features of what Paul Berlin is able to conjure in his imagination, but O'Brien makes it clear how the power of our dreams also creates what we call the real world.

Many early critics concentrated on the seemingly fantastic elements of the story without taking full account of the overall architecture and made comparisons based on that focus. Speaking for many, Richard Freedman in *The New York Times Book Review* (12 February 1978) asserted that "clearly we are dealing here with what the new South American novelists would call 'magical realism.' " There is, however, a large difference between O'Brien's novel and a work such as Gabriel García Marquez's *One Hundred Years of Solitude*, a novel in which supernatural and fantastic occurrences coexist in the same textual time and space with realistic happenings. Early in *Going After Cacciato*, Paul Berlin and Third Squad fall magically through a hole into an elaborate underground tunnel complex, a moment that may convince a reader that he or she is following Alice through a Vietnam wonderland. O'Brien carefully juxtaposes that apparently fantastic occurrence with Berlin's terrible memory of the destruction of a village called Hoi An. He remembers his and Third Squad's desire for revenge, the words "Kill it" coming from his lips. He remembers finally that "the village was a hole," a dark remnant of the war within his consciousness that Berlin "writes" anew as the tunnel sequence where imagination attempts to mediate and bargain with the unacceptable history of the war.

O'Brien rejects the "magical realism" tag for the novel, asserting that *Going After Cacciato* is truly about "the reality of our dreams, our day dreams in particular, the work of our imagination. There's nothing unreal or surreal about it." He is particularly amused by the suggestion that he was consciously or unconsciously airlifting the fictional technique and style of García Marquez to the jungles and mountains of Vietnam; of *One Hundred Years of Solitude* he said in 1984, "I just hated it. My wife read it and loved it, but I got through about three pages. . . . I remember the paragraphs were extraordinarily long, and I didn't like wending my way through long paragraphs." By wending their way through O'Brien's memory-dreamscape in *Going After Cacciato*, however, readers encounter O'Brien's familiar themes reconstituted and restated: the need to find personal courage in the face of overwhelming fear; the imperative to find a moral center within historical circumstances that consistently blunt such pretensions; the necessity of dreams, imagination, and stories as the protective flak jacket for everyone, whether in real combat zones or not.

The true battle in *Going After Cacciato* is not so much between memory and imagination as it is between the desire for freedom and safety and the terrible constraints of duty. Throughout the book O'Brien makes a dazzling display of both his and Paul Berlin's imaginations. Both write well — and creatively. At one juncture Cacciato rescues Third Squad from a Tehran prison using a 1964 Chevy Impala as a getaway car, but there are also drags and obstacles on the imagination throughout the narrative, and for a good thematic reason. The climax of the debate between duty and freedom occurs when Third Squad reaches Paris and Paul Berlin, the spokesperson for duty, and Sarkin Aung Wan, a mysterious female refugee who champions freedom, have their own dreamlike version of the Paris Peace Talks. Sarkin counsels Berlin to remain in Paris to make a separate peace, asserting, "For just as happiness is more than the absence of sadness, so is peace infinitely more than the absence of war. Even the refugee must do more than flee. He must arrive." From the beginning of the novel onward, Paul Berlin has been a fine creative writer of his own impulse toward freedom, asserting of his imaginative escape to Paris that "it could be done." At novel's end, however, his is a different voice, one that has tested through the power of story the limits of that narrative. Facing the attractive, powerful argument of Sarkin, he finally admits, "Even in imagination we must be true to our obligations, for,

Dust jacket for O'Brien's 1978 novel, in which a young soldier traces in his imagination a deserter's escape to Paris

even in imagination, obligation cannot be outrun. Imagination, like reality, has its limits."

Imagination is not vanquished, however, and O'Brien makes it clear that all of the other members of Third Squad will have to write their own personal "Goings After Cacciato." What both Paul Berlin and Tim O'Brien achieve in the novel is finally anything but fantastic: it is the real negotiation, the ongoing everyday dialectic, between dream and fact, the real and the possible, that constitutes what we call reality. Is Paul Berlin, as he pursues proper notions of duty and courage, Tim O'Brien himself? O'Brien in 1984 said, "he's more of a dreamer than I was, I think. He spends much more of his time in dream. . . . He's more frightened than I was – and I was very, very frightened." There are clear similarities, however, among the "Tim O'Brien" he creates in his memoir, Paul Perry from his first novel, and Paul Berlin in *Going After Cacciato*. All search seriously for a standard of courage that is not just intellectually and emotionally sound but historically applicable and livable. All achieve only partial, contingent, or qualified success in that quest. In *Going After Cacciato* both "writers" achieve clear victories on a certain level. Of the relationship of Tim O'Brien's storytelling to Paul Berlin's in the obser-

vation post by the South China Sea, perhaps Eric James Schroeder says it best: "O'Brien's own 'inner peace' is ultimately achieved in the writing of *Cacciato*. Paul Berlin's activity in the tower becomes a metaphor for O'Brien's own creative act." It is appropriate that at the end of the novel a new story is just beginning, this time by Third Squad's commanding officer, who, thinking of the impossibility of Cacciato's proposed walk to Paris, suggests, "And who knows? He might make it. He might do all right. . . . Miserable odds, but – ."

After the early critical reception to *Northern Lights* in 1975, many critics might have suggested there were also miserable odds against O'Brien's winning a National Book Award, at least so soon. But with *Going After Cacciato* he demonstrated that this, too, could be done, that events of the imagination could produce miracles both inside and outside the text. In his review Freedman suggested that "to call *Going After Cacciato* a novel about war is like calling *Moby-Dick* a novel about whales." Freedman soon found a large regiment of critics and readers that would nod to that assertion, but the novel produced for O'Brien another artistic irony. By producing the first novel of the Vietnam War that critics were calling an instant American classic comparable to the best of Crane or Hemingway, O'Brien wedded himself more solidly than ever to the term *war writer*. Three books into his career, he was being called by more and more critics America's best war writer on America's worst war.

It would be seven years before O'Brien would offer his critics and readers a new novel, this time one set on the American home front of nuclear paranoia, radical politics, and revolutionary terrorism. *The Nuclear Age* (1985) is in many ways O'Brien's most culturally ambitious work, a sprawling, darkly funny historical saga of what it meant to grow up with the persistent threat of the atomic flash, to reach intellectual and emotional maturity during the life and death of the antiwar movement, to see America's collective nervous breakdown of the 1960s and 1970s give way to the uneasy ennui and exhaustion of the 1980s. Some similarities exist between *The Nuclear Age* and *Going After Cacciato* in the way O'Brien handles time and history. Again there is a frightened protagonist, William Cowling, who is digging a hole to protect his poetic flight-attendant wife, Bobbi, his precocious daughter, Melinda, and himself from what he feels is imminent nuclear apocalypse. Like Paul Berlin in the observation post, William looks backward from the present time of the novel, 1995 in Montana, through turbulent American history and through his own comic-tragic evolution. If the immediate threats of history are less imminent to William Cowling than to Paul Berlin, they are also larger, for the hero of *The Nuclear Age* trembles not just for himself and his immediate peers but for mankind. Fear for the squad has been replaced by the nightmare of species suicide. In Vietnam, Paul Berlin surveys the damage from the elevated perspective of the tower and his creative imagination; at the end of the millennium in a chaotic American free-fire zone, William Cowling can only burrow deep below ground and wait for the end.

"Am I crazy?" William Cowling asks on the first page of the novel, and the reader must compare at all times contemporary historical hopes and fears to the "quality of obsession" that the hero personifies. O'Brien takes his protagonist from his boyhood fear of Soviet first strikes in 1958 – the young William attempts to build a bomb shelter from lead pencils in the family basement – to his final moments of sanity/insanity as he contemplates destroying himself and his family in 1995 in order to save them. Between those two fearful, obsessive moments, O'Brien offers the reader his hero's travelogue through the 1960s and 1970s, a comic-symbolic trek that features his involvement with a group of campus radicals who move from mild civil disobedience to violent revolutionary action. If Paul Berlin makes a poor foot soldier in Vietnam, William Cowling is a sorry terrorist, a disaffected figure who cannot buy into deathly tactics on the home front any more than O'Brien's protagonists can in the jungles and villages of Vietnam.

O'Brien's treatment of the New Left in *The Nuclear Age* is satiric, and the characters are often deliberate caricatures. With a homemade sign that says "THE BOMBS ARE REAL," Cowling becomes a one-student protest at Peverson State College – "Pevee State" – but he soon finds himself a member of "The Committee," a group of self-designated revolutionaries that includes a politicized former cheerleader, an activist linebacker, and an overweight young woman who combines leftist politics with the compulsive consumption of junk food. As the group drifts more and more toward irrevocable violence, William becomes less certain of his commitment, more fearful and alienated. The Committee eventually is trained for destructive imperatives in Cuba and participates in bombings, thefts of military weapons, and, finally, the absurd procurement of Cowling's worst nightmare, a live nuclear warhead, the ultimate tool for true apocalyptic terrorism. As his peers move toward inevitable meltdown and personal Armageddon, Cowling burrows deeper into his psychic hole. When revolutionary civil disobedience – years of what he calls "Kentucky Fried Terror" – finally kills all of his friends from the 1960s and 1970s, Cowling retreats more deeply, making his wife and daughter prisoners of contemporary history, concluding of his age, "The world has been sanitized. Passion is a metaphor. All we can do is dig."

What becomes clear in the novel is O'Brien's own ambivalence to the leftist politics, the civil disobedience, and the cultural upheaval of America in the 1960s and 1970s. Looking backward, his protagonist asks, "What *happened*? Was it entropy? Genetic decay? Even the villains are gone. . . . And who among us would become a martyr, and for what?" He describes the period as a time of great energy, but energy of a kind that is more pyrotechnic than useful or constructive – lots of flash and dazzle, questionable substance. The radicals in the novel are brave, driven, dedicated to their own manic mission, but depicted as more tragic than heroic. Indeed, there is a decidedly entropic feel to the book as O'Brien's own uncertainty toward his characters and their politics plays itself out in increasingly doomed enterprises.

It is tempting perhaps to read William Cowling as an imaginative variant of O'Brien himself,

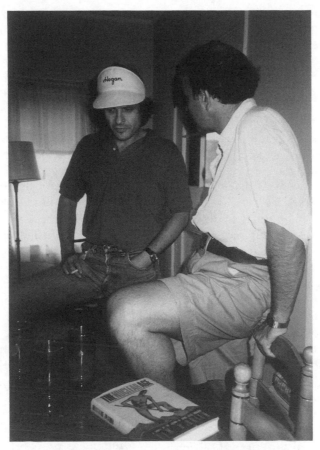

O'Brien and novelist Nicholas Delbanco at the 1986 Bread Loaf
Writers' Conference (collection of Tim O'Brien)

the domestic alternative to the young foot soldier who did go to Vietnam. Would he have been a different type of warrior, one fighting to stop a war rather than serve it? O'Brien uses a line from William Butler Yeats recurrently in the book – "*We had fed the heart of fantasies, the heart's grown brutal from the fare.*" Part of the enjoyment and the frustration of reading *The Nuclear Age* comes from the unresolved tensions that permeate the text, for O'Brien treats the social activism in the novel both satirically and respectfully. He both fears and admires the "quality of obsession" he creates, and, to his credit, does walk a fine, dangerous, fragile line between love and death, between affirmation and apocalypse.

At the end of the novel O'Brien offers an important debate. If Sarkin Aung Wan and Paul Berlin in *Going After Cacciato* enter into important negotiations involving freedom and duty, the final exchange in *The Nuclear Age* is potentially more crucial, even terminal. At the climax the hole beckons to the hero, "*I am, in modesty, Neverness. I am the be-all and end-all. I am you, of course. I am your inside-out – your Ace in the Hole.*" The voice of the end – the end of

fear, the end of uncertainty, the end of anxiety – the hole offers peace as nothingness. Cowling, however, a twitch of the finger from his loved ones' and his own personal apocalypse, chooses death's opposite, with all of the ongoing dangers that that choice entails. Asserts Cowling finally, "I will hold to a steadfast orthodoxy, confident to the end that E will somehow not quite equal mc^2, that it's a cunning metaphor, that the terminal equation will somehow not quite balance." This is a mature and sane response to questions raised in all of his works, but the answer is also complex and demanding: to live with fear, one must posit hope; to counter the certainty of death, one must traffic in the absurd, terrible substance called love.

When *The Nuclear Age* appeared, critical reaction was harsh, as if by leaving the literal combat zone of Vietnam behind, O'Brien had cut himself off from the wellspring of his imaginative power. Many critics were not willing to grant him true creative vision in the wider historical field of fire he chose to inhabit. Reviewers praised certain aspects of the book, but many felt it failed as a whole, primarily because O'Brien was not writing about what he knew best. David Montrose, for instance, praised "the lean clarity of O'Brien's prose" in *The Times Literary Supplement* of 28 March 1986; he also created a bandwagon of complaint other critics would climb aboard — "The principal flaw is O'Brien's inability to create believable urban guerrillas: Cowling's anti-war brothers and sisters come across as tepid cartoons."

O'Brien, however, says that many aspects of the novel are deliberately "cartoonlike, wildly exaggerated" and that those anticipating or demanding traditional realism are missing both the essence and the more subtle features of the novel. He wrote the novel as "a funny, comedic work," but he also describes it as "a meticulously structured book — a patterned book in which the lines increase on a mathematical scale." He likens *The Nuclear Age* to some of the novels of Jim Harrison and Tom McGuane, writers whose tough prose conceals a fragility, "a sense of the collapse all around us." Despite the panning by several critics, O'Brien calls *The Nuclear Age* "my strongest book by far," adding wryly that his reaction is certainly "what Melville would say about *Pierre*."

O'Brien admits to taking secret pleasure in the hidden structure of his apocalyptic comedy, and he also is interested in seeing how *The Nuclear Age* will meet the test of time. While enduring the confusion and disappointment the novel produced, O'Brien was already journeying back to the Vietnam killing ground of *If I Die in a Combat Zone* and *Going After Cacciato*, the imaginative territory of his greatest literary successes. Throughout his career O'Brien has published many stories or excerpts from his fiction that have become chapters or parts of the larger works; many of the best pieces originally appeared in *Esquire*. In 1981 that magazine published "The Ghost Soldiers," a striking Vietnam tale of revenge and expiation that also garnered an O. Henry award. Some of his most demanding, innovative, and critically praised stories appeared in the same magazine after the publication of *The Nuclear Age*: "The Things They Carried" in 1986, "How to Tell a True War Story" in 1987, "Sweetheart of the Song Tra Bong" and "The Lives of the Dead" in 1989. Although these individual tales were clearly some of O'Brien's finest short pieces, critics and readers were not fully prepared for what their effect would be in combination with other new stories. O'Brien was about to publish a work that would not only break new personal ground for him as a writer but also would test the ability of his critics to adhere to familiar generic distinctions.

In the chapter of *The Things They Carried* (1990) titled "Spin," a narrator and central charac-

ter named Tim O'Brien, "forty-three years old, and a writer now," offers a key assessment of the value of the "real" Tim O'Brien's challenging new work, of all great literary art: "Stories are for joining the past to the future. . . . Stories are for eternity, when memory is erased, when there is nothing to remember except the story." Creating a version of himself that is both real and imaginary, offering a group of stories that seem to be simultaneously a novel, a story collection, a literary autobiography, a personal confession of transgression and forgiveness, and a meditation on the art of fiction, *The Things They Carried* would be perceived as the most innovative and challenging book he had written to date. All of his established subjects and themes are here: the search for a workable definition of courage; the need to transmute terrible memory into a livable present; the responsibility of the living to the dead to keep them alive somehow; the wonderful, terrible nature of storytelling itself. Is the work a novel or a collection of stories? The answer would seem to be a simple — and ironic — yes. Characters appear and reappear in the different chapters, sometimes complementing, sometimes contradicting their own words and actions or those of other characters. Some of the stories are realistic and dramatic, some metafictional and philosophical, and all are spare, economical, ironic — live literary rounds that are both beautiful and brutal, terrible and true.

The most challenging feature of the book is the controlling narrator, the character named Tim O'Brien who both is and is not the "real" one. Many of Melville's commentators have noted how in *Moby-Dick* Ishmael at times seems merely the author himself, ruminating over and glossing his own creations and his own pretensions. Likewise in *The Things They Carried,* there is not only a pronounced metafictional feel — the implicit argument for the utter interchangeability and fluidity of life and art — but also the perception by the reader that finally any attempt to separate the author from the narrator-hero is a fool's errand. The work is the most serious literary game O'Brien had yet played, and throughout the strangely connected and affiliated chapters, which are also discrete tales, he preserves a weighty contradiction: that it is possible to revel in the glories of sheer imagination — storytelling in its purest, most shameless form — while revealing the most terrible truths about human beings.

Many critics were not certain how to appraise the book. In the 11 March 1990 *New York Times Book Review,* Robert R. Harris wrote, "This is a collection of interrelated stories. . . . The publisher calls the book 'a work of fiction,' but in no real sense can it be considered a novel. No matter. The stories cohere . . . he not only crystallizes the Vietnam experience for us, he exposes the nature of all war stories." Harris's arguments for coherence and universality do much to capture the unusual effects of *The Things They Carried,* for, in a radically different way from his earlier combat-zone narratives, the work depicts Vietnam as both "this war" and "any war"; O'Brien also achieves an organic unity among the tales that preserves their individual integrity while simultaneously displaying their interrelatedness. O'Brien confesses that the book is "all invented," that despite the presence of a version of himself as the narrative glue, the work is actually in the "form of the memoir as a way of telling a made-up story." The last comment suggests that the book should feel like *If I Die in a Combat Zone* at certain junctures, like *Going After Cacciato* at others. It does, but it also contains an affable quirkiness, a unique feel that belies the often dark events within its pages and makes the work a new point of departure for O'Brien even at the moments it appears to be a return to old fictional landscapes.

In the 2 April 1990 *Newsweek* Peter Prescott said of the book, "Wars seldom produce good short stories, but two or three of these seem as good as any short stories written about war." Some readers would contend that that number should be enlarged. The first chapter bears the book's title; it also bears the weight of the entire experience of the soldier in Vietnam, condensed and concentrated as a remarkable physical, emotional, and spiritual inventory. Some of what the men carry is visible, quantifiable, but the most important things are not. Creating one character who recurs in the early chapters, O'Brien writes, "As a first lieutenant and platoon leader, Jimmy Cross carried a compass, maps, code books, binoculars, and a .45-caliber pistol that weighed 2.9 pounds fully loaded. He carried a strobe light and the responsibility for the lives of his men." Because the psychological and spiritual inventories are offered matter-of-factly, without judgment, they gain significance and power. As O'Brien summarizes, "They carried all they could bear, and then some, including a silent awe for the terrible power of the things they carried."

Many of the characters gain form and feature as they appear and reappear in several stories. The chief carrier of evil in the text, for example, is a soldier named Azar: in "Spin" he straps a mine to another soldier's puppy and blows it to pieces, exclaiming to his disgusted peers, "What's everybody so upset about? . . . I mean, Christ, I'm just a *boy.*" In "The Man I Killed" Azar examines the enemy

soldier the fictional, traumatized Tim O'Brien has just killed and observes, "On the dead test, this particular individual gets A-plus." In "The Ghost Soldiers" Azar's brutality finally pushes the fictional Tim O'Brien and another soldier to contemplate killing him. As Azar gains definition and significance from story to story, so do evil, frustration, and loss.

Adjacent tales often do much more than enhance character. In "Speaking of Courage" Norman Bowker is the central figure in a painful coming-home story about the loss of a friend and O'Brien's prime theme, the failure to be courageous. In the next tale, "Notes," O'Brien creates a version of himself giving the history of the preceding story that is revealed as "a suggestion of Norman Bowker, who three years later hanged himself in the lockerroom of a YMCA in his hometown in central Iowa." The following story, "In the Field," however, complicates whatever conclusions the reader may have drawn, offering Bowker again at the scene of his friend's death, this time remarking of the loss, "Nobody's fault . . . Everybody's." Such accumulation of possibility is more than perverse gamesmanship on O'Brien's part, and in "How to Tell a True War Story," the key chapter in regard to his philosophy of storytelling, he argues strongly for a clear understanding of the difference between fact and truth. He states early in the chapter that "in any war story, but especially a true one, it's difficult to separate what happened from what seemed to happen"; he also contends that, for even the best of writers, a true war story sometimes "is just beyond telling." The effect of O'Brien's meditation is to bring the veracity of all of his stories into question at the very moment it makes such worries irrelevant. Is this puzzling, enchanting book finally memoir or fable? Again the answer is an emphatic yes. How can a reader know if a story is true? For O'Brien and his characters it comes down to a basic experience: "It comes down to gut instinct. A true war story, if truly told, makes the stomach believe." As storyteller, O'Brien in *The Things They Carried* discards once and for all concern with strict adherence to fact. As he has revealed in a 1991 interview in the *Missouri Review,* "Ninety percent or more of the material is invented, and I invented ninety percent of a new Tim O'Brien, maybe even more than that." More than ever, he is telling lies to get to the truth.

The "new" O'Brien is a wonderful teller of tales. Some of the stories remain in the imagination like strange inscriptions of terrible import. In "Sweetheart of the Song Tra Bong" O'Brien offers the American "girl next door" as an updated ver-

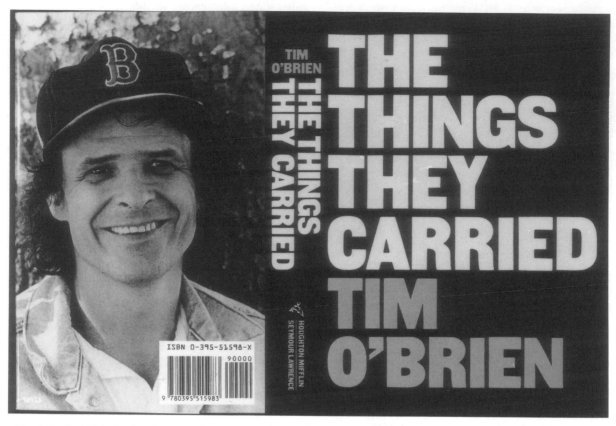

Dust jacket for O'Brien's 1990 short-story collection, in which a character named Tim O'Brien remarks, "Stories are for eternity, when memory is erased, when there is nothing to remember except the story"

sion of Conrad's Kurtz. When a soldier brings his girlfriend to Vietnam, she becomes involved in special duties with the Green Berets but soon becomes too attuned to the call of the wild even for them. At story's end O'Brien describes her as having "crossed to the other side. She was part of the land. She was wearing her culottes, her pink sweater, and a necklace of human tongues. She was dangerous. She was ready for the kill." The frequent descent into pure evil, however, is met in *The Things They Carried* by equally powerful salvational gestures. In the final chapter, a story called "The Lives of the Dead," the fictional Tim O'Brien – or is it the real one? – asserts simply, "But this too is true: stories can save us." Contemplating lost friends, fictional and real, living and dead, O'Brien lets the reader know that the person truly saved in the leap of faith called storytelling is most often the teller. *The Things They Carried* is yet another group of war stories by yet another war writer. But O'Brien transcends those categories to demonstrate once more that story is not an option but a need. As "The Lives of the Dead" and the book itself come to an end, the narrative loops back to its first word, to the begin-

ning of the writer's own creative consciousness. Like a Vietnam version of Joyce's Stephen Dedalus, O'Brien concludes, "I'll never die. I'm skimming across the surface of my own history, moving fast, riding the melt beneath the blades, doing loops and spins, and when I take a high leap into the dark and come down thirty years later, I realize it is as Tim trying to save Timmy's life with a story."

If *The Things They Carried* reveals O'Brien to be a stylistic risk taker and innovator with his own well-established themes, his newest work reveals that he is becoming an even more daring and compelling magician of postmodern fictional strategies. *In the Lake of the Woods* (1994) is a remarkable novel for a writer who has already delivered so many surprises in his writing, for in the newest book O'Brien offers a depiction of human mystery, secret sin, and the dark, tragic effects of contemporary American history that again rubs away the artificial line between the literary and historical imagination but does so in new, unexpected ways.

One main character is again a Vietnam veteran, John Wade, who has been a rising Minnesota politician but whose senatorial campaign and personal life have been derailed by disclosures of his participation with Lt. William Calley and his men in the My Lai massacre. A practitioner of magic since boyhood who gives himself the nickname "Sorcerer" in Vietnam, Wade attempts to cover up his participation in the evil of the My Lai episode, but *In the Lake of the Woods,* while exploring a contemporary Conradian scenario in Vietnam, is most truly about men and women: love, marriage, and the terrible, inevitable secrets husbands and wives keep from each other. Within a fictional landscape teeming with real historical personage, event, and voice – O'Brien's strategies often remind one of John Dos Passos's daring blends and collages of art and history in the *U.S.A.* trilogy – is a daring postmodern detective novel, a larger, even universal, exploration of what, says O'Brien, "deceit can do to the human heart."

In the Lake of the Woods is a striking achievement for many reasons. Another protagonist in the novel is Wade's wife, Kathy, whose sudden, strange disappearance is the story line that bears the weight of O'Brien's significant psychological and spiritual meditations on the nature of love and the difficulty, even the impossibility, of truly knowing another human being. John and Kathy Wade are both American secret sharers, and O'Brien combines in a truly masterful way the specifically historical, the daringly creative, and the richly universal threads of his intricate web of epistemological inquiry and emotional exploration. O'Brien serves as narrator and commentator in a set of intriguing author's notes, a uniquely American version of Conrad's Marlow, as he responds to the male and female hearts of darkness of John and Kathy Wade. A reader hears in the novel odd, compelling echoes of other great writers and texts – from Nathaniel Hawthorne's obsession with secret sin to Thomas Pynchon's concerns with postmodern cabal, conspiracy, and the problem of reading in a darkened American cultural landscape – but O'Brien's own originality is never diminished. While participating in the search for the missing Kathy Wade and learning more about the hidden recesses of her tormented husband and her own buried secrets, the reader also rewalks the dead land of national ethical and moral imperatives that extends from My Lai through the 1990s and moves back in time to other violent impulses and dark moments in American history: the massacres of Native Americans at Sand Creek and Wounded Knee; the brutal, vengeful British military action at Lexington and Concord.

In the Lake of the Woods is O'Brien's most daring and perhaps best book, for within its charged energy field of fictional and historical elements lies a story that remains compelling to all readers: the portrayal of well-intentioned hearts coming to terms with their own capacities for weakness, for deceit, for failure, and, sometimes, for real evil. In one of the important author's notes that gloss and complicate the motives of his protagonists, O'Brien makes the key revelation, a confession that speaks finally not just of *In the Lake of the Woods* but of his entire corpus of work: "What drives me on, I realize, is a craving to force entry into another heart, to trick the tumblers of natural law, to perform miracles of knowing. It's human nature. We are fascinated, all of us, by the implacable otherness of others." With this most recent work, O'Brien remains challenging and paradoxical, both diving and ascending within the heart and psyche, retracing familiar ground as he forges new and necessary trails through his creative imagination.

It has been a long, storied journey already for O'Brien: from the nine-year-old who wrote "Timmy of the Little League" to the mature, contemplative, innovative Tim O'Brien of *In the Lake of the Woods.* Readers and critics will wait eagerly to see what the war writer will create next, what new "miracles of knowing" he will achieve in his fictions. Living and working today in Cambridge, Massachusetts, he continues to play the role of the transplanted midwesterner, living a full-time writer's life that he feels to most people would appear "extremely boring." His work habits are disciplined and his outside diversions few and simple. He works from early morning to dinnertime, including weekends and holidays; his hobbies include golf and reading at night. Asked why he keeps his existence so basic and streamlined, he says, sounding like one of his own heroes, "the life of the imagination is enough."

Perhaps Tim O'Brien's career to date may be best summed up in two brief statements, one from himself and one from another notable contemporary writer. In "How To Tell a True War Story," striving to answer why the search for courage is so important and why the recording of that quest in story form is so crucial, O'Brien says it simply: "In the midst of evil you want to be a good man." Having experienced his fair share of contemporary historical evil, he has striven to find its opposite, and in addition to the quest for a fair and just definition of manhood, he has grown to become one of America's finest writers, one whose quirky humor and dazzling stylistic virtuosity cannot conceal the fact that he is a serious quester for truth, a creator of some of our finest and most important moral fiction.

Another contemporary novelist, Chaim Potok, has offered a good definition of what Tim O'Brien and other serious writers of imaginative moral fiction contribute to their culture. "Stories," Potok has said, "are maps that give shape to events which are shapeless." From the early 1970s onward, O'Brien has offered his readers some of the most interesting and necessary fictional charts possible. Like Cacciato leaving behind in the jungle his map for Third Squad to follow, O'Brien has created a corpus of work that has given shape to both American dream and reality — a remarkable, complex, and wonderful map for his readers to follow. In doing so, he has chronicled his war, his generation, his moment in American history like few other contemporary writers have done.

Few critics would argue with calling O'Brien the most important American fiction writer on the Vietnam conflict. Speaking for that consensus, Bates notes correctly that "his work is one of the happier outcomes of that unhappy war." While wearing with distinction the limiting tag of war writer, O'Brien continues to explore subjects and themes that demand of his critics larger classification and deeper vision. Whether his setting is a military combat zone where humans struggle just to survive or a domestic jungle whose casualties are often less obvious, he continues to feature protagonists who create and define themselves by the narratives they write, the dreams they imagine, the tales they pass on to others. Why the central concern with the power of the story to be told and retold well? O'Brien in 1992 said, "Stories, retold, carry the force of legend. . . . Huck is still going down that river, Ahab is still chasing that whale. Legends have to do with the repetition of things. Though there's a narrative end to *Moby-Dick,* there's a sense, as in all stories, that everyone is still out there, still doing these things, forever and ever."

What may lie ahead for Tim O'Brien? In a 1994 interview he said, "I don't know if I'll ever do another novel. . . . With *In the Lake of the Woods,* I feel like I've completed the things I have to say about myself and the world I've lived in, and I've also completed a kind of search. I can't see anywhere else to go beyond where John Wade is . . . I'm just gonna head north. See what happens." Many readers will hope that he will continue the artistic journey he began more than two decades ago: that he will offer his readers future stories and novels, "true or untrue," that will energize memory and imagination, conscience and fancy. O'Brien certainly knows the personal value of the well-told tale — "Good stories can be true or untrue," he said in 1992. "It doesn't really matter too much, provided that the story does to the spirit what stories should do, which is to entertain, but entertain in the highest way, entertain your brain and your stomach, and your heart, and your erotic zones, and make you laugh." One thing is certain of Tim O'Brien: whatever he writes in the future will be aimed at both head and heart, at both body and soul. And surely readers and critics will hope that a certain paradox will remain strangely valid — that his truth-filled lies will continue to make the stomach believe.

Interviews:

Larry McCaffery, "Interview with Tim O'Brien," *Chicago Review,* 33 (1982): 129–149;

Thomas LeClair and McCaffery, *Anything Can Happen: Interviews with Contemporary American Novelists* (Urbana: University of Illinois Press, 1983), pp. 262–278;

Eric James Schroeder, "Two Interviews: Talks with Tim O'Brien and Robert Stone," *Modern Fiction Studies,* 30 (Spring 1984): 135–164;

Martin Naparsteck, "An Interview with Tim O'Brien," *Contemporary Literature,* 32 (Spring 1991): i–ii;

Steven Kaplan, "An Interview with Tim O'Brien," *Missouri Review,* 14 (1991): 93–108;

"*Artful Dodge* Interviews Tim O'Brien," *Artful Dodge,* 22–23 (1992): 74–90;

John Mort, "The *Booklist* Interview: Tim O'Brien," *Booklist,* 90 (August 1994): 1990–1991.

Bibliography:

Catherine Calloway, "Tim O'Brien (1946-   ): A Primary and Secondary Checklist," *Bulletin of Bibliography,* 50 (September 1993): 223–229.

References:

Milton J. Bates, "Tim O'Brien's Myth of Courage," *Modern Fiction Studies,* 33 (Summer 1987): 263–279;

Philip D. Beidler, *American Literature and the Experience of Vietnam* (Athens: University of Georgia Press, 1982);

Beidler, *Re-Writing America: Vietnam Authors in Their Generation* (Athens: University of Georgia Press, 1991);

Maria S. Bonn, "A Different World: The Vietnam Veteran Novel Comes Home," in *Fourteen Landing Zones: Approaches to Vietnam War Literature,* edited by Philip K. Jason (Iowa City: University of Iowa Press, 1992), pp. 1–14;

Catherine Calloway, "Pluralities of Vision: *Going After Cacciato* and Tim O'Brien's Short Fiction," in

America Rediscovered: Critical Essays on Literature and Film of the Vietnam War, edited by Owen W. Gilman, Jr., and Lorrie Smith (New York: Garland, 1990), pp. 213–224;

G. Thomas Couser, "*Going After Cacciato:* The Romance and the Real War," *Journal of Narrative Technique,* 13 (Winter 1983): 1–10;

Toby Herzog, "*Going After Cacciato*: The Soldier-Author-Character Seeking Control," *Critique,* 24 (Winter 1983): 88–96;

Dale W. Jones, "The Vietnam of Michael Herr and Tim O'Brien: Tales of Disintegration and Integration," *Canadian Review of American Studies,* 13 (Winter 1982): 309–320;

John G. Leland, "Writing About Vietnam," *College English,* 43 (November 1981): 739–740;

Timothy J. Lomperis, *"Reading the Wind": The Literature of the Vietnam War* (Durham, N.C.: Duke University Press, 1987);

Gene Lyons, "Pieces of a Vietnam War Story," *Nation,* 224 (29 January 1977): 120–122;

Dean McWilliams, "Time in Tim O'Brien's *Going After Cacciato,*" *Critique,* 29 (Summer 1988): 245–255;

Thomas Myers, *Walking Point: American Narratives of Vietnam* (New York: Oxford University Press, 1988);

Edward F. Palm, "Falling In and Out: Military Idiom as Metaphoric Motif in *Going After Cacciato,*" *Notes on Contemporary Literature,* 22 (November 1992): 8;

Michael W. Raymond, "Imagined Responses to Vietnam: Tim O'Brien's *Going After Cacciato,*" *Critique,* 24 (Winter 1983): 97–104;

Arthur M. Saltzman, "The Betrayal of the Imagination: Paul Brodeur's *The Stunt Man* and Tim O'Brien's *Going After Cacciato,*" *Critique,* 22, no. 1 (1980): 32–38;

Eric James Schroeder, "The Past and the Possible: Tim O'Brien's Dialectic of Memory and Imagination," in *Search and Clear: Critical Responses to Selected Literature and Films of the Vietnam War,* edited by William J. Searle (Bowling Green, Ohio: Bowling Green State University Press, 1988), pp. 116–134;

Robert M. Slabey, "*Going After Cacciato:* Tim O'Brien's 'Separate Peace,'" in *America Rediscovered: Critical Essays on Literature and Film of the Vietnam War* (New York: Garland, 1990), pp. 205–212;

Gregory Stephenson, "Struggle and Flight: Tim O'Brien's *Going After Cacciato,*" *Notes on Contemporary Literature,* 14 (September 1984): 5–6;

Dennis Vannatta, "Theme and Structure in Tim O'Brien's *Going After Cacciato,*" *Modern Fiction Studies,* 28 (Summer 1982): 242–246;

Albert E. Wilhelm, "Ballad Allusions in 'Where Have You Gone, Charming Billy?,'" *Studies in Short Fiction,* 28 (Spring 1991): 218–222;

Daniel L. Zins, "Imagining the Real: The Fiction of Tim O'Brien," *Hollins Critic,* 23 (June 1986): 1–12.

Flannery O'Connor

(25 March 1925 – 3 August 1964)

Nancy K. Butterworth
Coker College

See also the O'Connor entries in *DLB 2: American Novelists Since World War II, First Series; DLB Yearbook: 1980;* and *Documentary Series 12: Southern Women Writers: Flannery O'Connor, Katherine Anne Porter, and Eudora Welty.*

BOOKS: *Wise Blood* (New York: Harcourt, Brace, 1952; London: Spearman, 1955);

A Good Man Is Hard To Find and Other Stories (New York: Harcourt, Brace, 1955); republished as *The Artificial Nigger and Other Tales* (London: Spearman, 1957);

The Violent Bear It Away (New York: Farrar, Straus & Cudahy, 1960; London: Longmans, Green, 1960);

Everything That Rises Must Converge (New York: Farrar, Straus & Giroux, 1965; London: Faber & Faber, 1966);

Mystery and Manners: Occasional Prose, edited by Sally and Robert Fitzgerald (New York: Farrar, Straus & Giroux, 1969; London: Faber & Faber, 1972);

The Complete Stories of Flannery O'Connor (New York: Farrar, Straus & Giroux, 1971);

The Presence of Grace and Other Book Reviews, compiled by Leo J. Zuber, edited by Carter W. Martin (Athens: University of Georgia Press, 1983);

Collected Works (New York: Library of America, 1988);

Flannery O'Connor: The Growing Craft – A Synoptic Variorum Edition of The Geranium, An Exile in the East, Getting Home, Judgement Day (Birmingham, Ala.: Summo, 1993).

OTHER: Dominican Nuns of Our Lady of Perpetual Help Cancer Home, *A Memoir of Mary Ann,* introduction by O'Connor (New York: Farrar, Straus & Cudahy, 1961), pp. 3–21.

Flannery O'Connor in 1962 (AP/Wide World)

Although Flannery O'Connor completed only a relatively small corpus of fiction during her brief life – two novels and thirty-one short stories between 1945 and her death at thirty-nine in 1964 – her stunning talent was immediately recognized, and her reputation has grown enormously since her death. This is not to imply, however, that her work has been universally applauded or even understood. Many readers have been disturbed by her bi-

158

zarre characters and pervasive use of violence; others have been confused by her confounding of traditional regional, religious, and literary categories. O'Connor's awareness of mixing modalities is shown by her sly comment in a 15 September 1955 letter to Andrew Lytle: "The only thing that keeps me from being a regional writer is being a Catholic and the only thing that keeps me from being a Catholic writer (in the narrow sense) is being a Southerner." She likewise wrote her anonymous Atlanta correspondent "A" on 24 September 1955, "everything funny I have written is more terrible than it is funny."

Both in her life and her art, O'Connor combined seemingly contradictory elements. In the introduction to *The Habit of Being,* her close friend and biographer Sally Fitzgerald characterizes O'Connor's complicated and demanding temperament through paradoxes, stating that she was extremely self-confident yet truly humble, sharply penetrating — even fierce — yet frequently filled with glee at the smallest absurdities of life, "devout but never pietistic." In titling the posthumous volume of O'Connor's essays and lectures *Mystery and Manners,* Robert and Sally Fitzgerald capture the twin threads of her uncompromisingly orthodox Roman Catholic faith and her delight in the comic details of social interaction. The core concern of her fiction is the fallen state of modern humanity unaware of its need for redemption. Writing of O'Connor's first novel, *Wise Blood* (1952), Caroline Gordon states, "In Miss O'Connor's vision of modern man — a vision not limited to Southern rural humanity — all her characters are 'displaced persons.' . . . 'off center,' out of place, because they are victims of a rejection of the Scheme of Redemption." Typically, her stories dramatize the climactic — and frequently fatal — proffering of grace to these prideful characters. The major technique she uses to present the resulting clash between secular and spiritual perspectives is an amalgam of comedy and satire based on the visual and literary arts of caricature, both of which she practiced as a young adult. Some readers have called this technique gothic or grotesque. In "The Fiction Writer and His Country" (1957), O'Connor defends her use of seemingly grotesque caricatures: "The novelist with Christian concerns will find in modern life distortions which are repugnant to him, and his problem will be to make these appear as distortions to an audience which is used to seeing them as natural; and he may well be forced to take ever more violent means to get his vision across to this hostile audience. . . . to the hard of hearing you shout, and for the almost-blind you draw large and

startling figures." As Anthony Di Renzo argues, O'Connor's grotesque caricatures are analogous to medieval gargoyles. Although they may offend because of their bizarre yoking of the sublime and the ridiculous, their ultimate purpose is therapeutic; they are a kind of "comic shock treatment."

Born 25 March 1925, Mary Flannery O'Connor was the only child of Edward F. O'Connor Jr. and Regina Cline O'Connor, both from established Georgia Catholic families. Until her early adolescence, the family resided in Savannah, Georgia, where she attended parochial schools. At five she gained fame when a New York newspaper reporter filmed her chicken that would walk backward or forward, begetting in her a lifelong obsession with breeding fowl, particularly peacocks. In an unpublished autobiographical fragment, she characterizes herself as "a pigeon-toed only child with a receding chin and a you-leave-me-alone-or-I'll-bite-you complex." Her stubborn, independent nature is illustrated in a 17 January 1956 letter by her recollection of a childhood practice she terms "anti-angel aggression." She would lock herself in her room and "with a fierce (and evil) face, whirl around in a circle with fists knotted, socking the angel" the nuns had told her guarded every person. During grade school she began drawing (mainly chickens) and writing verses and short narratives based on daily life experiences, which she illustrated with cartoons. The first page of a notebook written when she was twelve already exhibits her sharp tongue and idiosyncratic spelling, admonishing would-be snoopers, "I know some folks that don't mind thier own bisnis." Her father seems to have been the chief influence on her creative talents during this period. She notes in a 28 July 1956 letter that her father, a real estate broker, encouraged her artistic and literary productions because he "wanted to write but had not the time or money or training or any of the opportunities that I have had."

In 1938 her father's disseminated lupus, a hereditary autoimmune blood disease to which she would also succumb, forced the family to return to her mother's ancestral home in the central Georgia town of Milledgeville. They took up residence in the Cline House, which had been the interim governor's mansion until it was acquired by her maternal grandfather, Peter Cline, in 1886. Milledgeville's predominantly fundamentalist Protestant and rural milieu provided a strong counterpoint to Savannah's more Catholic and cosmopolitan social and intellectual environment. Because there were no parochial secondary schools in Milledgeville, she enrolled in the "progressive" Peabody High School, which she found disconcertingly eclectic. During her teen years she continued to write humorous literary sketches, to keep a journal defensively labeled "Don't Tuch," as well as to write satiric poetry and essays and to draw cartoons which she published in the high-school newspaper but was unsuccessful in placing elsewhere. An article in the 16 December 1941 *Peabody Palladium* cites "collecting rejection slips" as her hobby and notes that her ambition was "to keep on writing, particularly satire." Following her father's death when she was fifteen, O'Connor and her mother moved to Andalusia, the Cline family farm about five miles outside of Milledgeville.

In 1942 Mary Flannery (as she was still called) entered Georgia State College for Women (now Georgia College) at Milledgeville, where her creative interests remained about equally balanced between drawing and writing fiction. Her European-history professor, Helen Greene, recalled her love of James Thurber. She became art editor of the student newspaper, *The Colonnade,* which published many of her linoleum-cut cartoons. Sister Kathleen Feeley notes how their blending of visual caricature and trenchant verbal commentary presages her fiction. A typical cartoon depicts a student asking the librarian, "Do you have any books the faculty doesn't particularly recommend?" Her senior year she also edited *The Corinthian,* the campus literary quarterly, and was feature editor of the yearbook. The best of the unpublished college pieces in the collection at Georgia College are overwritten but evince her wry humor, interest in characters of all social classes, and attempt to capture dialogue and dialect. She was elected to the Phoenix Society and, by attending summers, graduated early, in June 1945.

At the conclusion of her college years, no one could have even remotely prophesied Mary Flannery's brilliant literary career. Her burgeoning ambition to become a writer is evidenced by a conversation with her mother during the summer of 1945 in which she requested permission to shorten her name to Flannery O'Connor for future publication purposes and haltingly discussed what direction her talent might take (she certainly did not want her mother to hold any illusions that she would become the next Margaret Mitchell). Her lack of practical knowledge about how to pursue a literary vocation is shown by the manner in which she entered the prestigious Iowa School for Writers in the fall of 1945. George Beiswanger, her philosophy professor, suggested she submit some of her *Corinthian* stories, and she was initially accepted into the graduate

program in journalism, not creative writing (her undergraduate major was changed to sociology from English). Indeed, her introductory interview with director Paul Engle for acceptance into the Writers' Workshop was nearly disastrous, for he humorously recalled later not having been able to understand a single syllable of her Southern dialect. He soon grew, however, to have a very high regard for her talent, noting that she profited enormously from the Iowa workshop experience because of her drive and diligence. Engle further recounted that she was reticent to read her work aloud and usually remained a silent observer during the group critiques: "The only communicating gesture she would make was an occasional amused and shy smile at something absurd." While in the Iowa program she also received encouragement and criticism from such renowned Southern visiting authors as Robert Penn Warren, John Crowe Ransom, and Andrew Lytle. Ransom edited the *Kenyon Review* and Lytle the *Sewanee Review,* which published several of her stories. She also met Allen Tate and his first wife, Caroline Gordon, who became her friend and mentor.

During her two-year residence in the Iowa School for Writers (fall 1945–June 1947), O'Connor wrote six stories – "The Geranium," "The Crop," "The Barber," "Wildcat," "The Turkey," and "The Train" – which became her master's thesis, titled "The Geranium: A Collection of Short Stories." On the basis of this work and Engle's recommendation, she won the Rinehart-Iowa Fiction Award, carrying a $750 honorarium and the publisher's option to purchase her first novel. These stories, together with four more written before 1950 – "The Peeler," "The Heart of the Park," "The Woman on the Stairs" (revised and retitled "A Stroke of Good Fortune"), and "Enoch and the Gorilla" – constitute her apprentice fiction, most of which was published in small magazines and remained uncollected until the posthumous *Complete Stories* (1971). Several of these "stories" were composed as part of her novel in progress, *Wise Blood,* though they were revised for that work: "The Train" (chapter 1), "The Peeler" (chapter 3), "The Heart of the Park" (chapter 5), and "Enoch and the Gorilla" (parts of chapters 11 and 12).

Overall, these apprentice works demonstrate neither the distinctive voice nor the vision that characterize her mature fiction. Rather, they are fairly superficial studies in social and psychological realism, conventional in form and derivative in style and technique. They are further marred by technical problems, such as inauthentic dialect, unintegrated flashbacks, and, most important, the failure

O'Connor (seated at center) and the 1944–1945 staff of The Corinthian, *the literary quarterly of the Georgia State College for Women (courtesy of Barbara Brannon)*

to separate the narrative voice from the protagonist's consciousness sufficiently to create the distance necessary for comic or ironic perspective – a technique Caroline Gordon would help O'Connor master in *Wise Blood*. The stories, however, do provide clues to her emerging character types, themes, and important influences, and certain passages foretell her future power.

Her first published story, "The Geranium" (*Accent,* Summer 1946), was revised and retitled three times, first as "An Exile in the East" in 1955, later as "Getting Home," and finally as "Judgement Day" in 1964. The original story dramatizes the plight of the prototypical O'Connor character, the displaced person (which O'Connor acutely felt herself to be during her first years in the North), anticipating such characters as Hazel Motes, the protagonist of *Wise Blood,* and The Misfit of "A Good Man Is Hard to Find." As Stuart Burns notes in "Literary Apprenticeship," however, Old Man Dudley's displacement is merely geographical and sociological, whereas in her later works displacement functions as a metaphor for man's estrangement from God. Having mistakenly moved from the South to his daughter's dismal New York apartment, Dudley

(like Aleck in Gordon's "Old Red," to which the story is indebted) spends his time in exile reminiscing about fishing and quail hunting with his Negro friend, Rabie. In one of the few dramatized scenes, Dudley confronts an urban black man with disastrous results. The story contains some convincing dialogue and striking imagery, particularly the concluding image of the inverted geranium lying in the alley below with its roots in the air, which serves as an powerful metaphor for Dudley's plight.

"The Turkey" (published in the November 1948 *Mademoiselle* as "The Capture") effectively combines a religious theme with comedy. The story presents the stages through which young Ruller McFarney progresses in his comic quest for a wounded turkey, which he sees as a sign of his spiritual election. The hilarious scene in which he thinks God has played a trick on him and alternately profanes God and giggles prefigures O'Connor's blasphemous rebel/prophets, such as Hazel Motes, The Misfit, young Tarwater of her second novel, *The Violent Bear It Away* (1960), and O. E. Parker of "Parker's Back," a story she completed less than three weeks before her death. The swift, violent revelation of the conclusion, in which the pursuer suddenly becomes the terrified prey of "Something Awful," is one of her classic dramatic devices. The story also contains the important motif of the neglected child. O'Connor's high regard for the story is shown by the fact that she rewrote it extensively in the early 1950s and seriously considered including it in *A Good Man Is Hard to Find* under the title "An Afternoon in the Woods."

The other thesis stories are far less successful. Her first forays into comic satire, "The Crop" and "The Barber," portray arrogant, alienated pseudo-intellectuals who are at least partially self-parodies: a spinster author of sentimental sociological fiction of the Erskine Caldwell school who lights on share-croppers as an appropriately "arty" subject and a frustrated Southern liberal college professor who unsuccessfully attempts to defeat the forces of racism in a local gubernatorial race through "reasoned" barbershop debate. Although "The Barber" evinces a degree of subtlety in handling colloquial speech, the setting and tone derive too directly from Ring Lardner's "Haircut." "Wildcat," O'Connor's only story featuring a black protagonist, is a melodramatic evocation of terror as though the gothic horror of Edgar Allan Poe was grafted onto a William Faulkner story. The climactic conjunction in "Wildcat" of violence, religious vision, and humor evoked by the protagonist's hubris becomes one of her hallmarks.

The last apprenticeship story in her thesis, "The Train" (*Sewanee Review,* April 1948), was also an early draft of the opening chapter of *Wise Blood.* The story focuses on the twenty-two-year-old veteran Hazel (or Haze) Wickers's inability to go home again because during his absence home has ceased to exist as a physical and emotional haven. During the train ride to Taulkinham, Tennessee, he returns to memories of his now-dead mother. The strong influence of Poe and Faulkner, especially *As I Lay Dying* (1930), is evident in his obsession with her death and the train-berth/coffin image. Haze heckles the Negro porter, convinced that he is old Cash Simmons from his hometown of Eastrod who is only pretending to be from Chicago — another avatar of the displacement motif. Haze's search for identity and his loneliness make him a pathetic but sympathetic character. The story lacks any references to religion.

O'Connor's increasingly subtle handling of narrative viewpoint, character, and theme during the late 1940s and early 1950s can be seen by comparing "The Train" with the extensively revised first chapter of *Wise Blood.* "The Train" opens with Haze's internal perceptions: "Thinking about the

porter, he had almost forgotten the berth." In contrast, *Wise Blood* dramatizes the scene, capturing him in an unconscious gesture of symbolic conflict: "Hazel Motes sat at a forward angle on the green plush train seat, looking one minute as if he might want to jump out of it, and the next down the aisle at the other end of the car." He has undergone a significant name change from the nonsymbolic Hazel Wickers to Hazel Motes. His namesake, Hazael in 1 and 2 Kings, was a king of Damascus who battled against God, and Hazel in Hebrew means "God sees." The shortened form Haze suggests his clouded vision of himself, and Motes recalls the mote of Matthew 7:3–5 (King James Version). The scene with Mrs. Wally Bee Hitchcock has also changed dramatically. Although the short-story version gently satirizes her porcine exterior and vacuous interior (she is the prototype for all the complacent, superficial, and spiritually void widows in O'Connor's subsequent fiction), Hazel Wickers "was glad to have someone there talking." In contrast, *Wise Blood* interjects the central theme of redemption right into the middle of Mrs. Hitchcock's prattle: "'I reckon you think you been redeemed,' he said." The background on Hazel's circuit-preacher grandfather and rejection of his calling were added to the novel version.

In her note prefacing the second edition of *Wise Blood,* O'Connor describes the book as "a comic novel about a Christian *malgré lui,* and as such, very serious, for all comic novels that are any good must be about matters of life and death." She then asserts that Hazel's integrity consists in his inability to evade the haunting figure of Jesus "moving from tree to tree in the back of his mind," which provides the central conflict of the novel. For resist it he does, from his first puritanical attempts to avoid Jesus by avoiding sin to his nihilistic program of proving the nonexistence of Christ by deliberately committing what traditionally would have been construed as sins: fornicating with Leora Watts and blaspheming. The central symbol of his futile attempt to escape culpability through mobility is his rat-colored Essex, from which he preaches the Church Without Christ: "there was no Fall because there was nothing to fall from and no Redemption because there was no Fall and no Judgment because there wasn't the first two." Haze begins to feel guilt only after murdering his pathetic double, Solace Layfield, who parodies modern commercialized religion by preaching a pablum self-help salvation for pay in the oxymoronic Holy Church of Christ Without Christ. It takes the destruction of Haze's beloved Essex by a policeman who functions as an externalized conscience to make Haze confront a vision of utter blankness necessary for his eventual salvation. Stages in his spiritual evolution include his rejection of the false Madonna, Sabbath Lily Hawks, and the desiccated mummy/Jesus figure, as well as various mortifications of the flesh, culminating in self-blinding. According to Burns in "The Evolution of Wise Blood," the paradoxical premise of his act of self-contrition is that "blindness is a prerequisite for insight."

Interspersed within this searing story of Haze's painful path toward salvation are the comic peregrinations of various alter egos, the most prominent of whom is Enoch Emery, a caricature of alienated modern urban man who can only communicate through his animal nature. Enoch, who works at the zoo, undergoes a kind of reverse evolution, finally becoming transformed into a gorilla and disappearing from the story, parodying Methuselah's son Enoch, who was translated into heaven (Genesis 5:24). Other characters comically satirized through animal and biblical imagery include Asa Hawks, a shrikelike preacher/con artist who pretends to be blind so that he can beg, and Hoover Shoates, a former radio evangelist on a show called Soulsease who, instead of exorcising sin onto swine (Matthew 8:28–34), preaches man's original sweetness (a parody of Original Sin). His alias, Onnie Jay Holy, is pig latin gibberish for John the Baptist, a role he burlesques as sidekick for his puppet-prophet Solace Layfield. Finally, Haze's landlady, Mrs. Flood, is satirized for her materialistic worldview which makes her almost totally incapable of comprehending spiritual reality. The novel concludes with a description of her staring into the dead Haze's eyes as he recedes "farther and farther into the darkness until he was the pin point of light."

Because of O'Connor's highly recursive method of writing, it is difficult to disentangle the personal, cultural, and literary influences that affected the radical reshaping of *Wise Blood*. As she wrote on 21 July 1948 to her literary agent, Elizabeth McKee: "I don't have my novel outlined and I have to write to discover what I am doing . . . I don't know so well what I think until I see what I say; then I have to say it over again." O'Connor conceived *Wise Blood* in late 1946 and remained at Iowa through autumn 1947 to continue working on it under Engle's guidance. Early in 1948 she took up residence at Yaddo, a private writers' colony in Sarasota Springs, New York, where she became friends with poet Robert Lowell, essayist Elizabeth Hardwick, and critic Alfred Kazin. Lowell introduced her to Robert Giroux, her future editor at Harcourt, Brace and later at Farrar, Straus & Giroux. During 1948 or early 1949, O'Connor wrote several undated "Plans for Work," one of which shows that Hazel's concept of home had expanded to stand "not only for the place and family, but for some absolute belief that would give him sanctuary in the modern world." O'Connor sent Rinehart nine chapters (108 pages) of the novel in January 1949 and received a reply from editor in chief John Selby conveying their criticisms. Affronted both by its tone and content, she wrote back on 18 February that she felt "whatever virtues the novel may have are very much connected with the limitations" he had mentioned of "peculiarity or aloneness." She noted emphatically that she was "not writing a conventional novel" and was "amenable to criticism but only within the sphere of what [she was] trying to do." Her determination to develop in her own way led to a divisive correspondence and release from Rinehart in October, allowing her to transfer publication rights to Harcourt, Brace.

Appalled by the organized leftist attack on Lowell when his call for the Yaddo director's dismissal was made public, O'Connor left the writing colony in March and spent a short time in New York, living in a drab Upper West Side apartment. Introduced to Robert and Sally Fitzgerald, she became a boarder in their rural Connecticut farmhouse in September 1949. The daily camaraderie over the next year and a half with the Fitzgeralds, with whom O'Connor shared a common Catholic and cultural perspective, provided a major influence on her writing. The Fitzgeralds sent her letters and works in progress on to Caroline Gordon.

O'Connor's reading of Nathanael West in the late 1940s, particularly *Miss Lonelyhearts* (1933), was probably the major catalyst that freed her to fuse elements of violence, the grotesque, and outrageous comedy with a serious theme of religious quest. Frederick Asals argues in "The Road to *Wise Blood*" that Hazel is a sort of "Miss Lonelyhearts in reverse" in that he seeks to flee rather than to pursue Christ. Suzanne Mannmeusel notes that although the ultimate effect of both works is quite different, they follow a similar structure based on the classic preconversion pattern delineated in William James's *The Varieties of Religious Experience:* "deadness, disorder, self-conscious sinning, flight from God, and submission." James's definition of the Sick Soul also applies to both characters: The Sick Soul defines evil as the core of reality, "which no alteration of the environment, or superficial rearrange-

*Dust jacket for O'Connor's first novel, a work she described in 1962 as
"about a Christian* malgré lui *[despite himself]"*

ment of the inner self, can cure, and which requires a supernatural remedy." This concept bears a striking resemblance to O'Connor's depiction of a spiritual hunger that only the Bread of Life can fill, which is apparent in *Wise Blood* as well as *The Violent Bear It Away*.

Other specific parallels between West's work and O'Connor's can also be drawn. Shrike, the False Prophet in *Miss Lonelyhearts,* probably influenced the characterizations of Asa Hawks and Solace Layfield in *Wise Blood* and may have provided the idea for the pervasive bird imagery/symbolism. Hoover Shoat's Soulease and Sabbath Lily's lewd letters and responses from the newspaper advice columnist probably derived both from Miss Lonelyhearts's parodies of such columns and Dr. George W. Crane's real one during the mid 1950s syndicated in the *Atlanta Constitution* titled "The Worry Clinic," which O'Connor in an 18 May 1955 letter characterized as "salvation by the compliment club."

Another seminal influence on *Wise Blood* was Sophocles' Oedipus plays. O'Connor read Robert Fitzgerald's translations of *Oedipux Rex* and *Oedipus at Colonus* in the summer of 1950, and he avers that Oedipus's self-blinding provided her with the powerful conclusion in which Haze successfully blinds himself, as Asa Hawks could not. Burns asserts that as O'Connor revised the novel, the alienation theme became subordinated to the religious one, and *Wise Blood* developed from a Freudian Oedipal to a Sophoclean Oedipus drama. Other possible sources for Hazel's conversion in *Wise Blood* include Saint Paul, Saint Anthony, as well as Dante's *The Divine Comedy* and John Bunyan's *Pilgrim's Progress*. O'Connor was also highly influenced during this period by European and Anglo-Catholic writers, especially Georges Bernanos (*The Diary of a Country Priest*), T. S. Eliot (*The Family Reunion* and his essay on Charles Baudelaire), Graham Greene (*Brighton Rock*), Romano Guardini (*The Lord*), James Joyce (*Dubliners*), and François Mauriac (*Therese Des-*

queroux), as well as by nineteenth-century American writers Edgar Allan Poe and Nathaniel Hawthorne.

The most important cultural and philosophical influences on O'Connor's thinking during these years were the emergence in Europe of the movement loosely termed existentialism and the Catholic Renaissance response. Brainard Cheney's assertion in a 1964 *Sewanee Review* article that *Wise Blood* is "a bitter parody on . . . atheistic Existentialism" is corroborated by O'Connor's lament in a 28 August 1955 letter, "If you live today you breathe in nihilism. . . . it's the gas you breathe." Certainly she would have opposed the nihilistic premise of ultimate Nothingness proposed by German philosopher Martin Heidegger and the French atheistic existentialists Jean-Paul Sartre and Albert Camus. However, she responded more positively to the ideas of Christian existentialists Gabriel Marcel and Søren Kierkegaard, whose works were frequently discussed both in the Catholic and the academic journals where she submitted her first stories. For example, she probably read neo-Thomist Jacques Maritain's essay "From Existential Existentialism to Academic Existentialism," which appeared in the same issue of *Sewanee Review* as "The Train." Maritain contrasts Kierkegaard's highly subjective agony of faith with the detached, theoretical searchings of the rationalist post-Cartesian academic existentialists, whom he castigates for positing "an insurmountable barrier between intelligence and mystery." O'Connor makes an almost identical point in "Catholic Novelists and Their Readers" (1964) when she laments the separations of fact from mystery, judgment "from vision, nature from grace, and reason from imagination" as inimical both to faith and art. Haze is also torn between these two contradictory modes of knowing. The title *Wise Blood* suggests both man's Original Sin of seeking too much knowledge and the higher wisdom of the primitive spiritual impulse associated with the heart rather than the head. Ironically, the animalistic Enoch thinks he has wise blood, whereas Haze's conflict between his willful intellect and his internalized image of the crucifixion associates the term more meaningfully with him. Throughout her career O'Connor continued to castigate intellectual atheists and rational secular humanists and to be drawn toward frenzied fundamentalists.

Christmas of 1950 commenced a series of devastating blows for O'Connor both personally and professionally. She began to experience a heaviness in her arms while typing, which was the first sign of lupus erythematosis. She was so stricken on the train ride home that she had to be hospitalized and was unable to return to Connecticut. The progressively debilitating effects of lupus confined her to semi-invalidism at Andalusia for the rest of her life. However, Sally Fitzgerald notes in her introduction to *The Habit of Being* that instead of becoming bitter, O'Connor accepted this limitation as a means to perfect what Maritain in *Art and Scholasticism* terms the "habit of art." Over the next two years she continued to rewrite drafts of what she facetiously called "Opus Nauseous No. 1," sending copies to Gordon and the Fitzgeralds for criticism.

The publication of *Wise Blood* in May 1952 was followed immediately by unsympathetic criticism reflecting almost total incomprehension of her intent. Critics deplored its bizarre plot and insane cast of characters, who were so repulsive that readers could not retain interest in them. Most saw Haze either as an unredeemed nihilist or a parody of Protestant fundamentalism and simply could not understand how she construed his fanatical asceticism as positive. None mentioned the humor, though some praised her vivid prose style. The contemporary reviewer who seemed best to apprehend what she was about was Cheney, whose long review in autumn 1952 *Shenandoah* led to their acquaintance. Among many insights, he noted that "she uses, under the face of naturalism, a theologically weighted symbolism." Slowly over the next forty years, most readers have come to understand – if not always to like – the work through rereading it based on a knowledge of her more accessible short fiction and the essays in *Mystery and Manners*. Contemporary critics are more likely to question the novel's structure, particularly the failure to integrate the Enoch subplot, rather than its intent. Yet a few otherwise astute readers continue to find *Wise Blood* appalling: Asals insisted in 1982 that Haze "receives no revelation" and calls *Wise Blood* "the most thoroughly grotesque and estranging work O'Connor ever wrote." On the opposite extreme, Richard Giannone eulogizes Haze as "a saint for our unbelieving age."

Soon after the publication of *Wise Blood*, O'Connor began working on a second novel, which would eventually become *The Violent Bear It Away*. She also returned to writing short stories, both to conserve her physical resources and to escape writing the novel, which she found increasingly difficult. Repeatedly during the 1950s she refers in her essays and correspondence to the necessity of accepting limitations imposed by vocation, vision, and individual circumstance. For example, in a 17 March 1953 letter to the Lowells she states, "I have enough energy to write with and as that is all I have business doing anyhow, I can with one eye squinted take it all as a blessing. What you have to measure out, you come to observe closer, (or so I tell myself)." Until the summer of 1952 she continued to hope she would be able to resume living with the Fitzgeralds. However, she was forced to shorten her July visit due to a virus, and the diagnosis of lupus was confirmed over the summer. She then adjusted to her restricted life at Andalusia, conforming to a simple daily schedule of writing two to three hours every morning. She would eat with her mother, occasionally entertain, read, write letters, and observe the doings of the myriad peafowl and hired help. Often she would watch the locals from the car while her mother ran errands in town. She did make several short trips, one to Nashville in July 1953 for a soiree at Brainard and Frances Cheney's, where she stunned guests into silence with her first public reading of "A Good Man Is Hard To Find," and others in October to visit the Fitzgeralds and Giroux. In May and June 1955 she journeyed to New York to be interviewed by Harvey Breit for the television serialization of "The Life You Save May Be Your Own" and to Connecticut to see Caroline Gordon. When her health permitted in the late 1950s and early 1960s, she lectured at various colleges and universities such as Chicago, Converse, Georgetown, Hollins, Minnesota, Notre Dame, Saint Louis, Sweet Briar, Texas, Vanderbilt, and Wesleyan. Upon the insistence of her cousin Katie, she even forayed as far as Lourdes for the healing baths and to Rome for an audience with Pope Pius XII in May 1958. But generally she stayed at home and wrote. With the stipends from the various fellowships and grants she was awarded – Kenyon fellowships in 1953 and 1954, a National Institute of Arts and Letters grant in 1957, and a Ford Foundation grant in 1959 – she paid for her medical treatments, books and journals, and growing brood of birds.

The three-year period between the fall 1952 and mid 1955 proved to be her most productive. On 11 November 1953 she wrote the Fitzgeralds that she had "seven good stories and two lousy ones for [her] collection." By Christmas 1954 the number was up to "[n]ine stories about original sin," which she dedicated to them. When the collection titled *A Good Man Is Hard to Find* was published in June 1955, it consisted of ten stories, including four among the finest she ever wrote: the title story, "The Displaced Person," and two superb newly completed ones, "The Artificial Nigger" and "Good Country People." On a slightly lower level are "The Life You Save May Be Your Own" and "A Circle in the Fire."

The stories show a major shift in narrative strategy from the novels by focusing on nominal Christians and nonbelievers (much like her audience) who are assaulted by a series of freaks and devil figures who often serve as unwitting instruments of spiritual revelation. Jack Ashley associates the latter with the scourges sent by God to chastise the Israelites. In her essay "In the Devil's Territory" (1961), O'Connor states, "From my experience in trying to make stories 'work,' I have discovered that what is needed is an action that is totally unexpected, yet totally believable. . . . frequently it is an action in which the devil has been the unwilling instrument of grace." Warren Coffrey delineates O'Connor's paradigm narrative as "a kind of morality story in which Pride of Intellect (usually Irreligion) has a shattering encounter with the Corrupt Human Heart (the Criminal, the Insane, sometimes the Sexually Demonic) and either sees the light or dies, sometimes both" (Friedman and Clark, *Critical Essays*).

"A Good Man Is Hard to Find" fits this paradigm perfectly. It treats the meeting between a too-garrulous Grandmother and a homicidal psychopath called The Misfit who undergo a mutual unmasking and catastrophic yet cathartic convergence. The Grandmother's illusions about her social and spiritual superiority are stripped away, leaving her sprawled crosslegged in a puddle of her own blood, while her unexpected gesture of genuine care toward The Misfit – "Why you're one of my babies. You're one of my own children" – challenges his defensive credos of total independence and sadistic pleasure in meanness. Despite obvious foreshadowing (the Grandmother dresses so "anyone seeing her dead on the highway would know at once that she was a lady," references to Toombsboro, an actual town in Georgia, and to six graves), some critics feel it is structurally and tonally disjunct, becoming The Misfit's story in the second half. Others question the necessity of the brutal murders and whether the Grandmother achieves salvation as she smiles up at the cloudless sky.

The last story in the collection, "The Displaced Person," seemingly inverts the paradigm when the Christlike Displaced Person, a hardworking tenant refugee from Poland, is run over by a tractor while the other farmhands and proprietress, Mrs. McIntyre, passively acquiesce. This "slaughter of an innocent," similar to the sacrifice of the angelic imbecile Lucynell in "The Life You Save May Be Your Own," plunges the nominally Catholic Mrs. McIntyre into purgatory. As Sister M. Joselyn notes, evil in "The Displaced Person" centers not in a demonic person or action but "the absence of love." The various characters' reactions to the Displaced Person and Christ, both of whom upset the balance, and the peacock, whose resplendent tail symbolizes the Transfiguration, serve as gauges of their failed spirituality.

"The Artificial Nigger," one of O'Connor's few stories that dramatize the healing effects of salvation on the characters, is a mock-heroic rendition of Dante's *Divine Comedy* and the Book of Tobit in the Apocrypha. Mr. Head, who grandiosely considers himself a wise spiritual guide like Virgil or Raphael, takes his uppity grandson, Nelson, to the evil city of Atlanta "so that he would be content to stay at home for the rest of his life." Instead, Head gets lost and rejects Nelson. Their symbolic circling of the hellish sewers and backstreets of Atlanta and reunion through the enigmatic "artificial nigger" statue initiate both characters into a recognition of their dependence on one another and God. The story is one of O'Connor's most intriguing treatments of doubling. Head is described as looking "like an ancient child and Nelson like a miniature old man." Likewise, "it was not possible to tell if the artificial Negro were meant to be young or old; he looked too miserable to be either." In a 4 May 1955 letter O'Connor states that it was meant to suggest "the redemptive quality of the Negro's suffering for us all."

O'Connor recounted that "Good Country People" was the easiest story she ever wrote and, along with "The Artificial Nigger," her personal favorite, perhaps because she identified so strongly with the homely, sour-tempered Joy/Hulga, who possesses both a Ph.D. in philosophy and a wooden leg. The final scene, in which the atheistic Hulga prepares to surrender herself to a fraudulent Bible salesman symbolically named Manly Pointer, climaxes with vintage O'Connor comic satire when he steals her assured belief in Nothing along with her wooden leg.

O'Connor herself was becoming increasingly crippled by her cortisone treatments, which by fall 1953 had deteriorated her hip joints to the degree that she was forced to begin using crutches. During the final nine years of her life O'Connor's writing slowed dramatically. In 1955 she published "You Can't Be Any Poorer Than Dead," the first chapter of *The Violent Bear It Away*, but the novel's composition thereafter was painstaking. At a pace of about one per year, she was able to complete the nine stories collected in the posthumous volume *Everything That Rises Must Converge* (1965) and a few others, as well as the introduction to *A Memoir of Mary Ann*

O'Connor in July 1953, during a visit to the Brainard Cheneys near Nashville, Tennessee (photograph by Ralph Morrissey, by permission of Eleanor F. Morrissey)

(1961) and fragments of an unfinished novel titled "Why Do the Heathen Rage?" Although O'Connor typically made light of her infirmities — referring to her crutches as "flying buttresses" — her stories written during the late 1950s and early 1960s show a darker tone, and her correspondence evinces periods of deep spiritual suffering, which she perceived as both personal and cultural. In a 6 September 1955 letter to "A," she acerbically asks why faith should be emotionally satisfying and avers that "there are long periods in the lives of all of us . . . when the truth revealed by faith is hideous, emotionally disturbing, downright repulsive. Witness the dark night of the soul in individual saints. Right now the whole world seems to be going through a dark night of the soul."

One reason for O'Connor's depression was her growing disillusionment with her general readership. She wrote "A" on 20 July 1955, "I am mighty tired of reading reviews that call *A Good Man* brutal and sarcastic. The stories are hard because there is nothing harder or less sentimental than Christian realism. . . . when I see these stories described as horror stories I am always amused because the reviewer always has hold of the wrong horror." Repeatedly in her lectures, essays, and book reviews, O'Connor refers to the difficulty of making the ultimate reality of the Incarnation real for an audience that has ceased to believe. She felt particularly compelled to explain her reasons for using distortion and violence. In "The Fiction Writer and His Country" (which gained a wide readership in Granville Hicks's *The Living Novel: A Symposium* in 1957), she argues that Christian writers must have "the sharpest eyes for the grotesque, for the perverse, and for the unacceptable" and that in order to dramatize these distortions as repugnant to a hostile audience that accepts them as natural, they may need to use shock techniques such as caricature. In "A Reasonable Use of the Unreasonable" (1962), however, she defines her technique as literal rather than grotesque, "in the same sense that a child's drawing is literal. When a child draws, he doesn't intend to distort but to set down exactly what he sees."

O'Connor defends violence not as an end in itself but as the only way to reach her hardheaded characters (and readers): "I have found that violence is strangely capable of returning my characters to reality and preparing them to accept their moment of grace. . . . This idea, that reality is something to which we must be returned at considerable cost, is one which is seldom understood by the casual reader." As she laments in a 1959 letter, "What people don't realize is how much religion costs. They think faith is a big electric blanket, when of course it is the cross." Likewise in a 1 October 1960 letter, she challenges the common misconception that the Christian novel should focus on healing rather than conflict: "This notion that grace is healing omits the fact that before it heals, it cuts with the sword Christ said he came to bring." In "Some Aspects of the Grotesque in Southern Fiction" (1960), she justifies the unsentimental detachment of her vision – "Certainly when the grotesque is used in a legitimate way, the intellectual and moral judgments implicit in it will have the ascendancy over feeling" – and satirizes "hazy compassion" that excuses any human weakness because it is human.

O'Connor explains the reasons for her repugnance toward sentimentality further in "The Church and the Fiction Writer" (1957) and her introduction to *A Memoir of Mary Ann,* where she states, "One of the tendencies of our age is to use the suffering of children to discredit the goodness of God. . . . In this popular pity, we mark our gain in sensibility and our loss in vision. If other ages felt less, they saw more, even though they saw with the blind, prophetical, unsentimental eye of . . . faith. In the absence of this faith now, we govern by tenderness." Her theological and artistic philosophies merge on the issue of vision, for following Saint Thomas Aquinas and Jacques Maritain, she believed both religion and art depend on a prophetic or visionary imagination, not morality or utility. She continually reiterates that her Catholic beliefs in no way limit her freedom as a writer; in fact, she maintains in 17 March 1956 that "it increases rather than decreases my vision. . . . [because] to believe nothing is to see nothing." Yet in "The Church and the Fiction Writer," she admits that "affirmative vision cannot be demanded of [the Catholic writer] without limiting his freedom to observe what man has done with the things of God."

Certainly O'Connor's satiric vision was modeled more on Juvenal's bitter and savage invective than Horace's genial and chiding corrective. As Ralph Wood points out in *The Comedy of Redemption,* she fits into the dark ironic traditions of the Old Testament jeremiad and Dante's *buona ira,* "the salutary wrath which seeks to laugh folly to scorn." Among American authors she was most drawn to the apocalyptic Poe and to Hawthorne, whose "great power of blackness" Melville ascribed to a "Calvinistic sense of Innate Depravity and Original Sin" very similar to O'Connor's own. So strong is O'Connor's satiric stance that many readers fail to perceive how much she identified with her characters (she wrote to "A" on 6 September 1955 that her own disposition was a combination of Hulga's and Nelson's).

O'Connor worked diligently to achieve the narrative detachment necessary for irony and satire. Gordon repeatedly counseled her to restrict her use of indirect discourse and to eliminate colloquial expressions from omniscient narration so that it sounded like the speech of Dr. Johnson – which O'Connor understandably found very difficult. Even as late as "Revelation" (1964), the omniscient narrator slips into Ruby Turpin's diction during an account of her ruminations: "some of the people with a lot of money were common and ought to be below she and Claud." O'Connor also learned much about narrative technique from Joseph Conrad, Gustave Flaubert, Henry James, and Joyce, as well as Cleanth Brooks and Robert Penn Warren's *Understanding Fiction* and Percy Lubbock's *The Craft of Fiction,* particularly to rely as much as possible on dramatic presentation (showing rather than telling).

O'Connor also felt many readers misunderstood her intentions as a Roman Catholic writer who chose predominantly to depict Southern Protestants. Although she greatly appreciated a few Catholic authors such as Léon Bloy, Bernanos, Mauriac, and Greene, she found the majority didactic and undramatic. In contrast, Protestants, especially the rural evangelical kind she encountered in backwoods Georgia, exhibited integrity and fervor that André Bleikasten notes were congenial with "the burning intransigence of her own faith." As she states in "Some Aspects of the Grotesque in Southern Fiction" (1960), the modern South remains "Christ-haunted," if no longer "Christ-centered." In an important 4 May 1963 letter to Sister Mariella Gable, she comments that one reason she writes about Protestants is that whereas Catholics with intense belief "join the convent and are heard from no more," fundamentalist Protestants "express their belief in diverse kinds of dramatic action which is obvious enough for [her] to catch." She was also drawn to Southern Protestants' dramatic sense that "everything is ultimately saved or lost," which some commentators term quasi-dualist or even Manichean or Gnostic, the heresies that polarize and give equal efficacy to the forces of God and the Devil in human history.

In "The Catholic Novelist in the Protestant South" (1963–1964) she expresses her disdain for "those politer elements for whom the supernatural is an embarrassment or for whom religion has become a department of sociology or culture or personality development." In contrast, members of what she terms "the invisible Church make discoveries that have meaning for us who are better protected from the vicissitudes of our own natures, and who are often too lazy and satisfied to make any discoveries at all." Despite conventional readers' discomfort (she wrote the Fitzgeralds that she sometimes feared that "a feeling for the vulgar is [her] natural talent"), she preferred the primitive prophet/freak protagonists of her two novels, the fiercely tattooed O. E. Parker and his fanatically heretical wife, and distorted visionaries such as Ruby Turpin of "Revelation" to tepid, respectable nominal Christians like Mrs. McIntyre and Mrs. May of "Greenleaf," who "thought the word, Jesus, should be kept inside the church building like other words inside the bedroom." O'Connor particularly approved of the former characters' unintellectualized ability to act upon their beliefs. Although many of her readers are as shocked as Mrs. Flood by Haze's self-immolation and other ascetic acts and by young Tarwater's fatal baptism of Bishop in the second novel, Albert Sonnenfeld, in an essay collected by Melvin J. Friedman and Beverly Lyon Clark in *Critical Essays on Flannery O'Connor*, shows how O'Connor was a true follower of John the Baptist's literal interpretation of baptism as exorcism. O'Connor's only major reservation about fundamentalists stems from their extreme individualism. Because they lack the structure of Church ritual, they frequently express their unconscious religious urges in bizarre, even monstrous acts. She wrote 13 September 1959 to John Hawkes, "Wise blood has to be these people's means of grace – they have no sacraments. The religion of the South is a do-it-yourself religion, something which I as a Catholic find painful and touching and grimly comic."

O'Connor's doctrinal differences from Protestants are more difficult to assess. In the letter to Hawkes, O'Connor emphasizes that she shares "the same fundamental doctrines of sin and redemption and judgment that they do." Likewise, in her 4 May 1963 letter she responds positively to Sister Gable's article on the ecumenical core of her fiction: "I am more and more impressed with the amount of Catholicism that fundamental Protestants have been able to retain. Theologically our differences with them are on the nature of the Church, not on the nature of God or our obligations to Him." Yet critics disagree about whether her views of Free Will versus Determinism and Grace versus Good Works place her on the Protestant or orthodox Catholic side. Whereas most Protestants, especially those in the Puritan/Calvinist tradition, believe in the doctrine of election and the assurance of salvation, O'Connor's letters and lectures stress both man's freedom to say no to God's commands and the anguishing struggle necessary to achieve and renew faith. For example, on 9 December 1958 she wrote that "All human nature vigorously resists grace because grace changes us and change is painful.... [Even the] Church is founded on Peter who denied Christ three times and couldn't walk on water by himself." In a 4 February 1961 letter she refers to the "deepening of conversion. I don't think of conversion as being once and for all and that's that. I think once the process is begun and continues that you are continually turning inward toward God and away from your own egocentricity." She repeatedly emphasizes humanity's fall and perfectibility only through God's Grace, not his own unaided efforts, views that she perceived herself as sharing with Southern but not mainstream Protestantism. Wood, though, in *Comedy of Redemption* notes the synergism between God's and man's actions in O'Connor's fiction and emphasizes the post–Vatican II Catholic core of her belief that God works through man's imperfect nature.

O'Connor also diverged from Protestants in her Catholic emphasis on pride as man's greatest sin. Whereas most Protestants strive to achieve goodness expressed through moral behavior and works, Catholics judge their innate human depravity more starkly against the ultimate standard of

*Katherine Anne Porter visiting O'Connor at Andalusia, the O'Connors'
farm, 27 March 1958 (Thomas Frank and Louise Young Gossett
Papers, Special Collections Library, Duke University)*

God's omnipotent goodness. What interested O'Connor as an artist was the radically disorienting process of stripping away the obstacles of self-sufficiency and pride necessary to make characters aware of their need for grace. As she states in "The Fiction Writer and His Country," "to know oneself is, above all, to know what one lacks, . . . to measure oneself against Truth. . . . The first product of self-knowledge is humility." The monumental pride of such characters as Mrs. Shortley in "The Displaced Person" and Ruby Turpin in "Revelation," which is comically mirrored in their robust physiques, must be diminished before they can achieve salvation. Mrs. Shortley is literally dismembered like the bodies of Holocaust victims in boxcars as she views for the first time the dimensions of her "true country." And Mrs. Turpin requires both the well-aimed blow of a book thrown by an acned Wellesley student and an angry colloquy with God outside her pig parlor before she is ready to receive her reductive revelation. In response to her audacious taunt at God, " 'Who do you think you are?,'"

resounds only an excoriating echo. Her dawning recognition of diminished stature is symbolically rendered by a scene of ultimate vulnerability as she mutely watches her husband Claud's tiny truck, "like a child's toy," and muses that at any moment it might be smashed by a bigger one.

The two short-story collections differ in structure, thematic emphasis, and tone. Leon Driskell and Joan Brittain observe that whereas most of the stories in the first collection concern horizontal quests in space, those in the second move vertically toward spiritual transcendence. The differences are reflected in their titles. *A Good Man Is Hard to Find* (which alludes to an Eddie Green blues tune first sung by Alberta Hunter and popularized by Sophie Tucker) counterpoints secular and religious definitions of good and evil, culminating in the redemptive "murder" of the Christlike Displaced Person; *Everything That Rises Must Converge* is structured around the conception of man's spiritual evolution paralleling the French paleontologist Pierre Teilhard de Chardin's vision of a divine centre of convergence. Teilhard de Chardin's *Le Phénomène humain* (1955; translated as *The Phenomenon of Man*, 1959) to which O'Connor refers in a 1960 book review as the most important book published in the prior three decades, foretells a future "convergence in which races, people and nations consolidate one another and complete one another in mutual fecundation."

It is difficult to reconcile this ecstatic prophecy with the social and racial realities of the South during the 1950s and early 1960s, which both short-story collections, but particularly the latter, treat in ways that progressive critics find distressing. Both personally and artistically, O'Connor sided with the Old South's manners and satirized the urban New South's misguided attempts at surface melioration. In a 1963 interview with C. Ross Mullins, Jr., she states, "The South has survived in the past because its manners, however lopsided or inadequate . . . provided enough social discipline to hold us together and give us an identity. Now these old manners are obsolete, but the new manners will have to be based on what was best in the old ones – in their real basis of charity and necessity." Like Eudora Welty, O'Connor portrays racial bigotry not to propound her own views but to illuminate her characters' limited perspectives. Thus, Nelson in "The Artificial Nigger" moves from utter ignorance of blacks, to hatred because of his ignorance, to unconscious attraction both to the Negro matriarch's emotional warmth and the artificial nigger statue's suffering, all without any diminution in impersonal prejudice. On the opposite extreme, "Everything That Rises Must Converge" satirizes the pseudo-liberal Julian's futile attempts to upset his mother by conspicuously sitting next to a well-dressed black man on the bus, the quintessential symbol of forced racial mixing in the newly integrated South. Although the mother's gesture of offering a penny to a little black boy elicits a fatal blow from her behemoth dark double, she dies recalling her loyal servant. The final story in the second collection, "Judgement Day," replaces the fondly remembered camaraderie between Old Dudley and his former Negro friend, Rabie, in the earlier "Geranium" with Tanner's hostile intellectual domination of his black counterpart, Coleman, whom he refers to as "a negative image of himself." The urban black tenant's attitude is also transformed from affable condescension into homicidal rage at the old Southern white's paternalistic racism. The only totally positive portrayal of a black in O'Connor's fiction is Buford Munson's redemptive burial of old Tarwater in *The Violent Bear It Away*.

"Everything That Rises Must Converge," "Greenleaf," and "Revelation" are O'Connor's most complex treatments of class convergence. Although the mother in the title story laments that "the bottom rail is on the top," she has adjusted because "if you know who you are, you can go everywhere." Ironically, Julian is most bothered by the loss of their former aristocratic status, symbolized by the decaying Godhigh mansion, which he "never spoke of without contempt or thought of without longing." Mrs. May in "Greenleaf" is outraged that the "scrub-human" tenant farmers, the Greenleafs, are becoming "Society" at the government's expense, while her own sons have deliberately dissipated the inheritance she worked so hard to maintain. The protagonist of "Revelation" has refined social delineation to an art of reading people's relative respectability by their shoes. Her shocking revelation is that she, a charitable, church going, white home owner and landowner, is targeted for God's well-aimed message which, following Matthew 19:30, "The last shall be first," comically inverts both her social and spiritual hierarchies.

Yet beneath the comedy, the stories in *Everything That Rises Must Converge* are troublingly reactionary. It is as though O'Connor deliberately set out to subvert the dominant progressive religious, economic, and social positions of the period. The stories satirize respectable social churchgoers (Mrs. May in "Greenleaf" and Mrs. Turpin in "Revelation"), abstract secular Jesuits and trendy pseudoexistential-Hindu nihilists (Father Ignatius Vogel and Goetz in "The Enduring Chill"), rapacious land developers (Tillman and Mark Fortune in "A View of the Woods"), naively liberal integrationists (Julian in "Everything That Rises" and Ashbury in "The Enduring Chill"), and social reformers who sentimentally sympathize with criminals (those who influence the gullible mother in "The Comforts of Home" and Sheppard, the aptly named social worker in "The Lame Shall Enter First," who receives O'Connor's most scathing scorn because he sanctimoniously "stuffed his own emptiness with good works like a glutton"). Perhaps our politically and socially sensitive age cannot appreciate such painful truths. Yet Woods in *Comedy of Redemption* counsels against sanitizing her views, for some of her seemingly most illiberal stories contain her most redemptive satire of the evil of "ethical self-righteousness," which he notes is "far subtler than injustice and far deeper than prejudice."

Except for the brilliantly comic "Revelation" and "Parker's Back," the stories in *Everything That Rises Must Converge* evince a darker tone and greater urgency than the earlier ones. Light comedy involving filial ill manners – usually ugly adolescent females who sass their mothers – is replaced in the second collection by caustic satire of psychologically impotent aging sons who vengefully plot to disturb and even destroy the mothers on whom they unconsciously depend. Martha Chew argues that the daughters in *A Good Man Is Hard To Find,* whether a docile imbecile like Lucynell Crater in "The Life You Save May Be Your Own" or a strident philosophy Ph.D. like Joy/Hulga, end up humiliatingly defeated by shrewder males. In contrast, the sons in the second collection rebel more violently, though equally self-destructively. The first six stories (written between 1956 and 1962) depict sometimes deadly confrontations between offspring and parents or other authority figures, culminating in pitched battles such as those between the grandfather and granddaughter in "A View of the Woods," Thomas and his mother in "The Comforts of Home," and Sheppard and the precocious juvenile delinquent Rufus Johnson in "The Lame Shall Enter First," the three stories that relate most directly to *The Violent Bear It Away.* (In a 1 February 1953 letter to the Fitzgeralds she notes that the novel contained "a nice gangster of 14 . . . named Rufus Florida Johnson.") The humor derives from primitive or unsophisticated characters such as the dirt-wallowing prayer-healer Mrs. Greenleaf and the "Nimpermaniac" Star Drake of "The Comforts of Home" or intellectual poseurs like Julian and Ashbury. Gone are the zany gossip and clichéd colloquies of "A Circle in the Fire" and "Good Country People," replaced in "Everything That Rises Must Converge," "Greenleaf," "The Enduring Chill," and "The Comforts of Home" by overt ironic foreshadowing and acid barbs.

Numerous critics have attempted to explain these negative parent-child dynamics psychoanalytically as a reflection of O'Connor's resentment of her mother, Regina. Most notoriously, Josephine Hendin sees O'Connor as resolving her own conflicts vicariously through what might be termed "literary matricide." The autobiographical basis for the large number of intellectual invalids and failed writers resentfully residing at home is evident. The recurrent figure of the practical widowed proprietress of a dairy farm also clearly derives from her mother's personality and situation. As Wood notes in *The Comedy of Redemption,* O'Connor and her mother were polar character types: an outgoing, hardworking woman who handled the hired help and purchased herd bulls with pragmatic acumen, and "a reflective, inward-turning, book-reading art-

ist whose prime focus was upon the unseen realm of the spirit." Sometimes Flannery was infuriated by her mother's inability to comprehend her vocation as a serious rather than a popular writer. For example, when her mother questioned why she did not write something people liked, she confided in a 3 April 1959 letter, "This always leaves me shaking and speechless, raises my blood pressure 140 degrees, etc." Yet despite O'Connor's and her mother's temperamental differences, their deep mutual devotion is shown by their daily correspondence during O'Connor's exile in the North. And Regina did attempt to read her daughter's fiction. O'Connor's bemused sympathy is evident in her depiction of her mother's ordeal reading *The Violent Bear It Away:* "All the time she is reading, I know she would like to be in the yard digging. I think the reason I am a short-story writer is so my mother can read my work in one sitting." Interestingly, despite their maddening manipulation, superficiality, complacence, and reactionary social stances, the mothers (excepting Mrs. May) are the most sympathetic characters O'Connor created during this time.

Another difference between the two short-story collections is the increasing violence required for redemption. All of the stories demonstrate O'Connor's "incarnational" or "sacramental vision," the Augustinian belief that spirit permeates the material universe as a direct manifestation of the divine, allowing the concrete to represent all levels from the actual to the anagogical. The primary task of both the artist and the prophet is to penetrate reality and reveal its inner spiritual essence, a view that O'Connor found corroborated by Teilhard de Chardin's scientific philosophy and Conrad's literary aesthetic of accurately depicting the visible universe, as set out in the preface to *The Nigger of the "Narcissus."* In a disorienting reversal of usual symbolic technique, metaphoric objects and actions in O'Connor's fiction frequently become literal. The sun not merely "stands for" the Son of God but actually bursts like a bloody wound through the tree line to destroy characters' defenses against salvation; baptism results in the second novel not in ritualistic but real drowning that kills as it redeems. Many of the vehicles of salvation in *Everything That Rises Must Converge* are no longer human but destructive animal and mechanical forces, such as the hostile yet amorous Dionysian/Christlike scrub bull that simultaneously gores/rapes and embraces Mrs. May at the conclusion of "Greenleaf," the fierce bird-shaped water stain that implacably descends upon the terrified Ashbury in "The Enduring Chill," the monstrous yellow bulldozer "gorging it-

O'Connor and Brainard Cheney in 1959 (photograph by Ralph Morrissey, by permission of Eleanor F. Morrissey)

self on clay" while Mark Fortune dies of a heart attack at the conclusion of "A View of the Woods," and Thomas's pistol shot "that would shatter the laughter of sluts" in "The Comforts of Home." Although O'Connor felt that she laid the dramatic groundwork for her characters' conversions, many readers place her less in the preparationist tradition of Thomas Hooker's and Thomas Shepard's Puritan sermons than the spiritual ravishment school of John Donne's holy sonnets, the Hebrew prophets, and early Christian saints and martyrs. In a 21 January 1961 letter O'Connor likens the shocking self-recognition at conversion to "a kind of blasting annihilating light." Similarly, Mrs. May finds "the light unbearable," and Thomas and Ashbury, like Julian, postpone as long as possible "entry into the world of guilt and sorrow."

However, a few of O'Connor's characters, such as Ruby Turpin and O. E. Parker, do unblinkingly accept the paradoxically "abysmal life-giving knowledge" of salvation. Although certainly not lacking in sternness nor intensity, "Revelation" and "Parker's Back" — the latter of which she was reworking in the hospital while she was dying — mark a shift to achieved spiritual serenity paralleling her own. Ruby's final vision perfectly modulates social comedy and spiritual awareness. Even though she realizes that respectable people like herself and her husband Claud are at the rear of the celestial procession, she still tries to justify their actions: "They were marching behind the others with great dignity, accountable as they had always been for good order and common sense and respectable behavior. They alone were on key." Finally she perceives from "their shocked and altered faces that even their virtues were being burned away." "Parker's Back" similarly manages to be funny without sacrificing any of its fierceness. O. E. Parker, whose initials mask his hieratic Old Testament name, Obadiah Elihue, is an exquisite exemplum of the capacity for spiritual vision within the apparently ordinary ("He was heavy and earnest, as ordinary as a loaf of bread"). This doubleness is also mirrored in his intense attraction-repulsion to his scrawny, straight-laced wife, whom he prophetically envisions as a "giant hawk-eyed angel wielding a hoary weapon." Although his attempt to win her love by having a Byzantine Christ with piercing eyes like hers tattooed on his back hilariously backfires because of her Docetism (the heresy that denies Christ's corporality), he is transfixed, like Moses, by an ecstatic vision of a tree of light "pouring through him, turning his spider web soul into a perfect arabesque of colors, a garden of trees and birds and beasts."

Fourteen-year-old Francis Marion Tarwater (whose surname refers to a common cathartic cure-all) in *The Violent Bear It Away* seems an equally unlikely candidate for seer. The protagonists of the two novels are quite similar in that both attempt unsuccessfully to escape the call to prophesy given them by their grandfather or granduncle. Whereas Haze in *Wise Blood* is pursued by an image in his mind of Christ, whom he fears will lure him off into the woods where he might attempt to walk on water and drown, young Tarwater is hounded by "the bleeding stinking mad shadow of Jesus," which can only be assuaged by baptizing his innocent/imbecile nephew, Bishop, whose literary antecedents include the mysteriously supernatural Pearl in Hawthorne's *The Scarlet Letter,* Lennie in John Steinbeck's *Of Mice and Men,* Benjy in Faulkner's *The Sound and the Fury,* and Stevie in Conrad's *The Secret Agent,* as well as Christ.

The differing ways O'Connor solved similar structural and narrative difficulties in her first and second novels demonstrate her artistic maturation during the 1950s. Whereas Haze's internal conflicts are revealed only indirectly through a series of encounters with Enoch and various false evangelists and whores, Tarwater's are dramatized in the literal fight for control of his psyche between his namesake prophet granduncle and his uncle Rayber, a rational secularist schoolteacher/psychologist. In contrast to the loose, episodic structure of *Wise Blood,* in which the comic Enoch subplot never quite coheres, *The Violent Bear It Away* follows a spare tripartite format (perhaps derived from the three scaffold scenes in Hawthorne's *The Scarlet Letter*). Part 1 sets up Tarwater's prophetic mission and his backwoods life at Powderhead, Tennessee, culminating in his drunken refusal to bury old Tarwater as promised and burning the cabin before hitchhiking to the city. Part 2 provides a counterweight through Rayber's equally unsuccessful attempt to indoctrinate him in the virtues of moderation and scientific rationalism. After the climactic baptism/drowning of Bishop, Tarwater returns to Powderhead in part 3, en route cathartically burning the woods where he was homosexually raped, before accepting his mission of preaching "the terrible speed of mercy" to the sleeping children of the corrupt cities.

O'Connor economically interconnects characters and themes in *The Violent Bear It Away* through an elaborate series of correspondences. The controlling metaphors of the novel are the parables of sowing the seed and the multiplication of loaves and fishes (Matthew 13:18–30 and 14:17–19). Old Tarwater disseminates the seed of his prophetic vision to both young Tarwater and Rayber. Although Tarwater admits the seed fell in deep, he deludes himself that "it fell on rock and the wind carried it away." In contrast, Rayber actively tries to weed it

out by anesthetizing his irrational terrifying love for Bishop. Old Tarwater is explicitly paralleled with Bishop, who "looked like the old man grown backwards to the lowest form of innocence." They are also linked by the recurrent motifs of bread and fish: Tarwater is described prematurely lying in his coffin with his stomach rising over the top "like over-leavened bread," and Bishop has fishlike "pale silver eyes like the old man's except . . . clear and empty." In contrast, young Tarwater, whose soul's emblem is a sleeping bat, is "not hungry for the bread of life." Rayber is related through his rational skepticism to Tarwater's internal "stranger friend," who turns out to be a devil surrogate. Other avatars of the devil include Meeks, the copper-flue salesman who attempts to reconcile selfishness and self-interest, the nihilistic truck driver from Detroit, and the smooth-talking homosexual rapist in a lavender shirt and panama hat, who steals the corkscrew Rayber gave to Tarwater. O'Connor also parallels recurrent actions (old Tarwater's baptism of the infant Tarwater is parodied by Rayber's blasphemous sprinkling of his bottom and the sexual violation of rape; the burnings of the cabin and woods frame the novel) and symbolic motifs (sun-moon; fire-water; blood and spiritual hunger as parodic consummations of fast food and liquor).

The Violent Bear It Away displays much more narrative control than *Wise Blood*. Whereas *Wise Blood* veers between farcical comedy and vindictive satire, the omniscient narrator in *The Violent Bear It Away* suspends judgment by recording Tarwater's rebellious ambivalence toward both old Tarwater and Rayber. Similar to Faulkner's use of multiple viewpoints in *As I Lay Dying* and *Absalom, Absalom!,* *The Violent Bear It Away* counterpoints different characters' perceptions of the same scene, for example Tarwater's and Rayber's differing views of the fountain episode that prefigures the central drowning/baptism of Bishop. *The Violent Bear It Away* also resembles *Absalom, Absalom!* in its progressive reiteration and reinterpretation of family history.

On the surface *The Violent Bear It Away* appears to fit the paradigms of both the classic bildungsroman, or novel of spiritual discovery, and the American adventure story, as well as archetypal heroic myths described in Joseph Campbell's *The Hero With A Thousand Faces.* For example, Tarwater recalls the typical American "good-bad boy" Huck Finn, who similarly rejects the advice both of his parental authority figures and teachers. Old Tarwater even resembles Pap Finn, the archetypal tyrant whose death liberates Huck. Yet *The Violent Bear It Away* inverts many readers' expectations about the hero's quest for freedom. As Robert Brinkmeyer Jr. notes, the typical reader is hoping Tarwater will successfully resist the strange pull of his granduncle's call to prophecy. Despite his "slip" of baptizing Bishop as well as drowning him, Tarwater seems to return to Powderhead secure in his independence: "It was no boy that he returned. He returned tried in the fire of his refusal, with all the old man's madness smothered for good." Yet, perplexingly, Tarwater is soon revealed to be more confused and tormented than ever. Many modern readers also misconstrue Tarwater's satanic "friend" as "the sanest voice in the novel." To miss the therapeutic shock of the ending, Brinkmeyer suggests, is to see Tarwater as perversely re-ensnared by the very forces he was attempting to escape, resulting in a misinterpretation of the novel as an existential negation of meaning. Stuart Burns in "Flannery O'Connor's *The Violent Bear It Away*: Apotheosis in Failure" provides another explanation for the apparent ambiguity of the conclusion. Whereas most initiation novels culminate in the protagonist's self-realization and achievement of psychic wholeness, Tarwater's prophetic mission requires the opposite: self-abnegation and psychic disintegration, which the novel paradoxically endorses.

The characterization of Rayber also causes confusion because he is much more complicated than many readers perceive. Like Tarwater, Rayber recognizes that he inherited "the stuff of which fanatics and madmen are made." He too has been baptized by old Tarwater, rebels at the age of fourteen, and attempts unsuccessfully to drown Bishop. But he manages until the end to balance a "very narrow line between madness and emptiness" by suppressing his mysterious "horrifying love" for Bishop, deluding himself that he can deafen himself to the voice of his inner feelings as simply as turning off his hearing aid. O'Connor struggled during the entire seven years of writing the novel to make Rayber more than a caricature of "an Atheist of Protestant descent," as she commented in a 25 February 1956 letter. At Gordon's suggestion, she greatly expanded the chapters dealing with Rayber, adding the scenes in which he is deeply affected by the child missionary Lucette Carmody's Pentecostal sermon and follows Tarwater barefoot through the streets like a mendicant friar. Ironically, although O'Connor despaired over her inability to animate a character so alien to her own sensibility, many modern readers prefer Rayber's tepid, life-denying rationalism to old Tarwater's intransigent, all-demanding faith. In an essay collected by Melvin J. Friedman

and Lewis A. Lawson in *The Added Dimension: The Art and Mind of Flannery O'Connor*, Louis Rubin Jr. laments that O'Connor fails to provide through Rayber a believable God of Love to counter Tarwater's God of Wrath. The author herself, however, endorsed old Tarwater's beliefs completely.

The widely varying interpretations of the novel's title reflect many contemporary readers' continuing struggle to comprehend her ideas. The title is an allusion to Matthew 11:12, which appears as the novel's epigraph: "From the days of John the Baptist until now, the kingdom of heaven suffereth violence, and the violent bear it away." O'Connor herself glosses the passage in somewhat different ways. In a 25 July 1959 letter to "A," she states that she follows Saint Thomas and Saint Augustine in emphasizing the unnaturalness of ascetics such as John the Baptist: "I am much more interested in the nobility of unnaturalness than in the nobility of naturalness. . . . The violent are not natural." In a 16 March 1960 letter to Ted Spivey, an English professor and longtime correspondent, she stresses that the passage gives Christ's approving assessment of asceticism: "this is the violence of love, of giving more than the [Old Testament] law demands." In general, she seems to justify violence for the sake of salvation, as she revealed to "A" in a 12 July 1957 letter: "more than ever now it seems that the kingdom of heaven has to be taken by violence, or not at all." In contrast, many readers and critics such as Stanley Hyman and Carter Martin emphasize the destructive aspects of the title. John May in *The Pruning Word*, though, shows how the novel represents the passage from the Old Covenant to the New, from austere justice to mercy and a New Testament vision of "unexpected graciousness." Likewise, Wood in "The Catholic Faith of Flannery O'Connor's Protestant Characters" minimizes the minatory meaning of the novel: "Tarwater does not violently bear away the Kingdom of God. His citizenship in that Eternal City is granted to him as an utter gratuity." He also notes that Tarwater's mission is not one of prophesying menace but the unmerited gift of mercy.

Although Gilbert Muller praised the novel in 1968 as a " perfect coincidence of the moral and the dramatic sense," many early reviewers castigated *The Violent Bear It Away* as "anti-Catholic" and psychologically if not theologically deterministic. Others found the characters bizarre and their motives incomprehensible. O'Connor, however, seems to have identified strongly with Tarwater (she even signed some of her letters to Maryat Lee with variations of his name, such as Tarlite and in her last let-

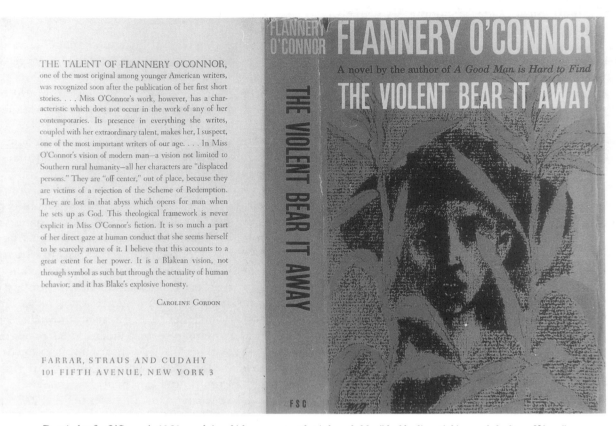

THE TALENT OF FLANNERY O'CONNOR, one of the most original among younger American writers, was recognized soon after the publication of her first short stories. . . . Miss O'Connor's work, however, has a characteristic which does not occur in the work of any of her contemporaries. Its presence in everything she writes, coupled with her extraordinary talent, makes her, I suspect, one of the most important writers of our age. . . . In Miss O'Connor's vision of modern man—a vision not limited to Southern rural humanity—all her characters are "displaced persons." They are "off center," out of place, because they are victims of a rejection of the Scheme of Redemption. They are lost in that abyss which opens for man when he sets up as God. This theological framework is never explicit in Miss O'Connor's fiction. It is so much a part of her direct gaze at human conduct that she seems herself to be scarcely aware of it. I believe that this accounts to a great extent for her power. It is a Blakean vision, not through symbol as such but through the actuality of human behavior; and it has Blake's explosive honesty.

CAROLINE GORDON

FARRAR, STRAUS AND CUDAHY
101 FIFTH AVENUE, NEW YORK 3

FLANNERY O'CONNOR

A novel by the author of *A Good Man is Hard to Find*

THE VIOLENT BEAR IT AWAY

THE VIOLENT BEAR IT AWAY

FSC

Dust jacket for O'Connor's 1960 novel, in which a young prophet is hounded by "the bleeding stinking mad shadow of Jesus"

ter Tarfunk), perhaps indicating that she resigned herself late in her career to a similar role as lone prophet in the modern wasteland of the spiritually asleep.

O'Connor's writing during the years surrounding the novel's publication reflects her psychic depletion. "The Enduring Chill" (1958) is a highly derivative satire of Joyce's *A Portrait of the Artist as a Young Man* and *Dubliners;* "The Comforts of Home" (1960), a shrill Oedipal melodrama parodying misguided sympathy for criminals and her own penchants for monasticism and violent climaxes; "The Partridge Festival" (1961), an admitted farce; and "The Lame Shall Enter First" (1962), a discursive reworking of early versions of the second novel in which Sheppard plays an even less appealing secular "savior" than Rayber, Rufus is "one of Tarwater's terrible cousins" disfigured by a clubfoot, and Norton is a gorging, seed-hoarding Bishop who commits suicide to be reunited with his dead mother. O'Connor's projected third novel, titled "Why Do the Heathen Rage?," about an agnostic failed writer named Walter Tilman who has the mentality of a medieval monk, foundered after its

initial conception as a sequel to "The Enduring Chill." O'Connor also expended much of her waning physical energy lecturing and writing journalism, such as the 1961 *Holiday* article on peacocks. Oddly, the unsolicited project to write an introduction for *A Memoir for Mary Ann* for the Dominican Nuns of Our Lady of Perpetual Help Cancer Home about a saintly girl who died of a grotesque face cancer at eleven did inspire her imaginatively, perhaps because the child's life, much like her own, demonstrated a positive acceptance of what Teilhard de Chardin in *Le Milieu divin* (1957; translated as *The Realm of the Divine,* 1960) calls "passive diminishments." The piece contains important critical comments on her views of genuine compassion as opposed to popular pity and how even the good may appear grotesque because it is still "under construction."

The final two years of O'Connor's life demonstrate Chardin's increasing influence on her beliefs and writing. She seems during this period to have achieved a sort of spiritual serenity burned clean through suffering. As Ruth Vande Kieft notes, O'Connor "carried the *momento mori* in her very bones, resulting in a vision which was 'essentially apocalyptic.' She herself was the prophet." Although she always accepted suffering graciously — even calling it an appropriate precursor to dying — her last days evinced unexpectedly exuberant humor. For example, during one of her final stays in the hospital she wrote "A" on 14 March 1964 about her nurse who was a "dead ringer for Mrs. Turpin. . . . She didn't know how funny she was and it was an agony to laugh and I reckon I increased my pain about 100%." As A. R. Coulthard comments, "pain not only failed to blunt her wonderful sense of humor but seems to have sharpened it. For all her theological profundity, the greatest affirmation of O'Connor's life and work may be her obvious delight in the human comedy." Until her death on 3 August 1964 O'Connor continued to rewrite "Judgement Day" and "Parker's Back," which is the most touchingly human story she wrote.

Although still not always accepted, O'Connor's views were fairly well understood by the time the posthumous collections *Everything That Rises Must Converge* (1965) and *The Complete Stories* (1970) were published, with excellent introductions by Robert Fitzgerald and Robert Giroux, respectively. Her ideas also became increasingly accessible through the publication of her literary lectures and essays in *Mystery and Manners* (1969), her letters in *The Habit of Being* (1979) and *The Correspondence of Flannery O'Connor and the Brainard Cheneys* (1986), and Catholic book reviews in *The Presence of Grace* (1983), as well as the listings of her personal library holdings (1985), interviews (1987), and manuscripts (1989). Since the 1960s scholars have produced at least twenty-five full-length studies, two hundred theses and dissertations, thousands of articles, and compilations of essays. Colloquiums such as the 1987 Denmark Conference and the April 1994 interdisciplinary celebration at Georgia College and the Southern Women Writers' Conference at Berry College continue to stimulate lively interchange. Excellent film versions of "The Displaced Person" (PBS telecast, 1977) and *Wise Blood* (1979; directed by John Huston and produced by some of the Fitzgerald children) have given her a popular audience. These new resources have resulted in more-informed, if still conflicting, readings.

Increasingly, many readers are finding narrowly religious interpretations of O'Connor's work repetitive and restrictive (O'Connor herself cited the need for a critique of her as more than a Catholic writer). At least four fairly distinct critical camps have evolved regarding the theological and aesthetic aspects of O'Connor's fiction. The first and most conservative group construes O'Connor as a thoroughly orthodox Catholic writer. During the 1960s and early 1970s, exegetical critics such as Sisters Kathleen Feeley, Mariella Gable, Barnetta Quinn, and Carter Martin sieved through the secondary sources to support traditional Catholic readings of her texts. These commentators stress how salvation in her stories is at least strongly implied, if not always achieved. A second group of religious scholars, including Robert Milder and Albert Sonnenfeld, ally her more strongly with pre-Reformation and Southern evangelical Protestant traditions than conventional Catholicism. Jill Baumgaertner links O'Connor's technique with medieval emblems, Anthony Di Renzo with grotesque bestiaries, and John May with New Testament parables. Other theological interpretations by David Eggenschwiler and Richard Gianonne attempt to temper her views to fit more conventional concepts of Christian humanism and brotherly love. Whereas critics such as May and Preston Browning find no incompatibility between art and belief in O'Connor's fiction, those in a third contingent, including Frederick Asals, Miles Orvell, Martha Stephens, and Ralph Wood, among many others, are often troubled by the harshness of her religious vision. Stephens is among the first to express reservations about O'Connor's tonal disjunctions and grim, literalistic, joyless faith. Asals and Di Renzo are likewise sometimes jarred by her extreme dialectics or tensions of opposites but explain them within the total dramatic context of her work. Finally, by far the most controversial are iconoclastic critics such as André Bleikasten, John Hawkes, Josephine Hendin, Irving Malin, and Carol Schloss who question whether O'Connor succeeds at her own dictum, "In the greatest fiction, the writer's moral sense coincides with his dramatic sense." Overall, these readers sense a discrepancy between her professed ideological stance and what Henry James terms the "felt life" of the works. They downplay or deny theological readings; some even perceive her vision as demonic. Hawkes, for example, in his 1962 essay "Flannery O'Connor's Devil," connects O'Connor's work with West's black comedies and Hawthorne's romances to show how her authorial attitude of judgment and victimization becomes in some measure diabolical. Bleikasten's poststructuralist study similarly describes how her dualistic vision results in a dramatic battle between the demonic and the divine in which the odds are about even — a stance strikingly similar to Brinkmeyer's and Marshall Bruce Gentry's recent Bakhtinian analyses of her narrative technique. Hendin and Claire Kahane, among others who eschew religious readings, delve into the psychoanalytic dynamics of the punishing parent–rebellious child motif in O'Connor's work as well as explore the previously taboo subject of her latent sexuality.

Further study is still needed in several areas, such as O'Connor's Jansenist repugnance to flesh (most apparent in early works such as *Wise Blood* and "The Temple of the Holy Ghost") but anti-Manichean incarnational view of matter. Her complex relations with both of her parents also await fleshing out by the forthcoming biographies of Sally Fitzgerald and Jean Cash. Additional studies are needed to refine O'Connor's enduring but evolving place within the concentric spheres of her gender (Lisa Babinec, Martha Chew, Josephine Hendin, Claire Kahane, Mary Morton, and Louise Westling), era (John Desmond and Thomas Schaub), region and race (Robert Coles, Janet Dunleavy, C. Hugh Holman, Lewis Lawson, Marion Montgomery, Louis D. Rubin Jr., and Ralph Wood), as well as broader American and European literary and philosophical traditions (Frederick Asals, Ashley Brown, David Eggenschwiler, John May, Miles Orvell, and Martha Stephens, among many others). Also useful would be additional thorough textual studies, following Karl-Heinz Westarp's lead, and extraliterary studies, such as Brian Ragen's book-length examination of her anti-Adamic treatment of the American automobile myth. As future readers necessarily turn to more specialized and revisionist approaches, one hopes that they will further elucidate O'Connor's entire complex vision, spanning the cosmic to the low comedic.

Letters:

The Habit of Being, edited by Sally Fitzgerald (New York: Farrar, Straus & Giroux, 1979);

The Correspondence of Flannery O'Connor and the Brainard Cheneys, edited by C. Ralph Stephens (Jackson: University Press of Mississippi, 1986);

The Collected Works (New York: Library of America, 1988), pp. 865–1234.

Interviews:

Conversations with Flannery O'Connor, edited by Rosemary M. Magee (Jackson: University Press of Mississippi, 1987).

Bibliographies:

Robert E. Golden and Mary Sullivan, *Flannery O'Connor and Caroline Gordon: A Reference Guide* (Boston: G. K. Hall, 1977);

David Farmer, *Flannery O'Connor: A Descriptive Bibliography* (New York: Garland, 1981);

Martha E. Cook, "Flannery O'Connor," in *American Women Writers: Bibliographic Essays,* edited by Maurice Duke, Jackson R. Bryer, and M. Thomas Inge (Westport, Conn.: Greenwood Press, 1983), pp. 269–296;

Stephen G. Driggers and Robert J. Dunn, with Sarah Gordon, *The Manuscripts of Flannery O'Connor at Georgia College* (Athens: University of Georgia Press, 1989);

R. Neil Scott, "UMI's Citations of Theses and Dissertations Related to Flannery O'Connor," *Flannery O'Connor Bulletin,* 19 (Autumn 1990): 77–99.

Biographies:

Lorine M. Getz, *Flannery O'Connor: Her Life, Library and Book Reviews* (New York: Edwin Mellen, 1980), pp. 3–82;

Linda Schlafer, "Monitum: Beware the Getz," *Flannery O'Connor Bulletin,* 11 (Autumn 1982): 43–57;

Harold Fickett and Douglas R. Gilbert, *Flannery O'Connor: Images of Grace* (Grand Rapids, Mich.: Eerdmans, 1986);

Sally Fitzgerald, "Chronology," in O'Connor's *Collected Works* (New York: Library of America, 1988), pp. 1237–1256.

References:

Frederick Asals, *Flannery O'Connor: The Imagination of Extremity* (Athens: University of Georgia Press, 1982);

Asals, "The Road to *Wise Blood,*" *Renascence,* 21 (Summer 1969): 181–194;

Lisa Babinec, "Cyclical Patterns of Domination and Manipulation in Flannery O'Connor's Mother-Daughter Relationships," *Flannery O'Connor Bulletin,* 19 (1990): 9–29;

Jill P. Baumgaertner, *Flannery O'Connor: A Proper Scaring* (Wheaton, Ill.: Shaw, 1988);

Harold Bloom, ed., *Flannery O'Connor: Modern Critical Views* (New York: Chelsea House, 1986);

Robert H. Brinkmeyer Jr., *The Art and Vision of Flannery O'Connor* (Baton Rouge: Louisiana State University Press, 1989);

Brinkmeyer, "Borne Away by Violence: The Reader and Flannery O'Connor," *Southern Review,* new series 15 (Spring 1979): 313–321;

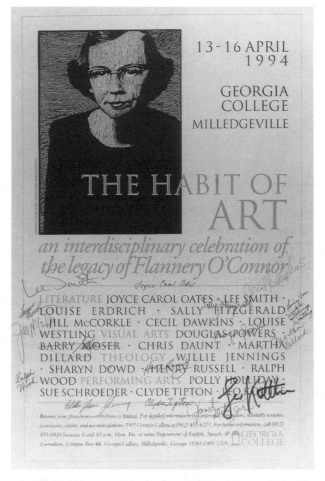

Poster, signed by the participants, for a 1994 symposium on O'Connor
(Collection of Barbara Brannon)

Preston M. Browning Jr., *Flannery O'Connor* (Carbondale: Southern Illinois University Press, 1974);

John J. Burke Jr., S.J., "Convergence of Flannery O'Connor and Chardin," *Renascence,* 19 (Fall 1966): 41–47, 52;

Stuart L. Burns, "The Evolution of *Wise Blood,*" *Modern Fiction Studies,* 16 (Summer 1970): 147–162;

Burns, "Flannery O'Connor's Literary Apprenticeship," *Renascence,* 22 (Autumn 1969): 3–16;

Burns, "Flannery O'Connor's *The Violent Bear It Away*: Apotheosis in Failure," 76 (Spring 1968): 319–336;

Brainard Cheney, "Flannery O'Connor's Campaign for Her Country," *Sewanee Review,* 72 (Autumn 1964): 555–558;

Cheney, Review of *Wise Blood, Shenandoah,* 3 (Autumn 1952): 55–60;

Martha Chew, "Flannery O'Connor's Double-Edged Satire: The Idiot Daughter versus the Lady Ph.D.," *Southern Quarterly,* 19 (Winter 1981): 17–25;

Robert Coles, *Flannery O'Connor's South* (Baton Rouge: Louisiana State University Press, 1980);

A. R. Coulthard, "From Sermon to Parable: Four Conversion Stories by Flannery O'Connor," *American Literature,* 55 (March 1983): 55–71;

John F. Desmond, *Risen Sons: Flannery O'Connor's Vision of History* (Athens: University of Georgia Press, 1987);

Anthony Di Renzo, *American Gargoyles: Flannery O'Connor and the Medieval Grotesque* (Carbondale: Southern Illinois University Press, 1993);

Robert Drake, *Flannery O'Connor: A Critical Essay* (Grand Rapids, Mich.: Eerdmans, 1966);

Leon V. Driskell and Joan T. Brittain, *The Eternal Crossroads: The Art of Flannery O'Connor* (Lexington: University Press of Kentucky, 1971);

David Eggenschwiler, *The Christian Humanism of Flannery O'Connor* (Detroit: Wayne State University Press, 1972);

Sister Kathleen Feeley, *Flannery O'Connor: Voice of the Peacock* (New Brunswick, N.J.: Rutgers University Press, 1972);

Melvin J. Friedman and Lewis A. Lawson, eds., *The Added Dimension: The Art and Mind of Flannery O'Connor* (New York: Fordham University Press, 1966);

Friedman and Beverly Lyon Clark, eds., *Critical Essays on Flannery O'Connor* (Boston: G. K. Hall, 1985);

Sister Mariella Gable, "The Ecumenical Core in the Fiction of Flannery O'Connor," *American Benedictine Review,* 15 (June 1964): 127–143;

Marshall Bruce Gentry, *Flannery O'Connor's Religion of the Grotesque* (Jackson: University Press of Mississippi, 1986);

Richard Giannone, *Flannery O'Connor and the Mystery of Love* (Urbana: University of Illinois Press, 1989);

Caroline Gordon, "Flannery O'Connor's *Wise Blood,*" *Critique,* 2, no. 2 (1958): 3–10;

Gordon, "Heresy in Dixie," *Sewanee Review,* 76 (Spring 1968): 263–297;

Josephine Hendin, *The World of Flannery O'Connor* (Bloomington: Indiana University Press, 1969);

Stanley Edgar Hyman, *Flannery O'Connor,* University of Minnesota Pamphlets on American Writers, no. 54 (Minneapolis: University of Minnesota Press, 1966);

Forrest L. Ingram, "O'Connor's Seven-Story Cycle," *Flannery O'Connor Bulletin,* 2 (Autumn 1973): 19–28;

Sister M. Joselyn, O.S.B., "Thematic Centers in 'The Displaced Person,'" *Studies in Short Fiction,* 1 (Fall 1965): 85–92;

Claire Kahane, "The Artificial Niggers," *Massachusetts Review,* 19 (Spring 1978): 183–198;

Arthur F. Kinney, *Flannery O'Connor's Library: Resources of Being* (Athens: University of Georgia Press, 1985);

Lewis A. Lawson, "Flannery O'Connor and the Grotesque: *Wise Blood,*" *Renascence,* 17 (Spring 1965): 137–147, 153;

Suzanne Maria Mannmeusel, "The Religious Quest in Nathanael West's *Miss Lonelyhearts* and Flannery O'Connor's *Wise Blood,*" M.A. thesis, University of South Carolina, 1988;

Carter W. Martin, "Flannery O'Connor's Early Fiction," *Southern Humanities Review,* 7 (Spring 1973): 210–214;

Martin, *The True Country: Themes in the Fiction of Flannery O'Connor* (Nashville: Vanderbilt University Press, 1969);

John R. May, *The Pruning Word: The Parables of Flannery O'Connor* (Notre Dame, Ind.: University of Notre Dame Press, 1976);

May, "*The Violent Bear It Away*: The Meaning of the Title," *Flannery O'Connor Bulletin,* 2 (Autumn 1973): 83–86;

Robert Milder, "The Protestantism of Flannery O'Connor," *Southern Review,* new series 11 (October 1975): 802–819;

Marion Montgomery, "Miss O'Connor and the Christ-Haunted," *Southern Review,* new series 4 (Summer 1968): 665–672;

Montgomery, "The Sense of Violation: Notes Toward a Definition of Southern Fiction," *Georgia Review,* 19 (Fall 1965): 278–287;

Mary L. Morton, "Doubling in Flannery O'Connor's Female Characters: Animus and Anima," *Southern Quarterly,* 23 (Summer 1985): 57–63;

Gilbert H. Muller, "*The Violent Bear It Away:* Moral and Dramatic Sense," *Renascence,* 22 (Autumn 1969): 17–25;

Loxley F. Nicholas, "Flannery O'Connor's Intellectual Vaudeville: Masks of Mother and Daughter," *Studies in the Literary Imagination,* 20 (Fall 1987): 15–29;

Miles Orville, *Flannery O'Connor: An Introduction* (Jackson: University Press of Mississippi, 1991);

Clara Claiborne Park, "Crippled Laughter: Toward Understanding Flannery O'Connor," *American Scholar,* 51 (Spring 1982): 249–257;

Suzanne Morrow Paulson, *Flannery O'Connor: A Study of the Short Fiction* (Boston: Twayne, 1988);

Sister M. Bernetta Quinn, O.S.F., "View from a Rock: The Fiction of Flannery O'Connor and J. F. Powers," *Critique,* 2 (1958): 19–27;

Brian Abel Ragen, *A Wreck on the Road to Damascus: Innocence, Guilt and Conversion in Flannery O'Connor* (Chicago: Loyola University Press, 1989);

Louis D. Rubin Jr., "Flannery O'Connor's Company of Southerners: or 'The Artificial Nigger' Read as Fiction Rather than Theology," *Flannery O'Connor Bulletin,* 6 (Autumn 1977): 47–71;

Carol Shloss, *Flannery O'Connor's Dark Comedies: The Limits of Inference* (Baton Rouge: Louisiana State University Press, 1980);

Martha Stephens, "Flannery O'Connor and the Sanctified Sinner Tradition," *Arizona Quarterly,* 24 (Autumn 1968): 223–239;

Stephens, *The Question of Flannery O'Connor* (Baton Rouge: Louisiana State University Press, 1973);

Diane Tolomeo, "Home in the True Country: The Final Trilogy of Flannery O'Connor," *Studies in Short Fiction,* 17 (Summer 1980): 335–341;

Clinton W. Trowbridge, "The Symbolic Vision of Flannery O'Connor: Patterns of Imagery in *The Violent Bear It Away,*" *Sewanee Review,* 76 (Spring 1968): 298–318;

Ruth Vande Kieft, "Judgment in the Fiction of Flannery O'Connor," *Sewanee Review,* 76 (Spring 1968): 337–356;

Alice Walker, "Beyond the Peacock: The Reconstruction of Flannery O'Connor," in her *In Search of Our Mothers' Gardens* (New York: Harcourt Brace Jovanovich, 1983), pp. 71–81;

Dorothy Walters, *Flannery O'Connor* (New York: Twayne, 1973);

Karl-Heinz Westarp, *Flannery O'Connor: The Growing Craft* (Birmingham, Ala.: Summa, 1993);

Westarp, " 'Parker's Back': A Curious Crux Concerning Its Sources," *Flannery O'Connor Bulletin,* 11 (Autumn 1982): 1–9;

Westarp, "Teilhard de Chardin's Impact on Flannery O'Connor: A Reading of 'Parker's Back,'" *Flannery O'Connor Bulletin,* 12 (Autumn 1983): 93–113;

Westarp and Jan Nordby Gretlund, eds., *Realist of Distances: Flannery O'Connor Revisited* (Aarhus, Denmark: Aarhus University Press, 1987);

Louise Westling, "Flannery O'Connor's Mothers and Daughters," *Twentieth Century Literature,* 24, no. 4 (1979): 510–522;

Westling, "O'Connor's Sacred Landscapes," in her *Sacred Groves and Ravaged Gardens: The Fictions of Eudora Welty, Carson McCullers, and Flannery O'Connor* (Athens: University of Georgia Press, 1985), pp. 133–174;

Ralph C. Wood, "The Catholic Faith of Flannery O'Connor's Protestant Characters: A Critique and Vindication," *Flannery O'Connor Bulletin,* 13 (Autumn 1984): 15–25;

Wood, *The Comedy of Redemption: Christian Faith and Comic Vision in Four American Novelists* (Notre Dame, Ind.: University of Notre Dame Press, 1988), pp. 80–132;

Wood, "The Heterodoxy of Flannery O'Connor's Book Reviews," *Flannery O'Connor Bulletin,* 5 (Autumn 1976): 3–29.

Papers:

Flannery O'Connor's manuscripts, letters, and private library are at the Ina Dillard Russell Library at Georgia College, Milledgeville, Georgia.

Cynthia Ozick

(17 April 1928 –)

Ruth Rosenberg
Brooklyn College

See also the Ozick entries in *DLB 28: Twentieth-Century American-Jewish Fiction Writers* and *DLB Yearbook: 1982.*

BOOKS: *Trust* (New York: New American Library, 1966; London: MacGibbon & Kee, 1967);

The Pagan Rabbi and Other Stories (New York: Knopf, 1971; London: Secker & Warburg, 1972);

Bloodshed and Three Novellas (New York: Knopf, 1976; London: Secker & Warburg, 1976);

Levitation: Five Fictions (New York: Knopf, 1982; London: Secker & Warburg, 1982);

Art and Ardor: Essays (New York: Knopf, 1983; London: Secker & Warburg, 1983);

The Cannibal Galaxy (New York: Knopf, 1983; London: Secker & Warburg, 1983);

The Messiah of Stockholm (New York: Knopf, 1987; London: Deutsch, 1987);

The Shawl (New York: Knopf, 1989; London: Cape, 1991);

Metaphor and Memory: Essays (New York: Knopf, 1989);

Epodes: First Poems, illustrated by Sidney Chafetz (Columbus, Ohio: Logan Elm, 1992);

What Henry James Knew, and Other Essays on Writers (London: Cape, 1993; revised edition, London: Vintage, 1994).

PLAY PRODUCTION: *Blue Light,* Sag Harbor, Long Island, Bay Street Theatre, August 1994.

OTHER: "We Are the Crazy Lady and Other Feisty Feminist Fables," in *Woman as Writer,* edited by Jeannette L. Webber and Joan Grumman (Boston: Houghton Mifflin, 1978), pp. 104–114.

SELECTED PERIODICAL PUBLICATIONS – UNCOLLECTED: "At Fumicaro," *New Yorker* (6 August 1984): 32–37, 40–41, 43–47, 50–58;

"Puttermesser Paired," *New Yorker* (8 October 1990): 40–52, 54, 56, 58–59, 62, 64–75;

Cynthia Ozick (photograph by Layle Silbert)

"Reflections: Alfred Chester's Wig," *New Yorker* (30 March 1992): 79–84, 86–98;

"More Than Just a Victorian," *New York Times Book Review* (1 January 1995): 1, 19, 21.

Cynthia Ozick's stature as a writer came through a long apprenticeship, during which she often read eighteen hours a day. Having so intensely lived within literature herself, she can by a few deft allusions weave a veil of bookish imaginings through which a character views the world. Her mastery of the entire canon has earned her a reputation as a writer's writer. Equally adept in any genre, she has achieved recognition as a poet, essayist, novelist, author of short fiction, and playwright. With an immense stylistic repertoire, she can parody the work of other writers.

The serious theme Ozick engages comically is the status of Jewish thought in a secular world. This concern has earned her a readership abroad and the translation of her work into eleven languages. Two recent critical assessments of her work – one by Sarah Blacher Cohen on her humor, the other by Elaine M. Kauvar on her metaphysics – demonstrate the difficulty of reconciling levity with liturgy. Admitting that commercial success has eluded her, Ozick said in a 1983 interview with Jean W. Ross, "I will never be a popular writer or a household name. I recognize that I'm not easy to read."

Some of the narrative challenges Ozick has adroitly resolved include the transformation of a muscular brute into a fragile spinster poetess, the metamorphosis of a Sunday *New York Times* into a naked sixteen-year-old girl who metamorphoses into a golem that seduces all the civil servants of New York, the forgery of a masterpiece destroyed by Nazis, a rendition of tree language, the levitation of a party of Jews, the invention of an African national culture, the transformation into a ship's figurehead, the conversion of a photographer into an old brown photograph, and the invention of a fantasy wife from one of Anton Chekhov's friends. Such challenges, she said in a 1983 interview with Catherine Rainwater and William J. Scheick, offer "a sensation akin, perhaps, to Houdini's. I'm locked in and have to figure out how to escape."

Often Ozick's subjects are adult "orphans" in search of an intellectual community. Finding no one who understands them, they are forced to invent families or to fashion fantasy companions with whom they can share their thoughts. They beget fictive disciples or conceive literary progeny. They enter others' minds or inhabit the biographies of famous writers.

The milieu from which these imaginary characters arise is always realized in a stylistically appropriate way that permits Ozick to play with the poetic resources of prose. Composing in fountain pen in her tiny handwriting, she places the same demands upon each sentence that she would upon a line of poetry. When the cadenced phrases, images, and internal assonances satisfy her, she types her first and only draft.

Ozick was born in the Yorkville neighborhood of New York City on 17 April 1928. Her parents, William and Shiphra Regelson Ozick, owned and worked fourteen-hour days in the Park View Pharmacy, often until one in the morning. Ozick helped by delivering prescriptions. This schedule shaped her later writing routine; she has always been a nocturnal author, beginning work at midnight and continuing until dawn.

In 1930 the family moved to Pelham Bay in the northeast Bronx, which was at that time still rural. Its woods, weeds, and wildflowers served as scenic background for Ozick's later fictions. Several of her stories also allude to landscapes her mother saw in Hlusk, in the province of Minsk, Belarus, from which she escaped at age nine. Ozick pays tribute to her father's Russian background as well in the story "Envy: or, Yiddish in America," collected in *The Pagan Rabbi and Other Stories* (1971). Asked by Tom Teicholz in 1987 at what age she first knew she would be a writer, she answered that she "was born into that condition," that she was destined to write "from the first moment of sentience."

From 1933 to 1941 Ozick attended public school in the Bronx and composed poems in emulation of her uncle Abraham Regelson, a Hebrew poet. In spite of her literary gifts, she was made to feel "stupid and inferior," she told Teicholz, by her elementary schoolteachers.

Ozick began to flourish academically in an all-girls high school at Hunter College in Manhattan, which she attended from 1942 to 1946. There she distinguished herself in Latin, mastering the poetry of Catullus, Ovid, Horace, and Virgil. She was also trained to eradicate her Bronx accent, "put through the wringer of speech repair," she writes in *Metaphor and Memory* (1989), by a relentless trio of phonetics coaches. Her keen awareness of nasalized *a*'s and elongated *i*'s persists in her characterizations, as in the counterfeiter who betrays his identity through his enunciation in *The Messiah of Stockholm* (1987).

From 1946 to 1949 Ozick studied at New York University, graduating Phi Beta Kappa and cum laude in English. What she remembered most was the intense competitiveness in her freshman composition class encouraged by the teacher. At Ohio State University in 1950 she wrote her master's thesis, "Parable in the Later Novels of Henry James." Her brother had first introduced her to James by bringing home a library book containing "The Beast in the Jungle" (1903). Reading it at seventeen, she felt herself summoned "to serve as a priest at the altar of literature," as she writes in *Art and Ardor* (1983).

On her return to New York in 1951 Ozick enrolled in a graduate seminar at Columbia University under Lionel Trilling. In "We Are the Crazy Lady and Other Feisty Feminist Fables" (1978) she describes herself as having been extremely shy, "bone-skinny, small, sallow and myopic." In 1952 she married Bernard Hallote, an attorney. They lived for a year in Boston, where she worked as advertising copywriter for a department store and published a feature article in the *Boston Globe* about the gilded dome of the statehouse. In 1953, when her husband was appointed an attorney for New York City, the couple moved into her parents' home. Using her childhood bedroom as a study, she began work on an ambitious philosophical novel. From that "tiny room, flowered with the do-it-yourself yellow wallpaper my mother had put up," her only excursions were "trips on the bus to the Westchester Square Public Library" to exchange stacks of books, she wrote in a 1992 essay in *The New Yorker*. She invested seven years on "Mercy, Pity, Peace, and Love," but feeling "futilely mired," she "finally had the sense to give up on it" after it reached three hundred thousand words. An excerpted chapter, "The Sense of Europe," was printed in *Prairie Schooner* in 1956. Of the poems she continued to write, some of which are still uncollected, twenty-six were published in a variety of scholarly journals.

At twenty-nine Ozick began work on *Trust,* determined to produce a masterpiece. It took six and a half years, except for a brief interlude. As she told Teicholz, "I stopped to write a shorter novel, which I did write in six sustained non-stop weeks. It was called *The Conversion of John Andersmall.* I conceived of it as a relief, a kind of virtuoso joke." Sent to several editors, it was eventually lost.

On 24 September 1965 Ozick's daughter, Rachel, was born. In that same year *Trust* was accepted for publication. Having the proofs and the baby come at the same time was an instance of life imitating art since the narrator of *Trust* had been born just as her mother finished her novel. She said to Teicholz, "I had the baby and the galleys together, and I sat at my desk . . . correcting the galleys with my right hand, and rocking the baby carriage with my left."

Begun as an apprenticeship to James and E. M. Forster, the book ended up "addressed to the Jews," Ozick writes in *Art and Ardor*. "I went into that book dazzled by [F. Scott] Fitzgerald, and came out attached to [the Talmudic scholar] Akiva." In a televised interview with Bill Moyers introducing the series *Heritage: Civilization and the Jews,* broadcast on 3 April 1986, Ozick noted that she had begun — like her protagonist, Enoch Vand — studying Jewish history and that in particular she had been "immensely influenced by an essay by Leo Baeck called 'Romantic Religion.' " At the end of *Trust* Enoch begins his education by studying Hebrew with a refugee, whose tattooed number was "daily covered by phylacteries." It takes them three years to read the Bible together. "Then he asked for the whole Talmud."

According to the Eriksonian scheme of developmental tasks, the achievement of trust is the initial psychological stage. "The eye — and the 'I' — of the novel," Ozick says in "We Are the Crazy Lady and Other Feisty Feminist Fables," were deliberately made anonymous so that the distrust she registered would be taken seriously. As she explains:

> So what I left out of my narrator entirely, sweepingly, with exquisite consciousness of what exactly I *was* leaving out, was any shred of "sensibility." I stripped her of everything, even a name. . . . She was for me a bloodless device, fulcrum or pivot, a recording voice, a language-machine. She confronted moment or event, took it in, gave it out . . . without ever influencing the story. My machine-narrator was there for efficiency only, for flexibility, for craftiness, for subtlety, but never, never as a "woman."

The novel begins in 1957 as the unnamed narrator, at twenty-two, describes her desolate college commencement, attended by neither of her parents. The second section is set in the destroyed Europe of 1946, where Enoch is recording a census of corpses. It moves another decade backward in the third section, to the cottage in Brighton, England, where the narrator was born; disowned by her biological father, who abandons them to sail toward a warmer climate; and repudiated by her legal father, William, who divorces her mother, with whom he had never consummated his marriage. The final section is set in Duneacres, an island estate in Westchester County on the grounds of her grandfather's now-ruined mansion. There history is again replayed: the narrator watches her mother's double, Stefanie, who is engaged to William's son, betray her fiancé with Nick. She relives, vicariously, her own conception.

Reviewer David Stevenson, in the 17 July 1966 *New York Times,* focused on "the sensibility of the narrator," who sees all her friends getting married and "longs to play some simple, easy feminine role herself" but "has been unable to define her role as a woman." Elinor Baumbach's 1966 review in the *Saturday Review of Literature* discussed the heroine's rejection by two of her fathers and her participation in a "carnal triumph" by her "young, Dionysian" actual father who "touches her sensually." Eugene Goodheart in *Critique* complained, "The source of the trouble with *Trust* is its heroine." Her misery is due to her being "the unprepossessing offspring of a moment of passion between two beautiful people."

Dust jacket for Ozick's first novel, in which a young woman's search for her father is juxtaposed with a young man's inquiries into the Holocaust

Ozick, he believes, "deprives the heroine of every grace a woman can have." Victor H. Strandberg, in "The Art of Cynthia Ozick" (1983), discusses her "portrait of the artist as a young woman." Her quest for a father leads her to the pagan "male muse" who initiates her and restores her trust in her own powers.

Feeling that she had remained too long a hermit during her ambitious undertaking, Ozick taught three sections of freshman composition at New York University from 1964 to 1965. She remarked in *Art and Ardor,* "After so long a retreat, my lust for the world was prodigious." Recognition finally came in 1968 with her election as a fellow of the National Endowment for the Arts. Then international recognition followed as she was invited to Israel in 1970, where she read a lengthy essay on the nature and history of literary culture. In contrast to the sparse reviews of her novel, the press coverage of her speech was extensive.

Ozick's next book brought her enduring acclamation. *The Pagan Rabbi and Other Stories* (1971) was nominated for a National Book Award, won the B'nai B'rith Jewish Heritage Award in 1971, and was given the Jewish Book Council Award in 1972 as well as the Edward Lewis Wallant Award. In 1973 it earned the American Academy of Arts and Letters Award. One of the stories, "Envy," was selected for *Best American Short Stories: 1970.*

"Usurpation," from her well-received collection, *Bloodshed and Three Novellas* (1976), won the first prize in the O. Henry contest of 1975 and received a good deal of critical commentary. In 1982 *Levitation: Five Fictions* was published. That same year Ozick was appointed Distinguished Artist in Residence at City College, received a Guggenheim Fellowship, and was invited to address an international conference in Bellagio, Italy. In 1983 she was notified that she had won the Strauss Living Award — thirty-five thousand dollars a year for five years;

she found the letter when she returned from Italy. The generous support freed Ozick to concentrate on writing, uninterrupted by the need to give lectures.

In 1983 Knopf issued a compilation of Ozick's essays, *Art and Ardor.* Her comments on Forster, James, Edith Wharton, Truman Capote, John Updike, Bernard Malamud, Harold Bloom, Isaac Bashevis Singer, and Maurice Samuel are fresh perspectives on significant writers. Her probing of Virginia Woolf's diary suggests the possibility that perhaps Ozick might one day release the journals she has kept since 1953, in which she has recorded responses to her reading and worked through problems with her writing. The lyrical reminiscence that concludes the collection suggests why she still writes "at that selfsame round glass table salvaged from the Park View Pharmacy" and how her writing was "buffetted into being by school hurts." It also suggests that writing keeps alive her father's "grieving over his mother in Moscow." Also, "mama's furnace-heart, her masses of mcmoirs," are kept alive for her through her fictions.

In 1983 Knopf published *The Cannibal Galaxy.* Originally intended for an earlier collection of novellas as "The Laughter of Akiva," it was pulled while already in galleys due to threatened litigation by the principal of a Westchester Yeshiva. Thus Ozick was forced for the first time to violate her own proscription against revision. Having to enlarge the frame made it a far more spiritually generous work. Instead of simply vindicating a wrongly assessed student, a new pattern emerged. Now the principal's own childhood suffering shadows the rest of his life, shown even in the shape of the buildings — a daily reminder of the Nazi extermination — over which he is meant to preside.

In the new introduction, Joseph Brill is the fifth and most brilliant of a Parisian fishmonger's nine children. The values of these Yiddish-speaking immigrants are taught by Rabbi Pult every afternoon in the back of the fish store. Joseph is warned against excursions into museums, explorations of French literature, and the teachings at the Sorbonne. Then one day he finds his entire world gone, his family deported. He hides first in the subcellar of a convent school, then in a peasant's hayloft. Now fifty-eight and still a displaced person, he runs a school housed in three brick and cinderblock buildings shaped like boxcars, the freight trains that deported his family. An abandoned stable beside these classrooms is to be remodeled into a residence for him. The benefactress makes his inhabiting the former hayloft a condition of her accepting the name of the school.

Brill feels an obligation to Edmond Fleg, the school's namesake, because he had inhabited his mind during his incarceration in the dark cellar. " 'I lost my mind,' he would describe it, 'but I didn't go mad. I only acquired someone else's mind for a while.' " It had not mattered to Brill that Fleg was both obscure and second-rate. What mattered was that a French Jew's books had been bought and annotated by a priest. That meant that even a priest could dwell inside a Jew's mind. And so was the Dual Curriculum conceived: Brill vowed, if he survived, to found a school dedicated to fusing the Aristotelian and Hebraic traditions.

Ozick's revision sharpened and refocused the extent to which this project is a violation of what Rabbi Pult had admonished against. The revised first encounter between Brill and Hester Lilt is an uncanny confrontation of doubles. The focus is on her reflection of what he might have become had he defined himself in terms of his own culture instead of adopting an alien culture's definitions. As Lilt registers her daughter at the school she is seen to be Brill's age. She speaks, as he does, in a refugee accent. She is single, as he is. Her voice is strikingly deep, masculine. She endorses the application forms with a male signature. Her presence evokes "some nameless familiarity," and he experiences a sense of déjà vu. Facing his alter ego, "he saw that they were unfailingly alike." She forcefully contradicts his perception that they are identical: "No, I'm not what you are." He is stung by her refusal "to recognize him as he had recognized her."

To teach him how he might still become what he intended to be, she invites him to a lecture. Were he able to concentrate, hc would discover that she is offering him the pedagogical theory the parents accuse him of lacking: a way of making the dual curriculum workable. However, he arrives late, is too distracted to follow, and loses the chance to redeem his lifc. What she demonstrates is the use of midrash, Talmudic wisdom tales, to resolve his deepest concerns. She speaks to him in stories he had heard from Rabbi Pult. For the swarm of mothers attacking him over their children's grades, she gives him the fable of the bees. To subdue his impatience with her daughter's slow development, she gives him the tale of the fox. For his own abandonment of ambition, she gives him the cannibal galaxy, which includes not only Jonah swallowed by the whale but also Joseph imprisoned by Pharaoh. Had he been able to listen, he would have heard that his own ancient tradition had survived dispersal in alien cultures. If he wished authenticity, he had only to reclaim his own heritage. Had he grasped her message's import, he would not have been shocked to see her daughter acclaimed as a world-famous artist.

Several of the critical discussions of this novel compared it with her essays "Bialik's Hint" (1989) and "Toward a New Yiddish" (1983). Naomi B. Sokoloff writes that Ozick has long been preoccupied with the question of sustaining "a cohesive Jewish life in Dispersion." One way to avoid being subsumed in the surrounding culture is to adopt the discourse modeled by Hester Lilt. "As she applies midrash to her own scholarly work, Lilt recalls Ozick's prescription for titanic intellectual efforts which, drawing on Jewish sources, may forge an American literature unlike any we have known so far." Janet Handler Burstein writes that "from the pedagogical equilibrium of Brill's Dual Curriculum comes only stasis" because he juxtaposes two discrete sets of texts, while Hester finds ways of fusing their "disparate insights." Her daughter's work also "opens out to riches: originality, the brilliance of the unexpected."

A. Alvarez notes in *Cynthia Ozick: Modern Critical Views* (1986), edited by Harold Bloom, that Brill's longing for a prodigy was "to vindicate his life, his methods, his private and intellectual aspirations, his own lack of originality." He found that the titles of Lilt's books "sound like the Dual Curriculum made print: philosophy from parable, metaphysics from midrash." While Alvarez deplores the proliferation of images "like tropical undergrowth," this aspect is praised by Edmund White, whose review in *The New York Times Book Review* consists of quotations of Ozick's "glorious" metaphors.

In 1984 Ozick was awarded honorary doctorates by the Hebrew Union College in Cincinnati and Yeshiva University of New York, and the Jewish Theological Seminary gave her the Distinguished Service in Jewish Letters Award. Her alma mater, New York University, conferred upon her its Distinguished Alumnus Award. She was also nominated for the P.E.N. Faulkner Award. That year her story "Rosa" won the O. Henry competition first prize. In 1985 she was invited to Harvard University to deliver the Phi Beta Kappa Oration, and in 1987 she was given an honorary doctorate by Hunter College.

In 1987 *The Messiah of Stockholm* was published. Ozick had been intrigued by the life and works of Bruno Schulz ever since 1977, when she had been invited to review his *The Street of Crocodiles,* a book of tales originally published in Polish in 1934 being reissued as part of a series introducing Eastern-European writers. She wove her own review, "The

Phantasmagoria of Bruno Schulz," into her novel. The fictional journalists in her book throw it away, but the protagonist, Lars Andemening, triumphantly fishes the review out of Anders Fiskyngel's trash basket and phones his bookseller to announce, "An American review! An amazement."

Ozick conceived the idea of writing about Schulz's lost *Messiah* in the fall of 1984 while in Sweden to launch the Swedish translation of *The Cannibal Galaxy.* It was rumored that Schulz's manuscript, lost when he was gunned down on 19 November 1942, had surfaced in Stockholm. Anxious not to betray Schulz, she said in a 1987 interview with Peggy Kaganoff, "I felt the Schulzian ghost angrily at my back — particularly when I saw I needed to reproduce the insides of *The Messiah* — saying, 'Who are you? Do you know Polish? Get out of my life!' "

To allay her anxiety, Ozick used privative definitions, describing what a character is not. Lars Andemening is not awake, but there is no one to notice — "Not that there was anyone to look for him." He does not look his age. He lives in a room "no bigger than a crack." He "had never learned his mother's name," and "neither wife had liked him." His secret is known by "no one — not his wives" and "none of his colleagues." His Monday column is not read. He has no sense of humor, tells no jokes. He is not in control of what he writes; he sees through an eye that is "not his own." He has cast out the two instruments most necessary to newspapermen, the telephone and the typewriter.

Gunnar Hemlig and Anders Fiskyngel analyze Lars's problem for him. His trouble is central Europe. The texts into which he is "drawn down by an undertow," through which he tries to swim with "the long weighted strokes of a drowning man," have their origins in Prague, Krakow, Budapest, and Bucharest. He had read Schulz a hundred times "like a tug dragging a river for a body." Believing himself to be Schulz's son, he studies Polish in order to hear his putative father's voice. He orders from his bookseller, Heidi Ecklund, those writers — Ludvík Vaculík, Bohumil Hrabal, Tadeusz Konwicki, Witold Gombrowicz — in whom he might find some trace of his origins. Heidi reels him in with these names.

The reason he sleeps in the daytime is "for the sake of catching sight of his father's eye." Nocturnally, seeing through that eye, he is able to penetrate the obscure books. Nightly he sees "his father's murdered eye." This vision enables him to understand what he had swum through with such effort. "He *saw*: what he saw, before he had formulated even a word of it, was his finished work."

A new novel
~her first in 17 years~by

Cynthia Ozick

The Cannibal Galaxy

TIME Magazine hails
"A commanding novel

[and its author's] commanding powers as a storyteller...
Though bursting with irony and wit, *The Cannibal Galaxy*
takes on a fearful seriousness when Ozick cites this fragment
from the Talmud: 'The world rests on the breath of the children in
the schoolhouses'...Hers is a triumph for the idiosyncrasy that
animates all art."
—from the review by PATRICIA BLAKE

The New York Times Book Review celebrates
"The best American writer
to have emerged in recent years

...Her artistic strength derives from
her moral energy...Judaism has given
to her what Catholicism gave to Flannery O'Connor—authority, penetra-
tion and indignation...Her shrewd
and second imagination inhabits the
details, the insights and especially
the astonishingly flexible and vital
language of this novel."
—from the review by EDMUND WHITE

"Glittering

...*The Cannibal Galaxy* sets forth the trifles and the grandeur of life and
bathes them in the magic light of common day."
—RHODA KOENIG,
New York Magazine

"An extraordinary piece of work.

It is about European traditions and American dreams, about astronomy,
Jewishness, fathering, mothering, love, pride, despair, ambition..."
—CATHLEEN MEDWICK, Vogue

"Tough, sad, funny,
beautiful in its design

...On every page she displays intelligence, wit, energy."
—PETER S. PRESCOTT, Newsweek

2nd printing • $11.95 • Just published by Knopf

*Advertisement for Ozick's 1983 novel, about a holocaust
survivor who establishes a school combining Hebrew and
classical traditions*

When this work is threatened Lars is forced to make a choice. His employer, Nilsson, warns him, "People complain, Lars — your reviews are practically theology. A little more wholesomeness for Monday, how about it? Soft-pedal the surreal, go easy on the existential dread, how about it?" Lars worries he will be fired "for the sins of unwholesomeness, theology, surrealism, existential dread." The threat of losing his last tenuous link with reality forces him to measure his existence. At first he pities his colleagues' normal lives. They have been denied access to "his father's eye, lit, steady, unmoving, strong and blatant, a violent white ray." By means of this string of adjectives Lars shows what he gains from his negations. Depriving himself of normality gives him the energizing brilliance and steadiness of purpose Gunnar and Anders lack.

But he counteracts his own first impulse; he surrenders. The next morning he sleepwalks into the newspaper office to the astonishment of his boss. He picks up a best-seller, a thick novel called *Illusion*. It takes an hour and a half to read, thirty minutes to write a review. Nilsson rewards him with the promise of his own cubicle and the offer of another column if he can keep up this kind of work. What the promotion costs Lars, as he had foreseen it would, is his guiding eye. "The author of *The Messiah* had withdrawn. Lars's father's eye did not return."

The irony is that the manuscript of Schulz's lost masterpiece is offered to him after he has been forced to make his commitment to reality. A woman claiming to be Schulz's daughter brings him the pages of *The Messiah* in a white shopping bag, symbolizing that its contents have become merchandise for sale.

The irony of how the dupers are duped is handled with cinematic flair. A long flashback details his four-year quest for the lost manuscript now being delivered to him. His bookseller had supplied him with scraps and shards: yellowed letters, faded photos, old periodicals, brittle fragments. Together they had sifted through these remnants, but the missing masterpiece continued to elude them. The conspirators want to manipulate him to legitimate their forgery. The well-rehearsed scenario they enact to get him involved in their scheme is played out in vain, however.

On the day he renounces his fantasy, he runs to the top of the stairwell to call down to the departing staff, "*The Messiah*'s turned up! Here! In Stockholm." He hears a woman say, "I think he's announcing the Second Coming." Laughter floats up the stairs.

The counterfeiter – Dr. Olle Eklund, born Alter Eckstein – performs an elaborate handwriting analysis to certify the authenticity of the document he himself has faked, but he has no way of knowing about the derision that had greeted Lars's news. It becomes increasingly evident to Lars that Adela, also known as Elsa, is Eklund's daughter and acts as his courier.

Syntactic shifts show Lars's change from passivity to action. In the beginning of the book Lars's "feet took him" past the Nobel Academy. The bookseller had hooked him with her bait and "reeled him back, a helpless fish on her line." After he is enraged by having been used by imposters, the syntax changes from passive to active. He "kicked Adela" and denounced them as "swindlers." Ferociously striking a match, he activates a conflagration.

Lars's awakening is like a recovery. "He was like a man in a coma who has unexpectedly come to, having been declared asleep for life." He moves to a spacious new apartment, acquiring not only a telephone but also an answering machine as well as a word processor. Not only is he accepted into the literary gossip of the office but also begins receiving more mail from readers. He had solidified from a phantom into a presence: "Lars was *there*."

The Messiah of Stockholm received extended critical discussion. In contrast to the relentless slowness of her first novel, this was fast-paced, wrote Earl Rovit. "Narrated at a pitch of intensity which constantly scintillates into the surreal, which lashes back and forth in time-sequences like an electric storm, it has the pace of exponential acceleration." Harold Bloom found in the plot a paradigm for what American Jews must do to authenticate themselves. The post-Holocaust world must reclaim its central European past and establish continuity with it. In *The New York Times Book Review* he commented, "In his powerfully rendered person, Lars is not only a student of losses, but is himself a grand loss, a blighted version of what would have been an eminent Jewish critic but for the sorrows of history." Anne Tyler in the *New Republic* called the hiatus between Lars's arrival at the bookshop and the resumption of his business there a "back-handed approach to narrative." She objected as well to having to "strain the story from a dense ragout of language," pointing to some "skewed images" and "strings of adjectives." She noted the fairy-tale elements as well as the parable aspects, "complete with a morally instructive ending." Alberto Manguel responded to the theme of creation, seeing reviewing as a "surrogate parenthood" in which Lars falls asleep impregnated by an author and awakes to deliver the result. The "paper-thin reality" of his invented ancestry is surrounded by the "meaner, tawdrier reality" created by the Eklunds. Surrounding these is the "spirit of murdered writers and or phaned men" created by Ozick. From this "web of creators and creations" comes the conviction that the entire creation is "pregnant with revelations." D. J. Enright read it as "a truly intriguing mystery" full of humor, welcoming the "jocularity" and "badinage" that brings Lars "down to earth" from his exalted flights. "No doubt to be a haunted man is a distinction, but we are bound to feel some relief when such a person sinks at last into relative normality."

In 1989 two related stories originally published in *The New Yorker* were reissued together. "Rosa" had won first prize in the 1984 O. Henry competition and was chosen for the 1984 *Best American Short Stories* volume. "The Shawl" had been selected for the 1981 edition of the same series.

Only eight pages long, "The Shawl" conveys a march to a death camp and the murder of an infant. The diction is constrained, repetitive, and nearly monosyllabic. The opening sentence, with its hypnotic rhythms, is an accusation by Rosa of her fourteen-year-old niece who walks beside her: "Stella, cold, cold, the coldness of hell." Ozick renders Rosa's thoughts as reported speech in the third person, past tense, in words consistent with her character. From this perspective the significance of the shawl emerges. During the trancelike walk it is used to cradle Rosa's baby, Magda, who sucks on it when her mother's milk dries up. It both keeps her from crying and conceals her, protecting her for fifteen months. One day the shawl disappears. Rosa cannot wrap her in it and hide her beside the barracks during the roll call, and Magda wails. Rosa flies into the dark barracks where "Stella was heaped under it, asleep in her thin bones," but it is too late. Magda, her thin arms outstretched toward her shawl, is flung against an electrified fence. Aware that she will be shot if she screams, Rosa stuffs the shawl into her own mouth.

The rage she could not vent against her baby's murderer is deflected against her niece. Rosa imagines Stella as a cannibal, "waiting for Magda to die so she could put her teeth into the little thighs." When Stella says "Aryan," referring to the baby's blue eyes and blonde hair, Rosa hears, "Let us devour her."

The sequel, "Rosa," opens with her having become "a madwoman," exiled to a dark room in a blazing Miami where she has been sent for having smashed up her own store. What incited her anger was her customers' inability to understand her story. "Whoever came, they were like deaf people. Whatever you explained to them, they didn't understand," she says. The story that no American could comprehend is the delusion of European Jewry that their assimilation would ensure their safety. This inherited belief in aristocratic manners and the acquisition of high culture, which Rosa finds to be incommunicable in her broken English, she confesses at length in unmailed letters to Magda in eloquent Polish.

On behalf of her parents, too well-bred to express their own anti-Semitism, she had spoken out in vigorous protest against the Zionists who had tried to take Stella to Palestine. Had Rosa not resisted, Stella would have been forced to live among "the Warsaw swarm" of people "of a particular kind, Persky and Finkelstein."

Rosa finally finds a sympathetic listener, who is not only impressed by her education but interested in every nuance of her story, which had so obsessed her that she had felt compelled to tell it to her customers. He introduces himself as Simon Persky, "a third cousin to Shimon Peres, the Israeli politician."

The agent of her redemption, met in a Laundromat, is an old man with gleaming false teeth, a red wig, and a Polish accent. As he helps her load the dryer, the prejudices she had inherited against everything he personifies are dismantled, one by one, in a series of ironically achieved insights. Rosa scornfully distances herself from the Yiddish paper Persky is reading, recalling how her mother had "despised the sounds" of the Yiddish lullabies crooned over her cradle by the grandmother from Minsk. As she mocks his immigrant cadences, she realizes that she is also constrained by her refugee's English. As she derides the bad-smelling, ancient alleys of Warsaw he must have inhabited, she inhales her own old woman's odors. As she ridicules his toupee, she catches a reflection of her own scraggly, uncombed gray hair. Back in her dark room, when she finds one pair of her underpants missing, she finally has a way of disavowing him — until she finds them tangled in a towel.

Persky's acceptance of her is due to long practice with his own wife: "If there's anything I know to understand, it's mental episodes." When the shawl arrives from Stella, she can see it as it really is — not magic, but a "colorless cloth" with "a faint saliva smell" that "lay like an old bandage." Rosa signals her willingness to live in the present by having her phone reconnected.

Many critics lauded this volume. Irving Halperin wrote, "In a time when the memory of the Holocaust is being trivialized by slick fiction, talk shows, and TV 'documentaries,' and when some social 'scientists' ('necrophiliacs' Rosa would call them) are doing 'research projects' written in atrocious psychobabble on the 'survivor,' Ms. Ozick's extraordinary volume is a particularly welcome achievement of the moral imagination." Elie Wiesel praised these "dazzling and staggering pages filled with sadness and truth."

Ozick's stage adaptation of The Shawl, titled Blue Light, premiered in August 1994 in a production directed by Sidney Lumet and featuring Dianne Wiest and Mercedes Ruehl. A revised version of the play, titled The Shawl, is scheduled to open under Lumet's direction in the fall of 1995.

Another collection of essays, Metaphor and Memory, was published in 1989. Ozick's analyses of James, Saul Bellow, Sholem Aleichem, S. Y. Agnon, J. M. Coetzee, and Italo Calvino show how passionately she engages herself with writers and how intensely she enters into their worlds. Even her confession of how she misread Cyril Connolly is instructive. "The Seam of the Snail" and "A Translator's Monologue" are invaluable insights into her own methods of composition, how she approaches "the terrible complexities of the craft." She compares her work to that of her carpenter ancestors. Her grandfather Yuda-Velvl Regelson had been an artisan who carved chairs; her uncle Jake built rosewood clocks. "I mitre every pair of abutting senten-

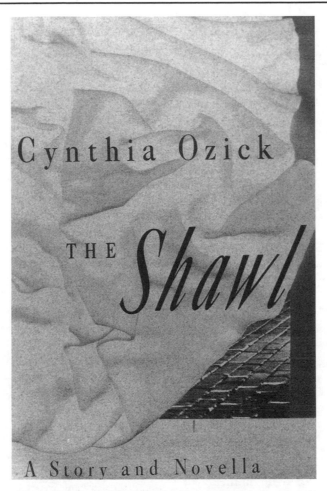

*Dust jacket for Ozick's 1989 book, two works of fiction about a
woman haunted by her experiences in the Holocaust*

ces as scrupulously as Uncle Jake fitted one strip of
rosewood against another."

An important preface, "Forewarning," pleads
with critics not to remove excerpts from the essays
with which to analyze her fiction: "The essays become the stories' interpreters: their clues, or cues,
or concordances, as if the premises of the essays
were incontrovertibly the premises of the stories as
well. As if the stories were 'illustrations' of the essays." When she was invited by editor Dan Walden
to respond to a collection of articles on her work,
she reiterated this same plea to assess her novels on
their own terms, but she conceded that she had
been pleased that notice had been taken of her
work.

In her next novella Ozick returned to one of
her favorite authors, George Eliot. Asked in 1982
by Rainwater and Scheick what she had been reading, she responded, "I will shamefacedly admit that
I am currently in *Middlemarch* again." She added, "I
find myself wishing I could write a contemporary
Middlemarch." Five years later she was still thinking
about Eliot's capacious work: as she said to Kaganoff, "I long to do a large, many charactered, many
placed, luxuriously voluptuous novel. I want to do
Middlemarch. But I don't know whether I have the
amplitude or whether the zeitgeist would, in fact,
permit that."

Introducing "Puttermesser Paired" as the first-
prize story of 1992 for the O. Henry Awards, William Abrahams wrote:

> We are in New York of the present, precisely and risibly
> caught in a wealth of realistic detail, where Puttermes-
> ser, "an elderly orphan," is to embark upon her quest
> for a suitable husband. It is the *fact* of New York that
> underlies and clarifies the irony of Puttermesser's *fiction,*
> and determines Ozick's presentation of it. As a seeming
> realist she leads us forward, reassured by the presence of
> an actual New York, persuading us that Puttermesser
> and her quest are as real as the ordinary everyday world
> in which they happen. Then, as the extraordinary re-
> veals its fateful contours, we find ourselves accepting the

solution Puttermesser produces for herself: that she will appropriate George Eliot's biography and reproduce it in her own life, not as a novelist but as a woman, even down to marrying a facsimile George Henry Lewes of her own.

The opening chapter, "An Age of Divorce," moves with virtuosity through a variety of epistolary forms, juxtaposing clips from legal tracts sent through the Municipal Building, an old letter of her mother's, personal ads, a questionnaire sent to her on "Aging and the Female Counselor," and a misdelivered announcement of "A Singles Event" – all sounding the carpe diem motif. Having retired from paperwork in order to live, Puttermesser's longing for a union of like-minded souls is intense. Her brief blundering into a failed singles party upstairs confirms the unlikelihood of ever finding a companion like Lewes. The irony of her seeking such a husband is also revealed through letters. She carries around and quotes from Eliot's correspondence. Lewes, the ideal mate, was already married, and "in an age of no divorce" the two Georges had to live together illicitly.

Wishing herself back in the Victorian era conjures up a dandy in a cape, slender, blond, serious-eyed, entering Morgenbluth's apartment just as she leaves. She sees him next at the Metropolitan Museum, rendering a copy of Socrates exhorting his disciples. A heated Platonic dialogue on the meaning of mimesis follows. Anxious for such discourse, she invites the man, Rupert Rabeeno, to join in her project: to read aloud, alternating chapters, all of Eliot's books. He moves in. The difference in their ages appears not to matter until they reach, in their reading of Eliot's biographies, the death of her consort. As far as Puttermesser is concerned they are finished. Rabeeno is so intent on continuing that he proposes marriage to gain her consent to go on with their reading.

Given his role as a copyist and his personal history, it is clear that he identifies with another man in Eliot's life, Johnny Cross, reenacting Cross's marriage to Eliot, twenty years his senior, eighteen months after Lewes's death. With the utmost fidelity, Rupert re-creates their honeymoon itinerary, retracing every step of an earlier trip taken by the two Georges. He even emulates Johnny's plunge out the window when his new wife tried to coax him into "conjugal intimacy."

As she told Ross, Ozick sees writing as an attempt to discover the truth through "a series of masks and disguises," through "a maze of schemes and strategies." One configuration for such fiction-

alized truth-telling is the "upraised pedagogical finger" fixed between Socrates and Eliot in "Puttermesser Paired." The Athenian quester for virtue and the Victorian seeker of morality point toward a type of literature envisioned by Ozick. Inherent in this symbol is the conception of creation portrayed on the ceiling of the Sistine Chapel, with humanity's aspiring finger reaching for the finger of the Creator. Rather than letting the reader see this aspiration from an ennobling distance, Ozick shows idealistic impulses in protagonists caught in such close-up views that their flawed humanity is evident.

Interviews:

Eve Ottenberg, "The Rich Visions of Cynthia Ozick," *New York Times Magazine* (10 April 1983): 47, 62–66;

Catherine Rainwater and William J. Scheick, "An Interview with Cynthia Ozick," *Texas Studies in Language and Literature,* 25 (Summer 1983): 255–265;

Jean W. Ross, "An Interview with Cynthia Ozick," in *Dictionary of Literary Biography Yearbook: 1983,* edited by Mary Bruccoli and Ross (Detroit: Gale, 1984), pp. 35–36;

Peggy Kaganoff, "*PW* Interviews Cynthia Ozick," *Publishers Weekly,* 27 (March 1987): 33–34;

Tom Teicholz, "Cynthia Ozick," *Paris Review,* 102 (Spring 1987): 154–190.

Bibliography:

Susan Currier and Daniel J. Cahill, "A Bibliography of the Writings of Cynthia Ozick," *Texas Studies in Literature and Language,* 25 (Summer 1983): 313–321.

References:

Elinor Baumbach, Review of Ozick's *Trust, Saturday Review of Literature* (9 July 1966): 34;

Harold Bloom, "The Book of the Father," *New York Times Book Review* (22 March 1987): 1, 36;

Bloom, ed., *Cynthia Ozick: Modern Critical Views* (New York: Chelsea House, 1986);

Janet Handler Burstein, "Cynthia Ozick and the Transgressions of Art," *American Literature,* 59 (March 1987): 85–101;

Sarah Blacher Cohen, *Cynthia Ozick's Comic Art: From Levity to Liturgy* (Bloomington: Indiana University Press, 1994);

D. J. Enright, "Visions and Revisions," *New York Review of Books* (28 May 1987): 18–20;

Eugene Goodheart, Review of Ozick's *Trust, Critique,* 9 (Winter 1967–1968): 99–102;

Irving Halperin, Review of Ozick's *The Shawl, Commonweal* (15 December 1989): 712;

Elaine M. Kauvar, *Cynthia Ozick's Fiction: Tradition and Invention* (Bloomington: Indiana University Press, 1993);

Joseph Lowin, *Cynthia Ozick* (Boston: Twayne, 1988);

Alberto Manguel, "Paternity Suite," *Village Voice,* 32 (21 April 1987): 45;

Ellen Pifer, "Cynthia Ozick: Invention and Orthodoxy," in *Contemporary American Women Writers: Narrative Strategies,* edited by Catherine Rainwater and William J. Scheick (Lexington: University of Kentucky Press, 1985), pp. 89–109;

Sanford Pinsker, *The Uncompromising Fictions of Cynthia Ozick* (Columbia: University of Missouri Press, 1987);

Ruth Rosenberg, "Covenanted to the Law: Cynthia Ozick," *MELUS,* 9 (Winter 1982): 39–44;

Rosenberg, "Cynthia Ozick," in *The Critical Survey of Short Fiction,* 7 volumes, edited by Frank N. Magill (Englewood Cliffs, N. J.: Salem, 1981), pp. 2035–2039;

Rosenberg, "The Ghost Story as Aggada: Cynthia Ozick's 'The Pagan Rabbi,' " in *Haunting the House of Fiction: Feminist Perspectives on Ghost Stories by American Women,* edited by Lynette Carpenter and Wendy K. Kolmar (Knoxville: University of Tennessee Press, 1991), pp. 215–228;

Earl Rovit, "The Two Languages of Cynthia Ozick," *Studies in American Jewish Literature,* 8 (Spring 1989): 34–49;

Naomi B. Sokoloff, "Interpretation: Cynthia Ozick's *Cannibal Galaxy,*" *Prooftexts,* 6 (September 1986): 239–257;

David L. Stevenson, "Daughter's Reprieve," *New York Times Book Review* (17 July 1966): 29;

Victor H. Strandberg, "The Art of Cynthia Ozick," *Texas Studies in Literature and Language,* 2 (Summer 1983): 266–311;

Strandberg, *Greek Mind / Jewish Soul: The Conflicted Art of Cynthia Ozick* (Madison: University of Wisconsin Press, 1994);

Anne Tyler, "The Mission," *New Republic,* 196 (6 April 1987): 39–41;

Daniel Walden, ed., *The World of Cynthia Ozick* (Kent, Ohio: Kent State University Press, 1987);

Edmund White, "Images of a Mind Thinking," *New York Times Book Review,* 11 September 1983, pp. 3, 46–47;

Elie Wiesel, "Ozick Asks Whether There Can Be Hope after Auschwitz," *Chicago Tribune Books* (17 September 1989): 6.

Sylvia Plath

(27 October 1932 – 11 February 1963)

Timothy Materer
University of Missouri – Columbia

See also the Plath entries in *DLB 5: American Poets Since World War II* and *DLB 6: American Novelists Since World War II, Second Series.*

BOOKS: *The Colossus* (London, Melbourne & Toronto: Heinemann, 1960; New York: Knopf, 1962);

The Bell Jar, as Victoria Lucas (London, Melbourne & Toronto: Heinemann, 1963); as Sylvia Plath (New York, Evanston, San Francisco & London: Harper & Row, 1971);

Ariel (London: Faber & Faber, 1965; New York: Harper & Row, 1966);

Crossing the Water (London: Faber & Faber, 1971; New York, Evanston, San Francisco & London: Harper & Row, 1971);

Crystal Gazer and Other Poems (London: Rainbow, 1971);

Winter Trees (London: Faber & Faber, 1971; New York, Evanston, San Francisco & London: Harper & Row, 1972);

Johnny Panic and the Bible of Dreams and Other Prose Writings (London & Boston: Faber & Faber, 1977);

The Collected Poems, edited by Ted Hughes (New York & London: Harper & Row, 1981);

The Journals of Sylvia Plath, 1950–62, edited by Frances McCullough (New York: Dial, 1982).

In his introduction to *The Journals of Sylvia Plath, 1950–62* (1982), her husband, poet Ted Hughes, wrote that she wore "many masks" but that he believes he knew her "real self" – "the self I had married, after all, and lived with and knew well." Yet this claim is as controversial as her biographers' claims to have given accurate accounts of her life. The controversy began soon after her suicide in 1963, when Hughes threatened a London magazine with legal action if it published the second part of A. Alvarez's account of the suicide. This incident set the tone for further dealings between the Plath estate and her biographers, who often com-

Sylvia Plath

plain that Hughes will tolerate only his version of the "real" Sylvia Plath. For Linda Wagner-Martin's *Sylvia Plath: A Biography* (1987), the first scholarly and critical biography, the estate's cooperation was withdrawn when the author refused to make several cuts.

The controversy peaked when the only biography to receive the estate's cooperation, Anne Stevenson's *Bitter Fame: A Life of Sylvia Plath* (1989), presented her as a spoiled product of the 1950s whose egoistic rage inspired brilliant but obsessive poetry. Stevenson's biography was meant to redress a too-sympathetic picture in Wagner-Martin's biography, and Paul Alexander's *Rough Magic: A Biography of Sylvia Plath* (1991) in turn tempered the harshness of Stevenson's book. Another recent biography, Ronald Hayman's *The Death and Life of Sylvia Plath* (1991), is as much a reflection on the difficulty of writing about her life as it is a conventional biography. Jacqueline Rose's *The Haunting of Sylvia Plath* (1991) and Janet Malcolm's *The Silent Woman: Sylvia Plath and Ted Hughes* (1994) are contentious but valuable accounts of the difficulties that the Plath estate has caused for critics and biographers.

The estate's strict control of copyright and its editing of such writings as Plath's journals and letters have caused the most serious problems for scholars. Yet even without these obstacles to interpretation Plath's identity would seem mysterious. Her life seems mythical rather than historical because she herself made her life the substance of her art. Her constant theme, the transformation and rebirth of the self, has given her readers multiple and sometimes contradictory versions of that self. Her critics have viewed her, for example, as the tragic victim of a childhood trauma when her father died and of an equally painful abandonment when her husband left her shortly before her death. Less-sympathetic critics have characterized her as the product of a generation of women who wanted too much: a perfect husband, home, and family as well as an independent career. Some view her as a feminist ahead of her time in fighting for a woman's independent identity. Perhaps the best-known persona is Plath the confessional poet whose "muse was rage," as Diane Middlebrook has said in "The Enraged Muse" (1989), and who finally expressed that rage in *The Bell Jar* (1963), her only novel, and *Ariel* (1965).

Plath's contradictory personality emerged from what at first seems an uncomplicated and conventional American background. Although her father died when she was a child, Plath's family life was otherwise comfortable. By the time she was a scholarship student at Smith College she was a popular, physically active, and talented young woman who won many prizes for her academic and creative achievements. As a graduate student she attended Cambridge University and married a brilliant English poet, Hughes, with whom she had two children, Nicholas and Frieda. Despite this record of achievements, she struggled continually against severe depression from at least her junior year of college — the same year that the autobiographical narrative of *The Bell Jar* begins. Although the depressed periods were matched by those of elation and creativity, the oscillation between these extremes was exhausting. She wrote in her journal for 20 June 1958, "it is as if my life were magically run by two electric currents: joyous positive and despairing negative — which ever is running at the moment dominates my life, floods it." As both her poetry and fiction suggest, her depression was related to the death of her father.

Otto Emil Plath was born in Germany in 1885 and came to America in 1900. By 1922 he was an instructor of German and then of biology at Boston University. Her mother, Aurelia Schober Plath, twenty-one years younger than her father, was his student in 1929. After Aurelia had graduated and was teaching high school, they married in January 1932. He insisted that his new wife quit her job and assist him in his research and in rewriting his dissertation, published as *Bumblebees and Their Ways* (1934). Sylvia was born in the Jamaica Plain section of Boston on 27 October 1932; her brother, Warren, was born in 1935. From 1935 on their father's health was poor, but he stubbornly refused to see a doctor, fearing that he would only learn he had cancer. (Plath later speculated that his refusal to do so was suicidal.) He steadily declined until he collapsed in 1940 from the effects of untreated diabetes. After an operation to amputate his leg in October 1940, he suffered an embolism and died on 5 November 1940. The eight-year-old Plath's response when her mother broke the news of her father's death was to say that she would never speak to God again. Thinking the children were too young, Mrs. Plath did not let them attend the funeral. They moved from their house near the ocean, which Plath missed deeply, to Wellesley, Massachusetts, in 1942. She recalled her love of the ocean in her essay "Ocean 1212–W" (1963), collected in *Johnny Panic and the Bible of Dreams and Other Prose Writings* (1977):

> My childhood landscape was not land but the end of the land — the cold, salt, running hills of the Atlantic. I sometimes think my vision of the sea is the clearest thing I own.... When I was learning to creep, my mother set me down on the beach to see what I thought of it. I crawled straight for the coming wave and was just through the wall of green when she caught my heels.

Her memories of moving away from the sea are briefly expressed: "My father died, we moved inland. Whereon those nine first years of my life sealed themselves off like a ship in a bottle — beauti-

*Plath with her mother, Aurelia Schober Plath, and her brother,
Warren, in 1950*

ful, inaccessible, obsolete, a fine, white flying
myth."

After the move to Wellesley, Aurelia Plath resumed her academic career with an appointment at
Boston University to develop and teach in a program for training medical secretaries. Plath entered
Smith College on a scholarship in 1950. Intent on
academic and social success, she pushed herself so
hard during her college years that a pattern of colds
and sinus infections at times of stress developed,
which also became characteristic of her adult life.
These illnesses in turn aggravated her recurrent depressions. In an entry of her journal for 20 February 1952 she confessed, "Small problems, mentions
of someone else's felicity, evidence of someone

else's talents frightened me, making me react hol-
lowly, fighting jealousy, envy, hate."

In 1952 Plath won a five-hundred-dollar first
prize for fiction from *Mademoiselle*. The next summer she was awarded a student editorship on *Mademoiselle* and spent June working in New York, an experience that provided the material for the first
chapters of *The Bell Jar*. Her anxiety to excel at
whatever she did made her frenetic stay in New
York particularly hard because she was competing
with other outstanding, prizewinning young
women. Returning home, the news that she had not
been accepted in Frank O'Connor's short-story
course at Harvard University further depressed
her, and she was placed in the care of a doctor who

prescribed electroshock treatments on an outpatient basis. The electroshocks, a drastic though not uncommon therapy at the time, were poorly administered and increased rather than relieved her anxieties. On 24 August 1953 she hid herself in the cellar of her home after taking about forty sleeping pills, prescribed for her, from a locked metal box where her mother kept them. She swallowed them and was found two days later when her brother heard her moans, and after her physical recovery she was admitted to the Massachusetts General Hospital (where poets Robert Lowell and Anne Sexton would also be patients) under the care of a competent psychiatrist, Dr. Ruth Beuscher. Although Beuscher also used electrotherapy, she won Plath's trust and was the model for Dr. Nolan in *The Bell Jar*. In the novel Dr. Nolan helps her patient foster the independence that allows her to face the hospital's examining board successfully and return to her life. Similarly, Plath returned to college in the spring of 1954 (at first under special supervision), completed her honors thesis on the motif of the double in the work of Fyodor Dostoyevsky, and graduated summa cum laude in 1955. She received a Fulbright grant and in October began her studies at Newnham College, Cambridge, England.

In Cambridge she met Hughes, whose poetry she already admired. In her journal for 5 May 1958 she remembered her first impression of his poems: "tough, knotty, blazing with color and fury, most eminently sayable." She described him in one of the letters collected in *Letters Home: Correspondence, 1950–63* (1975) as the "strongest man in the world," someone who commanded attention "like a blast of Jove's lightning." Their first meeting in a Cambridge pub in February 1956 was dramatic. Hughes snatched her hairband and earrings to keep as mementos, and Plath, to show that she also had a passionate nature, drew blood by biting his cheek. Their relationship developed as they met in London and Cambridge, and they married on 16 June 1956 and honeymooned in Spain. After Plath took her Cambridge exams for the B.A. degree they came to America, where Plath began teaching at Smith College. Typing his poems and sending them to periodicals and contests, she delighted to see his career thrive, but her own career languished. She felt inadequate as a teacher and found preparing for classes too stressful and time-consuming. She wrote in her journal for 8 March 1958, "I am living and teaching on rereadings, on notes of other people, sour as heartburn, between two unachieved shapes: between the original teacher and the original writer: neither." They moved to Boston in 1958 and tried

to live on their income as writers; Plath, however, took part-time jobs to help with their finances. A secretarial job at the Massachusetts General Hospital gave her the background for her best short story, "Johnny Panic and the Bible of Dreams" (published 1968), which also dealt with her traumatic memories of electroshock. She also attended Lowell's writing seminar at Boston University in 1958, where she became friendly with Sexton, and resumed treatments with Dr. Beuscher to cope with her recurrent depression. Despite the publication of her poems in magazines such as the *Nation, London Magazine,* and *The New Yorker,* her depressions centered on her low productivity, publishers' rejections of the manuscript that would eventually develop into *The Colossus* (1960), and her inability to make progress on a novel. After a summer touring and two months at the Yaddo writing colony, in December 1959 the Hugheses returned to England, where they hoped to live more cheaply as they advanced their careers.

Their first year in England was by all appearances successful. Plath gave birth to a daughter, Frieda Rebecca, in April 1960, and in October her much-revised first volume of poetry was published as *The Colossus,* a reference to her father as an "oracle" or "[m]outhpiece of the dead" that suggests she was finding her true inspiration through exploring her past. Although reviews of *The Colossus* were generally favorable, they were few. John Wain praised her verbal craft in the *Spectator,* although he thought her manner was not yet fully her own, but Roy Fuller attacked her poetry in the *London Magazine* for sounding derivative of other modern poets. In comparison to the reception of her husband's prizewinning volumes *The Hawk in the Rain* (1957) and *Lupercal* (1960), she felt her volume had made little impact on the literary world. In 1961 she made a new start on novel writing, which unlike poetry writing allowed her to write regularly as she carried out her household responsibilities. Despite a miscarriage and an appendectomy in 1961, she finished *The Bell Jar* in August. In the same month they bought a house in North Tawton, Devon, where their second child, Nicholas Farrar, was born in January 1962. During this time she wrote some of her finest poems, including "Blackberrying," "The Moon and the Yew Tree," "Little Fugue," and the long poem "Three Women." This period ended when she learned in July 1962 of Hughes's affair with another woman. The shock of this revelation is described in her poem "Words Heard, By Accident, Over the Phone," where the voice of the other woman is as "[t]hick as foreign coffee, and with a sluggy pulse."

Plath and her husband, British poet Ted Hughes, in 1956

After she and Hughes failed at an attempt at reconciliation, she moved with her two children into a London flat that once had been occupied by William Butler Yeats. Depressed by the separation, the hardships of a severe winter, and continual respiratory illnesses, she wrote the bitter poems that first appeared in *Ariel*. She wrote her mother on 16 October 1962, during a month when she wrote some thirty poems, "I am writing the best poems of my life; they will make my name."

In January 1963 *The Bell Jar* was published in England under the pseudonym Victoria Lucas. Although she told her brother that her novel was "a pot-boiler and no one must read it," she must have known that its harsh biographical portraits would soon come to her family's attention. Indeed, her mother tried to discourage Hughes from allowing its publication in America. The theme of *The Bell Jar*, and of the manuscript version of *Ariel* before Hughes rearranged it following her death, was rebirth after a period of suffering and despair. Yet on 11 February Plath committed suicide by inhaling gas from her kitchen oven. Questions that arose at the time, such as whether she hoped that someone

would also discover this suicide attempt in time to stop it and whether she left a suicide note, have remained unanswered.

The critical reactions to both *The Bell Jar* and *Ariel* were inevitably influenced by the manner of Plath's death at thirty. In addition to the autobiographical poems Plath had included in the manuscript of *Ariel*, Hughes included many of the poems written immediately before her death. The published volume's final poem, "Edge," is about a woman "perfected" in death; its composition date of 5 February 1963 puts it among the very last poems she wrote. Her own manuscript of *Ariel*, on the contrary, concluded with the poems on beekeeping, and the final poem, "Wintering," about a hive's survival, ends with the bees' anticipation of spring. However, the early reviewers of the pseudonymous *The Bell Jar*, before the publication of *Ariel* and before the novel's 1971 appearance in America, were favorable even though nothing was known of her identity or dramatic death. The review in the *Listener* praised it as a "brilliant and moving book," while the *New Statesman* review perceptively referred to it as a novel like J. D. Salinger's *The Catcher in the*

Rye (1951). Later critics have compared it to other novels of psychological crisis such as Ken Kesey's *One Flew over the Cuckoo's Nest* (1962), Saul Bellow's *Herzog* (1964), and Philip Roth's *Portnoy's Complaint* (1969). In writing a crisis novel about a young woman, Plath was seen as a feminist who analyzed the restrictive social roles of American women in the 1950s. Critics have compared her fiction to works by later feminist writers, such as Erica Jong's *Fear of Flying* (1973) and Joan Didion's *Play It as It Lays* (1970). More than thirty years after its first publication, critics generally place *The Bell Jar* in the context of Plath's achievement as a major writer of both poetry and prose. The voice of her fiction, with its strange combination of rage and comedy, is heard in the voice of many journal entries and poems such as "Daddy" – "Daddy, daddy, you bastard, I'm through" – and "Lady Lazarus" – "Out of the ash / I rise with my red hair / And I eat men like air." Her other writings of the times, which became *Letters Home,* are like *Ariel* too heavily edited – in this case by her mother rather than her husband – to reveal this angry, potent voice. Both poetry and prose express her anger at thinly veiled real-life models. This personal satire was seen as early as the *Mademoiselle* prize story, "Sunday at the Mintons" (1952), where the narrator imagines with liberating joy the death of her brother and her own suicide. Plath wondered in a letter to her mother if the model for the brother, a boyfriend, would recognize his "dismembered self." As in her poetry, the anger expressed in her fiction is cathartic and clears away the obstacles to the renewal of her life.

The Bell Jar is a finely plotted novel full of vivid characters and written in the astringent but engaging style one expects from a poet as frank and observant as Plath. The atmosphere of hospitals and sickness, of incidents of bleeding and electrocution, set against images of confinement and liberation, unify the novel's imagery. Liberation is often associated with the sea; for example, the happiest memory of Esther Greenwood, the main character, is being with her father on a sunny beach. Death seems to her a "sweeping tide, rush[ing] me to sleep," but the sea is also life-giving: "the water had spat me up into the sun, the world was sparkling all about me like blue and green and yellow semiprecious stones." The novel's major image is the bell jar in which Esther must breathe her "own sour air." This image is augmented by other images of confinement, such as boxes, cages, prison rooms, or vans, and the medical school's "big glass bottles full of babies that had died before they were born."

The plot of *The Bell Jar* closely follows the events of Plath's own life in 1953–1954. The New York chapters (chapters 1–9) lead to a second section (chapters 10–13), which concerns her breakdown and suicide attempts; the third and final section (chapters 14–20) describes the development of a new, independent self. The novel's tone is set as Esther, nineteen years old, agonizes over newspaper stories about the death by electrocution of Julius and Ethel Rosenberg on charges of spying. The heat of New York and her fashionable new clothes make her as uncomfortable as her relationships with her colleagues and her career-woman boss. Her introduction to supposedly adult sexuality occurs when she and her sophisticated friend Doreen visit a disc jockey's apartment. As Esther is dozing off and and Doreen is flirting with Lenny, the disc jockey, Esther is startled by Lenny's scream and sees Doreen "hanging on to Lenny's left earlobe with her teeth." As Lenny and the half-naked Doreen continue to laugh and scream, Esther leaves and walks the forty-three blocks back to her hotel. In a scene of ritual rebirth that recalls poems such as "Fever 103°" or "Lady Lazarus," Esther takes a bath after this tawdry incident to feel pure again. Wrapping herself in "one of the big, soft white hotel bath towels," she says, "I felt pure and sweet as a new baby." But the essential phoniness of the New York fashion career world is as poisonous as the spoiled crabmeat that sickens the young editors who attend a luncheon in their honor. Esther's rejection of this world is symbolized when she goes to the roof of the hotel and throws her clothes off: "flutteringly, like a loved one's ashes, the gray scraps were ferried off, to settle here, there, exactly where I would never know, in the dark heart of New York."

On her return home Esther's mother tells her, in a scene where the autobiographical parallel is painfully evident, that her application for a creative-writing class has been rejected. She had thought of the course as a "safe bridge" over the summer, but now she sees the bridge dissolve "and a body in a white blouse and green skirt plummet into the gap." She thinks of writing a novel that would "fix a lot of people" but makes progress on neither the novel nor her honors thesis. She, of course, rejects her mother's suggestions that she learn something practical, like shorthand: "My mother had taught shorthand and typing to support us ever since my father died, and secretly she hated it and hated him for dying and leaving no money because he didn't trust life insurance salesmen." Nor is her boyfriend, Buddy Willard, any help. An intelligent but conventional medical student whom her mother admires,

Plath's grave in Heptonstall, Yorkshire, with her married name obliterated by vandals. The epitaph is from the Bhagavad Gita.

his sexual double standard disgusts Esther when he tells her of an affair with a waitress. The tuberculosis that Buddy contracts soon after he begins his medical training symbolizes his diseased inner state. Esther resolves to commit suicide following a visit to her father's grave "to pay my father back for all the years of neglect."

The book's macabre humor is evident as, with the application of a good student, she explores the efficacy as suicide methods of shooting, drowning, hanging, and slashing her wrists. She tries to drown herself twice, but the first time, when she feels the ocean's "mortal ache," her "flesh winced, in cowardice, from such a death." The second time the water is warmer: "I fanned myself down, but before I knew where I was, the water had spat me up into the sun." When she tries to hang herself, she discovers that she is "poor at knots" and that her house has the "wrong kind of ceilings." She therefore walks through the house, "the silk cord dangling from my neck like a yellow cat's tail and finding no place to fasten it." Esther finally chooses the unreliable method of swallowing sleeping pills in exactly the manner Plath did during her own life.

After her failed suicide Esther's rebirth begins under the guidance of Dr. Nolan. There are two key developments in her therapy. First, Esther learns that it is acceptable and even wholesome to express her anger, however irrational, with her mother. Sec-

ond, she learns that her sexual life need not mean bondage to one man and a married life. (Dr. Nolan prescribes a diaphragm for her.) The "discarding" of her virginity, however, is as violent as the scene with Doreen and the disc jockey or another New York scene, in which Esther's odious blind date, Marco, assaults her. Esther first has sexual intercourse with a mathematics professor while she is out on a pass from the asylum. The hemorrhaging it causes sends her to a hospital emergency room. After this incident her new independence and her rage at the professor's callous behavior help her to overcome the fear of displeasing a male that developed from her relationship with her father. An example of her new resolve is her insistence that the mathematics professor pay her emergency room bill.

The character who plays the most crucial role in her rebirth is a young woman named Joan Gilling, a patient at Esther's hospital. Although she is wealthy, Joan's background is otherwise similar to Esther's; she is a friend of Buddy Willard and his family and an academically successful student at Esther's college. Esther describes Joan's room at the asylum as "a mirror image of my own." Joan treasures the newspaper clippings about Esther's attempted suicide and speaks of committing suicide herself. Esther once again feels she is competing with another woman as they both strive to recover and win release from the hospital. Both fascinated and repelled by Joan's lesbianism, Esther rejects her friendship until Joan helps when Esther is suffering from her hemorrhage. Soon after, however, Joan commits suicide by hanging, and the symbolic function of her character as Esther's double becomes clear. As Plath's honors thesis and such poems as "Death & Co." show, she was fascinated by the concept of the double as a shadow self that one might fear but must also understand. When Joan kills herself she seems to eliminate Esther's suicidal impulses. At Joan's funeral Esther "listened to the old brag of my heart. I am, I am, I am." She thinks there should be "a ritual for being born twice" as she waits to go before the examining board. As the novel's last sentence suggests, the board provides this ritual: "all turned themselves toward me, and guiding myself by them, as by a magical thread, I stepped into the room."

The Bell Jar concludes with a spiritual rebirth in the protagonist that Plath herself could not achieve in 1963. When she died she had written some of the finest lyrics in modern English-language poetry. She had also completed a draft of a second novel, "Double Exposure" (Hughes said the manuscript disappeared in 1970), that may have promised an achievement in fiction to match hers in poetry. She was the mother of two bright, healthy children and was forming new friendships in London, yet the fullness of her life could not hold back the tides of depression. In one of her last poems — "Words," dated 1 February 1963 — she wrote of the fatality of such recurrent and despairing moods:

> Words dry and riderless. . . .
> From the bottom of the pool, fixed stars
> Govern a life.

Letters:

Letters Home: Correspondence, 1950–63, edited by Aurelia Schober Plath (New York: Harper & Row, 1975).

Bibliographies:

Gary Lane and Maria Stevens, *Sylvia Plath: A Bibliography* (Metuchen, N.J.: Scarecrow, 1978);
Stephen Tabor, *Sylvia Plath: An Analytical Bibliography* (London: Mansell, 1987);
Linda Wagner-Martin, *Sylvia Plath: The Critical Heritage* (London: Routledge & Kegan Paul, 1988);

Sheryl Meyering, *Sylvia Plath: A Reference Guide, 1973–88* (Boston: G. K. Hall, 1990).

Biographies:

Linda Wagner-Martin, *Sylvia Plath: A Biography* (New York & London: Simon & Schuster, 1987);
Anne Stevenson, *Bitter Fame: A Life of Sylvia Plath* (Boston: Houghton Mifflin, 1989);
Paul Alexander, *Rough Magic: A Biography of Sylvia Plath* (New York & London: Viking, 1991);
Ronald Hayman, *The Death and Life of Sylvia Plath* (London: Heinemann, 1991);
Jacqueline Rose, *The Haunting of Sylvia Plath* (London: Virago, 1991).

References:

A. Alvarez, "Prologue: Sylvia Plath," in his *The Savage God: A Study of Suicide* (New York: Random House, 1972), pp. 3–41;
Steven Gould Axelrod, *Sylvia Plath: The Wound and the Cure of Words* (Baltimore & London: Johns Hopkins University Press, 1990);
Harold Bloom, ed., *Sylvia Plath* (New York: Chelsea House, 1989);
Mary Lynn Broe, *Protean Poetic: The Poetry of Sylvia Plath* (Columbia & London: University of Missouri Press, 1980);
Judith Kroll, *Chapters in a Mythology: The Poetry of Sylvia Plath* (New York & London: Harper & Row, 1976);
Janet Malcolm, *The Silent Woman: Sylvia Plath and Ted Hughes* (New York: Knopf, 1994);
Diane Middlebrook, "The Enraged Muse," *Times Literary Supplement* (October 27–November 1989): 1179;
Marjorie Perloff, "The Two Ariels: The (Re)Making of the Sylvia Plath Canon," in her *Poetic License: Essays on Modernist and Postmodernist Lyric* (Evanston, Ill.: Northwestern University Press, 1990), pp. 308–334;
Linda Wagner-Martin, *The Bell Jar: A Novel of the Fifties* (New York: Twayne, 1992).

Papers:

The major collections of Sylvia Plath's papers are at the Lilly Library, Indiana University, Bloomington, and the Rare Book Room at Smith College.

Chaim Potok

(17 February 1929 –   )

S. Lillian Kremer
Kansas State University

See also the Potok entries in *DLB 28: Twentieth-Century American-Jewish Fiction Writers* and *DLB Yearbook: 1984.*

BOOKS: *The Chosen* (New York: Simon & Schuster, 1967; London: Heinemann, 1967);

The Promise (New York: Knopf, 1969; London: Heinemann, 1970);

My Name Is Asher Lev (New York: Knopf, 1972; London: Heinemann, 1972);

In the Beginning (New York: Knopf, 1975; London: Heinemann, 1976);

The Jew Confronts Himself in American Literature (Hales Corners, Wis.: Sacred Heart School of Theology, 1975);

Wanderings: Chaim Potok's History of the Jews (New York: Knopf, 1978; London: Hutchinson, 1979);

The Book of Lights (New York: Knopf, 1981; London: Heinemann, 1982);

Davita's Harp (New York: Knopf, 1985);

Ethical Living for a Modern World: Jewish Insights (New York: Jewish Theological Seminary of America, 1985);

Theo Tobiasse: Artist in Exile (New York: Rizzoli, 1986);

The Gift of Asher Lev (New York: Knopf, 1990; London: Heinemann, 1990);

I Am the Clay (New York: Knopf, 1992; London: Heinemann, 1992);

The Tree of Here (New York: Knopf, 1993);

The Sky of Now (New York: Knopf, 1994).

Chaim Potok, rabbi and critical scholar of Judaic texts, has demonstrated in his literary career that the American novel is indeed a viable genre for writing about Jewish theology, liturgy, history, and scholarship. He has brought to American fiction a feeling for biblical exegesis, Talmudic study, and the mystical writings of the Cabala and Zohar. Born 17 February 1929 in New York to Polish Jewish immigrants Mollie Friedman and Benjamin Max

Potok, the novelist spent his formative years in a traditional Jewish home and parochial schools. A transformative experience of early adolescence, reading Evelyn Waugh's *Brideshead Revisited* (1945), provided major direction for his creative work. Potok recognized in Waugh's writing the capacity of literature to transport readers into cultural environments foreign from their own and determined that fiction would be his vehicle to present Jewish civilization in American literature. With that end in mind, he undertook a rigorous religious and secular education at Yeshiva University, where he earned a B.A. summa cum laude in 1950; at the Jewish Theological Seminary of America, where he received the Hebrew Literature Prize, Homiletics Prize, Bible Prize, the M.H.L. degree, and rabbinic ordination in 1954; and at the University of Pennsylvania, where he earned a Ph.D. in philosophy in 1965.

Unlike his fellow Jewish American novelists, to whom scholarship in Judaica has been of peripheral interest, Potok stands in the European tradition of Sholem Aleichem, Isaac Loeb Peretz, and Chaim Nachman Bialick, pursuing a Judaic professional role in conjunction with that of the creative artist. Following service as a U.S. Army chaplain in Korea with a front-line medical battalion and a combat engineer battalion in 1955–1957, Potok married Adena Sarah Mosevitzky and began a distinguished teaching and publication career in Jewish studies. He taught at the University of Judaism in Los Angeles (1957–1959); served as scholar in residence at Har Zion Temple in Philadelphia (1959–1963); and taught at the Jewish Theological Seminary Teacher's Institute (1963–1964). His publishing career has included positions as editor of *Conservative Judaism* (1964–1965) and associate editor for the Jewish Publication Society in 1965 and special projects editor since 1974. In his role as special projects editor for the Jewish Publication Society, he has collaborated with other scholars and rabbis to prepare the new authorized translation of *The Torah* (1962), *The Prophets* (1978), and *The Writings* (1982). Potok

Chaim Potok (photograph © Jerry Bauer)

acted as committee secretary for the final volume, coordinating the translation. *Wanderings: Chaim Potok's History of the Jews* (1978) is a compendium of scholarship about Jewish civilization and its relation to the myriad cultures with which Judaism has come into contact. As in the novels, Potok's structural scheme in this historic study is cultural encounter: exploring Jewish engagement with Egypt, Greece, Rome, Christianity, Islam, and modern secularism. The novelist's scholarly and critical articles have appeared in *Commentary,* the *Saturday Review of Literature, The New York Times, Conservative Judaism,* the *Reconstructionist,* and *American Judaism.*

Commitment to Judaism and the influence of Waugh, James Joyce, and Flannery O'Connor are evident in Potok's efforts to show characters in relation to God and to dramatize the importance of religion in a secular age and society. His characters, like Waugh's and Joyce's, display a strong sense of continuity with national history and are often presented against a backdrop of the demands of

family, community, and religion. Furthermore, the *Brideshead Revisited* interplay of two sensitive, intelligent young men of parallel yet divergent interests has become Potok's major character construct. The genesis and substance of every Potok novel, until *I Am the Clay* (1992), is Jewish religious, historic, and cultural experience in a non-Judaic world. Potok's philosophical and ethical views – his affirmative vision, veneration of life, positive assessment of human nature, and pervasive striving for meaning in the midst of chaos and for good in the face of evil – derive from Judaism. He joins other Jewish American novelists in advocating the Jewish view of a sanctified world and enduring and noble humanity, revealing a vital philosophy to counter twentieth-century alienation and despair. His characters are conversant with Jewish theology, liturgy, and rabbinic commentaries, and it is through these intellectual resources and their life experiences that they strive to comprehend the human condition. They are frequently presented in the context of synagogue, Yeshiva, and observant Jewish homes, occupied in prayer, study, and communal service. Unlike the assimilationist goals of the Jews about whom Saul Bellow and Philip Roth write, when Potok's Jews enter the secular world, they maintain orthodox private lives. That Potok stands alone among Jewish American novelists in the realm of Judaic studies becomes evident in comparison of his schoolroom scenes with those of other writers. Potok transforms Judaic scholarship to drama. Whether through Talmudic debate presented to an entire congregation or in private tutorial sessions or in the context of classroom discussion and dialogue, Potok's delineation of Hebrew higher education is superb. After many early education scenes limited to ineffectual instructors and recalcitrant young boys, it is refreshing to encounter Potok's able treatment of serious scholarship, progressing beyond the rudiments of Hebrew to Talmudic tractate and textual emendation.

The recurrent theme of Potok's fictional universe is, as he observed in an interview for *Studies in American Jewish Literature* (1984), "the interplay of the Jewish tradition with the secular twentieth-century." He writes of Jews "who are at the very heart of their Judaism and at the same time . . . encountering elements that are at the very heart of the umbrella civilization." Moreover, through the roles of artist and scholar, Potok also explores the tension inside the religious community. In *The Chosen* (1967) and *The Promise* (1969) two sets of core-to-core confrontations evolve: first within the context of Orthodox Judaism between traditionalists and Hasidim; and the second between religious orthodoxy and Western secular humanism. In *My Name Is Asher Lev* (1972) and *The Gift of Asher Lev* (1990) the confrontation is with Western art; in *In the Beginning* (1975), with scientific biblical criticism and modern Western anti-Semitism; in *The Book of Lights* (1981), with the Orient and the destructive implications of atomic physics; and in *Davita's Harp* (1985), with communism. Each of the novels considers whether American Jewry has succumbed to secularism or has used its freedom to reeducate itself, as Potok writes in *Wanderings: Chaim Potok's History of the Jews* (1978), "to rebuild its core from the treasures of our past, fuse it with the best in secularism, and create a new philosophy, a new literature, a new world of Jewish art, a new community, and take seriously the word *emancipation.*"

The Chosen examines contemporary Jewish American Orthodox identity. The Crown Heights–Williamsburg section of Brooklyn, an area heavily populated by Jews, is the setting for a religious conflict. The antagonists are Hasidim, known for their mystical interpretation of Judaic sources and intense devotion to their spiritual leaders, and Orthodox Jews, who emphasize a rational, intellectual approach to Judaic law and theology. The supportive relationship which later develops between two boys, one Hasidic and the other Orthodox, begins in strife, dramatized in a quintessentially American baseball rivalry. The Hasidic zealots are led by Danny Saunders, son of a charismatic leader, and the traditional Orthodox team is led by Reuven Malter, son of a modern scholar who applies textual explication to Talmud studies. An injury sustained by Reuven at Danny's hands is the catalyst which brings the boys together and exposes each to the other's father and to the antithetical religious practices of the other. The novel chronicles the boys' experiences and reactions as sons of fathers who strive to sustain religious life and tradition in a predominantly secular age and society. The elder Malter, patterned after the novelist's beloved father-in-law, Max Isaac Mosevitzsky, is the idealized Jewish teacher, a dedicated scholar and humanitarian. Just as he fuses the best in Judaic scholarship with the best in secular culture, his son combines intellectual excellence in sacred and secular studies, complementing Talmudic studies with forays into symbolic logic, mathematics, and secular philosophy. In marked contrast to the Malters' relationship is the strained silence between Reb Saunders and Danny, who is meant to succeed his father as Hasidic spiritual leader. Counterpointing the intellectual exploration Malter encourages is Reb Saunders's circumscribed grooming of Danny for his dynastic role. Convinced that it is dangerous to relegate the soul to the dominance of the mind, Saunders uses silence to teach Danny the value of heart and soul. When they are not engaged in Talmudic study, Saunders builds a wall of silence between them in an effort to strengthen Danny's soul through suffering and thereby help ready him to assume the burdens of his followers. Reb Saunders fails. Although Danny remains an observant Jew, he rejects the traditional role of spiritual guide and becomes instead its secular counterpart, a clinical psychologist.

In addition to using religious and scholarly interests to authenticate the Jewish milieu in *The Chosen*, Potok parallels his youths' inner quests for Jewish identity with historic events: the demonic Nazi mission to destroy Jewry and the search for physical and spiritual salvation in a Jewish national homeland. Although the Holocaust remains a muted topic in this first novel, it is presented as a hovering pestilence in the larger context of America at war.

Potok links the Holocaust and the creation of the State of Israel, a theme to which he will return in later works. The final third of the novel is narrated in the context of the Zionist struggle, and the experiences of the characters are intimately bound with that of Israel. Out of the ashes, Malter insists, new life must emerge. The only meaning to be derived from the destruction of one-third of world Jewry is the rebirth of a nation, the Zionist goal of the establishment of a Jewish state in its ancient territory. Beyond its thematic import, Zionism is integrated into the novel's dramatic conflict between the Malters and Reb Saunders, who predictably supports a post-Messianic Israel and bitterly denounces secular Zionism. The novel concludes emblematically with chapter 18. In Hebrew this number is transcribed *chai*, which also spells the word *life*. In this manner Potok symbolically suggests a renaissance for the Jewish people in the State of Israel and a new beginning for Danny in psychology and Reuven in rabbinic studies.

In *The Promise* the novelist continues to trace the careers of the two friends and the influence of their fathers. Reuven is preparing for rabbinical ordination at an Orthodox seminary while Danny is adjusting to secular life in pursuit of a psychology degree at Columbia University. Shorn of beard, earlocks, and Hasidic garb, Danny nevertheless remains a Hasid in spirit. Paralleling his separation from his traditional Hasidic role in *The Chosen* is his departure from orthodox psychiatric practice in the sequel. Reuven continues to work in Judaic studies but is faced with the dilemma of opposing his traditional instructor's insistence that he remain true to classic Talmudic scholarship and refrain from using modern textual criticism. Danny adapts Reb Saunders's technique for creative suffering through silence to clinical psychology, and Reuven adopts his father's critical method to elucidate the Talmud. Although Reb Saunders's dominating presence is somewhat diminished in *The Promise,* David Malter's parental and scholarly influence is extended. Just as the fathers defined themselves within the Jewish context, the sons find their elemental and existential purpose in Judaism, despite the incursion of secular interests in their lives. Every struggle is undertaken within the sphere of a dynamic Judaism, and the characters define and understand themselves as twentieth-century Jews.

As in the first novel, the dramatic conflict and thematic emphasis are in the arena of Judaic scholarship. *The Promise* explores the relationship and distinctions between Orthodox and Conservative Judaism. Using a structural scheme reminiscent of medieval morality drama, the novelist casts his rabbinical student at the center of discord. Reuven is at odds with a key member of his ordination committee, a fundamentalist who fears and resents the student's preference for his father's critical method of analyzing and emendating texts. The teacher views such critical emendation as sacrilege and enlists Reuven's assistance to help him understand the method so as to discredit it in the Orthodox scholarly press. Reuven is drawn into further conflict with his fundamentalist teachers when he challenges the rabbinic court's decree against studying the works of and befriending the radical scholar Abraham Gordon.

In addition to characters and themes, the sequel is also linked to its predecessor by its use of the structural device of a game to engage principal characters. Unfortunately, the device which served Potok so vibrantly in the first novel pales by comparison in the second, in which it is less carefully integrated. In *The Promise* a carnival pitch game is employed to introduce another father-and-son duet, the Gordons. Michael Gordon, an emotionally disturbed youngster who is to become Danny Saunders's patient, correlates a carnival barker's misrepresentation of his score with the unjust vilification his father has suffered in the Orthodox press and rabbinic court which has excommunicated him for heretical publications. The child relates the dishonest pitchman to the authors of vitriolic attacks against his father, critics who argue that the apostate Gordon is lethal to Judaism, a threat to scripture and religion. On a metaphoric level the game is emblematic of the core-to-core conflict within contemporary Judaism, a conflict between those who read scripture as divine revelation and those who insist on human attribution.

Potok further contrasts Hasidic and Conservative factions by juxtaposing their social and religious customs in the betrothal and marriage of Danny Saunders and Rachel Gordon. Accused by critics of having presented an unduly bleak portrayal of Hasidic life in *The Chosen,* Potok in *The Promise* writes about Hasidic joy and enthusiasm, the tumultuous song and dance of the betrothal and wedding feasts.

Potok's third novel, *My Name Is Asher Lev,* is a traditional initiation novel that charts the coming-of-age of an artist living in a Hasidic society inherently hostile to his vocation. As Danny Saunders abandons the role of Hasidic spiritual leader for that of secular healer, so Asher Lev rejects his designated role of Hasidic emissary for his career as an artist. Potok again uses the first-person narrative of his previous novels and achieves immediacy and vividness through the artist's retrospective portrait of his childhood. The pretext for the narrative is Lev's response to Hasidic detractors to whom he has become "the notorious and legendary Lev of the Brooklyn Crucifixion" due to a painting that particularly upset his community. The mature Lev offers a reexamination of his attitudes and the external forces that shaped his vision and judgment. Since artistic development is the subject of the novel, Asher's central position is juxtaposed with those who precipitate his nonconformity to Hasidic demands and discipline. Although Lev remains an observant Jew, the community judges him guilty of betraying his religious heritage and encroaching upon a tradition sacred to Christianity. He is labeled "a traitor, an apostate, a self-hater, an inflicter of shame" upon his family, his friends, and his people.

Juxtaposed to the self-absorbed artist are the Ladover Hasidim, a sect patterned on the Lubavitcher Jews, who, after fleeing European persecution, settled in the Crown Heights section of Brooklyn to rebuild their community. Among Asher's ancestors are the Rebbe of Berdichev, a celebrated Hasidic leader, and a grandfather recognized as a genius, "a dweller in the study halls and synagogues, and academies," who uprooted his family and journeyed to a distant Russian town to join the Ladover Hasidim and eventually became their Russian emissary. The artist's father, Aryeh Lev, continued his father's work and expanded it from national to international proportions as history warranted. In European cities, where Jews had suffered enormous losses, Aryeh created centers of Hasidic learning. Similarly, Asher's mother, Rivkeh, carries on the mission of her brother, killed in an accident while on a mission for the Rebbe. Beyond disappointment in their son's failure to work in behalf of Jewish causes, the Levs despair of his dedication to art, considering it blasphemous at worst and mere indulgence of personal vanity at best. Asher persistently defies his father's demand that he sacrifice art to religion, and a deep rift develops between them.

Consumed with self-doubt and guilt, the aspiring artist suffers nightmares in which his grandfather, the "mythic ancestor," accuses him of failing to continue the family tradition of service. The ancestor's nocturnal visits recur intermittently and in a manner reflecting Asher's transgressions, ranging from a mild admonition for "playing, drawing, wasting time" to a formidable rebuke for his refusal to join the family in Vienna on a Hasidic mission. Paradoxically, while most in the community associate the artist's gift with the demonic, the current Rebbe understands the magnitude of Asher's talent. Because the spiritual guide regards Asher's ability as a divine gift, he intervenes by forbidding the father to uproot the son and by engaging a mentor, Jacob Kahn, for the young artist. Under the sculptor-painter's tutelage Asher undergoes a program of expansion and discovery which introduces him to the subjects and modes of Western art and transports him from the religious to the secular world. Whereas to Asher progress toward self-realization as an artist demands that he learn to paint in the Western tradition of nudes and crucifixions, to his father that activity is an abomination, an abandonment of Torah and Talmud. Where the artist son sees the cross as an aesthetic mold stripped of Christological import, the father sees a river of Jewish blood replenished throughout a two-thousand-year history of Christian anti-Semitism.

The artist's torment, resulting from conflict between critical and public acclaim offset by family and Hasidic denunciation, is expressed in the "Brooklyn Crucifixion," a portrayal of his mother in a posture of agony, waiting for the warring husband and son to return home in peace. In the painter's mind "Brooklyn Crucifixion" expresses not religious martyrdom but the tragic division he has imposed upon the family. He uses the form of the cross because, as Potok remarked in a 1978 *Christianity Today* interview, he finds no comparable "aesthetic mold in his own religious tradition into which he could pour a painting of ultimate anguish and torment." "For Asher Lev," Potok explains, "the cross is the aesthetic motif for solitary protracted torment." Informed by the Rebbe that he must leave the community to which he has brought much pain, Asher envisions his Russian ancestor and experiences an epiphany of the divine and demonic possibilities of the creative impulse. He is now ready for a new beginning, ready to join forces with the ancestor and express the world's anguish, ready to use his artistic talents to give shape and form to human pain. Thus, Asher Lev shares with James Joyce's Stephen Dedalus the knowledge that his vocation as an artist demands a period of exile. Potok, like Joyce, treats the artist's isolation and alienation from family, school, and religious community, culminating in exile, as a progressive step that will lead to reconciliation of the artist's spiritual and aesthetic natures.

Potok's portrait of an artist as young Hasid reveals a powerful Joycean influence of subject, structure, and mythic patterning. His use of interior monologue, stream-of-consciousness techniques,

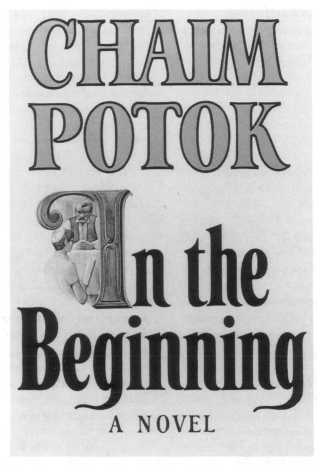

Dust jacket for Potok's 1975 novel, in which a young Jewish boy comes
to terms with American anti-Semitism and the Holocaust

and epiphany clearly reveal his indebtedness to Joyce. Corresponding to Joyce's fusion of the religionational perspective through Catholic Irish history and Greek mythology is Potok's incorporation of Jewish history and biblical and Joycean allusion and analogy. Not only does Potok satisfy the anticipated Daedalus-Icarus parallel with the analogous Kahn-Lev and mythic ancestor–Lev relationships, he further enriches the novel's symbolic implications by casting the biological father-son relationship in the Abraham-Isaac mold. Lev, like Stephen, is shaped by the religious and political beliefs of his community, yet he resists total absorption by the forces and values that define his community and expresses his reservation as artist-quester in exile.

Potok's autobiographical fourth novel, *In the Beginning,* fuses his interests in Jewish education and twentieth-century history, a history that has violently touched his family. The novelist's parents, described in *Wanderings* as "the bearded young man who hated Poles and Russians and the lovely young woman who was nearly raped by cossacks," mi-

grated to America "from the apocalypse that was eastern Europe after the Bolshevik Revolution and the First World War." Benjamin Max Potok, who "saw himself mirrored in the eyes of most American gentiles as a Jewish Caliban," is the model for Max Lurie, the novel's militant Jew who learned while serving as a Polish soldier that Gentile Poles wanted him, not as an equal, but as a scapegoat, ever ripe for persecution. A postwar pogrom, which was the elder Potok's reward for service to his country, is the fate of the fictional Lurie brothers and the occasion for the murder of the protagonist's uncle.

In this novel, as is typically the case in Potok's fictional universe, the young Jewish boy from whose perspective the tale is told has a broader view of international history than has generally been true of characters in American fiction. Reflective of Potok's own experience, David Lurie is a studious, thoughtful child, whose status as a child of immigrants makes him more sensitive to European influences on American life and policy than are Huck Finn and Holden Caulfield. Although *In the Begin-*

ning contains familiar Potokian material – an articulate friendship between two sensitive, intelligent boys and positive mentor-student and father-son relationships – it also explores new issues, closely examining anti-Semitic forces that impinge on the Jewish consciousness. Whereas contact with secular society was limited in the Hasidic and Orthodox enclaves of the early fiction's Williamsburg locale, this novel is set in a multiethnic Bronx neighborhood like that in which Potok was reared. Because Potok intends to show the violent gentile impact on his young protagonist, more often than not the settings are bustling sidewalks, schoolyards, commercial districts, and the zoo, with the short counterpoint scenes staged in the traditional Potokian environments of home, library, synagogue, and classroom.

Alternately bitter and melancholic in tone, *In the Beginning* reflects Jewish despair in the wake of Depression- and Holocaust-era anti-Semitism. The corresponding pathologies of Christian and Nazi anti-Semitic evils emerge from what Potok in 1978 called "the dark underbelly of Western civilization." David Lurie is the object of Polish American anti-Semitic outbursts that correspond, in a diminutive form, to the abuse his father suffered in Poland. David's childhood nemesis is Eddie Kulanski, the product of an evolutionary process whose "hatred bore the breeding of a thousand years." He hates Jews with a "kind of mindless demonic rage." Characteristic of Potok's historicity is his treatment of anti-Semitism in the Bronx Zoo ambush of the unsuspecting David. "For Christ's sake" is the rallying cry employed by Eddie Kulanski and his cousin as they unwittingly echo the Crusaders – who went about their sacred business of rampage, plunder, rape, and murder of European Jewry in the process of freeing the Holy Land from infidels – and of their descendants throughout the many centuries of Christian anti-Semitic rage. Through the microcosm of Kulanski's persecution of David that begins with boorish harassment and progresses to repeated attempts to push David and his tricycle into oncoming traffic, Potok suggests a parallel writ small to European anti-Semitic escalations from encroachment of civil rights to denial of human rights, culminating in genocide.

A measure of Potok's craftsmanship in the fourth novel is his integration of public event and private drama in a stream-of-consciousness segment. When David hears a graphic account of the 1929 Hebron Massacre, he is overwhelmed by visions of innocent Jewish scholars, "shot, stabbed, and chopped to pieces. . . . their eyes pierced and their hands cut off . . . burned to death inside their homes and inside the Hadassah Hospital." The irony of Jews fleeing European persecution only to be slaughtered in Palestine is the catalyst for a stream-of-consciousness reprisal vision in which the impotent child revels in his father's militant response to the Cossacks who had "Jewish blood on their sabers . . . Jewish flesh on their whips." In this sequence Potok skillfully fuses anti-Semitic references, David's recollection of a photograph of an armed secret Jewish self-defense league, allusions to the Lemberg Pogrom in which his uncle lost his life, and an attack on his father in the presence of fellow soldiers by a bandit confident that wounding a Jewish soldier would provoke no retribution from his Polish countrymen. These memories merge with David's own anti-Semitic encounters that parallel those of Potok's youth.

The natural blending of liturgy, political demonstration, and folkloric imagery patterns in this novel reflects the author's maturing talent. Exemplary is his introduction of the Holocaust in the context of a Yom Kippur memorial prayer in which David mourns the death of a Nazi victim as he chants the ancient lament for the martyrdom of Roman-era Torah sages. As Holocaust news is released, David enters an imaginary realm reflecting contemporary horrors. He retreats into the dark rectangle of a window shade containing his visions of Nazi demonstrations with flags, banners, and twenty thousand brown-shirted men shouting and saluting. The acceleration of wartime atrocities is evoked through Potok's deft fusion of nightmarish imagery with mythic legend. In the recesses of David's imagination he and the Golem of Prague, a legendary Jewish protector, heroically demolish demonstrations, quell the Nazi rage, and spy on Nazi strategy sessions. Finally, the boy becomes the dream hero, the savior of God's word. He battles smoke and flame to rescue endangered Torah scrolls from a burning synagogue. These fantasies, through their sharply etched contrast with reality, evocatively address the impotence of the Jews to halt Germany's genocidal endeavor. Potok effectively links the Holocaust with earlier historic manifestations of anti-Semitism through the integration of the golem legend with the traditional Passover liturgy. During the Passover Seder celebrating the historic deliverance of the Israelites from Egyptian bondage, David prays for another Moses, a historic deliverer to replace his weary, ineffectual imaginary warrior. These references to the mythology and history of the Jews are splendidly woven into the dramatic context of the novel.

Consistent with his John Dos Passos–style use of journalistic headline juxtaposed with private experience to render contemporary Jewish history in the earlier novels, Potok evokes the impact of the Holocaust through reference to newspaper photographs of Bergen-Belsen. David Lurie, as Potok describes his own experience in *Wanderings,* learned the truth of the camps from "newspaper photographs, memorial assemblies, the disbelief in the faces of friends, the shock as news came of death and more death." Like the novelist's own family, the Luries suffered enormous losses: more than 150 family members perished. Potok's "father's rage" and "mother's soft endless weeping" are the models for Max Lurie's anger and Ruth's grief. Although Potok has not yet confronted the Holocaust directly in his fiction, its ever increasing presence in the novels through the introduction of survivor characters and its impact on American Jews attests to the author's conviction, expressed in *Wanderings,* that "the Jew sees all his contemporary history through the ocean of blood that is the Holocaust." Only when he writes of the photographs of "hills of corpses, pits of bones, the naked rubble of the dead, and the staring eyes and hollow faces of the survivors" and when David imagines the trains that crossed Europe, behind whose sealed doors he sees "a multitude of writhing human beings packed together riding in filth and terror," does Potok treat Holocaust atrocities graphically.

Potok is one of a select group of American novelists who have related the Holocaust to the revitalization of Judaism. Two major aspects of this phenomenon, American Judaic scholarship and support for Israel as a Jewish nation, have been among Potok's recurring themes. *In the Beginning* presents both, exemplified in the son's dedication to biblical scholarship and the father's active support of Israel. David's motivation to pursue a career in biblical criticism employing techniques held suspect by fundamentalists is the same that Potok in 1978 attributed to his friends who entered the field "to change the attitude of the discipline toward Jews." Like the scholar-novelist himself, whose work in biblical studies and translation is acclaimed, the protagonist loves Torah and determines to use the tools of its detractors to prove them wrong, to demonstrate that the Hebrew Bible is, indeed, a light to the nations. The second component of the Potok equation for a revitalized Jewry, a vibrant Israel, is Max Lurie's cause. Like Potok's father, who supported the Revisionist Party and Vladimir Jabotinsky in efforts to gain home rule for Jews and Israeli independence from British

dominion, Max is a fervent supporter of the struggle to assert Jewish rights.

Attention to Potok's interest in post-Holocaust revival of Judaism clarifies the novel's biblical analogies. From its title, which is a translation of *Berashit,* the Hebrew word which begins Genesis, to the novel's structural parallel with the subject of Genesis, Potok draws thematic and allusive connections regarding the relationship of the Jewish people with surrounding Gentile societies. Similarly, Potok's portrayal of Judaism emerging from the Holocaust to rebirth in America and Israel parallels the conclusion of Genesis when Joseph recapitulates the lesson of his career, teaching that God brings good out of evil, that he will deliver the Jewish people out of Egypt and bring them to the land he promised the patriarchs. Significantly, it is during the worst period of Jewish suffering of the Holocaust that the nineteen-year-old David recalls his Bar Mitzvah Torah portion and its accompanying prophetic reading, passages recounting the entry of the Jews into Egypt and the promise of the restoration of Israel.

Although the characters are now older, *The Book of Lights* continues the Potokian pattern of exploring ideas through the juxtaposition of scholarly males. Two young rabbis, Gershon Loran and Arthur Leiden, are followed from their seminary studies at Riverside Hebrew Institute, a thinly veiled portrayal of Potok's old school, the Jewish Theological Seminary, through their search for meaning in the Judaic tradition while living in a secular society. The narrative is presented from the point of view of Gershon Loran, who started rabbinic study in the traditional Talmudic fashion and was drawn to Cabala, Jewish mysticism, by a brilliant teacher modeled on the famous scholar Gershom Scholem and by his readings in the Zohar, a thirteenth-century Jewish mystical text. Arthur Leiden travels the road to the rabbinate indirectly, by way of penance for what he perceives to be his father's sins.

The influence of Waugh's *Brideshead Revisited* on Potok's method of character interaction and thematic development is nowhere more evident than in this novel as Potok emulates Waugh's pattern of placing young men of divergent backgrounds in one another's paths. Loran, orphaned as a child when his parents were killed in Jerusalem, has been reared in an economically depressed Brooklyn neighborhood by an impoverished aunt and uncle who are mourning a son killed in World War II. His life is bleak until, at age sixteen, he experiences a vision of radiance, an epiphany that creates a feeling of being "all caught up in the life of heaven and

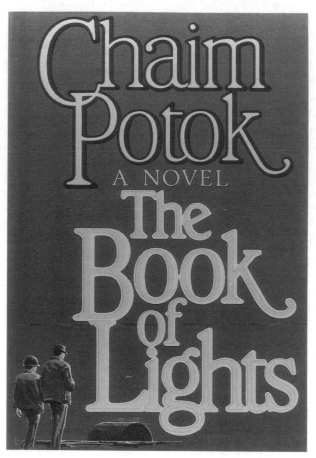

*Dust jacket for Potok's 1981 novel, in which a rabbi finds renewed
meaning through Cabala, Jewish mysticism*

earth, in the mystery of creation." He studies Cabala to recapture the awesome enlightenment of the epiphanal moment. While the Leidens are not members of a social aristocracy comparable to Waugh's upper-class Britons, they are members of an American aristocracy of talent, respected members of the intellectual and scientific elite. Mrs. Leiden is a professor of art history, and her husband is a prominent physicist. Among their friends are Albert Einstein, Edward Teller, Enrico Fermi, and Leo Szilard. Troubled by his father's role in atomic research, Arthur Leiden seeks the religious life not, like Loran, as a result of a transforming experience but in expiation for another's transgression. Leiden's dialogue provides a new discordant tone in Potok's fiction. Juxtaposed with moral introspection and exclamation are satiric barbs, invective, and vulgar colloquialism that register Leiden's fury at his atomic heritage – a legacy that fills him with memories of incinerated birds in his Los Alamos backyard and incinerated people in Hiroshima. Through Leiden's plight Potok grapples with the terrible truths of our time, the reality of a promising technological age which delivered devastation.

As Waugh's young men leave idyllic Oxford to make their way in the world, so do Potok's characters leave the haven of the Hebrew Institute to gain worldly knowledge. Like their creator, the characters begin their rabbinic careers by serving as army chaplains in Korea. Again mirroring Potok's experience, they find great beauty in the "pagan" world of Japan. Both are distraught by the bombing of Hiroshima, and Loran is further saddened by Leiden's death in an airplane crash. Although Leiden would have accepted his death as symbolic expiation for his father's nuclear weapons research, Loran is distressed by the capriciousness of the penitent's death and is unable to pray. His solace eventually comes from Cabala and the advice from a Talmudist who convinces him that the study of mystical texts also fulfills God's law. The adviser supports Loran's mystical and scholarly predilection by reiterating Potok's recurrent thesis: "the scientific study of sacred texts is a sacred act." Loran's ability to pray returns following a visit to the site of his epiphany, where he reaches the deepest recesses of self and hears the voice of his departed friend urging him to reject nothingness and search for meaning. Now, as at Hiroshima, the answer lies in the Jewish reverence for life expressed in the inspiring words of the Kaddish, the sacred public affirmation of God. He prays ardently for the broken people of his generation and for future generations and invokes the principle of *tikkun* (repair), the observant Jew's obligation to help mend a flawed world, thereby sharing in God's work. Appropriately, the novel concludes in the Jewish New Year season, a time of spiritual introspection, repentance, mercy, and forgiveness. The spiritual quester concludes his solemn New Year devotion with the decision to journey to Jerusalem, the religious center of Judaism, to study the mystical texts with his spiritual mentor.

In his search for the meaning of human experience, Potok has, in this novel, moved outward spatially, thematically, and technically from his traditional Orthodox environments of New York to the Orient, from the Talmudic intellectual core of traditional Judaism to the mystical sphere of Cabala. Although he employs the traditional literary convention of the spiritual quest, he situates the quest in new territory, having his protagonist experience the grandeur of God's creation in the Orient before furthering his quest in Jerusalem. Departing from his successful delineation of the dynamics of studying a page of Talmud, Potok undertakes the aesthetic challenge of rendering the dynamics of a page of Cabala, of creating visions and the interplay of people in the visions.

A significant departure from the Potokian male-dominated world of Judaic scholarship appears in *Davita's Harp* (1985). Although female scholars appear in Potok's fictional universe – Ruth Gordon of *The Promise,* Rivka Lev in *My Name Is Asher Lev,* and Elizabeth Leiden in *The Book of Lights* – and young women of intellectual promise are found – Rachel Gordon of *The Promise* and Karen Levin in *The Book of Lights* – it is not until *Davita's Harp* that Potok focuses on female characters and develops an intellectually gifted young woman's point of view. His protagonist, Ilana Davita Chandal, is influenced by contradicting philosophies of her father, Michael Chandal, a Gentile Yankee committed to the Communist Party and killed in the Spanish civil war at Guernica, and her mother, Channah (Annie), an apostate Jew who abandoned the ancestral faith of her stern Hasidic father for Marxism until the Hitler-Stalin nonaggression pact, Stalin's trials and purges,

and her daughter's interest provoked her return to Judaism. The novel focuses on Davita's intellectual and spiritual journey, exploring the young woman's responses to the political and religious forces that shape her: her encounter with communism during the Spanish civil war, the religious teaching of her missionary aunt and yeshiva teachers, and her subsequent adoption of and confrontation with patriarchal Orthodox Judaism. Following her exposure to Judaism through her Crown Heights Orthodox Jewish neighbors, Davita begins to attend the neighborhood synagogue and attends a Jewish parochial school, where she is a brilliant student and becomes increasingly observant.

Potok engages feminism as two generations of women, Davita and her mother, encounter discrimination in Orthodox Jewish practice that excuses or excludes women from obligatory prayer, ritual, and study that observant men must perform. Illustrative of the discrimination women experience in Orthodox Judaism is prohibition against women reciting the Kaddish, the mourner's prayer, an obligatory duty for men. This humiliation, paradoxically, accounts for Channah's return to Judaism and awakens Davita to the second-class status of women in Orthodox Judaism. While they defy one prohibition in the synagogue, Davita to recite the prayer for her father and Channah to recite it for her friend, they suffer defeat in the yeshiva. Davita's pivotal disillusionment with Orthodoxy occurs at the novel's climax. Modeled on the experience of Potok's wife, who was deprived of her earned position as yeshiva valedictorian, Davita is deprived of the Akiva Award for academic excellence on the grounds that girls cannot be seen to be more capable of academic performance in the yeshiva than are boys. Although she does not forsake the Jewish community for this indignity, she does decide to abandon her plans to attend a Jewish high school in favor of a secular school. Through the experience of Davita and her mother, Potok approaches the problem of contemporary Orthodox Judaism within which women are struggling to play an active and meaningful role. By his sympathetic rendition of the aggrieved woman's point of view and female characters who choose to remain religious despite sexist discrimination, Potok suggests that the rights of Jewish women must be accommodated from within the context of Judaism. Although he does not suggest that men and women will be equal in Orthodox Judaism, through Davita's continued affiliation to the Jewish community the possibility exists for either some level of accommodation or association with another branch of Judaism. Speculating about a sequel to the novel in a 1986 interview, Potok mused that Davita will become a writer, journey to the Soviet Union, experience a break with fundamentalism, but remain a traditional non-Orthodox Jewess.

In *The Gift of Asher Lev* (1990) the reader meets the artist during a midlife and midcareer crisis. By the beginning of the novel he has achieved a balance between his religious beliefs and the imperatives of art during his twenty-year exile in France. During this time he has been an observant member of the French Ladover community and a painter of international renown. Following the charge of his mythic ancestor in *My Name Is Asher Lev* to "Paint the anguish of all the world," Lev has learned something of anguish from his wife, who shares with him her Holocaust-wrought pain of years in a sealed apartment after her parents' arrest in the July 1942 roundup of Parisian Jews. In contrast to his earlier work, which mirrors the psychological pain of his family tensions, Lev's exilic paintings and drawings depict suffering produced by the century's political and social outrages. His subjects include the face of a student clubbed by the Parisian riot police, a terrorist on trial in Italy for assassinating the minister of justice, a survivor of Hiroshima, an Indian woman on a reservation in South Dakota, a homeless black man in New York, and a legless man in his hovel in South Africa. Yet, despite decades of critical acclaim, he has arrived at an artistic impasse, and reviewers are now faulting his work as repetitious.

Returning to Brooklyn for his beloved Uncle Yitzchok's funeral, Lev is once again plunged into communal and familial conflict. The balance he achieved between his religious and artistic loyalties in France is threatened by the New York community's disapproval. As he wrestles with his own artistic block, Asher's crisis is compounded by his uncle's directive that he, rather than his cousins, control the uncle's formidable art collection and by the enigmatic demands of the community's spiritual leader. The "gift," which had signified the painter's artistic talent in the first Lev novel, assumes a new connotation in the sequel. Since the childless Rebbe will appoint Lev's father as his successor only if he is assured that a dynastic line will follow, he asks for the gift of Lev's son for the Hasidic community. Descendant of maternal grandparents who perished in the Holocaust and of paternal ancestors who escaped Russian anti-Semitic persecution and dedicated their lives to establishing Jewish houses of study and worship, the child will preserve and enrich the heritage and the people by succeeding to the role of spiritual leader.

Just as the Rebbe had earlier found an artistic mentor for Lev and arranged his exile, he now intervenes to foster the artist's reconciliation with the community and his artistic revitalization. Reconciliation with self, family, and community is achieved through Lev's capitulation to the Rebbe's wisdom. After much agonizing, he grasps the parallel between his own artistic anointment by Jacob Kahn and the Rebbe's need for continuity. Signifying his acceptance of the Rebbe's request, Asher hands the six-year-old child to his father and the Rebbe during a joyous holiday celebrating Torah learning. Just as the holiday signifies the continuation of Jewish devotion to Torah, so Asher's "gift" to the Rebbe signifies the harmonious continuation of the Ladover Hasidim.

Resolution of the painter's personal and professional crises stem from Lev's agreement to allow his son to be raised as successor to the next Rebbe. He exercises stewardship of his uncle's art collection by placing the treasures in storage until his son, who has demonstrated sensitivity to art, will, as Rebbe, determine how to manage it. Lev's artistic block is resolved when he begins work on the Holocaust, a new subject and a new mode of expression for him. Heretofore he avoided artistic confrontation with the Holocaust despite being moved by his wife's history of suffering stemming from the years she spent hiding in a sealed apartment. Although the sequel falls short of Potok's original intention of showing the artist wrestling with the aesthetic problem of Holocaust interpretation, in the final paragraph we learn that Lev is painting "strange images in sealed rooms," and the work now flows. By bequeathing his son to the mission of Jewish regeneration Asher Lev is freed to interpret the century's Jewish calamity and thereby fulfill his mythic ancestor's injunction that he paint the suffering of humanity. Lev's decision will lead to redemption for the pain he has caused the Ladover community and to his own immortality in Hasidic circles as the son and father of Ladover spiritual leaders.

Potok's most recent novel, *I Am the Clay* (1992), is a significant departure from his previous work since it concerns the lives of Koreans during the Korean War and is set entirely in that country. Written during the Persian Gulf conflict when Potok was once again troubled by the terrors of war, the novel portrays the struggles of an elderly childless peasant couple and a severely wounded boy, the sole survivor of his village, whom the wife insists on taking with them as they flee the war. Whereas the old woman takes the boy, the last of a long line of poets and scholars, as a son and generously nurtures him, the old man, uprooted from the social order he understands and the farming that sustains him, initially resists accepting him as his own, until he is convinced that he brings good fortune. The old man eventually believes that the child is mysteriously responsible for the survival of their village despite the ravages of war and economic upheavals. To have him in their home, therefore, is to share in his "magical" power.

Potok celebrates these dislocated Korean farmers who endure and achieve meaning in their lives despite their experience of disruption and chaos in a world different from the one they have known in their farming village. Taking the characters, literally and figuratively, through various terrains, from ditch, to riverbank, to cave, to mountain, to plain, Potok dramatizes their suffering cold, hunger, and illness as they outwit enemy and friendly soldiers alike.

Potok's decision to have the old woman blend Christian and folk beliefs manifests the family's resignation to supernatural powers and reflects the author's continued interest in the meeting of differing cultures. To foster the good spirits and propitiate the evil ones that afflict them, the old woman prays to the spirits of her Korean religion, makes the sign of the cross, and recites lines from a Christian hymn, "Have thine own way, Lord . . . Thou art the potter, I am the clay." Although for the old woman the rituals and incantations serve to placate the spirits that influence human fate, on another level, as J. Martin Holman observes, "The words [of the hymn] state a truth that the Korean people hold dear: They are the clay. The Korean people, who sprang from the soil of the Korean peninsula, have suffered through centuries of domination by foreign powers" – yet maintain their cultural identity. Notwithstanding the new cultural identity of his characters, Potok's abiding interest in the breadth and depth of the human spirit as it confronts political, social, or cultural disruption remains intact.

Whereas the Holocaust has been a presence since Potok's earliest fiction, it only comes to the forefront in "The Trope Teacher" (1992) and "The Canal" (1993). These works, which appear in Dutch translation but have not yet been published in the United States, show the destructive aftereffects of the Holocaust experience on their protagonists, neither of whom is any longer an observant Jew. Benjamin Walter, the central character of "The Trope Teacher," is a sociologist specializing in military history who has been labeled by the media as the Professor of War. As he begins to write his memoirs, Walter discovers that he cannot recall sig-

nificant periods of his youth. He enters a strange liaison with a renowned writer living next door who extracts stories from his past that revive his childhood years and stories about his trope teacher, an eccentric who taught him a sacred melody echoing the terrors of World War I. The stories also revive his memories of World War II, his role as an infantryman with the U.S. Army, and the death camp his unit liberated. Returned to his heritage by the stories, the professor regrets his life of forsaken loyalty to the sacred world of the trope teacher. "The Canal" deals with an Auschwitz survivor, Amos Brickman, who has become a wealthy and famous American architect. Commissioned to design a church, Brickman recalls a church in the city of his birth – Kraków, Poland – where a beloved cousin was slain during World War II. Plagued by dreams, he decides to return to the places of his youth: Warsaw, Kraków, Auschwitz, forests, a canal. His journey is a descent into the past to confront the terrifying memory.

Critical response to Potok's writing has ranged from denunciation to acclaim. Potok's detractors frequently center their criticism on the novelist's style, charging him with composing banal speech and employing a pompous tone. Others have complained about the predictability and lack of complexity in his characters. In the November 1967 *Midstream,* Curt Leviant judges the dialogue between the young men of *The Chosen* "more like a mature man's bookish presumption of what their talk should sound like than authentic speech itself" and objects to Potok's rendition of Hasidim void of humor and zest for life. In his fall 1967 review of *The Chosen* in *Judaism,* Judah Stampfer also rejects Potok's description of a joyless, rigid Hasidic lifestyle, seeing in it "only the most superficial resemblance of its outer behavior," but he lauds Potok's rendition of yeshiva life and regards that aspect as the novel's strongest asset. Most often Potok is extolled for examining serious social, philosophical, and theological problems and praised for his concern with ideas and issues.

Criticism of the subsequent novels has largely followed lines similar to those which characterized the reception of *The Chosen,* though several critics have perceived maturation and growth in Potok's work. A notable exception is Ruth Wisse's March 1982 review of *The Book of Lights* for *Commentary* in which she takes Potok to task, charging that "the historicity of the novel is selective," that Potok has superimposed "current attitudes and cultural trends on events of three decades ago." Further, Wisse attacks Potok for Judaizing the atomic bomb and indulging in a "drama of Jewish self-accusation and expiation." Wisse laments Potok's departure from his original authentic representation of Jewish life, "validating traditional Judaism" and taking "his cues from the culture at large." Excepting the charge leveled by Wisse, most knowledgeable critics assess Potok's treatment of Jewish life and thought as among the finest in American literature. Sanford Marovitz speaks for many in his 1986 article in *Studies in American Jewish Literature,* where he describes Potok as a "highly learned and intellectual writer, a novelist of ideas," whose books merit careful reading.

In his article on the popularity of *The Chosen,* Sheldon Grebstein identifies the elements which assure Potok a significant place in Jewish American fiction. Among these are "moral fervor, strong emotions experienced by sensitive characters, the portrayal of ancient and deeply felt traditions, the depiction of intimate family life, and an essentially affirmative view of human nature." Edward A. Abramson, author of the first critical book on Potok's fiction, concludes:

> While his work has not reached the very highest level, there have been parts of individual work that have. He has shown the ability to create characters who remain with the reader long after the novel is closed, to tackle difficult issues and complex situations, and to illuminate previously untreated areas of Jewish life. He has extended the range of Jewish-American literature. These are no mean achievements, and he is still writing.

Supplanting popular fiction's satiric and stereotypical Jewish characters, vulgar Yiddishisms, and pop psychology and sociology, Potok has created an enduring body of work that is centrally Jewish, erudite in its presentation of Jewish values and liturgy. Yet, like Saul Bellow, Bernard Malamud, and Phillip Roth, Potok too rejects the label and pigeonhole of "Jewish American writer" as reductionist. Potok considers himself an American writing about a particular New York American world, just as William Faulkner wrote about his particular Mississippi world and Joyce wrote about his particular Irish world. The appeal of his work to diverse readers demonstrates how the universal can exist within the particular and how religious and ethnic themes need not be barriers to understanding and acceptance. At the same time, his absorption in Jewish learning makes Potok an important voice in Jewish American writing since his knowledge and commitment to Judaism have enriched his fiction by moving religion and culture from the periphery, where it exists in many novels, to the center.

Dust jacket for Potok's 1992 novel, set in Korea during the Korean War, his first work focusing on non-Jews

Interviews:

Cheryl Forbes, "Judaism Under the Secular Umbrella," *Christianity Today,* 22 (8 September 1978): 14–21;

Harold Ribalow, "Chaim Potok," in *The Tie That Binds: Conversations With Jewish Writers* (New York: Barnes, 1980);

Martin Bookspan, "A Conversation with Chaim Potok," in *The Eternal Light,* no. 1453, transcript of NBC Radio Network broadcast, 22 November 1981 (New York: Jewish Theological Seminary of America, 1981);

Alan Abrams, "When Cultures Collide," *Jewish News* (22 June 1984): 13ff.;

S. Lillian Kremer, "Interview With Chaim Potok, July 21, 1981," *Studies in American Jewish Literature,* 4 (1984): 84–99;

Kremer, "A Conversation with Chaim Potok, July 1983," in *Dictionary of Literary Biography Yearbook: 1984,* edited by Jean W. Ross (Detroit: Gale, 1985), pp. 83–87;

Elaine Kauvar, "An Interview with Chaim Potok," *Contemporary Literature,* 27 (Fall 1986): 291–317;

Wendy Herstein, "An Interview with Chaim Potok," *The World & I* (August 1992): 309–313;

Aviva Kipen, "The Odyssey of Asher Lev," *Jewish Quarterly* (Spring 1993): 1–5.

Bibliography:

Cynthia Fagerheim, "A Bibliographic Essay," *Studies in American Jewish Literature,* 4 (1985): 107–120.

References:

Edward A. Abramson, *Chaim Potok* (Boston: Twayne, 1986);

Sam Bluefarb, "The Head, the Heart, and the Conflict of Generations in Chaim Potok's *The Chosen,*" *College Language Association Journal,* 14 (June 1971): 402–409;

Joan Del Fattore, "Women as Scholars in Chaim Potok's Novels," *Studies in American Jewish Literature,* 4 (1984): 52–61;

Leslie Field, "Chaim Potok and the Critics: Sampler From a Consistent Spectrum," *Studies in American Jewish Literature,* 4 (1985): 3–12;

Michael T. Gilmore, "A Fading Promise," *Midstream,* 16 (January 1970): 76–80;

Sheldon Grebstein, "Phenomenon of the Really Jewish Best-Seller: Potok's *The Chosen,*" *Studies in American Jewish Literature,* 1 (1975): 23–31;

Allen Guttman, *The Jewish Writer in America: Assimilation and the Crisis of Identity* (New York: Oxford University Press, 1971);

Jay Halio, "American Dreams," *Southern Review,* 13 (Autumn 1977): 837–844;

J. Martin Holman, "A Voice From the Earth," *The World & I* (August 1992): 303–308;

S. Lillian Kremer, "Dedalus in Brooklyn: Influences of *A Portrait of an Artist as a Young Man* on *My Name is Asher Lev,*" *Studies in American Jewish Literature,* 4 (1985): 26–38;

Kremer, "Encountering the Other," *The World & I* (August 1992): 315–325;

Kremer, "Eternal Light: The Holocaust and the Revival of Judaism and Jewish Civilization in the Fiction of Chaim Potok," in her *Witness Through the Imagination: Jewish American Holocaust Literature* (Detroit: Wayne State University Press, 1989), pp. 300–323;

Curt Leviant, "The Hasid as American Hero," *Midstream,* 13 (November 1967): 76–80;

Edward Margolies, "Chaim Potok's *Book of Lights* and the Jewish American Novel," *Yiddish,* 6, no. 4 (1987): 93–98;

Sanford Marovitz, "*The Book of Lights:* Jewish Mysticism in the Shadow of the Bomb," *Studies in American Jewish Literature,* 4 (1985): 62–83;

Marovitz, "Freedom, Faith, and Fanaticism: Cultural Conflict in the Novels of Chaim Potok," *Studies in American Jewish Literature,* 5 (1986): 129–140;

Sanford Pinsker, "The Crucifixion of Chaim Potok/The Excommunication of Asher Lev: Art and the Hasidic World," *Studies in American Jewish Literature,* 4 (1985): 39–51;

William F. Purcell, "Potok's Fathers and Sons," *Studies in American Literature,* 26 (1989): 75–92;

Dorothy Rabinowitz, "Sequels," *Commentary,* 50 (May 1970): 104–108;

Shelly Regenbaum, "Art, Gender, and the Jewish Tradition in Yezierska's *Red Ribbon on a White Horse* and Potok's *My Name Is Asher Lev,*" *Studies in American Jewish Literature,* 7 (1988): 55–66;

Ellen Schiff, "To Be Young, Gifted, and Oppressed: The Plight of the Ethnic Artist," *MELUS,* 6 (1979): 73–80;

Will Soll, "Chaim Potok's *Book of Lights:* Reappropriating Kabbalah in the Nuclear Age," *Religion and Literature,* 21 (Spring 1989): 111–135;

Judah Stampfer, "The Tension of Piety," *Judaism,* 16 (Fall 1967): 494–498;

David Stern, "Two Worlds," *Commentary,* 54 (October 1972): 102, 104;

Sam Sutherland, "Asher Lev's Visions of His Mythic Ancestor," *Re: Artes Liberales,* 3 (Spring 1977): 51–54;

Warren True, "Potok and Joyce: The Artist and His Culture," *Studies in American Jewish Literature,* 2 (1982): 181–190;

Ellen Uffen, "*My Name Is Asher Lev:* Chaim Potok's Portrait of the Young Hasid as Artist," *Studies in American Jewish Literature,* 2 (1982): 174–180;

Daniel Walden, "Chaim Potok: A *Zwischenmensch* ('Between-Person') Adrift in the Cultures," *Studies in American Jewish Literature,* 4 (1985): 19–25;

Ruth Wisse, "Jewish Dreams," *Commentary,* 73 (March 1982): 45–48;

Joan Zlotnick, "The Chosen Borough: Chaim Potok's Brooklyn," *Studies in American Jewish Literature,* 4 (1985): 13–18.

Robert Stone

(21 August 1937 –   )

Robert Solotaroff
University of Minnesota

BOOKS: *A Hall of Mirrors* (Boston: Houghton Mifflin, 1967; London: Bodley Head, 1968);
Dog Soldiers (Boston: Houghton Mifflin, 1974; London: Secker & Warburg, 1975);
A Flag for Sunrise (New York: Knopf, 1981; London: Secker & Warburg, 1981);
Children of Light (London: Deutsch, 1986; New York: Knopf, 1986);
Outerbridge Reach (New York: Ticknor & Fields, 1992; London: Deutsch, 1992).

MOTION PICTURES: *WUSA,* screenplay by Stone, Paramount, 1970;
Who'll Stop the Rain, screenplay by Stone and Judith Rascoe, United Artists, 1978.

OTHER: "Portrait," in *Legacy of Light,* edited by Constance Sullivan (New York: Knopf, 1987), pp. 59–63;
The Best American Short Stories: 1992, edited by Stone and Katrina Kenison (Boston: Houghton Mifflin, 1992).

SELECTED PERIODICAL PUBLICATIONS – UNCOLLECTED:

FICTION
"Porque No Tiene, Porque Le Falta," *New American Review,* 6 (April 1969): 198–226;
"Aquarius Obscured," *American Review,* 22 (February 1975): 144–151;
"Helping," *New Yorker,* 63 (8 June 1987): 28–47;
"Absence of Mercy," *Harper's,* 275 (November 1987): 61–68.

NONFICTION
"We Couldn't Swing with It: The 'Intrepid Four,'" *Atlantic,* 221 (June 1968): 57–64;
"There It Is," *Guardian,* 17 July 1971, p. 9;
"A Higher Horror of the Whiteness: Cocaine's Coloring of the American Psyche," *Harper's,* 273 (December 1986): 49–54;
"Me and the Universe," *Triquarterly,* 65 (Winter 1986): 229–234;

Robert Stone (photograph © Kelly Wise)

"The Reason for Stories: Toward a Moral Fiction," *Harper's,* 276 (June 1988): 71–76;
"Keeping the Future at Bay: Republicans and Their America," *Harper's,* 277 (November 1988): 57–66;
"Havana Then and Now," *Harper's,* 284 (March 1992): 36–46.

The beginning of A. Alvarez's review of Robert Stone's fourth novel, *Children of Light* (1986), stands as the best concise summary of Stone's achievement that has yet been published:

In just four novels in almost twenty years Robert Stone has established a world and style and tone of voice of

216

great originality and authority. It is a voice without grace or comfort, bleak, dangerous, and continually threatening.... Stone has a Hobbesian view of life – nasty, brutish and short – but it is also fiercely contemporary and not just because he has a marvelous ear for the ellipses and broken rhythms and casual obscenity of the way people talk now. Stone is contemporary because he takes for granted the nihilism that seems to be a legacy of the Vietnam War, that fracturing of the sensibility which began in the Sixties with disaffected young and continues, in these more conservative times, out there in the streets with the hustlers and junkies, the random violence and equally random paranoia. He is one of the few writers who are at once culturally sophisticated – full of sly quotes and literary references, strong on moral ambiguities – and streetwise.

Stone's tonal range and vision of existence are more various than Alvarez suggests, but the reviewer's emphasis upon the importance of the Vietnam experience holds true in Stone's next and best novel, *Outerbridge Reach* (1992). Although set in the years 1988 and 1989, more than fifteen years after the last American troops left Vietnam, the protagonist's experience in that country helps to shape his fate, as it does the fates of half the principals in the two Stone novels that are closest in achievement to *Outerbridge Reach – Dog Soldiers* (1974) and *A Flag for Sunrise* (1981) – as well as in "Helping" (1987), the best of the four stories Stone has so far published. The malign, shaping presence of Vietnam and the more widespread social dissonances which characterize his work place Stone among that continuity of American writers – such as Herman Melville, Stephen Crane, John Dos Passos, Ernest Hemingway, and Norman Mailer – who believe that, at bottom, life is war. Indeed, when Stone first saw combat, as a nineteen-year-old radioman on an American AKA (attack troop carrier) at Port Said during the Suez Crisis of 1956, he was not surprised at the spectacle of mutilated bodies and shattered structures. As he reflected in his 1986 article "Me and the Universe," "I always thought that the world was filled with evil spirits, that people's minds teemed with depravity and craziness and murderousness, that that basically was an implicit condition, an uncurable condition of mankind." Stone's formative years perhaps explain how this nineteen-year-old had come to this Hobbesian appraisal.

Robert Anthony Stone was born in Brooklyn on 21 August 1937 to C. Homer Stone, a former railroad detective, and Gladys Catherine Grant, a member of a family that had been involved for several generations in the tugboat business of New York harbor. The difference between his parents' surnames is telling: Homer Stone worked on a tug-

boat, impregnated Gladys Grant, and with that act passed out of his son's life. Robert Stone knows nothing of his father's life after 1937, in good part because he has never felt any interest in learning anything about him. The consequences of his father's absence were unusually severe, for though Gladys Stone was relatively refined and well-educated – for a while a schoolteacher – she was schizophrenic, with symptoms severe enough to hospitalize her for the three and a half years just following Stone's turning six.

Stone has several times asserted the distance between the verbal constructions of language and the structures of the real world. In a 1985 interview with William Crawford Woods, he traced his sense of this distance "to the curious luck to be raised by a schizophrenic, which gives one a tremendous advantage in understanding the relation of language to reality." This remark puts too positive a cast on his desperate childhood situation: when he briefly spoke of his mother's symptoms during an October 1991 interview with Robert Solotaroff (published in 1993), his voice betrayed an uncharacteristic anger, which hinted at how much his mother's delusions must have threatened him. Since his mother's accounts of the world that she saw were often obviously incorrect, terrifying, or both, Stone had to come up with his own versions of reality. The intensity of the young Stone's need for a more accurate account of the external world than those his mother offered perhaps explains the singular clarity and vividness of both his fiction and nonfiction. Paul Gray's description in *Time* (11 November 1974) of Stone's prose in *Dog Soldiers* – "as precise as the cross hairs on a rifle sight" – applies to most of what he has published.

In the interview with Woods, Stone spoke of his sense, from an early age, of the interpenetration of his internal and external worlds. At age seven, under the influence of the radio stories he listened to, he would walk "through Central Park, describing aloud what I was doing, becoming both the actor and the writer setting the scene." The ability to enter into such fantasy, while enjoyable, had a more serious and needful aspect. Stone has said that he had to become a writer, to create someone significant. Without his self-created identity as a writer, he "would have been swept away" – into the severe emotional disturbance that pervaded his environment and constantly threatened him. This sense of urgency, the imperative to create, contributes proportionately to the impact of his fictions.

"Cross hairs on a rifle sight" captures the sense of menace, of impending violence, in Stone's work and world. Saint Ann's, a school run by brothers of the Marist Order, brought physically realized menace, the sense of life as war, to Stone as a first grader. His mother had moved from Brooklyn to the Yorkville section of Manhattan when Stone was two, and, when he was five, Stone began kindergarten at Saint Ann's, less than a mile from their home. The school accepted boarders, and when Gladys Grant was hospitalized, the family court system placed her son in a setting with "the social dynamic of a coral reef," where "a good beating was forever at hand" — descriptions Stone used in a 1987 story, "Absence of Mercy." Stone has vouched for the accuracy of the story's accounts of the beatings by other students, by teachers, and, above all, by a prefect who at night, after keeping terrified boys as young as six waiting outside his room, would call them in and, like an appalling force of nature, "as implacable as a shark or a hurricane," lash their palms. Stone transferred the basic situation of Saint Ann's — in which sufferers were pitted against overwhelming, unfairly empowered antagonists — to the settings of his first three novels, the New Orleans of *A Hall of Mirrors* (1967), the American locales of *Dog Soldiers,* and the Central American country of *A Flag for Sunrise.* In his last two novels Stone has finally worked beyond his projection of Saint Ann's upon the world.

Gladys Grant was released from the hospital shortly before Stone's tenth birthday, but, no longer able to gain a teaching position, she supported herself and her son with such low-paying jobs as working as a hotel maid and addressing envelopes. The comfortable apartments in which Stone and she had lived before the hospitalization were replaced by rented rooms in seedy hotels on the West Side of Manhattan. Around the time that Stone once again became a day student and not a boarder at Saint Ann's, he wrote a science-fiction story, and from time to time over the next five or six years he would turn out stories. When he was a junior he won a contest for a story that he remembers as being heavily influenced by a recent reading of J. D. Salinger's *The Catcher in the Rye* (1951). Other aspects of his adolescence were less genteel. When he was fifteen he joined a West Side gang but quit a year later when a collision with members of another gang in Central Park resulted in drawn knives and cuttings. He would also sometimes try to impress his friends at Saint Ann's by drinking four or five cans of beer and showing up at school drunk. By the time he was seventeen, he had reasoned his way into atheism, and, though he had recently been awarded a New York State Regents' Scholarship, he was thrown out

of school a few months before graduation for converting a classmate to his atheistic stance. Of this experience, Stone said in his 1991 interview with Solotaroff that he "felt pretty good when they called me on the carpet and were accusing me. I felt like Martin Luther."

Stone then indulged his love of the sea by enlisting in the navy, which at that time — the summer of 1955 — offered a three-year hitch for enlistees under eighteen. As Stone recalled in the interview with Solotaroff, boot camp in Bainbridge, Maryland, was "too familiar; absolute hell." He had a terrible time keeping his gear, particularly his summer whites, acceptable. More significant was the consequence of being again submerged in an authoritarian setting for twenty-four hours a day: the fearful cringe he had picked up at Saint Ann's reasserted itself, and it took his drillmasters' considerable effort to cajole and insult him out of it. The post–boot camp service was much more pleasurable. For a bit over a year Stone was a radioman through two Mediterranean cruises. By spring 1956 he had passed a high-school equivalency test as well as a competitive examination to become a navy journalist, a third-class petty officer. He wrote a story on the Marine residence station in Beirut, but his main reportage began with his third cruise, in December 1957 in Antarctica with Operation Deep Freeze III, a scientific mission to trace cosmic rays. His three months there were to provide essential background for the splendid chapters in *Outerbridge Reach* that are set south of the forty-fifth latitude. Stone would later feel that his writing was much enriched by his "being thrown together with a whole lot of people from all over the country, especially since this was at a time, in the midfifties, when the country was much less homogenous, when for example, the South was still the South and all that it entailed. . . . It was very interesting and tremendously helpful."

Discharged, as he likes to remember, on Bastille Day, 1958, Stone returned to Manhattan, to enroll in New York University and to try out a journalistic career by getting a job as a copyboy with the *Daily News.* He was allowed to write captions, report on some sporting events, and make preliminary inquiries at places reporters did not want to go, such as morgues, and he was fascinated by some of the hard-boiled reporters who had been newspapermen since the 1920s. Still, he was in retrospect grateful to the *News* for having enough repellent aspects to scare him off a newspaper career forever. In particular, he found at the paper the working class authoritarianism that he had loathed at Saint Ann's. As for his academic career, he was at first more interested in the characters at the *Daily News* and in his new career as a late-fifties beatnik, hanging out at and reading his poems in coffeehouses. But during his second semester at New York University, in a creative-writing course, Stone wrote a story drawn from a brief Navy stint as a prisoners' guard that so impressed the instructor, M. L. Rosenthal, that he suggested to Stone that he apply for a fellowship to the Wallace Stegner Writing Program at Stanford, which required no prior degrees.

Two years passed before Stone could follow Rosenthal's advice. He met Janice Burr in his writing course, and they married on 11 December 1959. Intelligent, energetic, and supportive, Janice Burr Stone has contributed greatly to the transformation of the young man who seemed slated for a marginal existence into one of America's outstanding fiction writers. About a month after the wedding, Stone quit his job at the *Daily News,* and as Janice Stone recalls, with barely enough money for bus fare, the couple traveled to New Orleans, arriving a few days before the 1960 Mardi Gras. A singular city, percolating with impending violence, simultaneously seedy and exotic – "like a cross between Paterson, N.J. and Port-au-Prince," as A. J. Liebling put it in *The Earl of Louisiana* (1961) – New Orleans cried out to Stone for fictional rendering when he sat down two years later to begin his first novel.

Stone wrote no fiction during the eight months he stayed in New Orleans. He thought about writing drama and did write some poems that he read for contributions in coffeehouses – one of the many ways he tried to support himself, his wife, and their daughter Deidre, who was delivered free of charge at the Huey Long Charity Hospital on 15 June 1960. Some of the jobs – repairing drums, trying to sell encyclopedias, and working on the docks – would not figure in his first novel, *A Hall of Mirrors,* which Stone published seven years later, but others did. Like Stone, the novel's protagonist, Rheinhardt, has a job for a week or two on the assembly line of a soap factory. Stone's work for the 1960 census during May and June was particularly significant to the prospective novelist. He knocked on the doors of houses, apartments, and rented rooms, mostly in black sections of the city. Some of the people he called on would talk to him at length, and as he listened to the accounts of their lives his sense of the unfairness of American society grew. The tone and essence of these conversations are conveyed in much of *A Hall of Mirrors.* As Stone reminisced in "Keeping the Future at Bay: Republicans and Their America" (November 1988), black speech in 1960 was "ringing my young literary bells ... the

rhythms and raps ... were sounding in my dreams; I [thought] I'm ready to signify." Stone was also able to integrate into his novel what he learned from the whites he tracked down for the census: "the hard cases – the brothels, skid row, the B-girl dorms, the transvestites who scared the last census taker away."

In his 1991 interview with Solotaroff, Stone reflected that in 1960 he really saw the horrid side of white Louisiana and the sweet side of black Louisiana. His introduction to the least amiable face of the Deep South came a few weeks after he arrived, when he was twice arrested while trying to sell encyclopedias. The charge was peddling door to door without a license, but the real cause was the consequence of his northern accent: police suspected that he was trying to organize blacks to vote. Stone's faculty for finding his way to where the action was or was going to be – a sense that had earlier led him to the Suez and would later lead him to Vietnam and Central America – had brought him to New Orleans just a few days after the first sit-in occurred in Greensboro, North Carolina. By late March the attempts to integrate segregated public places or businesses had spread to Louisiana, and the ferocity of white resistance to the sit-ins and especially to the demands of a federal judge to integrate the public schools of the state was not lost on Stone, who responded intensely to actual or threatened violence. Nor did he miss the purging on supposedly moral grounds of more than twenty two thousand children, most of them black, from the welfare rolls, or the riot that followed the entrance of four black girls, escorted by U.S. marshals, into two previously all-white New Orleans schools in November. Stone had returned to New York in the preceding month, and so, like tens of millions of other Americans, he learned through the media of the screaming crowds confronting the young women and of the ensuing riot. Both a race riot and the purging of welfare rolls appear in *A Hall of Mirrors.*

In New York Stone got a job that he hated, writing copy for a low-end-furniture store, staying only long enough to qualify for unemployment compensation (at that time about thirty-five dollars a week). Janice worked as a waitress and then learned keypunch operation, a skill often needed to support the Stone family over the next half-decade. As he remembered in an interview with Solotaroff, one day late in 1961 the twenty-four-year-old Stone put down *The Great Gatsby,* which he had been rereading, and said to himself, "This is what I want to do; I want to write novels." In the next few months the college dropout who seemed destined for a lifetime of low-paying jobs took a long step toward transforming his life by writing and then sending to the Stanford writing program some thirty pages of what would become his first novel.

The acceptance came in the spring of 1962, and that autumn found the Stones in an inexpensive apartment in a section of Menlo Park that served as Stanford's bohemian quarter. With the flora, the great climate, the weekend parties, and stimulating young artists as neighbors, life was sweet. As Stone recalled to interviewer Charles Ruas (1985), "When I went to California it was like everything turned Technicolor." Stone soon became one of the visitors swallowing LSD at the residence Ken Kesey had just purchased in La Honda, fifteen miles to the south. His LSD experiments (and also his reading of Louis-Ferdinand Céline) led to the expressionistic and surrealistic sections in the last third of *A Hall of Mirrors*. To LSD alone Stone attributed a return to the religious concerns he thought he had put permanently behind him when he was seventeen. The religious experiences he had on drugs, remembered in a interview with Steve Chapple (1984), were far more significant to his later work than the temporary stylistic excursions from realism:

> What I witnessed or thought I witnessed in my stoned state was an enormously powerful, resolving presence within which all phenomenology was contained. It wasn't a God that said you're good and you're bad. . . . But there was a suggestion that everything was all right. In spite of all the horrors, way down deep, everything was all right. . . . I don't know if that dimension really exists. I suspect so. . . . Agnosticism is literally true in my case: *I don't know.* . . . I'm temperamentally inclined to religion. I do not have faith. I don't. . . . I feel it as a lack.

God's presence as a form of absence is to varying degrees inscribed into each of Stone's five novels.

There were also less ambiguous benefactions in Stone's California experience. For one, the writing workshop that brought him to Stanford was extremely supportive. According to Wallace Stegner in "Hard Experience Talking," an August 1967 article for *Saturday Review,* the other members "listened to the successive chapters with an enthusiasm that grew by the week and that was curiously untouched by envy. . . . He was the one who would not only publish his book — they all expected [him] to do that — but publish it big." Stone's sense of his worth and potential was also heightened when, toward the end of the school year, he received a Houghton Mifflin Literary Fellowship and signed a contract (including an advance) with the Boston publisher.

In the latter part of 1963, he and Janice decided that he would never get his novel completed in the perpetual party of Ken Kesey California. Moreover, their long-range economic pressures had intensified with the birth of their second child, Ian, on 24 May 1963, and Janice wanted to return to working on her degree in psychology at City College in New York so that she could pursue a career in social work that might be gratifying and relatively profitable. And so the spring of 1964 found Stone and the two-thirds-completed first draft of his novel back in New York, where for the next two years he returned to the routine of holding jobs long enough to collect unemployment compensation. He finally finished the novel during the summer of 1966 and then, for the year until it was published, held a rather pleasant job as an assistant at an art gallery in midtown Manhattan.

Stone told Ruas that he had not been able to start a novel until he had gained a coherent sense of "the shape of peoples' lives" and of "the pattern . . . in things." The political and experiential vision that emerges in *A Hall of Mirrors* could be seen as a product of Stone's beatnik period, similar to the standard of 1950s counterculture, Allen Ginsberg's *Howl*. In both works Moloch rules America, and decent people are inevitably damaged. Those in control are power-mad and corrupt, and it is foolish to think that any individual can change the order of things for the better. In *A Hall of Mirrors* the counterculture characters anticipate only a worsening of the hellish social conditions. When Morgan Rainey, an idealistic census taker, realizes that his job is a cover for a scheme to strike blacks from the welfare rolls, he seeks information and support from the novel's frequently amoral protagonist, Rheinhardt. Rheinhardt gives him neither and instead defends his job as a disc jockey for a racist radio station: "things are taking a cold turn. . . . One by one the warm weather creatures will topple dead with frosted eyelids. . . . The creatures of the cold will proliferate. The air will become thin and difficult to breathe. . . . Very shortly it will start to snow." Rainey argues, "But there is such a thing as a gift of life. Humanness is given. Clay was raised to consciousness. Blood was made warm." Rheinhardt's opinion, however, is the one that gains support from two beatnik neighbors present at this encounter. Bogdanovich counters Rainey with "All that gift of life and humanness is a trip. . . . [B]lood was made warm to keep a scene circulating . . . that's the only reason blood is warm." Marvin adds that they all know about "warm blood and gifts and humanness. . . . But it doesn't apply now, you dig?" A fairly sustained pattern of water and fish imagery relates this new moral ice age to what Melville, in *Moby-Dick,* called "the universal cannibalism of the sea, all whose creatures prey upon each other, carrying on eternal war since the world began." The vision of the survival of the cold-blooded over the warm is fulfilled as the principals who are capable of love and concern for others, Rainey and Geraldine Crosby, are killed off, and Rheinhardt – who takes pride in his ability to survive in the cold new world, and who claims that he is really "Jack Frost, baby, I'm the original" – lives on.

If the absence of benign alternatives in American life seemed obvious enough to Stone when he began his novel in 1961, it must have seemed a good deal less so as the 1960s unfolded. Having received the inciting animus of the civil rights movement, many aspects of the American counterculture were by 1963 aflame with the possibilities of social transformation, both individual and collective. As Morris Dickstein observes in *Gates of Eden* (1977), "the spirit of the sixties witnessed the transformation of utopian religion into the terms of sexual humanism. . . . [T]he sixties translated the Edenic impulse once again into political terms." Stone dates the span of the novel's dramatized present – about six months – by having Rainey date a journal entry 16 April 1963. In his 1991 interview with Solotaroff, Stone conceded that he had inserted the 1963 date in an attempt to make the novel more contemporary but had throughout its writing been thinking of the New Orleans he knew in the far less hopeful year of 1960.

The descriptions of New Orleans experienced from the social underside usually emphasize the city's tawdry or grimy aspects, and the novel's grim social vision culminates with a race riot engineered by a right-wing multimillionaire. When we first meet the twenty-four-year-old Geraldine, a psychopathic lover disfigures her face with an oyster shucker. In her passage through life the healthy, loving young woman is psychically as well as physically scarred, and her last act is to hang herself in a jail cell. The novel's title suggests that if the reader would look at a mirror with enough perception, he or she would see someone similarly scarred by cruel attackers.

Yet more than half of the novel's pages have about them a lightness, even a gaiety, that flows from the inventiveness and wit of the narrative voice; from the antics of the novel's con men; and, most of all, from the sensibility of Rheinhardt. During her affair with Rheinhardt, Geraldine tells him, "You're sick, you're nervous, you're a drunk, you're cowardly, you're a mouthoff" – only a par-

A Hall of Mirrors
A Houghton Mifflin Literary Fellowship Award Novel
Robert Stone

Dust jacket for Stone's first novel, set in New Orleans during the early 1960s

tial list of his vices. Nevertheless, he remains appealing, with charm and insight woven through his flaws. The workings of his mind are always interesting and his gestures endearing. Although his circumstances are sometimes desperate, he seldom takes himself seriously and views the deepening of his alcoholic pathology as casually as if he were paring his nails. The reader's response to him is interestingly complicated by the way his most hateful performances are suffused with a zany humor that is sometimes irresistible. Most notable is a madly funny speech he makes to tens of thousands of right-wing zealots at the rally that culminates the novel. Rheinhardt's cadenza is the culmination of a good many comic strategies that Stone employs to ridicule the radical right. Of course, this ridicule runs counter to the novel's warnings about the imminence of right-wing takeover, and one suspects that the comic undermining of the radical right as well as the expressionistic and surrealistic flights in the last third of the novel are Stone's concession to the social eruptions that occurred during the five years in which he wrote the book.

A Hall of Mirrors was published in August 1967 to mixed but predominantly positive reviews. An anonymous reviewer for the 31 July 1967 issue of *Publisher's Weekly* called it "a pretentiously written novel that does achieve a certain nightmare power at times, but never rises to the heights one expects of a winner of a Houghton Mifflin Literary Fellowship." However, two other reviews in the same trade journal were positive. More widely read publications – *Newsweek, The New York Times, Commonweal,* and the *New Republic* – published reviews praising such elements of the novel as the brilliant prose, the vivid evocation of the New Orleans setting, the strength of its characterizations, and the depth of the author's imagination. In 1968 Stone received the William Faulkner Award for best first novel and also sold the movie rights to *A Hall of Mirrors.* Over the next year he was well paid for turning his novel into a screenplay, which was produced by Paramount as *WUSA* in 1970. With these earnings, along with an advance on his second novel, Stone and his family were able to live in England for four years (1967–1971). When they returned to the United States, Stone became writer in residence at Princeton for one year (1971–1972) and then taught at Amherst College for three years (1972–1975). The writing of *A Hall of Mirrors* had lifted him from the world of short-lived assembly-line and loading-dock jobs to which his origins seemed at times to have doomed him.

Stone did not write much in the five years after he completed *A Hall of Mirrors,* and one kind of dissatisfaction or another attended most of what he did complete. In 1968 he wrote "We Couldn't Swing with It," a nonfiction piece about four opponents of the Vietnam engagement who, while on liberty in Japan, deserted the U.S. Navy. Stone's own appraisal of the article, given in an interview with Eric James Schroeder (1984), was self-critical: "It's me trying to be a good supporter of the movement. It's boring and it's pretentious and (in my opinion) it's essentially false." The "falseness" arises from his attempt to glorify the four sailors instead of subjecting them to the usual corrosive irony he drops upon decent but limited idealists. However, the piece is of considerable interest to a reader interested in Stone's style, for it shows how stiff his writing is when his subjects are not given the shadings of irony or allusiveness they might deserve. Stone described himself well when he told Woods, "Irony is my friend and brother."

In "Porque No Tiene, Porque Le Falta," Stone's first published short story, irony returns and helps to make the vivid story about a paranoid, cuckolded American writer in Mexico the only clear triumph among all the work Stone did between August 1966 and the early summer of 1971, when he wrote "There It Is," an account of his recent two-week visit to Vietnam. Until his Vietnam visit he had not felt sure enough about what he wanted to do with his second novel to start writing it. As Stone told Schroeder, "It seemed to me that these people – my characters – must have been in Vietnam, even though I didn't know quite who they were. I thought, 'What is their relationship to this Vietnam situation that is filling everybody's life now, that is so much on everybody's mind?' It's all anybody would talk about when I was with other Americans. It was so present, looming large in everybody's consciousness."

Accredited by *Ink,* a London paper which was soon to go out of business, Stone found Saigon in late May 1971 even more vivid than New Orleans eleven years earlier. In addition to the American and Vietnamese military presence, there were, as Stone recollected to Schroeder, "all sorts of adventurers and wanderers and hippies [many of whom dealt in dope or gold or cinnamon] . . . Saigon was just full of Americans and Europeans of any possible description." Saigon also contained a good deal more that fired Stone's urge to get back to his desk in England and start writing. His piece for the *Guardian* (*Ink* having folded) details bizarre acts of violence, including helicopter pilots gunning down herds of elephants and a hotel guest crushing a dozen lizards into the walls and floor with "a framed tintype of Our Lady of Lourdes." While he was in the city, the Saigon tax office was bombed, killing six, including three children. But who was the detonator – an angry taxpayer, the ARVN (the Army of the Republic of Vietnam), the Vietcong, or some other malevolent individual or group? Stone's title "There It Is" was the operative phrase of the American troops in Vietnam, as well as the bemused response of many Americans to the absurdity and uncertainty that arose from the country's participation in a nondeclared war. "There it is" – observe, but do not try to organize, explain, or understand experience. Stone indeed noted so much of the material in Saigon so precisely in "There It Is" that he was able to transfer ten vignettes from the piece to the first forty-one pages of *Dog Soldiers* – the ones that are set in Vietnam.

In the novel Stone offers no political background, no informative explanations for the civil war in Vietnam, though there is the ironic touch of John Converse's explaining to his wife no one can ever understand human motivation: " 'Nobody knows,' he told her confidently. 'That's the principle we were defending over there. That's why we fought the war.' " As Frank Shelton has observed, the novel "assumes the war as a given and traces its effects on the noncombatants both in Vietnam and the United States." Beneath the sharply rendered, realistic representation of narrative and dialogue is an almost allegorical examination of the effects of the Vietnam involvement on the American psyche. Instead of employing the usual allegorical strategy of parallel realistic and symbolic lines of action, Stone offers up a broadside of correspondences that assert that the United States is becoming, like Vietnam, an amoral combat zone. To take a few of the many examples: Ngon Loc, a province inhabited by supposed worshipers of Satan, is said to look much like northern California; one character likes Saigon because it reminds her so much of Washington; John Wayne movies play in both locales, *True Grit* at the Vietnamese base, where the gravitational center of the novel – three kilos of heroin – is transferred, and *The Searchers* in a Brooklyn theater, where one character earlier caved in the head of an usher who had humiliated him. All of the correspondences speak in different ways for the collapse of traditional ethical directives, for the pervasive energy of evil.

Dog Soldiers, a violent and fast-paced novel, commands strong reactions from readers and reviewers. In the *New Republic* (4 January 1975), reviewer Joan Joffe Hall wrote that "despite my profound moral disgust at this novel, my utter inability to sympathize with the characters, and my suspicion that my good liberal notion that the Vietnam war is as American as apple pie is cheaply manipulated, I have to admit I read the book straight through, addictively flipping pages." But *Dog Soldiers* is not at all a conventional adventure novel in which readers know that the imperiled, admirable hero will win out in the end. No character is consistently admirable, and one of the book's singular achievements is the way in which more-sympathetic readers than Hall can find themselves, by novel's end, strongly, strangely moved by the saga of Raymond Hicks. It is profitable to consider *Dog Soldiers* as a grim descendant of James Fenimore Cooper's capture-escape-pursuit affairs that helped to shape the European conception of the American. After reading the five volumes of Cooper's Natty Bumppo saga, D. H. Lawrence wrote in *Studies in Classic American Literature* (1923) that the series contains "the myth of the essential white America . . . The essential American soul is hard, isolate, stoic, a killer." Whether or not the whole of the statement is true, it certainly captures a fair part of the psyche and reality of Hicks, the former Marine who agrees to help smuggle several million dollars' worth of heroin from Vietnam to Berkeley. Because of a double cross, Hicks flees with the heroin and Marge Converse, the drug-addicted wife of a former Marine buddy, to a former counterculture commune in invented terrain – Stone described it as Northern New Mexico lifted up and placed on the Rio Grande. They are pursued by the corrupt employee of the unnamed federal agency (obviously the Federal Narcotics Bureau) and the agent's two hirelings as the novel culminates in a shootout in and near the former commune.

A singular texture is drawn tight over the novel's suspenseful foundation. Taut, ominous language is sustained from the opening page of *Dog Soldiers,* in which Marge's husband, John, observes "the progress of his fever" as he sits across the street from menacing Vietnamese who lounge "sleepy-eyed, rousing themselves now and then to hiss after the passing of a sweating American," to its closing page, in which the federal agent achieves his objective – the heroin left by the fleeing Converses – but must deal with the possibility that his assistant may kill him. Believable vulnerability and menace exude from action, description, and a type of dialogue that William Pritchard compared in the *Hudson Review* (Spring 1975) to the workings of a switchblade: "the flick and spring of exchange – hardly conversation."

Blended in with the heightened aspects of a conventional thriller is a subtle philosophical inquiry concerning the generation of value. With the collapse of the ethical, all value derives from the realm of sensation, and so it is appropriate that the novel's ground of value (and central symbol) is the heroin, a drug offering many kinds of sensation, which is treated as a sacred object. Hicks, a self-styled American samurai and Nietzschean, embodies the most conscious and most evolved version of the monism to which the German philosopher reduced all motivation: the will to power. As he tells Marge as they escape from Berkeley with the heroin, "It belongs to whoever controls it." In a brilliant interior monologue near the end of the novel, the wounded, dying Hicks exercises his radically limited options for control as he tries to carry the heroin through a terrifying salt waste. Hicks tries to control with his mind this splendidly rendered wasteland as well as the pain and the eruption of past vulnerabilities within him. For intertwined with the sordidness of Stone's fictions are riveting accounts of characters' struggles for transcendence.

Surely many readers who, like Hall, were repelled by some of Hicks's earlier actions accepted the author's intentions for his character. As Stone told Schroeder, Hicks "is really extending – he is actually having a shot at greatness, at power, at true virtue, the old Roman *virtus*." A fascinating multiplicity of emotions emerges in Hicks's final characterization: stoicism, love, aggression, obscenity, pride, spite, irony, humor, the lust for *virtus*.

Correspondingly, the characterization of Converse – the ultimate dog soldier of the novel, the man who would do anything to be a living dog rather than a dead lion – is so subtle and precise that it is hard for the attentive reader not to feel compromised as he identifies with Converse's indulgences and futile assertions. Indeed, the present (1971) stances and narrated pasts of all of the principals of the novel – both Converses and Hicks – as well as those of Dieter Bechstein, the founder of the commune, combine to form a penetrating critique of the indulgences of self-proclaimed soldiers of the new order of the 1960s. The response of most reviewers to this perfectly realized novel was generally more positive than Jean Joffe Hall's. Clive Jordan spoke for the consensus of critical judgment when he wrote in the September 1975 issue of *Encounter* that because of the novel's "mastery of contemporary American dialogue, its evocation of dark forces at work in that society, its modes, its relevance to public events of the present and recent past, it strikes this British observer as a truly American work of fiction." And perhaps the most significant reviewers of all, those for the National Book Awards, chose *Dog Soldiers* as the best extended work of fiction published by an American in 1974.

Stone took two years off from academia to work on the shooting of *Who'll Stop the Rain* (1978), the film version of *Dog Soldiers,* and to begin writing another novel. After only about thirty pages of this effort, Stone abandoned it. The subject, the Münster Anabaptists, whom Stone described to Solotaroff as "a kind of scatological sect of apocalyptic proto-Mennonites," proved intractable: "I just couldn't handle the diction; how was I going to get these sixteenth-century Germans to talk? I had no idea." After a March 1976 reading in Alabama, Stone's wanderlust took over, and he found his way to Central America, traveling for six weeks in Costa Rica, Nicaragua, and Honduras. Here he found the environment in which his current interest in the conjunction of religious fervor and social unrest could mesh with his mastery of colloquial language. As he revealed to Ruas, "I became aware that there was a lot going on down there that was extraordi-

narily interesting. . . . The situation began to remind me of Vietnam. I was sensing the American presence in the underdeveloped world, and I was again seeing this vaguely irrational sense of mission which Americans are consumed with when they are about their business in the underdeveloped world: anthropologists, missionaries, deserters, crazies, druggies – various people." Among its many achievements, the novel that grew out of this sense, *A Flag for Sunrise,* traces the negative consequences of American meddlers – whether government officials or isolated American romantics – upon some of the people of Central America.

Stone's narrative strategies are consistent. All of his five novels and four published stories are written in the third person, and, since Stone writes within the impressionist tradition, the reader experiences the great majority of the works' locales and happenings through the sensibilities of the main characters. Each of the stories has only one center of consciousness, and four of the five novels have three principals: two male and one female, though it could be argued that Father Charles Egan, of *A Flag for Sunrise,* is the novel's fourth principal. Stone's practice is to introduce the main characters into the narrative one at a time and then bring them into painful, sometimes fatal, conflict.

When Stone returned to Massachusetts late in 1976 to begin his Central American novel, he created Tecan, a country – like Nicaragua and the setting of Joseph Conrad's Central American political novel, *Nostromo* – bordered by the Pacific to the west and the Caribbean to the east. Tecan blends the geography, customs, and political conditions of Nicaragua and Honduras. On its Caribbean coast, across the country from the capital, he placed the mission of a nursing order, the Devotionists, which is run by Egan and Sister Justin. The beautiful, idealistic nun, who is in her late twenties, has been at the mission for six or seven years. In his sixties and an alcoholic, Egan has been there for about twice that long and, as the novel opens, is working on the seventh draft of a book that seems to endorse standard Gnostic doctrine. This would assert that God did not create the world and does not govern it. Instead, humans and everything else in the visible universe were created by the demiurge, flawed in all Gnostic teachings and, in some, malevolently opposed to all manifestations of divine goodness. Gnostic thought constitutes a thorough rejection of mundane existence. As Hans Jonas writes in *Gnostic Religion* (1958), "The universe . . . is like a vast prison whose innermost dungeon is the earth, the scene of man's life. . . . in gnostic thought the world takes the place of the traditional underworld and is itself already the realm of the dead, that is, of those who have to be raised to life again." This possibility of a new life exists because Gnostics believed that each person contains a part of the Godhead and that destiny is to rejoin and help reconstitute Him somehow.

In one account of why Central America fired his creative powers, Stone wrote in "The Reason for Stories" (1988), "This band of republics between the Andes and the Grijalva seemed placed by its gods in a very fateful situation. The region seemed to have attracted the most violent conquistadors and the most fanatical inquisitors. When they arrived, the Spaniards found holy wells of human sacrifice. Here, racial and social oppression had always been most severe." In the novel the oppression is meticulously, often painfully detailed, but Stone pushes beyond social criticism to make much of Tecan seem like the irrevocably fallen world the Gnostics saw. One of these blasted sites is the clearing behind the mission. On one side of the clearing is a hill covering a burial pyramid; centrally located are three stelae, whose inscriptions and hieroglyphs tell of the human sacrifice that once occurred in that very space. To the clearing come Egan and his bizarre congregation (about forty, often drugged, North American and European wandering hippies); Weitling, a psychotic who hears and obeys the voice of a fertility god telling him to murder children; and two more Americans: Frank Holliwell, an anthropologist, and Pablo Tabor, a deserter from the Coast Guard who arrives a few hours after he has murdered three companions on the ship that brought him to the Tecanese coast. As Egan tells him, "You understand, Pablo? there's a charge upon the place. It draws people like Weitling and people like you. The field of blood. The place of the skull. . . . Can that be? A temple? A temple of the demiurge?"

Holliwell and Pablo are, with Justin and possibly Egan, the novel's principals. A professor at what seems to be the University of Delaware, Holliwell is strongly built, handsome, and intelligent. He has been scorched by his experience in Vietnam and is presently a self-indulgent alcoholic, wallowing in midlife crisis. In large part Holliwell comes to Tecan to encounter Egan and Justin, who, in their reported involvement with revolutionary factions, might live in an ethical realm that Holliwell feels is closed to him. For in *A Flag for Sunrise,* particularly with the relationship that develops between Justin and Holliwell, Stone continues the Kierkegaardian inquiry into the differences between aesthetic and ethical modes of existence which he wove into *Dog Soldiers.* Stone created in Sister Justin the most idealistic principal of any of his fictions. At the beginning of the ten-day space into which the author crams almost all of the novel's action, Justin is undergoing a severe crisis of faith, which leads her to accept the request of a left-wing priest to help in the impending revolution. To an interestingly qualified degree, Marx temporarily replaces Christ for Justin, but she dies a devout Christian, experiencing Christ's presence as she is tortured for her role in the revolution. Whether the Christ she experiences objectively exists is an unanswered question. Holliwell's week in Tecan leaves him, on the last page of the novel, an apparent convert to Gnosticism who has lost all sense of himself as an essentially decent person. But with the characterization of Justin, Stone offers an admittedly tentative alternative – the possibility of Christ's valorizing, redeeming presence – to the Gnosticism which largely pervades the book.

Critics of the novel found both Holliwell and Justin subtly and fully realized, but as memorable characterizations they are at least equaled by Stone's rendering of Pablo Tabor. The author told Woods in a 1985 interview, "What I'm always trying to do is define that process in American life that puts people in a state of anomie, of frustration. The national promise is so great that a tremendous bitterness is evoked by its elusiveness. That was Fitzgerald's subject, and it's mine." The majority of Stone's characters do not appear to be particularly embittered by their distance from the prized goals of society, but Pablo Tabor certainly is. In fact, Stone's comment applies more to Pablo – embittered by what he considers his degrading past, obsessed with making "the big score" – than to any of his other creations.

The more various the parts of a character, the more effective the character is if the author can somehow make the parts cohere. The different strands of psychopathy, moral outrage, innocence, feral cunning, bizarre inventiveness, and moving pathos convincingly entwine in this amphetamine addict who prays for a Dexadrine rush that will make him one of Jesus' sunbeams. The complex intensity of these often potentially dangerous elements creates the character's exciting unpredictability, which contributes powerfully to the novel. Stone's control of Pablo's actions, thought processes, and speech is remarkable.

Critics were impressed with the characterizations, the skillfulness with which the many strands of the plot are interwoven, and the seri-

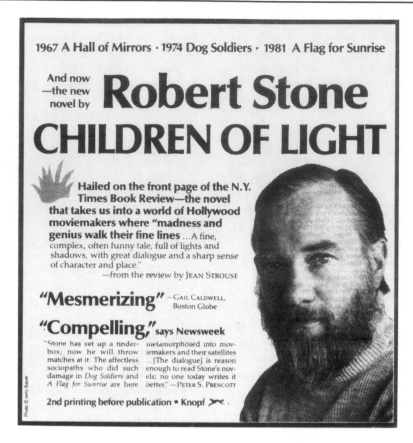

1967 A Hall of Mirrors · 1974 Dog Soldiers · 1981 A Flag for Sunrise

And now
—the new
novel by
**Robert Stone
CHILDREN OF LIGHT**

Hailed on the front page of the N.Y. Times Book Review—the novel that takes us into a world of Hollywood moviemakers where "madness and genius walk their fine lines ...A fine, complex, often funny tale, full of lights and shadows, with great dialogue and a sharp sense of character and place."
—from the review by JEAN STROUSE

"Mesmerizing" —GAIL CALDWELL, Boston Globe

"Compelling," says Newsweek

"Stone has set up a tinderbox; now he will throw matches at it. The affectless sociopaths who did such damage in *Dog Soldiers* and *A Flag for Sunrise* are here metamorphosed into moviemakers and their satellites ...[The dialogue] is reason enough to read Stone's novels; no one today writes it better." —PETER S. PRESCOTT

2nd printing before publication • Knopf

Advertisement for Stone's 1986 novel, in which he meticulously depicts the stages of a young woman's schizophrenia

ousness and ambition of the novel's ideas and politics. There were, of course, exceptions: Robert Towers in *Atlantic Monthly* and David Pritchard in *Library Journal* found it hard to separate Holliwell's garrulousness and sentimentality from the author's personality, and Joseph Epstein in *Commentary* complained that Stone had opinions, not a genuine political vision. Yet such negative responses seem to follow from the critics' failing to register the author's ironic disapproval of Holliwell's often florid and/or sentimental assertions. Then again, it could be argued that the failure to make this distance more apparent was Stone's fault, not his readers'.

Stone taught at five universities, including Stanford and Harvard, from 1979 through 1983, when he accompanied some friends who were traveling to the Santa Cruz Shakespeare Festival to read for parts. Since the director was impressed with Stone's elegant speaking voice and obvious love and control of the English language, she asked the novelist to read for the part of Kent. After what must have been a successful reading, Stone acted for the rest of the summer in *King Lear*. The Stones

had recently moved from western Massachusetts to Westport, Connecticut, and the novelist was so moved by the immersion in *King Lear* that he stopped work on a novel set in New England and began a new one. The new effort was largely filtered through the sensibility of Gordon Walker, a screenwriter and actor who, though only in his forties, had spent three of the four months before the approximately eighty-two-hour dramatized presentation of *Children of Light* playing the lead in Shakespeare's masterpiece. Like his creator, Walker professes himself overwhelmed by the bottomlessness of the play. Lines from the drama find their way into his speech, which is "chockablock with cheerless dark and deadly mutters, little incantations from the text. They were not inappropriate to his condition; during the run of the show his wife had left him."

In his interview with Solotaroff Stone discussed the origins of the novel:

> I got into the notion of a relationship between two people who know that nothing good can happen to them from each other and who know that they have nothing

but trouble and even potential destruction to give to each other but who willfully – and one of them more willfully than the other – out of nostalgia, out of weakness, out of perversity, out of a desire for generalized destruction, for his own destruction, out of a combination of self-destructiveness and selfishness, makes this pilgrimage. I thought once of calling this *Death and the Lover*. I always felt this was a knight on a pilgrimage to bring death. I had the image of a skeleton in armor, death as a knight errant, going after this enchanted princess and bringing her nothing but destruction.

Children of Light is distinguished from Stone's other novels in many ways. It has only two main characters instead of three or four, as in the other novels, and the action follows not from a concatenation of individual and social forces but from the decision of one principal, Walker, to seek out the other: the actress Lu Anne Bourgeois, who acts under the name of Lee Verger. While he was having an affair with Lu Anne a decade earlier, Walker wrote a screenplay of Kate Chopin's 1899 novel *The Awakening*. The novel follows Walker as he travels from Los Angles to Bahía Honda, in the Baja, where Lu Anne is now starring in the filming of his screenplay. His contemplations of the journey south and the journey itself, interrupted by sections that develop what is waiting for him in Mexico, occupy more than half of the novel. As a reader watches the protagonists of Stone's earlier novels approaching each other, he or she may feel more or less like a host presiding over the first interaction between two people he has gotten to know (like Rheinhardt and Geraldine) or between a pair he has gotten to know very well (like Holliwell and Justin). In contrast, the detailing of Walker's and Lu Anne's symptoms – which follow from his alcohol and cocaine addictions and from her schizophrenia – is so elaborate that, awaiting the collisions of the two damaged but energized characters, the reader might feel more like a member of the audience waiting for the curtain to go up on the plays the Marquis de Sade staged at Charenton Asylum.

Unlike his previous works, *Children of Light* has almost no overt or covert cultural commentary and no subplots. The characters' many brief internal and spoken articulations create what is for Stone a certain narrative thinness. All of this creates a narrative speed unusual in a novel in which there is so much pain, but the pace is in keeping with Walker's and Lu Anne's antic, suffering dance toward the three scenes that culminate the novel: Lu Anne's hallucinations turn an already hilarious cast party into a display of breakdown reminiscent of the mad scenes of playwright John Webster; having, with

her behavior at the party, torn herself from the restraints of the movie community, Lu Anne acts out on a hilltop an assortment of agonized or demented roles; and finally, she drowns in a half-suicidal gesture. By the end of the novel one realizes that the central action – the collision of Walker and Lu Anne – itself exists to give Stone reason to pursue Lu Anne's schizophrenic eruptions to the fullest. In his interview with Solotaroff, Stone admitted that some of Lu Anne's delusions are similar to those his mother had. It is possible that Stone's deepest motivation in the novel was to confront and transcend through art the schizophrenia that had overpowered him as a boy.

Stone's claim to Woods that all of his novels are "about America" does not hold for *Children of Light*. There is no "larger scheme of things" that subordinates or controls his characters' lives and decisions; Walker's and, particularly, Lu Anne's intentions and afflictions *are* the scheme of things. In Stone's other novels, obstacles prevent the characters from reaching their goals. Here Stone arranges the story so that roadblocks are swept away as the principals rush toward the fatal collision of their personalities. Ten days before the beginning of the dramatized present, Lu Anne conveniently stops taking the medication that controls her schizophrenic eruptions because the medication's side effects prevent her from fully inhabiting the role of Edna Pontillier, the heroine of the movie and of Chopin's novel. Her eminently decent physician-husband might have reasoned her back onto the medication as the symptoms accelerated, and surely he would have interfered with the liaison with Walker. But Stone takes him out of the novel by having him leave for his native South Africa with his and Lu Anne's two children. Although the director, Walter Drogue, is warned about the need to keep Walker away from Lu Anne, he overconfidently feels he can "swallow that asshole with a glass of water."

One might describe schizophrenia as the leaking of unconscious structures into the conscious mind. Lu Anne's medications impede leakage, while alcohol and particularly cocaine accelerate it. Walker's arrival with the cocaine that he shares with her permits the fullest disclosure of Lu Anne's complex, delusional systems as well as her struggle to transcend her damaged condition. Certainly Stone denies to Lu Anne the transcendence she seeks. Her ascent of Monte Carmel is an extremely painful, even grotesque, parody of the journey described in the great mystic poem of the most famous Carmelite of them all: Saint John of the Cross's "Dark Night of the Soul." After moving through maddened roles – Lear, Eve, and a version of the murderous Great White Goddess among them – Lu Anne sleeps through a passing storm and awakens to the beauty of a bright rainbow, arching from an adjoining peak. Apparently exhausted emotionally, she weeps as she watches the rainbow fade and struggles to interpret it as a positive sign from God: "I know it all must mean something, Gordon, because it hurts so much . . . I think there's a mercy. I think there must be." This is the novel's closest approach to one of Stone's favorite themes: the unavailability of God. Pressed by Lu Anne for his honest opinion of the rainbow as a portent of mercy, Walker replies, "Mercy? In a pig's asshole." At this point, in the author's ironic commentary on the accessibility of divine mercy or the possibilities of the miraculous, a herd of pigs appears, a manifestation which soon triggers yet another maddened eruption from Lu Anne.

Children of Light received the most unfavorable critical reception of Stone's five novels, in large part because critics failed to understand or appreciate his meticulous cataloguing of the workings of Lu Anne's pathology. What attention was paid tended to be given to the benign, but rather spectacular, group of attendants Lu Anne hallucinated – the "Long Friends." Critics found the Long Friends too melodramatic – ignoring the fact that Lu Anne's world is a melodramatic one – and repeatedly mistook Lu Anne's deranged account of the acquiring of her schizophrenia as Stone's explanation. Even Jean Strouse, one of the novel's most sympathetic reviewers, wrote in *The New York Times Book Review* that Lu Anne's "memory" of acquiring the Long Friends while playing in a crypt as a child was "contrived, called upon to explain too much." While Strouse found the culminating Monte Carmel scene "wildly sad and clever," Alvarez called the scene "the exact point where the narrative unravels into histrionics, as if Stone had lost patience with the harsh and unsavory world he has so elegantly created and settled for something more stagy but less demanding." This otherwise fine review misses the point that the Monte Carmel scene is actually the main event, the grand finale of the novel's show: the spectacular and open display of Lu Anne's symptoms.

Stone discussed the inspiration for his fifth novel, *Outerbridge Reach,* in a radio interview with Steve Benson and Robert Solotaroff (1 May 1992). Late on a 1986 November afternoon, as a part of his gathering of material for a piece on the waterways of New York City, Stone motored south on the Arthur Kill, the channel between Staten Island and New Jersey, when he came on the prospect of

this old yard named Woodie's, filled with all these skeletons of old steam tugs piled on each other so that the proportion was lost, and because of their shape – the old straight stacks, instead of raked ones – they looked like little kids' bathtub toys piled on each other. And on the other side was a tank farm: these oil storage tanks, almost as far as you could see. And then in the middle of the reach were these blue herons that were feeding so that there was at the same time a kind of marine landscape and a blighted landscape. When I looked at the chart and saw Outerbridge Reach, it suggested so many things to me. It suggested a crossing; it suggested extending, stretching, trying for something, trying to get across something. All of the weight of the name came to me; it was coming on that on the chart that made me decide to put down what I was working on and write this.

As he sought a way to dramatize a nautical and terrestrial tale of the expanse and its decay, both social and individual, Stone remembered the true story of Donald Crowhurst. In 1968 Crowhurst, an English electrical engineer who was a small-time inventor and entrepreneur, entered an around-the-world sailing race, using a trimaran he had mostly designed himself. Leaving Devon in October, Crowhurst soon found that his boat was too unstable to make the trip, and instead of circumnavigating the globe in the proper course from the Cape of Good Hope to Cape Horn, he never went farther east than his point of departure. Between December and June he sailed surreptitiously down and then up the coast of South America. In April, after a radio silence of eleven weeks, he reported that he was approaching Cape Horn from the west (when in fact he was three thousand miles northeast of the cape). A hero's welcome awaited him eighteen hundred miles away in England – mixed with some acute suspicion. Crowhurst, whose trip had apparently been accompanied by a deepening insanity, almost certainly jumped off his boat and drowned. When his boat was found, his logs gave an account of a trip that never left the Atlantic and revealed that he had started faking his positions less than six weeks into the voyage.

The revelation of Crowhurst's attempted hoax, disordered mind, and probable suicide was sensationally aired in the papers in late July 1969, and Stone, then living outside of London, devoured these accounts. He told Solotaroff during the radio interview that when he originally read the account in the London *Times,* "it seemed like such a wonderful example of the connection between heroism and folly, which are never too far separated, and often the line between them is very fine." In answer to the question of why he transformed the wildly extroverted Crowhurst into the often rigid, idealistic Owen Browne, Stone explained:

> I wasn't all that taken with who Crowhurst himself was or Crowhurst's individual circumstances. The human dimension of the story is wonderful, but it was the more universal aspect than the particular world of Crowhurst that interested me, and it seemed to me that the points I wanted to make are not necessarily the same points that are brought to the fore by the people who handled the Crowhurst story. I wanted to illustrate a theme of mine, which is how difficult it is for people to behave well and how even a good person in certain circumstances can trap himself in something like a lie. . . . So I had my own agenda, very much my own agenda, but I really loved the idea of reducing their circumstances to the ocean, and the sky and the boat, and of course their own mind, and having to live it out to the most intense degree.

Although the social orders of *Outerbridge Reach* are flawed, they are not malevolent, as are those of Stone's first three novels. Moreover, the social centrality of Owen Browne and his wife Anne, and the latter's psychic health, stand in sharp contrast against Stone's existing gallery of self-destructive and/or socially marginal protagonists: alcoholics, drug addicts, drug smugglers, psychopaths, candidates for martyrdom, and a schizophrenic. (Sister Justin of *A Flag for Sunrise* is, admittedly, a relatively healthy candidate for martyrdom.) Stone returned to his usual triad of main characters – two men and a woman. The second man, Ron Strickland, a documentary director whose origins are interestingly similar to Stone's, is twisted and troubled. Still, for a Stone character he remains an uncharacteristically fine functioner: his films are the products of a hardworking, talented, and shrewd man.

John Leonard describes Browne as "someone new to Stone's fiction: Northeast Middle-Class Normal, Dick Tracy Square, Wonderbread WASPy, as if wandering in from a Cheever or an Updike: monogamous husband, worried father, Navy pilot, sailboat salesman. He seldom drinks, never drugs and listens to the music of Russ Columbo." Although Browne is not as bland or square as Leonard would have him, Browne does, without too much hypocrisy, present himself to the world as a dignified and disciplined man. Sixteen years after his successive four-year stints in Vietnam and Annapolis, the forty-two-year-old Browne lives in a small city on Long Island Sound and appears to be a perfect match for his employer, Altan Marine Corporation. He writes the company's copy, and his good looks and articulateness enable him to act in the promotional films he scripts.

Browne's self-presentation is impressive, especially to women. However, as the novel opens, Browne is in a state that he will later describe as "paralysis and despair," for his unfulfilled romantic yearnings are breaking through the armature he has created to encase them. The vapid weather seems a correlative to alert some people to the vapidity of their inner lives. Browne, "stirred by the weather and some obscure guilt" at the beginning of the novel, travels to Annapolis to visit two old Navy buddies, one of whom tells him that "the heroic age of the bourgeoisie is over" – to which Browne adds, "So is the cold war. . . . We're all redundant." Having committed himself to heroic goals as a boy, Browne had been able to regard his service in Vietnam as a holy war against the Communist monolith, one that offered him opportunity to fulfill his desires to serve his country and to prove himself in heroic struggle. (Though implicated in the carnage as a guider of Navy planes to Vietnamese targets and, in a later duty, a defender of the process of the war to the press, Browne has always escaped feeling any guilt about his involvement.)

A few days after Browne's comment about his sense of redundancy, he thinks over his situation more cogently. The decisive war against communism "would never be fought because the enemy had proved false. All his fierce alternatives were lies. Surely, Browne thought sleepily, this was a good thing. Yet something was lost. For his own part, he was tired of living [only] for himself and for those who were him by extension. It was impossible, he thought. Empty and impossible." Between Browne and the heroic collectivity that he still yearns for is what he sees as the presiding national spirit of "No Can Do. It was everywhere lately, poisoning life and the country." When the opportunity for the single-handed circumnavigation offers itself, Browne sees it as an opportunity to join the brotherhood of morally disciplined adventurers, some of whom have written the memoirs he likes to read.

In Browne, Stone does a splendid job of creating a character who is enough of a tweedy, conscientious WASP to represent convincingly that part of American culture but who is filled with enough loathing for his present life and enough impulsiveness to set out around the world with little single-handed sailing experience and in a dangerous boat. Stone gives his protagonist enough gung-ho idealism and competence to make his way to what his creator has waiting for him in the southern latitudes, where his potentials of emotion and articulation combine with circumstances and his vulnerability to generate commanding eloquence and pathos.

Alternating with the chapters that trace Browne's assertions and deteriorations are those that document Strickland's unwilling love for Anne Browne and her fascination with the twisted moviemaker, obsessions that propel the other two principals into psychic terrains that are almost as frightening to them as the annihilating seas that Browne traverses are to him.

Of all Stone's novels, *Outerbridge Reach* states his negative criticism of America most generally, least obliquely. To take just three of many examples, Browne's own initial malaise is representative: the unseasonable warmth might be the result of the greenhouse effect, to Browne one of the many symptoms of the wrong turn his country has made. The "South Korean fuckup," the faulty hose that aborts Browne's initial sail to Annapolis, speaks of the immense amount of manufacturing farmed out by American companies to Third World countries. And Browne relates the fateful shoddiness of the boat in which he tries to circumnavigate to the way the United States has "[s]old our pottage, overheated the poles, poisoned the rain, burned away the horizon with acid. Despised our birthright. Forgot everything, destroyed and laughed away our holy things." As Pritchard observes in *The New York Times Book Review* of 23 February 1992, Stone's prose is extraordinarily precise and suggestive:

> The novel's movement is leisurely but the narrative has shapeliness and great cumulative power. The source of that power – and pleasure – is of course, Mr. Stone's language as it creates a style. On every page something verbally interesting happens: the insolent voice of a Hylan executive "suggested gulls over India Wharf"; Strickland's 1963 Porsche has rusty fittings, but "the engine reported like a Prussian sailor on the first turn of the key"; Captain Riggs-Bowen "had a brick-red blood-pressure mask around his eyes which resembled those of a raptor"; Anne's father, who disapproves of Browne, calls the sea a desert ("Nothing there but social cripples and the odd Filipino") while his sixty-year-old secretary, Antoinette Lamattina looks "As though she thrived on chaste bereavement, frequent communion and the occasional excursion to Roseland Ballroom."

Leonard asserts that the last half of the novel is "as dazzling as anything in American literature." This estimation may be excessive – one thinks of the level of the prose sustained in *The Sound and the Fury* or *The Great Gatsby* – but certainly the last half of the novel, which begins with Browne finally at sea, is impressive. The expansiveness of both locale and concern justifies the title, and the novel is close to being a great one.

The four short stories that Stone has published can be divided into two groups of two. The earlier stories, the 1969 "Porque No Tiene, Porque Le Falta" and the 1975 "Aquarius Obscured," are largely comic performances that, like Stone's first three novels, trace the liabilities of drugs, alcohol, and paranoia. The second story acts as a rebuttal of contemporary beliefs in the coming of Aquarius, when – as the authors of the musical *Hair* would have it – the benign conjunction of planets will enable us to live with the fullest honesty, empathy, and harmony. At the center of "Aquarius Obscured" is a brilliantly conceived encounter at an aquarium between a woman who has just swallowed a handful of hallucinatory pills and a porpoise to whom the woman attributes the power of speech and the desire to conquer the world. The two later stories, "Absence of Mercy" and "Helping," both published in 1987, are in tone and theme much more serious: both detail the pervasive effects of a damaging past.

Both "Porque No Tiene, Porque Le Falta" and "Helping" were included in yearly collections of best stories, and the other two stories are not significantly inferior to these two. Moreover, Stone's work as a novelist has brought him significant recognition. He has received Guggenheim and NEH fellowships, the five-year Mildred and Harold Strauss Living Award, the John Dos Passos Prize for Literature, the American Academy and Institute of Arts and Letters Award; the *Los Angeles Times* Book Prize for *A Flag for Sunrise,* and in 1993 he replaced John Barth as the "star" of the creative-writing program at Johns Hopkins University. In his illuminating summary of the contemporary fictional scene, Sven Birkerts ranks Stone highly: "Among our writers, only Robert Stone, Don DeLillo, and Thomas Pynchon have found ways to incorporate the period, its energies and contradictions, into their fiction. They have all recognized in the brief cultural interlude a condensation of our fundamental nature" (*American Energies,* 1992). But something should be added. In perhaps half of DeLillo's novels and all of Pynchon's, characterization is so flat that it often verges on caricature. There is nothing surprising about this: the more a work is illustrative, the more characterizations are flattened or universalized, as the work's agents increasingly serve as conduits for the author's ideas or moral precepts. Among these three significant social critics, only Stone has consistently created singular, arresting characters – both principals and supporting players – and achieved such compelling pace and compression in each novel that, as Pritchard wrote in the 1994 *Norton Anthology of American Literature,* "once entered, the book is impossible to put down. A confirmed storyteller like Stone would probably demand no further tribute."

Interviews:

Kay Bonetti, "An Interview with Robert Stone," *Missouri Review,* 6 (Fall 1982): 91–114;

Maureen Karagueuzian, "Interview with Robert Stone," *Triquarterly,* 53 (Winter 1983): 249–258;

Eric James Schroeder, "Two Interviews: Talks with Tim O'Brien and Robert Stone," *Modern Fiction Studies,* 30 (Spring 1984): 135–164;

Steve Chapple, "Robert Stone Faces the Devil," *Mother Jones,* 9 (May 1984): 35–41;

William Crawford Woods, "The Art of Fiction XX: Robert Stone," *Paris Review,* 27 (Winter 1985): 26–57;

Charles Ruas, *Conversations with American Writers* (New York: Knopf, 1985);

Steve Benson and Robert Solotaroff, "Talking Sense," Minneapolis, KUOM, 1 May 1992;

Robert Solotaroff, "An Interview with Robert Stone," *South Carolina Review,* 26 (Fall 1993): 27–49.

Bibliography:

Ken Lopez and Bev Chaney, *Robert Stone: A Bibliography, 1960–1992* (Hadley, Mass.: Numinous Press, 1992).

References:

A[lfred] Alvarez, "Among the Freaks," *New York Review of Books,* 33 (10 April 1986): 23–26;

David West Furniss, "Making Sense of the War: Vietnam and American Prose," Ph.D. dissertation, University of Minnesota, 1989, pp. 80–99;

Maureen Karagueuzian, "Irony in Robert Stone's *Dog Soldiers,*" *Critique: Studies in Modern Fiction,* 24 (Winter 1983): 65–73;

Sharon Lee Ladin, "Spirit Warriors: The Samurai Figure in Current American Fiction," Ph.D. dissertation, University of California, Santa Cruz, 1979, pp. 165–199;

John Leonard, "Leviathan," *Nation,* 254 (13 April 1992): 489–494;

Eileen Taylor McClay, "Images of Latin America in Contemporary U.S. Literature," Ph.D. dissertation, George Washington University, 1987, pp. 134–187;

L. Hugh Moore, "The Undersea World of Robert Stone," *Critique: Studies in Modern Fiction,* 11 (1969): 43–56;

Hugh O'Haire, "The Search for Transcendence in the Novels of Robert Stone," M.A. thesis, City University of New York, Queens campus, n.d.;

John G. Parks, "Unfit Survivors: The Failed and Lost Pilgrims in the Fiction of Robert Stone," *CEA Critic,* 53 (Fall 1990): 52–57;

Roger Sale, "Robert Stone," in his *On Not Being Good Enough* (New York: Oxford University Press, 1979), pp. 66–73;

Frank W. Shelton, "Robert Stone's *Dog Soldiers:* Vietnam Comes Home to America," *Critique: Studies in Modern Fiction,* 24 (Winter 1983): 74–81;

Robert Solotaroff, *Robert Stone* (New York: Twayne, 1994);

Bruce Weber, "An Eye for Danger," *New York Times Magazine,* 19 January 1992, pp. 19–24.

Gore Vidal

(3 October 1925 –)

Robert F. Kiernan
Manhattan College

See also the Vidal entry in *DLB 6: American Novelists Since World War II, Second Series*.

BOOKS: *Williwaw* (New York: Dutton, 1946; London: Panther, 1965); republished as *Dangerous Voyage* (New York: Signet/New American Library, 1953);

In a Yellow Wood (New York: Dutton, 1947; London: New English Library, 1967);

The City and the Pillar (New York: Dutton, 1948; London: Lehmann, 1949; revised and enlarged edition, New York: Dutton, 1965; London: Heinemann, 1965);

The Season of Comfort (New York: Dutton, 1949);

A Search for the King: A Twelfth-Century Legend (New York: Dutton, 1950; London: New English Library, 1967);

Dark Green, Bright Red (New York: Dutton, 1950; London: Lehmann, 1950; revised edition, New York: Signet/New American Library, 1968; London: New English Library, 1968);

Death in the Fifth Position, as Edgar Box (New York: Dutton, 1952; London: Heinemann, 1954);

The Judgment of Paris (New York: Dutton, 1952; London: Heinemann, 1953; revised and abridged edition, New York: Ballantine, 1961; revised edition, Boston: Little, Brown, 1965; London: Heinemann, 1966);

Death Before Bedtime, as Edgar Box (New York: Dutton, 1953; London: Heinemann, 1954);

Death Likes It Hot, as Edgar Box (New York: Dutton, 1954; London: Heinemann, 1955);

Messiah (New York: Dutton, 1954; London: Heinemann, 1955; revised edition, Boston: Little, Brown, 1965; London: Heinemann, 1968);

A Thirsty Evil: Seven Short Stories (New York: Zero Press, 1956; London: Heinemann, 1958; enlarged edition, London: New English Library, 1967);

Visit to a Small Planet and Other Television Plays (Boston: Little, Brown, 1956);

Visit to a Small Planet: A Comedy Akin to a Vaudeville (Boston: Little, Brown, 1957; revised edition, New York: Dramatists Play Service, 1959);

The Best Man: A Play of Politics (Boston: Little, Brown, 1960; revised edition, New York: Dramatists Play Service, 1977);

On the March to the Sea: A Southron Tragedy (New York: Grove, n.d.; London: Heinemann, 1962);

Romulus: A New Comedy, Adapted from a Play by Friedrich Dürrenmatt (New York: Dramatists Play Service, 1962);

Rocking the Boat (Boston: Little, Brown, 1962; London: Heinemann, 1963);

Three Plays (London: Heinemann, 1962);

Julian: A Novel (Boston: Little, Brown, 1964; London: Heinemann, 1964);

Washington, D.C.: A Novel (Boston: Little, Brown, 1967; London: Heinemann, 1967);

Myra Breckinridge (Boston: Little, Brown, 1968; bowdlerized edition, London: Blond, 1968); revised and enlarged as *Myra Breckinridge & Myron* (New York: Random House, 1986);

Sex, Death and Money (New York & London: Bantam, 1968);

Weekend: A Comedy in Two Acts (New York: Dramatists Play Service, 1968);

Reflections Upon a Sinking Ship (Boston: Little, Brown, 1969; London: Heinemann, 1969);

Two Sisters: A Memoir in the Form of a Novel (Boston: Little, Brown, 1970; London: Heinemann, 1970);

An Evening with Richard Nixon (New York: Random House, 1972);

Homage to Daniel Shays: Collected Essays, 1952–1972 (New York: Random House, 1972); published as *Collected Essays, 1952–1972* (London: Heinemann, 1974); republished as *On Our Own Now* (St. Albans, U.K.: Panther, 1976);

Burr: A Novel (New York: Random House, 1973; London: Heinemann, 1974);

Gore Vidal

Myron: A Novel (New York: Random House, 1974;
London: Heinemann, 1975); enlarged as *Myra
Breckinridge & Myron* (New York: Random
House, 1986);

Great American Families, by Vidal and others (New
York: Norton, 1975), pp. 7–27;

1876: A Novel (New York: Random House, 1976;
London: Heinemann, 1976);

Matters of Fact and of Fiction: Essays 1973–1976 (New
York: Random House, 1977);

Kalki: A Novel (New York: Random House, 1978;
London: Heinemann, 1978);

Creation: A Novel (New York: Random House, 1981;
London: Heinemann, 1981);

*The Second American Revolution and Other Essays (1976–
1982)* (New York: Random House, 1982);
published as *Pink Triangle and Yellow Star, and
Other Essays (1976–1982)* (London: Heinemann, 1982);

Duluth (New York: Random House, 1983; London:
Heinemann, 1983);

Lincoln: A Novel (New York: Random House, 1984;
London: Heinemann, 1984);

Vidal in Venice, edited by George Armstrong, photographs by Tore Gill (New York: Summit

Books, 1985; London: Weidenfeld & Nicolson, 1985);

Armageddon? Essays, 1983–1987 (London: Deutsch,
1987); enlarged as *At Home: Essays 1982–88*
(New York: Random House, 1988),

Empire: A Novel (New York: Random House, 1987;
London: Deutsch, 1987);

The Best Man: A Screen Adaptation of the Original Play,
edited by George P. Garrett and others (New
York: Irvington, 1989);

Hollywood: A Novel of America in the 1920s (London:
Deutsch, 1989; New York: Random House,
1990);

A View from the Diner's Club: Essays 1987–1991 (London: Deutsch, 1991);

The Decline and Fall of the American Empire (Berkeley,
Cal.: Odonian Press, 1992);

Live from Golgotha (New York: Random House,
1992; London: Deutsch, 1992);

Screening History, The William E. Massey Sr. Lectures in the History of American Civilization
(Cambridge: Harvard University Press,
1992);

United States – Essays, 1951–1991 (New York: Random House, 1992);

PLAY PRODUCTIONS: *Visit to a Small Planet,* New York, Booth Theatre, 7 February 1957;

The Best Man, New York, Morosco Theatre, 31 March 1960;

On the March to the Sea: A Southron Comedy, Hyde Park, N.Y., summer 1960;

Romulus, New York, Music Box Theatre, 10 January 1962;

Weekend, New York, Broadhurst Theatre, 13 March 1968;

An Evening with Richard Nixon and . . . , New York, Schubert Theatre, 30 April 1972.

MOTION PICTURES: *The Catered Affair,* screenplay by Vidal, adapted from Paddy Chayefsky's teleplay *Wedding Breakfast,* M-G-M, 1956;

I Accuse!, screenplay by Vidal, M-G-M, 1958;

The Scapegoat, screenplay by Vidal and Robert Hamer, M-G-M, 1959;

Suddenly, Last Summer, screenplay by Vidal and Tennessee Williams, adapted from Williams's play, Columbia, 1959;

The Best Man, screenplay by Vidal, adapted from his play, United Artists, 1964;

Is Paris Burning?, screenplay by Vidal and Francis Ford Coppola, adapted from the book by Gary Collins and Dominique Lapierre, Paramount, 1966;

The Last of the Mobile Hot-Shots, screenplay by Vidal, adapted from Tennessee Williams's *The Seven Descents of Myrtle,* Warner Bros., 1970.

TELEVISION: *Dark Possession,* teleplay by Vidal, *Studio One,* CBS, 15 February 1954;

Smoke, teleplay by Vidal, adapted from the story by William Faulkner, *Suspense,* CBS, 4 May 1954;

Barn Burning, teleplay by Vidal, adapted from the story by William Faulkner, *Suspense,* CBS, 17 August 1954;

A Sense of Justice, teleplay by Vidal, *Philco Television Playhouse,* NBC, 6 February 1955;

The Turn of the Screw, teleplay by Vidal, adapted from the novel by Henry James, *Omnibus,* CBS, 13 February 1955;

The Blue Hotel, teleplay by Vidal, adapted from the story by Stephen Crane, *Danger,* CBS, 22 February 1955;

Stage Door, teleplay by Vidal, adapted from the drama by George S. Kaufman and Edna Ferber, *The Best of Broadway,* CBS, 6 April 1955;

Summer Pavilion, teleplay by Vidal, *Studio One,* CBS, 2 May 1955;

Visit to a Small Planet, teleplay by Vidal, *Goodyear Television Playhouse,* NBC, 8 May 1955;

A Farewell to Arms, teleplay by Vidal, adapted from the novel by Ernest Hemingway, *Climax,* CBS, 26 May 1955;

The Death of Billy the Kid, teleplay by Vidal, *Philco Television Playhouse,* NBC, 24 July 1955;

Dr. Jekyll and Mr. Hyde, teleplay by Vidal, adapted from the novel by Robert Lewis Stevenson, *Climax,* CBS, 28 July 1955;;

Portrait of a Ballerina, teleplay by Vidal as Edgar Box, adapted from his novel *Death in the Fifth Position,* CBS, 1 January 1956;

Honor, teleplay by Vidal, *Playwrights 56,* NBC, 19 June 1956;

The Indestructible Mr. Gore, teleplay and narration by Vidal, *Sunday Showcase,* NBC, 13 December 1959;

Dear Arthur, teleplay by Vidal, adapted from the drama by Ferenc Molnar, *Ford Startime,* NBC, 22 March 1960;

Dress Gray, teleplay by Vidal, adapted from the novel by Lucian K. Truscott IV, NBC, 9–10 March 1986;

Vidal in Venice, text and narration by Vidal, WNET, 30 June 1986;

Gore Vidal's Billy the Kid, teleplay by Vidal, adapted from his screenplay *The Death of Billy the Kid,* TNT, 10 May 1989.

OTHER: *Best Television Plays,* volume 1, edited by Vidal (New York: Ballantine, 1956);

Roloff Beny, *Roloff Beny in Italy,* epilogue by Vidal (New York: Harper & Row, 1974), pp. 408–409.

"Gore Vidal wasn't what I set out to be. . . ," Gore Vidal quipped in the 18 November 1974 *Newsweek,* "but I don't mind what I've become." What he has become is one of America's preeminent novelists, a prolific writer whose novels and collections of essays have sold in excess of thirty million copies. His historical novels, especially the novels of the American Chronicle, are among the most accomplished and artful work in the genre by a living author. His Myra/Myron novels are classic works of camp sensibility, and his essays perfectly express his role of American cultural critic. These considerable achievements tend to be underestimated

Warrant Officer, J.G., Gore Vidal at the wheel of Army Freight Supply Ship 35, winter 1944–1945 (Collection of Gore Vidal). His experiences as first mate on supply runs in the Aleutian Islands provided the background for his first novel,
Williwaw *(1946).*

largely because of the variety of Vidal's writerly impulses, as if he had somehow failed to fix upon his essential being as a writer. He is viewed by Mitchell S. Ross as a "detoured politician," by Russell Jacoby as a last intellectual, and by Bernard E. Dick as an "apostate angel." Such tags have their value, but Vidal has said that he is simply a professional writer, asserting in 1975 that he would like to be remembered as "the person who wrote the best sentences in his time."

Although Vidal styles himself a populist, he grew up in a patrician world that explains a great deal of who and what he is as a writer. His mother, Nina Gore Vidal Auchincloss Olds (1903–1978), was a Washington socialite who traced her American roots to the eighteenth century, and his father, Eugene Vidal (1895–1969), was an aviation expert who taught aeronautics at the United States Military Academy, founded several unsuccessful airlines, and from 1933 to 1937 served President

Franklin D. Roosevelt as director of air commerce. Vidal was born at the United States Military Academy at West Point, New York, but the family lived for the first ten years of his life in the Washington establishment of his maternal grandfather, Sen. Thomas Pryor Gore of Oklahoma (1870–1949). In the senator's parlors, the young Vidal became accustomed to such visitors as Huey Long and Eleanor Roosevelt. After Vidal's parents divorced in 1935, his mother married the wealthy and socially prominent financier Hugh D. Auchincloss, and from 1936 until 1941 Vidal lived at the Auchincloss estate on the Potomac River when not at a succession of boarding schools, among them the spartan Los Alamos Ranch School in New Mexico. After separating from Vidal's mother, Auchincloss went on to marry Janet Lee Bouvier, the mother of Jacqueline Bouvier Kennedy Onassis, bringing Vidal into future orbit with the Kennedy family. Vidal apparently felt abandoned by his parents as a result of these several domestic upheavals and based his sense of family in Senator Gore. As a student at Phillips Exeter Academy in New Hampshire, he was an America Firster in imitation of his grandfather's populism, and by the time he graduated from Exeter in 1943 he had changed his name from Eugene Luther Vidal, after his father, to Gore Vidal. In 1959 he was further to commemorate his grandfather by scripting and narrating a television play titled *The Indestructible Mr. Gore,* in which he played the role of himself.

Vidal's cynicism about American politics and the insider's perspective he likes to claim in writing about American history as well as his taste for luxury and his stated pride in avoiding salaried employment would all seem to have originated in his patrician background. To understand Vidal's political ideology, however, one must give special importance to the idiosyncratic populism of Senator Gore that Vidal adopted as his own. This populist legacy impelled him in 1960 to seek election to the House of Representatives from New York's heavily Republican Twenty-ninth Congressional District on a platform of taxing wealth; to cofound with Dr. Benjamin Spock the short-lived New Party (later refounded briefly as the People's Party) at the Democratic National Convention of 1968; and to seek in 1982 a California Democratic nomination to the United States Senate on a platform that included taxing church income and nationalizing natural resources.

The advantages of a privileged youth ended for Vidal with graduation from Phillips Exeter Academy. Enlisting in the wartime army on 30 July 1943, he trained as an engineer and served in 1945 as a maritime warrant officer aboard a ship patrolling the Aleutian Islands. During this period he developed severe rheumatoid arthritis that led to his hospitalization. After demobilization, he worked as an editor for the firm of E. P. Dutton, which that same year published his first novel, *Williwaw* (1946). The novel was begun while Vidal was in uniform and is the story of seven men caught up in a web of mutual antagonisms while they serve on an army transport vessel cruising the Aleutian waters during World War II. The novel is obviously influenced by Ernest Hemingway's style, and its central event is a storm (or williwaw), an echo of Joseph Conrad. The men fail the test of camaraderie that the storm sets, and the novel thus deflates wartime clichés. If *Williwaw* is derivative and constituted something of a false start for Vidal, it bears remembering that he was a teenage author, nineteen years old when it was written. Surprisingly, the novel was well received. Indeed, encomiums in the *Saturday Review of Literature, The New York Times,* and *The New York Times Book Review* spoke of its palpable authenticity in such a way as to persuade the young editor to resign immediately his position at Dutton and to chance full-time in New York City the life of a literary wunderkind.

A second novel, *In a Yellow Wood* (1947), appeared quickly and drew upon Vidal's stint as a Dutton editor to tell the story of one day in the life of Robert Holton, a young veteran who chooses to embrace the dull routine of his days in a New York brokerage firm rather than to follow "the road not taken" in the yellow wood of Robert Frost's famous poem. While there are glimmers of artfulness in the novel, it is made tedious on the whole by Holton's unearned ennui. It received some favorable notice on its publication, but it was dismissed by its author in a 1974 interview with the *Paris Review* as "in limbo forever."

In his third novel, *The City and the Pillar* (1948), Vidal boldly told a story of homosexual self-discovery. A literary sensation in its day, it was generally considered to be of a piece with the Kinsey report, which came out the same year. The 10 January 1948 *New Yorker,* offended at words it thought proper to "a metropolitan police blotter," called it "tabloid writing." Other reviews called the novel a "social tract," and "clinical." The sensational plot traces a young man named Jim Willard and his adolescent homosexual passion for a friend he thinks of as a lost twin, until it culminates in a *crime passionnel* – murder in the first edition of the novel, homosexual rape in a 1965 revision. Reviewers found the plotting melodramatic and the tone inappropriately dispassionate, but particularly disturbing at the time was the depiction of Jim Willard as an all-American boy. Indeed, Willard is one of those boy-men almost prototypical in American literature, and his passion for his lost twin recalls not only Aristophanes' myth of creation in Plato's *Symposium* but also the mainstream pattern of Natty Bumppo's affection for Chingachgook, Ishmael's love for Queequeg, and Huck Finn's concern for Jim. Today, the novel is less striking for this audacious stance in relation to figures of the literary canon than for its authentic, unsentimental depiction of a coming-out experience in the 1940s. It survives the period of its writing better than any other American novel of comparable subject for the poise of its understandings and for the credibility of Jim Willard's confusions.

While residing primarily in Antigua, Guatemala, Vidal completed three more novels: *The Season of Comfort* (1949), *Dark Green, Bright Red* (1950), and *A Search for the King* (1950). If none of these works has a claim to literary distinction, each can be understood as an incremental step toward Vidal's mature work. *The Season of Comfort* is something of an autobiographical self-indulgence, a novel about the psychic damage done young Bill Giraud in a dysfunctional southern family whose personae correspond unmistakably to those of Vidal's own family. It attempts unsuccessfully the archness of tone that distinguishes much of Vidal's mature work, but it is entirely successful in throwing off the Hemingway style that until then had straitjacketed Vidal's prose.

Dark Green, Bright Red is a quite different endeavor from *The Season of Comfort*. Inspired by Vidal's residence in Guatemala, it is a novel of tropical intrigue and failed revolution with a cast of characters adapted from the novels of Graham Greene and Joseph Conrad, among them Gen. Jorge Alvarez Asturias, a former president of the republic; José Alvarez, his playboy son; and Peter Nelson, an American mercenary. Like Greene and Conrad, Vidal envelops the adventure-story elements of his plot in a pervasive weltschmerz, but the novel is weakened by inadequate character development.

The most interesting and certainly the most narratively competent of these three novels is *A Search for the King*, a straightforward retelling of the thirteenth-century tale of the troubadour Blondel de Néel and his search for Richard the Lion-Hearted. If the straightforwardness of the novel points backward to the Hemingway manner, its historical elements point forward to the novels of Vidal's maturity. And its two central male figures, one of whom grounds his existence in the other, is an effective treatment of a twin motif that haunts Vidal's work.

The Judgment of Paris (1952) is the first work of Vidal's artistic maturity. Based on the incident in Greek mythology in which Paris is forced to choose among Hera, Athena, and Aphrodite, it depicts a young man sojourning in Europe who must choose among three women offering him variously a political career, an intellectual life, and physical intimacy. So entirely unimportant is this structure in the novel's development, however, that one is compelled to wonder if Vidal is parodying the modernist tendency to find in mythology a gloss for every human situation. Far more interesting than the mythic parallel is the wealth of invention that Vidal expends on minor characters. Indeed, Vidal seems to have discovered in writing *The Judgment of Paris* the narrative power of anecdotes rendered wittily, of character sketches that approach caricature, and of a fine, enveloping insouciance — all hallmarks of

his mature art. Presciently, the critic John W. Aldridge was moved to declare Vidal's long apprenticeship at an end.

Having purchased in 1950 an 1820 Greek Revival mansion in Barrytown, New York, Vidal was under increasing financial pressure. Three inconsequential if pleasant detective stories that he wrote under the pseudonym Edgar Box were the immediate result: *Death in the Fifth Position* (1952), *Death Before Bedtime* (1953), and *Death Likes It Hot* (1954). To augment his income further, Vidal began writing screenplays in the mid 1950s — some twenty or thirty, he avers, for television drama series such as *Omnibus* and *Studio One,* and about a dozen screenplays for Hollywood, among them *The Catered Affair* (1956), *I Accuse!* (1958), and an adaptation of Tennessee Williams's *Suddenly, Last Summer* (1959). His play *Visit to a Small Planet,* an engaging science-fiction fantasy, was successful in different versions on television in 1955 and on Broadway in 1957, where it ran for a respectable 338 performances. In the wake of its success, Vidal began to review stage productions as well as books, and he served in the late 1950s as a drama critic for the *Reporter*. *The Best Man* (1960), a topical election-year drama about character assassination in a presidential campaign, repeated the success of *Visit to a Small Planet* and enjoyed a Broadway run of 520 performances. Later works such as *Romulus* (1962), adapted from Friedrich Dürrenmatt's *Romulus der Grosse*; *Weekend* (1968); and *An Evening with Richard Nixon* (1972) did not gain large audiences. Briefly in the late 1950s, however, Vidal enjoyed a reputation as a scriptwriter superior to his reputation as a novelist. By 1960 he could command on occasion nearly five thousand dollars for a one-hour television script. "What became of our postwar hopes?" lamented the 29 July 1962 *New York Times Book Review,* believing that Vidal and other postwar writers had abandoned the novel.

Aside from a handful of short stories collected as *A Thirsty Evil* (1956), Vidal had published only one novel, *Messiah* (1954), in the decade preceding the *New York Times Book Review* lament. An undistinguished but in some ways seminal work, its putative subject is the origin of an imaginary messianic cult as recorded in a memoir and some diaristic passages set down in the year 2000 by Eugene Luther, a man who helped to launch the cult in the early 1950s. The novel's real subjects are religious revisionism and the merchandising of messiahs — subjects to which Vidal would return several times in his career. Having discovered his best voice in *The Judgment of Paris*, Vidal discovered his best genre in *Mes-*

Vidal with Anaïs Nin (University of California at Los Angeles)

siah, for the fictive memoir lends itself to Vidal's ideological revisionism and accommodates well his penchant for anecdote, quick character sketches, and incidental grotesquery.

These discoveries of voice and genre culminated in 1964 in *Julian,* a novel about the fourth-century Roman emperor known as Julian the Apostate in the Christian church, which the emperor rejected for Mithraism. Ostensibly Julian's autobiographical memoir and his private journal as written in the year of his death and introduced and annotated seventeen years later by the philosophers Libanius of Antioch and Priscus of Athens, the novel is a rich, many-layered tale of Julian the Christian becoming Julian the Apostate, of Julian the philosopher becoming Julian the warrior, and of Julian the heir-unapparent becoming Julian the emperor – all critiqued with entertaining volubility by Priscus and Libanius. The historical authenticity of the novel is impressive. Vidal had occupied himself for five years with voluminous source material on the emperor and for several more years with a general study of the fourth century, developing a discipline of serious research that he would bring to all of his historical fictions. *Julian* is also contemporaneously edged: Vidal's recent experiments in form and voice had provided him with a technique for turning the fourth-century triumph of Christianity over Mithraism into a diagnosis of present-day cultural ills. This latter achievement of the novel's historicity was not generally recognized at the time. Critics tended to seek in Vidal's novel the high drama of Robert Graves's reconstructions of history but missed his effort to pinpoint in ancient history a moment of crisis for the modern world.

Shortly after Vidal's unsuccessful bid for a congressional seat in 1960, he began to channel his political views into a series of articles for the magazine *Esquire.* Since then he has discoursed many times on politics and other cultural matters in the pages of the *New York Review of Books,* the *New Statesman,* and similar organs of opinion. A frequent guest on television talk shows since the early 1960s, he can be counted upon to turn the conversation to American politics, often in a confrontational way. Although not considered a weighty or original thinker, Vidal has earned considerable stature as a critic of the American establishment through his aphoristic style. The essays collected in *Reflections Upon a Sinking Ship* (1969), *Homage to Daniel Shays* (1972), and several other collections are in general less interesting for their large arguments than for their incidental disparagements and flashes of wit.

Julian led the way to the great endeavor of Vidal's maturity: a loosely coordinated, multivolume narrative that highlights figures and periods of American history. Not written or published in temporal sequence (not talked about at all and probably not conceived as a sequence until the mid 1970s), Vidal's chronicle of America includes to date the novels *Washington, D.C.* (1967), *Burr* (1973), *1876* (1976), *Lincoln* (1984), *Empire* (1987), and *Hollywood* (1989). The sequence employs as an organizing motif an imaginary family dynasty, the Schuyler-Sanfords, but is not in any important sense a unified whole. The novels of the American Chronicle were creatively nourished, it would seem, by Vidal's selling his Barrytown mansion in the early 1960s and settling with his longtime companion Howard Austen in Rome and in Ravello, on Italy's Amalfi coast. He quipped, in the epilogue to Roloff Beny's *Roloff Beny in Italy* (1974), that "a city which calls itself 'eternal' is obviously the best place to watch eternity go down the drain." James Tatum observes, in Jay Parini's 1992 work, that Vidal recovered the model for America as a second Rome in Italy and also recovered there a distinctively Roman way of attacking the American Rome.

Washington, D.C., the first-written, temporally last novel in Vidal's American Chronicle, is a comedy of political manners that unfolds between the years 1937 and 1956, with Pearl Harbor, Roosevelt's death, the McCarthy hearings, and the Korean War figuring prominently in the background. It focuses on the Washington families of James Burden Day, an influential senator, and of Blaise Sanford, owner of the *Washington Tribune*. It also traces the unscrupulous rise to power of Clay Overbury, a rise to power so ripely gothic that it imparts a humorous cast even to the seamiest aspects of political life. Vidal's spokesman for his own, seriocomic point of view is young Peter Sanford, who thrills to the melodrama of both familial and political life without losing his bearings in reality. He differs from Senator Day, whose overactive imagination leads him into madness, and from Overbury, who knows nothing of the thrill that gothic imaginings impart to Peter's life.

With little taste for the cynicism of *Washington, D.C.,* many reviewers were curtly negative. Josh Greenfeld wrote dismissively in the 30 April 1967 *New York Times Book Review* that "Vidal picks an assortment of on-target political themes, adds several pinches of off-beat sex, and cooks it all over a good melodramatically licking flame." Having achieved best-seller status with *Julian* and *Wash-*

ington, D.C., Vidal decided to exploit the reputation as a cultural critic that he had begun to foster not only in his novels but also in his ideologically provocative essays. His novel *Myra Breckinridge* (1968) would outstrip in sexual daring *The City and the Pillar,* using the freedom of the form of the fictive journal, which had worked so well in *Julian,* to challenge the regnant culture like no other Vidal work.

An uninhibited disquisition by the eponymous Myra (who was Myron before a sex-change operation), *Myra Breckinridge* recounts Myra's establishment of herself in Hollywood, where she works as an instructor in an academy of drama and modeling. Like Vidal, she is a cinema enthusiast, erudite in Hollywood lore and unstinting in her esteem for Hollywood's golden age. "*In the decade between 1935 and 1945, no irrelevant film was made in the United States,*" she boldly avers. But Myra's goal is not only the inculcation in students of correct cinematic understandings; her psychosexual circumstances make her resolved as by a holy mission to realign the sexes. To that end she subjugates and finally rapes a virile young student. Myra also seduces his girlfriend.

It was immediately clear to aficionados of the genre that *Myra Breckinridge* is a masterpiece of camp, that form of humor that delights in the exaggerated and artificial sexuality celebrated by Myra both in her person and in her rhetoric. Fancying herself an archetypal femme fatale, even something of a goddess, she experiences a continual ravishment by her own beauty that is communicated in majestically allusive idiom. The effect is so rhetorically overripe that it belongs clearly to the realm of linguistic conceit on one level of understanding, to psychological pathology on another, while beggaring moral censure on both levels. Even the pornographic clichés of the novel have a kind of innocence in that they spring uncensured from Myra's hyperbolic consciousness of her mission. A segment of reviewers thought the novel in woeful taste, but more than any previous Vidal novel it elicited widespread admiration.

Myra Breckinridge spawned a sequel in *Myron* (1974), which finds the libidinous Myra and her repressed alter ego alternately possessing the Breckinridge psyche in dizzying convolutions of time and space. Accidentally transported back to the original M-G-M set of the 1948 Maria Montez film *Siren of Babylon,* Myra tampers creatively with the film and actually becomes Montez, while the Latin film star inhabits ten-year-old Myron. Myra does not shrink for a moment from altering history and attempts to save M-G-M from its future insolvency. A fervent Malthusian, she even finds the opportunity to reduce the 1973 population by attempting the 1948 castration of a young actor – in the midst of which Myron comes to the fore of the Breckinridge persona. The fun of such scenes is Myra's battling for dominance over Myron in a fireworks of invective, Myron's invective priggish and demotic, Myra's funky and garish. This stylistic élan of the novel falters only in Vidal's replacing references to genitalia with the names of the five Supreme Court justices who in 1973 linked obscenity to community standards – a gimmick eliminated in the 1986 revision.

As is usually the fate of sequels, *Myron* has been found inferior to *Myra Breckinridge* although it is the more complexly imagined work of the two and Vidal's favorite. Whatever their relative merits, the two novels are an important pairing, as much a plateau of Vidal's art as the novels of his American Chronicle. If it is only occasionally observed that *Myra Breckinridge* and *Myron* contain serious diagnoses of the relationship between power and sex and between politics and cinema – diagnoses that link the two novels to major themes of the American Chronicle and of the essays – it is because their unabashed campiness is triumphant over all else.

Having shared a stepfather with Jacqueline Kennedy, Vidal was briefly taken up by the Kennedys when they came to power in the White House. In the April 1967 *Esquire* Vidal asserts that he admired John F. Kennedy as "an ironist in a profession where the prize usually goes to the apparent cornball," but in a April 1975 interview he said he detested Robert Kennedy as "a child of Joe McCarthy, a little Torquemada." After a contretemps with the younger Kennedy at a White House reception in 1961, Vidal was no longer on good terms with the family. Of particular note from the period, therefore, are two iconoclastic essays Vidal subsequently wrote on the Kennedys titled "The Best Man, 1968" (*Esquire,* March 1963) and "The Holy Family" (*Esquire,* April 1967). There ensued also *Two Sisters* (1970), a novel irreverent in incidental ways to the mystique of Jacqueline Kennedy.

Two Sisters is narrated by a Vidalian "V." who reminisces with a former mistress named Marietta Donegal about Eric and Erika Van Damm, twins whom they knew in Paris in the 1940s. At the heart of the novel is Eric's putative screenplay "Two Sisters of Ephesus," which concerns a rivalry of the fourth-century widows Helena and Artemisa and their efforts to outshine each other and their half-brother Herostratus on the world's great stage – efforts with unmistakable relevance to the apparent relationship of Jacqueline Kennedy and her sister Lee Radziwill in the 1960s. Marietta is a gratuitous portrait of the diarist Anaïs Nin, who was once Vidal's confidante and who wrote indiscreetly of him in her 1944–1947 diary. Correspondences of all kinds proliferate in the novel in a postmodern interplay of reality with fiction and of fictions with fictions. The most undervalued of Vidal's novels, *Two Sisters* continues today to suffer critical neglect.

To many readers the publication of *Burr* in 1973 signaled Vidal's coming of age as a major novelist. Chronologically the first installment in the American Chronicle, the novel is set in the 1830s and is narrated by Charlie Schuyler, a junior law clerk employed by the aged Aaron Burr. When Schuyler is hired by others to write a scurrilous pamphlet alleging that Martin Van Buren is Burr's bastard son, he discovers ironically that he and Van Buren are both sons of the great man. But more important than this secret of biological paternity is the scandal of national paternity that Schuyler discovers via a memoir that Burr has entrusted to him and that he presents in alternation with his own narrative. Indeed, Burr's memoir suggests that the Founding Fathers were despoilers of the infant republic and that Aaron Burr alone was innocent of their lust for empire. The actual Burr was probably guilty of that failing – some historians accept as fact Thomas Jefferson's charge that Burr attempted to separate the western territories from the Union in order to rule over them – but Vidal endorses the fictive Burr's self-image.

If the portraits of the Founding Fathers are revisionist good fun in the novel, the characterization of Burr as a charming, patrician adventurer is the text's very considerable entertainment. Nothing is more central to Burr's charm than his verbal elegance. Of his impending death, he can say casually to Schuyler, "If you should hear that I have died in the bosom of the Dutch Reformed Church, you will know that either a noble mind was entirely overturned at the end or a man of the cloth has committed perjury." Such poise of mind and language vindicate character in the world of *Burr,* as in the world of *Myra Breckinridge* beforehand and in the Vidalian world at large. The great majority of critics found *Burr* an entertaining raconteur, and they were charmed by the novel's incidental pleasures. Writing in the 28 October 1973 *New York Times Book Review,* John Leonard described Vidal admiringly as a craftsman "for whom wit is not a mechanical toy that explodes in the face of the reader but a feather that tickles the bare feet of the imagination."

*Dust jacket for Vidal's novel about Aaron Burr, one of five novels
Vidal has set during various periods of American history*

With the publication of *1876* in America's bicentennial year, the American Chronicle began to take shape and to be promoted for the first time as an entity. The narrator of *1876* is once again Charlie Schuyler, now sixty-two years old and returning to New York from France for the first time in thirty-eight years. He is accompanied by his widowed daughter Emma, the Princess d'Agrigente, who eventually marries William Sanford and becomes the grandmother of Peter Sanford, Vidal's spokesman in *Washington, D.C.* The novel affects to be a workbook, a scribbled journal of impressions that Schuyler keeps from his arrival in New York until his death in 1877, in hopes, he says, of hacking from it "a monument or two to decorate the republic's centennial." Effectively, it is a Cook's tour of American life and politics in the centennial year, for the inconsequential plot of the novel functions almost entirely as scaffolding for a survey of the American scene and the satiric commentary that it

occasions. Its satire of the year 1876 seemed to some readers to take on a contemporary edge with Samuel Jones Tilden functioning as a persona of George McGovern and Rutherford B. Hayes as a persona of Gerald Ford. Dark memories in *1876* of the Civil War, of the Lincoln assassination, and of the corrupt Grant administration seemed to foreshadow in 1976 memories of Vietnam, the Kennedy assassination, and the Watergate scandal of the Nixon presidency.

The Cook's tour through American life and politics in *1876* crystallized two ongoing questions about Vidal's art. To what extent, reviewers asked, can the reader's pleasure in Vidal's mandarin style and satiric eye compensate for the more ordinary novelistic pleasures of plot and character development? Vidal had proven himself able to create richly egocentric characters, but he seemed incapable of developing such characters in a workmanlike plot. And to what extent, some reviewers asked, can the historical novel tolerate Vidal's revisionism without vitiating its claim to historicity?

The popular success of *Myra Breckinridge, Burr,* and *1876* should have demonstrated conclusively to Vidal that the fictive journal is his best narrative mode since it can accommodate his anecdotes and incidental wit while requiring little in the way of plot. But Vidal has never been one to admit the limitations of his art, certainly not one to relax into the proven formula. And so the novel *1876* was followed in 1978 by *Kalki,* an unsuccessful and heavily plotted doomsday tale about a mad Vietnam veteran, James J. Kelly, who styles himself "Kalki," the last avatar of the Hindu god Vishnu.

Vidal purchased a home in Los Angeles in 1976, intending to live there half of each year in deference to new Italian tax laws. The purchase drew attention to what has come to be his love/hate relationship with Hollywood: love, because the movies are one of his great interests; hate, because he often remarks on Hollywood's decline from the golden age of his youth. It had not improved Vidal's esteem for modern-day Hollywood that his screenplay for *The Last of the Mobile Hot-Shots* (1970), based on Tennessee Williams's *The Seven Descents of Myrtle,* was judged a "cruel parody" in the 15 January 1970 *New York Times.* Nor was he pleased that the disastrously tasteless films *Myra Breckinridge* (1970) and later *Caligula* (1979) were linked to his name even though he had nothing to do with them. Vidal was also displeased to discover in 1964 that *The Best Man,* a film he had thought wholly his own, was advertised at the Cannes Film Festival as "un film de Franklin Schaffner." Such irritations were vented in a 25 November 1976 *New York Review of Books* essay titled "Who Makes the Movies?" in which Vidal attacked the so-called auteur theory of filmmaking, a theory that asserts that a film has an author in the same way that a book has an author and that a film's author is not the screenwriter but the director.

With the 510-page *Creation* (1981) Vidal returned to the form of the fictive historical memoir. His period is the fifth century B.C., and his protagonist is Cyrus Spitama, a putative grandson of Zoroaster, who dictates to his own grandson a disjointed memoir that details his career as a roving ambassador for Persia. The narrative encompasses four ancient civilizations – Athens, China, India, and Persia – but Cyrus's journeys are telescoped, and the landscapes through which he passes are barely sketched in deference to the novel's ingathering of such fifth-century notables as Confucius,

Master Li, and Themistocles. In service to the novel's title, Cyrus concerns himself intermittently with a quest for the secret of creation and inquires into the various creation myths of the East but never with a convincing show of interest. Like *1876, Creation* is essentially a Cook's tour of a remote world.

Much of the charm of *Creation* is the prosaism of Cyrus's point of view. The Buddha's bared teeth, he tells us, were "mottled and yellow, disconcertingly suggestive of fangs." Confucius he sums up as "a nag." "Protocol was particularly strict at the court of Darius," he recalls, "as it tends to be whenever a monarch is not born to the throne." Such observations take on at their best an aphoristic edge that is quintessentially Vidalian. "It is odd," Cyrus says, " – and charming – to talk to an intelligent woman who is not a prostitute." "For the Greek, what is not Greek is not," he quips. And like other Vidalian spokespersons, Cyrus is an observer of the emperor's new clothes. "At the core of the Buddhist system," he says, "there is an empty space which is not just the sought-after nirvana. It is perfect atheism." Elsewhere he says, "I have yet to know of a state that does not so misrepresent its military strength and wealth that, in time, the state ends by deceiving itself."

Such mordant observations crowd the pages of *Creation,* rendering the novel something of a sociological and ideological treatise as well as a geographical and historical travelogue. But Cyrus is a camp follower of greatness who rarely sits at campfires with the camel drivers, only at the feet of kings and sages. Typically, he proclaims, "I have no intention of revealing to the Greeks *any* details of my journey to Cathay," a remark which has the advantage for Vidal of occasioning an ellipsis in the narrative that propels Cyrus expeditiously from one celebrity to the next. Reviewers found fault with several matters of historical accuracy and with the novel's cardboard characterizations but tended to admire its compass. "As a novel of ideas, its ambition and its cast of characters could not possibly be bolder," observed Paul Theroux in the 29 March 1981 *New York Times Book Review.*

As a man who lives by the income from his writing, Vidal has not scrupled on occasion to publish work inferior to his best, but neither the Edgar Box novels nor the labored *Kalki* prepared readers for the meretricious *Duluth* (1983). One critic speculated that it was the world's first campaign-debt-retirement novel, its purpose to pay for the author's failed campaign in 1982 to win a senatorial nomination. Whatever its purpose, *Duluth* freewheelingly burlesques America as a land of yahoos — that is to say, a land of venal politicians, socially ambitious matrons, sadomasochistic police, angry blacks, and Chicanos whose barrios are "alive with mariachi music and joyous laughter because illegal aliens are essentially life-enhancing." Incidental objects of satire in the novel include Harlequin romances, racially balanced television news teams, and deconstructionist literary criticism as it approaches the millennium of "*après* post-structuralism."

Duluth is akin to *Myron* and to *Two Sisters* in its obsession with the octopus embrace of media and in its postmodern layering of realities with fictions, but its satire is far bleaker than that of the earlier novels — Swiftian, some have argued. The vast majority of critics found it mean-spirited in its humor where *Myron* is zestful and saw its narrative experimentation as plodding. A notable exception in a general chorus of disdain is Angela McRobbie, who wrote in the 6 May 1983 *New Statesman* that *Duluth* is "one of the most brilliant, most radical and most subversive pieces of writing to emerge from America in recent years."

Vidal wrote *Duluth* in two years while also occupied with research for the much more ambitious novel *Lincoln,* chronologically the second work in his American Chronicle. A daunting, 657-page study of America's sixteenth president from his inauguration in 1861 until his assassination in 1865, the novel depicts Lincoln from several different points of view: that of his wife Mary Todd Lincoln, of Secretary of State William H. Seward, of Secretary of the Treasury Salmon P. Chase, of the conspirator David Herold, and, most important, of the twenty-three-year-old John Hay, Lincoln's private secretary, to whom is given the climactic insight of the novel that Lincoln "not only put the Union back together again, but he made an entirely new country, and all of it in his own image." Refracted through these and other points of view, Lincoln is a shadowy figure, narratively only watched and judged, as around him swirl the politicians, the generals, and the bankers who constitute a sort of malarial miasma arising from the Potomac swampland.

Vidal's portrait of Lincoln is as respectful as it is compatible with his rendering him as a complete and accomplished politician, a self-mythologizer who encourages the legend of the naive rail-splitter while quietly subverting the Constitution in order to preserve the Union. Indeed, Vidal's Lincoln is the founder of what historians call the Imperial Presidency in that he broadly interprets the doctrine of the presidency's "inherent powers," empowers his secretary of the treasury with extraordinary

latitude to raise funds for the war, and assists Maryland's decision to remain in the Union by suspending several constitutional liberties, among them the rights of assembly and habeas corpus. Without giving the reader access to Lincoln's mind or heart and without challenging seriously the mystique of the sixteenth president, Vidal revives questions that historians have generally dismissed. Was Lincoln indulgent of his wife because he knew he had passed on to her a syphilitic infection that destroyed her mind and killed their sons? Did he superstitiously look to his own assassination as atonement for the war's terrible slaughter of young men? In his transformation of the presidency, did Lincoln foresee and will into being what Vidal likes to call the American Imperium? Vidal does not applaud Lincoln's reinvention of the republic, certainly, but he admires the audacity of Lincoln's single-minded devotion to the Union in the same way that he admires the imperiousness of Myra Breckinridge.

The most interesting historical fictions are often those that illumine a moment in the past when the modern age or some dominant aspect of it came into existence. If *Julian* is marginally more successful as a novel than *Lincoln,* it is possibly for the reason that remote history lends its events and personae to fiction more readily than recent history, whose familiarity tends to inhibit a novelist's imagination. Such is a point made repeatedly by reviewers who found that Vidal's imagination had not adequately dominated the source material on Lincoln. Even enthusiastic reviewers such as Joyce Carol Oates in the 13 June 1984 *New York Times Book Review* found the novel thinly imagined: "*Lincoln,*" she noted, "is not so much an imaginative reconstruction of an era as an intelligent, lucid, and highly informative transcript of it."

The Schuyler-Sanford dynasty takes center stage again in *Empire,* chronologically the fourth installment in the American Chronicle. The central character of *Empire* is Caroline Sanford, a daughter of the French-born Emma of *1876.* In the course of the novel, Caroline is engaged to the son of the John Hay in *Lincoln* and has an affair with the James Burden Day of *Washington, D.C.* She also makes a success of a moribund newspaper by modeling it on the yellow journalism of the Hearst papers.

Vidal focuses in *Empire* on the years 1895–1906, a period during which the William McKinley and Theodore Roosevelt administrations indulged dreams of empire with interventions in Cuba, the Philippine Islands, and Panama. It is a story without important villains as Vidal tells it — a story, rather, of political happenstance and jour-

*Dust jacket for Vidal's 1992 novel, a treatment of the Crucifixion
as it would have been covered by a television
news crew*

nalistic mendacity. The aged John Hay views his "Open Door" pronouncement not as a logical capstone to the foreign policy of post–Civil War America but as a triumph of the imagination. William McKinley is simply perplexed by the consequences of what he has authorized in the Philippines. And Theodore Roosevelt is a blustering boy elevated to the presidency by William Randolph Hearst. If there is any villain at all in the novel, it is Hearst, who boasts of the Spanish-American War as his creation, but Vidal seems to view Hearst less as an evil genius than as an imaginative force inseparable from the republic's transformation. Indeed, reality surrenders increasingly to the inventions of the journalistic imagination in *Empire,* and Vidal links that surrender to the drift from isolationist republic to arrogant empire. This lack of meaningful villains adds to the novel's tone of sadness. The reader might prefer to have a villain to blame for the lost

honor of the republic, but *Empire* is an elegy, not a *J'accuse.*

After Vidal's tentative reach for the sublime in *Lincoln, Empire* seemed to some reviewers an unfortunate reversion to cynicism. "*Lincoln* has been Vidal's one concession that something other than tawdriness and hypocrisy might have been present in American political life," observed Andrew Delbanco; *Empire,* he said, "is one long expression of disgust." Some newspaper reviewers were put off by the novel's conceit that newspapers invent national issues. "Surely Vidal blows his own cover," complained the 20 July 1987 *Christian Science Monitor;* "He spells out the Hearst formula. Sensationalism, scandal, invented news. And then he follows it himself." But most reviewers found Vidal's mix of the fictive and the historical to be highly entertaining – a feast of confected and configured moments. And many reviewers were not at all put off by

Vidal's confident cynicism. Richard Poirier went so far as to point out that "part of Vidal's originality derives from his attendant assurance that he can create and command the American history of his novels, as much as he can their imaginary components. No other American writer . . . has Vidal's sense of national proprietorship."

Vidal had ceased writing for television drama after the demise of its so-called golden age and did not return to the medium in a creative capacity until the mid 1980s. Still, he had not wholly spurned the medium he so often castigated in print. He wrote and narrated a television documentary entitled *Vidal in Venice* (1986) and appeared on innumerable television talk shows. Finally he was persuaded in 1986 to adapt for television Lucien K. Truscott IV's novel *Dress Gray,* a screenplay for which he won an Emmy nomination. In 1989 he adapted anew for Turner Network Television his early teleplay *The Death of Billy the Kid,* which was adapted with unhappy results for Warner Bros. as *The Left-Handed Gun* in 1955. The title of the teleplay's third incarnation is *Gore Vidal's Billy the Kid.*

In *Hollywood,* temporally the fifth installment in the American Chronicle, Vidal deals with the years 1917 to 1923, a period dominated in American politics by World War I and the scandal-ridden administration of Warren G. Harding. The bit players in the novel comprise a veritable Who's Who of the age, including not only Woodrow Wilson and Harding but also the young Franklin and Eleanor Roosevelt, Alice Roosevelt Longworth, William Randolph Hearst and Marion Davies, W. D. Griffith, and such film stars as Douglas Fairbanks, Mary Pickford, Charlie Chaplin, and Fatty Arbuckle. There is even a cameo appearance by Vidal's grandfather Sen. Thomas Gore.

The major player and the author's primary spokesperson is once again Caroline Sanford. An owner of the influential *Washington Tribune,* she discovers still another realm of power in Hollywood, where she aids in recruiting the embryonic "photo play" industry to the war effort and where she discovers Hollywood's ability not just to invent the news, like the Hearst newspapers, but actually to script reality. "Reality could now be entirely invented and history revised," she realizes with shock; "Suddenly, she knew what God must have felt when he gazed upon chaos, with nothing but himself upon his mind."

Its title notwithstanding, *Hollywood* focuses more on Washington than it does on the film industry. Organized around the fall in different ways of two very different presidents, it chronicles in detail the controversies that swirled around the proposed League of Nations, the course of Wilson's physical decline, the corruptions of the Harding administration, and the orchestrated rhetoric by which an America sympathetic toward Germany and hostile toward England had its sympathies precisely reversed. As much as in any novel of the series, the story in *Hollywood* is one of a nation too easily forced onto the paths of empire by the dream merchants of Washington and Hollywood and doomed to suffer too willingly its own corruption. Like his main characters, Vidal casts a cool eye on what Caroline knows to be "the prevailing fact of force in human affairs" but in this, his twenty-third novel, with less overt cynicism than heretofore toward all things American. "A wonderfully literate and consistently impressive work of fiction," opined Joel Conarroe in the 21 January 1990 *New York Times Book Review.* The general praise for *Hollywood* was tempered only by the commonplace criticism that Vidal's approach to writing novels indulges too many different impulses.

Among the several urgencies of Vidal's craft would seem to be a return periodically to messianic figures like Myra, Kalki, and Lincoln and a return periodically to Rabelaisian satire. The two impulses meet, not for the first time, in *Live from Golgotha* (1992), a freewheeling burlesque of the New Testament. Set near the close of the second millennium, the novel postulates that the technology exists for sending holograms, objects, and even persons into the past in such a way as to allow NBC-TV to film the historical Crucifixion and to hire Timothy, the first bishop of Ephesus, to anchor the broadcast. At the same time, a computer virus orchestrated by a master hacker has corrupted the extant Gospels, making it imperative for Timothy to set down the "true" story of Judas crucified in lieu of Jesus even as the Crucifixion is so corrupted by contact with the future that Saint Paul, Shirley MacLaine, Oral Roberts, and Mary Baker Eddy are enabled to attend on Golgotha. There is in actuality no "true" story at all, for *Live from Golgotha* is a series of false bottoms. That the events occur only in Timothy's dream-life is a possibility Vidal keeps open.

The largest point of Vidal's satire would seem to be the corruptibility of religious texts, but that point barely survives his crediting an undeveloped technology for so many of the actual corruptions in *Live from Golgotha.* Lesser points of Vidal's satire (for example, corrupt religious fund-raising, the idea that Saint Paul was homosexual) fail to shock. Wilfrid Sheed suggests in the 26 October 1992 *New Yorker* that such whimsies of the text are not blasphemies or even satire but only "roguish impieties."

Vidal is a writer, then, of uneven but substantial development. Throwing off early the influence of Hemingway and the modernists, he adapted to his own uses the genres of camp, historical fiction, and apocalyptic fantasy, and he helped to bring those genres into the literary mainstream by making them vehicles for his distinctive modes of auctorial audacity. In the best mode of that audacity, the indecorous and the demotic overlay his elegantly lucid prose. In another mode, a wit recognizably Vidalian underlies his artifices of time and person, tending to render such artifices a celebration of his authorial selfhood – which is to say, a celebration of his political and psychosexual agendas. It is generally recognized that these modes are both the limitation and the achievement of his art, irritating some readers while delighting others.

Interviews:

Eugene Walter, "Conversations with Gore Vidal," *Transatlantic Review,* 4 (Summer 1960): 5–17;

Eve Auchincloss and Nancy Lynch, "Disturber of the Peace: Gore Vidal," *Mademoiselle,* 53 (September 1961): 132–133, 176–179;

"*Playboy* Interview: Gore Vidal," *Playboy,* 16 (June 1969): 77–96, 238;

Daniel Halpern, "Interview with Gore Vidal," *Antaeus,* 1 (1971): 67–76;

Gerald Clarke, "Petronius Americanus: The Ways of Gore Vidal," *Atlantic,* 229 (March 1972): 44–51;

Clarke, "The Art of Fiction," *Paris Review,* 15 (Fall 1974): 130–165;

Arthur Cooper, "Gore Vidal on . . . Gore Vidal," *Newsweek,* 84 (18 November 1974): 97–99;

Michael S. Lasky, "The Complete Works on Gore Vidal: His Workings," *Writer's Digest,* 55 (March 1975): 20–26;

Ken Kelly, "*Penthouse* Interview: Gore Vidal," *Penthouse,* 6 (April 1975): 97–98, 104–106;

Diane Johnson, "Gore Vidal: Scorekeeper," *New York Times Book Review,* 17 April 1977, p. 47;

Michael Segell, "The Highbrow Railings of Gore Vidal," *Rolling Stone,* no. 317 (15 May 1980): 40–43;

Robert J. Stanton and Gore Vidal, *Views from a Window: Conversations with Gore Vidal* (Secaucus, N.J.: Lyle Stuart, 1980);

Charles Ruas, "Gore Vidal," in his *Conversations with American Writers* (New York: Knopf, 1985), pp. 57–74;

Claudia Dreifus, "Gore Vidal: The Writer as Citizen," *Progressive,* 50 (September 1986): 36–39;

Robert Katz, "Gore Goes to War," *American Film,* 13 (November 1987): 43–46;

Carole Mallory, "Mailer and Vidal: The Big Schmooze," *Esquire,* 15 (May 1991): 105–112;

Martha Duffy, "A Gadfly in Glorious, Angry Exile," *Time,* 140 (28 September 1992): 64–66;

David Hutchings, "Gospel According to Gore," *People,* 38 (2 November 1992): 103–106;

Jay Parini, "An Interview with Gore Vidal," in his *Gore Vidal: Writer Against the Grain* (New York: Columbia University Press, 1992), pp. 278–290.

Bibliography:

Robert J. Stanton, *Gore Vidal: A Primary and Secondary Bibliography* (Boston: G. K. Hall, 1978).

References:

John W. Aldridge, "Gore Vidal: The Search for a King," in his *After the Lost Generation: A Critical Study of the Writers of the Two World Wars* (New York: McGraw-Hill, 1951), pp. 170–183;

Earl P. Bargainnier, "The Mysteries of Edgar Box (aka Gore Vidal)," *Clues: A Journal of Detection,* 2 (Spring–Summer 1981): 45–92;

David Barton, "Narrative Patterns in the Novels of Gore Vidal," *Notes on Contemporary American Literature,* 7 (September 1981): 3–9;

Harold Bloom, "The Central Man," *New York Review of Books,* 31 (19 July 1984): 5–8;

Purvis E. Boyette, " 'Myra Breckinridge' and Imitative Form," *Modern Fiction Studies,* 17 (Summer 1971): 229–238;

William F. Buckley, Jr., "On Experiencing Gore Vidal," *Esquire,* 72 (August 1969): 108–113;

Walter Clemons, "Gore Vidal's Chronicle of America," *Newsweek,* 103 (9 June 1984): 74–75, 78–79;

Peter Conrad, "Hall of Mirrors: The Novels of Gore Vidal," *London Sunday Times,* 27 March 1977, p. 35;

Conrad, "Look at Us," *New Review,* 2 (July 1975): 63–66;

Conrad, "Re-inventing America," *Times Literary Supplement,* 26 March 1976, pp. 347–348;

Andrew Delbanco, "The Bad and the Ugly," *New Republic,* 197 (14 and 21 September 1987): 49–55;

Bernard E. Dick, *The Apostate Angel: A Critical Study of Gore Vidal* (New York: Random House, 1974);

Owen Dudley Edwards, "Fiction as History: On an Earlier President," *Encounter,* 64 (January 1985): 33–42;

Joseph Epstein, "What Makes Vidal Run," *Commentary,* 63 (June 1977): 72–75;

M. D. Fletcher, "Vidal's *Duluth* as 'Post-Modern' Political Satire," *Thalia: Studies in Literary Humor,* 9 (Spring–Summer 1986): 10–21;

Samuel M. Hines, Jr., "Political Change in America: Perspectives from the Popular Historical Novels of Michener and Vidal," in *Political Mythology and Popular Fiction,* edited by Ernest J. Yanarella and Lee Sigelman (New York: Greenwood Press, 1988), pp. 81–99;

Michiko Kakutani, "Gore Vidal," in her *The Poet at the Piano: Portraits of Writers, Filmmakers, Playwrights, and Other Artists at Work* (New York: Times Books, 1988), pp. 89–92;

Robert F. Kiernan, *Gore Vidal* (New York: Ungar, 1982);

Seymour Krim, "Reflections on a Ship That's Not Sinking at All," *London Magazine,* new series 10 (May 1970): 26–43;

Marvin J. LaHood, "Gore Vidal: A Grandfather's Legacy," *World Literature Today,* 64 (Summer 1990): 413–417;

John Mitzel and Steven Abbot, *Myra & Gore: A New View of Myra Breckinridge and a Candid Interview with Gore Vidal. A Book for Vidalophiles* (Dorchester, Mass.: Manifest Destiny Books, 1974);

Mitzel and others, "Some Notes on Myra B," *Fag Rag,* 6 (Fall 1973): 21–25;

Anaïs Nin, *The Diary of Anaïs Nin, Volume IV, 1944–1947,* edited by Gunther Stuhlmann (New York: Harcourt Brace Jovanovich, 1971), pp. 106, 113, 121;

Jay Parini, ed., *Gore Vidal: Writer Against the Grain* (New York: Columbia University Press, 1992);

Richard Poirier, "American Emperors," *New York Review of Books,* 34 (24 September 1987): 31–33;

Mitchell S. Ross, "Gore Vidal," in his *The Literary Politicians* (Garden City, N.Y.: Doubleday, 1978), pp. 247–300;

John Simon, "The Good and Bad of Gore Vidal," *Esquire,* 88 (August 1977): 22–24;

Catherine R. Stimpson, "My O My O Myra," *New England Review: Middlebury Series,* 14 (Fall 1991): 102–115;

Claude J. Summers, " 'The Cabin and the River,' Gore Vidal's *The City and the Pillar,*" in his *Gay Fictions: Wilde to Stonewall: Studies in a Male Homosexual Literary Tradition* (New York: Continuum, 1990), pp. 112–129;

Ray Lewis White, *Gore Vidal* (Boston: Twayne, 1968);

John F. Wilhelm and Mary Ann Wilhelm, " 'Myra Breckinridge': A Study of Identity," *Journal of Popular Culture,* 3 (Winter 1969): 590–599;

Theodore Ziolkowski, *Fictional Transfigurations of Jesus* (Princeton, N.J.: Princeton University Press, 1972), pp. 250–257.

Papers:

The largest collection of Vidal's papers is held by the State Historical Society of Wisconsin at Madison. The libraries associated with the University of Florida, Yale University, Boston University, Syracuse University, and the University of Texas also have some of his papers.

Kurt Vonnegut

(11 November 1922 –   )

Peter J. Reed
University of Minnesota

See also the Vonnegut entries in *DLB 2: American Novelists Since World War II; DLB 8: Twentieth-Century American Science-Fiction Writers; DLB Yearbook 1980;* and *DLB Documentary Series 3: Saul Bellow, Jack Kerouac, Norman Mailer, Vladimir Nabokov, John Updike, Kurt Vonnegut.*

BOOKS: *Player Piano* (New York: Scribners, 1952; London: Macmillan, 1953); republished as *Utopia 14* (New York: Bantam, 1954);

The Sirens of Titan (New York: Dell, 1959; London: Gollancz, 1962);

Canary in a Cat House (Greenwich, Conn.: Fawcett Gold Medal, 1961);

Mother Night (Greenwich, Conn.: Fawcett Gold Medal, 1962; London: Cape, 1968);

Cat's Cradle (New York, Chicago & San Francisco: Holt, Rinehart & Winston, 1963; London: Gollancz, 1963);

God Bless You, Mr. Rosewater; or, Pearls Before Swine (New York, Chicago & San Francisco: Holt, Rinehart & Winston, 1965; London: Cape, 1965);

Welcome to the Monkey House (New York: Seymour Lawrence/Delacorte, 1968; London: Cape, 1969);

Slaughterhouse-Five; or, The Children's Crusade (New York: Seymour Lawrence/Delacorte, 1969; London: Cape, 1970);

Happy Birthday, Wanda June (New York: Seymour Lawrence/Delacorte, 1971; London: Cape, 1973);

Breakfast of Champions; or, Goodbye Blue Monday! (New York: Seymour Lawrence/Delacorte, 1973; London: Cape, 1973);

Wampeters, Foma and Granfalloons (Opinions) (New York: Seymour Lawrence/Delacorte, 1974; London: Cape, 1975);

Kurt Vonnegut

Slapstick; or, Lonesome No More! (New York: Seymour Lawrence/Delacorte, 1976; London: Cape, 1977);

Jailbird (New York: Seymour Lawrence/Delacorte, 1979; London: Cape, 1979);

Sun Moon Star, by Vonnegut and Ivan Chermayeff (New York: Harper & Row, 1980);

Palm Sunday: An Autobiographical Collage (New York: Seymour Lawrence/Delacorte, 1981; London: Cape, 1981);

Deadeye Dick (New York: Seymour Lawrence/ Delacorte, 1982; London: Cape, 1983);

Nothing Is Lost Save Honor: Two Essays (Jackson, Miss.: Nouveau, 1984);

Galápagos (New York: Seymour Lawrence/ Delacorte, 1985; London: Cape, 1985);

Bluebeard (New York: Delacorte, 1987; London: Cape, 1988);

Hocus Pocus (New York: Putnam, 1990; London: Cape, 1990);

Fates Worse Than Death: An Autobiographical Collage of the 1980s (New York: Putnam, 1991: London: Cape, 1991).

PLAY PRODUCTION: *Happy Birthday, Wanda June,* New York, Theatre de Lys, 7 October 1970.

OTHER: Anonymous, *Between Time and Timbuktu,* introduction by Vonnegut (New York: Seymour Lawrence/Delacorte, 1972; St. Albans, U.K.: Panther, 1975).

Though Kurt Vonnegut had been a widely read short-story writer throughout the 1950s and though his novels had developed a cult following in the 1960s, it was in 1970, when his novel *Slaughterhouse-Five; or, The Children's Crusade* (1969) caught the mood of a country disillusioned with the Vietnam War, that he achieved widespread acclaim. Since then his earlier novels have been studied with increased attention, while his steady production has continued to keep his name before the public. Besides his popularity in the United States, Vonnegut's work has been widely translated, achieving particular success in Britain, Germany, and Russia. All thirteen of his novels remain in print, a remarkable feat considering that they cover a career of some forty years. The novels and short stories continue to be adapted for film, television, and theater. His nonfiction works – including *Wampeters, Foma and Granfalloons (Opinions)* (1974), *Palm Sunday: An Autobiographical Collage* (1981), and *Fates Worse Than Death: An Autobiographical Collage of the 1980s* (1991) – underline his role as an American literary icon and respected social observer, and he frequently is sought out for speeches, interviews, and commentary.

Vonnegut has come to be recognized as a thoughtful social critic who ponders the impact of technology, science, and social behavior. A skeptical observer with a light touch, he charms and amuses readers with his humor and irreverence while unflinchingly exposing society's foibles. The technique in much of his work may be characterized as postmodern; rather than revering classical prose models, it instead uses choppy, vernacular sentences and deemphasizes traditional conventions of plot, theme, time, and character development. Like postmodern buildings, which may unite the architecture of disparate styles and eras, his novels combine comedy with pathos, fantasy with history, and didacticism with farce. Such forms as poetry, science fiction, satire, drama, graffiti, lyrics, drawings, and even recipes appear in the novels. They deconstruct the social myths on which society often thoughtlessly runs and repeatedly defamiliarize the commonplace daily world to make their audience reexamine its habits of thinking. Vonnegut cuts quickly to the issue, actions are reported succinctly, and the prose is geared toward moving the story along and holding the reader's attention. His style, conspicuous for its short sentences and paragraphs, owes much to his background in journalism. As a satirist he acknowledges his debt to Voltaire and Jonathan Swift, while his brand of humor is influenced by Mark Twain and comedians such as Laurel and Hardy, W. C. Fields, and Bob and Ray. Vonnegut's enduring themes – social injustice, economic inequality, environmental exploitation, and militaristic barbarity – spring from his experiences growing up in the Depression and surviving World War II. Through his usually damaged, faltering antiheroes his stories search for what gives life meaning in a society bereft of cultural certainties.

Vonnegut was born in Indianapolis, Indiana, on 11 November 1922. His forebears came to the United States as part of the heavy wave of German immigration of the mid nineteenth century, two of his great-grandfathers – Clemens Vonnegut Sr. and Peter Lieber – arriving in 1848. They both eventually found their way to Indianapolis, where Lieber bought into a brewery in the 1860s and with a combination of business acumen and political awareness made his fortune. By the end of the century he had retired in style to Germany, leaving his son, Albert, to run the brewery and to indulge his extravagant tastes. Meanwhile, Clemens Vonnegut's son, Bernard, had become an architect, as did in turn his son Kurt. They were cultured men who revered the arts, especially poetry and music.

Both families became well established professionally and socially and were joined on 22 November 1913 by the marriage of Kurt Vonnegut and Albert Lieber's daughter, Edith Sophia Lieber. From this marriage came three children: Bernard in 1914, Alice in 1917, and Kurt Jr. in 1922. As Vonnegut reflects in the introduction to *Slapstick; or, Lonesome No More!* (1976), the children were born into a large, prosperous family that offered the support of many close relatives and the security of a preserved cultural heritage, things for which he later yearned nostalgically.

Anti-German sentiment after World War I and the general erosion of distinctions of place and heritage in an increasingly mobile, homogenized America contributed to the cultural decline of German American society in Indianapolis. Financial blows also fell. Prohibition ended the Lieber income from brewing, and the Depression brought a halt to building and hence unemployment to Vonnegut's architect father. Looking back on those years Vonnegut has said that during the Depression his family never went hungry, and although they moved to a new, somewhat smaller house, designed by his father, their lifestyle was not crimped. But his father found no work for ten years and became increasingly withdrawn and tentative. The experience was something Vonnegut seems never to have forgotten, and his fiction abounds with characters who fall into self-doubt when they lose productive social roles. The strains on Edith Vonnegut were also considerable, and she perhaps felt the family's financial decline most acutely, having known her flamboyant father's lifestyle before the war. With the goal of bringing in money, Edith began taking writing courses in an attempt to become a short-story writer. None of her stories was published, but her attempt seems to have made an impression on her younger son.

Bernard and Alice had governesses and attended private schools, but because of the family's financial decline Kurt Jr. went to public schools, graduating from Shortridge High School. Shortridge was the first high school in America to have a daily newspaper, the *Echo,* and he became one of its correspondents and later an editor. This connection with newswriting continued when Vonnegut went to Cornell University in 1941 and wrote for the *Cornell Sun.* He majored in biochemistry more because his scientifically minded family expected it of him, he says, than from any great interest. In the *Sun* he wrote against American involvement in the European war, but after the bombing of Pearl Harbor he enlisted, and by March 1943 he was in the army. Vonnegut's enlistment came as a final blow to his mother, who had already become increasingly prone to depression. He sought a special leave to return home for Mother's Day the following year, only to have her commit suicide by an overdose of sleeping pills while he was there. His most direct references to this event come in *Breakfast of Champions; or, Goodbye Blue Monday!* (1973), but there are other indications of its impact in his recurring references to the mental health of his characters and himself and conceivably in his portrayals of women and marriages.

In 1944 Vonnegut was sent to Europe and shortly thereafter was captured during the famous Battle of the Bulge of December 1944, becoming a prisoner of war in Dresden, Germany. He survived the firebombing of Dresden on the night of 13 February 1945 in an underground meat-storage cellar used as an air-raid shelter, emerging the next morning to find only smoking ruins. For the next several days he and other prisoners were employed pulling corpses from the debris and cremating them. These events became the basis of his best-known novel, *Slaughterhouse-Five.* In April 1945 Russian troops occupied Dresden, and he was liberated.

After a period in a military hospital in Europe, trying to rebuild his already lean frame after losing thirty-four pounds while a prisoner, he returned to Indianapolis with the Purple Heart. He married his high-school sweetheart, Jane Marie Cox, on 1 September 1945, and they moved to Chicago. There he pursued graduate work in anthropology at the University of Chicago while working for the Chicago News Bureau. He left Chicago without a degree when his master's thesis, "Fluctuations between Good and Evil in Simple Tales," was rejected. By this time he had attended four colleges (two of them for military training while in the army) without earning a degree from any of them, a feat of which he often enjoyed boasting. Years later the University of Chicago accepted his novel *Cat's Cradle* (1963) as a thesis and granted him a master of arts in anthropology.

In 1947 Vonnegut moved to Schenectady, New York, to work as a public-relations writer for General Electric, where his brother, Bernard, already worked as a scientist. The job, the plant, the town, and the people he encountered there provided settings, characters, and situations for many of his stories. Initially, though, the job provided well-paid employment that enabled him to draw on both his journalistic experience and the scientific emphasis of his education. These elements combined when he began writing fiction. Many of his colleagues from the public-relations department at General Electric would describe how they aspired to become writers, but Vonnegut dedicated long hours after work and on weekends to his writing. The bombing of Dresden was the subject about which he felt compelled to write, but finding the form through which to approach it proved difficult. It was to be twenty years before he actually came to it.

Vonnegut's childhood home in Indianapolis. During the Depression the family was forced to sell the house, which his father had designed.

In the meantime Vonnegut began more modestly with short fiction and then with the novel *Player Piano* (1952), which drew heavily on his Schenectady environment. His first story, "Report on the Barnhouse Effect," was accepted by *Collier's* in 1949 and appeared in the February 1950 issue. As its title suggests, the story combines the reportorial and the scientific, as does much of his fiction that followed. The combination led to his being categorized as a science-fiction writer, an appellation that he regretted but that was hard to avoid given his use of distanced, objectified narrative perspectives and his recognition of the social, cultural, and psychological implications of technological innovation.

Years later Vonnegut spoke disparagingly of being a public-relations man, enjoying the salary but not the frequent need to camouflage truth and mislead newspaper reporters, with whom he readily identified. In some of his novels public-relations writing is presented as the artist's ultimate prostitution of his talent and as the philistine's vision of a writer's highest achievement. Such reservations, along with his success in placing short stories, led to his decision to leave General Electric to devote himself full-time to writing.

In 1951 Vonnegut moved to Provincetown, Massachusetts, and later to West Barnstable, living on Cape Cod for almost twenty years. During this time he and Jane had three children; Mark, Nan-

nette, and Edith. In 1957 they adopted three of the four children orphaned when his sister died of cancer within forty-eight hours of her husband's death in a train crash. This bizarre and painful incident, compounding the impact of his mother's suicide and his own wartime experiences, appears to have contributed to his attitudes toward life and the strange and often brutal twists it can take. There are references to couples who die within hours of each other in several of his novels.

Vonnegut quickly came to enjoy success as a short-story writer. Prominent magazines of the time, including *Collier's, Cosmopolitan, Esquire, Ladies' Home Journal,* and the *Saturday Evening Post,* accepted his work, often illustrated by some of the best artists in the business. He later called the short stories work sold in order to finance the writing of his novels. Among the forty-six stories there are many that do not deserve such easy dismissal, but the short fiction has attracted little critical attention and remains less important artistically than the novels. Their place in Vonnegut's literary career should not be overlooked, however, since they were his primary works through the 1950s. Bringing in as much as $2,700 a story, they provided most of his income and brought him into contact with experienced figures in the publishing world such as *Collier's* editor Knox Burger and literary agent Kenneth Littauer, who aided and influenced him. Littauer encouraged

Vonnegut in the direction of telling well-made stories, shaped narratives with beginnings, middles, and ends. The origin for this kind of writing also suggests his earlier journalism.

The range of subjects in Vonnegut's short stories is remarkably varied. Some deal with the fantastic and futuristic, others with the homespun, yet some characteristics remain constant. They are thematically consistent in espousing traditional middle-class values. The future and the fantastic invariably serve to vindicate these values, while the struggler's dreams of an exotic, charmed life always fade to reassert the solid worth of the mundane one. Perhaps inevitably such stories are frequently tinged with sentimentality and nostalgia, traits that reappear in the novels, where they are more controlled. These traits continue to have an important function in Vonnegut's writing, contributing to the humor and to the feeling of human warmth that is frequently strengthened by its contrast to the coldness of an alien world. Though their quality may be uneven, the short stories are rich in variety as well as in entertainment. They are more unified than some of the novels, yet one reason that the novels surpass them is that as Vonnegut's career progresses, it becomes increasingly apparent that he flourishes in the looser, more comfortably digressive narrative of the novel.

Because of the place of technology, science, and the future in many of the stories and because a few of the later tales were published in *Galaxy* and *The Magazine of Fantasy and Science Fiction,* Vonnegut came to be pigeonholed as a science-fiction writer. It is a label he never relished, partly because it was not respected and meant that most of his early writing was thus dismissed from serious review, and partly because he believed that it simply misrepresented his work. He regards himself not simply as a science-fiction writer but as a novelist who, rather unusually, takes full account of modern science and technology in his depiction and analysis of his world.

Player Piano, Vonnegut's first published novel, enjoyed a mixed success, the original Scribners edition being followed within two years by the 1953 Doubleday Science Fiction Book Club edition and a Bantam paperback with a new title, *Utopia 14,* in 1954. These editions increased sales but furthered the tendency to categorize him as a science-fiction writer, thus excluding him from consideration as a mainstream American novelist. The novel depicts a technologically advanced, highly regulated society set in a future United States. While everyone is provided for, only an elite of technicians and managers

has any real purpose, and eventually the protagonist, Paul Proteus, joins with those made useless by technology in a rebellion against the system. The title derives from the fact that the player piano, with its key-punched paper rolls displacing the pianist, is one of the earliest applications of automation.

In some respects *Player Piano* appears autobiographical, reflecting Vonnegut's resignation from General Electric to become a full-time writer. The implied commentary is divided between the protagonist, who rebels against the Ilium Works, and a minor character known simply as Ed, whose wife has turned to prostitution rather than have him compromise his artistic integrity by writing a book that will sell. By a kind of comic inversion Vonnegut makes Ed's situation say much about his own. Ed writes "beautifully" and works on anti-machinery novels, whereas Vonnegut tells self-deprecating jokes about his own style. Obviously Vonnegut had made some of the compromises that Ed refuses: he had written public-relations material, he was now aiming short stories at a commercial market, and at times financial security must have seemed precarious enough to raise questions about the integrity that led him from General Electric to full-time fiction writing. In Ed, then, is the forerunner of Kilgore Trout and other personae that Vonnegut uses to mock his own role.

Yet Paul Proteus may actually reflect Vonnegut's situation more searchingly. Paul questions his own motives, suspecting that he may be going through a period of personal uncertainty rather than a real revaluation of his social and professional environment. Such doubts possibly worked in Vonnegut's mind while the novel was being written. He had, after all, made an abrupt change in lifestyle that proved economically risky and that involved turning away from his involvement in a technological society and breaking with former friends and their world to become an iconoclastic outsider. There is even the suggestion that Paul's social rebellion in fact expresses a wish to destroy his father. Father/son relationships are a continuing motif in Vonnegut's work. Just as Paul turns away from emulating his engineer-manager father, Vonnegut has departed from the scientific educations and professions of the males in his family.

In other respects *Player Piano* is derivative, admittedly drawing on its widely popular dystopian forebear, Aldous Huxley's *Brave New World* (1932). In its themes and techniques, however, *Player Piano* points the way to Vonnegut's later novels in its treatment of scientific ethics, technology as a two-edged sword, the individual's need not simply for a comfortable existence but for purpose, and the search to overcome loneliness when friendships and marriages fail. Similarly, in ending with scenes of destruction, the novel sets a pattern for the apocalyptic visions in the other novels leading up to Vonnegut's final confrontation with the Dresden firestorm in *Slaughterhouse-Five*.

One significant thematic and structural pattern in *Player Piano* involves the classical and religious mythic pattern of the hero's descent into a netherworld in order to be resurrected, rejuvenated and enlightened, and often hailed as a messianic figure. In this instance a hesitant Paul Proteus is literally taken underground to undergo conversion and surface as the messiah of the rebellion. Variations of this pattern, which also echoes Vonnegut's personal experience in his descent into the underground shelter in Dresden, recur in most of the novels.

There are also patterns in the techniques through which Vonnegut's persistent themes are approached. Evident in this novel are the beginnings of Vonnegut's technique of defamiliarizing the everyday — sometimes through hyperbole; sometimes through naive, almost childlike depiction; and sometimes by the use of an outside observer, such as the bewildered Shah of Bratpuhr here. A triangle of two male characters and one female character — here Paul, his wife Anita, and antagonist Dr. Lawson Shepherd — also becomes a repeated structure in Vonnegut's fiction, seemingly echoing his family situation with his siblings. The interweaving of several subplots that serve his various social commentaries also is now a familiar technique. Here the central "PP" (Paul Proteus/Player Piano) plot becomes an axis around which the "II" subplots (Homestead/Hacketts/Hagstrohm/Haycox/Halyard) rotate. The tone, of a weary but forgiving cynicism nevertheless able to laugh at absurdities, grows more confident in his subsequent novels.

In the years following the publication of *Player Piano* Vonnegut worked on another novel, the unfinished "Upstairs and Downstairs." His second novel, *The Sirens of Titan*, was not published until 1959. The popular story of the book's genesis — that at a cocktail party Burger asked Vonnegut why he did not write another novel, and Vonnegut responded that he was doing so and proceeded extemporaneously to spin off the plot of *The Sirens of Titan* — is scarcely more interesting than its actual background.

By the mid 1950s Vonnegut was placing short stories frequently in the better-paying magazines. His career seemed to be developing successfully, although not as a novelist. As the decade advanced, however, he experienced some setbacks. The failure of *Collier's* in 1957 presaged a decline, under the mounting onslaught of television, in the market for short fiction that the weekly family magazines had provided generously. There were also sharp personal setbacks. In October 1957 Vonnegut's father died. For a year he found it difficult to write; then in 1958 occurred the almost simultaneous deaths of his sister and her husband. After adopting three of the orphaned sons, thus doubling the size of his family, he found himself faced with greater responsibilities at a time when his market was beginning to decline.

One response was to devote more attention to the science-fiction magazines, which remained active in publishing short fiction. Another was to return to the novel, this time writing specifically for the prosperous paperback market. Here he was aided by Burger, who had also moved to paperback publishing. *The Sirens of Titan* and *Mother Night* (1962) were both written to paperback contracts. Another paperback publication was *Canary in a Cat House* (1961), a collection of twelve previously published stories. Although these paperbacks helped ease Vonnegut's financial plight, they did little at the time to advance his career. They went unreviewed, and whatever notice they received served only to entrench his reputation as a science-fiction writer. *The Sirens of Titan* was reissued in hardcover in 1961 but went largely unnoticed except by a small college underground.

Vonnegut's second novel reads quite differently from the first. While *Player Piano* constantly moves the reader back and forth between its subplots, *The Sirens of Titan* has a more relaxed, linear movement. Borrowing on the space-opera form, it moves on from one plot, with its underlying theme or social commentary, to another simply by moving its protagonist from one planet to the next. While the dystopian vision of *Player Piano* deals with the potential impact of technology upon society, *The Sirens of Titan* is closer to conventional science fiction. Again loneliness and purposelessness are dominant themes. Fraternal, marital, and parental relationships are constantly tested in a setting where the yearning for human warmth is set off against the cold recesses of space. As in other novels Vonnegut finds romantic love wanting and affirms the value of "common human decency," which emerges as a recognition of and respect for others free of the passions, possessiveness, and coerciveness of romantic love. The recurrent theme of people being replaced by machines or becoming machinelike is embodied by the robotized Martian army, while the compassion and loyalty demonstrated by the outside observer, the robot Salo, gives that theme emphasis by inversion.

The Sirens of Titan is thus more philosophical and psychological where *Player Piano* is sociological, and it makes its comments metaphorically through the use of science-fiction tropes. The Tralfamadorian robots in control, for instance, show a mechanistic universe. As a consequence of these philosophical ponderings, *The Sirens of Titan* seems more profound. Yet the fantastic world of the novel instructs easily, like Lewis Carroll's *Alice's Adventures in Wonderland* (1865) – which it resembles from the time its protagonist, Malachi Constant, steps through the tiny door in the wall of the Rumfoord estate until the last smile of Winston Niles Rumfoord fades, like that of a Cheshire cat, into the "chrono-synclastic infundibulum."

Of the characteristic patterns noted in *Player Piano,* the one that most obviously undergoes development in *The Sirens of Titan* is that of the mythic descent and return, which is no longer implicit but is presented directly and literally. Malachi is tested on Mars and descends into the caves of Mercury, from which he returns as the messiah of the Church of God the Utterly Indifferent, only to be condemned and made its scapegoat. Many characters, images, and motifs in this novel reappear in later ones, including Tralfamadorians, physical handicaps to create equality, and above all religion. Rumfoord's Church of God the Utterly Indifferent is the first of Vonnegut's experiments in the creation of a religion that is practical in intent but ludicrous.

The Sirens of Titan has won the admiration of many readers for its imagination, its often-poetic language, and its ability to find affirmation in the face of its bleak universe. Malachi, the Space Wanderer, undergoes almost endless abuse and hardship but outgrows his egocentrism to proclaim the value of learning to love "whoever is around to be loved." His once-embittered son, Chrono, comes in the end to make shrines to Titan's beautiful giant bluebirds and to say, "Thank you, mother and father, for the gift of life." While the protagonist changes, however, there is a sense that the world cannot be changed, that existence is governed by inevitability. It may not be Tralfamadorians who control human existence, the book seems to say, but there is a great deal that is as beyond human control as if they did, and this makes it all the more imperative for people to treat each other "with common human decency," to find a way to love each other. Despite the strong element of fatalism in the book, it contains more humor than *Player Piano.* It is rich in contrasts, its

humor and its pathos mutually sharpened by their juxtaposition, its portrayals of scarcely relieved suffering and the cold wastes of space heightening its affirmation of loyalty, decency, and compassion.

The first two novels use omniscient third-person narration. With the novels that follow Vonnegut moves closer to including himself directly through the introduction of first-person narration. In *Mother Night* Howard W. Campbell, Jr., is both first-person narrator and lead character. But Vonnegut also intrudes as the "editor" of Campbell's confessions. In an introduction written for the 1966 edition he adds an autobiographical commentary on the relevance of the novel's content, personalizing the novel directly. This paves the way for the intrusion of himself as narrative voice, commentator, and even character, a hallmark of many of the novels that follow. This change is coincident with his accepting, in 1965, a two-year appointment to the Writers' Workshop at the University of Iowa. Vonnegut's stay brought him into contact with other novelists such as Verlin Cassill, Richard Yates, William Murray, and Vance Bourjaily and academic critics such as Robert Scholes. Vonnegut claims that one of the things he learned there was that it was not, as early editors had told him, wrong to speak directly of himself in his fiction.

The plot and form of *Mother Night* are strikingly different from those of the preceding two novels. The story of Campbell, an American playwright who remains in Nazi Germany as an American spy while outwardly working as a Nazi propagandist, follows the pattern of the confessional novel. Here there is no emphasis on technology, no fictional future, no science fiction. Its first-person narration helps to deepen the characterization of its protagonist and to intensify the inward searching, on both his part and the author's. Vonnegut's wartime experiences as a German American in Germany, first fighting Germans then being in a German city bombed by British and Americans, and his thoughts on what might have been had his family remained in Germany, inform many of the issues raised in this novel.

Once again, and with considerable emphasis, Vonnegut returns to examining the role of the writer, and particularly the writer's ethics. Campbell, as a playwright who creates fictional worlds peopled by characters played by actors, is godlike yet a false creator, making audiences believe fictions. The "editor" in *Mother Night* says that Campbell's being a writer meant that "the demands of art alone were enough to make him lie, and to lie without seeing any harm in it. To say that he was a

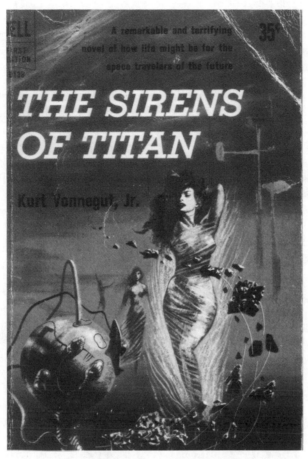

*Cover for Vonnegut's 1959 novel, a paperback original, which
deals comically with the insignificance of humanity in the universe*

playwright is to offer an even harsher warning to
the reader, for no one is a better liar than a man
who has warped lives and passions onto something
as grotesquely artificial as a stage." Vonnegut returns to this topic of the writer as trickster several
times in his later work. Campbell is also a propagandist, a role Vonnegut is acutely aware of having
approached as a public-relations writer. And in
Campbell's coming to be used as a pornographer
there may be sensitivity to the notion that in some
of the short stories Vonnegut has also compromised
to write what would sell. Doubts about the role of
writers within their own fiction is not a new phenomenon starting with Vonnegut, but it is persistent in his work, often with a uniquely autobiographical emphasis. At the time of writing *Mother
Night,* as he encountered a changing market, a continuing lack of recognition, and an inability to address the Dresden experience squarely, Vonnegut
may have felt some doubts about his role.

In content the three novels that precede
Slaughterhouse-Five, starting with *Mother Night,* move
progressively closer to the author's traumatic Dresden experience. The primary setting of *Mother Night*
is wartime Germany, and perhaps some of the ambiguities that wrack Campbell have to do with the
feelings of an author of German descent who wonders how he might have acted had he been on the
other side. "If I'd been born in Germany,"
Vonnegut reflects in the introduction, "I suppose I
would have been a Nazi, bopping Jews. . . ."

In *Mother Night,* particularly after the addition
of the 1966 introduction, Vonnegut was able to create a kind of dialogic narration. First there is the
ambiguity of the first-person narrator, the Howard
Campbell that was and the one that is, the playwright and the spy. But outside Campbell's narration is the editorial Kurt Vonnegut and then the authorial Kurt Vonnegut of the introduction, one en-
closing another like Russian dolls. His next novel,
Cat's Cradle, extends the technique through Bokonon, who as a character continues Rumfoord's
role as inventor of religions and thus is a super-
playwright manipulating real characters and who as

author of the books that are at the heart of the novel and its philosophy becomes another narrative presence. The first-person narrator is John (or "Jonah"), while allusions within the text remind the reader of Vonnegut's presence. Bokonon voices some of the novel's most important, yet most cynical, ideas, allowing both John and the author to remain at some distance from this cynicism and preserve the book's comic tone.

Though written with the paperback market in mind, *Cat's Cradle* first appeared in hardcover. But the book was easily labeled science fiction, and sales were small. In form, however, *Cat's Cradle* marks a point of departure. The first three novels had all been derivative – the dystopian novel, the space opera, the confessional novel – but *Cat's Cradle* was something new and signaled that Vonnegut was finding his own voice.

Cat's Cradle is all self-declared fictionality, from its beginning – "Call me Jonah" – echoing the opening of Herman Melville's *Moby-Dick* (1851) to its location on a rectangular island copied from the table-mounted model in a toy shop. Its politics derive from a magazine ad for Charles Atlas's "Dynamic Tension," and its religion of Bokononism is founded on *foma* (defined as "harmless untruths"). The first sentence of the Books of Bokonon reads, "All of the true things I am about to tell you are shameless lies." One of Vonnegut's significant themes here is artifice. The repeated response to its title image, a tangle of string signifying nothing, is the phrase "No damn cat, no damn cradle." Its premises and situations are jokes, its characters are caricatures, and its language, with its comical-sounding invented vocabulary and its Bokononist calypsos, is hilarious. The narration of the story – with its many chapters, satiric epigraphs, and fragmentary paragraphs, which often amount to a succession of one-liners – is an amusing parody of the novel form.

The origins of the novel are equally amusing. One of the stars of the research team at General Electric was Irving Langmuir. He was reputed to have absentmindedly left a tip for his wife under his breakfast plate and at one time to have become preoccupied with whether turtles buckle or compress their spines when they retract their heads, both of which Vonnegut attributes to the father, Felix Hoenikker, in *Cat's Cradle*. Vonnegut also has told the story that when H. G. Wells, the British novelist who was one of the fathers of science fiction, came to visit the Schenectady laboratory "Langmuir thought he might entertain Wells with an idea for a science-fiction story – about a form of ice that was stable at room temperature. Wells was uninterested, or at least never used the idea. And then Wells died, and then, finally, Langmuir died. I thought to myself: 'Finders, keepers – the idea is mine.'" "Ice-nine" becomes the cause of the end of the world in this novel, which begins with John/Jonah setting out to write a book called "The Day the World Ended," about the day Hiroshima was bombed.

The narrative form of *Cat's Cradle*, with an author standing behind a narrator (John/Jonah) retailing the words of another writer (Bokonon), proved liberating for Vonnegut. His comic impulses flourish in the eccentric voices the narrative device affords, but his more serious purposes are also served. Behind all the hilarity of the situation there is pain – in the personal relationships of the Hoenikker family, in the reminders of the Holocaust and Hiroshima, in the hopeless plight of the impoverished islanders, and in the constant threat existing in the "real" world of this time of nuclear annihilation. The "dynamic tension" of the novel, to use its own term, heightens the impact of both the comedy and the underlying dark warning by their juxtaposition.

In the destruction of Dresden, in the technical and moral ability of human beings to commit such an act, Vonnegut saw the potential for ultimate destruction. This vision underlies *Cat's Cradle*, in which John/Jonah sets out to write a book on Hiroshima and ends up witnessing the doom wrought by ice-nine. In his next novel, *God Bless You, Mr. Rosewater; or, Pearls Before Swine* (1965), the theme of apocalypse, particularly connecting social and physical cataclysm with individual psychological collapse, reappears in Eliot Rosewater's vision of the destruction of Indianapolis by firestorm at the moment of his breakdown. In his 1975 account of his own mental illness, *The Eden Express*, Vonnegut's son Mark describes a vision of the destruction of Seattle.

God Bless You, Mr. Rosewater, also published in hardcover, moves away from direct authorial expression in form, but the content compensates for this. There may be much of Vonnegut in Eliot Rosewater – in his wide-ranging observations on American society and the lives of individuals within it, in the almost childlike freshness of his way of looking at things, and even perhaps in the mixture of compassion and frustration expressed in Eliot's characteristic expression, "Goddamn it, you've got to be kind." Another Vonnegut surrogate, Kilgore Trout, has a major and largely serious role in the ending of this book and provides the author with another voice, especially where he explains the sanity of Eliot's actions within the context of a society pervaded by mental and physical malaise.

God Bless You, Mr. Rosewater places a heavy emphasis upon economic issues and their effects on psychology, a reminder of the financial erosion of the Vonnegut family and its impact on its psychological well-being. Neurosis and economics often become connected phenomena in his work. He shows how unemployment and the loss of status and purpose can lead to depression and suicide, as with his mother, and withdrawal, as with his father. The novel is perhaps Vonnegut's most direct statement on the need for social responsibility and compassion for the less fortunate, and it gains emotional force by drawing on personal experience.

Vonnegut had not stopped writing shorter prose entirely as his production of novels increased. In the mid 1960s he began to write essays, reviews, short travel accounts, and human-interest stories. "Brief Encounters on the Inland Waterway" (1966) recounts a journey from Massachusetts to Florida on the Kennedy yacht crewing for their captain, Frank Wirtanen (whose name had been borrowed for the character of an American intelligence officer in *Mother Night*). "Oversexed in Indianapolis" (1970) is a review of a novel, *Going All the Way,* written by Dan Wakefield, another graduate of Shortridge High School. A couple of pieces published in 1969 deal with witnessing rocket launchings. Many of these compositions were collected in *Wampeters, Foma and Granfalloons.* A characteristic of this short nonfiction is that Vonnegut frequently includes himself directly, as he starts to do in his novels from the 1960s. He may write reportage, but he is open about who is reporting and how he feels about what he is reporting. One of the most interesting aspects of this material for the reader is the emergent relationship between observer-writer and subject. By revealing his attitudes to the subject he reveals much of himself. Vonnegut's association with the short story was far from over, however, and he prepared and introduced a new collection, *Welcome to the Monkey House* (1968), which included eleven of the twelve stories from *Canary in a Cat House* and fourteen others.

At this point in his career Vonnegut's fortunes began to turn. The first printing of *God Bless You, Mr. Rosewater* (six thousand copies) in March 1965 was quickly followed by a second printing, of seven thousand copies, in May. The Dell paperback edition, published in April 1966, ran to 177,855 copies. Dell also reissued *Cat's Cradle* in September 1965, with 150,000 copies printed, and in 1966 *The Sirens of Titan,* with 201,703 copies. Avon came out with

paperback printings of *Player Piano* and *Mother Night.* In addition to this mounting commercial success, in 1967 he received a Guggenheim Fellowship to travel to Dresden and gather material for the novel on that experience, which was to emerge as *Slaughterhouse-Five.* In the course of preparing the novel Vonnegut visited his old friend Bernard O'Hare, who had been a scout, then a prisoner, with him in Germany, and who was now an attorney in Pennsylvania, to see whether they could together uncover more specific recollections. It was then, as Vonnegut notes in the introduction to *Slaughterhouse-Five,* that Mary O'Hare objected to the conception of the story, which could have been turned into a movie starring John Wayne and Frank Sinatra. Vonnegut recalls, "She freed me to write about what infants we really were: 17, 18, 19, 20, 21. We were baby-faced, and as a prisoner of war I don't think I had to shave very often. I don't recall that was a problem."

Later Vonnegut sought to put the Dresden experience into perspective, claiming that it had less influence on his life than *Slaughterhouse-Five* would suggest. Perhaps it was easier for him to make such a disclaimer after writing about the experience. Perhaps, too, his characteristic modesty urged him to back away from something he might have felt was being sensationalized. Nevertheless, the importance of the event for his fiction, if not his life, seems undeniable, as apocryphal disasters, visions that embody the symbolism of Dresden, haunt novel after novel. His resistance to exaggerating the importance of a short-term event does reinforce the point, though, that earlier, less dramatic experiences influence his fiction just as significantly.

Despite Vonnegut's claim in the first chapter that the book is a failure, *Slaughterhouse-Five* succeeds remarkably well both in encompassing the personal trauma he experienced in Dresden and in emphasizing its universal human significance. To do so demanded an artistic innovation evolving from the form of the previous three novels that is most apparent in the unusual narrative perspective of the book. The novel is a first-person narration, although glancing at any page in the middle chapters may make it seem to be third-person omniscient. Vonnegut speaks as himself about his experiences and the writing of *Slaughterhouse-Five* not in a separate preface or introduction but in the first chapter. He returns in the tenth and final chapter. In between he declares himself periodically as someone present in the action of the novel by saying "that was me" or "I said that."

This narrative presence makes a crucial impact on the novel's tone. Vonnegut's reminiscences and his openness in declaring his difficulties with the subject all authenticate his role as narrator. The narrative presence is established as an emotionally involved and compassionate one, recounting the story not with objectified detachment or stern moralizing but with an understanding yet urgent resignation. Injunctions such as "Listen" reveal the narrator's compulsion to tell his story, yet an apparent acceptance of the inevitable emerges in the repetitive, weary, but not unfeeling "So it goes," said whenever anyone or anything dies.

The use of the first person affords Vonnegut the kind of direct expression necessary to authenticate the novel and doubtless to satisfy his need for catharsis. Yet clearly he wants the emphasis to fall not simply on himself, on his experience, or even on Dresden alone, but on the symbolic, universal meaning of Dresden. An omniscient third-person narrator might serve well the description and analysis of social aspects of the human condition, as it does in *Player Piano*. But that perspective remains too distant and detached to achieve the combination of the personal and the symbolic relevance of the event that he now wishes to portray. So Vonnegut creates a first-person frame to which he can allude throughout and that builds a narrative presence into the novel; he then has the narrator use an omniscient third-person voice throughout most of the story.

On the title page of *Slaughterhouse-Five* Vonnegut invites the reader to see the book as "a novel somewhat in the telegraphic schizophrenic manner of tales of the planet Tralfamadore." With its short chapters and paragraphs, its short sets of sentences or paragraphs with spaces between them, the novel has a physical resemblance to the Tralfamadorian model. Many of the juxtaposed segments do not relate sequentially or thematically but together build a total impression like a montage. Events from two periods (1944–1945 and 1968) and from other points in the life of the protagonist, Billy Pilgrim, are intermixed. His life is not revealed chronologically, by beginning in medias res, or by flashback; rather, the reader knows its end from the start, and the parts are filled in, from all segments of his life, as the novel progresses.

Vonnegut cannot use the traditional form of the novel in presenting life viewed in contemporary terms because the conventional novel conforms to assumptions of cause and effect and rigidities of time and substance that he questions. For him the apparently pointless firebombing of Dresden, with its destruction of beautiful art and architecture and the killing of thousands of innocents, epitomizes the illogical. Consequently he needs a form that, while providing the reader with an intelligible account, does not appear to rationalize the events. In particular he needs a form that recognizes duration as a fourth dimension. He has sought to incorporate this view of reality into his fiction from the start. It means that each object or character is its history, not something that exists and has a history. In contrast to the portrayals of Proteus and Constant in *Player Piano* and *The Sirens of Titan*, the nonlinear characterization of Billy Pilgrim emphasizes that he is not simply an established identity who undergoes a series of changes but all the different things he is at different times.

The same principles that govern characters govern events as well. Dresden is led up to, as it were, by events that precede and follow it. It is surrounded by allusions to other catastrophes and to other events with comparable victims. Its being is its history, so that it ceases to be a single event with a single explanation or meaning. It is as Vonnegut and Billy Pilgrim see it, as the stunned German guards see it, as the weeping civilian couple sees it, in all the ambiguity this implies. The relationship between parts in the novel resembles relationships in life — relative, ambiguous, and frequently subjective.

Part of Vonnegut's artistry shows in his giving his peculiar brand of realism a strong pattern in its apparent randomness. The novel is described as "A Duty Dance with Death," which seems appropriate since there is a kind of sweeping circularity in its movement. Dresden, symbol of death, is always at the center; it begins where it ends, with the author speaking; and throughout characters appear and reappear. In confronting in this novel the specter of death — the deaths of many others and his own near death — it is as if he is at last performing an obligatory "Dance with Death."

If war serves as his metaphor for the larger human condition and apocalpyse functions as its ultimate consequence, in Dresden Vonnegut finds the quintessential embodiment of these perceptions. It becomes the keystone of all he has to say about human behavior or the nature of human existence. The combination of personal involvement, historical authenticity, and symbolic meaning invests the Dresden of *Slaughterhouse-Five* with an impact more profound than any of his previous world-ending catastrophes. *Slaughterhouse-Five* integrates the personal and the public to achieve a unique richness; it remains its author's most intensely cathartic novel but also carries perhaps his most compelling social message.

*Cover for Vonnegut's 1962 paperback original, a novel in the form
of the memoirs of an American spy who worked as a Nazi
propagandist*

That *Slaughterhouse-Five* appeared at a time when antiwar feeling over Vietnam was increasing in America no doubt helped its sales. The first printing in March 1969 ran to ten thousand copies, the first Delta printing a year later was twenty-five thousand copies, and the first Dell edition of 1971 was seven hundred thousand copies. The 1972 Universal Pictures film adaptation, directed by George Roy Hill, also contributed to the popularity of both book and author. Rather suddenly, twenty years into his career as a writer, Vonnegut found himself famous, prosperous, and even something of a guru figure to the Woodstock generation. Simultaneously he was at last earning the acclaim of academics, led by Leslie A. Fiedler, Tony Tanner, and Scholes, and of reviewers.

With the success of *Slaughterhouse-Five* Vonnegut emerged from a following of largely young audiences to wider recognition. Much of the developing interest in him was not simply in his role as writer but as so-

cial observer and popular philosopher. Many of his views struck a sympathetic chord in this era, not just about the war but on such issues as overpopulation, ecology, civil rights, and consumer protection. This popularity grew even greater in the next few years. In January 1970 he flew into Biafra, a part of Nigeria fighting for independence, accompanying an aircraft load of medical and food supplies. His visit was scarcely over when Biafra fell. His moving account of the suffering of the Biafrans and of the beauty and strength of their family system was published in *McCall's* and later included in *Wampeters, Foma and Granfalloons,* though these impressions emerge most profoundly in *Slapstick*.

With this public recognition came disruptions in Vonnegut's personal and literary life. His six children were old enough to leave home, and his melancholy at the scattering of the family coincided with a sense of depression after finishing *Slaughterhouse-Five,* which left him fulfilled yet drained. "I felt after

I finished *Slaughterhouse-Five* that I didn't have to write at all anymore if I didn't want to," he says in *Wampeters, Foma, and Granfalloons.* "It was the end of some sort of career." Pleased with the film, he spoke of being "through with novels," with "spooks in a novel" rather than flesh-and-blood characters, announcing, "It's plays from now on." In the prologue to his play, *Happy Birthday, Wanda June* (1971), he tells of his effort to write himself a new family in a company of actors. The play, which opened on 7 October 1970 and ran Off Broadway until 14 March 1971, was based on one he had written some fifteen years earlier. It derives in part from his aversion to the Hemingwayesque hero who demonstrates his manhood by killing beautiful rare animals that never hurt him and by abusing women. It also stems from his interest in Penelope in Homer's *Odyssey,* one of the works included in the Great Books program that Vonnegut and his wife conducted on Cape Cod. Indeed, the earlier play was called "Penelope." While *Slaughterhouse-Five* makes the point that all people need to feel that they retain some dignity, *Happy Birthday, Wanda June* shows a proud "hero" whose false sense of dignity denies any kind of dignity to women, nonwhites, and a good many other men.

By 1971 Vonnegut had separated from his wife and moved to New York. The next year brought another personal trauma when his son Mark suffered the onset of schizophrenia while living in a commune in British Columbia. In 1975 Mark published his account of this episode, *The Eden Express.* Vonnegut meanwhile seemed uncertain about the direction of his work. In 1972 a television screenplay based on his fiction, *Between Time and Timbuktu,* was produced by National Educational Television, and the illustrated script was published that year with an introduction by Vonnegut. His popularity was by now at its height, and he had achieved more serious critical and scholarly recognition as well. Two critical quarterlies, *Summary* and *Critique,* ran special Vonnegut issues in 1971, and two books – *Kurt Vonnegut Jr.* (1972) by Peter J. Reed and *The Vonnegut Statement* (1973), edited by Jerome Klinkowitz and John Somer, emerged from academe. Vonnegut received honorary degrees from Indiana University in 1973 and from Hobart and William Smith College in 1974, an appointment as Distinguished Professor of English Prose by the City University of New York in the fall of 1973 (he left in February 1974), and election as vice-president of the National Institute of Arts and Letters in 1975.

Despite Vonnegut's proclamation that he would devote himself to plays, a new novel, *Breakfast of Champions,* soon followed. He described this seemingly whimsical book as a self-indulgent fiftieth birthday present to himself and claimed that he intended it as a clearing out of old ideas, obsessions, and characters. It did look like an attempt at a new start, but although it enjoyed better sales than any of his previous books – a first edition of 100,000 copies, followed by a Delta edition of 200,000, and then a Dell first printing of almost a million copies – it drew generally weak reviews.

Breakfast of Champions appears heavily autobiographical. It includes some forthright rumination and his anxieties about depression and suicide. He writes, " 'You're afraid you'll kill yourself the way your mother did,' I said. 'I know,' I said." There are affectionate allusions to his father and his grandfather. Vonnegut even includes himself as a character, so that he exists both outside and within the fiction and participates in its creation in both roles. At one point Vonnegut the character-novelist sits in a bar in the fictional Midland City, Ohio, watching his own characters and debating what to do with them. Such passages comment on the roles of writer and fiction in the contemporary artistic world (an arts festival comprises the novel's central public event) and particularly on his own changed role. Contemporary criticism tends to see the author as a product of the fiction, and Vonnegut may sometimes have felt this to be literally true, at least in as much as the public perception of him as a person was shaped by his writing. This may be true of almost any author, but in Vonnegut's case his direct introduction of himself into his fiction and his explicit relation of personal experience increasingly had the effect of making him a character of his own creation as much as any of the other characters.

One of the main characters in this book is Kilgore Trout, who appeared in the two preceding novels as a comic surrogate for the author. Trout now shares the dilemma of his creator, being suddenly both "fabulously well to do" and famous. Both find the new situation difficult. In the past Trout had embodied a comic vision of what might be Vonnegut's worst fears: of writing endlessly and achieving no recognition, of not making a living, of being dismissed as little more than a pornographer, and so on. Now both seem to find that the adjustment to fame has its burdens, and Vonnegut once again lampoons his situation through Trout. Like Vonnegut, Trout often views things afresh by reducing them to their simplest terms, and they often share the technique of taking one of these simplified perceptions to an extreme. Vonnegut calls this technique "solipsistic whimsy." One consequence of Trout's indulging in this tendency is that another character in the novel, Dwayne Hoover, believes that everyone but him is a robot he can attack at will. All of this relates to Vonnegut's uncertainties about being taken as a guru and his concerns with the moral responsibilities of writers, of being (like Trout) taken seriously when he is trying to be funny and vice versa.

Hoover perhaps represents the solid middle-class origins with which Vonnegut never loses touch, and he may also reflect some of the author's anxieties about mental stability, sharing with him the disturbing suicide of a close female relative. Even the fraudulent artist Rabo Karabekian becomes a mouthpiece for Vonnegut, expressing the ideal of recognizing individual worth that counters the novel's pervasive solipsism. That solipsism, which leads to seeing others as mere robots or as characters in fiction to be conveniently dismissed, constitutes the personal and social malaise this novel attacks.

On several occasions Vonnegut has spoken of the tendency for people to fictionalize their lives. He also warns of the danger of imposing such fictions upon other people's lives. He has observed, for example, that one reason why Americans are so prone to solving situations by killing the opposing character, notably by shooting, is that this is how things are resolved in the archetypal American folktale, the Western. *Breakfast of Champions* shows the broader implications of this tendency. In the area of race relations he speaks of the old perception of African American laborers as merely pieces of machinery to perform work. At one point in the novel a machine that replaces manual laborers becomes known as "the fifty thousand nigger machine." He then goes further, connecting "woman's work" with "nigger work." Hoover, when he goes berserk, calls his mistress, Francine Pefko, "the fucking machine." In this blunt fashion Vonnegut demonstrates that when groups of people are discriminated against they are dehumanized and reduced to the status only of their functions or to being mere machines or tools. Just as Hoover, in his madness, feels liberated to do whatever he wants to anyone because he believes they are all only robots anyway, so in general people and societies feel free to abuse individuals or groups to whom they have granted less than full human status. *Breakfast of Champions* is thus Vonnegut's most outspoken work on racism and especially gender equity.

Breakfast of Champions is notable for its staccato style and its irreverent, deflating glances at every aspect of American life. Sometimes the perspective is almost perversely childlike; this means of defamiliarizing the commonplace is accompanied by the novel's other dramatic innovation, a series of naive felt-tip-pen drawings. The drawings contribute to an apparent breeziness that characterizes much of the novel but that also has been misunderstood, since it works as part of a serious and carefully constructed moral framework. Once again Vonnegut needs the appearance of randomness to emphasize his postmodern vision of a society "without a culture." In retrospect the frank commentary on American society and the clever structure have earned *Breakfast of Champions* more respect from critics and readers, but at the time many viewed it as a facile self-parody that was irreverent, whimsical, and generally disappointing after *Slaughterhouse-Five*.

During this period Vonnegut began a relationship with photographer Jill Krementz, who became his second wife in November 1979. Though he was a widely recognized author and public figure, he also experienced a difficult period in terms of his creativity. Speaking of the problems of revitalizing himself as a writer, in a 1976 interview he told Robert Short, "I think it's just Puritanism now that keeps me writing, as I simply . . . I don't know, whatever I was born to do I completed after I completed *Slaughterhouse-Five*. After that, I just had to start a new career somehow, you know. All I say is that I had a feeling of *completion* after that. . . . It's just something was finished when I finished that." This interview came just before the publication of *Slapstick* in October 1976 and before he began work on his next novel, *Jailbird* (1979).

Slapstick is the memoir of a one-hundred-year-old former president named Dr. Wilbur Daffodil-11 Swain, who earlier, with his twin sister, had written the most popular child-care book ever. His presidential program consists of giving everyone new middle names so that they will become members of elaborate extended families. Unfortunately, a plague and other disasters such as variable gravity turn the United States into an anarchic collection of balkanized nations and make the plan and his presidency meaningless. The novel's dominant theme is implicit in its subtitle, *Lonesome No More!* In the introduction Vonnegut talks about the large German family in Indianapolis in which he grew up and how it gave love, comfort, and stability to all its members. Most Americans once had such families, but now the generations are separated, and the remaining nuclear family is overloaded with burdens once assumed by a larger and more versatile unit. The main problem with modern Americans, he concludes, is that they are lonely. This is an old theme for him, though it was not thus brought to the fore in his previous novels, where it was expressed mainly in characters' feelings of purposelessness and of being unwanted. In *Breakfast of Champions* people viewed as slaves and robots lose value for themselves and others. In *Slapstick* the two main characters are dehumanized because they are seen as freaks. Vonnegut posits that in a large family or clan such people are still treated with common human decency, cared for, and valued.

The two central characters, Wilbur Swain and his sister, Eliza, are hideous Neanderthaloids, fantastic creatures about whom everything is exaggerated – age, height, numbers of nipples and fingers – yet Vonnegut describes the novel as "the closest I will ever come to writing an autobiography." This declaration of its autobiographical nature may be misleading, and he adds the qualification that it describes "what life feels like to me." The casting of himself and his sister (whom he acknowledges as an influence and the imaginary audience to whom he writes) in the form of Neanderthaloids may represent the kind of intimacy in separation from the rest of the world that young siblings can achieve. Other things – sharing the same jokes and discoveries, feeling brighter as a pair than alone, the inevitable separation, the sense of loss in the other's death, even perhaps the distance from parents who have trouble communicating love – may all reasonably have an autobiographical basis.

But the depiction of "how life feels" remains foremost: a sense of being continually confronted, like Laurel and Hardy, with tests of one's agility and inventiveness, "bargaining in good faith with destiny." It is a painful world, one characterized by his dying sister's saying, on hearing of the death of her husband, "Slapstick." And it is a lonely world, against which Vonnegut poses a solution drawn from his childhood and his experiences visiting Biafra – the extended family. Proclaimed on campaign buttons, "Lonesome No More!" becomes the motto of Swain's presidency, to be enacted through a system that Vonnegut had proposed to vice-presidential candidate Sargent Shriver in 1972 and recollected in an essay published in *Wampeters, Foma, and Granfalloons*:

> I wanted Sarge Shriver to say, "You're not happy, are you? Nobody in this country is happy but the rich people. Something is wrong. I'll tell you what's wrong: We're lonesome! We're being kept apart from our neighbors. Why? Because the rich people can go on taking our money away if we don't hang together. They can go on taking our power away. They want us lone-some; they want us huddled in our houses with just our wives and kids, watching television, because they can manipulate us then. . . . Here's a war cry for the American people: 'Lonesome no more!'" That's the kind of demagoguery I approve of.

However, the reviewers once again charged that the energy had gone out of Vonnegut's writing and that he was repeating surface characteristics without effect. Sales of *Slapstick* reflected a disappointed audience, with paperback printings running at half those of *Breakfast of Champions*.

The three novels that followed *Slaughterhouse-Five* focus on related aspects of contemporary American life. *Breakfast of Champions* reflects the spirit preceding the nation's bicentennial in pondering what America had been and has become. In characteristic Vonnegut style it reexamines with childlike simplicity national emblems, symbols, songs, and mottoes, creating hyperbolic distinctions between pretense and reality, intention and achievement. *Slapstick* examines the social malaise in broad terms, using a futuristic setting of a balkanized America. Vonnegut's next novel, *Jailbird* (1979), repeats this theme but again narrows the focus, observing a particular real presidency and the effects of the American system on two elderly people. It anticipates the 1980s world of conglomerates and mergers and arbitrageurs yet at the same time presents a world of the lonely, the dispossessed, and the homeless.

Thematically *Jailbird* is related to *God Bless You, Mr. Rosewater* in looking at the economic circumstances of society from a moral standpoint. Nicola Sacco and Bartolomeo Vanzetti serve *Jailbird* much as *Slapstick* uses Laurel and Hardy – as a recurrent refrain that embellishes the theme of the novel. These two immigrants were tried as anarchist murderers and executed despite their certain innocence because they spoke eloquently for the working poor and because their socialist and unionist beliefs threatened rich and powerful men. Vonnegut reveres them much as he does the unionist from his native Indiana who in the early decades of the twentieth century ran for president five times on the Socialist ticket, Eugene Debs. There are other glimpses of the turbulent history of the formation of American unions, and various episodes debate the achievement of socio-economic equality. The prologue makes clear that just as Laurel and Hardy came out of Vonnegut's childhood memories during the Depression, so do Sacco and Vanzetti. The economic circumstances that colored his childhood less by deprivation than by their psychological impact on his parents reappear.

Dust jacket for Vonnegut's 1963 novel, in which a substance called ice-nine destroys all life on earth

In the first chapter the narrator-protagonist, Walter F. Starbuck, says that years as well as people are characters in the book, "which is the story of my life," and goes on to elaborate dates, such as 1929, that shape his story. The first half of the prologue is autobiographical, in part devoted to explaining the wellsprings of the novel's theme. It recalls a day in 1945 when Vonnegut, freshly returned from the war, met with his father, his Uncle Alex, and a union officer named Powers Hapgood to discuss his finding work with a union. Hapgood serves as the prototype for one of the novel's fictional characters, Kenneth Whistler, who affirms the Sermon on the Mount as the basis of morality.

The second half of the prologue is fictional, providing an invented background for events in the novel. It tells the story of the McCones, a family of rich industrialists. Alexander McCone selects his chauffeur's son as a protégé, offering him wealth, privilege, and a Harvard education. To fit the part the boy's name is changed from Walter Stankiewicz to Walter Starbuck. While at Harvard, Starbuck turns toward socialism and the example of Whistler, consequently losing McCone's patronage. His career as a government bureaucrat crumbles soon after he exposes his friend Leland Clewes to the

House Un-American Activities Committee as a former Communist. Committee member Richard Nixon remembers Starbuck for this service, and years later President Nixon makes Starbuck a White House staffer. His basement office becomes a repository for Nixon's slush funds, and for his unwitting role in the Watergate affair Starbuck goes to jail. The other main line of the plot concerns Mary Kathleen O'Looney, a college lover of Starbuck's who as Mrs. Jack Graham becomes the owner of the fabulous RAMJAC conglomerate. Like Howard Hughes, she becomes a recluse, hiding her identity as a bag lady. Starbuck's efforts to carry forward her business after her death, which he conceals, lead to his return to prison at the end of the novel.

Jailbird appeared at the time when some of those convicted in the Watergate scandal were publishing their stories, so a parody of those confessional pleas of innocence might be predicted. But Vonnegut is not vindictive; he lampoons rather than villainizes, and his satire reaches back past Watergate to the McCarthy era, the House Un-American Activities Committee, and the "brightest and best" Harvard population in Washington during the Kennedy administration, while public fascination with the life and death of bizarre billionaire

Hughes influenced the characterization of Mary Kathleen O'Looney. The novel, then, mixes fact and fiction; Nixon, Roy Cohen, Charles Colson, and others from the news of the time join with fictional characters. Events and places undergo a similar mixture. Finally – another innovation – there is an index that lists the real and the invented with like authenticity. This mixing of forms is an aspect of the novel's postmodernism, although a few years earlier Vonnegut recounted visiting a university where he talked to some literary critics in the English department: "They called me a postmodernist," he said, "whatever the hell that is."

As is typical of Vonnegut's novels, the mosaic of vignettes, jokes, sketches, and analyses in *Jailbird* supersedes the importance of the story line per se. Vonnegut observed this direction in his fiction in the 1976 interview with Short:

> There'll be more and more to complain about in my fiction. People will say it's not fiction any more, it's editorializing. And, you know, the stories are getting sketchier and sketchier and sketchier. But I like stories because they allow you to digress. I'm not capable of logic, really a paragraph to paragraph logic. And so the story form allows me to make statements that I know intuitively are true. I can't begin to buttress with arguments.

In part the novels of this period are less narrative and more editorial in nature. Also, like the "nonfiction novel" – for example, Truman Capote's *In Cold Blood* (1966) or Norman Mailer's *The Armies of the Night* (1968) – in which fiction is created out of real historical events, his novels acknowledge the unreality of the factual and the inevitability of reality being given artistic form in its recounting. At the same time there is recognition of the fictiveness of fiction. Reader and writer both know that while a novel is being told as if it were reality, it remains a fiction. Many readers in the present era find themselves uncomfortable with artifice presented as reality, thus a metal sculptor may leave girders showing to reveal the true artistic medium. Vonnegut exposes authorial presence and acknowledges the fictiveness of his novels most dramatically by the inclusion of himself in *Slaughterhouse-Five* – "that was me" – and by his direct involvement as character-author in *Breakfast of Champions*.

Such direct authorial declaration, and the combinations of the documentary and the fantastic, cosmic distortion and social realism, science fiction and history, and even real and fictional persons in the index, typifies the mixed character of postmodern fiction. Postmodernism rejects the im-

plication in earlier writing that patterns can be found in chaos, that the world, however absurd it may appear, is explainable. Even depicting life in a narrative sequence implies cause and effect rather than randomness or chance. Postmodernists try not to make the contingency of life comfortable in the process of narrating it, hence their concern with constant shifts and changes that keep readers off guard. Vonnegut has moved increasingly in this direction. As he said in *Breakfast of Champions,* "Let others bring order to chaos. I would bring chaos to order, instead, which I think I have done." The postmodernist does this believing that this "order" is a false imposition upon the true nature of a contingent world.

After *Jailbird* Vonnegut wrote the text for a children's book called *Sun Moon Star* (1980), a Christmas story recounting the first visual perceptions of the infant Jesus. This new treatment of an age-old story is paired with striking color illustrations by Ivan Chermayeff. Then came *Palm Sunday,* like *Wampeters, Foma and Granfalloons* a collection of assorted short pieces. Among these are his self-interview for the *Paris Review* and his Palm Sunday sermon delivered at Saint Clement's Episcopal Church, New York, on 30 March 1980. Contributions written by others include "An Account of the Ancestry of Kurt Vonnegut, Jr.," by his uncle, John Rauch; the lyrics of two songs by the Statler Brothers; a letter by his daughter Nannette; and a speech made by his great-grandfather, Clemens Vonnegut. *Palm Sunday* is an interesting source of biographical information with a personal touch, and it includes a good blend of humor and thoughtful commentary on many aspects of contemporary life.

Shortly after his sixtieth birthday Vonnegut published his tenth novel, *Deadeye Dick* (1982). There is less direct infusion of autobiographical fact or authorial voice than in the preceding novels. The short introduction contains little personal rumination, nor is the story framed by authorial declaration or punctuated by interjections as in *Slaughterhouse-Five,* but the introduction firmly announces the way in which this book fictionalizes autobiography:

> I will explain the main symbols in this book.

> There is an unappreciated, empty arts center in the shape of a sphere. That is my head as my sixtieth birthday beckons me.

> There is a neutron bomb explosion in a populated area. This is the disappearance of so many people I cared about in Indianapolis when I was starting out to

be a writer. Indianapolis is there, but the people are gone.

> Haiti is New York City, where I live now.

> The neutered pharmacist who tells the tale is my declining sexuality. The crime he committed in childhood is all the bad things I have done.

In effect, the events and characters of the book are frequently metaphorical equivalents of those in Vonnegut's life. He gives a warning about this as well: "This is fiction, not history, so it should not be used as a reference book." And *Deadeye Dick* abounds in fictions. Fictions are the provisional realities by which the characters live. Author, narrator, and characters invent their own stories to describe what life feels like to them.

This emphasis on subjective impressions of reality is underlined in the way the narrator, Rudy Waltz, describes life: "I was a wisp of undifferentiated nothingness, and then a little peephole opened quite suddenly. Light and sound poured in. Voices began to describe me and my surroundings. Nothing they said could be appealed." Throughout the novel people are born, and voices go on describing them until they die. Sometimes the fictions these voices invent hardly fit the character. Rudy never even sees the woman he accidently shoots, but the people of Midland City call him "Deadeye Dick" for most of his life. Rudy also invents fictions. Besides writing his play based on the life of his father's old friend, he punctuates his narrative with dramatic scenes that reenact key episodes between the people in his life. Beyond that, Rudy believes (as Vonnegut has suggested previously) that people make their lives into stories. In general he suspects that a good deal of mischief results from people's trying to invent for themselves interesting fictions.

Deadeye Dick itself is a fiction inhabiting a fiction. As if to emphasize the point about fiction being only a provisional reality, this novel is set, in effect, in another one – *Breakfast of Champions*. Names, places, dates, and events are all the same from that novel to this. For instance, Celia Hildreth becomes Celia Hoover, Dwayne's wife, who has a homosexual son named Bunny and who kills herself by imbibing Drano. There are also allusions to other Vonnegut books.

The metafictional highlight comes when, at Celia Hoover's funeral, Rudy finds himself inappropriately smiling. "I glanced around to see if anyone had noticed. One person had. He was at the other end of our pew, and he did not look away when I caught him gazing at me. He went right on gazing, and it was I who faced forward again. I had not rec-

ognized him. He was wearing large sunglasses with mirrored lenses. He could have been anyone." The man is Kurt Vonnegut, author and character, described as he appears in *Breakfast of Champions*.

Vonnegut has made himself a character in this story in other ways as well. Rudy is ten years younger than Vonnegut, so he goes through some experiences that might be equivalents of the author's own a decade later. For example, Rudy's traumatizing shock, the shooting, happens when he is twelve, the suicide of Vonnegut's mother when he was twenty-two. These events occur on the same date: Mother's Day 1944. Rudy's play bombs on 14 February; Dresden was bombed on the night of 13–14 February. Like the events, the characters are reinventions of those in Vonnegut's life. The mother whose "story ended when she married the handsomest rich man in town" and who cannot cope with crumbling fortunes later might stand for his own mother, as might Celia in her suicide. Elsewhere, however, Celia seems to represent his sister, especially in completing the threesome with Rudy and his brother Felix, who, like Vonnegut's brother, is seven years his senior.

While Vonnegut clearly is engaged in a new fiction, one should remember his admonition that this "is fiction, not history" and not read it simply as a roman à clef. More important is how Vonnegut uses this autobiographical material – the fictionalizing process at work in this particular novel and, more broadly, in the continuation of his canon. In this process he has evolved new descriptions of what experience feels like to him and new forms of the novel to match modern society's changing ways of understanding itself.

One curiosity of *Deadeye Dick* is the inclusion of recipes. Some of the recipes seem hilarious simply in the telling, others by their content. In some ways the recipes are reminiscent of the calypsos in *Cat's Cradle*. There are other echoes of previous works, especially in the general notion that language itself fictionalizes. In *Deadeye Dick,* for instance, Haitian Creole is presented as having only a present tense, so that time and existence are transformed by the telling, as in this discussion of Rudy's late father:

> "He is dead?" he said in Creole.
> "He is dead," I agreed.
> "What does he do?" he said.
> "He paints," I said.
> "I like him," he said.

Deadeye Dick ranks as one of Vonnegut's funniest books, noticeably lacking the bleakness imparted to *Slapstick* by deformed characters and blasted landscapes. Its critical acclaim was qualified. For some the experiments in form were a distraction, the evocation of previous work mistaken for mere repetition, and the lack of an engrossing, connected plot line a limitation. Technically it remains one of his most innovative books, however, and for that reason, as well as the autobiographical elements, may continue to grow in interest.

A visit to the Galápagos Islands was the inspiration for Vonnegut's next novel. That he would make the journey, furthering not just his general scientific interests but in particular his interest in fauna and their evolution, seems appropriate. Many years before, when he had made a field trip west with a group of teachers and students from Shortridge High School, Vonnegut had been the expedition's "biologist," collecting and annotating samples. Three years in the making, *Galápagos* (1985) shows the labor in its polish and density. The axis around which the novel revolves is Charles Darwin and the evolutionary theory of natural selection. One of the reasons for the slow evolution of the novel itself was Vonnegut's great concern to have it be scientifically sound, which involved research and thought. He was consequently highly gratified to be told by the famous evolutionary biologist, Stephen Jay Gould of Harvard University, that he had gotten it right.

Vonnegut has always had a warm spot for animals – in his high-school writing he took the pen name "Ferdy" from the children's book *Ferdinand the Bull* – and has frequently drawn on the deep impressions made by his visit to the Galápagos. Also, Darwin has always fascinated Vonnegut. He never has liked the notion of "survival of the fittest" (a precept upon which he casts doubt), in which every death is a triumph of progress, and he dislikes any doctrine that might be used even to imply that there is justification for the subjugation of the weak. Darwinian evolution as a rational and logical progression toward superiority, whether in the survival of species or as a social metaphor, is something he has consistently rejected on both moral and scientific grounds. He rejects it morally as a justification for oppression and scientifically as simply not supported by the more random and convoluted sequences the facts reveal.

The story has two parts, "The Thing Was" and "And the Thing Became." The thirty-eight chapters of the first part trace the baroque interplay of the random and the inevitable whereby a cast of ten comes to be the Noah's Ark of human survival. The fourteen chapters of the second part take these characters to Santa Rosalia, one of the Galápagos Islands. They evade the insidious virus that ends the rest of the human race, not with the usual apocalyptic bang but with the whimper of infertility. That the fifty-two chapters equal the weeks of the year fits much else in this book, which at every turn manifests evolution over periods of time.

A million years later humans have evolved to have fur, flippers, and streamlined heads like seals, a consequence of a typical mix of freak circumstance and gradual adaptation. They are much happier because without hands they cannot use tools or weapons. Additionally, they no longer have the large, overactive brains that invented lies, caused other trouble, and were generally as burdensome and lethal as any other evolutionary overadaptation.

The theme of evolution permeates the book, even governing the form. Vonnegut has described his books as mosaics in which each tile is a joke. This description certainly fits in this case, where chapter after chapter ends with the punch line of a joke. But each joke evolves from the last, and the larger joke of the whole situation – be it the first step of selecting the final ten survivors and getting them to the island or evolution one million years in the future – evolves out of a sea of coincidence and happenstance, as if everything conspires to thwart an inevitable destiny. The longer, first part of the novel, with its many names and complications, initially seems confusing because of this technique. But this confusion of characters and events proves effective, illustrating the nature of evolution: that it is not all triumph of the fittest or grand design, but that it sifts itself out of chance and coincidence. Life's evolutionary processes, Vonnegut insists, are contingent.

Another form of evolution in *Galápagos* comes in the narration. Vonnegut does not enter this novel to speak directly, as he does in many previous novels. Instead his narrator turns out to be the son of his fictional alter ego Kilgore Trout. This intertextual device makes it seem as if Vonnegut's novel has evolved out of his own earlier writing, as if characters from a fiction are making a fiction. This implies the contemporary perception of the artist as a product of his or her art rather than the traditional opposite view. Vonnegut uses other techniques associated with postmodernism: fragmentation through short chapters and subdivisions; shifts in setting, time, and character; random, noncausal events; Darwin's biography mixed with Trout's science fiction; and the use of the fictive worlds of Vonnegut's earlier novels.

Vonnegut frequently has used distancing devices such as looking at the earth through the eyes

Dust jacket for Vonnegut's best-known novel, which combines his experiences during World War II with science-fiction elements

of an extraterrestrial or from another planet or assessing society from the perspective of another age or culture. These distances are used to great effect in *Galápagos*. Human social behavior is measured against timeless evolutionary adaptations. The narrator views everything from the perspective of the year A.D. 1001986. As a result Vonnegut achieves the kinds of distances and fresh perspectives that Swift created through remote locations and changing scales in *Gulliver's Travels* (1726). Vonnegut thus examines current issues such as the imbalances of the world's economies or the dangers implicit in accelerating armament procurement in striking new terms.

One way in which Vonnegut conceives of his task as a writer is to view it as being like a scientist who asks, "What if ?" The scientist conducts experiments to see what might happen given certain conditions. So can the writer, says Vonnegut, and he enjoys this because it is also a playful process. In *Slapstick* he asks, "What if gravity were not a constant force?" In *Galápagos* he asks, "What if everyone died except an isolated group? How would they evolve?" There is, as he has admitted, a certain sophomoric naiveté about such questions, but that is the source of their freshness and vigor. *Galápagos* shows that, in his sixties, Vonnegut still had that sense of lively irreverence. It fuels his humor and arms his attacks on often-specious platitudes and conventional wisdom.

Galápagos warns against the arrogance of humanity's self-assurance in its own intelligence and its dogmatic opinionatedness. This arrogance emerges in the self-righteousness with which people impose opinions, subjugate others, abuse animals, and devastate the planet. Even the assumption that humans will end the world with their own weapons is undercut when the species is brought to extinction by a humble virus. Out of the irreverence of the book, finally, emerges the kindly but rather weary avuncular voice, so frequent in Vonnegut's work, that speaks the novel's moral warnings. Evolution allows him to take the long view and look at human endeavors with his characteristic mix of detached amusement and compassion, despite seeing cause for pessimism. After all, he takes as his epigraph Anne Frank's stubborn assertion, "In spite of everything, I still believe people are really good at heart."

Galápagos was generally well received. Vonnegut's own view was that he remained popular with a wide readership on the one hand (since all his novels remained in print) and respected by literary scholars and academic writers on the other but was resisted by some reviewers in the popular presses. Some magazines and newspaper reviews were grudging about *Galápagos* and Vonnegut in general, but he continued to be taught, anthologized, and written about in universities, where the novel often won praise. Some reviewers, including novelist John Irving, called *Galápagos* Vonnegut's best novel since *Slaughterhouse-Five,* and it received favorable treatment in the British press.

As it announces, Vonnegut's next novel, *Bluebeard* (1987), is "The Autobiography of Rabo Karabekian (1916–1988)." Karabekian previously appeared as the painter who attends the Midland City Arts Fair in *Breakfast of Champions*. There his painting consists of a plain canvas with a single vertical stripe, which represents "the unwavering band of light" that is the unique individual core of each person. While Karabekian is dismissed in that novel as "a vain and weak and trashy man," he nevertheless provides the affirmation that breaks the narrator out of his bleak view of a mechanistic world in which people are really no more than robots.

In *Bluebeard* Karabekian is not at all the abrasive, self-assured snob he was in *Breakfast of Champions*. He is a one-eyed veteran and widower, most of whose friends have died (frequently by suicide) and whose paintings have fallen apart, so that if he is remembered as an artist at all it is as an object of derision. In the novel's present he encounters Circe Berman, a pushy forty-three-year-old widow who persuades him to write an autobiography. *Bluebeard* is divided between his autobiography and the present in which he is writing it. To a degree the two accounts are complementary, and they are punctuated by signals such as "Back to the Great Depression" or "To return to the past." Inevitably, the autobiography and the daily diary converge at the end.

Two worlds dominate this novel. One is the world of art, or specifically of painting, and the other is a world of massacre and war. From the account of the Karabekians' escape from the Turkish massacre of the Armenians to the references to World War II, there is a backdrop of violence and inhumanity that sets in context the dialogue between representational and expressionist painting in this novel. It suggests that these modern horrors are in part responsible for the rise of Abstract Expressionism. While Vonnegut professes to be not much drawn to the Abstract Expressionists, he presents a case for their technique in a December 1983 *Esquire* article called "Jack the Dripper," collected in *Fates Worse Than Death*. In it he asks whether "any moralists [could] have called for a more apt reaction by painters to World War II, to the death camps and Hiroshima and all the rest of it, than pictures without persons or artifacts, without even allusions to the blessings of nature? A full moon, after all, had come to be known as 'a bomber's moon.' . . . It had seemed impossible that any real artist could honorably create harmonious pictures for a European and North American civilization whose principal industry had become the manufacture of ruins and cripples and corpses." Pollock's answer had been to turn inward in order to express the unconscious. Rabo's vertical stripes, which represent the souls of beings, presumably seek to evade the corrupted physical world in the same way.

The title refers to the folktale of Bluebeard, who forbade each of his wives in turn to enter one chamber of his castle. Such a prohibition proved irresistible, and when each wife after the first entered she found there the remains of her predecessors and a foretaste of her own doom. In Vonnegut's tale the forbidden room is the potato barn behind Rabo's East Hampton home. Yet in the end Rabo opens it willingly to Circe, and it holds no horrors for her. It turns out to contain a sixty-four-by-eight-foot painting depicting a scene Rabo recalled from the end of the war when refugees, soldiers, released prisoners, and others by the thousands found themselves together in one valley. The painting is perfect representationalism, each of its many characters depicted with photographic accuracy and each having his or her own story. A curiosity is that the only young and healthy women are all depicted hiding in root cellars because they know the conquering armies are advancing and they will all be raped. The painting is called *Now It's the Women's Turn*.

The painting's title is a revelation of horror to come for women, much like the ending of the old folktale. This kind of horror is ever present in this novel – from the murder of Armenian women and children by the Turks, to illustrator Dan Gregory's battering of his mistress Marilee Kemp, to Marilee's telling of being raped by the football team after her junior prom to the women she later employs in her Italian villa, who have all been brutalized by men during the war. Marilee becomes the voice of this novel's pacifist and feminist conscience. She sees war as "always men against women, with the men only pretending to fight among themselves." Men plant mines, women plant seeds. In this book the women are nurturers, and the postwar men are all – like Rabo and the suicidal Abstract Expressionists – damaged, inadequate, and self-destructive. In this context, *Now It's the Women's Turn* could have completely different implications. It could be seen as addressing this sea of war-dislocated souls and saying, "Now it is time women had a turn running things. Men have wrought war. Perhaps women can do better."

Certainly the strongest characters are women, even though women, including Circe and Marilee, are frequently victims. Marilee has been responsible for Rabo's start in art and nurtures his growth; Circe brings a washed-up recluse back to life, encouraging him to share his art and to write an autobiography. Many of the men in the novel are physically or emotionally crippled. Several commit suicide, as did some of the Abstract Expressionists in reality, and others are physically impaired, as is the one-eyed Rabo. Men who are hale and hearty are real-life dictators, such as Benito Mussolini, or bullies, such as Gregory. Women are exploited in patriarchal society, and most men are left crippled and inadequate by it. It is epitomized by war, yet war is also the sign of its failure. Perhaps, *Bluebeard* seems to say, humanity is due for a new, androgynous world where art can once again tell its human story. In this sense the novel develops a feminist theme also strongly present in *Galápagos*.

Vonnegut has long entertained a strong interest in the visual arts and frequently relates the problems of the writer to those of the painter. *Bluebeard* is especially interesting from this perspective. It is characteristic of his work in its attention to themes of war and suffering, of neurosis and suicide, and of failed marriages and reclusive widowers. It is also typical in its inclusion of commentary on the contemporary social scene, much of it deprecatory and cynical. Yet the tone of the novel is predominantly affirmative. Its relationships are mostly positive, much of its humor is lighthearted, and its ending is strongly upbeat. The life-affirming energies within the story seem to survive despite the lethal forces. The image of jewels spilling from the mouth of a dead person, like fruit from a cornucopia, recurs in the novel, which is fitting in a book where new life – and new art – comes out of death and destruction.

The narrator and protagonist of Vonnegut's next novel, *Hocus Pocus* (1990), Eugene Debs Hartke, is a less happy soul than Rabo Karabekian, although he follows in the mold of Walter F. Starbuck, Rudy Waltz, and Rabo. Like them, he is a man in his later years looking back over life who might exclaim, as did Malachi Constant of *The Sirens of Titan,* "I WAS A VICTIM OF A SERIES OF ACCIDENTS, AS ARE WE ALL." The effect, however, is quite different in that there is little self-pity in Hartke, and he is resolute enough and self-deprecatingly humorous enough to endow his story with a milder tone than its plot's bleak circumstances would appear to invite.

The setting for the novel echoes that of *Player Piano,* with Scipio and its Tarkington College and Athena and its penitentiary set across a lake from each other, which is similar to Ilium and Homestead straddling the river in *Player Piano.* Geography is not the only reminder, because like that first novel, this includes a great deal of direct social commentary and traces the decline of America from World War II into a fictional future, when contemporary society's problems reach their nightmarish logical extremes. There is even a final futile and violent rebellion, which the protagonist is falsely accused of leading, and, as a final echo, the return of the Shah of Bratpuhr.

These echoes of the first novel become less surprising when one realizes that in *Hocus Pocus* one can find some echo of virtually every preceding book. In this way, perhaps, it reveals its own evolution, for this is a book as concerned with evolution as *Galápagos.* Hartke's life and, more important, his character evolve before the reader's eyes, created out of a succession of coincidences, random happenings, and trivia that subsequently shape major decisions. The same is true in the theme of social and institutional evolution that permeates the novel. As Hartke says, "Accident after accident has made Tarkington what it is today. Who would dare to predict what it will be in 2021, only 20 years from now? The 2 prime movers in the Universe are Time and Luck." Several episodes begin with "If." *If* the timing had been different, *if* this or that had not happened, *if* a certain person had not been here or there, Hartke would have been different.

The form Vonnegut has chosen is perfect for the message. In this case the tiles of his fictional mosaic are short fragments separated by lines. An editor's note explains that Hartke "wrote this book in pencil on everything from brown wrapping paper to the backs of business cards. The unconventional lines separating passages within chapters indicate where one scrap ended and the next began. The shorter the passage, the smaller the scrap." Besides making possible some interesting comic tricks, this method allows the story, and Hartke's character, to emerge from an accumulation of little things. Just as this novel suggests happens in life, little things later prove significant. This device also allows Vonnegut to splice recollection and present, as in *Bluebeard.* This device is an important element in the revelation of Hartke's personality.

Like his fictional forebears, Hartke is battered and physically marked (he has tuberculosis). As he looks back he makes lists of the women he has loved and the people he has killed. This may sound like bombast and chauvinism and perhaps was in the younger Hartke, but it is now done with feeling. Hartke's compassion constantly shows, and he is philosophically nonjudgmental of a range of bizarre or vicious people. His harshest words are reserved for the very rich, who have ravaged the country and dispossessed its people. By the end his views have moved closer to those of his namesake, Socialist Eugene Debs.

The mosaic of short passages also serves the social commentary well. The observations, though often damning, are short and sharp, with no chance to turn heavily didactic. Often the form also makes possible a comic twist. Just as Hartke's character evolves from these scraps, so too do they reveal social evolution. One might reasonably have expected Scipio, with its college, to grow and evolve and the isolated Athena prison to stagnate. By the end the penitentiary literally explodes and incorporates the college. Social evolution is compared to microbiological evolution:

> My body, as I understand it, is attempting to contain the TB germs inside me in little shells it builds around them. The shells are calcium, the most common element in the walls of many prisons, including Athena. This place is ringed by barbed wire. So was Auschwitz.
>
> If I die of TB, it will be because my body could not build prisons fast enough and strong enough.
>
> Is there a lesson there? Not a cheerful one.

Indeed, the vision of America's future implied in *Hocus Pocus* is not cheerful, and the narrator is unjustly accused, yet the novel retains a kind of resigned cheerfulness. The title perhaps implies that hocus pocus is what life amounts to — a slapstick journey moved by time and luck. The design on the cover and the dust jacket of two wheels alludes to the perpetual-motion machines Elias Tarkington had attempted to build, which Hartke has exhibited with the sign, "THE COMPLICATED FUTILITY OF IGNORANCE." Much human behavior shown in the book is summed up in this phrase. The concept of perpetual motion captures a world constantly evolving, always changing.

Hartke admires the craftsmanship in these futile machines and the dedication and care of those who, knowing they were futile, nevertheless made them. What one senses in Vonnegut's fiction, what one hears in his lectures, and what emerges here through the character of Hartke is that Vonnegut believes in caring, in trying, in taking pride and showing compassion despite the constantly defeating twists of a contingent world. In fact, it is the nature of this chaotic, random universe that makes the human virtues the more important. This is what Hartke has learned.

Hocus Pocus was followed by another collection, what Vonnegut called "a sequel, not that anyone has clamored for one, to a book called *Palm Sunday*." *Fates Worse Than Death* is described as "An Autobiographical Collage of the 1980s." Like *Wampeters, Foma and Granfalloons* and *Palm Sunday* it is a collection of assorted writings and speeches by Vonnegut and by others, several of which had appeared previously in less available places. In this collection, as compared with the previous ones, Vonnegut has provided more connections between the component parts. Rather than the separate items making separate chapters, as in the earlier books, here they are more often blended into a continuing commentary and become parts of its chapters, making the text more linear and unified. It also includes an appendix with various supporting documents and even a few photographs.

Vonnegut's dedication of *Fates Worse Than Death* to his father signals the personal tone of the book. In various places he speaks intimately of his father, his grandfather, and his children, is frank about his mother's suicide, and in his reminiscences of his earlier life includes his wives and other relatives. He also talks about public figures he has known. Some of the other essays involve his usual social commentary and, especially when taken from speeches, exemplify a balance of lightness and edge that is the key to his success as a satirist. The emphasis of this collection, though, is not on social commentary nearly as much as it is on himself, his family, the bases for his beliefs, and the people he has known. It is therefore a satisfying book for the reader attracted to the type of persona who emerges from the novels and wishing to feel closer to the author.

Vonnegut has proven a remarkably durable author. The recent novels demonstrate that his skills have matured while his imagination has remained fresh. Such a long, steady career is rare in American letters. In addition to his stories, novels, plays, and nonfiction, he has written many introductions, essays, and commentaries in every conceivable type of book and magazine. He has also continued to be in demand as a speaker and to draw large audiences. The heading Vonnegut commonly uses for these engagements is "How to Get a Job Like Mine," which serves to launch him into an evening of entertainment in which he may talk about absolutely anything but what that title suggests. Typically he will start with something relating to the place in which he is speaking and to current events, then read from things he has written but that have not been widely published if published at all, interspersing these with extemporaneous remarks, jokes, and outrageous asides. He usually ends with a chalkboard demonstration of how story plots can be graphed that recalls his refused anthropology thesis but that now provides him with a popular comic apparatus.

Another activity in which Vonnegut has become increasingly involved is art. What began as

*Vonnegut at the University of South Carolina, February 1979,
with photographer Jill Krementz, whom he married in November
1979, and novelist William Price Fox (photograph
by Steve Hunt)*

felt-tip-pen doodles and a spin-off from the line drawings in *Breakfast of Champions* has become a series of drawings of faces. He was delighted to sell one for $850 and held a one-man exhibition at the Margo Fine Galleries in New York in October 1980. More recently he has begun using color in these works, and some have been silk-screened by Joseph Pietro III of Lexington, Kentucky. There was an exhibition of Vonnegut's work on Long Island in the summer of 1994. He enjoys this medium for his creativity, its spontaneity a release from the rigors of long periods of daily writing and revising demanded by the novel.

The work ethic he learned as a journalist remains undiminished, and he continues to live as a working writer. He still composes on a manual typewriter and sends the manuscripts to a typist who has worked loyally with him for many years. After *Hocus Pocus* he began work on a fourteenth novel, which has the working title "Timequake"; like *Galápagos,* it has a fairly complex scientific premise and has proved a challenging subject for him. He now spends more of his time at his home on Long Island than he does in Manhattan. His wife continues her own career as a photographer and writer, and they have an adopted daughter, Lily, who was born in 1983.

Interviews:

Robert Scholes, "A Talk with Kurt Vonnegut, Jr.," in *The Vonnegut Statement,* edited by Jerome Klinkowitz and John Somer (New York: Seymour Lawrence/Delacorte, 1973), pp. 90–118;

David Standish, "*Playboy* Interview," *Playboy,* 20, no. 7 (1973): 57ff; reprinted in *Wampeters, Foma and Granfalloons (Opinions)* (New York: Seymour Lawrence/Delacorte, 1974), pp. 237–285;

Robert Short, "Robert Short Interviews Kurt Vonnegut, Chicago – June 8, 1976," in his *Something to Believe In: Is Kurt Vonnegut the Exorcist of Jesus Christ Superstar?* (San Francisco: Harper & Row, 1976), pp. 283–308;

David Hyman, David Michaelis, George Plimpton, and Richard L. Rhodes, "The Art of Fiction LXIV: Kurt Vonnegut," *Paris Review,* 18 (Spring 1977): 56–103;

Conversations with Kurt Vonnegut, edited by William Rodney Allen (Jackson: University Press of Mississippi, 1988).

Bibliographies:

Betty L. Hudgens, *Kurt Vonnegut, Jr.: A Checklist* (Detroit: Gale Research, 1972);

Jerome Klinkowitz and Asa B. Pieratt, *Kurt Vonnegut, Jr.: A Descriptive Bibliography and Annotated Secondary Checklist* (Hamden, Conn.: Archon, 1974);

Pieratt, Klinkowitz, and Julie Huffman-Klinkowitz, *Kurt Vonnegut: A Comprehensive Bibliography* (Hamden, Conn.: Archon, 1987);

Donald M. Fiene, "Kurt Vonnegut in the USSR: A Bibliography," *Bulletin of Bibliography,* 45, no. 4 (1988): 223–232;

Peter J. Reed and Paul Baepler, "Kurt Vonnegut: A Selected Bibliography, 1985–1992," *Bulletin of Bibliography,* 50, no. 2 (1993): 123–128.

References:

William Rodney Allen, *Understanding Kurt Vonnegut* (Columbia: University of South Carolina Press, 1991);

William Bly, *Kurt Vonnegut's Slaughterhouse-Five* (Woodbury, N.Y.: Barron's Educational Series, 1985);

Lawrence R. Broer, *Sanity Plea: Schizophrenia in the Novels of Kurt Vonnegut* (Ann Arbor, Mich.: UMI Research Press, 1988);

Critique, special issue on Vonnegut, 12, no. 3 (1971);

Draftings in Vonnegut: The Paradox of Hope, edited by Loree Rackstraw (Cedar Falls: University of Northern Iowa Press, 1988);

Leslie A. Fiedler, "The Divine Stupidity of Kurt Vonnegut, Jr.," *Esquire,* 74 (September 1970): 195–197, 199–200, 202–204;

Richard Giannone, *Vonnegut: A Preface to His Novels* (New York: Kennikat Press, 1977);

David H. Goldsmith, *Kurt Vonnegut: Fantasist of Fire and Ice* (Bowling Green, Ohio: Bowling Green State University Popular Press, 1972);

Charles B. Harris, *Contemporary American Novelists of the Absurd* (New Haven, Conn.: College and University Press, 1971), pp. 51–75;

John Irving, "Kurt Vonnegut and His Critics," *New Republic,* 181 (22 September 1979): 41–49;

Jerome Klinkowitz, *Kurt Vonnegut* (London & New York: Methuen, 1982);

Klinkowitz, *Slaughterhouse-Five: Reforming the Novel and the World* (Boston: Twayne, 1990);

James Lundquist, *Kurt Vonnegut* (New York: Ungar, 1977);

Clark Mayo, *Kurt Vonnegut: The Gospel from Outer Space* (San Bernardino, Cal.: Borgo Press, 1977);

Donald E. Morse, *Kurt Vonnegut* (San Bernardino, Cal.: Borgo Press, 1992);

Peter J. Reed, *Kurt Vonnegut, Jr.* (New York: Warner, 1972);

Stanley Schatt, *Kurt Vonnegut, Jr.* (Boston: Twayne, 1977);

Summary, special issue on Vonnegut (1971);

Tony Tanner, "The Uncertain Messenger: A Study of the Novels of Kurt Vonnegut, Jr.," *Critical Quarterly,* 11 (Winter 1969): 297–315;

Vonnegut in America, edited by Klinkowitz and Donald L. Lawler (New York: Seymour Lawrence/Delacorte, 1977);

The Vonnegut Statement, edited by Klinkowitz and John Somer (New York: Seymour Lawrence/Delacorte, 1973).

Margaret Walker

(7 July 1915 –   )

Jane Campbell
Purdue University – Calumet

See also the Walker entry in *DLB 76: Afro-American Writers, 1940–1955.*

BOOKS: *For My People* (New Haven: Yale University Press, 1942);

Jubilee (Boston: Houghton Mifflin, 1966; London: Hodder & Stoughton, 1967);

Prophets for a New Day (Detroit: Broadside Press, 1970);

How I Wrote Jubilee (Chicago: Third World Press, 1972);

October Journey (Detroit: Broadside Press, 1973);

A Poetic Equation: Conversations between Nikki Giovanni and Margaret Walker, by Walker and Nikki Giovanni (Washington, D.C.: Howard University Press, 1974);

For Farish Street Green (Jackson, Miss., 1986);

Richard Wright: Daemonic Genius (New York: Dodd, Mead, 1987);

This Is My Century: New and Collected Poems (Athens: University of Georgia Press, 1989);

How I Wrote Jubilee and Other Essays on Life and Literature, edited by Maryemma Graham (New York: Feminist Press, 1990);

God Touched My Life: The Inspiring Autobiography of the Nun Who Brought Song, Celebration, and Soul to the World, by Walker and Thea Bowman (San Francisco: Harper & Row, 1992);

Margaret Walker's "For My People": A Tribute, by Walker and Roland L. Freeman (Jackson: University of Mississippi Press, 1992).

OTHER: "New Poets," in *Black Expression,* edited by Addison Gayle Jr. (New York: Weybright & Talley, 1969), pp. 89–100;

"Religion, Poetry, and History: Foundations for a New Educational System," in *The Black Seventies,* edited by Floyd B. Barbour (Boston: Sargent, 1970), pp. 284–295;

"On Being Female, Black, and Free," in *The Writer on Her Work,* edited by Janet Sternburg (New York: Norton, 1980), pp. 95–106;

Margaret Walker

"Dr. Nick Aaron Ford: A Man in the Classic Tradition," in *Swords Upon This Hill,* edited by Burney J. Hollis (Baltimore: Morgan State University Press, 1984), pp. 116–120;

Langston Hughes, *I Wonder As I Wander: An Autobiographical Journey,* foreword by Walker (New York: Thunder's Mouth Press, 1986).

SELECTED PERIODICAL PUBLICATIONS – UNCOLLECTED: "Black Studies: Some Personal Observations," *Afro-American Studies* (1970): 41–43;

273

"The Humanistic Tradition of Afro-American Literature," *American Libraries,* 1 (October 1970): 849–854;

"Some Aspects of the Black Aesthetic," *Freedomways,* 16 (Winter 1976): 95–102.

Poet, novelist, essayist, orator, and literary critic, Margaret Abigail Walker Alexander has lived a full, long life, seeking personal and professional acquaintances with writers from virtually every literary period of the twentieth century. She counts among those significant to her, and whose work she admires, Langston Hughes, Arna Bontemps, Richard Wright, Gwendolyn Brooks, Nikki Giovanni, Sonia Sanchez, Amiri Baraka, and Alice Walker.

Margaret Walker was born in 1915 in Birmingham, Alabama, and her educated parents expected her to excel. Her father, Sigismund Walker, immigrated from Jamaica Buff Bay, Jamaica, to study for the ministry; he attended Tuskegee Institute for a time but left because of his disagreement with Booker T. Washington's conservative philosophy that industrial and vocational education was the best that African Americans should hope to attain. In 1913 he received a degree from Gammon Theological Seminary in Atlanta. Both he and Walker's mother – Marion Dozier, a music teacher – propelled their four children toward the highest academic achievements possible. At fourteen Margaret completed high school in New Orleans and enrolled in New Orleans University, now Dillard University. Two years later, with the encouragement of Langston Hughes, she left the South, finishing her bachelor's degree at Northwestern University in 1935 only a few months after her twentieth birthday. Soon after graduation she joined the Federal Writers Project in Chicago, where she met Wright, Nelson Algren, Willard Motley, and other promising young writers. In 1939 she left the project, and by 1940 she had received her M.A. from the University of Iowa. In 1942 she married Firnist James Alexander, with whom she had four children. She later returned to the University of Iowa, receiving her Ph.D. in 1965.

Beginning with her first collection of poetry, *For My People* (1942), selected by Stephen Vincent Benét for the Yale Younger Poets Series, Walker's writing has been infused with her humanism. Her work is animated by her desire to champion African American heroism and her belief that despite racism, poverty, and oppression, African Americans will continue to work toward a better world. As a writer, she takes seriously her role in this process of bringing about social justice. In a 1993 interview she told Maryemma Graham, "It has always been my understanding from my school days that the writer's responsibility is the same as that of the social scientist or philosopher: to be like God and show the way."

Walker has written eloquently of her creative process in her essay *How I Wrote Jubilee,* first published as a book in 1972: "Long before *Jubilee* had a name, I was living with it and imagining its reality. Its genesis coincides with my childhood, its development grows out of a welter of raw experiences and careful research, and its final form emerged exactly one hundred years after its major events took place." Based on stories that her grandmother told her during her childhood, *Jubilee* (1966) is also a scrupulously researched historical novel fictionalizing slavery, emancipation, and Reconstruction in the years between 1839 and 1870. Vyry, its heroine, is a fictional re-creation of Walker's maternal great-grandmother. Besides crafting a panorama about slavery and Reconstruction, Walker has created a memorable character in Vyry, who epitomizes the courage and optimism of Walker's ancestor and of Walker herself. "I'm interested in the black woman in fiction," she told Nikki Giovanni in *A Poetic Equation: Conversations between Nikki Giovanni and Margaret Walker* (1974), "perhaps because I'm a black woman and feel that the black woman's story has not been told, has not been dealt with adequately."

In *How I Wrote Jubilee* Walker relates that the novel took her thirty years to write. Although she wrote the first three hundred pages when she was nineteen, she put the project aside when she joined the Federal Writers Project, and for the next three decades each effort to complete the book ended in delay. In 1942, at about the same time she married Alexander, she began her career as an English professor, first at West Virginia State College, then at Livingstone College in Salisbury, North Carolina, where she stayed until 1946. From 1949 to 1979 she taught at Jackson State University, also directing the Institute for the Study of the History, Life, and Culture of Black People. Not surprisingly, the demands of motherhood, marriage, and career interfered with the completion of *Jubilee* until 1966. While raising four children and supporting the family (her husband was disabled) she managed to do extensive research and to compose the novel's early drafts. During this same period she also wrote poems, speeches, and essays; received the Rosenwald Fellowship for Creative Writing in 1944 and a Ford Fellowship at Yale University in 1954; and completed her Ph.D. at the University of Iowa, with

Walker in the early 1940s (courtesy of the Schomberg Center for Research in Black Culture, New York Public Library, Astor, Lenox and Tilden Foundations)

Jubilee serving as her dissertation. *How I Wrote Jubilee* testifies to the obstacles women face while writing; at the same time, the essay explores the creative process, arguing that experience and maturity are central to the novel's depth and to its artistic vision. *Jubilee* received the Houghton Mifflin Literary Fellowship in 1966.

In writing this novel Walker transcribed her family's oral history passed along to her from her grandmother, who often enthralled her "way past bedtime" with stories of her forebears. When her mother objected to these "tall tales," Walker's grandmother insisted that she was telling the truth. Many of the chapter headings are transcriptions of her grandmother's words. Thus does Walker take on the role of African griot, or oral historian.

Jubilee opens with Vyry's birth on a Georgia plantation. Vyry has been fathered by her master, John Dutton. Her mother, Sis Hetta, dies while giving birth to Vyry, her fifteenth child. Vyry is relegated to the role of cook for the family and maid to her white half-sister, Lillian. Physically, Vyry is nearly identical to Lillian, and Marse John's wife, Missy Salina, despises and abuses Vyry, who serves

as a reminder of her husband's sexual relations with Sis Hetta. *Jubilee* recounts Vyry's sad childhood as a slave, her marriage to Randall Ware, and her attempt to flee the plantation, which does not succeed because she will not abandon her two children. After emancipation the novel chronicles Vyry's relationship with her second husband, Innis Brown, and their agonizing bouts with poverty, sharecropping, Klan terrorism, and virulent bigotry. Just as *Jubilee* began with a birth, it ends with Vyry's announcement that she is expecting another child, thus underscoring the theme of motherhood in the novel.

The significance of motherhood in its various manifestations underpins Walker's celebration of black women in the novel. Vyry also embodies other characteristics associated with strong African American women. Although *Jubilee* is a realistic novel, Vyry is a type of conjurer. She nurtures and heals, going so far as to turn her skills as a midwife into a profession. Her spirituality allows her to survive slavery and Reconstruction without bitterness and to influence people to a remarkable degree. Her inner strength rarely falters, giving her a nearly superhuman quality.

Jubilee illustrates how slavery robbed African American women of motherhood. The death of Vyry's mother at the beginning of the novel inaugurates Walker's theme that black women have historically suffered exploitation as sexual objects and mothers. To satisfy the boy's adolescent lust, Marse John's father gives John Hetta when she is prepubescent. John's desire springs partly from her extreme youth and partly from his hormones. He clearly enjoys his complete power over her, likening her to "a wild colt" he has the opportunity to "break in." This sexual arrangement, a fixture of plantation life, ensures that John will not "spoil a pure white virgin girl."

When John marries Salina, who is in his estimation "a beautiful young lady of quality," he maintains his sexual relationship with Hetta until her death. Once John has impregnated Hetta, he gives her to another slave, Jake, reflecting his attitude that she is his pet. As the novel opens, Hetta is literally "broken" beyond repair from bearing fifteen children by age twenty-nine, most of whom have been sold away from the plantation. Despite Walker's obvious rage and sadness over Hetta's victimization, *Jubilee* also begins with a sense of hope. From the beginning of the novel Walker emphasizes Vyry's strength, for despite a life filled with losses and abuse Vyry manages to surmount virtually every situation.

Orphaned at birth, Vyry suffers the loss not only of her biological mother but of her two adopted mothers, Mammy Sukey and Aunt Sally. Yet she grieves these tragedies and moves on. Raised by Mammy Sukey, Vyry cries for an entire day when her adopted mother dies. Vyry is only a child, but her life of drudgery as a house servant demands that she put her grief aside. Just as Hetta was given to John as a child, Vyry has been given to Miss Lillian, Vyry's half-sister, the daughter of John and Salina.

The strong resemblance between Vyry and Lillian reinforces John and Salina's cruelty and inhumanity in enslaving her. Salina treats Vyry with particular sadism. The evening before Mammy Sukey's death Salina, known as "Big Missy," douses Vyry with urine for forgetting to empty Lillian's chamber pot. Not long afterward Big Missy hangs Vyry by her wrists in a closet for breaking a dish, nearly killing her in the process. These incidents not only represent the kinds of atrocities African Americans in general suffered during slavery; they also signify the violence inflicted on black women in particular, for Vyry is being punished for her mother's rape and enforced motherhood by her master.

Abusing Vyry for her mother's victimization, Salina represents the profound viciousness of "the peculiar institution." When John sells Aunt Sally, Vyry's other adopted mother, it is at the urging of Salina. As Aunt Sally is led away Vyry begins to sob; instead of comforting her, Salina slaps her nearly unconscious.

Vyry's intrinsic humanity and spirituality emerge from her refusal to harbor bitterness. Despite Salina's efforts to dehumanize her, Vyry develops into a nurturing, maternal woman. She refuses to retaliate, remaining loyal to Lillian even after emancipation. When Lillian goes insane after her father, mother, brother, and husband die during the Civil War and she herself is beaten by Union soldiers, Vyry refuses to abandon her. Although Lillian has never really acknowledged Vyry as her sister, Vyry cannot ignore their blood ties or their childhood friendship. Vyry cares for Lillian until Lillian's relatives arrive to take her home with them to Alabama.

Walker's portrayal of Vyry's loyalty to Lillian and Vyry's lack of bitterness has inspired much anger and bewilderment from readers and critics. Walker responds that her maternal great-grandmother "realized that hatred wasn't necessary and would have corroded her spiritual well-being." In her depiction of Vyry's belief in sisterhood she adheres to the nurturing, spiritual vision of her grandmother's tales. In Vyry's words, "keeping hatred inside makes you git mean and evil inside. . . . Folks with a loving heart don't never need no doctor."

Walker's portrayal of Vyry as a woman dedicated to mothering and nurturing appears early in the novel, at Vyry's first menstruation. Calming Vyry's fears, Aunt Sally explains the significance of womanhood: "It's what makes you a woman. Makes you different from a no-good man. It's what makes you grow up to have younguns and be a sho-nuff mammy all your own. Man can't have no youngun. Takes a sho-nuff woman. A man ain't got the strength to have younguns. He's too puny-fied." Aunt Sally clearly suggests that Vyry's ability to mother affirms her superiority.

Vyry internalizes this message. During a time of total despair she miscarries, symbolizing her loss of hope and vitality. Moreover, her children are the center of her life. In one of the most memorable episodes of *Jubilee,* her first husband tries to persuade her to leave Jim and Minna, their children, so that she can escape slavery unencumbered. He promises her that they will get the children back later, but she instinctively knows that this will never happen. She walks miles to meet Randall in the night, staggering

Participants at the Festival of Negro Poets held in October 1952 in Jackson, Mississippi: (seated) Sterling Brown, Zora Neale Hurston, Walker, Langston Hughes; (standing) Arna Bontemps, Melvin Tolson, Jacob Reddix, Owen Dodson, and Robert Hayden (courtesy of the Schomberg Center for Research in Black Culture, New York Public Library, Astor, Lenox and Tilden Foundations)

in exhaustion because she is carrying Minna and trying to keep Jim quiet. Collapsing from fatigue, she never meets him and is recaptured and given seventy-five lashes. The episode, epitomizing Vyry's courageous loyalty to her children, also highlights African American women's double oppression during slavery.

Vyry's nurturing, maternal role constitutes a redemptive, humanitarian vision throughout *Jubilee*. Her only rift with her second husband occurs when he beats Jim for accidentally killing their sow and her brood. She refuses to countenance violence, especially against her children, because she connects it with the horrifying abuse she has witnessed. She views his violence as no more justified than that of Grimes, the overseer, who beats the field hands to death; brands the forehead of Lucy, a runaway slave; and murders

slaves too old to work. "It was part of all the turbulence of the Ku Klux Klan and the fire and all the evil hatred she had felt before the house was built here. Now this awful hatred and violence was threatening to destroy her happy home and her loving family." For Vyry, as for Walker, violence does not solve but only creates problems.

Walker has described one of her goals in *Jubilee* as telling a "simple folk story" that accurately portrays history and at the same time celebrates ordinary yet remarkable people such as Vyry, Randall, and Innis. Vyry is heroically faithful to her children; at the same time, she extends her maternal qualities to the community. When she offers her services as a midwife and saves a white baby's life without asking for remuneration, her family receives its first safe haven during the terrifying, Klan-dominated years of Reconstruction.

Vyry's ability to midwife signals her conjuring role in the novel. Conjure women — the wise women of African, African American, and Caribbean culture — possess powers that emanate from nature but at times transcend earthly confinement, reaching into supernatural realms of healing and knowledge. Vyry learns midwifery during Minna's and Jim's births, but when she brings her second son, Harry, into the world, no midwife is at hand to help her. Resisting Innis's desires to procure a doctor, Vyry instead teaches him how to help her deliver. Later her midwifery, the most ancient and creative of women's healing arts, turns around racist sentiment and causes the white inhabitants of Greenville, Alabama, to welcome her family into the community, which offers protection in exchange for her skill as a "granny," for, she is told, "colored grannies are the best."

Vyry's conjuring extends to other forms of healing. While yet a child she learns to use roots and herbs for maladies from foot swelling to dysentery. Claiming she "never needs no doctor," Vyry cures her children of malaria and ministers to every ailment in the family. In addition to her healing arts, she embodies the more traditional domestic skills of canning, candle making, toy making, and cooking.

Descriptions of cooking abound in *Jubilee*. At age fifteen Vyry becomes the head cook on the plantation because she possesses superior culinary skills. Walker subtly juxtaposes Vyry's preparation of potted pheasant in cream, wild turkey, and wild duck for her owners with the occasional treats of raccoon, opossum, rabbit, and squirrel she prepares for her own family. After emancipation, cooking for her family takes on a kind of sacramental quality, inspiring intimacy and joy. As with her midwifery, Vyry's cooking extends to the community. When she and Innis move into a house that starving white sharecroppers are vacating, she feeds the white family before they set out on their journey.

Walker also uses Vyry to celebrate the African American survival tactic and creative art of singing. Vyry's singing heals herself and her family. Simultaneously, singing passes along her personal and racial history: "When she sang, the children would stop their playing and come closer to listen, for they loved all her songs — the old slave songs Aunt Sally used to sing, and the tender, lilting ballads of the war, too." Singing conveys her state of mind, varying from her songs of jubilee when the family begins their new life after leaving the plantation to her hymns of despondency when she confronts repeated instances of racism and discrimination.

Vyry's conjuring role derives in part from her abilities to heal and in part from her intuitive knowledge and inner strength. Her intuition becomes particularly apparent when the family flees from a corrupt landlord who seeks to cheat and reenslave them as sharecroppers in Alabama. Running for their lives, the Browns land by accident in Troy, Alabama, when their wagon breaks down. From the beginning Vyry senses danger, and her fears materialize when the Klan torches their house. Soon thereafter they move to Luverne, Alabama, where Vyry adamantly refuses to rebuild until she feels the incident will not repeat itself. Not until the whites in nearby Greenville offer to protect the Browns in exchange for Vyry's midwifery does Vyry agree to build there. Throughout *Jubilee* Innis respects his wife's intuition and wisdom, admitting that her decisions are usually right.

Vyry's spirituality emerges in her refusal to take credit for her premonitions or her wisdom. This spirituality informs her life and is part of Walker's vision as well. Even able to forgive Big Missy for mistreating her, Vyry epitomizes Walker's humanistic vision. The tranquillity Innis notices in Vyry stems from her refusal to remain mired in rage and hatred, despite her psychic and physical scars from the hideous mistreatment she suffered at the hands of whites. As in all of Walker's poetry and essays, *Jubilee* conveys Walker's insistence that blacks and whites must work together to erase bigotry and ignorance.

Walker's hope for social justice based on understanding between the races pervades *Jubilee*. Repeatedly the novel stresses the class connections between poor "buckrah" (whites) and African Americans. Landlords exploit and cheat white and black sharecroppers alike. Vyry learns to her amazement that one hundred thousand poor whites starved during the Civil War and that mass illiteracy affected not only African Americans but also whites in Alabama during the late nineteenth century. At the conclusion of *Jubilee*, when Randall returns to provide Jim with an education, Randall's militancy and separatism disturb Vyry. She admonishes Randall, "White folks needs what black folks got just as much as black folks needs what white folks is got, and we's all got to stay here mongst each other and git along."

At the same time, Walker never downplays the virulence of racism or the brutality of white people. *Jubilee* resounds with abuses inflicted on African Americans. She juxtaposes Lillian's decadently elaborate wedding with the hideous branding of Lucy's forehead; she vividly describes the Fourth of

*Cover for the first paperback edition of Walker's only novel,
based on the life of her great-grandmother from slavery
to emancipation*

July barbecue where whites celebrate by publicly hanging two slaves. "On the faces of some of the men and boys there was an unnatural look, neither human nor sane, a look of pleasurable excitement, a naked look of thrills born from cruel terror." The Browns suffer repeated injury and cruelty, including insults and Klan terrorism. Even while Walker chronicles the ugliness of white brutality, recording its savagery, she maintains the hope that the races can come to understand each other.

A Poetic Equation reflects Walker's insistence on a humanitarian, loving solution to racism. "I don't know that that's necessarily great spiritual strength," Walker asserts, "to have deep hatred and . . . kill some of those honkies." Rather, Walker believes that Vyry's inner peace and spiritual transcendence point the way to racial harmony.

Walker believes just as adamantly in harmony between the sexes. Despite her awareness of sexism,

she offers positive portrayals of black men, both in her poetry and in *Jubilee*. Randall Ware and Innis Brown are kind, decent, hardworking, sensitive men who love Vyry and remain loyal to her. The two men represent different responses to slavery and racism, but Walker treats both characters respectfully.

Randall Ware, freeborn, literate, and propertied, is a skilled artisan. Never having been a slave, he possesses notions of revolt and rebellion throughout the novel. He is politically active, failing to return to the plantation to reunite with Vyry after emancipation because he is attending the First Convention of Colored People in Georgia. Although some critics have suggested that Randall was ahead of his time, representing the radical politics of the 1960s, Walker insists that such a view reflects ignorance of African American history. "We make a mistake to think that the protest movement of the

'60s was an isolated decade in itself. Protest, for Black people in this country, is more than a century old."

Walker also points out that Randall Ware is not merely a fictional creation but is based on a real person: "My mother says she knows – according to my grandmother and great uncle – that Randall Ware was a militant man in his lifetime. I have not used him to place the words and ideas of the 1960s and a Nationalist in his head." When Randall and Vyry meet toward the end of the novel, he rebukes her for her docility, and she chastises him for his lack of Christian charity. But ultimately she allows him to take their son away from the farm so that he can be educated, announcing her awareness that Randall can transform Jim's life in ways that she never can.

Innis Brown, although he can never inspire Vyry with the passion and romance that she associates with Randall, is unfailingly gentle, supportive, and uncomplaining. Born a slave, illiterate, and fearful of Randall's notions of resistance, Innis, like Vyry, is a product of plantation life. He does not dream of social revolution but of owning a farm and caring for his wife and children. Walker creates in Innis a hero without apology, delineating him as emblematic of the gentle, hardworking, wise black man rarely found in literature.

In her effort to create a folktale Walker relies on plot rather than on psychology; rarely does she delve into the inner lives of her characters. Barbara Christian writes, "needing to cover so much territory to render Vyry's story, Walker ... created characters who are not subjects so much as they are the means by which we learn about the culture of slaves and slave holders and the historical period."

Walker seeks to embody history in her folktale; she also views her role as that of social historian. While doing the research for *Jubilee* she encountered three principal views of the Civil War and the history of slavery: the white Southern viewpoint; the white Northern viewpoint; and the African American viewpoint. During the years she spent writing the novel, she gradually realized that she must create her own view. *Jubilee* is based on folk songs, folk sayings, and folk beliefs; it synthesizes historical background, gleaned both from library research and from her grandmother's oral narrative, with Walker's humanistic vision. Walker visited the Dutton plantation and the site of Randall Ware's smithy and gristmill. She found her mother's last surviving sister, who showed her the chest her great-grandmother had carried from the plantation. She also spent six months in North Carolina perusing the Nelson Tift papers, a collection of bills of sale, diaries, letters, and other documents owned by a wealthy planter who lived near the Dutton plantation.

Based on all these elements, *Jubilee* successfully presents a realistic depiction of slavery and Reconstruction. At the same time the novel encapsulates Walker's vision. Like her poetry, *Jubilee* enshrines African Americans, both ordinary and heroic. It demonstrates her belief that African Americans, despite having been victimized, have been not victims but agents, actively shaping history and preserving a complex culture. Walker's novel encapsulates her confidence in biblical values, as typified by the title: in the Old Testament, the jubilee is the slaves' release from bondage every fifty years. Despite the agonizing hardships Walker fictionalizes in her novel, *Jubilee* ends with Vyry feeling "a peace in her heart she could not express."

Although *Jubilee* is Walker's only novel, its historical focus affects her entire canon. In her words, "the body of my work . . . springs from my interest in an historical point of view that is central to the development of Black people as we approach the twenty-first century." Her urge to write continues to inform her life, and her retirement from Jackson State University has afforded her the opportunity to pursue many new writing projects. At age seventy-nine she completed a manuscript about Jesse Jackson and his relationship to politics. Other projects include her autobiography, a sequel to *Jubilee* titled "Minna and Jim," and another novel, "Mother Broyer." Margaret Walker is indeed a visionary who has dedicated her life to preserving and applauding the folkways, voice, and history of black women and men.

Interviews:

Charles H. Rowell, "Poetry, History, and Humanism: An Interview with Margaret Walker," *Black World,* 25 (December 1975): 4–17;

Phanuel Egejuru and Robert Elliot Fox, "An Interview with Margaret Walker," *Callaloo,* 2 (1979): 29–35;

John Griffith Jones, "Margaret Walker Alexander," in his *Mississippi Writers Talking,* volume 2 (Jackson: University Press of Mississippi, 1983), pp. 121–146;

Claudia Tate, "Margaret Walker," in *Black Women Writers at Work,* edited by Tate (New York: Continuum, 1983), pp. 188–204;

Lucy M. Freibert, "Southern Song: An Interview with Margaret Walker," *Frontiers,* 9 (1987): 50–56;

Jerry W. Ward Jr., "A Writer for Her People: An Interview with Dr. Margaret Walker Alexander," *Mississippi Quarterly*, 41 (Fall 1989): 515–527;

Maryemma Graham, "The Fusion of Ideas: An Interview with Margaret Walker Alexander," *African American Review*, 27 (Summer 1993): 279–286.

References:

Bernard W. Bell, *The Afro-American Novel and Its Tradition* (Amherst: University of Massachusetts Press, 1987);

Jane Campbell, "Margaret Walker," in *African American Writers*, edited by Valerie Smith, Lea Baechler, and A. Walton Litz (New York: Scribners, 1991), pp. 459–471;

Barbara Christian, " 'Somebody Forgot to Tell Somebody Something': African-American Women's Historical Novels," in *Wild Women in the Whirlwind: Afra-American Culture and the Contemporary Literary Renaissance*, edited by Joanne M. Braxton and Andree Nicola McLaughlin (New Brunswick, N.J.: Rutgers University Press, 1990), pp. 326–341;

Minrose C. Gwin, *Black and White Women of the Old South: The Peculiar Sisterhood in American Literature* (Knoxville: University of Tennessee Press, 1985);

Phyllis R. Klotman, " 'Oh Freedom': Women and History in Margaret Walker's *Jubilee*," *Black American Literature Forum*, 11 (Winter 1977): 139–145;

James E. Spears, "Black Folk Elements in Margaret Walker's *Jubilee*," *Mississippi Folklore Register*, 14 (Spring 1980): 13–19;

Melissa Walker, *Down from the Mountaintop: Black Women's Novels in the Wake of the Civil Rights Movement, 1966–1989* (New Haven: Yale University Press, 1991);

Delores S. Williams, "Black Women's Literature and the Task of Feminist Theology," in *Immaculate and Powerful: The Female in Sacred Image and Social Reality*, edited by Clarissa W. Atkinson, Constance H. Buchanan, and Margaret Ruth Miles (Boston: Beacon Press, 1985), pp. 88–110.

Papers:

Galley sheets of *Jubilee* and an uncorrected copy of *A Poetic Equation* are collected at Millsaps-Wilson Library, Millsaps College, Jackson, Mississippi. A Margaret Walker Alexander Room and Collection is housed at Jackson State University; the bulk of the author's papers are in her personal possession.

Robert Penn Warren

(24 April 1905 – 15 September 1989)

Randolph Paul Runyon
Miami University

See also the Warren entries in *DLB 2: American Novelists Since World War II, First Series; DLB 48: American Poets, 1880–1945, Second Series; DLB Yearbook: 1980;* and *DLB Yearbook: 1989.*

BOOKS: *John Brown: The Making of a Martyr* (New York: Payson & Clarke, 1929);

Thirty-Six Poems (New York: Alcestis, 1935);

Night Rider (Boston: Houghton Mifflin, 1939; London: Eyre & Spottiswoode, 1940);

Eleven Poems on the Same Theme (Norfolk, Conn.: New Directions, 1942);

At Heaven's Gate (New York: Harcourt, Brace, 1943; London: Eyre & Spottiswoode, 1943);

Selected Poems, 1923–1943 (New York: Harcourt, Brace, 1944; London: Fortune, 1951);

All the King's Men (New York: Harcourt, Brace, 1946; abridged edition, London: Eyre & Spottiswoode, 1948);

Blackberry Winter (Cummington, Mass.: Cummington, 1946);

The Circus in the Attic and Other Stories (New York: Harcourt, Brace, 1947; London: Eyre & Spottiswoode, 1952);

World Enough and Time: A Romantic Novel (New York: Random House, 1950; London: Eyre & Spottiswoode, 1951);

Brother to Dragons: A Tale in Verse and Voices (New York: Random House, 1953; London: Eyre & Spottiswoode, 1954);

Band of Angels (New York: Random House, 1955; London: Eyre & Spottiswoode, 1956);

Segregation: The Inner Conflict in the South (New York: Random House, 1956; London: Eyre & Spottiswoode, 1957);

To a Little Girl, One Year Old, In a Ruined Fortress (New Haven: Yale School of Design, 1956);

Promises: Poems 1954–1956 (New York: Random House, 1957; London: Eyre & Spottiswoode, 1959);

Selected Essays (New York: Random House, 1958; London: Eyre & Spottiswoode, 1964);

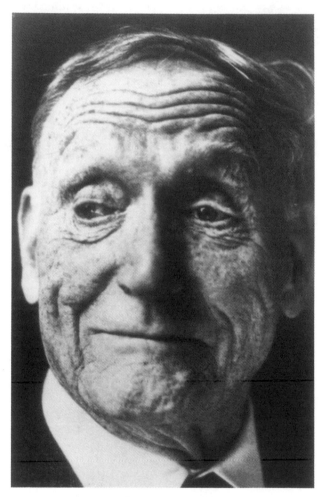

Robert Penn Warren (photograph by Robert A. Ballard Jr.)

Remember the Alamo! (New York: Random House, 1958);

How Texas Won Her Freedom: The Story of Sam Houston and the Battle of San Jacinto (San Jacinto Monument, Tex.: San Jacinto Museum of History, 1959);

The Cave (New York: Random House, 1959; London: Eyre & Spottiswoode, 1959);

The Gods of Mount Olympus (New York: Random House, 1959; London: Muller, 1962);

All the King's Men: A Play (New York: Random House, 1960);

You, Emperors, and Others: Poems 1957–1960 (New York: Random House, 1960);

The Legacy of the Civil War: Meditations on the Centennial (New York: Random House, 1961);

Wilderness: A Tale of the Civil War (New York: Random House, 1961; London: Eyre & Spottiswoode, 1962);

Flood: A Romance of Our Time (New York: Random House, 1964; London: Collins, 1964);

Who Speaks for the Negro? (New York: Random House, 1965);

A Plea in Mitigation: Modern Poetry and the End of an Era (Macon, Ga.: Wesleyan College, 1966);

Selected Poems: New and Old, 1923–1966 (New York: Random House, 1966);

Incarnations: Poems 1966–1968 (New York: Random House, 1968; London: Allen, 1970);

Audubon: A Vision (New York: Random House, 1969);

Homage to Theodore Dreiser: August 17, 1871–December 28, 1945, On the Centennial of His Birth (New York: Random House, 1971);

Meet Me in the Green Glen (New York: Random House, 1971; London: Secker & Warburg, 1972);

Or Else: Poem/Poems 1968–1974 (New York: Random House, 1974);

Democracy and Poetry (Cambridge: Harvard University Press, 1975);

Selected Poems: 1923–1975 (New York: Random House, 1977; London: Secker & Warburg, 1977);

A Place to Come To (New York: Random House, 1977; London: Secker & Warburg, 1977);

Now and Then: Poems 1976–1978 (New York: Random House, 1978);

Brother to Dragons: A Tale in Verse and Voices (A New Version) (New York: Random House, 1979);

Being Here: Poetry 1977–1980 (New York: Random House, 1980; London: Secker & Warburg, 1980);

Jefferson Davis Gets His Citizenship Back (Lexington: University Press of Kentucky, 1980);

Rumor Verified: Poems 1979–1980 (New York: Random House, 1981; London: Secker & Warburg, 1982);

Chief Joseph of the Nez Perce (New York: Random House, 1983);

New and Selected Poems 1923–1983 (New York: Random House, 1985);

Portrait of a Father (Lexington: University Press of Kentucky, 1988);

New and Selected Essays (New York: Random House, 1989).

Edition and Collection: *A Robert Penn Warren Reader,* edited by Albert Erskine (New York: Random House, 1987).

OTHER: "The Briar Patch," in *I'll Take My Stand: The South and the Agrarian Tradition,* by Twelve Southerners (New York: Harper, 1930), pp. 246–264;

An Approach to Literature: A Collection of Prose and Verse with Analyses and Discussions, edited by Warren, Cleanth Brooks, and John Thibault Purser (Baton Rouge: Louisiana State University Press, 1936);

A Southern Harvest: Short Stories by Southern Writers, edited by Warren (Boston: Houghton Mifflin, 1937);

Understanding Poetry: An Anthology for College Students, by Warren and Brooks (New York: Holt, 1938);

Understanding Fiction, by Warren and Brooks (New York: Crofts, 1943);

"A Poem of Pure Imagination: An Experiment in Reading," in *The Rime of the Ancient Mariner,* by Samuel Taylor Coleridge (New York: Reynal & Hitchcock, 1946), pp. 59–117;

Modern Rhetoric, by Warren and Brooks (New York: Harcourt, Brace, 1949);

Fundamentals of Good Writing: A Handbook of Modern Rhetoric, by Warren and Brooks (New York: Harcourt, Brace, 1950; London: Dobson, 1952);

An Anthology of Stories from the Southern Review, edited by Warren and Brooks (Baton Rouge: Louisiana State University Press, 1953);

Short Story Masterpieces, edited by Warren and Albert Erskine (New York: Dell, 1954);

Six Centuries of Great Poetry: From Chaucer to Yeats, edited by Warren and Erskine (New York: Dell, 1955);

A New Southern Harvest: An Anthology, edited by Warren and Erskine (New York: Bantam, 1957);

The Scope of Fiction, edited by Warren and Brooks (New York: Appleton-Century-Crofts, 1960);

Dennis Devlin, *Selected Poems,* edited by Warren and Allen Tate (New York: Holt, Rinehart & Winston, 1963);

Faulkner: A Collection of Critical Essays, edited by Warren (Englewood Cliffs, N. J.: Prentice-Hall, 1966);

Randall Jarrell, 1914–1965, edited by Warren, Robert Lowell, and Peter Taylor (New York: Farrar, Straus & Giroux, 1967);

Selected Poems of Herman Melville: A Reader's Edition, edited by Warren (New York: Random House, 1970);

John Greenleaf Whittier's Poetry, edited by Warren (Minneapolis: University of Minnesota Press, 1971);

American Literature: The Makers and the Making, 2 volumes, edited by Warren, Brooks, and R. W. B. Lewis (New York: St. Martin's Press, 1973);

Katherine Anne Porter: A Collection of Critical Essays, edited by Warren (Englewood Cliffs, N. J.: Prentice-Hall, 1979);

The Essential Melville, edited by Warren (New York: Ecco, 1987).

The importance of Robert Penn Warren has made itself felt in almost equal measure in American literary criticism, poetry, and fiction. Expounding a home-grown New Criticism, Warren and Cleanth Brooks, through their textbook *Understanding Poetry* (1938), changed the way poetry was taught in American universities. Warren's characteristic yoking of high and low diction in his early poems, of the tragic and the risible, the English metaphysical and the southern down-home, constituted a new and influential poetic voice; the sublimity of his later poetry, its direct appeal to the human heart, brought him fresh recognition. Perhaps no better novel of American politics has been written than *All the King's Men* (1946). Yet Warren wrote nine others between 1939 and 1977, none as openly political but all of them deeply rooted in the American experience. His importance as a novelist has perhaps not been fully recognized, having been overshadowed by both the enormous popular and critical success of his most well-known efforts and the more recent high regard his late poetry enjoyed.

Warren was the first child, followed by Thomas and Mary, of Ruth Penn and Robert Franklin Warren, a banker in Guthrie, Kentucky. Located in the southwest part of the state just a few miles north of the Tennessee line, Guthrie was, as Warren told Floyd Watkins for *Then and Now,* "anything but the usual older southern town, being on the order of a real estate project, having been put there when two railroads crossed." Though not far from the monument to Jefferson Davis in Fairview, it was hardly rich in history, nor did it live up to the speculative promise of its youth. In the poem "Whistle of the 3 A.M.," Warren recalls hearing the train go by and being consumed "With the thought that some night in your own dark cubicle, / You would whirl, in sleep or in contempt, / Past some straggle of town." Alienated from Guthrie in part because his intellectual precocity turned his schoolmates against him, young Warren nevertheless adored the surrounding countryside, whose woods he wandered and streams he swam. "I loathed the town," he told Watkins. "I couldn't wait to get out of it and loved to go to the country." Some of those rural excursions were spent at the farm of his maternal grandfather Gabriel Penn, who entranced the boy with firsthand accounts of the Civil War. Equally influential would be the memory of having at the age of eleven or twelve stumbled across some poems his father had written, and even published, in a vanity anthology. "The discovery," he wrote in *Portrait of a Father* (1988), "was, in itself, a profound and complex surprise." When he presented it to his father, the elder Warren "took it, examined it, and wordlessly walked away with it." That taciturn response would have a long echo in the novels. It was the last Warren ever saw of the book.

Already three grades ahead of his contemporaries, Warren commuted by train the twelve miles to high school in Clarksville, Tennessee, graduating at age fifteen. His father had managed to secure a place in the Annapolis naval academy for Warren, who had fixed upon the vocation of ship's captain. But fate decided otherwise. Lying on his back alongside a hedge and gazing at the evening sky, his hands behind his head, Warren was suddenly blinded in one eye by a cinder his brother had thrown up in the air, in total ignorance of Robert Penn's presence on the other side of the hedge. He could not then go to Annapolis. Vanderbilt beckoned, and a career in electrical engineering. These plans changed when he entered John Crowe Ransom's English class and quickly abandoned the sciences for poetry. In college he likewise made the acquaintance of Allen Tate and Donald Davidson, who were starting a magazine they called *The Fugitive,* seeing themselves as refugees from the impending industrialization of the South. Warren published poems for the literary magazine, of which one, "To a Face in a Crowd" (1923), would conclude each of his *Selected Poems* volumes (right down to the last in 1985).

In 1925 Warren began graduate studies at the University of California at Berkeley, where he met Emma Brescia, daughter of an Italian orchestra conductor, who would become his bride in 1930. Missing the intellectual excitement to which Vanderbilt had accustomed him, he switched to Yale. A Rhodes Scholarship took him to Oxford in 1928,

Warren as a student at Vanderbilt (Vanderbilt University Photographic Archives)

where he earned a B. Litt. two years later. He accepted a teaching position at Southwestern College in Memphis in 1930, followed by a post at Vanderbilt the following year, where he remained until 1934.

Meanwhile, Allen Tate, who was writing biographies of Stonewall Jackson and Jefferson Davis, introduced Warren to a literary agent through whom he received a publisher's commission to write *John Brown: The Making of a Martyr,* which appeared in 1929. It is remarkable that Warren could have carried out such an enormous project while at the same time pursuing his graduate studies. The subtitle declares his thesis: that the author of the Harper's Ferry raid was a martyr only as he made himself up to be one; Warren's aim was to deconstruct the fiction Brown and his admirers had invented. Like the historical Brown, Warren's is a murderer, particularly in the incident at Pottawatomie Creek, but the narrator's anti-Yankee bias is distressingly evident throughout. The flavor of

what James Justus later characterized as a "breezily irreverent" style is apparent, for example, when Warren says of William Lloyd Garrison and his followers that they were not only against slavery but "were regularly against most things," including "having Sunday in the week. . . . On the whole they must have been very unhappy people; one sometimes suspects that such unhappy people must also have been just a little wicked." Such flippancy would serve him well when he transformed it into the wise-guy voice of the narrator of *All the King's Men.* But in *John Brown: The Making of a Martyr* it was symptomatic of the shortcoming he would later own up to, that the book was, as admitted to Charles Bohner, "shot through with Southern defensiveness." Unfortunately for sales, the book's appearance in 1929 coincided with the stock market crash; by Warren's estimate, only about five hundred copies were sold. Warren's apparent decision to allow Random House consistently to list *John Brown: The Making of a Martyr* at the beginning of the list of

"Books by Robert Penn Warren" facing every title page (up to forty titles by 1989, with *New and Selected Essays*) suggests that as far as he was concerned it was part of the canon of his works. Thickness of description and mastery of detail would remain strong points of Warren's both in such later historical essays as *The Legacy of the Civil War* (1961) and *Jefferson Davis Gets His Citizenship Back* (1980) and in such historically based novels as *Night Rider* (1939), *World Enough and Time: A Romantic Novel* (1950), *Band of Angels* (1955), and *Wilderness: A Tale of the Civil War* (1961). John Brown himself would find his later incarnations in Perse Munn and Jeremiah Beaumont of *Night Rider* and *World Enough and Time*: men caught up in social upheaval who take matters into their own hands for private reasons.

In 1930 Warren published "The Briar Patch," his contribution to the Agrarians' collection *I'll Take My Stand,* a title whose evident endorsement of the Confederate cause was not to his taste. Collectively, the book urged a return to rural southern values in the face of northern industrialization; Warren's essay, which the book's editors, according to Justus, found alarmingly "progressive," argued that blacks would be better off remaining a fixture of southern agricultural life than becoming wage slaves for northern capitalists.

By this time Warren had published more than fifty poems, though his first collection would not appear until *Thirty-Six Poems* in 1935. In his years as assistant professor of English at Vanderbilt University (1931–1934), Warren worked on two novel manuscripts, of which the first was alternately named "The Apple Tree" and "God's Own Time" and the second bore no title. Both were set in his native western Kentucky-Tennessee; the first centered around a farm, the second a school. Though never published as novels, these manuscripts were mined for material for short stories that were included in his 1947 collection of fourteen stories, *The Circus in the Attic and Other Stories*. The ninth chapter of the first novel became "Christmas Gift" (*Virginia Quarterly Review,* Winter 1937), later the fourth story of the collection. Chapters from the second novel were reworked into "When the Light Gets Green" (*Southern Review,* Spring 1936), "The Love of Elsie Barton" (*Mademoiselle,* January 1947), and "Testament of Flood" (*The Magazine,* March–April 1935), the collection's third, eighth, and ninth stories.

Warren's first published story, however, had a separate origin, though it proved to be the initial exploration of material he would later use in his first published novel, *Night Rider*. Separated by

thousands of miles from his native Black Patch region – named after the tobacco raised there, as Joseph Millichap explains, "because its dark green leaf becomes even darker when cured with wood smoke" – Warren at Oxford in the spring of 1930 responded to an invitation from an editor to write a story about Kentucky. The result was "Prime Leaf," (*American Caravan,* 1931), later published as the final story in *The Circus in the Attic and Other Stories*. The title could be taken as a self-referential allusion to its being the first page of what would turn out to be an extraordinary career in narrative, but it more directly refers to a grade of tobacco. For this first story Warren turned not only to his home section but to events in the year of his birth. Guthrie witnessed a rally of five thousand growers in the fall of 1904 (a scene that would be recounted in the opening pages of *Night Rider*), when Ruth Warren was pregnant with her son. The farmers were rallying against the pricing policies of the tobacco trusts, a protest that turned into "tobacco wars" that would rage there between 1907 and 1911. Convinced that the big tobacco companies were conspiring to lower the value of their crop, growers banded together for a boycott to drive up the price. It was in effect a local civil war, as "night riders" sought to enforce the boycott by destroying tobacco beds and burning barns; towns were invaded, trains were seized, and considerable blood was spilled.

"Prime Leaf " focuses on the Hardin family – patriarchal Joseph, his son Thomas, Thomas's wife Edith, and their son Tommy. With the triple perspective that would characterize his novels, it is at the same time a political story, a family drama with oedipal resonances, and a meditation on textuality. Joseph Hardin had been among the first to oppose the oppression of the tobacco buyers by joining the association and had persuaded his son to come along. Now that the association is starting to burn the barns and destroy the crops of those who refuse to join, the elder Hardin is the first to make a moral point of leaving it and is having difficulty persuading his son to follow his example once more. The struggle between father and son for moral authority is played out before the latter's wife and son. The oedipal stakes for which it is played become at certain moments particularly clear: staring "into the depth of the embers" of the family hearth like "a man who sees something he desires but may not have," Joseph's son realizes that he may not have his wife's prime affections. Not only does Edith laugh at her husband, but she teasingly confirms his suspicion that she prefers her father-in-law to him and then remarks, "I do believe you're jealous of your own father." The textual stakes emerge when the elder Hardin sits down at his desk to write his letter of resignation from the association, in the knowledge that his son is not willing to follow his lead. He begins by taking a sheet of his embossed stationery. "Carefully he drew a single line through the '& Son' of the caption, but he did not begin to write again." He doesn't have to begin again, for by that single stroke of the pen he has accomplished what he set out to do, which was to obliterate his son. Penning the letter of resignation itself was, evidently, of but secondary importance. In the end both father and son are satisfied, in a way, as the son gets to kill the father in a symbolic way, while the father contributes materially to the actual death of the son. Thomas tells his father that he is wrong to resign from the board of the association because it is like starting something and then not seeing it through: "Papa, you're on horseback now, you're on horseback, and it's a wild piece of horseflesh." The story reaches its denouement when Thomas goes out and shoots a night rider off his horse (for having burned down their barn), symbolically striking at the father whom he had so pointedly said was on horseback. In what Millichap calls "perhaps the most interesting development of this section," the elder Hardin talks his son into riding to town to give himself up to the sheriff and accompanies him for a distance. But then, to the son's surprise, at a branch in the road he halts to announce that he's turning off. He will pay a visit to the man his son had wounded. The son continues his way alone — to his death, as events prove, falling to an assailant's bullet before he can make it to town. Had the father not abandoned him he would not have died, for the ambusher was seeking vengeance for a crime of which only the son, not the father, had been guilty and would not have risked making the father a witness to his crime.

Though originally not a separately composed story like "Prime Leaf," "Christmas Gift" nevertheless stands on its own rather well. At the same time it offers a rare glimpse of the texture of Warren's first attempt at a novel. It is a bleak winter's tale of a ten-year-old boy's errand to find a doctor to attend to his half-sister, who is about to give birth. In the novel the unmarried girl had been made pregnant by a naive young man from another town who, as Millichap points out, may represent, together with his friend, "a more worldly wise aesthete," the two sides of the author. Though the story ends before the doctor arrives to deliver the baby, the motif of childbirth evident in Warren's first known novel resonates in his published novels, from which the image of an unborn or stillborn or still-to-be-born child is rarely absent. Not used in the novel, the story's title alludes to the exchange at its close between the doctor, who offers tobacco and cigarette paper, and the poor sharecropper's son, who responds with half a stick of his red-striped candy.

Of the three stories Warren carved from his second unpublished novel, "When the Light Gets Green" is a strongly autobiographical reminiscence of his grandfather Penn. The story's boy protagonist hears the dying man complain that it is time to die because nobody loves him. The boy tries to say " 'Grandpa, I love you.' And then I did say it all right, feeling like it hadn't been me said it, and knowing all of a sudden it was a lie, because I didn't feel anything." A similar moment of distancing concludes "Testament of Flood," when young Steve Adams, smitten with a girl who has given her heart to a flashier and older rival, forms with his lips the words of John Webster's line from the *Duchess of Malfi,* "Cover her face: mine eyes dazzle: she died young" and then wonders if he actually said them out loud. He experiences what Millichap calls "an epiphany worthy of Joyce's [similarly first-named] Stephan Daedelus. . . .: 'He felt the veins of the neck throb, and heard, in his ears, the mounting blood that roared, then gradually diminished as when one rides away from the sea.' When he recovers, he feels 'himself far away from her, and much older,' distanced in space and time. He has discovered this ironic distance in art, for in a sense Helen has 'died young,' lost in her love" for his rival. Preceding the "Testament of Flood" in the collection, "The Love of Elsie Barton: A Chronicle" was not published until 1946, though Millichap believes it was written and circulated in the mid 1930s. A loosely constructed story, it features the same characters as those of *Testament of Flood,* plus those of the prior generation.

This second novel was written during his tenure at Vanderbilt, which may have provided the academic setting that inspired "The Unvexed Isles" (*The Magazine,* July–August 1934), later the penultimate story of *The Circus in the Attic.* The professor protagonist, however, teaches at a much less prestigious college, in Illinois — perhaps on the order of Southwestern in Memphis, where Warren had been before Vanderbilt. Offering a student a glass of whiskey, Professor Dalrymple discovers to his shock that the young man's cigarette bears the red trace of his wife's lipstick and then meditates on the discovery "as a child sucks candy," thereby recalling to the reader the child-adult exchange that concluded "Christmas Gift." Unlike the earlier story,

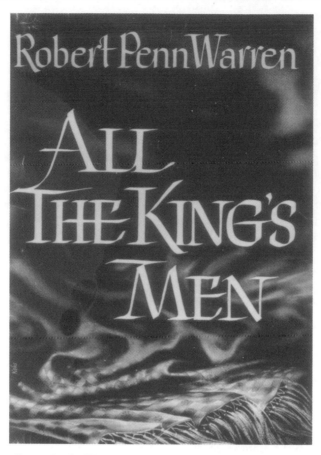

Dust jacket for Warren's best-known novel, which according to the author was not about corrupt Louisiana governor Huey Long

the encounter here is at least mildly oedipal, while hearth imagery anticipates the scene of father-son conflict in the concluding story of the collection, "Prime Leaf," and links the professor's wife with Edith Hardin. Academia would also provide the setting for "The Life and Work of Professor Roy Millen" (*Mademoiselle,* February 1943), where again an older man is pitted against a younger, with the difference that this time the former gets to act out his jealousy of the latter by writing a damning letter of reference. At about the same time Warren would publish "The Ballad of Billie Potts" (*Partisan Review,* Winter 1944), in which an innkeeper in the habit of murdering his guests for their money fails to recognize his returning son and dispatches him with a hatchet.

One more story emerged from the Vanderbilt years. "Her Own People" (*Virginia Quarterly Review,* April 1935) is set among young exurban professionals in Tennessee, likely near Nashville, anticipating the setting and some of the characters of the Nashville chapters of Warren's last novel, *A Place to Come To* (1977). The sense of the title is that the Allens'

maid Viola, having rejected her African American origins but enjoying no hope of social acceptance on the part of her racist white employers, has no one she can call her own people. The story marks an important moment in the evolution of Warren's attitudes on race, which still had a far way to go between the segregationism of "The Briar Patch" and the commitment to civil rights evident in *Segregation: The Inner Conflict in the South* (1956).

In 1934 Warren was appointed assistant professor of English at Louisiana State University (L.S.U.), where he and Cleanth Brooks, with Huey Long's help, founded the influential *Southern Review* in 1935. The same year also saw the publication of *Thirty-Six Poems*. Brooks and Warren were to collaborate on *Understanding Poetry: An Anthology for College Students* (1938) and *Understanding Fiction* (1943), textbooks that revolutionized the teaching of literature by encouraging students to clear away the deadwood of a facile biographical approach in order to focus on the text itself. By 1936 Warren was writing what would prove to be a remarkably accomplished first published novel. In *Night Rider* he returned to what had worked so well in his first piece of fiction, the tobacco wars he had heard tales of as a child. Along the lines traced in the story, but more complex, the first novel can be read at the same time as a political conflict, a struggle between father and son, and a dramatization of the relationship between reader and text.

Politically, *Night Rider* takes up the cause of the small local tobacco growers oppressed by large and distant corporations. In an attempt at a kind of unionization, the farmers form an "Association" to pool their product in the hope of forcing a better price from the corporate buyers. But the latter can always divide and conquer, bribing enough individual farmers with a temptingly high price to break up their solidarity. The Association then resorts to violence to enforce the boycott, first directed not at men but tobacco beds and barns; but men defend their property, and bloodshed ensues. Perse Munn is swept into all this almost against his will, finding himself on the speakers' platform, listening to the "full, compelling voice" of Senator Tolliver and then suddenly propelled to the podium to address the crowd, with no idea of what he is going to say. Like Warren, Munn has found his audience, but what content does he have to convey? "My friends," he begins, "You came here . . . because you thought you could get something here to help you. But there is nothing here to help you . . . nothing here except what you have brought with you." His is a speech about nothing, the nothing the farmers can count on but themselves, the nothing Munn has to say except to make it the theme of his speech. It is an interesting way to begin a novel – is the novel, too, to be about nothing? – and to begin a novelist's career.

What the novel is about is not nothing so much as the nothing the protagonist feels he can contribute to what has already been said. It was the full-voiced patrician Tolliver who had had the first word, the Tolliver who becomes Munn's symbolic father, laying a paternal hand on his shoulder as he draws him into the Association – as Thomas Hardin's father had drawn his son into the growers' association in "Prime Leaf." And as Joseph Hardin would subsequently resign from his political involvement, frustrating the son who then takes his revenge on a substitute rider, so too will Senator Tolliver resign from the Association when it turns too violent for him, and Munn will try to slay the father who betrayed his commitment. To make sure the oedipal reference will not be missed, Warren locates this failed attempt at patricide in the neighborhood of a fictive "Thebes," Kentucky.

The second and third of the perspectives through which Warren's novels invite themselves to be read are here, as elsewhere, inextricably mixed, for Munn is to Tolliver not only as a son confronting a problematic father but also as a reader confronting a problematic text. Tolliver's speech, to which Munn must respond, is followed, later in the novel, by Tolliver's letter of resignation from the Association. The board members puzzle over it intently, especially Munn, who believes he has found in one sentence "the key" to its interpretation, basing his conclusion on an apparent discrepancy with the rest of the letter. The only mention in the entire novel of Munn's biological father, as it happens, will be through his recollection of "one of his father's books." An avowedly biographical reading of Warren's novels might well see here a fictional transposition of the boy's discovery, "profound and complex," of his father's "book," and in the son's anger at his father's abandonment of the cause of the young Warren's feeling that his father had betrayed his calling.

Not quite all these themes are present in Warren's second novel, *At Heaven's Gate* (1943), but most are. Both novels are principally concerned with the decline and fall of a corporate enterprise – literally a corporation, in the case of Bogan Murdock's financial empire – and with what happens to a young man who has been seduced by a fatherly figure to hitch his wagon to the star of that enterprise when it descends into illegality and collapses. Perse Munn is hunted down and slain by agents of the law; Jerry Calhoun is arrested and imprisoned for being in Murdock's employ. Although Calhoun is allowed to go home on bail, his legal situation is by no means resolved at the end of the novel. In both novels, incidentally, an innocent black man is arrested for someone else's crime. In both, a bizarre and haunting dream is recounted: Munn dreams of a fetus borne toward him in the arms of his wife, wrapped in newspaper that flakes away to reveal the face of Bunk Trevelyan, whom Munn had defended in court from a charge of murder but at the cost of unknowingly condemning an innocent black sharecropper. After Munn realizes his error, he kills Trevelyan under cover of Association business. In the second novel, literary aesthete Slim Sarrett, whose pronouncements somewhat echo Warren's own in his essay "Pure and Impure Poetry," claims (falsely) to have had a recurring nightmare of his father's death in an explosion, his progenitor's severed head drifting his way trailing a piece of dirty white string (recalling the sodden white newspaper hanging from Munn's dreamed fetus). Elements of each dream will continue to recur throughout Warren's novels – in Jack Burden's meditation on the "sad little fetus you carry around inside yourself" in *All the King's Men*, in the fetus to which Rachel Beaumont gives premature birth in *World Enough and Time*, a misfortune that likewise happens to Mary Tillyard in *The Cave* (1959) and to Miss Pettifew in *Flood: A Romance of Our Time* (1964) and in the "soaked and disintegrating newspaper parcel" with which *Meet Me in the Green Glen* (1971) begins.

Warren drew upon his knowledge of both Nashville and Memphis for the setting of *At Heaven's Gate*, which has both a university (Nashville's Vanderbilt) and an important river (Memphis being situated on the banks of the Mississippi). Bogan Murdock, corrupt financier, has some traits in common with Luke Lea, a notorious Tennessee businessman whose career peaked during Warren's undergraduate years at Vanderbilt. One structural peculiarity of the novel is that it tells two stories – the second is the tale of displaced and religion-bit mountaineer Ashby Wyndham – in alternating chapters, uniting them in the conclusion when their characters come together. *Night Rider* is a more tightly focused work; *At Heaven's Gate* sprawls. Warren worked from an elaborate outline, based in part on Dante's Seventh Circle (with respect to such "violators of nature" as homosexuals and usurers); in a 1969 interview with Roger Sale he confessed that by the time he had finished outlining every paragraph and began to write, some of the freshness was gone.

Warren's acquaintance with Louisiana politics gave him the material for his third novel, *All the King's Men* (1946), the masterpiece his preceding works could not have prepared anyone to expect. Warren always denied that Willie Stark was Huey Long, but this was to stave off the notion that his novel was an apologia for the corrupt but progressive Louisiana governor. The novel makes a philosophical issue out of whether it is nobler to make good out of evil materials than to do no good at all. Willie adopts this line, but so does Ellis Burden, the putative father of the narrator Jack, who in a theological tract declares that "the creation of man whom God in His foreknowledge knew doomed to sin was the awful index of God's omnipotence.... The creation of evil is therefore the index of God's glory and His power." Likewise, henchman Tiny Duffy, whom Stark took apart and put back together again, was the "index of the Boss's own success." Stark used graft for the good of the people, building highways, schools, and hospitals.

When his son Tom is seriously, ultimately fatally, injured playing football for his father's greater glory (in the equivalent of Louisiana State University's Huey P. Long Field House), Willie Stark decides to dedicate the hospital he is building to his son, and thus he reneges on a commitment to let a crony of Tiny Duffy's build it. He wants it free of taint, but this departure from his normal Machiavellian philosophy of creative government turns out to be a tragic mistake. Duffy retaliates by telling Dr. Adam Stanton of his sister Anne's affair with Willie. Dr. Stanton then assassinates Stark (as a Dr. Weiss had done Long in 1935, for reasons still unknown).

The focus of the novel is really on its narrator Jack Burden, who is engaged in a search for a father. Ellis Burden, he eventually learns, is not his biological sire. That honor belongs to Judge Irwin, though Jack discovers this fact only after he, on a mission for Stark, presents the judge with the incriminating information from his past that makes him, in guilt at being found out by his son (who does not yet realize he is the son), put a bullet through his heart. Similarly, in the embedded Civil War–era tale (the subject of Burden's unwritten history Ph.D. dissertation), which William Faulkner once said was so good that Warren ought to have kept it and thrown the rest of the novel away, Cass Mastern brings about Duncan Trice's suicide by sleeping with his wife. As Jonathan Baumbach has pointed out, Duncan and Annabelle Trice were surrogate parents to the younger Mastern. Thus, what is embedded in the novel is an oedipal tale, Burden behaving like Oedipus in assiduously digging up the truth from the past (as Oedipus made it his business to get to the bottom of what was afflicting Thebes), whether it be the Cass Mastern incident he uncovered in his graduate student days or the skeleton in Judge Irwin's closet.

But Willie Stark, too, is Jack's father, his instructor in politics and life. Their relationship began with an ambiguous sign from Stark, an indecipherable gesture whose correct interpretation Jack demands but Stark refuses to give. Back in 1922, when Stark had not yet become a man of power, Jack thought he had winked at him but could not be sure. Twelve years later, he asked Stark if it had been a wink for real. " 'Boy,' he said, 'if I was to tell you, then you wouldn't have anything to think about.'" Like the letter from Senator Tolliver that Munn puzzled over, the wink is a problematic text for the filial protagonist to read, if he can. Burden's last glimpse of Stark is like this first one, an ambiguous wink: "Perhaps he piled up his greatness and burnt it in one great blaze in the dark like a bonfire

Participants at 1956 Fugitive reunion: (first row) Allen Tate, John Crowe Ransom, Donald Davidson; (second row) Alfred Starr, Alec Stevenson, Warren; (third row) William Yandell Elliott, Merrill Moore, Jesse Wills, Sidney M. Hirsch (Vanderbilt University Photographic Archives)

and then there wasn't anything but dark and the embers winking." In New Mexico once, on his way back from an attempt to escape Stark's paternal eyes (consequent upon his realization that Anne Stanton had become the Boss's mistress), Jack met an old man with a strange twitch on the side of his "mummy's jaw," a twitch that would make "you . . . think he was going to wink, but he wasn't." A clue to the meaning of all this mysterious winking may lie in Jack's outburst to Tiny Duffy, when he lets him know he knows how Stark was led to his death: "My name is Jack and I'm the wild jack and I'm not one-eyed." Warren, however, was one-eyed and evidently turned his disability into a motif in his famous novel.

The idea for what would become *All the King's Men* — which he first wrote as a verse play — came to

Warren in the winter of 1937–1938 at L.S.U., and his visit to Italy in 1939 allowed him to see in Mussolini a second, and darker, model for corrupting power. When L.S.U. refused to match the modest raise and promotion offered by the University of Minnesota, Warren went to Minneapolis in 1942, where he would remain until 1950, except for his tenure as chair of poetry at the Library of Congress in 1944. In exile from the South, as he had been in England when he wrote "Prime Leaf," Warren turned once more to the short-story form, completing the collection *The Circus in the Attic* (1947) with the title story (*Cosmopolitan,* September 1947), "Blackberry Winter" (1946), undoubtedly his best effort in the genre, and "The Patented Gate and the Mean Hamburger" (*Mademoiselle,* January 1947). All three stories are set in the southwest Kentucky and middle Tennessee region he had known so well.

"The Circus in the Attic" recounts the wasted life of Bolton Lovehart, whose oppressive mother manipulates him into staying at home, so that in his life he has realized no greater ambition than to construct a miniature circus in his attic while pretending to write the history of the county. While "The Circus" limns small-town life, "Blackberry Winter" is a rural tale of young Seth, who likes to go barefoot, even if his mother says it's too cold, in order to make a perfect footprint in the mud and then pretend someone else had made it. That way he can pretend to have "suddenly come upon that single mark on the glistening auroral beach of the world" — and have the pleasure of creation ex nihilo, as if it came into being on its own, he having for the moment erased the memory of his authorship of the mark. Creating out of nothing was clearly on Warren's mind at the time, for he had Jack Burden make the discovery "that the reality of an event, which is not real in itself, arises from other events which, likewise, in themselves are not real." And in the contemporaneous critical essay "Pure and Impure Poetry" (*Kenyon Review,* Spring 1943), he asked, "Does this not, then, lead us to the conclusion that poetry does not inhere in any particular element but depends upon the set of relationships, the structure, which we call the poem?" The poetry, or in Burden's terms the reality, that arises not from a single element or event but some combination of them, is evidenced in the collection itself in Warren's decision to place "Blackberry Winter" immediately after the title story. For when young Seth walked up to his father, who is on horseback, and his father "leaned over and reached a hand" to pull him up onto the horse in a loving way the reader may experience an unsettling sense of déjà vu, because another Seth in "The Circus in the Attic" performed the same act with a quite different outcome. In a Civil War prologue to Bolton Lovehart's life story, a Seth Sykes, defending his corn from the invading Yankees, walked up to a Union officer on horseback, who then "leaned from the saddle" and grabbed him by the hair, "jerked his head back, and carefully put the muzzle of a pistol against the head" and shot him dead. The poetry or the reality that emerges from these two contiguous stories is rather different from that which arises from either taken separately. The same oedipal resonance arises from the novels taken together, particularly when combined with the filicide enacted in the 1943 "Ballad of Billie Potts."

If "Blackberry Winter," in which the boy Seth that cold spring morning encounters not only his father but his black playmate Little Jebb, Jebb's par-

ents, and perhaps most importantly a nameless, knife-wielding tramp whom his father sends packing, is the best story in the collection, "The Circus in the Attic" is not the second best. As Bohner observes, "it seems more a synopsis of a Warren novel than a fully realized short story" — though it is too bad the novel was never written. The next best story, apart from "Prime Leaf," is probably "The Patented Gate and the Mean Hamburger," written in the chilly Minneapolis spring of 1946, at the same time as "Blackberry Winter," a season according to Bohner "when thoughts of his southern boyhood were much in Warren's mind." The gate was the pride of Jeff York, allowing him to enter the dirt road leading up to his farmhouse without getting off his horse; it was, Warren writes, "the seal Jeff York had put on all the years of sweat and rejection" that he had put into acquiring the house and farm. The hamburger was his downfall, the "mean" (that is, tasty) ones served at Slick Hardin's Dew Drop Inn Diner that corrupted his wife with the desire not only to eat them but to talk her husband into selling his farm so that she could take over the business. As Bolton Lovehart's mother is said to have controlled him by a "thousand invisible threads," Jeff York's wife was emblematically attired in a coat that had "a scrap of fur at the collar which looked like some tattered growth of fungus feeding on old wood." Her husband, of course, was the wood, having wrists like a "stove-length of a hickory sapling." In the end the encircling growth wins out, for York hangs himself from the patented gate.

For some time a source of trouble, Warren's marital problems came to a head in these years, culminating in his divorce from Emma Brescia in 1951; there were no children from this marriage. In 1952 he married the writer Eleanor Clark; daughter Rosanna was born in 1953, son Gabriel in 1955. Though primarily a poet and novelist, Warren had always had a strong interest in drama; *All the King's Men* had originally been a play and was produced as such in New York in 1947. Already at work on the drama *Brother to Dragons: A Tale in Verse and Voices* (1953), Warren in 1951 was awarded the post of professor of playwriting at the Yale Drama School, though he would teach literature courses as well. The Warrens took up residence in a converted barn in nearby Fairfield, Connecticut, where he lived until the end of his life. He resigned his Yale position in 1956 but returned in 1961, serving as professor of English until 1973.

When they were both working in the Library of Congress in 1944, Katherine Anne Porter introduced Warren to the historical documents on which he would base *World Enough and Time: A Romantic Novel* (1950), set in Kentucky in the 1820s. Despite his later denials that he ever wrote historical romances, Warren's subtitle does situate this novel in the genre. *Band of Angels* and *Wilderness* also could have born similar subtitles but didn't. Commenting on why it is that Warren's novels have so often achieved best-seller status, Leslie Fiedler points out that they "were based not on the models of high Modernism" written by such authors as Henry James, Virginia Woolf, or James Joyce, but "seem more indebted to the example of the Historical Romance: a disreputable sub-genre still despised by elitist critics though it is at the present [one of] the most widely read of all Pop forms." Warren's decision to tell the story through a twentieth-century narrator who comments upon the (fictive) historical documents does, however, break the convention of the historical novel and the melodramatic spell; the novel's philosophical depth and universal significance allow it to transcend whatever it shares with popular genres.

There is a political dimension to *World Enough and Time,* but it is perhaps less compelling than the issues of labor organizing, aggressive capitalism, and demagogy found in the previous three novels. Kentucky political opinion in the 1820s was split by the Old Court/New Court factions, the former arguing for fiduciary integrity, the latter for debt relief. In the novel Col. Cassius Fort is at first for relief, then switches sides. In this regard he follows in the footsteps of Warren's previous father figures, Joseph Hardin of "Prime Leaf" and Senator Tolliver of *Night Rider.* Jeremiah Beaumont plays the disappointed son, for he had studied law under Fort and regarded him as a father. When Jeremiah succeeds in winning the hand of Rachel Jordan, whom Fort had once seduced and impregnated, Rachel makes him swear upon the grave of her stillborn fetus to avenge her disgrace by killing Fort. Blocked by Fort's refusal to fight a duel, Beaumont does not fulfill the promise until he is manipulated into assassinating the man (as Adam Stanton was provoked into killing Willie Stark) by some unscrupulous Reliefers who send him a copy of a handbill purporting to clear Fort's name with the claim that the fetus had been black and thus could not have been Fort's. Beaumont thinks Fort wrote the handbill. Reading it, he felt "the gratitude of a good son to a father. He was grateful because Fort, with the last outrage, had showed him the truth" — not the truth about the fetus, of course, but of the extent of the evil of which he was capable. Like Perse Munn, Jeremiah Beaumont thinks he knows how to read

the text from the father, and for this hoax of a father's text the father is slain. For Fort did not write it (nor did Jeroboam Beauchamp, Beaumont's historical original, ever say Solomon Sharp – Fort's prototype – had); in fact, it was not even a handbill in the sense Beaumont took it to be, for only one copy was ever printed, and thus it was not, as he had thought, a public besmirching of Rachel's name.

Warren pursued his deep interest in Kentucky history with the book-length narrative poem *Brother to Dragons* (1953), which details the ax-murder of a slave by Thomas Jefferson's nephew in western Kentucky in 1811. Despite its considerable fidelity, as in Jeremiah Beaumont's story, to the historicity of the event, Warren's recurring fetal nightmare returns even here, as the victim "Drew up his knees to make himself all little . . . sidewise, and his eyes squinched shut," like fetal mummies recalled in *At Heaven's Gate,* "hunched . . . eyelids squinting."

In his next novel, *Band of Angels* (1955), published not long after the birth of his daughter, Warren decided to tell a story from a woman's point of view. At the same time he continued his immersion in the rich history of his native Kentucky. Based on historian Winston Coleman's account of just such an event, the novel is the story of a young woman who discovers she is both black and a slave only upon the death of her father. Returning from Oberlin College to Danville, Kentucky, for the funeral, Amantha Starr is seized by a slave trader and hustled downriver to New Orleans to be sold for her father's debts. Had her father written out and signed her manumission papers, which he could not bring himself to do because he could not stop denying what they would have acknowledged, all this would have been quite unnecessary — so that once more the plot turns on what the father does (or does not) write. The novel begins with Amantha recalling the grave of her mother, who died when Amantha was an infant, meditating in particular upon the inscription on the stone, which in addition to the dates of her mother's brief life bore "the word *Renie.*" It is her mother's name of course, but Warren curiously uses "word" instead of "name," reminding the reader that it is in fact a word in addition to being a name, the second person singular imperative of the French verb *renier,* "deny" (as in to deny or renounce one's origins) — a one-word message from the mother, or from the father who had it carved and whose own denial had such disastrous results, that Amantha spends most of her life obeying, until her ultimate reconciliation with her identity.

Band of Angels did not enjoy a warm critical reception. That it quickly became a movie (starring Clark Gable, Sidney Poitier, and Yvonne De Carlo as Amantha) only confirmed, for some, the suspicion that Warren was trying to write in the tradition of Margaret Mitchell. The film, though now a staple of late-night television, was less successful than Robert Rossen's Academy Award–winning 1949 version of *All the King's Men*. Critics of the novel found fault with the weakness of Warren's heroine and narrator, who seemed less a protagonist than a person to whom things happened.

In 1959 Warren took a more successful step in this direction, for *The Cave* is, as Justus has pointed out, a novel without a protagonist. Set in contemporary Tennessee but in part inspired by events near Mammoth Cave, Kentucky, in the 1920s, the novel centers around a character the reader never even sees ("except," writes Justus, "in the flashbacks of other characters"). Jasper Harrick remains trapped in a cave while the inhabitants of Johntown scramble to save him or, more typically, to make a profit. The story bears more than a passing resemblance to Billy Wilder's 1951 film *Ace in the Hole,* starring Kirk Douglas as a newspaperman who stumbles across the story of a man trapped in a cave near Albuquerque, New Mexico. In the movie the newspaperman persuades the local sheriff to grant him exclusive rights to the story as well as to take the more cumbersome course of drilling from above instead of going in directly through the mouth of the cave. Isaac Sumpter does the same in Warren's novel, with the same result as in the film, the trapped man needlessly dying before help can reach him. Isaac in fact takes the place of the novel's absent protagonist, not only spinning a fiction to claim to speak in his name, pretending to relay Jasper's thoughts to the audience, but also taking over as Warren's typically oedipal hero, a man in deep conflict with the father yet puzzling over the correct interpretation of a message left for him. As in the immediately preceding novel, where the text was a name, the "Renie" on the gravestone, in *The Cave* it is the name the Reverend MacCarland Sumpter gave his son. "Why did you name me Isaac? . . . There wasn't any Isaac in the family, ever," he complains, having looked in the family Bible (where, by custom, the generations of the family were recorded). Isaac is convinced his father was thinking of Abraham's willingness to sacrifice his son at God's command, and he takes his name as evidence of his father's filicidal intent. The father, in response, insists upon God's providential mercy in putting a ram in the bushes, entangled by his horns, so that at

the last minute a saving substitution could be made. This is what happens in the novel, as Isaac's father, having discovered his son's treachery toward Jasper Harrick, covers for him by rearranging articles in the cave to correspond to Isaac's fictional version and save him from the legal consequences of having prevented a timely rescue. Jasper Harrick, entangled among the rocks in the cave, becomes the sacrificial ram. Filicidal feelings are admitted in the parallel father and son, as Jack Harrick confesses that he actually wanted Jasper to die so that he would not have to.

From its subtitle, *Wilderness: A Tale of the Civil War* (1961) may give the appearance of being a pièce d'occasion, written to coincide with the nation's centenary observance of the events of 1861–1865, but Warren's interest in the American nineteenth century had been genuine and longstanding. Furthermore, as in the other novels, the inner drama is just as important as the exterior historical context. On the surface this is the story of an idealistic Bavarian Jew (the European setting of the opening chapter is unique among Warren's novels) who, handicapped by a deformed left foot, struggles to find a way to enlist in the Union army to fight to free the slaves. Yet it is at the same time a variation on a now-familiar story in the Warren canon, that of a son who (like Thomas Hardin, Perse Munn, and Jeremiah Beaumont) finds fault with a father for having reneged on a commitment to a certain set of ideals (the tobacco farmers' association, the Reliefers' cause). In the case of Adam Rosenzweig's father Leopold, he renounces the revolutionary effort that erupted in the 1848 uprising in Berlin, electing shortly before his death to return to an obedience to the Mosaic Law that precluded placing any hope in secular social progress. Warren gets the closest he has so far to the incident from his own life that seems to have so strongly influenced his recurring narrative, the discovery of his father's poetry and apparent shame at having had to give it up. For Adam's father was a poet too, and Adam meditates (as Amantha and Isaac had before him) on a single word from the father's text, one that sums up the whole situation of ideals abandoned and the problem of forging one's identity: "worthy" — three times repeated in the three lines preserved from Leopold's poem ("If I could only be worthy . . ."). Adam asks, for example, Mose Talbutt, an escaped slave, to call him Adam (instead of "Slew," on account of his lameness) to "help me be worthy of my name." Adam, of course, is seeking to be worthy of his father's original revolutionary spirit by fighting to free the slaves. By a wonderful irony, it is on the

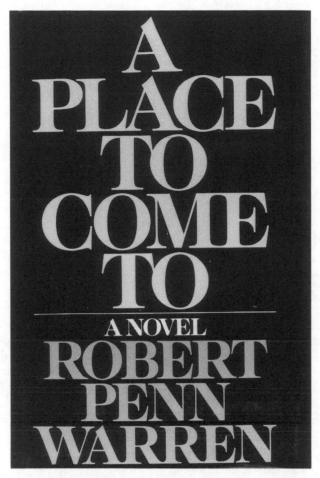

Dust jacket for Warren's last novel, in which a son comes to terms with the ambiguous circumstances surrounding his father's death

skin of a former slave that he discovers a fragment of the very word he retained from his father's poem and that had so governed his life, but when he finds it there its meaning has turned into just the opposite of its original one. For having been caught deserting the Union army, Mose Talbutt had been branded on the thigh with the letter *W,* for "worthless." If this Mose is without worth, his name makes him the perfect counterpoint to the text that had led Adam's father to betray his own original text about worth, the Mosaic Law to which he yielded at the end of his life.

The Cave and *Wilderness* elicited tepid critical response; *Flood: A Romance of Our Time* (1964) suffered worse reviews. As Bohner writes, the novel seemed like a parody of southern writing, "the ultimate anthology of decayed aristocracy, blood taint, miscegenation, hapless chivalry, and lost causes." With a subtitle that recalled that of *World Enough*

and Time, Warren almost seemed to be confessing to melodrama, the past dredged up into the present. It is fair to say that at this time Warren was devoting his best energies to poetry, and his novels may have suffered thereby. At least on the surface there was not a great deal that was new. Read, however, as part of the recurring and still unfolding "buried narrative" (a term borrowed from one of his later poems) about fathers and sons, *Flood* has its story to tell.

As a thirteen-year-old the novel's protagonist, Brad Tolliver, had fought to stop his unlettered father from idly destroying the books that had come into his possession as a result of his foreclosure of the property of Dr. Amos Fiddler, a man his son admired. Although he received a blow on the head for his pains, the son through his perseverance at last impressed his father, who snatched the last book from the fire, flung it in front of the boy, and left the house to weep in the mud of the swamp. Later in his life, as a native southerner who had left for the north, written successful short stories about his youth, and worked in Hollywood, Tolliver, as Bohner points out, has much in common with Warren, who won an award from the Screen Writers Guild in 1949. He even signs something like Warren's own name to a motel register, for since Warren was known to his friends as "Red," an appropriately filial Warren is evoked by the first name of "Redfill Tellfer," while the last lies halfway between Tolliver and the Christian name of another of his symbolic fathers in the novel, Telford Lott. Instrumental to Tolliver's career, Lott had edited the young author's story collection and given him a handsome advance for a novel on his experiences in the Spanish civil war that Tolliver found he could not write. In his fantasy of returning to Spain, Tolliver eventually realized that the "faceless enemy" he was aiming at actually "wore the face of Telford Lott." The father's text in this instance was the one he required the son to write but that would belong to the father because he had paid for it. The father-son motif is also repeated in the present of the novel, as Tolliver and his new "father," film director Yasha Jones, arrive in Fiddlersburg to make a movie about its intentional flooding. In the melodramatic climax, the late Dr. Fiddler's son Calvin, freshly escaped from the penitentiary, accidentally shoots Brad in the neck in a violent struggle and then miraculously experiences an eidetic memory of the relevant medical text of his father's so that he might successfully perform an emergency tracheotomy on him with a ballpoint pen belonging to Jones. Warren's writer hero is saved by the pen of one father and the text that had belonged to another.

In *Meet Me in the Green Glen* (1971) Warren returns once more to middle Tennessee, which by now had come to overshadow Kentucky as his favorite setting, fictional Fiddlersburg and its environs becoming for him something along the order of Thomas Hardy's Wessex and Faulkner's Yoknapatawpha. The penitentiary from which Calvin Fiddler had escaped is where Italian immigrant Angelo Passetto will be executed for the murder of Sunderland Spottwood, a crime actually committed by Sunderland's wife, Cassie, who had become Angelo's lover. She had taken him in as a resident handyman, as Sunderland had been rendered inert by a stroke years before, the only sign of life a twitch on the side of his face, a phenomenon familiar to Warren readers since the twitch on the face of the old man in New Mexico in *All the King's Men.* Passetto is familiar too, for he is the knife-wielding tramp encountered by the boy Seth and his father in

"Blackberry Winter," though Passetto, like Seth, will prove to be fascinated by the footprints his shoes can make. Indeed, the two coalesce into one, the boy becoming the tramp, who grows up to become the wandering stranger who is taken in, sleeps with his mother, and causes his father's death (Cassie kills her husband with Angelo's switchblade knife out of despair when Angelo rejected her). The cooling touch of Cassie's hand becomes for Angelo "his mother's . . . on his forehead"; for Cassie his was the face of "a little boy asleep." Warren's oedipal scenarios are always enriched by the addition of the element, taken from his own life story, of an intervening paternal text; one of its manifestations here is the collection of detective magazines Angelo devours from cover to cover and uses as inspiration for eroticizing Cassie Spottwood. Interestingly, he found these old magazines of Sunderland's upstairs in what had originally been the Spottwoods' bedroom, in a wardrobe behind a mirror in which he was startled to discover his own reflection. Passetto as the passing stranger who turns out to be the son is a reincarnation of Billie Potts, whose last name anagrammatically presages most of his own. Potts just did not make it as far as Passetto, unaware as he contemplated his reflection in a forest stream that the axe was about to fall.

Critics were almost evenly divided on the merits of *Meet Me in the Green Glen,* some faulting Warren for writing yet another old-fashioned romance of the South, others praising him for having tightened up his prose since *Flood,* having jettisoned his philosophical baggage, and, in the words of John W. Aldridge, for having adopted "a hard texture of language very like his poetry." If *Flood* suffered because Warren was becoming a better poet than novelist, his fiction could only benefit from a deeper integration of the two domains.

In *A Place to Come To* (1977) Warren brought his career as a novelist to a glorious close, writing what some consider his best work since *All the King's Men.* Like *Flood,* its protagonist is a Southerner in exile; if Bradwell Tolliver in some ways resembled Warren as artist, Jediah Tewksbury may reflect him as academic. A literature professor of international renown, Jed progresses from Dugton, Alabama, to graduate studies at the University of Chicago, a teaching position in Nashville, and then a more prestigious career up North, crowned with honorary degrees. The novel opens with the spectacular and mythologically resonant death of Jed's father, who while standing on his mule-drawn wagon one starlit night with his hand on his member, lost his balance and fell off, the wheel crushing his neck.

Like Jasper Harrick's father in *The Cave,* Buck Tewksbury was locally renowned for his sexual prowess, and thus his last gesture was variously interpreted by his acquaintances: was it urination or masturbation? Infusing the novel with imagery drawn from his poems – in particular the contemporaneous "No Bird Does Call," where the poet lies down on a carpet of gold leaves, cradled in the roots of a beech, and identifies his resting place as "Danaë's lap lavished with gold by the god" – Warren makes both interpretations coincide: in Zeus's case the golden shower is also seminal; the undecidability of Jed's father's last gesture, that it was somehow both at once (in Jed's various retellings), allows the father to incarnate the god. That would make Jed into the offspring of Zeus's golden shower, Danaë's son Perseus, a mythological figure who has been hiding in the wings at least since Adam Rosenzweig beheld a bronze of the Medusa-slayer in Aaron Blaustein's house, perhaps ever since Warren's choice of a first name for Perse Munn. In a scene paralleling the one in *Wilderness* in which Rosenzweig, having arrived in New York but not yet having achieved his goal of joining the Union forces, turns down Blaustein's plea that he become his adopted child, Jed Tewksbury discovers "a matching copy of the Discobolus" – an allusion to Perseus's accidentally slaying his grandfather with a discus – in the apartment of Heinrich Stahlmann, the Chicago classics professor who takes him in as a son. The discus surfaces twice elsewhere in the novel, once as the life preserver that could have saved Rozelle Hardcastle's first husband from drowning had her lover thrown it, and in the opening pages as the wagon wheel that killed Jed's father.

Warren's last novel achieves a closure to the continuous story all have been telling of sons trying to become their fathers with the singular event of its protagonist siring a son. Only in the first novel had such an event taken place, yet all Perse Munn ever saw of his child was the dream of a dead fetus with the face of the man he killed; Brad Tolliver and his wife conceive, but the pregnancy miscarries. In Jed's eyes, his son Ephraim has the grace of a knife-wielding purse snatcher who stabs him near the site of Stahlmann's apartment in Chicago, a thief who poses momentarily, "beautifully balanced there with the purse" on the hood of a car, like "Cellini's Perseus." Through this by no means home-grown myth, Warren universalizes the particularities of the deeply southern setting of his opening scene. In his graduate-school years, Jed Tewksbury turns the circumstances of his father's death into a rousingly good story, winning friends, fame, and women by

telling it in an increasingly entertaining way. "I should have been grateful," he confesses, echoing the words Jeremiah Beaumont spoke when he read what he thought was the handbill Fort had composed: "the gratitude of a good son to a father." The echo is genuine, for in Jed's case too a son has been given by his father what he can make into a text, to do with what he will.

Robert Penn Warren died 15 September 1989 after a long illness. Joseph Blotner is at work on an authorized biography, which is scheduled to appear in 1995. At that time, we should learn much more about this writer who has been singularly reticent in revealing details of his private life. In his last new book, *Portrait of a Father* (1988), Warren took a step toward autobiography, recounting, among other reminiscences, the scene of his discovery of his father's poems, and later his realization of why his father had not objected when he chose to abandon a surer vocation for the study of literature at Vanderbilt: "My father had known what it was to sweat over poems. I had long since seen the hidden book."

By *All the King's Men* alone Warren would be ranked among the century's best novelists; though undeniably of lesser stature, his other nine novels are nevertheless underrated in part because of the realization that in the last decades of his life his greatest achievements lay in his poetry – in such works as *Audubon* (1969), *Or Else* (1974), *Now and Then* (1978), *Being Here* (1980), *Rumor Verified* (1981), and *Altitudes and Extensions* (in *New and Selected Poems 1923–1985*). Yet if his novels were to be read afresh from the perspective of his poetry, less for their sociological content, or as "southern novels," than for their symbolic depth, for the beauty and cohesion of their construction out of "pure and impure" elements, their reputation would surely rise.

Interviews:

Talking with Robert Penn Warren, edited by Floyd C. Watkins, John T. Hiers, and Mary Louise Weaks (Athens: University of Georgia Press, 1990).

Bibliographies:

Neil Nakadate, *Robert Penn Warren: A Reference Guide* (Boston: G. K. Hall, 1977);

James A. Grimshaw Jr., *Robert Penn Warren: A Descriptive Bibliography 1922–1979* (Charlottesville: University Press of Virginia, 1981).

References:

John W. Aldridge, "The Enormous Spider Web of Warren's World," in *Critical Essays on Robert Penn Warren,* edited by William Bedford Clark (Boston: G. K. Hall, 1981), pp. 64–70;

Jonathan Baumbach, "The Metaphysics of Demagoguery: *All the King's Men* by Robert Penn Warren," in *Twentieth Century Interpretations of All the King's Men: A Collection of Critical Essays,* edited by Robert H. Chambers (Englewood Cliffs, N. J.: Prentice-Hall, 1977), pp. 126–142;

Harold Bloom, ed., *Robert Penn Warren* (New York: Chelsea House, 1986);

Charles Bohner, *Robert Penn Warren, Revised Edition* (Boston: Twayne, 1981);

John Burt, *Robert Penn Warren and American Idealism* (New Haven: Yale University Press, 1988);

Leonard Casper, *Robert Penn Warren: The Dark and Bloody Ground* (Seattle: University of Washington Press, 1960);

William Bedford Clark, *The American Vision of Robert Penn Warren* (Lexington: University Press of Kentucky, 1991);

Walter B. Edgar, ed., *A Southern Renascence Man: Views of the Robert Penn Warren* (Baton Rouge: Louisiana State University Press, 1984);

Leslie Fiedler, "Robert Penn Warren: A Final Word," in *To Love So Well The World: A Festschrift in Honor of Robert Penn Warren,* edited by Dennis L. Weeks (New York: Peter Lang, 1992), pp. 19–28;

Richard Gray, ed., *Robert Penn Warren: A Collection of Critical Essays* (Englewood Cliffs, N. J.: Prentice-Hall, 1980);

James A. Grimshaw Jr., ed., *Time's Glory: Original Essays on Robert Penn Warren* (Conway: University of Central Arkansas Press, 1986);

Barnett Guttenberg, *Web of Being: The Novels of Robert Penn Warren* (Nashville: Vanderbilt University Press, 1975);

Mark Jancovich, *The Cultural Politics of the New Criticism* (New York: Cambridge University Press, 1995);

James H. Justus, *The Achievement of Robert Penn Warren* (Baton Rouge: Louisiana State University Press, 1981);

Robert Koppelman, *Robert Penn Warren's Modernist Spirituality* (Columbia: University of Missouri Press, 1995);

Joseph R. Millichap, *Robert Penn Warren: A Study of the Short Fiction* (New York: Twayne, 1992);

Neil Nakadate, ed., *Robert Penn Warren: Critical Perspectives* (Lexington: University Press of Kentucky, 1981);

Randolph Paul Runyon, *The Braided Dream: Robert Penn Warren's Late Poetry* (Lexington: University Press of Kentucky, 1990);

Runyon, *The Taciturn Text: The Fiction of Robert Penn Warren* (Columbus: Ohio State University Press, 1990);

Hugh Ruppersburg, *Robert Penn Warren and the American Imagination* (Athens: University of Georgia Press, 1990);

Southern Quarterly, special issue on Warren, 31 (Summer 1993);

Katherine Snipes, *Robert Penn Warren* (New York: Ungar, 1983);

Marshall Walker, *Robert Penn Warren: A Vision Earned* (Edinburgh: Harris, 1979);

Floyd C. Watkins, *Then and Now: The Personal Past in the Poetry of Robert Penn Warren* (Lexington: University Press of Kentucky, 1982);

Dennis L. Weeks, ed., *To Love So Well the World: A Festschrift in Honor of Robert Penn Warren* (New York: Peter Lang, 1992);

Harold Woodell, *All the King's Men: The Search for a Usable Past* (New York: Twayne, 1993).

Papers:

Most of Warren's manuscripts, correspondence, and other papers are held at the Beinecke Library at Yale University. Other important collections are those at the University of Kentucky, Western Kentucky University, and Vanderbilt University.

Tom Wolfe

(2 March 1931 –   )

Barbara Lounsberry
University of Northern Iowa

BOOKS: *The Kandy-Kolored Tangerine-Flake Streamline Baby* (New York: Farrar, Straus & Giroux, 1965; London: Cape, 1966);

The Pump House Gang (New York: Farrar, Straus & Giroux, 1968); republished as *The Mid-Atlantic Man and Other New Breeds in England and America* (London: Weidenfeld & Nicolson, 1969);

The Electric Kool-Aid Acid Test (New York: Farrar, Straus & Giroux, 1968; London: Weidenfeld & Nicolson, 1969);

Radical Chic & Mau-Mauing the Flak Catchers (New York: Farrar, Straus & Giroux, 1970; London: Joseph, 1971);

The Painted Word (New York: Farrar, Straus & Giroux, 1975);

Mauve Gloves & Madmen, Clutter & Vine, and Other Stories, Sketches, and Essays (New York: Farrar, Straus & Giroux, 1976);

The Right Stuff (New York: Farrar, Straus & Giroux, 1979; London: Cape, 1979);

In Our Time (New York: Farrar, Straus & Giroux, 1980; London: Picador, 1980);

From Bauhaus to Our House (New York: Farrar, Straus & Giroux, 1981; London: Cape, 1982);

The Purple Decades: A Reader (New York: Farrar, Straus & Giroux, 1982; London: Cape, 1983);

The Bonfire of the Vanities (New York: Farrar, Straus & Giroux, 1987; London: Cape, 1988).

OTHER: *The New Journalism,* edited by Wolfe and E. W. Johnson (New York: Harper & Row, 1973; London: Pan, 1975);

Marie Cosindas: Color Photographs, edited by Susan Feldman, with an essay by Wolfe (Boston: New York Graphic Society, 1978).

SELECTED PERIODICAL PUBLICATION –
UNCOLLECTED: "Stalking the Billion-Footed Beast," *Harper's,* 279 (November 1989): 45–56.

Tom Wolfe (photograph by Thomas Victor)

Tom Wolfe might be called the literary son of Mark Twain. Famous for his white suits and his high-speed, highly exclamatory, highly italicized delivery, Wolfe is one of America's leading prose stylists and satirists, although he demurs at the latter label. A brilliant phrasemaker, Wolfe's own labels, such as *radical chic* and *the right stuff,* have stuck, becoming part of the cultural landscape, as has his name for the 1970s, "the me decade." After more than twenty years as one of the leading advocates and practitioners of the New Journalism, Wolfe succeeded in 1987 with his first novel, *The Bonfire of the Vanities.* First published serially in *Rolling Stone* from August 1984 to August 1985 and revised for book publication, the novel rode both the hardcover and paperback best-seller lists for weeks, garnering critical praise as well as attacks.

It was the kind of beginning one might expect from a boy whose first idols were Napoleon Bonaparte and Wolfgang Amadeus Mozart. Thomas Kennerly Wolfe, Jr., was born 2 March 1931 on Confederate Avenue in Richmond, Virginia, the son of Thomas Kennerly Wolfe, an agronomist and editor of the *Southern Planter,* and Helen Hughes Wolfe, who encouraged young Tom to be an artist. In his spring 1991 *Paris Review* interview Wolfe revealed that he decided to become a writer at the age of six or seven in simple imitation of his father, whom he always saw writing at a desk. The volumes of Thomas Wolfe, the famous southern writer, were included on the family bookshelves, and Wolfe's parents had a hard time convincing Tom that he was not related to the author of *Look Homeward, Angel* (1929) and *You Can't Go Home Again* (1940). Wolfe said in the interview that he has been a "tremendous fan" of Thomas Wolfe's work throughout his life. Nevertheless, the name similarity was a problem. After graduating from Saint Christopher's prep school in Richmond in 1947, he experimented with a variety of pen names in his early writings at Washington and Lee University in Lexington, Virginia. He began with "Tom Wolfe" as his freshman byline but abandoned that quickly for "Tekay Wolfe" in his sophomore and junior years. As a senior he traded that for the more conservative "T. K. Wolfe."

Wolfe's undergraduate years were rife with literary struggles and sports humiliations. The name problem was merely one dilemma. The other was Wolfe's yearning to become a great pitcher at the university where Cy Young was the best-known alumnus. "I had tremendous stuff," recalls Wolfe, who actually pitched briefly in semiprofessional baseball, in a 1965 interview. "I could make the ball do anything – but the trouble was, I gave the batters too long to look at it. I was not fast, you might say." Wolfe's failure to become the world's greatest pitcher opened his eyes to status – and to humiliation. He has never stopped writing about these subjects since. The prologue of *The Bonfire of the Vanities* depicts the mayor of New York City undergoing humiliation in Harlem. When the book's hero, Sherman McCoy, first appears, he is on his knees. A later image of McCoy tangled in his dog's leash becomes an emblem of his plight.

Wolfe wrote three short stories while at Washington and Lee, but he was primarily a sportswriter for the university's student newspaper. Upon graduating cum laude in 1951, he enrolled in Yale University's doctoral program in American studies, but unlike New Journalist Hunter S. Thompson,

who has attached a fictitious "Dr." to his name, Wolfe rarely flaunts his legitimate Ph.D. After completing his dissertation, "The League of American Writers: Communist Activity among American Writers, 1929–1942" in 1957, Wolfe sought work as a journalist, writing one hundred letters of application. Only three editors responded, and two of them said no. Thus Wolfe began his journalistic career at the *Springfield* (Mass.) *Union,* where he worked from 1956 to 1959. In 1959 Wolfe took a job with the *Washington Post,* which he exchanged in 1962 for a position at the *New York Herald Tribune.* There he had the chance to write for its Sunday supplement, *New York,* which would later become an independent magazine. Wolfe remains a contributing editor to *New York* and to *Esquire,* which published "There Goes (Varoom! Varoom!) That Kandy-Kolored Tangerine-Flake Streamline Baby" (1963), Wolfe's first article in his dazzlingly punctuated, colorful, and kinetic style.

Wolfe's long career as a New Journalist should not be seen as laying the groundwork for his emergence as a novelist. Rather, his nonfiction and fiction are two sides of the same coin. As a New Journalist Wolfe applies the techniques of a novelist to factual or journalistic subjects. As a novelist he employs a journalist's exhaustive legwork to gather the rich details, and even whole scenarios, for his imagined tale. In both, the distinctive Wolfe style remains virtually the same.

The components of this style derive from Wolfe's early reading. Emil Ludwig's 1906 biography of Napoleon, which Wolfe read at age eight, not only fired his ambition but taught him to use the historical present for its sense of immediacy. Wolfe borrowed another narrative technique and his dynamic punctuation from a group of Soviet writers of the early twentieth century, whom he read in translation at Yale. Yevgeny Zamyatin, Boris Pilnyak, and the Serapion Brothers wrote about the Soviet revolution, employing the techniques of the French symbolists. In *We* (1924), the novel upon which George Orwell based his *1984* (1949), Zamyatin often breaks off thoughts with a dash in midsentence. Zamyatin also uses many exclamation points. This style attempts to imitate the human mind, which operates not in elegant sentences but in fragmentary, often emotional, fits and starts.

Wolfe's kinetic style should be seen as his attempt not only to imitate mental and sensory processes but also to decrease the distances between author, subject, and reader. Through frenetic fragments and picturesque punctuation he tries to give readers a vicarious sense of the rush of psychedelic drugs in *The Electric Kool-Aid Acid Test* (1968), of supersonic space travel in *The Right Stuff* (1979), and of mob violence in *The Bonfire of the Vanities*. This highly sensory style matches best with highly sensory subjects.

In his introduction to *The New Journalism* (1973) Wolfe acknowledges that he learned to write scenes from nonfiction writer Gay Talese and dialogue from Jimmy Breslin. His penchant for what he calls "status detail" can be traced to Honoré de Balzac, who enjoyed dropping the names of furniture into his novels. Wolfe delights in quoting French critic Charles-Augustin Sainte-Beuve's denunciation of Balzac: "If this little man is so obsessed with furniture why doesn't he open up a shop and spare us these so-called novels of his?" Modern society is dominated by brand names, Wolfe rejoins.

Wolfe's most brilliant and original stylistic trait, however, is his adoption of Henry James's notions of point of view. Wolfe has acknowledged that he tries to create his scenes from a triple perspective: the subject's point of view, that of other people watching, and his own. His technical virtuosity in shifting among these conflicting perspectives, often from sentence to sentence, invigorates his writing. The opening of *The Bonfire of the Vanities* illustrates this virtuosity, as the reader is thrust headlong into the action:

> "And then say what? Say, 'Forget you're hungry, forget you got shot inna back by some racist cop – Chuck was here? Chuck come up to Harlem – ' "
>
> "No, I'll *tell* you what – "
>
> " 'Chuck come up to Harlem and – ' "
>
> "I'll *tell* you what – "
>
> "Say, 'Chuck come up to Harlem and gonna take care a business for the black community'?"
>
> That does it.
>
> Heh-heggggggggggggggggggghhhhhhhhhhhhhhhh!
>
> It's one of those ungodly contraltro cackles somewhere out there in the audience. It's a sound from down so deep, from under so many lavish layers, he knows exactly what she must look like. Two hundred pounds if she's an ounce! Built like an oil burner!

Wolfe's opening line presents not just one person talking but one angry Harlem woman imitating the mayor of New York. The sixth paragraph, which seems at first to introduce the voice of a third-person narrator commenting on the preceding dialogue, is not that at all, for here Wolfe suddenly begins narrating the action from the point of view of the hassled mayor, who thinks, "That does it." Not until the eleventh paragraph does the reader encounter an actual third-person narrator who might

be associated with Wolfe – the voice that says in historical present, "The Mayor leans into the microphone."

No one switches point of view more rapidly than Wolfe. However, this rapid-fire multiple perspective carries with it certain risks. It tends to frustrate readers seeking to isolate Wolfe's own view of his subjects. Questions about his views have been raised regarding *The Bonfire of the Vanities* and about his earlier nonfiction as well. He relishes such confusion. As John Hellmann has noted in *Fables of Fact* (1981), Wolfe's "insistent choices of hyperbolic, kinetic, or baroque words and phrases make his descriptions as much an assault as a representation. . . . These stylistic traits work like those of the cubists to break up the reader's usual modes of perception."

Wolfe has made a career of challenging establishment views, of being the bad boy of arts and letters. His early assault on *The New Yorker* and its venerable former editor, William Shawn, in two 1965 articles, "Tiny Mummies" and "Lost in the Whichy Thicket," occasioned a spirited defense of the magazine, just as his attacks on the art and architectural worlds in *The Painted Word* (1975) and *From Bauhaus to Our House* (1981) stirred debates. Wolfe even admitted in a November 1987 *Rolling Stone* interview that he began wearing his trademark vanilla suits to annoy people: "Why I wanted to annoy people is another question. You'll have to call Dr. Freud's night line to get an answer to that!"

In his introduction to *The New Journalism* Wolfe takes aim at the contemporary novel, announcing that "the most important literature being written in America today is in nonfiction" and that artful nonfiction "would wipe out the novel as literature's main event." Why then would Wolfe choose to become a novelist a decade later? Wolfe offers two answers in "Stalking the Billion-Footed Beast," his provocative manifesto for the novel of social realism, which appeared in the November 1989 issue of *Harper's* after the success of *The Bonfire of the Vanities*. Subconsciously, Wolfe says, he was trying to prove to himself that, in devoting himself to nonfiction, he was not "merely ducking the big challenge – The Novel." On a conscious level, he asserts, he was trying to show that "the future of the fictional novel would be in a highly detailed realism based on reporting, a realism more thorough than any currently being attempted, a realism that would portray the individual in intimate and inextricable relation to the society around him."

Reviewers of *The Bonfire of the Vanities* have been virtually unanimous in praising the extensive research and reporting so apparent in the rich de-

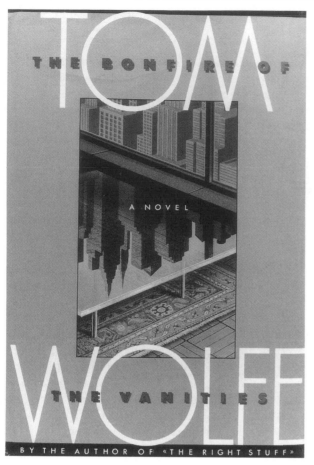

Dust jacket for Wolfe's 1987 novel, a contemporary morality play about a New York stockbroker

tails of New York life in Wolfe's novel. *The Bonfire of the Vanities* is the story of a privileged thirty-eight-year-old WASP, Sherman McCoy, who at the novel's beginning thinks of himself as "master of the Universe." McCoy is the top bond salesman at a Wall Street brokerage house and lives in a $2.6-million, thirteen-room luxury apartment on Fifth Avenue with his wife, Judy, an interior decorator, and six-year-old daughter, Campbell. He also has a twenty-six-year-old mistress named Maria. Lust and overweening pride are clearly McCoy's vanities, and they soon precipitate his downfall. One evening, after picking up Maria at the airport, McCoy makes a wrong turn in his $60,000 Mercedes roadster, and instead of returning to the safe haven of Manhattan, he and Maria find themselves in the alien land of the Bronx. In one of the most artful chapters in the novel, two young black men approach the car, which is stalled at a barricade. In the confusion Maria hits one of the young men with the rear of the car as she and Sherman attempt to escape. This hit-and-run accident changes McCoy's

life – and rights his vision. He is thrust into the New York criminal justice system, is exposed to the media, and becomes a political pawn as "the great white defendant" in a system sick to death of prosecuting minorities.

Wolfe realized that the criminal-justice system could serve as the meeting ground for the haves and the have-nots of New York City. A sensational court case could involve the media, politicians, and religious leaders as well. Like Balzac, who visited the French bankruptcy courts to research a novel, in the early 1980s Wolfe began attending trials at the Manhattan Criminal Court Building. Once there he began to hear stories of amazing incidents that occurred in the Bronx; he then began visiting the Bronx County Courthouse, which is the setting of many of the most pivotal scenes in the novel.

Wolfe has said that only two characters in the novel are based on actual people. McCoy's flashy-dressing Irish lawyer, Tommy Killian, is modeled on a counselor named Eddie Hayes, and the righteous Judge Kovitsky is based on Judge Burton Roberts. Although various reviewers have suggested that the Reverend Bacon, the activist minister from Harlem, is modeled on Al Sharpton or Jesse Jackson, Wolfe declared in the 1991 *Paris Review* interview that, aside from Killian and Kovitsky, he "steered clear of the roman à clef game." He insisted, in fact, that the Reverend Bacon is based on "the sort of figure I had begun seeing as early as 1969, shortly after the poverty program had gotten started."

Wolfe has also been forthright about the many details in his novel derived from pure reporting. He began riding the subway in order to be able to write about it. There he found an old friend who worked on Wall Street wearing tattered running shoes and carrying his expensive leather shoes in an A&P bag to lessen the chances of being mugged. In the novel this is the memorable practice of assistant district attorney Larry Kramer. Wolfe swears that the Bronx Courthouse practices of ordering out for lunch and leaving the building in groups when cases run after dark are simply accurate reporting. After spending time in the courthouse holding pens himself, he realized that he could only get an authentic sense of the experience by interviewing former prisoners. From one of these interviews he gleaned the basis for the humiliating incident in which Sherman is passed repeatedly through the courthouse metal detector, only to discover that the fillings in his teeth are setting off the machine.

Despite this wealth of material derived from his research, Wolfe acknowledges that he was initially intimidated by the challenge of writing a novel. "For eight months I . . . sat at my typewriter every day, intending to start this novel and nothing happened," he told the *Paris Review*. "I felt that the only way I was ever going to get going on it was to put myself under deadline pressure." Wolfe contacted Jann Wenner, the editor of *Rolling Stone,* who agreed to serialize the novel. Serialization unblocked him, but the deadline pressures also made him want to make extensive revisions of his novel before publishing it as a book. Wolfe changed McCoy's occupation from writer to Wall Street financier, a more colorful career, and he changed the critical Bronx incident from a minor felony to the ambiguous automobile accident.

Despite Wolfe's disingenuous demurrals, *The Bonfire of the Vanities* is best understood as literary satire. He likes to say that he is not intentionally engaged in satire, that he is just trying to write down what people do. Nevertheless, he constructs his characters as caricatures and gives them satiric names to boot. The greasy minister is Reverend Bacon; the shallow, drunken journalist, Peter Fallow; the rapacious real estate agent, Mrs. Rawthrote; and the tragic accident victim, Henry Lamb. Occupations also fall prey to Wolfe's wit. Sherman's father is a member of the prestigious law firm of Dunning, Sponget, and Leach, and Sherman's own brokerage house is called Pierce & Pierce.

Save Sherman McCoy, Wolfe's characters are not constructed as complex, realistic human beings but rather to represent specific vanities for the bonfire. The Jewish mayor in the prologue is concerned only about his image. Sherman is also a pathetic figure, although he does not know it at first. His vices are arrogance and lust, and he shares the latter sin with Larry Kramer, the ambitious young Jewish assistant district attorney introduced in the second chapter. Though Kramer is on a different economic level, his fall parallels Sherman's own, which makes their adversarial position as prosecutor and defendant especially absurd.

Lust, pride, greed, and ambition are the primary vanities upon which Wolfe focuses in this novel. The unnamed mayor of New York and Abe Weiss, the district attorney of the Bronx, are both ambitious to retain their power. The Reverend Bacon also wants power, but he is greedy for money as well. The most extensive female portrait in the novel is that of Maria Raskin, Sherman's mistress, who exudes greed and lust. Through most of the novel Sherman's wife is a social climber who is eager to make her way with the other "social X-rays," society women who seem interested only in money and appearance. In fact, only six characters in the novel seem the least bit honorable: the courageous but vitriolic Jewish Judge Kovitsky; the honorable Irish lawyers, Tommy Killian and Bernie Fitzgibbon; the innocent young Campbell McCoy; and the African American victims, Henry Lamb and his mother. With these few exceptions, all is vanity in *The Bonfire of the Vanities.*

Despite his denials, therefore, one can easily suggest that Wolfe assumes the role of satirist in his first novel as well as in his nonfiction. Instead of declaring outright his own moral or intellectual positions, he prefers to expose the vices and follies of others through their own outrageous voices. A certain tension exists, however, between his call for social realism in fiction and his own satiric practice. In fact, Wolfe's characters are more allegorical than realistic. They tend to represent types impervious to change. Only Sherman McCoy undergoes change in this novel, and his fall and renewal stand in high relief against the stasis of the other characters. This works as satire; indeed, the comic exaggeration accounts for much of the novel's pleasure. If one holds Wolfe to his claims for social realism, however, one asks where "the Laboratory of Human Relations" is in this novel. In the best scenes the realism is there, as in the confrontation between rich whites and poor blacks on the Bronx ramp way, with all the fears, doubts, guilt, and miscommunication that Wolfe insightfully evokes, and in the courthouse scenes in which Sherman repudiates his former way of life.

A similar tension exists between the old-fashioned religious vision of the novel and its new-fangled prose style. One effect of this tension is that Wolfe's Swiftian abhorrence of the human vices he tolls is camouflaged, cloaked in the exuberance of his comic presentation. One senses that Wolfe yearns to be Judge Kovitsky, the self-righteous Jehovah figure spitting in the eyes of sinners and cowing them with his thunderous wrath. One can also see him in the character of poet Aubrey Buffing, prophesying the doom of the socialites in the pivotal fifteenth chapter, titled "The Masque of the Red Death."

Wolfe draws deftly on Edgar Allan Poe to underscore the moral corruption and impending destruction of the New York culture he exposes. Buffing is dying of AIDS, and as critic Myles Raymond Hurd notes, "For . . . Buffing, who silences guests into embarrassment with his synopsis of Poe's tale, the Red Death bears a painful personal reference to the 'gay menace,' and the description of the Red

Death's telltale markings are suggestive of Kaposi's sarcoma, a rare skin cancer that ravages . . . victims of the syndrome." Sherman appears to be the only person at the exclusive party to recognize the warning of this Jeremiah: "That mannered, ghostly English voice had been the voice of an oracle. Aubrey Buffing had been speaking straight to him, as if he were a medium dispatched by God Himself. Edgar Allan Poe! – *Poe!* – the ruin of the dissolute! – in the Bronx – *the Bronx!*" Wolfe also draws on Poe's story "The Tell-Tale Heart" to enhance the reader's sense of Sherman's increasing panic. Alluding to the biblical writing on the wall, the eleventh chapter is revealingly titled "The Words on the Floor," and from this moment on Wolfe records the palpitations of Sherman's heart and his urge to confess.

A major theme of *The Bonfire of the Vanities* is the moral corruption of the American metropolis. "We are suffering fundamentally from a moral deficit. That's why this is such an important book," said New York writer Richard Vigilante during a spirited panel discussion on the novel, "Tom Wolfe's New York." To this, attorney Peter Huber responded, "The problem with all these folks is that they think that money or power is sufficient, in fact the entire object of existence." A corollary to this theme of human corruption is the lament of Wolfe, raised in the Presbyterian Church, for waning Protestant morality and his implicit call for its renewal. In the twenty-first chapter Sherman recognizes his father's frailty and the diminishment of the former world of Calvinist morality that he represents. John Campbell McCoy's world is being superseded. A new office building "had cast his father's little office into a perpetual gloom." Sherman observes that his father's skin "seemed thin and delicate, as if at any moment his entire leonine hide might crumple inside all the formidable worsted clothes. . . . And all at once Sherman felt sad, not so much for himself as for this old man before him, clinging to a power of connections that meant something back in the 1950s and early 1960s." Sherman himself thinks often of moving to Knoxville, named for the Calvinist John Knox. His fall and renewal, his redirection toward better values, demonstrates the spiritual rededication Wolfe desires.

Sherman's journey has also been seen as a reactionary fantasy of white male triumph. In "Tom Wolfe's New York" Myron Magnet suggests that "*Bonfire*'s recurrent theme [is] the white man who is restored to primal maleness by taking on and triumphing over a young black man." This observation points to Wolfe's daring. Many reviewers have noted that in the novel Wolfe dares to give voice to

the racial hostilities simmering beneath the polite surface of New York liberal politics. Another panel member, Terry Teachout, observes that Wolfe "is saying publicly things that most people in New York are only willing to say behind closed doors and not for quotation." Racial hostilities exist, Wolfe's novel proclaims. Indeed, an important theme is the changing social order. In an often-quoted passage from the prologue, the mayor of New York silently addresses the white elite:

> Do you really think this is *your* city any longer? Open your eyes! . . . Come down from your swell co-ops, you general partners and merger lawyers! It's the Third World down there! Puerto Ricans, West Indians, Haitians, Dominicans, Cubans, Colombians, Hondurans, Koreans, Chinese, Thais, Vietnamese, Ecuadorians, Panamanians, Filipinos, Albanians, Senegalese, and Afro-Americans! . . . You don't think the future knows how to cross a *bridge*?

Among the liberal pieties Wolfe's novel demolishes are the myths that the rich can insulate themselves from this new New York and that they can always get what they want from the legal system.

Wolfe has been accused of racism in his presentation of racial hostilities. Helle Porsdam suggests that Wolfe has "enlisted in the ranks of scared whites who, feeling they are losing their white supremacy and that something has to be done about it, tend toward bigotry and racism, and this seriously mars his otherwise very interesting account of life in contemporary New York." Porsdam believes that Wolfe's fears also tend to obscure "the *real* issue, that of assuring justice to *every* citizen, regardless of gender, race, and class." Teachout has asserted that Wolfe simplifies the New York black community into an "opinion monolith," obscuring its complex reality, and other critics have noted Wolfe's reluctance to enter the mind of any black character other than that of one of his targets, the Reverend Bacon. Those defending Wolfe from such charges point out that his sinners include Christians, Muslims, and Jews, blacks as well as whites. Indeed, the structural and character parallels between Sherman and Kramer suggest that lust is both a Christian and Jewish burden. Also, the six most admirable characters in the book include two blacks and four whites – two Catholics, one Protestant, and one Jew. Vigilante has insisted that rather than being a racist novel, *The Bonfire of the Vanities* is "a book about the fact of racial animosity and the opportunities that it gives people like Bacon."

Reviewers have also stressed the importance of Wolfe's novel as an attack on New York media

Wolfe in one of his trademark ice-cream suits (photograph by Charles Ford)

and on the city's legal and political institutions. New York City writer Charles Olson argued in "Tom Wolfe's New York" that the Reverend Bacon is in some ways a creation of the "white establishment." He points to the failure of the press to act as a watchdog for injustice and suggests, "Possibly there is symbolic significance in the fact that the one character who had the responsibility of blowing the whistle at each stage of injustice in the novel [Peter Fallow] was the one whose mind had been quite thoroughly, and by self-infliction, befogged. . . . This suggests the greatest guilt belongs to the people who should be calling attention to the nature of the system." Vigilante concurs, noting that the press "accepts New York's desperate condition with remarkable equanimity."

Huber describes Wolfe's novel as a devastating indictment of lawyers and the legal system. He notes that Wolfe dramatizes the "core problem" of today's legal system: its loss of the Kantian notions of justice and morality. According to Huber:

> The legal system has come to operate for purposes other than doing individual justice according to norms rooted in history and longstanding practice. The legal system is

now trying to do something else. In the case of *Bonfire,* it happens to be trying to soothe black-white relations. . . . Granted, Wolfe's particular caricature may not be all that common. But the picture he paints of the legal system co-opted for other purposes – increasing safety or redistributing income or what have you – is very accurate.

Porsdam explores other legal issues in *The Bonfire of the Vanities,* asserting that it "successfully – even if provokingly – draws the reader's attention to certain problems relating to the litigiousness of American society." Indeed, she notes that Wolfe sides with those critical of America's current mania for litigation. The adversary system, she notes, fails to function in the novel in its historical role of ensuring that all the facts are brought out in the trial. Similarly, he depicts the jury system as failing in its historical function of protecting citizens from unscrupulous members of the legal profession. Juries in *The Bonfire of the Vanities* are putty in Kramer's hands; as exemplified by the character of Miss Shelly Thomas, they are as corrupt as he is. "By pointing to the deteriorioration of such key institutions of the Anglo-American legal tradition as the adversary system and the trial by jury, and to the accompanying loss of justice and fairness so fundamental to the common law," Porsdam says, "Tom Wolfe voices the key concerns of the critics of . . . [America's] litigiousness."

When the press fails to blow the whistle and the legal system abdicates its historic roles, city life falls back upon the "favor bank," the informal but powerful political system depicted in the novel. Vigilante calls the favor bank the "modern social contract," and Olson notes that Wolfe's hinging his ironic denouement on New York's system of rent control provides a perfect illustration of how easily such systems can be corrupted.

A final theme recurrent in *The Bonfire of the Vanities* concerns the fragmentation of New York. In Wolfe's vision New York consists of a mass of unconnected groups. Given this reality and the lack of civic virtue in group leaders, progress is slow at best and impossible at worst. Magnet remarks on Wolfe's difference from Charles Dickens in this regard:

> Everybody is saying that *Bonfire* is a "Dickensian" novel. But one of the things that Charles Dickens does so successfully is show how this ragged boy and that respectable middle-class member of the community are in labyrinthine and hidden ways closely connected with each other. That's the weakest part of *Bonfire,* the fact that Wolfe is not interested in exploring these direct connections. Instead, he anatomizes a variety of little subcultures. He's brilliant on each one, but they don't come together to form the large coherent whole which is New York. That may actually be Wolfe's message – that what we've got is a bunch of little groups, all coherent in themselves, and all capable of banging up against the other groups.

In such a world, suffering such as Sherman undergoes seems the only path to goodness.

The Bonfire of the Vanities was a popular triumph and a qualified critical success. (The 1990 film version, in contrast, was a financial and critical failure, with critics faulting the casting and the narration from Fallow's point of view.) The most consistent criticism of Wolfe as a novelist relates to his creation of characters and to the tension between his methods as a satirist and his calls for social realism in fiction. Magnet's remarks on the lack of inner lives of characters in the book and his belief that Wolfe offers a shrunken conception of self have been noted. Joseph Epstein writes that "Tom Wolfe is pre-eminently the chronicler of those people who do not so much live lives as they live lifestyles – which is to say, of people who do not live life very deep down or authentically." Indeed, Wolfe does not seem to be introspective. His concerns are external rather than internal, focusing on matters of surface appearance rather than depth. Epstein, Jonathan Alter, and others call for greater depth, empathy, and commitment from Wolfe as a novelist, in effect asking him to temper his broad satiric strokes and develop his range as a realist. Alter writes, "Cervantes and Shakespeare proved that humor and commitment can coexist; they love the men they made fun of."

Whether Wolfe will take this advice in his next work remains to be seen. What is clear is that he has been buoyed sufficiently by the success of *The Bonfire of the Vanities* to continue as a novelist. Immediately after its 1987 publication he reportedly went to San Francisco to begin researching that city as the site for his second novel. In 1988, however, he announced that his next novel would describe life in the working-class bedroom communities of the American East Coast. Wolfe may also deliver another nonfiction work. Among the recent topics of interest he has listed are college sports and religion.

The confusing and seemingly contradictory tensions in Wolfe's art are no longer confusing once he is understood as a wary twentieth-century Jeremiah. Surrounded by unbelievers in a pluralistic culture, he can assert his Calvinistic zeal only through mock sophistication and satire. Nevertheless, the rhetorical forms he employs in his art — tableaux of pandemonium, the tolling of vices, speaking in tongues, and social denunciation — reveal him to be an American Jeremiah in camouflage, both criticizing vice and encouraging American expansion and revolution toward grace.

Interviews:

"Tom Wolfe! Terrific!," *Washington and Lee Alumni Magazine,* 40 (June 1965): 21;

Dorothy M. Scura, ed., *Conversations with Tom Wolfe* (Jackson & London: University Press of Mississippi, 1990);

Anthony Plimpton, "The Art of Fiction," *Paris Review,* 33 (Spring 1991): 93–121.

References:

Jonathan Alter, "Two Cheers for Tom Wolfe," *Washington Monthly,* 20 (March 1988): 42–46;

Chris Anderson, "Tom Wolfe: Pushing the Outside of the Envelope," in his *Style as Argument: Contemporary American Nonfiction* (Carbondale: Southern Illinois University Press, 1987), pp. 8–47;

James Card, "Tom Wolfe and the 'Experimental' Novel," *Journal of American Culture,* 14 (Fall 1991): 31–34;

Ed Cohen, "Tom Wolfe and the Truth Monitors: A Historical Fable," *Clio,* 16 (Fall 1986): 1–11;

Sheri F. Crawford, "Rebel-Doodle Dandy," *Journal of American Culture,* 14 (Fall 1991): 13–18;

Crawford, "Tom Wolfe: Outlaw Gentleman," *Journal of American Culture,* 13 (Summer 1990): 39–50;

Hal Crowther, "Clinging to the Rock: A Novelist's Choices in the New Mediocracy," *South Atlantic Quarterly,* 89 (Spring 1990): 321–336;

Joseph Epstein, "Tom Wolfe's Vanities," *New Criterion,* 6 (February 1988): 5–16;

Marshall W. Fishwick, "Introduction," *Journal of American Culture,* 14 (Fall 1991): 1–10;

Ronald L. Goldfarb, "Tom Wolfe's Jurisprudence," *Criminal Justice Ethics,* 9 (Winter–Spring 1990): 2+;

Lisa Grunwald, "Tom Wolfe Aloft in the Status Sphere," *Esquire,* 114 (October 1990): 39, 146–152+;

John Hellmann, "Reporting the Fabulous: Representation and Response in the Work of Tom Wolfe," in his *Fables of Fact: The New Journalism as New Fiction* (Urbana: University of Illinois Press, 1981), pp. 101–125;

Myles Raymond Hurd, " 'The Masque of the Red Death' in Wolfe's *The Bonfire of the Vanities,*" *Notes on Contemporary Literature,* 20 (May 1990): 4–5;

Barbara Lounsberry, "Tom Wolfe's American Jeremiad," in her *The Art of Fact: Contemporary Artists of Nonfiction* (Westport, Conn.: Greenwood Press, 1990), pp. 37–64;

Lounsberry, "Tom Wolfe's Negative Vision," *South Dakota Review,* 20 (Summer 1982): 15–31;

Helle Porsdam, "In the Age of Lawspeak: Tom Wolfe's *The Bonfire of the Vanities* and American Litigiousness," *Journal of American Studies,* 25 (April 1992): 39–57;

Parke Rouse, "Tom Wolfe Unchanged by Fame," *Journal of American Culture,* 14 (Fall 1991): 11–13;

James F. Smith, "Tom Wolfe's *Bonfire of the Vanities:* A Dreiser Novel for the 1980s," *Journal of American Culture,* 14 (Fall 1991): 43–51;

Lisa Stokes, "Tom Wolfe's Narratives as Stories of Growth," *Journal of American Culture,* 14 (Fall 1991): 19–24;

James N. Stull, "The Cultural Gamesmanship of Tom Wolfe," *Journal of American Culture,* 14 (Fall 1991): 25–30;

"Tom Wolfe's New York," *Society,* 25 (September–October 1988): 67–78;

Robert Towers, "The Flap over Tom Wolfe: How Real Is the Retreat from Realism?," *New York Times Book Review,* 95 (28 January 1990): 15–16;

Jerry A. Varsava, "Tom Wolfe's Defense of the New (Old) Social Novel: Or, the Perils of the Great White-Suited Hunter," *Journal of American Culture,* 14 (Fall 1991): 35–41;

Kathleen J. Weatherford, "Tom Wolfe's Billion-Footed Beast," *American Studies in Scandinavia,* 22, no. 2 (1990): 81–93;

Mas'ud Zavarzadeh, "The Contingent *Donnee:* The Testimonial Nonfiction Novel," in his *The Mythopoeic Reality: The Postwar American Nonfiction Novel* (Urbana: University of Illinois Press, 1976), pp. 131–153.

Books for Further Reading

This is a selective list of general studies relating to the contemporary novel. Fuller bibliographies can be found in Lewis Leary, *Articles on American Literature, 1950–1967* (Durham, N.C.: Duke University Press, 1970); the annual MLA International Bibliography; and *American Literary Scholarship: An Annual* (Durham, N.C.: Duke University Press, 1965–   ).

Aldridge, John W. *Classics and Contemporaries.* Columbia: University of Missouri Press, 1992.

Aldridge. *The Devil in the Fire: Retrospective Essays on American Literature and Culture, 1951–1971.* New York: Harper's Magazine Press, 1972.

Aldridge. *In Search of Heresy: American Literature in an Age of Conformity.* New York: McGraw-Hill, 1956.

Aldridge. *Talents and Technicians: Literary Chic and the New Assembly-Line Fiction.* New York: Scribners, 1992.

Aldridge. *Time to Murder and Create: The Contemporary Novel in Crisis.* New York: McKay, 1966.

Allen, Mary. *The Necessary Blankness: Women in Major American Fiction of the Sixties.* Urbana: University of Illinois Press, 1976.

Alter, Robert. *After the Tradition: Essays on Modern Jewish Writing.* New York: Dutton, 1969.

Auchincloss, Louis. *Pioneers or Caretakers: A Study of Nine American Women Novelists.* Minneapolis: University of Minnesota Press, 1965.

Bachelard, Gaston. *The Poetics of Space.* New York: Orion, 1964.

Baker, Houston A. *Blues, Ideology, and Afro-American Literature: A Vernacular Theory.* Chicago: University of Chicago Press, 1984.

Baker, ed. *Three American Literatures: Essays in Chicano, Native American, and Asian-American Literature for Teachers of American Literature.* New York: Modern Language Association of America, 1982.

Balakian, Nona, and Charles Simmons, eds. *The Creative Present: Notes on Contemporary American Fiction.* Garden City, N.Y.: Doubleday, 1963.

Baumbach, Jonathan. *The Landscape of Nightmare: Studies in the Contemporary American Novel.* New York: New York University Press, 1965.

Bell, Bernard W. *The Afro-American Novel and Its Tradition.* Amherst: University of Massachusetts Press, 1987.

Bellamy, Joe David. *The New Fiction: Interviews with Innovative American Writers.* Urbana: University of Illinois Press, 1974.

Bercovitch, Sacvan, ed. *Reconstructing American Literary History.* Cambridge, Mass.: Harvard University Press, 1986.

Bergman, Ronald. *America in the Sixties: An Intellectual History.* New York: Free Press, 1968.

Bigsby, C. W. E., ed. *The Black American Writer*. De Land, Fla.: Everett/Edwards, 1969.

Blotner, Joseph. *The Modern American Political Novel, 1900–1960*. Austin: University of Texas Press, 1966.

Boelhower, William. *Through a Glass Darkly: Ethnic Semiosis in American Literature*. New York: Oxford University Press, 1987.

Bone, Robert A. *The Negro Novel in America,* revised edition. New Haven: Yale University Press, 1965.

Bradbury, John M. *Renaissance in the South: A Critical History of the Literature, 1920–1960*. Chapel Hill: University of North Carolina Press, 1963.

Bradbury, Malcolm. *The Modern American Novel,* revised edition. New York: Viking, 1992.

Bredahl, A. Carl Jr. *New Ground: Western American Narrative and the Literary Canon*. Chapel Hill: University of North Carolina Press, 1989.

Bryant, Jerry H. *The Open Decision: The Contemporary American Novel and Its Intellectual Background*. New York: Free Press, 1970.

Byerman, Keith E. *Fingering the Jagged Grain: Tradition and Form in Recent Black Fiction*. Athens: University of Georgia Press, 1985.

Campbell, Jane. *Mythic Black Fiction: The Transformation of History*. Knoxville: University of Tennessee Press, 1986.

Carr, John, ed. *Kite-Flying and Other Irrational Acts: Conversations with Twelve Southern Writers*. Baton Rouge: Louisiana State University Press, 1972.

Chametzky, Jules. *Our Decentralized Literature: Cultural Mediations in Selected Jewish and Southern Writers*. Amherst: University of Massachusetts Press, 1986.

Christian, Barbara. *Black Women Novelists: The Development of a Tradition, 1892–1976*. Westport, Conn.: Greenwood Press, 1980.

Conversations with Writers, 2 volumes. Detroit: Bruccoli Clark/Gale, 1977–1978.

Cook, Bruce. *The Beat Generation*. New York: Scribners, 1971.

Cook, M. G., ed. *Modern Black Novelists: A Collection of Critical Essays*. Englewood Cliffs, N. J.: Prentice-Hall, 1971.

Core, George, ed. *Southern Fiction Today: Renascence and Beyond*. Athens: University of Georgia Press, 1969.

Cowan, Louise. *The Fugitive Group: A Literary History*. Baton Rouge: Louisiana State University Press, 1959.

Cowley, Malcolm. *The Literary Situation*. New York: Viking, 1954.

Cunliffe, Marcus, ed. *American Literature Since 1900*. London: Penguin, 1993.

Darby, William. *Necessary American Fictions: Popular Literature of the 1950s*. Bowling Green, Ohio: Bowling Green State University Popular Press, 1987.

Dekker, George. *The American Historical Romance*. Cambridge: Cambridge University Press, 1987.

Drake, Robert, ed. *The Writer and His Tradition*. Knoxville: University of Tennessee Press, 1969.

Eco, Umberto. *Travels in Hyperreality*. San Diego: Harcourt Brace Jovanovich, 1983.

Eisinger, Chester E. *Fiction of the Forties*. Chicago: University of Chicago Press, 1963.

Elliott, Emory, ed. *The Columbia History of the American Novel*. New York: Columbia University Press, 1991.

Elliott, ed. *The Columbia Literary History of the United States*. New York: Columbia University Press, 1988.

Etulain, Richard W., and Michael T. Marsden, eds. *The Popular Western: Essays toward a Definition*. Bowling Green, Ohio: Bowling Green State University Popular Press, 1974.

Federman, Raymond, ed. *Surfiction: Fiction Now and Tomorrow*. Chicago: Swallow Press, 1975.

Feldman, Gene, and Max Gartenberg, eds. *The Beat Generation and the Angry Young Men*. New York: Citadel, 1958.

Folsom, James K. *The American Western Novel*. New Haven: Yale University Press, 1966.

Fox, Robert Elliott. *Conscientious Sorcerers: The Black Postmodernist Fiction of LeRoi Jones/Amiri Baraka, Ishmael Reed, and Samuel R. Delany*. New York: Greenwood Press, 1987.

French, Warren, ed. *The Fifties: Fiction, Poetry, Drama*. De Land, Fla.: Everett/Edwards, 1970.

Friedman, Melvin J., and John B. Vickery. *The Shaken Realist*. Baton Rouge: Louisiana State University Press, 1970.

Fuller, Edmund. *Man in Modern Fiction: Some Minority Opinions on Contemporary American Writing*. New York: Random House, 1958.

Gado, Frank, ed. *First Person: Conversations on Writers and Writing*. Schenectady, N.Y.: Union College Press, 1973.

Galloway, David D. *The Absurd Hero in American Fiction: Updike, Styron, Bellow, Salinger*, revised edition. Austin: University of Texas Press, 1970.

Gass, William H. *Fiction and the Figures of Life*. New York: Knopf, 1970.

Gass. *On Being Blue: A Philosophical Inquiry*. Boston: Godine, 1976.

Gates, Henry Louis Jr. *The Signifying Monkey: A Theory of Afro-American Literary Criticism*. New York: Oxford University Press, 1988.

Gayle, Addison Jr. *The Way of the New World: The Black Novel in America*. Garden City, N.Y.: Anchor/Doubleday, 1975.

Gayle, ed. *Black Expression: Essays by and about Black Americans in the Creative Arts*. New York: Weybright & Talley, 1969.

Geismar, Maxwell. *American Moderns: From Rebellion to Conformity*. New York: Hill & Wang, 1958.

Gerstenberger, Donna, and George Hendrick. *The American Novel, 1789–1959: A Checklist of Twentieth Century Criticism*. Chicago: Swallow Press, 1970.

Gilman, Richard. *The Confusion of Realms.* New York: Random House, 1969.

Glicksberg, Charles I. *The Sexual Revolution in Modern American Literature.* The Hague: Nijhoff, 1971.

Gold, Herbert, ed. *First Person Singular: Essays for the Sixties.* New York: Dial, 1963.

González Echevarría, Roberto. *The Voice of the Masters: Writing and Authority in Modern Latin American Literature.* Austin: University of Texas Press, 1985.

Gossett, Louise Y. *Violence in Recent Southern Fiction.* Durham, N.C.: Duke University Press, 1965.

Green, Martin. *Re-appraisals: Some Commonsense Readings in American Literature.* London: Hugh Evelyn, 1963.

Gruen, John. *The Party's Over Now: Reminiscences of the Fifties.* New York: Viking, 1972.

Guttmann, Allen. *The Jewish Writer in America: Assimilation and the Crisis of Identity.* New York: Oxford University Press, 1971.

Hamilton, Cynthia S. *Western and Hard-Boiled Detective Fiction in America: From High Noon to Midnight.* Iowa City: University of Iowa Press, 1987.

Handy, William J. *Modern Fiction: A Formalist Approach.* Carbondale: Southern Illinois University Press, 1971.

Harap, Louis. *In the Mainstream: The Jewish Presence in Twentieth-Century American Literature, 1950s–1980s.* New York: Greenwood Press, 1987.

Hardwick, Elizabeth. *A View of My Own: Essays in Literature and Society.* New York: Noonday Press, 1962.

Harper, Howard M. Jr. *Desperate Faith: A Study of Bellow, Salinger, Mailer, Baldwin, and Updike.* Chapel Hill: University of North Carolina Press, 1967.

Harris, Charles B. *Contemporary American Novelists of the Absurd.* New Haven: Yale University Press, 1971.

Haslam, Gerald W., ed. *Western Writing.* Albuquerque: University of New Mexico Press, 1974.

Hassan, Ihab. *Contemporary American Literature, 1945–1972: An Introduction.* New York: Ungar, 1973.

Hassan. *The Postmodern Turn.* Columbus: Ohio State University Press, 1987.

Hassan. *Radical Innocence: Studies in the Contemporary American Novel.* Princeton: Princeton University Press, 1961.

Hassan. *The Right Promethean Fire: Imagination, Science, and Cultural Change.* Urbana: University of Illinois Press, 1979.

Hauck, Richard Boyd. *A Cheerful Nihilism: Confidence and "The Absurd" in American Humorous Fiction.* Bloomington: Indiana University Press, 1971.

Hicks, Granville. *The Living Novel: A Symposium.* New York: Macmillan, 1957.

Hicks, Jack. *In the Singer's Temple: Prose Fictions of Barthelme, Gaines, Brautigan, Piercy, Kesey, and Kosinski.* Chapel Hill: University of North Carolina Press, 1981.

Hilfer, Tony. *American Fiction Since 1940.* London & New York: Longman, 1992.

Hill, Herbert, ed. *Anger and Beyond: The Negro Writer in the United States*. New York: Harper & Row, 1966.

Hobson, Fred. *Tell about the South: The Southern Rage to Explain*. Baton Rouge: Louisiana State University Press, 1983.

Hoffman, Daniel, ed. *Harvard Guide to Contemporary American Writing*. Cambridge, Mass.: Belknap Press of Harvard University Press, 1979.

Hoffman, Frederick J. *The Art of Southern Fiction: A Study of Some Modern Novelists*. Carbondale: Southern Illinois University Press, 1967.

Hurm, Gerd. *Fragmented Urban Images: The American City in Modern Fiction*. Frankfurt am Main & New York: Peter Lang, 1991.

Jackson, Blyden. *The History of Afro-American Literature,* 1 volume to date. Baton Rouge: Louisiana State University Press, 1989– .

Johnson, Charles R. *Being and Race: Black Writing Since 1970*. Bloomington: Indiana University Press, 1988.

Jones, Peter G. *War and the Novelist: Appraising the American War Novel*. Columbia: University of Missouri Press, 1976.

Karl, Frederick Robert. *American Fictions, 1940–1980: A Comprehensive History and Critical Evaluation*. New York: Harper & Row, 1983.

Kazin, Alfred. *Bright Book of Life: American Novelists and Storytellers from Hemingway to Mailer*. Boston & Toronto: Atlantic/Little, Brown, 1973.

Kazin. *Contemporaries*. Boston: Little, Brown, 1962.

Kazin. *An Interpretation of Modern American Prose Literature*. Garden City, N.Y.: Doubleday, 1956.

Kennard, Jean E. *Number and Nightmare: Forms of Fantasy in Contemporary Fiction*. Hamden, Conn.: Archon, 1975.

Kim, Elaine H. *Asian American Literature: An Introduction to the Writings and Their Social Contexts*. Philadelphia: Temple University Press, 1982.

Klein, Marcus. *After Alienation: American Novels in Mid-century*. Cleveland & New York: World, 1964.

Klein, ed. *The American Novel Since World War II*. Greenwich, Conn.: Fawcett, 1969.

Klinkowitz, Jerome. *The Life of Fiction*. Urbana: University of Illinois Press, 1977.

Klinkowitz. *Literary Disruptions: The Making of a Post-contemporary American Fiction*. Urbana: University of Illinois Press, 1975.

Klotman, Phyllis Rauch. *Another Man Gone: The Black Runner in Contemporary Afro-American Literature*. Port Washington, N.Y.: Kennikat Press, 1977.

Kort, Wesley A. *Shriven Selves: Religious Problems in Recent American Fiction*. Philadelphia: Fortress, 1972.

Kostelanetz, Richard. *The End of Intelligent Writing: Literary Politics in America*. New York: Sheed & Ward, 1974.

Kostelanetz. *Master Minds: Portraits of Contemporary American Artists and Intellectuals*. New York: Macmillan, 1969.

Kostelanetz, ed. *The New American Arts*. New York: Horizon, 1965.

Kostelanetz, ed. *On Contemporary Literature: An Anthology of Critical Essays on the Major Movements and Writers of Contemporary Literature*. New York: Avon, 1964.

Kostelanetz, ed. *The Young American Writers: Fiction, Poetry, Drama, and Criticism*. New York: Funk & Wagnalls, 1967.

Krim, Seymour. *Shake It for the World, Smartass*. New York: Dial, 1970.

Lebowitz, Naomi. *Humanism and the Absurd in the Modern Novel*. Evanston, Ill.: Northwestern University Press, 1971.

Lehan, Richard. *A Dangerous Crossing: French Literary Existentialism and the Modern American Novel*. Carbondale: Southern Illinois University Press, 1973.

Ling, Amy. *Between Worlds: Women Writers of Chinese Ancestry*. New York: Pergamon Press, 1990.

Lipton, Lawrence. *The Holy Barbarians*. New York: Messner, 1959.

Litz, A. Walton, ed. *Modern American Fiction: Essays in Criticism*. New York: Oxford University Press, 1963.

Lord, William J. Jr. *How Authors Make a Living: An Analysis of Free Lance Writers' Incomes, 1953–1957*. New York: Scarecrow Press, 1962.

Ludwig, Jack. *Recent American Novelists*. Minneapolis: University of Minnesota Press, 1962.

Lutwack, Leonard. *Heroic Fiction: The Epic Tradition and American Novels of the Twentieth Century*. Carbondale: Southern Illinois University Press, 1971.

Madden, Charles F., ed. *Talks with Authors*. Carbondale: Southern Illinois University Press, 1968.

Madden, David. *American Dreams, American Nightmares*. Carbondale: Southern Illinois University Press, 1970.

Madden. *Rediscoveries: Informal Essays in Which Well-Known Novelists Rediscover Neglected Works of Fiction by One of Their Favorite Authors*. New York: Crown, 1971.

Malin, Irving. *New American Gothic*. Carbondale: Southern Illinois University Press, 1962.

Margolies, Edward. *Native Sons: A Critical Study of Twentieth-Century Negro American Authors*. Philadelphia & New York: Lippincott, 1968.

May, John R. *Toward a New Earth: Apocalypse in the American Novel*. Notre Dame, Ind.: University of Notre Dame Press, 1972.

McHale, Brian. *Postmodernist Fiction*. New York & London: Methuen, 1987.

Milton, John R. *The Novel of the American West*. Lincoln: University of Nebraska Press, 1980.

Moore, Harry T., ed. *Contemporary American Novelists*. Carbondale: Southern Illinois University Press, 1964.

Myers, Carol Fairbanks. *Women in Literature: Criticism of the Seventies*. Metuchen, N.J.: Scarecrow Press, 1976.

Newman, Charles. *The Post-modern Aura: The Act of Fiction in an Age of Inflation.* Evanston, Ill.: Northwestern University Press, 1985.

Newquist, Roy. *Counterpoint.* Chicago: Rand McNally, 1964.

Nin, Anaïs. *The Novel of the Future.* New York: Macmillan, 1968.

O'Brien, John, ed. *Interviews with Black Writers.* New York: Liveright, 1973.

Olderman, Raymond M. *Beyond the Waste Land: A Study of the American Novel in the Nineteen-Sixties.* New Haven: Yale University Press, 1972.

Olster, Stacey Michele. *Reminiscence and Re-creation in Contemporary American Fiction.* Cambridge: Cambridge University Press, 1989.

Panichas, George A. *The Politics of Twentieth-Century Novelists.* New York: Hawthorn, 1971.

Parkinson, Thomas, ed. *A Casebook on The Beat.* New York: Crowell, 1961.

Pearce, Richard. *Stages of the Clown: Perspectives on Modern Fiction from Dostoyevsky to Beckett.* Carbondale: Southern Illinois University Press, 1970.

Peden, William. *The American Short Story: Front Line in the National Defense of Literature.* Boston: Houghton Mifflin, 1964.

Pinsker, Sanford. *The Schlemiel as Metaphor: Studies in the Yiddish and American Jewish Novel.* Carbondale: Southern Illinois University Press, 1971.

Podhoretz, Norman. *Doings and Undoings: The Fifties and After in American Writing.* New York: Farrar, Straus, 1964.

Rocard, Marcienne. *The Children of the Sun: Mexican-Americans in the Literature of the United States,* translated by Edward G. Brown Jr. Tucson: University of Arizona Press, 1989.

Rosenblatt, Roger. *Black Fiction.* Cambridge, Mass.: Harvard University Press, 1974.

Rubin, Louis D. Jr. *The American South: Portrait of a Culture.* Baton Rouge: Louisiana State University Press, 1980.

Rubin. *The Faraway Country: Writers in the Modern South.* Seattle: University of Washington Press, 1963.

Rubin and Robert D. Jacobs, eds. *South: Modern Southern Literature in Its Cultural Setting.* Garden City, N.Y.: Doubleday, 1961.

Rubin and others, eds. *The History of Southern Literature.* Baton Rouge: Louisiana State University Press, 1985.

Ruoff, A. Lavonne Brown, and Jerry W. Ward Jr. *Redefining American Literary History.* New York: Modern Language Association of America, 1990.

Scholes, Robert. *The Fabulators.* New York: Oxford University Press, 1967.

Scholes and Robert Kellogg. *The Nature of Narrative.* New York: Oxford University Press, 1966.

Schraufnagel, Noel. *From Apology to Protest: The Black American Novel.* De Land, Fla.: Everett/Edwards, 1973.

Schulz, Max F. *Black Humor Fiction of the Sixties: A Pluralistic Definition of Man and His World.* Athens: Ohio University Press, 1973.

Schulz. *Radical Sophistication: Studies in Contemporary Jewish-American Novelists.* Athens: Ohio University Press, 1969.

Scott, Nathan A. Jr. *Three American Moralists: Mailer, Bellow, Trilling.* Notre Dame, Ind.: University of Notre Dame Press, 1973.

Sherzer, Joel, and Anthony Woodbury. *Native American Discourse: Poetics and Rhetoric.* New York: Cambridge University Press, 1987.

Simonson, Harold P. *Beyond the Frontier: Writers, Western Regionalism and a Sense of Place.* Fort Worth: Texas Christian University Press, 1989.

Smith, Valerie. *Self-Discovery and Authority in Afro-American Narrative.* Cambridge, Mass.: Harvard University Press, 1987.

Sollors, Werner. *Beyond Ethnicity: Consent and Descent in American Culture.* New York: Oxford University Press, 1986.

Spiller, Robert, ed. *A Time of Harvest: American Literature, 1910–1960.* New York: Hill & Wang, 1962.

Stark, John. *The Literature of Exhaustion: Borges, Nabokov, and Barth.* Durham, N.C.: Duke University Press, 1974.

Stepto, Robert. *From Behind the Veil: A Study of Afro-American Narrative.* Urbana: University of Illinois Press, 1979.

Stuckey, William J. *The Pulitzer Prize Novels: A Critical Backward Look.* Norman: University of Oklahoma Press, 1966.

Sutherland, William O. S., ed. *Six Contemporary Novels: Six Introductory Essays in Modern Fiction.* Austin: University of Texas Department of English, 1962.

Tanner, Tony. *City of Words: American Fiction, 1950–1970.* New York: Harper & Row, 1971.

Tanner. *The Reign of Wonder: Naivety and Reality in American Literature.* Cambridge: Cambridge University Press, 1965.

Tate, Claudia. *Black Women Writers at Work.* New York: Continuum, 1983.

Taylor, J. Golden, and Thomas J. Lyon, eds. *A Literary History of the American West.* Fort Worth: Texas Christian University Press, 1987.

Tilton, John W. *Cosmic Satire in the Contemporary Novel.* Lewisburg, Pa.: Bucknell University Press, 1977.

Turner, Darwin T. *Afro-American Writers.* New York: Appleton-Century-Crofts, 1970.

Tuttleton, James W. *The Novel of Manners in America.* Chapel Hill: University of North Carolina Press, 1972.

Tytell, John. *Naked Angels: The Lives and Literature of the Beat Generation.* New York: McGraw-Hill, 1976.

Waldmeir, Joseph J., ed. *Recent American Fiction: Some Critical Views.* Boston: Houghton Mifflin, 1963.

Watkins, Floyd C. *The Death of Art: Black and White in the Recent Southern Novel.* Athens: University of Georgia Press, 1970.

Watson, Carole McAlphine. *Prologue: The Novels of Black American Women, 1891–1965.* New York: Greenwood Press, 1985.

Weber, Ronald, ed. *America in Change: Reflections on the 60's and 70's.* Notre Dame, Ind.: University of Notre Dame Press, 1972.

West, James L. W. *American Authors and the Literary Marketplace Since 1900.* Philadelphia: University of Pennsylvania Press, 1988.

Westbrook, Max, ed. *The Modern American Novel: Essays in Criticism.* New York: Random House, 1966.

Whitlow, Roger. *Black American Literature: A Critical History.* Chicago: Nelson Hall, 1973.

Wiget, Andrew. *Native American Literature.* Boston: Twayne, 1985.

Wiget, ed. *Critical Essays on Native American Literature.* Boston: G. K. Hall, 1985.

Wilde, Alan. *Middle Grounds: Studies in Contemporary American Fiction.* Philadelphia: University of Pennsylvania Press, 1987.

Williams, John A., and Charles F. Harris, eds. *Amistad I: Writings of Black History and Culture.* New York: Knopf, 1970.

Williams and Harris, eds. *Amistad II.* New York: Knopf, 1971.

Writers at Work: The "Paris Review" Interviews, 4 volumes. New York: Viking, 1958–1976.

Contributors

Edwin T. Arnold ....*Appalachian State University*
Nancy K. Butterworth ....*Coker College*
Keith E. Byerman ....*Indiana State University*
Jane Campbell ....*Purdue University – Calumet*
Sandy Cohen ....*Albany State College*
R. H. W. Dillard ....*Hollins College*
Philip K. Jason ....*United States Naval Academy*
Robert F. Kiernan ....*Manhattan College*
Victor A. Kramer ....*Georgia State University*
S. Lillian Kremer ....*Kansas State University*
Leon Lewis ....*Appalachian State University*
Barbara Lounsberry..*University of Northern Iowa*
Timothy Materer..*University of Missouri – Columbia*
Thomas Myers ....*Saint Norbert College*
Peter J. Reed...*University of Minnesota*
Ruth Rosenberg...*Brooklyn College*
Randolph Paul Runyon...*Miami University*
Joel Salzberg ....*University of Colorado at Denver*
Robert Solotaroff...*University of Minnesota*
Cynthia Tompkins ....*Arizona State University West*

Cumulative Index

Dictionary of Literary Biography, Volumes 1-152
Dictionary of Literary Biography Yearbook, 1980-1994
Dictionary of Literary Biography Documentary Series, Volumes 1-12

Cumulative Index

DLB before number: *Dictionary of Literary Biography,* Volumes 1-152
Y before number: *Dictionary of Literary Biography Yearbook,* 1980-1994
DS before number: *Dictionary of Literary Biography Documentary Series,* Volumes 1-12

D

E

J

N

O

ISBN 0-8103-5713-5

(Continued from front endsheets)

Documentary Series